Lecture Notes in Computer Science   11893

More information about this series at http://www.springer.com/series/7408

Anthony Widjaja Lin (Ed.)

Programming Languages and Systems

17th Asian Symposium, APLAS 2019
Nusa Dua, Bali, Indonesia, December 1–4, 2019
Proceedings

 Springer

Editor
Anthony Widjaja Lin 🆔
University of Kaiserslautern
Kaiserslautern, Germany

ISSN 0302-9743   ISSN 1611-3349   (electronic)
Lecture Notes in Computer Science
ISBN 978-3-030-34174-9   ISBN 978-3-030-34175-6   (eBook)
https://doi.org/10.1007/978-3-030-34175-6

LNCS Sublibrary: SL2 – Programming and Software Engineering

This Springer imprint is published by the registered company Springer Nature Switzerland AG
The registered company address is: Gewerbestrasse 11, 6330 Cham, Switzerland

Preface

This volume contains the papers presented at the 17th Asian Symposium on Programming Languages and Systems (APLAS 2019), held in Bali, Indonesia, between December 1–4, 2019. APLAS aims to stimulate programming language research by providing a forum for the presentation of the latest results and the exchange of ideas in programming languages and systems. APLAS is based in Asia but is an international forum that serves the worldwide programming languages community.

This year we solicited contributions in the forms of regular research papers and tool papers. The conference solicts contributions in, but is not limited to, the following topics: semantics, logics, and foundational theory; design of languages, type systems, and foundational calculi; domain-specific languages compilers, interpreters, and abstract machines; program derivation, synthesis, and transformation; program analysis, verification, and model-checking; logic, constraint, probabilistic, and quantum programming; software security; concurrency and parallelism; tools and environments for programming and implementation; and applications of SAT/SMT to programming and implementation.

APLAS 2019 employed a light weight double-blind reviewing process with an author-response period. More precisely, we had a two-stage reviewing process, wherein each paper received at least three reviews before the author-response period, which was followed by a two-week Program Committee (PC) discussion taking into account initial impressions of the papers as well as the author responses.

This year APLAS received 50 submissions, out of which 22 papers (21 regular papers and 1 tool paper) were accepted after thorough reviews and discussions by the PC. After a rigorous reviewing process and PC discussion, we decided to award a Distinguished Paper Award to the paper titled "Dissecting Widening: Separating Termination from Information" by Graeme Gange, Jorge Navas, Peter Schachte, Harald Sondergaard, and Peter Stuckey. We were also honored to include three invited talks by distinguished PL researchers:

- Nate Foster (Cornell University, USA): "Network Verification: Past, Present, and Future"
- Annabelle McIver (Macquarie University, Australia): "Proving that Programs are Differentially Private"
- Philipp Rümmer (Uppsala University, Sweden): "On Strings in Software Model Checking"

I am indebted to many people who helped make APLAS 2019 possible. First and foremost, I sincerely thank the PC, who gave a lot of time and effort throughout the entire reviewing process. I am also grateful to the sub-reviewers and expert reviewers for their thorough and constructive reviews. I thank Mirna Adriani (University of Indonesia, Indonesia) who served as a general chair and worked out every detail of the conference well in advance. I thank Jens Dietrich (Victoria University of Wellington,

New Zealand) who served as a publicity chair and spent a lot of time (through posters, social media, mailing list, among others) advertising APLAS 2019. I am also grateful to the APLAS Steering Committee (especially Wei-Ngan Chin, National University of Singapore, Singapore, and Atsushi Igarashi, Kyoto University, Japan) who provided a lot of helpful advice and leadership. I thank recent APLAS PC chairs, especially Bor-Yuh Evan Chang (University of Colorado Boulder, USA) and Sukyoung Ryu (KAIST, South Korea) for their helpful advice. Finally, I thank Eelco Visser and Elmer van Chastelet for their very helpful conf.researchr.org conference management system, as well as Andrei Voronkov for the very helpful EasyChair conference management system.

Last but not least, I would like to thank the organizers of associated events that helped make APLAS 2019 a success: (1) The Poster and Student Research Competition, organized by Andreea Costea (National University of Singapore, Singapore) and (2) Workshop on New Ideas and Emerging Results (Wei-Ngan Chin and Atsushi Igarashi).

September 2019   Anthony W. Lin

Organization

General Chair

Mirna Adriani   University of Indonesia, Indonesia

Publicity Chair

Jens Dietrich   Victoria University of Wellington, New Zealand

Program Chair

Anthony W. Lin   Technische Universität Kaiserslautern, Germany

Program Committee

Timos Antonopoulos	Yale University, USA
Sandrine Blazy	University of Rennes 1, Irisa, France
Yu-Fang Chen	Academia Sinica, Taiwan
Silvia Crafa	Università di Padova, Italy
Vijay D'Silva	Google, USA
Jens Dietrich	Victoria University Wellington, New Zealand
Rayna Dimitrova	University of Leicester, UK
Julian Dolby	IBM, USA
Jeremy Gibbons	University of Oxford, UK
Matthew Hague	Royal Holloway University of London, UK
Philipp Haller	KTH Royal Institute of Technology, Sweden
Ichiro Hasuo	National Institute of Informatics, Japan
Aquinas Hobor	National University of Singapore, Singapore
Ohad Kammar	University of Edinburgh, UK
Johannes Kinder	Bundeswehr University Munich, Germany
Ekaterina Komendantskaya	Heriot-Watt University, UK
Laura Kovacs	TU Wien, Austria
Quang-Loc Le	Teesside University, UK
Martin Lester	University of Reading, UK
Hongjin Liang	Nanjing University, China
Roland Meyer	TU Braunschweig, Germany
Alexandra Silva	University College London, UK
Makoto Tatsuta	National Institute of Informatics, Japan
Tachio Terauchi	Waseda University, Japan
Peter Thiemann	Universität Freiburg, Germany
Alwen Tiu	Australian National University, Australia
Takeshi Tsukada	University of Tokyo, Japan

Hiroshi Unno	University of Tsukuba, Japan
Tomas Vojnar	Brno University of Technology, Czech Republic
Lijun Zhang	Institute of Software, Chinese Academy of Sciences, China
Damien Zufferey	MPI-SWS, Germany
Florian Zuleger	TU Wien, Austria

Workshop on New Ideas and Emerging Results Organizers

Wei-Ngan Chin	National University of Singapore, Singapore
Atsushi Igarashi	Kyoto University, Japan

Poster and Student Research Competition Organizer

Andreea Costea	National University of Singapore, Singapore

Additional Reviewers

Peter Chini
Jeremy Dawson
Hendra Gunadi
Vojtěch Havlena
Lukas Holik
Zhe Hou
Jens Katelaan
Daisuke Kimura
Ondrej Lengal
Yong Li
Hsin-Hung Lin

Duncan Mitchell
Koji Nakazawa
James Patrick-Evans
Long H. Pham
Hernan Ponce-De-Leon
Gabriel Radanne
Adam Rogalewicz
Andrea Turrini
Jannik Vierling
Sebastian Wolff

Network Verification: Past, Present, and Future (Invited Paper)

Nate Foster

Cornell University, Ithaca, NY, USA

Abstract. Networks today achieve robustness not by adhering to precise formal specifications but by building implementations that tolerate modest deviations from correct behavior. This philosophy can be seen in the slogan used by the Internet Engineering Task Force, "we believe in rough consensus and running code," and by Jon Postel's famous dictum to "be conservative in what you do, be liberal in what you accept from others." But as networks have grown in scale and complexity, the frequency of faults has led to new interest in techniques for formally verifying network behavior.

This talk will discuss recent progress on practical tools for specifying and verifying formal properties of networks. In the first part of the talk, I will present p4v, a tool for verifying the low-level code that executes on individual devices such as routers and firewalls. In the second part of the talk, I will present NetKAT, a formal system for specifying and verifying network-wide behavior. In the third part of the talk, I will highlight some challenges and opportunities for future research in network verification.

Contents

Language Design and Implementation

Concurrency

Verification

Logic and Automata

Invited Papers

Proving that Programs Are Differentially Private

Annabelle McIver[1($\boxtimes$)] and Carroll Morgan[2]

[1] Department Computing, Macquarie University, Sydney, Australia
`annabelle.mciver@mq.edu`
[2] University of New South Wales and Data61, Sydney, Australia

Abstract. We extend recent work in Quantitative Information Flow (QIF) to provide tools for the analysis of programs that aim to implement differentially private mechanisms. We demonstrate how differential privacy can be expressed using loss functions, and how to use this idea in conjunction with a QIF-enabled program semantics to verify differentially private guarantees. Finally we describe how to use this approach experimentally using Kuifje, a recently developed tool for analysing information-flow properties of programs.

Keywords: Quantitative Information Flow · Probabilistic program semantics · verification · privacy · Differential privacy

1 Introduction

This paper concerns the verification of privacy properties of programs. Our particular focus is *differential privacy* and how to prove that implementations of privacy-style mechanisms satisfy a differentially private property. Whilst differential privacy has been much studied as a mathematical theory there is further work to be done in ensuring that its properties are faithfully implemented in a programming language. This is particularly important because implementations are rarely transcriptions of mathematical functions, and program code could present very differently from the mathematical function it purports to compute. There are several important approaches for tackling this problem [9,13] from a programming languages perspective. In this paper we study it as a verification exercise using a programming semantics based on the *Quantitative Information Flow* (QIF) paradigm.

Quantitative information flow is designed to model the severity of risks associated with any information leaks in systems that process confidential information. QIF consists of three components. The first is a model for confidential information (or "secrets") based on probability distributions over possible values that a secret could take. The second is a model of a mechanism (or program)

This research was supported by the Australian Research Council Grant DP140101119.

A. W. Lin (Ed.): APLAS 2019, LNCS 11893, pp. 3–18, 2019.
https://doi.org/10.1007/978-3-030-34175-6_1

which describes how the mechanism's external outputs affect the flow of information about the secret. The third is a model of an adversary (as a gain or loss function) operating within a specific scenario describing how an adversary could exploit any flow that has occurred. A QIF analysis takes these elements and then interprets the severity of the information leak relative to the given adversarial scenario.

Elsewhere [3] it has been shown how to model differential privacy as a QIF mechanism and here we extend that idea by introducing an adverarial scenario (or loss function) that can be used to verify whether a mechanism satisfies a differential privacy guarantee. We also show how it can be applied directly to a QIF-enabled semantics of a sequential programming language [16,17] to verify differential privacy. Finally we describe how a QIF-enabled interpreter Kuifje [15] is able to verify experimentally that sequential programs satisfy differentially private properties.

In Sect. 2 we review the fundamentals of QIF, and in Sect. 3 we show how to express a the notion of differential privacy as an adversarial scenario. In Sect. 4 we recall how to use the basic QIF ideas in a QIF-enabled program semantics and illustrate how to use it to verify a small example based on the familiar random-response protocol of Warner [21].

2   Review of Quantitative Information Flow

The informal idea of a secret is that it is something about which there is some uncertainty, and the greater the uncertainty the more difficult it is to discover exactly what the secret is. For example, the name of one's first primary school teacher might not be generally known, but if the gender of the teacher is leaked, then it might rule out some possible names and make others more likely. Similarly, when some information about a secret becomes available to an observer (often referred to as an adversary) the uncertainty is reduced, and it becomes easier to guess its value. If that happens, we say that information (about the secret) has leaked, or equivalently that information flow has occurred.

Quantitative Information Flow (QIF) makes this intuition mathematically precise. Given a range of possible secret values of (finite) type $\mathcal{X}$, let $\mathbb{D}\mathcal{X}$ be the space of probability distributions over $\mathcal{X}$. We model a secret as a probability distribution of type $\mathbb{D}\mathcal{X}$, because it ascribes "probabilistic uncertainty" to the secret's exact value. Given $\pi: \mathbb{D}\mathcal{X}$ we write π_x for the probability that π assigns to $x: \mathcal{X}$ with the idea that the more likely it is that the real value is some specific x then the closer π_x will be to 1. Normally the uniform distribution over $\mathcal{X}$ models a secret which with equal likelihood could take any one of the possible values drawn from its type and we might say that, beyond the existence of the secret, nothing else is known. There could, of course, be many reasons for using some other distribution, for example if the secret was the height of an individual then a normal distribution might be more realistic. In any case, once we have a secret, we are interested in analysing whether an algorithm, or protocol, that uses it might leak some information about it. To do this we define a measure for uncertainty, and use it to compare the uncertainty of the secret before and after executing the algorithm. If we find that the two measurements are different then we can say that there has been an information leak.

The original QIF analyses of information leaks in computer systems used Shannon entropy [18] to measure uncertainty because it captures the idea that more uncertainty implies "more secrecy", and indeed the uniform distribution corresponds to maximum Shannon entropy (corresponding to maximum "Shannon uncertainty"). More recent treatments have shown however that Shannon entropy is not the best way to measure uncertainty in security contexts because it does not necessarily model scenarios relevant to the goals of the adversary. In particular there are some circumstances where a Shannon analysis gives a more favourable assessment of security than is actually warranted if the adversary's motivation is taken into account [19].

Alvim et al. [5] proposed a more general notion of uncertainty based on "gain functions". Here we shall use its dual formulation namely *loss functions*. A *loss function* measures a secret's uncertainty according to how it affects an adversary's actions within a given scenario. We write $\mathcal{W}$ for a (usually finite) set of actions available to an adversary corresponding to an "attack scenario" where the adversary tries to guess something (e.g. some property) about the secret. For a given secret $x\colon \mathcal{X}$ an adversary's choice of $w\colon \mathcal{W}$ results in the adversary losing something beneficial to his objective[1]. This loss can vary depending on the adversary's choice (w) and the exact value of the secret (x). The more effective is the adversary's choice in how to act, the more he is able to overcome any uncertainty concerning the secret's value thereby losing less compared to his losses in the same scenario but without the benefit of the leaked information.

Definition 1. *Given a type $\mathcal{X}$ of secrets, a* loss function $\ell\colon \mathcal{W}\times\mathcal{X} \to \mathbb{R}$ *is a real-valued function such that $\ell(w,x)$ determines the loss to an adversary if he chooses w and the secret is x.*

A simple example of a loss function is given by br, where $\mathcal{W}:=\mathcal{X}$, and

$$\mathsf{br}(x,x') \quad := \quad 0 \ \ if \ \ x=x' \ \ else \ \ 1. \tag{1}$$

For this scenario, the cost to the adversary if he correctly guesses the value of a secret is 0, but 1 if he guesses incorrectly. Elsewhere the utility and expressivity of loss functions for measuring various attack scenarios relevant to security have been explored in more detail [4,5]. Given a loss function we define the *uncertainty* of a secret in $\mathbb{D}\mathcal{X}$ relative to the scenario it describes: it is the minimum average loss to an adversary.

Definition 2. *Let $\ell\colon \mathcal{W}\times\mathcal{X} \to \mathbb{R}$ be a loss function, and $\pi\colon \mathbb{D}\mathcal{X}$ be a secret. The uncertainty $U_\ell[\pi]$ of the secret wrt. ℓ is:*

$$U_\ell[\pi] \quad := \quad \min_{w\in\mathcal{W}} \sum_{x\in\mathcal{X}} \ell(w,x)\times\pi_x.$$

---

[1] Alvim et al. explained this as a gain to benefit the adversary; couching the interpretation as losses is mathematically equivalent but the formulation as losses turns out to be more convenient for reasoning about programs [17].

For a secret $\pi: \mathbb{D}\mathcal{X}$, the uncertainty wrt. br in particular is $U_{\mathsf{br}}[\pi]:= 1 - \max_{x:\,\mathcal{X}} \pi_x$, i.e. the complement of the maximum probability assigned by π to possible values of x. The adversary's best strategy for minimising his loss would therefore be to choose the value x that corresponds to the maximum probability under π.

A *mechanism* is an abstract model of a protocol or algorithm that uses secrets. As the mechanism executes we assume that there are a number of observables that can depend on the actual value of the secret. We define $\mathcal{Y}$ to be the type for observables. The model of a mechanism now assigns a probability that $y: \mathcal{Y}$ can be observed given that the secret is x. Such observables could be sample timings in a timing analysis in cryptography, for example.

Definition 3. *A mechanism is a* stochastic matrix[2] $C: \mathcal{X} \times \mathcal{Y} \to [0, 1]$. *The value C_{xy} is the probability that y is observed given that the secret is x. Given a (prior) secret $\pi: \mathbb{D}\mathcal{X}$ we write $\pi\rangle C$ for the* joint distribution *over $\mathcal{X} \times \mathcal{Y}$ defined*

$$(\pi\rangle C)_{xy} \quad := \quad \pi_x \times C_{xy}.$$

For each $y: \mathcal{Y}$, the marginal probability *that y is observed is $p_y := \sum_{x:\,\mathcal{X}} (\pi\rangle C)_{xy}$. And for each observable y the corresponding* posterior probability *of the secret is the conditional $\pi|^y : \mathbb{D}\mathcal{X}$ defined $(\pi|^y)_x := (\pi\rangle C)_{xy}/p_y$.[3] (It is undefined if p_y is zero.)*

Now consider the secret space with only two values, $\mathcal{X} := \{\mathsf{c}, \neg\mathsf{c}\}$ and the channel inc given below which produces two observations A and B. If the secret is c then A will be observed with probability $1/4$ and B will be observed with probability $3/4$. Alternatively if the secret is $\neg$c then A will be observed with probability $3/4$ and B will be observed with probability $1/4$.

$$\text{inc}:= \quad \begin{array}{c} \\ \mathsf{c} \\ \neg\mathsf{c} \end{array} \begin{array}{c} \mathsf{A} \quad \mathsf{B} \\ \left(\begin{array}{cc} 1/4 & 3/4 \\ 3/4 & 1/4 \end{array} \right) \end{array} \tag{2}$$

Intuitively, given a prior secret π, the entry $\pi_x \times C_{xy}$ of the joint distribution $\pi\rangle C$ is the probability that the actual secret value is x and the observation is y. This joint distribution contains two pieces of information: the probability p_y of observing y and the corresponding posterior $\pi|^y$ which would then represent the adversary's updated view about the uncertainty of the secret's value. In our example above, if π is the uniform distribution over $\{\mathsf{c}, \neg\mathsf{c}\}$ then $p_A = p_B = 1/2$. On the other hand the posterior $\pi|^A$ assigns a probability of $1/4$ that the secret is c, an event to which $\pi|^B$ assigns a probability of $3/4$. This implies that if A is observed the adversary is likely to decide that the secret is $\neg$c, whereas if he observes B then he will most likely determine that the secret is c. The extent to which the adversary can use the leaked information can be understood by

---

[2] Stochastic means that the rows sum to 1.

[3] We use p_y and $\pi|^y$ for typographical convenience. Notation suited for calculation would need to incorporate C and π.

comparing the uncertainties of the posteriors with the uncertainty of the prior. For example if $U_\ell[\pi|^A]$ is strictly less than $U_\ell[\pi]$ then the adversary is indeed able to use the information leaked by inc to benefit himself within the scenario defined by the loss function ℓ.

More generally if the risk of the posterior decreases wrt. a scenario defined by ℓ, then information about the secret has leaked and the adversary can use it to decrease his loss by changing how he chooses to act. The adversary's average overall loss, taking the observations into account, is defined to be the average posterior uncertainty (i.e. the posterior distribution, weighted according to their respective marginals):

$$U_\ell[\pi\rangle C] := \sum_{y\in\mathcal{Y}} p_y \times U_\ell[\pi|^y] \,, \qquad \text{where } p_y, \ \pi|^y \text{ are defined at Definition 3.} \quad (3)$$

Now that we have Definitions 2 and 3 we can start to investigate whether the information leaked through observations $\mathcal{Y}$ actually have an impact in terms of whether it is useful to an adversary. It is easy to see that for any loss function ℓ, prior π and mechanism C we have that $U_\ell[\pi] \geq U_\ell[\pi\rangle C]$. In fact the greater the difference between the prior and posterior vulnerability, the more the adversary is able to use the leaked information within the scenario defined by ℓ. In a mechanism that leaks no information at all, its prior and posterior vulnerabilities are the same under any scenario.

In our example above, can compare the overall losses without the benefit of inc's leaks and with them as follows. Since $U_{br}[\pi] = 1/2$ and $U_{br}[\pi\rangle\text{inc}] = 1-3/4 = 1/4$, we can see that with the benefit of inc's leaked information the adversary is able to halve his losses (in the Bayes' Risk scenario).

Using the idea of quantifying losses, we can define a robust qualitative comparison between mechanisms. We say that one mechanism M' is more secure than another M exactly when the adversary's losses under M' are always at least those under M in every possible scenario defined by a prior and a loss function.

Definition 4. *Given mechanisms M, M' we say that M' is more secure than M, or $M \sqsubseteq M'$ if for all loss functions ℓ and priors π we have that*

$$U_\ell[\pi\rangle M] \quad \leq \quad U_\ell[\pi\rangle M'].$$

Given the observation above that $U_\ell[\pi] \geq U_\ell[\pi\rangle C]$ we can say (now formally) that the mechanism that releases no information is the most secure amongst all mechanisms.

In the next section we will review how to specialise the above ideas to obtain a QIF formulation of differential privacy which can then be applied directly to verify programs.

3 Differential Privacy as a Problem in QIF

Dwork's original definition of differential privacy [12] relates to databases and protections for individuals whose data might or might not be contained in the database. We generalise the definition for the context of secrets described above.

Given a (privacy) mechanism $\mathcal{M} : \mathcal{X} \to \mathbb{D}\mathcal{Y}$ and $\epsilon > 0$, we say that $\mathcal{M}$ is ϵ-differentially private with respect to secrets x, x' if:

$$\int_{\mathcal{M}.x} \zeta \;\; \leq \;\; e^\epsilon \times \int_{\mathcal{M}.x'} \zeta, \tag{4}$$

where $\zeta : \mathcal{Y} \to \mathbb{R}$ is any (measurable) function, and we write $\int_\gamma \zeta$ for the weighted average of ζ with respect to the distribution $\gamma \in \mathbb{D}\mathcal{Y}$. More general definitions of differential privacy [11] include a metric between secrets which are incorporated in constraints such as (4), so that:

$$\int_{\mathcal{M}.x} \zeta \;\; \leq \;\; e^{\epsilon \times d(x,x')} \times \int_{\mathcal{M}.x'} \zeta \tag{5}$$

must hold, where $d(\cdot, \cdot)$ is a metric on values. Here the metric provides a measure of similarity between alternative values, with a greater divergence between values implying a possible greater variation in the distributions over outputs. In our definitions below we use the simpler (4), but note here that they can easily be extended to include a metric as in (5).[4]

Alvim et al. [3] show that when a mechanism is modelled as a channel the above Definition (4) is equivalent to comparing rows of channels relating to x, x'. In particular (4) applied to a channel M says that M is ϵ-differentially private for x, x' if

$$M_{xy} \leq e^\epsilon M_{x'y} \quad and \quad M_{x'y} \leq e^\epsilon M_{xy} \tag{6}$$

for all $y \in \mathcal{Y}$. Notice that (6) compares two channel rows corresponding to secret values x, x'. It turns out that we can do the same thing using loss functions. Given a pair $v := (v_1, v_2) \in \mathcal{X} \times \mathcal{X}$ we write $\overleftarrow{v}$ for the left component v_1 and $\overrightarrow{v}$ for the right component v_2. We say that a subset of pairs $\mathcal{V} \subseteq \mathcal{X} \times \mathcal{X}$ is *symmetric* and *irreflexive* if whenever $(x, x') \in \mathcal{V}$ then also $(x', x) \in \mathcal{V}$ and $(x, x) \notin \mathcal{V}$ for any x.

Definition 5. *Given are $\epsilon > 0$, and $\mathcal{W} := \mathcal{V} \cup \{\star\}$, where $\mathcal{V} \subseteq \mathcal{X} \times \mathcal{X}$ is symmetric and irreflexive. We define dp_ϵ, the ϵ-differentially private loss function relative to $\mathcal{W}$:*

$$
\begin{aligned}
dp_\epsilon(w, x) &= -1, & \text{if } w \neq \star \;\; \wedge \;\; \overleftarrow{w} = x \\
dp_\epsilon(w, x) &= e^\epsilon, & \text{if } w \neq \star \;\; \wedge \;\; \overrightarrow{w} = x \\
dp_\epsilon(w, x) &= 0, & \text{if } w \neq \star \;\; \wedge \;\; \overleftarrow{w} \neq x \neq \overrightarrow{w} \\
dp_\epsilon(\star, x) &= 0.
\end{aligned}
$$

Note that for $\pi \in \mathbb{D}\mathcal{X}$ we see that $U_{dp_\epsilon}[\pi] = \min_{x \neq x'}(\pi_x \times e^\epsilon - \pi_{x'}) \min 0$, where the minimisation is over the relevant pairs (x, x') defined by $\mathcal{V}$. This means that if $U_{dp_\epsilon}[\pi] \geq 0$ then for each $x \neq x'$ we must have that $\pi_x \times e^\epsilon - \pi_{x'} \geq 0$,

---

[4] The revised definition would change the second line of Definition 5 to be

$$dp_\epsilon(w, x) \;\; = \;\; e^{\epsilon \times d(\overleftarrow{w}, \overrightarrow{w})}, \quad \text{if } w \neq \star \;\; \wedge \;\; \overrightarrow{w} = x.$$

which is reminiscent of (4). It turns out that this idea can indeed be applied to privacy, as follows.

Theorem 1. *Given are $\epsilon > 0$, and M a mechanism interpreted as a channel, and let υ be the uniform distribution in $\mathbb{D}\mathcal{X}$. Then M satisfies ϵ-differential privacy if and only if*

$$U_{dp_\epsilon}[\upsilon \rangle M] = 0.$$

Proof. It is clear that $U_{dp_\epsilon}[\upsilon \rangle M] \leq 0$, since the adversary is always able to choose action $\star$ for a loss of zero to the adversary. If it turns out that $U_{dp_\epsilon}[\upsilon \rangle M] < 0$, it implies by (3) that there is some observation y such that the adversary can choose some $w \in \mathcal{V}$ that gives an average negative loss, i.e. that $U_{dp_\epsilon}[\upsilon | ^y] < 0$ for some observation y. Let $(x, x') = w$ be the action that produces that negative minimum loss for this y. We reason as follows:

$U_{dp_\epsilon}[\upsilon | ^y] < 0$

$\Rightarrow \sum_{x'' \in \mathcal{X}} dp_\epsilon(w, x'') \times M_{x'' y}/|\mathcal{X}| < 0$ "Definition 3 for $\upsilon | ^y$ and choice of w Definition 5"

$\Rightarrow e^\epsilon M_{x' y}/|\mathcal{X}| - M_{xy}/|\mathcal{X}| < 0$, "Definition 5, with $w = (x, x')$"

implying from (6) that M is not differentially private.

On the other hand if $U_{dp_\epsilon}[\upsilon \rangle M] \geq 0$, it must mean that $e^\epsilon M_{x'y}/|\mathcal{X}| - M_{xy}/|\mathcal{X}| \geq 0$ for all choices of x, x', y and so M is ϵ-differentially private.

A simple corollary is that any mechanisms that are more secure than some ϵ-differentially private mechanism M, must also be ϵ-differentially private.

Lemma 1. *If M, M' are two mechanisms and $M \sqsubseteq M'$, then if M is ϵ-differentially private, so is M'.*

Proof. We reason as follows:

$U_{dp_\epsilon}[\upsilon \rangle M']$

$\geq U_{dp_\epsilon}[\upsilon \rangle M]$ "$M \sqsubseteq M'$, Definition 4"

≥ 0, "Theorem 1 for M"

implying that M' is ϵ-differentially private, also by Theorem 1.

Observe that when M fails to be ϵ-differentially private it is because the adversary is able to reason that the secret is more likely to be one value rather than another by an amount distinguishable by e^ϵ.

Recall the mechanism `inc` from (2). Now from Definition 5 and Theorem 1 we see that `inc` is $\log 3$ differentially private[5] but not $\log 2$ differentially private, since

$$U_{dp_{\log 2}}[\upsilon \rangle \text{inc}] \quad < \quad 0 \quad \leq \quad U_{dp_{\log 3}}[\upsilon \rangle \text{inc}].$$

Next we prove the familiar additive law for differentially-private mechanisms. Recall that the additive law determines that if the secret is accessed first by M and then by M' then the combined access represents a mechanism with

---

[5] We use logs base e throughout.

(differential privacy) parameter the sum of those of M and M'. From (3) we can see that $U_\ell[v\rangle M]$ is determined by the posteriors, and Theorem 1 teaches us that whether or not a mechanism satisfies a differentially private property is therefore determined by the "unpredictability" of its posteriors, defined next.

Definition 6. *Let π be a (prior/posterior) distribution in $\mathbb{D}\mathcal{X}$, and let $\epsilon > 0$. We say that π is dp_ϵ-unpredictable if $U_{dp_\epsilon}[\pi] \geq 0$.*

The uniform distribution v of the whole type is dp_0-unpredictable, and a consequence of Theorem 1 is that a mechanism is ϵ-differentially private if and only if all posteriors in $u\rangle M$ are dp_ϵ-unpredictable. In cases where the prior π is known, and it is not uniform, we can see that unpredictability of the posteriors $\pi\rangle M$ are bounded by π's unpredictability and the ϵ-privacy of M.

Lemma 2. *Let $\pi \in \mathbb{D}\mathcal{X}$ be dp_ϵ-unpredictable, and let M be ϵ'-differentially private. Then $U_{dp_{\epsilon+\epsilon'}}[\pi\rangle M] = 0$.*

Proof. (Sketch.) We observe first that by assumption we have that for (relevant) $x, x' \in \mathcal{X}$ and any $y \in \mathcal{Y}$, we know that $\pi_x - e^\epsilon \pi_{x'} \geq 0$ and $M_{xy} - e^{\epsilon'} M_{x'y} \geq 0$. Rearranging, we have:

$$\pi_x \geq e^\epsilon \pi_{x'} \wedge M_{xy} \geq e^{\epsilon'} M_{x'y}$$
$$\Rightarrow \quad \pi_x \times M_{xy} \geq e^{\epsilon+\epsilon'} \pi_{x'} \times M_{x'y} , \qquad\qquad \text{"arithmetic"}$$

from which we deduce that $\pi_x \times M_{xy} - e^{\epsilon+\epsilon'} \pi_{x'} \times M_{x'y} \geq 0$. This implies that $U_{dp_{\epsilon+\epsilon'}}[\pi|^y] = 0$ for the posterior $\pi|^y$. Hence by (3) we must have $U_{dp_{\epsilon+\epsilon'}}[\pi\rangle M] = 0$ as well.

For the composition of two differentially private mechanisms, if the posteriors of the composition written $(v\rangle(M; M'))$ are formed from the posteriors of $(v|^y\rangle M')$, where $v|^y$ is any posterior of $(v\rangle M)$, then it follows that the unpredictability of all the posteriors $(v\rangle(M; M'))$ are determined by Lemma 2. In fact we shall see in our semantics for programming language this is case (see Section 4), thus for such a composition we have the following additive law.

Corollary 1. *Let M be ϵ-differentially private, and M' be ϵ'-differentially private. The composition $M; M'$ is $\epsilon+\epsilon'$-differentially private.*

Proof. (Sketch.) This follows if all posteriors of $(v\rangle(M; M'))$ are $dp_{\epsilon+\epsilon'}$-unpredictable. But each such posterior is exactly one of the posteriors of $v|^y\rangle M'$ for some posterior $v|^y$ of $(v\rangle M)$ (see discussion above). Since M is ϵ-differentially private we have that $v|^y$ must be dp_ϵ-unpredictable; therefore by Lemma 2 it must be that all posteriors of $(v|^y\rangle M')$ are $dp_{\epsilon+\epsilon'}$-unpredictable since M' is ϵ'-differentially private.

In the remainder of the paper we show how to apply these ideas to the verification of programs that implement differential privacy.

4 QIF in Programming Languages

Elsewhere [16] we introduced a probabilistic semantics applicable to a small sequential programming language. It embeds QIF ideas within a probabilistic semantics based on the well known probability monad [14].

4.1 The Probabilistic Monad for Information Flow

Standard models of (sequential) probabilistic programs are normally based on Markov Processes with type $\mathcal{A} \to \mathbb{D}\mathcal{A}$. In this sense programs can be thought of as mapping a base type $\mathcal{A}$ to a probability distribution (also) over type $\mathcal{A}$. In QIF however, as has been noted, the mathematical essentials for understanding information flows are priors, posteriors and marginals. Setting $\mathcal{A}$ to $\mathbb{D}\mathcal{X}$ that gives the type of a QIF-enabled model for programs as $\mathbb{D}\mathcal{X} \to \mathbb{D}(\mathbb{D}\mathcal{X})$, or $\mathbb{D}\mathcal{X} \to \mathbb{D}^2\mathcal{X}$.

We call an object of type $\mathbb{D}^2\mathcal{X}$ a *hyper-distribution* over $\mathcal{X}$. It turns out that hyper-distributions exactly match the structure of posteriors and marginals discussed above. Recall the mechanism inc described at (2) and that the observations labelled A and B both occurred with probability $1/2$ (in the given scenario of a uniform prior) with corresponding posteriors $\pi|^A$ and $\pi|^B$. Formatted as a hyper-distribution, this scenario can be presented as:

$$\frac{1}{2}(\pi|^A) \quad \oplus \quad \frac{1}{2}(\pi|^B), \tag{7}$$

where we use the operator $\oplus$ to indicate addition at the level of $\mathbb{D}\mathcal{X}$ considered as a "vector space", so that a hyper-distribution is a weighted $\oplus$-sum of posteriors considered as individual (1-summing) vectors.

In (7) the outer distribution corresponds to the marginal and the inner distributions corresponds to posteriors. Moreover for a hyper-distribution $\Delta \in \mathbb{D}^2\mathcal{X}$, we write Δ_δ for the outer probability corresponding to inner δ; we can therefore define the average uncertainty relative to Δ as:

$$U_\ell(\Delta) \quad := \quad \sum_\delta U_\ell[\delta] \times \Delta_\delta.$$

If we let $[\pi\rangle M]$ be formatted as a hyper-distribution as sketched above, we can see clearly that $U_\ell[\pi\rangle M]$ returns exactly the same value as (3) for $\pi\rangle M$ as a joint distribution, showing that the average posterior uncertainty does not depend on the names of the observations, but only on how a mechanism determines marginals and posteriors [5,6]. With this in mind we can define a QIF-enabled semantic space.

Definition 7 ([16,17]). *Let $\mathcal{X}$ be a (finite) state space. The space of programs is defined to be the set of functions from priors to hyper-distributions $\mathbb{D}\mathcal{X} \to \mathbb{D}^2\mathcal{X}$. If $P, P' : \mathbb{D}\mathcal{X} \to \mathbb{D}^2\mathcal{X}$ are programs then we say that $P \sqsubseteq P'$ if $U_\ell(P.\pi) \leq U_\ell(P'.\pi)$ for all loss functions ℓ and priors π.*

Once a program is modelled as a function $\mathbb{D}\mathcal{X} \rightarrow \mathbb{D}^2\mathcal{X}$, it turns out that a standard Giry Monadic setting provides the basic functionality for sequencing and assignments. We summarise the semantics for three important operators here, and refer elsewhere for full details [16]. Recall the Giry Monad defined by the triple $(\mathbb{D}, \eta, \mathsf{avg})$, where the type constructor $\mathbb{D}$ is a functor, η maps an object of type $\mathcal{A}$ to a point distribution in $\mathbb{D}\mathcal{A}$ and $\mathsf{avg} : \mathbb{D}^2\mathcal{A} \rightarrow \mathbb{D}\mathcal{A}$ takes the weighted average of a hyper-distribution, defined

$$(\mathsf{avg}.\Delta)_a \quad := \quad \sum_{\delta \in \mathbb{D}\mathcal{X}} \Delta_\delta \times \delta_a.$$

Here we use $+$ and $\sum$ to mean the normal summation between numbers.

We can interpret a programming language in terms of Definition 7 as follows, where we use $[\![\cdot]\!]$ to map a program fragment to a function $\mathbb{D}\mathcal{X} \rightarrow \mathbb{D}^2\mathcal{X}$.

1. **Assignment.** Let $f : \mathcal{X} \rightarrow \mathbb{D}\mathcal{X}$ be a function that maps states in $\mathcal{X}$ to distributions over states in $\mathcal{X}$.[6]

$$[\![\mathtt{x}:=\mathtt{f}(\mathtt{x})]\!].\pi \quad := \quad (\eta \circ \mathsf{avg} \circ \mathbb{D}f).\pi.$$

2. **Sequence.** Let P, Q be program fragments.

$$[\![P; Q]\!].\pi \quad := \quad (\mathsf{avg} \circ \mathbb{D}[\![Q]\!] \circ [\![P]\!]).\pi.$$

3. **Print statement.** Let g be a function from $\mathcal{X}$ to $\mathcal{Y}$.

$$[\![\mathtt{Print}\ g]\!].\pi \quad := \quad \bigoplus_y p_y(\pi|^y),$$

where $p_y := ((\mathbb{D}g).\pi)_y$, and $\pi|^y$ is the posterior probability distribution, given that y is an output of g, and $\oplus$ is the summation over 1-summing vectors described above.

The assignment statement is used to assign a value to a variable x according to a distribution, where informally we assume that the value of the variable x is value $\mathtt{x} \in \mathcal{X}$. We use the unit of the Giry Monad to produce a point hyper-distribution. Sequence is defined in the standard monadic manner, by first applying $[\![P]\!]$ to the input and then $\mathbb{D}[\![Q]\!]$ is applied to $[\![P]\!]$'s output hyper-distribution, with a final application of avg applied to amalgamate equivalent posteriors. The action of $\mathbb{D}[\![Q]\!]$ is to apply $[\![Q]\!]$ to each of the posteriors in the output of $[\![P]\!]$, thus satisfying the condition for Corollary 1. Finally, notice that the **Print** statement acts like a channel but without creating the joint distribution between the observables and the prior. Instead it formats the (equivalent) result directly as a hyper-distribution. A full description of the QIF-aware program semantics is detailed elsewhere [16].

---

[6] This is essentially a Markov update of the state.

5   Example: Implementing Plausible Deniability

Consider the small program in Fig. 1 which forms the basis for a random-response program. A participant in a survey is asked to input a response *resp* to a yes/no question. If they are concerned about the security of the method of collection, in particular whether their answer will be leaked, they might decline to participate. In order to encourage participation, Warner [21], devised a random response protocol which gives participants "plausible deniability" in regards to their responses, if the results of the survey are published.

In Fig. 1 we see the details of the algorithm `SingleRespondent` implemented as a sequential program. The participant's answer is stored in a variable *resp* (1 for "yes" and 0 for "no"). The variable *count* is used to store and then publish the result of the data collection. First a random result is stored in a variable *coin*, where we use "$0[1/2]1$" to mean that the value is randomised between 0 or 1, using an unbiased "coin toss". Next the variable *count* is updated, and again the update is randomised between either incrementing *count* with the value stored previously in *coin*, or with the participant's choice *resp*. The last act is then to publish the final value of *count*.

A participant worried about the collection procedure might wonder whether the data collected is an accurate recording of their real response *resp*. The answer is "it depends", in the sense that the final value of *count* could be either 1 or 0 whatever the value of *resp*, with the difference between the initial values of *resp* observed through the probabilities ascribed to the possible values of *count* observed. However that difference is bounded by a differentially private guarantee. This fact can be proven by showing that `SingleRespondent` is $\log 3$ differentially private with respect to the two conditions defined by *resp*.

A traditional QIF analysis would construct an explicit channel for the random response protocol to describe how information about the secret (in this case *resp*) can leak. The result of this exercise turns out to be the the of the channel inc at (2). From, this we can initialise *resp* to be either 0 or 1 with probability 1/2 each; finally we can compute $U_{dp_{\log 3}}[\upsilon\rangle\text{inc}]$ and observe that it is 0.

An alternative approach is to interpret `SingleRespondent` directly in the QIF semantics above. First we define a mechanism over the secret *resp* as follows. Let $\delta \in \mathbb{D}\{0,1\}$. Define a mechanism $\mathcal{M} : \mathbb{D}\mathcal{X} \to \mathbb{D}^2\mathcal{X}^7$

$$\mathcal{M}.\delta \quad := \quad [\![\text{SingleRespondent}]\!].\delta.$$

Now we examine $U_{dp_{\log 3}}(\mathcal{M}.\upsilon) = 0$, showing similarly that the difference in *resp* = 0 and *resp* = 1, is that for any observation of *count*, the corresponding posteriors differ in probability according to the multiplicative contstraint $e^{\log 3} = 3$.

---

[7] Strictly speaking the state is determined by the values of all the program variables. However the only secret that we worry about for this example is the value of *resp*. These details can all be handled by adjusting the definition of dp_ϵ.

```
// Assume resp is either 0 or 1 initially

count:= 0;
        coin:= 0 [1/2] 1;          // Random response
        count:= (count + coin
                [1/2]              // Randomly include resp or not
                count + resp);
Print count;      // Announce the approximate count
```

The value resp is either added to the variable count or not; in the case that it is not included, a random response *coin* for that participant is delivered instead.

Fig. 1. Randomised response, `SingleRespondent`

5.1 Random Response Protocol

An implementation of a full random response protocol is set out in Fig. 2. For N participants, each participant executes the single response protocol defined at Fig. 1.

```
// Assume resp is an array of length N set to
// participants' responses, to a survey question.
i := 0;
count:= 0;
while (i<N) {
        coin:= 0 [1/2] 1;          // Random response
        count:= (count + coin
                [1/2]              // Randomly include participant i or not
                count + resp[i]);
        i++;
}
Print count;    // Announce the approximate count
```

On each iteration, the participant i is randomly selected for inclusion in the count or not. In the case that the participant's true response *resp[i]* is not included, a random response *coin* for that participant is delivered instead.

Fig. 2. Randomised response with N participants

The privacy for each individual is whether their specific response is private. For that we can use the results above to show that their individual response is protected through Fig. 1 considered as a log 3 differentially private mechanism. Moreover within the context of the other responses, we are able to show that the other respondents do not affect that privacy level. For example, for the final participant in Fig. 2, the other participants' responses reveals nothing about the final participant's response, thus the protocol is equivalent to $R; R'$ where R corresponds to the collection of the first $N-1$ participants responses and R to the collection of the final participant's response. We have that R is 0-differentially private with respect to the final participant's response and that R' is log 3-differentially private. Hence by the additive law Corollary 1 we have that the full random response protocol in Fig. 2 is also log 3-differentially private (for that participant). This argument can be generalised to apply to any participant taking part in the random response.

6   Experiment and Exploration

The experiments described above were carried out using the tool Kuifje [10, 15] which interprets a small programming language in terms of the QIF semantics alluded to above. Kuifje supports the usual programming constructs (assignment, sequencing, conditionals and loops) but crucially it takes into account information flows consistent with QIF. In particular the `Print` statements used in our examples correspond exactly to the observations that an adversary could make during program execution. This allows a direct model for eg. known side channels that potentially expose partially computation traces during program execution.

The basic assumption built into the semantics of Kuifje is that no variable can be observed unless revealed fully or partially through a `Print` statement. For example `Print x` would print the value of variable x and so reveal it completely at that point of execution, but `Print(x>0)` would reveal only whether x is strictly positive or not. As usual, we also assume that the adversary knows the program code.

Kuifje is implemented in Haskell and makes extensive use of the Giry monad [14] for managing the prior, posterior and marginal probabilities in the form of "hyper-distributions".

In order to use Kuifje to analyse Figs. 1 and 2, we assume a uniform input for $resp$ ($resp[i]$). Kuifje then generates the hyper-distribution output, which can then be evaluated against dp_ϵ for a chosen $\epsilon > 0$. Since we are only interested in a specific response, we can assume that the secret is determined by $resp(resp[i])$. We can then adjust the details of dp_ϵ by setting $\mathcal{V}$ to be sensitive only to different values of $resp$ ($resp[i]$).

Finally, we note that since Kuifje computes the output hyper-distribution, other properties of Figs. 1 and 2 can also be explored, such as the Bayes Risk of the $resp$, and the true average number of "yes" respondents.

7   Related Work

Differential privacy was proposed by Dwork [12] to provide mechanisms that satisfy strong privacy guarantees for individuals. Alvim et al. [2] were the first to explain the relationship between information-flow channels and differential privacy, and to investigate leakage properties of differentially-private mechanisms modelled as channels [1].

There has been recent interest in verification techniques for proving differential-privacy properties, with the intention of providing programmers with the capability to certify privacy guarantees, and to support reasoning. Wang et al. have [20] proposed a technique called "Shadow execution" to enable the verification of implementations of differentially private algorithms using traditional program logics. Adaptations of Hoare Logic have been proposed [7] based on reasoning about product programs. Bathe et al. [8] use a technique based on probabilistic couplings to enable differential privacy to be treated as a program-verification problem. More generally Barthe et al. [9] describe three verification and programming-language techniques for certifying that programs satisfy the more general (ϵ, γ) differential privacy guarantees, as in:

$$\int_{\mathcal{M}.x} \zeta \;\leq\; e^{\epsilon} \times \int_{\mathcal{M}.x'} \zeta \;+\; \gamma. \tag{8}$$

All of these techniques are supported by automation. Zhang and Kifer [22] use a relational type system to decompose privacy verification into two parts, one for relational reasoning and the other to compute the "privacy budget". A privacy budget is related to the fact that every query to a database, even one protected by differential privacy, leaks some information about the data. A privacy budget denotes an upper limit on information leakage that is insufficient to identify individuals. Finally, Ebadi and Sands [13] have implemented a system based similarly on reasoning rules to keep track of the privacy budget related to datasets.

8   Conclusions

We have shown how to use a loss function combined with a QIF-enabled programming semantics to verify privacy properties for programs. We have used the interpreter Kuifje to enable experimental investigation of differential privacy for small sequential programs.

We described the simplest and most restrictive version of differential privacy (4), but note that the weaker (ϵ, γ) notion of differential privacy can also be modelled using loss functions. To see this, we note that if M is not ϵ-differentially private for some particular $x, x' \in \mathcal{X}$, we must have:

$$\sum_{y \in \mathcal{Y}} (M_{x'y}e^{\epsilon} - M_{xy}) \min 0 \;<\; 0. \tag{9}$$

In fact each individual summand is non-zero exactly when $M_{x'y}/M_{xy}$ can be distinguished by more than the "allowed" e^{ϵ} multiplier. Observe that the sum of those summands is equal to some value $-\gamma'$, and if it is at least $-\gamma$ in (8) then M is (ϵ, γ) differentially private. We can formalise this observation using loss functions as follows.

As in Definition 5 we formulate a loss function dp_{ϵ}^*, this time letting $\mathcal{V} := \{(x, x'), \star\}$. If we let υ be the uniform distribution over x, x', we see that $U_{dp_{\epsilon^*}}[\upsilon \rangle M]$ is equal to half the sum in (9). Thus we can conclude that M is (ϵ, γ) differentially private if $U_{dp_{\epsilon^*}}[\upsilon \rangle M] \geq -\gamma/2$ for all such pairs x, x'. More investigation is required to determine whether this provides a useful characterisation.

Finally we observe that a QIF model is rich enough to capture many other other kinds of risks related to information flow. For example a participant in the random response survey might be more interested in whether their response can be determined with some likelihood, and the response gatherer might be interested in how the output *count* is related to the real "yes" count. Both of these properties can be analysed using loss functions and the QIF interpretation [15, 16].

Acknowledgements. I thank Tom Schrijvers for having the idea of embedding these ideas in Haskell, based on Carroll Morgan's talk at IFIP WG2.1 in Vermont, and for carrying it out to produce the tool Kuifje. Together with Jeremy Gibbons all four of us wrote the first paper devoted to it [15]. (It was Jeremy who suggested the name "Kuifje", the Dutch name for TinTin — and hence his "QIF".)

References

1. Alvim, M.S., Andrés, M.E., Chatzikokolakis, K., Degano, P., Palamidessi, C.: On the information leakage of differentially-private mechanisms. J. Comput. Secur. **23**(4), 427–469 (2015)
2. Alvim, M.S., Andrés, M.E., Chatzikokolakis, K., Palamidessi, C.: On the relation between differential privacy and quantitative information flow. In: Aceto, L., Henzinger, M., Sgall, J. (eds.) ICALP 2011. LNCS, vol. 6756, pp. 60–76. Springer, Heidelberg (2011). https://doi.org/10.1007/978-3-642-22012-8_4
3. Alvim, M.S., Chatzikokolakis, K., Degano, P., Palamidessi, C.: Differential privacy versus quantitative information flow. CoRR, abs/1012.4250 (2010)
4. Alvim, M.S., Chatzikokolakis, K., McIver, A., Morgan, C., Palamidessi, C., Smith, G.: Additive and multiplicative notions of leakage, and their capacities. In: IEEE 27th Computer Security Foundations Symposium, CSF 2014, Vienna, Austria, 19–22 July 2014, pp. 308–322. IEEE (2014)
5. Alvim, M.S., Chatzikokolakis, K., Palamidessi, C., Smith, G.: Measuring information leakage using generalized gain functions. In: Proceedings 25th IEEE Computer Security Foundations Symposium, CSF 2012, pp. 265–279, June 2012
6. Alvim, M.S., Scedrov, A., Schneider, F.B.: When not all bits are equal: worth-based information flow. In: Abadi, M., Kremer, S. (eds.) POST 2014. LNCS, vol. 8414, pp. 120–139. Springer, Heidelberg (2014). https://doi.org/10.1007/978-3-642-54792-8_7
7. Barthe, G., Gaboardi, M., Arias, E.J.G., Hsu, J., Kunz, C., Strub, P.-Y.: Proving differential privacy in Hoare logic. In: IEEE 27th Computer Security Foundations Symposium, CSF 2014, Vienna, Austria, 19–22 July 2014, pp. 411–424 (2014)
8. Barthe, G., Gaboardi, M., Grégoire, B., Hsu, J., Strub, P.-Y.: Proving differential privacy via probabilistic couplings. In: Proceedings of the 31st Annual ACM/IEEE Symposium on Logic in Computer Science, pp. 749–758 (2016)
9. Barthe, G., Gaboardi, M., Hsu, J., Pierce, B.: Programming language techniques for differential privacy. ACM SIGLOG News **3**(1), 34–53 (2016)
10. Bognar, M., Schrijvers, T.. Kuifje: a prototype for a quantitative information flow aware programming language. https://github.com/martonbognar/kuifje
11. Chatzikokolakis, K., Andrés, M.E., Bordenabe, N.E., Palamidessi, C.: Broadening the scope of differential privacy using metrics. In: De Cristofaro, E., Wright, M. (eds.) PETS 2013. LNCS, vol. 7981, pp. 82–102. Springer, Heidelberg (2013). https://doi.org/10.1007/978-3-642-39077-7_5

12. Dwork, C.: Differential privacy. In: Bugliesi, M., Preneel, B., Sassone, V., Wegener, I. (eds.) ICALP 2006. LNCS, vol. 4052, pp. 1–12. Springer, Heidelberg (2006). https://doi.org/10.1007/11787006_1
13. Ebadi, H., Sands, D.: Featherweight PINQ. J. Priv. Secur. **7**(2) (2017)
14. Giry, M.: A categorical approach to probability theory. In: Banaschewski, B. (ed.) Categorical Aspects of Topology and Analysis. LNM, vol. 915, pp. 68–85. Springer, Heidelberg (1982). https://doi.org/10.1007/BFb0092872
15. Gibbons, C.M.J., Mciver, A., Schrijvers, T.: Quantitative information flow with monads in haskell. In: Foundations of Probabilistic Programming. CUP (2019, to appear)
16. McIver, A., Meinicke, L., Morgan, C.: Compositional closure for Bayes risk in probabilistic noninterference. In: Abramsky, S., Gavoille, C., Kirchner, C., Meyer auf der Heide, F., Spirakis, P.G. (eds.) ICALP 2010. LNCS, vol. 6199, pp. 223–235. Springer, Heidelberg (2010). https://doi.org/10.1007/978-3-642-14162-1_19
17. McIver, A., Morgan, C., Rabehaja, T.: Abstract hidden Markov models: a monadic account of quantitative information flow. In: Proceedings LiCS 2015 (2015)
18. Shannon, C.E.: A mathematical theory of communication. Bell Syst. Tech. J. **27**(379–423), 623–656 (1948)
19. Smith, G.: On the foundations of quantitative information flow. In: de Alfaro, L. (ed.) FoSSaCS 2009. LNCS, vol. 5504, pp. 288–302. Springer, Heidelberg (2009). https://doi.org/10.1007/978-3-642-00596-1_21
20. Wang, Y., Ding, Z., Wang, G., Kifer, D., Zhang, D.: Proving differential privacy with shadow execution. In: Proceedings of the 40th ACM SIGPLAN Conference on Programming Language Design and Implementation, PLDI 2019, New York, NY, USA, pp. 655–669. ACM (2019)
21. Warner, S.L.: Randomized response: a survey technique for eliminating evasive answer Bias. J. Am. Stat. Assoc. **60**, 63–69 (1965)
22. Zhang, D., Kifer, D.: Lightdp: towards automating differential privacy proofs. In: Proceedings of Principles of Programming Languages, pp. 1–17 (2017)

On Strings in Software Model Checking

Hossein Hojjat[1], Philipp Rümmer[2(✉)], and Ali Shamakhi[1]

[1] University of Tehran, Tehran, Iran
{hojjat,ali.shamakhi}@ut.ac.ir
[2] Uppsala University, Uppsala, Sweden
philipp.ruemmer@it.uu.se

Abstract. Strings represent one of the most common and most intricate data-types found in software programs, with correct string processing often being a decisive factor for correctness and security properties. This has led to a wide range of recent research results on how to analyse programs operating on strings, using methods like testing, fuzzing, symbolic execution, abstract interpretation, or model checking, and, increasingly, support for strings is also added to constraint solvers and SMT solvers. In this paper, we focus on the verification of software programs with strings using model checking. We give a survey of the existing approaches to handle strings in this context, and propose methods based on algebraic data-types, Craig interpolation, and automata learning.

1 Introduction

The analysis of program operating on strings has received a lot of attention in the past years, motivated by the observation that correct string handling is crucial to achieve functional correctness, and that even innocent-looking mistakes related to strings (for instance, incorrect input validation or sanitisation) can open severe security vulnerabilities in programs [10]. In this paper, we consider the analysis of software programs with the help of model checking, and provide a survey of the methods used in model checkers to handle strings. We observe that several bounded model checkers and tools for symbolic execution use "native" methods for solving string constraints, in particular inbuilt string support in SMT solvers, whereas unbounded model checkers tend to represent strings using data-types like arrays and stay closer to the runtime implementation of strings. We then outline ongoing work to handle strings natively in the Horn clause-based software model checker JayHorn.

1.1 Strings in Programming Languages

Given a finite, non-empty alphabet Σ, strings are elements of the set Σ^* or finite sequences of characters over Σ. In practice, alphabets are, e.g., ASCII or Unicode. Relevant operations on strings include functions to access individual characters or substrings, to concatenate strings, to split strings, to compute the length of strings or the number of character occurrences, to check membership in

© Springer Nature Switzerland AG 2019
A. W. Lin (Ed.): APLAS 2019, LNCS 11893, pp. 19–30, 2019.
https://doi.org/10.1007/978-3-030-34175-6_2

regular or context-free languages, to replace all or some occurrences of substrings, or more generally transformations like sanitisation or encoding/decoding.

In programming languages, strings are partly given the status of a primitive data-type with inbuilt notation for literals ("..."), but the full set of string operations is typically provided through libraries, such as `string.h` in C, and `java.lang.String` and related classes in Java. The internal representation of strings as a character array is fully exposed in C, but usually hidden in more high-level languages.

Strings are in programs often used to store *data* such as addresses, usernames, or passwords, whose correct processing is critical. Strings can also represent *code,* for instance when interfacing databases (SQL commands) or in the context of the web (JavaScript embedded in HTML), leading to the possibility of injection attacks when a programs fails to correctly isolate code from data [10].

2   Survey of Existing Methods for String Analysis

In this section, we focus on strings in model checking while only touching upon some of the methods in other areas. For a more complete survey of string methods we refer the reader to the recent book [10].

2.1   Bounded Methods

Bounded analysis methods, for instance, bounded model checking or symbolic execution, typically only have to check *satisfiability (SAT)* of constraints extracted from a program, usually testing path feasibility. In our case, such constraints will contain variables ranging over strings. SAT checks on string constraints are at this point supported relatively well by existing constraint and SMT solvers (as a result of extensive research over the past years) and string theories have in particular been added to state-of-the-art SMT solvers like Z3 [16] and CVC4 [7]. There is also a larger number of dedicated string solvers, for instance ABC [6], Hampi [20], Kaluza [37], Norn [3], Ostrich [11], Sloth [26], Trau [1], Z3-str [41]. Scalability to handle real-world constraints and support for more complex string operations (e.g., transduction) are still a concern with the existing solvers, however.

As a representative set of state-of-the-art software model checkers, we survey the tools that participated at SV-COMP 2019 [8], the most recent competition of automatic software verifiers. In the competition, 31 tools participated, of which 27 were verifiers for C and 4 for Java. It is observable that purely bounded analysis is applied by 7 of the C verifiers[1] and 3 of the Java verifiers,[2] while the other tools attempt exhaustive verification without imposing any bound on the number of execution steps (Sect. 2.2).

---

[1] CBMC, CBMC-Path, Map2Check, Pinaka, VeriFuzz, Yogar-CBMC, Yogar-CBMC-Parallel.

[2] JBMC, JPF, SPF.

Following the actual C semantics of strings, the predominant approach applied by the bounded C verifiers is to consider strings as zero-terminated arrays, and rely on decision procedures for the theory of arrays (for instance, via encoding to Boolean SAT) to perform feasibility checks. There exists some initial work in CBMC to target native string solvers, but does not seem to be used in the competition versions.

The situation is different in the bounded Java verifiers, where the symbolic tools use native string solvers to analyse path constraints. JBMC [14] comes with its own string solver that works through an encoding to Boolean SAT, while SPF [36] can use multiple different string solvers as its back-end.

2.2 Unbounded Methods

In addition to SAT checks, unbounded (infinite-state) program verification methods also require artefacts like loop invariants or function summaries, which can be provided manually or be computed automatically. For the latter purpose, a wider range of techniques has been proposed that could be listed here; to get a full picture, we refer to the recent handbook on model checking [13]. A general observation, however, is that strings can be handled only by few of the existing invariant generation methods; in particular, to the best of our knowledge, no interpolation procedures are known for any (relevant) theory of strings.

The few invariant generation methods specifically supporting strings include the randomised search approach in [38], and the SAT-based automata learning approach in [2], which we employ in Sect. 3.3.

Software Model Checking. We survey again the tools that participated at SV-COMP 2019 [8]: 20 tools performing unbounded verification for C programs, and one model checker for unbounded Java verification. Like in the bounded case, most of the C model checkers see strings as character arrays, and execute string operations as code; this means that invariant generation relies on existing methods for the theory of arrays. 2LS encodes data structures (including string) using invariants describing heap configuration [33], PredatorHP models memory using Symbolic Memory Graph (SMG) and defines certain manipulations of zero-terminated strings over SMG [18], and SMACK models the behaviour of `string.h` functions. The handling of strings in the Java model checker JayHorn, an ongoing implementation effort, is discussed in Sect. 3.

Deductive Verification. In deductive verification systems, invariants and method contracts usually have to be provided manually, but their correctness is verified automatically. To be able to handle strings, deductive verification systems include axiomatic models of strings. For instance, in Dafny [31] strings are encoded as sequences, which are in turn mapped to arrays, together with a set of operations modelled using quantified axioms that are heuristically instantiated by the underlying SMT solver. The KeY system [4], a verification tool for Java programs, includes a formalisation of Java strings and the Java string constant pool in terms of algebraic data-types [9]. This formalisation partly inspires the techniques discussed in Sect. 3.2. Like [9], we propose to represent strings using ADTs while targeting the fully-automatic setting of a software model checker, including automatic invariant inference.

Static Analysis and Abstract Interpretation. A number of abstract domains have been proposed to analyse programs with strings, see for instance [10] for an overview. A related approach [12] translates Java programs to (data) flow graphs, extracts context-free grammars characterising the possible strings in the program, and then over-approximates those sets using regular languages.

Dedicated Analysis Methods. Several approaches exist to specifically analyse loops that iterate over or manipulate strings; such methods are usually restricted to loops of a particular syntactic shape, or to loops written in domain-specific languages. Bek is a language and system to write and analyse string sanitisers that internally uses symbolic transducers [27]. An extended version of Bek, named Bex, targets the more general case of string decoders [39]. A summarisation (or acceleration) method for string-manipulating loops is given in [40].

3   Towards String Handling in a Java Model Checker

We now describe ideas and techniques to handle strings natively in an unbounded model checker for Java. The work is inspired by the implementation of JayHorn tool [29], a Java verifier that works by translating Java bytecode to sets of constrained Horn clauses [23].

As observed in the previous section, and as with any other theory in software model checking, one of the main challenges with strings is the inference of inductive invariants. This aspect is particularly pronounced with strings, for which already decidability of SAT checks is sometimes open (depending on the precise set of operations considered [21]), and implementation even of known decision procedures can be hard. Logical methods used in other domains for invariant generation, for instance Craig interpolation [34] or abduction [17], have so far not been carried over for strings, to the best of our knowledge.

We consider two main paradigms to compute invariants in this setting:

- A *reduction-based* approach, in which string constraints are translated to algebraic data-types (ADTs), which can then be handled using known techniques, and are in particular amenable to Craig interpolation [24]. The reduction also requires an encoding of the string operations, which is in our setting done by formulating constrained Horn clauses, i.e., through an operational encoding. This is possible for all computable operations on strings, but does not always make it easy for an ADT solver to discover sufficiently general invariants.
- A *learning-based* approach, which performs an exhaustive search for Craig interpolants (as building blocks of inductive invariants) through SAT-based construction of finite-state automata [2].

Those two approaches have quite complementary properties. Reduction to other theories can in principle support all string operations, and handle the combination of strings with other theories (e.g., integers, arrays, or bit-vectors), but might not lead to useful predicates or invariants. The reduction approach is also similar in flavour to the representation of strings as arrays in existing software model checkers, though considering a different target theory, and using tailor-made operational encodings also of the string operations. Learning and systematic search can find concise predicates that pinpoint the reason why a program behaves correctly, but the approach might be computationally expensive, restricted to invariants of particular syntactic shape, and (depending on the algorithm used) difficult to combine with other theories. In our case, the learning procedure attempts to construct Craig interpolants that are regular expression membership constraints, which means that formulas like equality of two strings cannot be expressed or found.

3.1   Dealing with Implementation Artefacts

As a prerequisite for applying native string solving technology, it is necessary to bridge the gap between the programming language semantics of strings (in Java, the view of strings being instances of the class `java.lang.String`, and the string constant pool [22]) and the algebraic view on strings (strings constituting the set Σ^* of finite sequences over some alphabet Σ). The architecture of JayHorn offers a natural solution for this: deviating from the standard runtime implementation, object references in JayHorn are treated as *tuples* that consist of the object address (an integer), but also include other (immutable) information about an object [28]. For instance, a reference can store the precise dynamic type of the referenced object, the allocation site, constructor parameters, or values of immutable fields. The additional information contained in a reference has the purpose of increasing the expressive power of the class invariants used to represent heap data-structures.

This approach turns out to be particularly useful for boxed data-types like `java.lang.Integer`, since those classes are immutable and their contents do not change after object creation. This means that a reference to an object of `java.lang.Integer` can be defined to store the actual value (the boxed integer number) as well, using the native data-type for integers; since the boxed data can now be retrieved directly from the reference, without having to access any fields of the object, verification with boxed data becomes very similar to the handling of native data-types and local variables.

The same encoding can be used for strings: the reference tuple pointing to a `java.lang.String` object can be defined to contain the actual string contents as one of the components, represented using a native data-type, for instance, an ADT as in Sect. 3.2. Since the semantics of most of the string operations (for instance, `String.equals` and `String.concat`) can be modelled purely in terms of the string contents, this means that programs can then be analysed treating strings as a native data-type, assuming the idealised algebraic semantics of the string stored in the reference tuple.

3.2   Strings as an Algebraic Data-Type

Algebraic data-types (with fully-free constructors) is a theory increasingly supported by Horn solvers, for instance by Eldarica [25], Spacer [30], and a version of VeriMAP [15]. While ADT support in the mentioned solvers is still somewhat limited and an active area of research (e.g., in case of Eldarica, only quantifier-free solutions are computed), ADTs are significantly simpler to handle than a full theory of strings, since methods like Craig interpolation and quantifier elimination are available.[3]

We define the theories of recursive algebraic data types (ADTs) as it is done in [24]. The signature of an ADT is defined by a sequence $\sigma_1, \ldots, \sigma_k$ of sorts and a sequence $f_1, \ldots, f_m$ of constructors. The type of an n-ary constructor is of the form $f_i : \sigma_1 \times \cdots \times \sigma_n \to \sigma_0$. Zero-ary constructors are also called constants. In addition to constructors, formulas over ADTs can use *variables* (with some type from the sorts $\{\sigma_1, \ldots, \sigma_k\}$); *selectors* f_i^j (which extract the jth argument of an f_i-term) and *testers* is_{f_i} (which determine whether a term is an f_i-term).

ADTs enable a natural representation of strings as lists of characters. Here, nil is a constant, cons is a binary constructor, and Character is a sort:

$$\text{String} \ ::= \ \text{nil} \ | \ \text{cons(Character, String)}$$

This representation still leaves a number of choices open; exploration of this space is ongoing work, so that we only discuss the parameters in the scope of this paper, without evaluating the implications experimentally.

Encoding Choice 1: *The character domain.* In our current implementation in JayHorn, the Character is a synonym for the mathematical integers, which are handled well by most Horn solvers. This domain does obviously not model ASCII or Unicode characters accurately, and might lead to spurious verification counterexamples; a more precise encoding could be using bit-vectors or an interval of the integers.

Encoding Choice 2: *The character order.* The encoding of lists leaves open in which order the characters of a string should be stored: starting with the first character or starting with the last (or choosing an order individually for each string variable). The current JayHorn implementation uses the more natural order of storing the first string character as the first element of a list; but given that it is more common in Java programs to *append* to strings, it is quite possible that reverse order would perform better for static analysis.

After choosing the string representation, the Java API string operations have to be defined. One approach for this would be to execute the bytecode implementing the methods, for instance the methods of `java.lang.String`. This would not yield the most efficient definition for the purpose of model checking, however, since the bytecode would assume the internal representation of strings as

---

[3] In this sense, ADTs also have better properties than the theory of arrays.

```
package java.lang;
public class String {
   [...]
   public String concat(String that) { [...] };
   [...]
}
```

Fig. 1. The Java string concatenation method

Table 1. Different Horn encodings of concatenation of two strings

Recursive encoding $\mathcal{H}_{rec}$:
$$C_{rec}(\mathsf{nil}, x, x) \leftarrow true$$ $$C_{rec}(\mathsf{cons}(c, x), y, \mathsf{cons}(c, z)) \leftarrow C_{rec}(x, y, z)$$
Recursive encoding with pre-condition $\mathcal{H}_{prec}$:
$$C_{prec}^{post}(\mathsf{nil}, x, x) \leftarrow C_{prec}^{pre}(\mathsf{nil}, x)$$ $$C_{prec}^{pre}(x, y) \leftarrow C_{prec}^{pre}(\mathsf{cons}(c, x), y)$$ $$C_{prec}^{post}(\mathsf{cons}(c, x), y, \mathsf{cons}(c, z)) \leftarrow C_{prec}^{pre}(\mathsf{cons}(c, x), y) \wedge C_{prec}^{post}(x, y, z)$$
Iterative encoding $\mathcal{H}_{it}$:
$$C_{it}^1(\bar{z}, x, \mathsf{nil}, y) \leftarrow C_{it}^{entry}(\bar{z}, x, y)$$ $$C_{it}^1(\bar{z}, a, \mathsf{cons}(c, b), y) \leftarrow C_{it}^1(\bar{z}, \mathsf{cons}(c, a), b, y)$$ $$C_{it}^2(\bar{z}, b, y) \leftarrow C_{it}^1(\bar{z}, \mathsf{nil}, b, y)$$ $$C_{it}^2(\bar{z}, a, \mathsf{cons}(c, b)) \leftarrow C_{it}^2(\bar{z}, \mathsf{cons}(c, a), b)$$ $$C_{it}^{exit}(\bar{z}, r) \leftarrow C_{it}^2(\bar{z}, \mathsf{nil}, r)$$

character arrays, running counter to the chosen algebraic list representation. In the context of JayHorn, a more efficient path is to encode each string operation using a set of Horn clauses tailored to static analysis. As a case study in the scope of this paper, we consider the method to perform concatenation of two strings (Fig. 1). Other Java string operations can be handled in a similar way.

Encoding Choice 3: *The concatenation function.* Table 1 shows some of the different encodings of the concatenation function as a set of constrained Horn clauses, operating on the ADT string representation: using a total function defined recursively, and represented using a summary predicate C_{rec}; using a partial function defined recursively by a summary predicate C_{prec}^{post} and a domain predicate C_{prec}^{pre}; and using a purely iterative encoding with entry predicate C_{it}^{entry} and exit predicate C_{it}^{exit}.

A clause with a concatenation constraint on natively represented strings,

$$H \leftarrow z = \mathsf{concat}(x, y) \wedge B(\bar{a})$$

can then be translated using the different encodings, leading to three different but equisatisfiable sets of clauses:

$$\{H \leftarrow C_{rec}(x, y, z) \wedge B(\bar{a})\} \cup \mathcal{H}_{rec} \tag{1}$$

$$\{H \leftarrow C_{prec}^{post}(x, y, z) \wedge B(\bar{a}), \ C_{prec}^{pre}(x, y) \leftarrow B(\bar{a})\} \cup \mathcal{H}_{prec} \tag{2}$$

$$\{H \leftarrow C_{it}^{exit}(\bar{a}, z), \ C_{it}^{entry}(\bar{a}, x, y) \leftarrow B(\bar{a})\} \cup \mathcal{H}_{it} \tag{3}$$

In the last encoding $\mathcal{H}_{it}$, the arity of the predicates has to be adjusted so that all variables $\bar{a}$ occurring in the clause body $B(\bar{a})$ can be passed through.

Only experiments can tell which of those encodings performs best in a software model checker. Initial results indicate that the iterative encoding, although it requires the largest number of clauses, might be easiest to handle for existing Horn solvers, probably because only linear clauses are generated.

In cases where the length of the left string x is known to be bounded (and small), it is, of course, most efficient to unwind the recursive/iterative definition of the concatenation function sufficiently often.

Encoding Choice 4: *Clause sharing.* In the iterative version of concatenation, it is always necessary to introduce fresh predicates and clauses $\mathcal{H}_{it}$ for each occurrence of concatenation concat in a program. This is not the case for the recursive versions, however, where the same predicates and clauses could be used for multiple occurrences of concat. Whether such clauses sharing has advantages for Horn solving is so far unclear, however.

Encoding Choice 5: *Ghost data.* In addition to just working with the string contents represented using an ADT, it can be meaningful to also explicitly pass around ghost data obtained by applying some homomorphism to string values. For instance, the *length* of a string is a feature that is frequently useful for invariants; the function that maps a string to its length is a homomorphism of the concatenation function, and the clauses shown in Table 1 can easily be augmented to keep track of string length as well.

3.3   Learning Invariants over Strings

The encoding of strings using ADTs is quite flexible, and can be expected to work well when the correctness of a program can be shown using invariants on the level of ADTs: that means, using quantifier-free formulas that talk about a finite number of characters of the involved strings. Depending on the applied Horn solver, and the encoding choices with respect to ghost data, also invariants are feasible that can be expressed using recursive functions like the string length function.[4] However, ADTs do not suffice for programs that demand more intricate invariants about strings; for instance, the statement that an unbounded string only contains characters in the range a-z.

We propose the use of learning-based interpolation, as defined in [2], to find such more expressive invariants. Interpolation is used by many Horn solvers to construct building blocks for invariants. A *(binary) interpolation problem* is a conjunction of formulas $A[\overline{x}_A, \overline{x}] \wedge B[\overline{x}, \overline{x}_B]$ over disjoint variables $\overline{x}_A$, $\overline{x}_B$ local to A, B and common variables $\overline{x}$. An *interpolant* is a formula $I[\overline{x}]$ over the common variables such that $A[\overline{x}_A, \overline{x}] \Rightarrow I[\overline{x}]$ and $B[\overline{x}, \overline{x}_B] \Rightarrow \neg I[\overline{x}]$ hold.

In [2], it is assumed that $\bar{x} = \langle x_1, x_2, \ldots, x_n \rangle$ only contains string variables; a SAT solver is then used to systematically search for interpolants of the form

$$I[\overline{x}] \quad = \quad x_1 | x_2 | \cdots | x_n \in \mathcal{R} \tag{4}$$

where $|$ is a fresh separator character, and $\mathcal{R}$ a regular expression. $\mathcal{R}$ is for the search represented as a finite-state automaton using a set of Boolean variables. The search procedure itself uses a refinement loop in which the SAT solver guesses interpolant candidates, and a string solver checks the correctness of the candidates. Counterexamples produced by the string solver are used to refine the Boolean constraints. The procedure, therefore, has a lot of similarities with methods in syntax-guided synthesis [5], and could be generalised to interpolant patterns other than (4); it could also be changed to compute inductive invariants instead of just interpolants directly.

SAT-based learning has in the past also been used for a number of related applications, for instance to compute finite-state automata describing regions or strategies of games on infinite graphs [32, 35], or to synthesise transition systems that satisfy given LTL specifications [19]. This illustrates the flexibility of this form of learning; the challenge, however, is usually scalability, since a SAT solver essentially carries out a systematic search over all automata up to a certain size.

In practice, it appears most useful to combine the ADT-based method from Sect. 3.2 with the learning method. This could be done, for instance, by using the ADT method by default, but switching to the learning method when the computed ADT interpolants start to contain too complex ADT expressions. As a further criterion, when analysing programs that combine strings and other data-types (the most common case), it should be checked prior to starting the learning process whether the conjunction $A[\overline{x}_A, \overline{x}] \wedge B[\overline{x}, \overline{x}_B]$ is unsatisfiable for reasons pertaining to strings. This is a necessary (though not sufficient) criterion for the existence of an interpolant of the form (4). To check whether strings are responsible for any inconsistency, the common non-string variables in $\bar{x}$ can be renamed to local variables x_i' in A and x_i'' in B.

---

[4] For instance, Eldarica has built-in support for the ADT size function, which corresponds to string length.

4   Conclusions

We have given a survey of string handling in software model checkers, and proposed a combination of methods for model checking of Java programs. The paper presents work in progress, and at the moment the impact of the different design and encoding choices has not been evaluated experimentally yet; we do believe, however, that the outlined combination of string methods can significantly improve the usability of a Java model checker like JayHorn.

Acknowledgements. This research is supported by the Swedish Research Council (VR) under grant 2018-04727, and by the Swedish Foundation for Strategic Research (SSF) under the project WebSec (Ref. RIT17-0011).

References

1. Abdulla, P.A., et al.: Trau: SMT solver for string constraints. In: FMCAD. IEEE (2018)
2. Abdulla, P.A., et al.: String constraints for verification. In: Biere, A., Bloem, R. (eds.) CAV 2014. LNCS, vol. 8559, pp. 150–166. Springer, Cham (2014). https://doi.org/10.1007/978-3-319-08867-9_10
3. Abdulla, P.A., et al.: Norn: an SMT solver for string constraints. In: Kroening, D., Păsăreanu, C.S. (eds.) CAV 2015. LNCS, vol. 9206, pp. 462–469. Springer, Cham (2015). https://doi.org/10.1007/978-3-319-21690-4_29
4. Ahrendt, W., Beckert, B., Bubel, R., Hähnle, R., Schmitt, P.H., Ulbrich, M. (eds.): Deductive Software Verification—The KeY Book—FromTheory to Practice. Springer, Heidelberg (2016). https://doi.org/10.1007/978-3-319-49812-6
5. Alur, R., et al.: Syntax-guided synthesis. In: Dependable Software Systems Engineering. IOS Press (2015)
6. Aydin, A., Bang, L., Bultan, T.: Automata-based model counting for string constraints. In: Kroening, D., Păsăreanu, C.S. (eds.) CAV 2015. LNCS, vol. 9206, pp. 255–272. Springer, Cham (2015). https://doi.org/10.1007/978-3-319-21690-4_15
7. Barrett, C., et al.: CVC4. In: Gopalakrishnan, G., Qadeer, S. (eds.) CAV 2011. LNCS, vol. 6806, pp. 171–177. Springer, Heidelberg (2011). https://doi.org/10.1007/978-3-642-22110-1_14
8. Beyer, D.: Automatic verification of C and Java programs: SV-COMP 2019. In: Beyer, D., Huisman, M., Kordon, F., Steffen, B. (eds.) TACAS 2019. LNCS, vol. 11429, pp. 133–155. Springer, Cham (2019). https://doi.org/10.1007/978-3-030-17502-3_9
9. Bubel, R., Hähnle, R., Geilmann, U.: A formalisation of Java strings for program specification and verification. In: Barthe, G., Pardo, A., Schneider, G. (eds.) SEFM 2011. LNCS, vol. 7041, pp. 90–105. Springer, Heidelberg (2011). https://doi.org/10.1007/978-3-642-24690-6_8
10. Bultan, T., Yu, F., Alkhalaf, M., Aydin, A.: String Analysis for Software Verification and Security. Springer, Cham (2017). https://doi.org/10.1007/978-3-319-68670-7
11. Chen, T., Hague, M., Lin, A.W., Rümmer, P., Wu, Z.: Decision procedures for path feasibility of string-manipulating programs with complex operations. In: PACMPL, no. POPL (2019)

12. Christensen, A.S., Møller, A., Schwartzbach, M.I.: Precise analysis of string expressions. In: Cousot, R. (ed.) SAS 2003. LNCS, vol. 2694, pp. 1–18. Springer, Heidelberg (2003). https://doi.org/10.1007/3-540-44898-5_1
13. Clarke, E.M., Henzinger, T.A., Veith, H., Bloem, R. (eds.): Handbook of Model Checking. Springer, Heidelberg (2018). https://doi.org/10.1007/978-3-319-10575-8
14. Cordeiro, L., Kesseli, P., Kroening, D., Schrammel, P., Trtik, M.: JBMC: a bounded model checking tool for verifying Java bytecode. In: Chockler, H., Weissenbacher, G. (eds.) CAV 2018. LNCS, vol. 10981, pp. 183–190. Springer, Cham (2018). https://doi.org/10.1007/978-3-319-96145-3_10
15. De Angelis, E., Fioravanti, F., Pettorossi, A., Proietti, M.: Solving Horn clauses on inductive data types without induction. TPLP **18**(3–4), 452–469 (2018)
16. de Moura, L., Bjørner, N.: Z3: an efficient SMT solver. In: Ramakrishnan, C.R., Rehof, J. (eds.) TACAS 2008. LNCS, vol. 4963, pp. 337–340. Springer, Heidelberg (2008). https://doi.org/10.1007/978-3-540-78800-3_24
17. Dillig, I., Dillig, T., Li, B., McMillan, K.L.: Inductive invariant generation via abductive inference. In: OOPSLA. ACM (2013)
18. Dudka, K., Peringer, P., Vojnar, T.: Byte-precise verification of low-level list manipulation. In: Logozzo, F., Fähndrich, M. (eds.) SAS 2013. LNCS, vol. 7935, pp. 215–237. Springer, Heidelberg (2013). https://doi.org/10.1007/978-3-642-38856-9_13
19. Faymonville, P., Finkbeiner, B., Rabe, M.N., Tentrup, L.: Encodings of bounded synthesis. In: Legay, A., Margaria, T. (eds.) TACAS 2017. LNCS, vol. 10205, pp. 354–370. Springer, Heidelberg (2017). https://doi.org/10.1007/978-3-662-54577-5_20
20. Ganesh, V., Kieżun, A., Artzi, S., Guo, P.J., Hooimeijer, P., Ernst, M.: HAMPI: a string solver for testing, analysis and vulnerability detection. In: Gopalakrishnan, G., Qadeer, S. (eds.) CAV 2011. LNCS, vol. 6806, pp. 1–19. Springer, Heidelberg (2011). https://doi.org/10.1007/978-3-642-22110-1_1
21. Ganesh, V., Minnes, M., Solar-Lezama, A., Rinard, M.: What is decidable about strings? Technical report MIT-CSAIL-TR-2011-006, March 2011
22. Gosling, J., Joy, B., Steele, G.L., Bracha, G., Buckley, A.: The Java Language Specification, Java SE 8 Edition, 1st edn. Addison-Wesley Professional, Boston (2014)
23. Grebenshchikov, S., Lopes, N.P., Popeea, C., Rybalchenko, A.: Synthesizing software verifiers from proof rules. In: PLDI. ACM (2012)
24. Hojjat, H., Rümmer, P.: Deciding and interpolating algebraic data types by reduction. In: SYNASC. IEEE Computer Society (2017)
25. Hojjat, H., Rümmer, P.: The ELDARICA Horn solver. In: FMCAD. IEEE (2018)
26. Holík, L., Janku, P., Lin, A.W., Rümmer, P., Vojnar, T.: String constraints with concatenation and transducers solved efficiently. In: PACMPL, no. POPL (2018)
27. Hooimeijer, P., Livshits, B., Molnar, D., Saxena, P., Veanes, M.: Fast and precise sanitizer analysis with BEK. In: 20th USENIX Security Symposium, San Francisco, CA, USA, 8–12 August 2011, Proceedings. USENIX Association (2011)
28. Kahsai, T., Kersten, R., Rümmer, P., Schäf, M.: Quantified heap invariants for object-oriented programs. In: LPAR, EasyChair (2017)
29. Kahsai, T., Rümmer, P., Sanchez, H., Schäf, M.: JayHorn: a framework for verifying Java programs. In: Chaudhuri, S., Farzan, A. (eds.) CAV 2016. LNCS, vol. 9779, pp. 352–358. Springer, Cham (2016). https://doi.org/10.1007/978-3-319-41528-4_19
30. Komuravelli, A., Gurfinkel, A., Chaki, S.: SMT-based model checking for recursive programs. Formal Methods Syst. Des. **48**(3), 175–205 (2016)

31. Leino, K.R.M.: Dafny: an automatic program verifier for functional correctness. In: Clarke, E.M., Voronkov, A. (eds.) LPAR 2010. LNCS (LNAI), vol. 6355, pp. 348–370. Springer, Heidelberg (2010). https://doi.org/10.1007/978-3-642-17511-4_20

32. Lin, A.W., Rümmer, P.: Liveness of randomised parameterised systems under arbitrary schedulers. In: Chaudhuri, S., Farzan, A. (eds.) CAV 2016. LNCS, vol. 9780, pp. 112–133. Springer, Cham (2016). https://doi.org/10.1007/978-3-319-41540-6_7

33. Malík, V., Martiček, Š., Schrammel, P., Srivas, M., Vojnar, T., Wahlang, J.: 2LS: memory safety and non-termination. In: Beyer, D., Huisman, M. (eds.) TACAS 2018. LNCS, vol. 10806, pp. 417–421. Springer, Cham (2018). https://doi.org/10.1007/978-3-319-89963-3_24

34. McMillan, K.L.: Interpolation and SAT-based model checking. In: Hunt, W.A., Somenzi, F. (eds.) CAV 2003. LNCS, vol. 2725, pp. 1–13. Springer, Heidelberg (2003). https://doi.org/10.1007/978-3-540-45069-6_1

35. Neider, D., Topcu, U.: An automaton learning approach to solving safety games over infinite graphs. In: Chechik, M., Raskin, J.-F. (eds.) TACAS 2016. LNCS, vol. 9636, pp. 204–221. Springer, Heidelberg (2016). https://doi.org/10.1007/978-3-662-49674-9_12

36. Noller, Y., Păsăreanu, C.S., Fromherz, A., Le, X.-B.D., Visser, W.: Symbolic pathfinder for SV-COMP. In: Beyer, D., Huisman, M., Kordon, F., Steffen, B. (eds.) TACAS 2019. LNCS, vol. 11429, pp. 239–243. Springer, Cham (2019). https://doi.org/10.1007/978-3-030-17502-3_21

37. Saxena, P., Akhawe, D., Hanna, S., Mao, F., McCamant, S., Song, D.: A symbolic execution framework for JavaScript. In: IEEE. IEEE Computer Society (2010)

38. Sharma, R., Aiken, A.: From invariant checking to invariant inference using randomized search. Formal Methods Syst. Des. **48**(3), 235–256 (2016)

39. Veanes, M.: Symbolic string transformations with regular lookahead and rollback. In: Voronkov, A., Virbitskaite, I. (eds.) PSI 2014. LNCS, vol. 8974, pp. 335–350. Springer, Heidelberg (2015). https://doi.org/10.1007/978-3-662-46823-4_27

40. Xie, X., Liu, Y., Le, W., Li, X., Chen, H.: S-looper: automatic summarization for multipath string loops. In: ISSTA. ACM (2015)

41. Zheng, Y., Zhang, X., Ganesh, V.: Z3-str: a Z3-based string solver for web application analysis. In: SIGSOFT. ACM (2013)

Types

Manifest Contracts with Intersection Types

Yuki Nishida$^{(\boxtimes)}$ and Atsushi Igarashi

Graduate School of Informatics, Kyoto University, Kyoto, Japan
{nishida,igarashi}@fos.kuis.kyoto-u.ac.jp

Abstract. We present a *manifest contract system* PCFvΔ_H with *intersection types*. A manifest contract system is a typed functional calculus in which software contracts are integrated into a refinement type system and consistency of contracts is checked by combination of compile- and run-time type checking. Intersection types naturally arise when a contract is expressed by a conjunction of smaller contracts. Run-time contract checking for conjunctive higher-order contracts in an untyped language has been studied but our typed setting poses an additional challenge due to the fact that an expression of an intersection type $\tau_1 \wedge \tau_2$ may have to perform different run-time checking whether it is used as τ_1 or τ_2.

We build PCFvΔ_H on top of the Δ-calculus, a Church-style intersection type system by Liquori and Stolze. In the Δ-calculus, a canonical expression of an intersection type is a *strong pair*, whose elements are the same expressions except for type annotations. To address the challenge above, we relax strong pairs so that expressions in a pair are the same except for type annotations and casts, which are a construct for run-time checking.

We give a formal definition of PCFvΔ_H and show its basic properties as a manifest contract system: preservation, progress, and value inversion. Furthermore, we show that run-time checking does not affect essential computation.

1 Introduction

Manifest contract systems [1, 10–13, 15, 19, 24–26, 31], which are typed functional calculi, are one discipline handling *software contracts* [18]. The distinguishing feature of manifest contract systems is that they integrate contracts into a type system and guarantee some sort of satisfiability against contracts in a program as type soundness. Specifically, a contract is embedded into a type by means of *refinement types* of the form $\{x{:}\tau \mid M\}$, which represents the subset of the *underlying type* τ such that the values in the subset satisfy the *predicate* M, which can be an arbitrary Boolean expression in the programming language. Using the refinement types, for example, we can express the contract of a division function, which would say "... the divisor shall not be zero ...", by the type int $\rightarrow \{x{:}$int $\mid x \neq 0\} \rightarrow$ int. In addition to the refinement types, manifest

© Springer Nature Switzerland AG 2019
A. W. Lin (Ed.): APLAS 2019, LNCS 11893, pp. 33–52, 2019.
https://doi.org/10.1007/978-3-030-34175-6_3

contract systems are often equipped with *dependent function types* in order to express more detailed contracts. A dependent function type, written $(x{:}\sigma) \to \tau$ in this paper, is a type of a function which takes one argument of the type σ and returns a value of the type τ; the distinguished point from ordinary function types is that τ can refer to the given argument represented by x. Hence, for example, the type of a division function can be made more specific like $(x{:}\texttt{int}) \to (y{:}\{x'{:}\texttt{int} \mid x' \neq 0\}) \to \{z{:}\texttt{int} \mid x = z \times y\}$. (Here, for simplicity, we ignore the case where devision involves a remainder, though it can be taken account into by writing a more sophisticated predicate).

A manifest contract system checks a contract dynamically to achieve its goal—as many *correct* programs as possible can be compiled and run; while some studies [16, 23, 27, 28, 30, 33], which also use a refinement type system, check contract satisfaction statically but with false positives and/or restriction on predicates. The checks are done in the form of explicit casts of the form $(M : \sigma \Rightarrow \tau)$; where M is a subject, σ is a source type (namely the type of M), and τ is a target type.[1] A cast checks whether the value of M can have the type τ. If the check fails, the cast throws an uncatchable exception called *blame*, which stands for contract violation. So, the system does not guarantee the absence of contract violations statically, but it guarantees that the result of successful execution satisfies the predicate of a refinement type in the program's type. This property follows subject reduction and a property called *value inversion* [26]—*if a value V has a type $\{ x{:}\tau \mid M \}$, then the expression obtained by substituting V for x in M is always evaluated into* true.

1.1   Motivation

The motivation of the integration of intersection types is to enrich the expressiveness of contracts by types. It naturally arises when we consider a contract stated in a conjunctive form [3, 9, 14]. Considering parities (even/odd) of integers, for example, we can state a contract of the addition as a conjunctive form; that is

> "An even integer is returned if both given arguments are even integers; **and** an odd integer is returned if the first given argument is even integer and the second given argument is odd integer; **and** ..."

Using intersection types, we can write the contract as the following type.[2]

$$(\texttt{even} \to \texttt{even} \to \texttt{even}) \wedge (\texttt{even} \to \texttt{odd} \to \texttt{odd})$$
$$\wedge (\texttt{odd} \to \texttt{even} \to \texttt{odd}) \wedge (\texttt{odd} \to \texttt{odd} \to \texttt{even})$$

In fact, a semantically equivalent contract could be expressed by using dependent function types found in existing systems as follows, where $\texttt{evenp} := \lambda x{:}\texttt{nat}.x \bmod 2 = 0$ and $\texttt{oddp} := \lambda x{:}\texttt{nat}.x \bmod 2 = 1$.

---

[1] Many manifest contract systems put a unique label on each cast to distinguish which cast fails, but we omit them for simplicity.

[2] $\texttt{even} := \{x{:}\texttt{nat} \mid x \bmod 2 = 0\}$ $\texttt{odd} := \{x{:}\texttt{nat} \mid x \bmod 2 = 1\}$.

$$(x{:}\mathtt{nat}) \to (y{:}\mathtt{nat}) \to \{z{:}\mathtt{nat} \mid \qquad\qquad \mathtt{if\ evenp}\, x$$
$$\mathtt{then}\, (\mathtt{if\ evenp}\, y\ \mathtt{then\ evenp}\, z\ \mathtt{else\ oddp}\, z)$$
$$\mathtt{else}\, (\mathtt{if\ evenp}\, y\ \mathtt{then\ oddp}\, z\ \mathtt{else\ evenp}\, z)\}$$

Thus, one might think it is just a matter of taste in how contracts are represented. However, intersection types are more expressive, that is, there are contracts that are hard to express in existing manifest contract systems. Consider the following (a bit contrived) contract for a higher-order function.

$$((\mathtt{int} \to \{x{:}\mathtt{int} \mid x \neq 0\}) \to \{z{:}\mathtt{int} \mid z = 1\}) \wedge ((\mathtt{int} \to \mathtt{int}) \to \{z{:}\mathtt{int} \mid z = 0\})$$

The result type depends on input as the parity contract does. This time, however, it cannot be written with a dependent function type; there is no obvious way to write a predicate corresponding to $\mathtt{evenp}$ (or $\mathtt{oddp}$). Such a predicate must check that a given function returns non-zero for all integers, but this is simply not computable.

1.2   Our Work

We develop a formal calculus PCFv$\varDelta_\mathrm{H}$, a manifest contract system with intersection types. The goal of this paper is to prove its desirable properties: preservation, progress, value inversion; and one that guarantees that the existence of dynamic checking does not change the "essence" of computation.

There are several tasks in constructing a manifest contract system, but a specific challenge for PCFv$\varDelta_\mathrm{H}$ arises from the fact—manifest contract systems are intended as an intermediate language for *hybrid type checking* [10]. Firstly, consider the following definition with a parity contract in a surface language.

$$\mathtt{let}\ succ'{:}\mathtt{odd} \to \mathtt{even} = \lambda x.\mathtt{succ}(x).$$

Supposing the primitive operator $\mathtt{succ}(x)$ has the type $\mathtt{nat} \to \mathtt{nat}$, we need to check subtyping relation $\mathtt{odd} <: \mathtt{nat}$ and $\mathtt{nat} <: \mathtt{even}$ to check well-typedness of the definition. As we have mentioned, however, this kind of subtyping checking is undecidable in general. So, (when the checking is impossible) we insert casts to check the contract at run-time and obtain the following compiled definition.

$$\mathtt{let}\ succ'{:}\mathtt{odd} \to \mathtt{even} = \lambda x{:}\mathtt{odd}.(\mathtt{succ}((x : \mathtt{odd} \Rightarrow \mathtt{nat})) : \mathtt{nat} \Rightarrow \mathtt{even}).$$

A problem arises when we consider the following definition equipped with a more complicated parity contract.

$$\mathtt{let}\ succ'{:}(\mathtt{odd} \to \mathtt{even}) \wedge (\mathtt{even} \to \mathtt{odd}) = \lambda x.\mathtt{succ}(x).$$

The problem is that we need to insert different casts into code according to how the code is typed; and one piece of code might be typed in several essentially different ways in an intersection type system since it is a polymorphic type system. For instance, in the example above, $\lambda x{:}\mathtt{odd}.(\mathtt{succ}((x : \mathtt{odd} \Rightarrow \mathtt{nat})) :$

nat $\Rightarrow$ even) is obtained by cast insertion if the function is typed as odd $\rightarrow$ even; while λx:even.(succ((x : even $\Rightarrow$ nat)) : nat $\Rightarrow$ odd) is obtained when the body is typed as even $\rightarrow$ odd. However, the function must have both types to have the intersection type. It may seem sufficient to just cast the body itself, that is, ((λx:nat.succ(x)) : nat $\rightarrow$ nat $\Rightarrow$ (odd $\rightarrow$ even) $\wedge$ (even $\rightarrow$ odd)). However, this just shelves the problem: Intuitively, to check if the subject has the target intersection type, we need to check if the subject has both types in the conjunction. This brings us back to the same original question.

Contributions. Our contributions are summarized as follows:

– we design a manifest contracts calculus with *refinement intersection types* [27, 33], a restricted form of intersection types.
– we formalize the calculus PCFvΔ_H; and
– we state and prove type soundness, value inversion, and dynamic soundness.

The whole system including proofs is mechanized with Coq.[3] We use locally nameless representation and cofinite quantification [5] for the mechanization.

Disclaimer. To concentrate on the PCFvΔ_H-specific problems, we put the following restrictions for PCFvΔ_H in this paper compared to a system one would imagine from the phrase "a manifest contract system with intersection types".

– PCFvΔ_H does not support dependent function types. As we will see, PCFvΔ_H uses nondeterminism for dynamic checking. The combination of dependent function types and nondeterminism poses a considerable challenge [19].
– We use *refinement intersection types* rather than general ones. Roughly speaking, $\sigma \wedge \tau$ is a refinement intersection type if both σ and τ refine the same type. So, for example, (even $\rightarrow$ even) $\wedge$ (odd $\rightarrow$ odd) is a refinement intersection types since types of both sides refine the same type nat $\rightarrow$ nat, while (nat $\rightarrow$ nat) $\wedge$ (float $\rightarrow$ float) is not.

2   Overview of Our Language: PCFvΔ_H

Our language PCFvΔ_H is a call-by-value dialect of PCF [20], extended with intersection types (derived from the Δ-calculus [17]) and manifest contracts (derived from λ_H [10,12]). So, the baseline is that any *valid* PCF program is also a valid PCFvΔ_H program; and a PCFvΔ_H program should behave as the same way as (call-by-value) PCF. In other words, PCFvΔ_H is a conservative extension of call-by-value PCF.

---

[3] The Coq scripts are available through the following URL: https://www.fos.kuis. kyoto-u.ac.jp/~igarashi/papers/manifest-intersection.html.

2.1   The Δ-Calculus

To address the challenge discussed in Sect. 1, PCFvΔ_{H} is strongly influenced by the Δ-*calculus* by Liquori and Stolze [17], an intersection type system à la Church. Their novel idea is a new form called *strong pair*, written $\langle M, N \rangle$. It is a kind of pair and used as a constructor for expressions of intersection types. So, using the strong pair, for example, we can write an identity function having type (even $\rightarrow$ even) $\wedge$ (odd $\rightarrow$ odd) as follows.

$$\langle \lambda x{:}\mathsf{even}.x,\ \lambda x{:}\mathsf{odd}.x \rangle$$

Unlike product types, however, M and N in a strong pair cannot be arbitrarily chosen. A strong pair requires that the *essence* of both expressions in a pair be the same. An essence $\wr M \wr$ of a typed expression M is the untyped skeleton of M. For instance, $\wr \lambda x{:}\tau.x \wr = \lambda x.x$. So, the requirement justifies strong pairs as the introduction of intersection types: that is, computation represented by the two expressions is the same and so the system still follows a Curry-style intersection type system. Strong pairs just give a way to annotate expressions with a different type in a different context.

We adapt their idea into PCFvΔ_{H} by letting an essence represent the *contract-irrelevant part* of an expression, rather than an untyped skeleton. For instance, the essence of $\lambda x{:}\mathsf{odd}.(\mathsf{succ}((x\ :\ \mathsf{odd}\ \Rightarrow\ \mathsf{nat}))\ :\ \mathsf{nat}\ \Rightarrow\ \mathsf{even})$ is $\lambda x{:}\mathsf{nat}.\mathsf{succ}(x)$ (the erased contract-relevant parts are casts and predicates of refinement types). Now, we can (ideally automatically) compile the *succ'* definition in Sect. 1 into the following PCFvΔ_{H} expression.

$$\texttt{let } succ'{:}(\mathsf{odd} \rightarrow \mathsf{even}) \wedge (\mathsf{even} \rightarrow \mathsf{odd}) =$$
$$\langle \lambda x{:}\mathsf{odd}.(\mathsf{succ}((x : \mathsf{odd} \Rightarrow \mathsf{nat})) : \mathsf{nat} \Rightarrow \mathsf{even}),$$
$$\lambda x{:}\mathsf{even}.(\mathsf{succ}((x : \mathsf{even} \Rightarrow \mathsf{nat})) : \mathsf{nat} \Rightarrow \mathsf{odd}) \rangle$$

This strong pair satisfies the condition, that is, both expressions have the same essence.

2.2   Cast Semantics for Intersection Types

Having introduced intersection types, we have to extend the semantics of casts so that they handle contracts written with intersection types. Following Keil and Thiemann [14], who studied intersection (and union) contract checking in the "latent" style [12] for an untyped language, we give the semantics of a cast *to* an intersection type by the following rule:

$$(V : \sigma \Rightarrow \tau_1 \wedge \tau_2) \longrightarrow \langle (V : \sigma \Rightarrow \tau_1), (V : \sigma \Rightarrow \tau_2) \rangle$$

The reduction rule should not be surprising: V has to have both τ_1 and τ_2 and a strong pair introduces an intersection type $\tau_1 \wedge \tau_2$ from τ_1 and τ_2. For the original cast to succeed, both of the split casts have to succeed.

A basic strategy of a cast *from* an intersection type is expressed by the following two rules.

$$(V : \sigma_1 \wedge \sigma_2 \Rightarrow \tau) \longrightarrow (\pi_1(V) : \sigma_1 \Rightarrow \tau)$$
$$(V : \sigma_1 \wedge \sigma_2 \Rightarrow \tau) \longrightarrow (\pi_2(V) : \sigma_2 \Rightarrow \tau)$$

The cast tests whether a nondeterministically chosen element in a (possibly nested) strong pair can be cast to τ.

One problem, however, arises when a function type is involved. Consider the following expression.

$$(\lambda f{:}\mathsf{nat} \rightarrow \mathsf{nat}.f\,0 + f\,1)\,M_{\mathrm{cast}}$$

where

$$M_{\mathrm{cast}} := (V : (\mathsf{even} \rightarrow \mathsf{nat}) \wedge (\mathsf{odd} \rightarrow \mathsf{nat}) \Rightarrow \mathsf{nat} \rightarrow \mathsf{nat}).$$

V can be used as both $\mathsf{even} \rightarrow \mathsf{nat}$ and $\mathsf{odd} \rightarrow \mathsf{nat}$. This means V can handle arbitrary natural numbers. Thus, this cast should be valid and evaluation of the expression above should not fail. However, with the reduction rules presented above, evaluation results in blame in both branches: the choice is made before calling $\lambda f : \mathsf{nat} \rightarrow \mathsf{nat}. \cdots$, the function being assigned into f only can handle either even or odd, leading to failure at either $f\,1$ or $f\,0$, respectively.

To solve the problem, we delay a cast into a function type even when the source type is an intersection type. In fact, M_{cast} reduces to a wrapped value V_{cast} below

$$V_{\mathrm{cast}} := \langle\!\langle V : (\mathsf{even} \rightarrow \mathsf{nat}) \wedge (\mathsf{odd} \rightarrow \mathsf{nat}) \Rightarrow \mathsf{nat} \rightarrow \mathsf{nat}\rangle\!\rangle,$$

similarly to higher-order casts [8]. Then, the delayed cast fires when an actual argument is given:

$$
\begin{aligned}
&(\lambda f{:}\mathsf{nat} \rightarrow \mathsf{nat}.f\,0 + f\,1)\,M_{\mathrm{cast}} \\
\longrightarrow\ &(\lambda f{:}\mathsf{nat} \rightarrow \mathsf{nat}.f\,0 + f\,1)\,V_{\mathrm{cast}} \\
\longrightarrow\ &V_{\mathrm{cast}}\,0 + V_{\mathrm{cast}}\,1 \\
\longrightarrow^*\ &(V : \mathsf{even} \rightarrow \mathsf{nat} \Rightarrow \mathsf{nat} \rightarrow \mathsf{nat})\,0 + (V : \mathsf{odd} \rightarrow \mathsf{nat} \Rightarrow \mathsf{nat} \rightarrow \mathsf{nat})\,1 \\
\longrightarrow^*\ &1
\end{aligned}
$$

$$
\begin{aligned}
\sigma, \tau &::= \mathsf{nat} \mid \mathsf{bool} \mid \sigma \rightarrow \tau \\
L, M, N &::= \mathsf{0} \mid \mathsf{succ}(M) \mid \mathsf{pred}(M) \mid \mathsf{iszero}(M) \mid \mathsf{true} \mid \mathsf{false} \mid \mathsf{if}\,L\,\mathsf{then}\,M\,\mathsf{else}\,N \mid \\
&\quad x \mid M\,N \mid \lambda x{:}\tau.M \mid \mu f{:}\sigma_1 \rightarrow \sigma_2.\lambda x{:}\tau.M \\
\bar{n} &::= \mathsf{0} \mid \mathsf{succ}(\bar{n}) \\
V &::= \bar{n} \mid \mathsf{true} \mid \mathsf{false} \mid \lambda x{:}\tau.M \\
\mathcal{E} &::= \mathsf{succ}(\square) \mid \mathsf{pred}(\square) \mid \mathsf{iszero}(\square) \mid \mathsf{if}\,\square\,\mathsf{then}\,M\,\mathsf{else}\,N \mid \square\,M \mid V\,\square
\end{aligned}
$$

Fig. 1. Syntax of PCFv.

3   Formal Systems

In this section, we formally define two languages PCFv and PCFvΔ_{H}, an extension of PCFv as sketched in the last section. PCFv is a call-by-value PCF. We only give operational semantics and omit its type system and a type soundness proof, because we are only interested in how its behavior is related to PCFvΔ_{H}, the main language of this paper.

3.1   PCFv

The syntax of PCFv is shown in Fig. 1. Metavariables x, y, z, f, and g range over term variables (f and g are intended for ones bound to functions); σ and τ range over types; L, M, and N range over expressions; V ranges over values; and $\mathcal{E}$ ranges over evaluation frames. The definition is fairly standard, except for one point: instead of introducing a constant for the general fix-point operator, we introduce a form $\mu f{:}\sigma_1 \to \sigma_2.\lambda x{:}\tau.M$ for recursive functions.

Definition 1 (Bound and free variables). *An occurrence of x in M of $\lambda x{:}\tau.M$ and f in M of $\mu f{:}\sigma_1 \to \sigma_2.\lambda x{:}\tau.M$ is called* bound. *The set of* free *variables in M is the variables of which there are free occurrence in M. We denote the free variables by* $\mathtt{fv}(M)$.

Convention. We define α-equivalence in a standard manner and identify α-equivalent expressions.

Definition 2 (Substitution). *Substitution of N for a free variable x in M, written $M[x \mapsto N]$, is defined in a standard capture-avoiding manner.*

Definition 3 (Context application). *Given an evaluation frame $\mathcal{E}$ and an expression M, $\mathcal{E}[M]$ denotes the expression obtained by just replacing the hole $\square$ in $\mathcal{E}$ with M.*

A small-step operational semantics of PCFv is inductively defined by the rules in Fig. 2. Those rules consist of standard (call-by-value) PCF axiom schemes and one rule scheme (PCF-CTX), which expresses the call-by-value evaluation strategy using the evaluation frames.

3.2   PCFvΔ_{H}

PCFvΔ_{H} is an extension of PCFv. Through abuse of syntax, we use the metavariables of PCFv for PCFvΔ_{H}, though we are dealing with the two different languages.

The syntax of PCFvΔ_{H} is shown in Fig. 3. We introduce some more metavariables: I ranges over *interface types*, a subset of types; B ranges over *recursion bodies*, a subset of expressions; C ranges over *commands*; and Γ ranges over typing contexts. Shaded parts show differences (extensions and modifications) from PCFv. Types are extended with intersection types and refinement types;

$$\text{pred}(0) \longrightarrow_{\text{PCF}} 0 \qquad\qquad (\text{PCF-Pred-Z})$$

$$\text{pred}(\text{succ}(\overline{n})) \longrightarrow_{\text{PCF}} \overline{n} \qquad\qquad (\text{PCF-Pred})$$

$$\text{iszero}(0) \longrightarrow_{\text{PCF}} \text{true} \qquad\qquad (\text{PCF-IsZero-T})$$

$$\text{iszero}(\text{succ}(\overline{n})) \longrightarrow_{\text{PCF}} \text{false} \qquad\qquad (\text{PCF-IsZero-F})$$

$$\text{if true then } M \text{ else } N \longrightarrow_{\text{PCF}} M \qquad\qquad (\text{PCF-If-T})$$

$$\text{if false then } M \text{ else } N \longrightarrow_{\text{PCF}} N \qquad\qquad (\text{PCF-If-F})$$

$$(\lambda x{:}\tau.M)\, V \longrightarrow_{\text{PCF}} M[x \mapsto V] \qquad\qquad (\text{PCF-Beta})$$

$$\mu f{:}\sigma_1 \to \sigma_2.\lambda x{:}\tau.M \longrightarrow_{\text{PCF}} (\lambda x{:}\tau.M)[f \mapsto \mu f{:}\sigma_1 \to \sigma_2.\lambda x{:}\tau.M] \quad (\text{PCF-Fix})$$

$$\frac{M \longrightarrow_{\text{PCF}} M'}{\mathcal{E}[M] \longrightarrow_{\text{PCF}} \mathcal{E}[M']} \qquad\qquad (\text{PCF-Ctx})$$

Fig. 2. Operational semantics of PCFv.

$$\sigma, \tau ::= \textbf{nat} \mid \textbf{bool} \mid \sigma \to \tau \mid \sigma \wedge \tau \mid \{x{:}\tau \mid M\}$$

$$I ::= \sigma \to \tau \mid I_1 \wedge I_2$$

$$L, M, N ::= 0 \mid \text{succ}(M) \mid \text{pred}(M) \mid \text{iszero}(M) \mid \textbf{true} \mid \textbf{false} \mid \text{if } L \text{ then } M \text{ else } N \mid$$
$$\qquad x \mid M\, N \mid \lambda x{:}\tau.M \mid \mu f{:}I.B \mid \langle M, N \rangle \mid \pi_1(M) \mid \pi_2(M) \mid (M : \sigma \Rightarrow \tau) \mid$$
$$\qquad \langle\!\langle V : \sigma \Rightarrow \tau_1 \to \tau_2 \rangle\!\rangle \mid \langle\!\langle M \;?\; \{x{:}\tau \mid N\} \rangle\!\rangle \mid \langle\!\langle M \Longrightarrow V : \{x{:}\tau \mid N\} \rangle\!\rangle$$

$$B ::= \lambda x{:}\tau.M \mid \langle B_1, B_2 \rangle$$

$$\overline{n} ::= 0 \mid \text{succ}(\overline{n})$$

$$V ::= \overline{n} \mid \textbf{true} \mid \textbf{false} \mid \lambda x{:}\tau.M \mid \langle V_1, V_2 \rangle \mid \langle\!\langle V : \sigma \Rightarrow \tau_1 \to \tau_2 \rangle\!\rangle$$

$$C ::= M \mid \textbf{blame}$$

$$\mathcal{E} ::= \text{succ}(\Box) \mid \text{pred}(\Box) \mid \text{iszero}(\Box) \mid \text{if } \Box \text{ then } M \text{ else } N \mid \Box M \mid V \Box \mid$$
$$\qquad \pi_1(\Box) \mid \pi_2(\Box) \mid (\Box : \sigma \Rightarrow \tau) \mid \langle\!\langle \Box \;?\; \{x{:}\tau \mid M\} \rangle\!\rangle$$

$$\Gamma ::= \emptyset \mid \Gamma, x{:}\tau$$

Fig. 3. Syntax of PCFvΔ_{H}.

the restriction that a well-formed intersection type is a refinement intersection type is enforced by the type system. The variable x in N of $\{x{:}\tau \mid N\}$ is bound. An interface type, which is a single function type or (possibly nested) intersection over function types, is used for the type annotation for a recursive function. Expressions are extended with ones for: strong pairs (namely, pair construction, left projection, and right projection); casts; and run-time expressions of the form $\langle\!\langle \ldots \rangle\!\rangle$ that can occur at run time for dynamic checking and not in source code. Recursion bodies are (possibly nested strong pairs) of λ-abstractions.

Run-time expressions deserve detailed explanation. A *delayed check* $\langle\!\langle V : \sigma \Rightarrow \tau_1 \to \tau_2 \rangle\!\rangle$ denotes a delayed cast into a function type, which is used in cases such as those discussed in Sect. 1 for instance. A *waiting check* $\langle\!\langle M \;?\; \{x{:}\tau \mid N\} \rangle\!\rangle$ denotes a state waiting for the check M against N until M is evaluated into a value. An *active check* $\langle\!\langle M \Longrightarrow V : \{x{:}\tau \mid N\} \rangle\!\rangle$ is a state running test M to see if V satisfies N. The variable x in N of $\langle\!\langle M \;?\; \{x{:}\tau \mid N\} \rangle\!\rangle$ and $\langle\!\langle M \Longrightarrow V : \{x{:}\tau \mid N\} \rangle\!\rangle$ is bound.

We do not include **blame** in expressions, although existing manifest contract systems usually include it among expressions. As a consequence, the evaluation relation for PCFvΔ_{H} is defined between commands. This distinction will turn out to be convenient in stating correspondence between the semantics of PCFvΔ_{H} and that of PCFv, which does not have **blame**.

Convention. We assume the index variable i ranges over $\{1, 2\}$ to save space.

Definition 4 (Terms). *We call the union of the sets of types and expressions as* terms.

Notation. $M \preceq N$ denotes that M *is a sub-expression of* N.

Convention. We define α-equivalence in a standard manner and identify α-equivalent terms.

$$
\begin{aligned}
\lfloor\mathsf{nat}\rfloor &= \mathsf{nat} & \lfloor\mathsf{if}\ L\ \mathsf{then}\ M\ \mathsf{else}\ N\rfloor &= \mathsf{if}\ \lfloor L\rfloor\ \mathsf{then}\ \lfloor M\rfloor\ \mathsf{else}\ \lfloor N\rfloor \\
\lfloor\mathsf{bool}\rfloor &= \mathsf{bool} & \lfloor x\rfloor &= x \\
\lfloor\sigma \to \tau\rfloor &= \lfloor\sigma\rfloor \to \lfloor\tau\rfloor & \lfloor M\ N\rfloor &= \lfloor M\rfloor\lfloor N\rfloor \\
\lfloor\sigma \wedge \tau\rfloor &= \lfloor\sigma\rfloor & \lfloor\lambda x{:}\tau.M\rfloor &= \lambda x{:}\lfloor\tau\rfloor.\lfloor M\rfloor \\
\lfloor\{x{:}\tau \mid M\}\rfloor &= \lfloor\tau\rfloor & \lfloor\langle M, N\rangle\rfloor &= \lfloor M\rfloor \\
\lfloor 0\rfloor &= 0 & \lfloor\pi_i(M)\rfloor &= \lfloor M\rfloor \\
\lfloor\mathsf{succ}(M)\rfloor &= \mathsf{succ}(\lfloor M\rfloor) & \lfloor\mu f{:}I.B\rfloor &= \mu f{:}\lfloor I\rfloor.\lfloor B\rfloor \\
\lfloor\mathsf{pred}(M)\rfloor &= \mathsf{pred}(\lfloor M\rfloor) & \lfloor(M : \sigma \Rightarrow \tau)\rfloor &= \lfloor M\rfloor \\
\lfloor\mathsf{iszero}(M)\rfloor &= \mathsf{iszero}(\lfloor M\rfloor) & \lfloor\langle\!\langle V : \sigma \Rightarrow \tau_1 \to \tau_2\rangle\!\rangle\rfloor &= \lfloor V\rfloor \\
\lfloor\mathsf{true}\rfloor &= \mathsf{true} & \lfloor\langle\!\langle M\ ?\ \{x{:}\tau \mid N\}\rangle\!\rangle\rfloor &= \lfloor M\rfloor \\
\lfloor\mathsf{false}\rfloor &= \mathsf{false} & \lfloor\langle\!\langle M \Longrightarrow V : \{x{:}\tau \mid N\}\rangle\!\rangle\rfloor &= \lfloor V\rfloor
\end{aligned}
$$

Fig. 4. Essence of a PCFvΔ_{H} term.

Convention. We often omit the empty environment. We abuse a comma for the concatenation of environments like Γ_1, Γ_2. We denote a singleton environment, an environment that contains only one variable binding, by $x{:}\tau$.

Definition 5 (Free variables and substitution). *Free variables and substitution are defined similarly to PCFv; and we use the same notations. Note that since the types and expressions of PCFvΔ_{H} are mutually recursively defined, the metaoperations are inductively defined for terms.*

Definition 6 (Domain of typing context). *The* domain *of* Γ, *written* $\mathrm{dom}(\Gamma)$, *is defined by:* $\mathrm{dom}(\emptyset) = \emptyset$ *and* $\mathrm{dom}(\Gamma, x{:}\tau) = \mathrm{dom}(\Gamma) \cup \{x\}$. *We abbreviate* $x \notin \mathrm{dom}(\Gamma)$ *to* $x \# \Gamma$.

The essence of a PCFvΔ_{H} term is defined in Fig. 4, which is mostly straightforward. The choice of which part we take as the essence of a strong pair is arbitrary because for a well-typed expression both parts have the same essence. Note that the essence of an active check $\langle\!\langle M \Longrightarrow V : \{x{:}\tau \mid N\}\rangle\!\rangle$ is V rather than M. This is because V is the subject of the expression.

3.3   Operational Semantics of PCFvΔ_{H}

The operational semantics of PCFvΔ_{H} consists of four relations $M \rightharpoonup_{\mathsf{p}} N$, $M \rightharpoonup_{\mathsf{c}} C$, $M \longrightarrow_{\mathsf{p}} N$, and $M \longrightarrow_{\mathsf{c}} C$. Bearing in mind the inclusion relation among syntactic categories, these relations can be regarded as binary relations between commands. The first two are basic reduction relations, and the other two are contextual evaluation relations (relations for whole programs). Furthermore, the relations subscripted by p correspond to PCFv evaluation, that is, *essential evaluation*; and ones subscripted by c correspond to dynamic contract checking. Dynamic checking is nondeterministic because of (RC-WEDGEL/R), (EC-PAIRL), and (EC-PAIRR).

$$\mathtt{pred}(\mathtt{succ}(\overline{n})) \rightharpoonup_{\mathsf{p}} \overline{n} \qquad \text{(RP-PRED)}$$

$$\mathtt{iszero}(0) \rightharpoonup_{\mathsf{p}} \mathtt{true} \qquad \text{(RP-IsZERO-T)}$$

$$\mathtt{iszero}(\mathtt{succ}(\overline{n})) \rightharpoonup_{\mathsf{p}} \mathtt{false} \qquad \text{(RP-IsZERO-F)}$$

$$\mathtt{if\,true\,then}\ M\ \mathtt{else}\ N \rightharpoonup_{\mathsf{p}} M \qquad \text{(RP-IF-T)}$$

$$\mathtt{if\,false\,then}\ M\ \mathtt{else}\ N \rightharpoonup_{\mathsf{p}} N \qquad \text{(RP-IF-F)}$$

$$(\lambda x{:}\tau.M)\,V \rightharpoonup_{\mathsf{p}} M[x \mapsto V] \qquad \text{(RP-BETA)}$$

$$\mu f{:}I.B \rightharpoonup_{\mathsf{p}} B[f \mapsto \mu f{:}I.B] \qquad \text{(RP-FIX)}$$

$$\frac{M \rightharpoonup_{\mathsf{p}} N}{M \longrightarrow_{\mathsf{p}} N}\ \text{(EP-RED)} \qquad \frac{M \longrightarrow_{\mathsf{p}} N}{\mathcal{E}[M] \longrightarrow_{\mathsf{p}} \mathcal{E}[N]}\ \text{(EP-CTX)}$$

$$\frac{M \longrightarrow_{\mathsf{p}} M' \qquad N \longrightarrow_{\mathsf{p}} N'}{\langle M, N \rangle \longrightarrow_{\mathsf{p}} \langle M', N' \rangle}\ \text{(EP-PAIRS)}$$

Fig. 5. Operational semantics of PCFvΔ_{H} (1): essential evaluation.

Essential Evaluation $\longrightarrow_{\mathsf{p}}$. The essential evaluation, defined in Fig. 5, defines the evaluation of the essential part of a program; and thus, it is similar to $\longrightarrow_{\mathsf{PCF}}$. There are just three differences, that is: there are two relations; there is no reduction rule for $\mathtt{pred}(0)$; and there is a distinguished contextual evaluation rule (EP-PAIRS), which synchronizes essential reductions of the elements in a strong pair. The synchronization in (EP-PAIRS) is important since a strong pair requires the essences of both elements to be the same. The lack of predecessor evaluation for 0 is intentional: Our type system and run-time checking guarantee that 0 cannot occur as an argument to $\mathtt{pred}$.

Dynamic Checking $\longrightarrow_{\mathsf{c}}$. Dynamic checking is more complicated. Firstly, we focus on reduction rules in Fig. 6. The side-conditions on some rules are set so that an evaluation is less nondeterministic (for example, without the side conditions, both (RC-FORGET) and (RC-DELAY) could be applied to one expression).

The rules irrelevant to intersection types ((RC-NAT), (RC-BOOL), (RC-FORGET), (RC-DELAY), (RC-ARROW), (RC-WAITING), (RC-ACTIVATE), (RC-SUCCEED), and (RC-FAIL)) are adopted from Sekiyama et al. [26], but

$$\pi_i(\langle V_1, V_2 \rangle) \twoheadrightarrow_c V_i \qquad \text{(RC-Proj)}$$

$$(V : \mathtt{nat} \Rightarrow \mathtt{nat}) \twoheadrightarrow_c V \qquad \text{(RC-Nat)}$$

$$(V : \mathtt{bool} \Rightarrow \mathtt{bool}) \twoheadrightarrow_c V \qquad \text{(RC-Bool)}$$

$$(V : \{x{:}\sigma \mid M\} \Rightarrow \tau) \twoheadrightarrow_c (V : \sigma \Rightarrow \tau) \qquad \text{(RC-Forget)}$$

$$\frac{(\forall x \tau M.\sigma \neq \{x{:}\tau \mid M\})}{(V : \sigma \Rightarrow \tau_1 \to \tau_2) \twoheadrightarrow_c \langle\!\langle V : \sigma \Rightarrow \tau_1 \to \tau_2 \rangle\!\rangle} \qquad \text{(RC-Delay)}$$

$$\langle\!\langle V_1 : \sigma_1 \to \sigma_2 \Rightarrow \tau_1 \to \tau_2 \rangle\!\rangle\, V_2 \twoheadrightarrow_c (V_1\,(V_2 : \tau_1 \Rightarrow \sigma_1) : \sigma_2 \Rightarrow \tau_2) \quad \text{(RC-Arrow)}$$

$$\langle\!\langle V_1 : \sigma_1 \wedge \sigma_2 \Rightarrow \tau_1 \to \tau_2 \rangle\!\rangle\, V_2 \twoheadrightarrow_c (\pi_i(V_1) : \sigma_i \Rightarrow \tau_1 \to \tau_2)\, V_2 \quad \text{(RC-Wedgel/R)}$$

$$(V : \sigma_1 \wedge \sigma_2 \Rightarrow \mathtt{nat}) \twoheadrightarrow_c (\pi_1(V) : \sigma_1 \Rightarrow \mathtt{nat}) \qquad \text{(RC-WedgeN)}$$

$$(V : \sigma_1 \wedge \sigma_2 \Rightarrow \mathtt{bool}) \twoheadrightarrow_c (\pi_1(V) : \sigma_1 \Rightarrow \mathtt{bool}) \qquad \text{(RC-WedgeB)}$$

$$\frac{(\forall x \tau M.\sigma \neq \{x{:}\tau \mid M\})}{(V : \sigma \Rightarrow \tau_1 \wedge \tau_2) \twoheadrightarrow_c \langle\!\langle (V : \sigma \Rightarrow \tau_1), (V : \sigma \Rightarrow \tau_2) \rangle\!\rangle} \qquad \text{(RC-WedgeI)}$$

$$\frac{(\forall x \tau M.\sigma \neq \{x{:}\tau \mid M\})}{(V : \sigma \Rightarrow \{x{:}\tau \mid M\}) \twoheadrightarrow_c \langle\!\langle (V : \sigma \Rightarrow \tau)\ ?\ \{x{:}\tau \mid M\} \rangle\!\rangle} \qquad \text{(RC-Waiting)}$$

$$\langle\!\langle V\ ?\ \{x{:}\tau \mid M\} \rangle\!\rangle \twoheadrightarrow_c \langle\!\langle M[x \mapsto V] \Longrightarrow V : \{x{:}\tau \mid M\} \rangle\!\rangle \quad \text{(RC-Activate)}$$

$$\langle\!\langle \mathtt{true} \Longrightarrow V : \{x{:}\tau \mid M\} \rangle\!\rangle \twoheadrightarrow_c V \qquad \text{(RC-Succeed)}$$

$$\langle\!\langle \mathtt{false} \Longrightarrow V : \{x{:}\tau \mid M\} \rangle\!\rangle \twoheadrightarrow_c \mathtt{blame} \qquad \text{(RC-Fail)}$$

Fig. 6. Operational semantics of PCFvΔ_H (2): reduction rules for dynamic checking.

there is one difference about (RC-Delay) and (RC-Arrow). In the original definition delayed checking is done by using lambda abstractions, that is,

$$(V : \sigma_1 \to \sigma_2 \Rightarrow \tau_1 \to \tau_2) \longrightarrow \lambda x{:}\tau_1.(V\,(x : \tau_1 \Rightarrow \sigma_1) : \sigma_2 \Rightarrow \tau_2).$$

The reason we adopt a different way is just it makes technical development easier. Additionally, the way we adopt is not new—It is used in the original work [8] on higher-order contract calculi.

The other rules are new ones we propose for dynamic checking of intersection types. As we have discussed in Sect. 2, a cast into an intersection type is reduced into a pair of casts by (RC-WedgeI). A cast from an intersection type is done by (RC-Delay), (RC-Wedgel/R) if the target type is a function type. Otherwise, if the target type is a first order type, (RC-WedgeN) and (RC-WedgeB) are used, where we arbitrarily choose the left side of the intersection type and the corresponding part of the value since the source type is not used for dynamic checking of first-order values.

The contextual evaluation rules, defined in Fig. 7, are rather straightforward. Be aware of the use of metavariables, for instance, the use of N in (EC-Ctx); it implicitly means that M has not been evaluated into blame (so the rule does not overlap with (EB-Ctx)). The first rule lifts the reduction relation to the evaluation relation. The next six rules express the case where a sub-expression is successfully evaluated. The rules (EC-ActiveP) and (EC-ActiveC) mean that evaluation inside an active check is always considered dynamic checking, even

$$\frac{M \rightharpoonup_c C}{M \longrightarrow_c C} \text{ (EC-Red)} \qquad \frac{M \longrightarrow_c N}{\mathcal{E}[M] \longrightarrow_c \mathcal{E}[N]} \text{ (EC-Ctx)}$$

$$\frac{M \longrightarrow_p M'}{\langle\!\langle M \Longrightarrow V : \{x{:}\tau \mid N\}\rangle\!\rangle \longrightarrow_c \langle\!\langle M' \Longrightarrow V : \{x{:}\tau \mid N\}\rangle\!\rangle} \text{ (EC-ActiveP)}$$

$$\frac{M \longrightarrow_c M'}{\langle\!\langle M \Longrightarrow V : \{x{:}\tau \mid N\}\rangle\!\rangle \longrightarrow_c \langle\!\langle M' \Longrightarrow V : \{x{:}\tau \mid N\}\rangle\!\rangle} \text{ (EC-ActiveC)}$$

$$\frac{M \longrightarrow_c M'}{\langle M, N \rangle \longrightarrow_c \langle M', N \rangle} \text{ (EC-PairL)} \qquad \frac{N \longrightarrow_c N'}{\langle M, N \rangle \longrightarrow_c \langle M, N' \rangle} \text{ (EC-PairR)}$$

$$\frac{M \longrightarrow_c \texttt{blame}}{\mathcal{E}[M] \longrightarrow_c \texttt{blame}} \text{ (EB-Ctx)}$$

$$\frac{M \longrightarrow_c \texttt{blame}}{\langle\!\langle M \Longrightarrow V : \{x{:}\tau \mid N\}\rangle\!\rangle \longrightarrow_c \texttt{blame}} \text{ (EB-Active)}$$

$$\frac{M_i \longrightarrow_c \texttt{blame}}{\langle M_1, M_2 \rangle \longrightarrow_c \texttt{blame}} \text{ (EB-PairL/R)}$$

Fig. 7. Operational semantics of PCFvΔ_{H} (3): contextual rules for dynamic checking.

when it involves essential evaluation. The rules (EC-PairL) and (EC-PairR) mean that dynamic checking does not synchronize because the elements in a strong pair may have different casts. The other rules express the case where dynamic checking has failed. An expression evaluates to `blame` immediately— in one step—when a sub-expression evaluates to `blame`. Here is an example of execution of failing dynamic checking.

$$(0 : \texttt{nat} \Rightarrow \{x{:}\texttt{nat} \mid x > 0\}) + 1 \longrightarrow \langle\!\langle 0 \mathbin{?} \{x{:}\texttt{nat} \mid x > 0\}\rangle\!\rangle + 1$$
$$\longrightarrow \langle\!\langle 0 > 0 \Longrightarrow 0 : \{x{:}\texttt{nat} \mid x > 0\}\rangle\!\rangle + 1$$
$$\longrightarrow \langle\!\langle \texttt{false} \Longrightarrow 0 : \{x{:}\texttt{nat} \mid x > 0\}\rangle\!\rangle + 1$$
$$\longrightarrow \texttt{blame}$$

Definition 7 (Evaluation). *The one-step evaluation relation of PCFvΔ_{H}, denoted by $\longrightarrow$, is defined as $\longrightarrow_p \cup \longrightarrow_c$. The multi-step evaluation relation of PCFvΔ_{H}, denoted by $\longrightarrow^*$, is the reflexive and transitive closure of $\longrightarrow$.*

$$\emptyset \text{ ok (V-Empty)} \qquad \frac{\Gamma \text{ ok} \qquad \Vdash \tau \qquad (x \mathbin{\#} \Gamma)}{\Gamma, x{:}\tau \text{ ok}} \text{ (V-Push)}$$

$$\Vdash \texttt{nat} \text{ (W-Nat)} \qquad \Vdash \texttt{bool} \text{ (W-Bool)} \qquad \frac{\Vdash \sigma \qquad \Vdash \tau}{\Vdash \sigma \to \tau} \text{ (W-Arrow)}$$

$$\frac{\Vdash \sigma \qquad \Vdash \tau \qquad (\lfloor\sigma\rfloor = \lfloor\tau\rfloor)}{\Vdash \sigma \wedge \tau} \text{ (W-Wedge)} \qquad \frac{x{:}\tau \vdash M : \texttt{bool}}{\Vdash \{x{:}\tau \mid M\}} \text{ (W-Refine)}$$

Fig. 8. Type system of PCFvΔ_{H} (1): well-formedness rules.

3.4   Type System of PCFvΔ_H

The type system consists of three judgments: Γ ok, $\Vdash \tau$, and $\Gamma \vdash M : \tau$, read "Γ is well-formed", "τ is well-formed", and "M has τ under Γ," respectively. They are defined inductively by the rules in Figs. 8, 9 and 10.

The rules for well-formed types check that an intersection type is restricted to a refinement intersection type by the side condition $\langle\sigma\rangle = \langle\tau\rangle$ in (W-WEDGE) and that the predicate in a refinement type is a Boolean expression by (W-REFINE). Note that, since PCFvΔ_H has no dependent function type, all types are closed and the predicate of a refinement type only depends on the parameter itself.

The typing rules, the rules for the third judgment, consist of two more subcategories: compile-time rules and run-time rules. Compile-time rules are for checking a program a programmer writes. Run-time rules are for run-time expressions and used to prove type soundness. This distinction, which follows, Belo et al. [1], is to make compile-time type checking decidable.

$$\frac{\Gamma \text{ ok}}{\Gamma \vdash 0 : \mathbf{nat}}\ (\text{T-ZERO}) \qquad \frac{\Gamma \vdash M : \mathbf{nat}}{\Gamma \vdash \mathbf{succ}(M) : \mathbf{nat}}\ (\text{T-SUCC})$$

$$\frac{\Gamma \vdash M : \{x{:}\mathbf{nat} \mid \mathbf{if\ iszero}(x)\ \mathbf{then\ false\ else\ true}\}}{\Gamma \vdash \mathbf{pred}(M) : \mathbf{nat}}\ (\text{T-PRED})$$

$$\frac{\Gamma \vdash M : \mathbf{nat}}{\Gamma \vdash \mathbf{iszero}(M) : \mathbf{bool}}\ (\text{T-ISZERO}) \qquad \frac{\Gamma \text{ ok}}{\Gamma \vdash \mathbf{true} : \mathbf{bool}}\ (\text{T-TRUE})$$

$$\frac{\Gamma \text{ ok}}{\Gamma \vdash \mathbf{false} : \mathbf{bool}}\ (\text{T-FALSE})$$

$$\frac{\Gamma \vdash L : \mathbf{bool} \qquad \Gamma \vdash M : \tau \qquad \Gamma \vdash N : \tau}{\Gamma \vdash \mathbf{if}\ L\ \mathbf{then}\ M\ \mathbf{else}\ N : \tau}\ (\text{T-IF})$$

$$\frac{\Gamma \text{ ok} \qquad (x{:}\tau \in \Gamma)}{\Gamma \vdash x : \tau}\ (\text{T-VAR}) \qquad \frac{\Gamma, x{:}\sigma \vdash M : \tau}{\Gamma \vdash \lambda x{:}\sigma.M : \sigma \to \tau}\ (\text{T-ABS})$$

$$\frac{\Gamma \vdash M : \sigma \to \tau \qquad \Gamma \vdash N : \sigma}{\Gamma \vdash M\,N : \tau}\ (\text{T-APP})$$

$$\frac{\Gamma \vdash M : \sigma \qquad \Gamma \vdash N : \tau \qquad (\langle M\rangle = \langle N\rangle) \qquad (\langle\sigma\rangle = \langle\tau\rangle)}{\Gamma \vdash \langle M, N\rangle : \sigma \wedge \tau}\ (\text{T-PAIR})$$

$$\frac{\Gamma \vdash M : \sigma \wedge \tau}{\Gamma \vdash \pi_1(M) : \sigma}\ (\text{T-FST}) \quad \frac{\Gamma \vdash M : \sigma \wedge \tau}{\Gamma \vdash \pi_2(M) : \tau}\ (\text{T-SND}) \quad \frac{\Gamma, f{:}I \vdash B : I}{\Gamma \vdash \mu f{:}I.B : I}\ (\text{T-FIX})$$

$$\frac{\Gamma \vdash M : \sigma \qquad \Vdash \tau \qquad (\langle\sigma\rangle = \langle\tau\rangle)}{\Gamma \vdash (M : \sigma \Rightarrow \tau) : \tau}\ (\text{T-CAST})$$

Fig. 9. Type system of PCFvΔ_H (2): compile-time typing rules.

A large part of the compile-time rules are adapted from PCF, Sekiyama et al. [26], and Liquori and Stolze [17]. Here we explain some notable rules. As an intersection type system, (T-PAIR), (T-FST), and (T-SND) stands for introduction and elimination rules of intersection types (or we can explicitly introduce and/or eliminate an intersection type by a cast). The rule (T-PAIR) checks a strong pair is composed by essentially the same expressions by $\langle M \rangle = \langle N \rangle$. The rule (T-Pred) demands that the argument of predecessor shall not be zero. The premise $\langle \sigma \rangle = \langle \tau \rangle$ of the rule (T-Cast) for casts requires the essences of the source and target types to agree. It amounts to checking the two types σ and τ are compatible [26].

The run-time rules are from Sekiyama et al. [26] with one extra rule (T-Delayed). The rule (T-Delayed) is for a delayed checking for function types, which restrict the source type so that it respects the evaluation relation (there is no evaluation rule for a delayed checking in which source type is a refinement type), and inherits the condition on the source and target types from (T-Cast). The side condition $N[x \mapsto V] \longrightarrow^* M$ on (T-Active) is an invariant during evaluation, that is, M is an intermediate state of the predicate checking. This invariant lasts until the final (successful) run-time checking state $\langle\!\langle \mathtt{true} \Longrightarrow V : \{x{:}\tau \mid N\} \rangle\!\rangle$ and guarantees the checking result V (obtained by (RC-Succeed)) satisfies the predicate N by (T-Exact).

$$\frac{\Gamma \ \mathrm{ok} \quad \vdash V : \sigma \quad \Vdash \tau_1 \to \tau_2 \quad (\forall x \tau M. \sigma \neq \{x{:}\tau \mid M\}) \quad (\langle \sigma \rangle = \langle \tau_1 \to \tau_2 \rangle)}{\Gamma \vdash \langle\!\langle V : \sigma \Rightarrow \tau_1 \to \tau_2 \rangle\!\rangle : \tau_1 \to \tau_2} \quad \text{(T-Delayed)}$$

$$\frac{\Gamma \ \mathrm{ok} \quad \vdash M : \tau \quad \Vdash \{x{:}\tau \mid N\}}{\Gamma \vdash \langle\!\langle M \ ? \ \{x{:}\tau \mid N\} \rangle\!\rangle : \{x{:}\tau \mid N\}} \quad \text{(T-Waiting)}$$

$$\frac{\Gamma \ \mathrm{ok} \quad \vdash M : \mathtt{bool} \quad \vdash V : \tau \quad \Vdash \{x{:}\tau \mid N\} \quad N[x \mapsto V] \longrightarrow^* M}{\Gamma \vdash \langle\!\langle M \Longrightarrow V : \{x{:}\tau \mid N\} \rangle\!\rangle : \{x{:}\tau \mid N\}} \quad \text{(T-Active)}$$

$$\frac{\Gamma \ \mathrm{ok} \quad \vdash V : \{x{:}\tau \mid N\}}{\Gamma \vdash V : \tau} \quad \text{(T-Forget)}$$

$$\frac{\Gamma \ \mathrm{ok} \quad \vdash V : \tau \quad \Vdash \{x{:}\tau \mid N\} \quad N[x \mapsto V] \longrightarrow^* \mathtt{true}}{\Gamma \vdash V : \{x{:}\tau \mid N\}} \quad \text{(T-Exact)}$$

Fig. 10. Type system of PCFvΔ_{H} (3): run-time typing rules.

4 Properties

We start from properties of evaluation relations. As we have mentioned, $\longrightarrow_{\mathsf{p}}$ is essential evaluation, and thus, it should simulate $\longrightarrow_{\mathsf{PCF}}$; and $\longrightarrow_{\mathsf{c}}$ is dynamic checking, and therefore, it should not change the essence of the expression. We formally state and show these properties here. Note that most properties require that the expression before evaluation is well typed. This is because the condition of strong pairs is imposed by the type system.

Lemma 1. *If* $M \longrightarrow_{PCF} N$ *and* $M \longrightarrow_{PCF} L$, *then* $N = L$.

Proof. The proof is routine by induction on one of the given derivations.   □

Lemma 2. *If* $\vdash M : \tau$ *and* $M \longrightarrow_p N$, *then* $\wr M \wr \longrightarrow_{PCF} \wr N \wr$.

Proof. The proof is by induction on the given evaluation derivation.   □

The following corollary is required to prove the preservation property.

Corollary 1. *If* $\vdash M : \sigma$, $\vdash N : \tau$, $M \longrightarrow_p M'$, $N \longrightarrow_p N'$, *and* $\wr M \wr = \wr N \wr$; *then* $\wr M' \wr = \wr N' \wr$.

Lemma 3. *If* $\vdash M : \tau$ *and* $M \longrightarrow_c N$, *then* $\wr M \wr = \wr N \wr$.

Proof. The proof is by induction on the given evaluation derivation.   □

Now we can have the following theorem as a corollary of Lemma 2 and Lemma 3. It guarantees the essential computation in $\mathrm{PCFv}\Delta_H$ is the same as the PCFv computation as far as the computation does not fail. In other words, runtime checking may introduce blame but otherwise does not affect the essential computation.

Theorem 1. *If* $\vdash M : \tau$ *and* $M \longrightarrow N$, *then* $\wr M \wr \longrightarrow^*_{PCF} \wr N \wr$.

4.1   Type Soundness

We conclude this section with type soundness. Firstly, we show a substitution property; and using it, we show the preservation property.

Lemma 4. *If* $\Gamma_1, x{:}\sigma, \Gamma_2 \vdash M : \tau$ *and* $\Gamma_1 \vdash N : \sigma$, *then* $\Gamma_1, \Gamma_2 \vdash M[x \mapsto N] : \tau$.

Proof. The proof is by induction on the derivation for M.   □

Theorem 2 (Preservation). *If* $\vdash M : \tau$ *and* $M \longrightarrow N$, *then* $\vdash N : \tau$.

Proof. We prove preservation properties for each $\longrightarrow_p$ and $\longrightarrow_c$ and combine them. Both proofs are done by induction on the given typing derivation. For the case in which substitution happens, we use Lemma 4 as usual. For the context evaluation for strong pairs, we use Corollary 1 and Lemma 3 to guarantee the side-condition of strong pairs.   □

Next we show the value inversion property, which guarantees a value of a refinement type satisfies its predicate. For $\mathrm{PCFv}\Delta_H$, this property can be quite easily shown since $\mathrm{PCFv}\Delta_H$ does not have dependent function types, while previous manifest contract systems need quite complicated reasoning [19,24,26]. The property itself is proven by using the following two, which are for strengthening an induction hypothesis.

Definition 8. *We define a relation between values and types, written* $V \models \tau$, *by the following rules.*

$$\frac{V \models \tau \qquad M[x \mapsto V] \longrightarrow^* \mathbf{true}}{V \models \{x{:}\tau \mid M\}} \qquad \frac{(\tau \neq \{x{:}\sigma \mid M\})}{V \models \tau}$$

Lemma 5. *If $\vdash V : \tau$, then $V \models \tau$.*

Proof. The proof is by induction on the given derivation.   □

Theorem 3 (Value inversion). *If $\vdash V : \{x{:}\tau \mid M\}$, then $M[x \mapsto V] \longrightarrow^*$* true.

Proof. Immediate from Lemma 5.   □

Remark 1. As a corollary of value inversion, it follows that a value of an intersection type must be a strong pair and its elements satisfy the corresponding predicate in the intersection type: For example, if $\vdash \langle V_1, V_2 \rangle : \{x{:}\sigma \mid M\} \wedge \{x{:}\tau \mid N\}$, then $M[x \mapsto V_1] \longrightarrow^*$ true and $N[x \mapsto V_2] \longrightarrow^*$ true. In particular, for first-order values, every element of the pair is same. That means the value satisfies all contracts concatenated by $\wedge$. For example, $\vdash V : \{x{:}\mathtt{nat} \mid M_1\} \wedge \cdots \wedge \{x{:}\mathtt{nat} \mid M_n\}$, then $M_k[x \mapsto \wr V \wr] \longrightarrow^*$ true for any $k = 1..n$. This is what we have desired for a contract written by using intersection types.

Lastly, the progress property also holds. In our setting, where $\mathtt{pred}(M)$ is partial, this theorem can be proved only after Theorem 3.

Theorem 4 (Progress). *If $\vdash M : \tau$, then M is a value or $M \longrightarrow C$ for some C.*

Proof. The proof is by induction on the given derivation. Since the evaluation relation is defined as combination of $\longrightarrow_\mathsf{p}$ and $\longrightarrow_\mathsf{c}$, the proof is a bit tricky, but most cases can be proven as usual. An interesting case is (T-PAIR). We need to guarantee that if one side of a strong pair is a value, another side must not be evaluated by $\longrightarrow_\mathsf{p}$ since a value is in normal form. This follows from Lemma 2 and proof by contradiction because the essence of a PCFvΔ_H value is a PCFv value and it is normal form.   □

5   Related Work

Intersection types were introduced in Curry-style type assignment systems by Coppo et al. [6] and Pottinger [21] independently. In the early days, intersection types are motivated by improving a type system to make more lambda terms typeable; one important result towards this direction is that: *a lambda term has a type iff it can be strongly normalized* [21,29]. Then, intersection types are introduced to programming languages to enrich the descriptive power of types [2,7,22].

Intersection Contracts for Untyped Languages. One of the first attempts at implementing intersection-like contracts is found in DrRacket [9]. It is, however, a naive implementation, which just enforces all contracts even for functional values, and thus the semantics of higher-order intersection contracts is rather different from ours.

Keil and Thiemann [14] have proposed an untyped calculus of blame assignment for a higher-order contract system with intersection and union. As we have mentioned, our run-time checking semantics is strongly influenced by their work, but there are two essential differences. On the one hand, they do not have the problem of varying run-time checking according to a typing context; they can freely put contract monitors[4] where they want since it is an untyped language. On the other hand, their operational semantics is made rather complicated due to blame assignment.

More recently, Williams et al. [32] have proposed more sorted out semantics for a higher-order contract system with intersection and union. They have mainly reformed contract checking for intersection and union "in a uniform way"; that is, each is handled by only one similar and simpler rule. As a result, their presentation becomes closer to our semantics, though complication due to blame assignment still remains. A similar level of complication will be expected if we extend our calculus with blame assignment.

It would be interesting to investigate the relationship between their calculi and PCFvΔ_{H} extended with blame labels, following Greenberg et al. [12].

Gradual Typing with Intersection Types. Castagna and Lanvin [3] have proposed gradual typing for set-theoretic types, which contain intersection types, as well as union and negation. A framework of gradual typing is so close to manifest contract systems that there is even a study unifying them [31]. A gradual typing system translates a program into an intermediate language that is statically typed and uses casts. Hence, they have the same problem—how casts should be inserted when intersection types are used. They solve the problem by *type-case* expressions, which dynamically dispatch behavior according to the type of a value. However, it is not clear how type-case expressions scale to a larger language. In fact, the following work [4], an extension to parametric polymorphism and type inference, removes (necessity of) type-case expressions but imposes instead a restriction on functions not to have an intersection type. Furthermore, the solution using type-case expressions relies on strong properties of set-theoretic types. So, it is an open problem if their solution can be adopted to manifest contract systems because there is not set-theoretic type theory for refinement types and, even worse, dependent function types.

Nondeterminism for Dependently Typed Languages. As we have noted in Sect. 1, PCFvΔ_{H} has no dependent function types. In fact, no other work discussed in this section supports both dependent function contracts and intersection contracts. To extend PCFvΔ_{H} to dependent function types, we have to take care of their interaction with nondeterminism, which we studied elsewhere [19] for a manifest calculus $\lambda^{H\|\Phi}$ with a general nondeterministic choice operator.

---

[4] A kind of casts in their language.

A technical challenge in combining dependent function types and nondeterminstic choice comes from the following standard typing rule for (dependent) function applications:

$$\frac{\Gamma \vdash M : (x{:}\sigma) \to \tau \qquad \Gamma \vdash N : \sigma}{\Gamma \vdash M\,N : \tau[x \mapsto N]}$$

The problem is that the argument N, which may contain nondeterministic choice, may be duplicated in $\tau[x \mapsto N]$ and, to keep consistency of type equivalence, choices made in each occurrence of N have to be "synchronized." To control synchronization, $\lambda^{H\|\Phi}$ introduces a named choice operator so that choice operators with the same name make synchronized choice. However, $\lambda^{H\|\Phi}$ puts burden on programmers to avoid unintended synchronization caused by accidentally shared names.

If we incoporate the idea above to PCFvΔ_{H}, it will be natural to put names on casts so that necessary synchronization takes place for choices made by (RC-WEDGEL) and (RC-WEDGER). It is not clear, however, how unintended synchronization can be avoided systematically, without programmers' ingenuity.

6   Conclusion

We have designed and formalized a manifest contract system PCFvΔ_{H} with refinement intersection types. As a result of our formal development, PCFvΔ_{H} guarantees not only ordinary preservation and progress but also the property that a value of an intersection type, which can be seen as an enumeration of small contracts, satisfies all the contracts.

The characteristic point of our formalization is that we regard a manifest contract system as an extension of a more basic calculus, which has no software contract system, and investigate the relationship between the basic calculus and the manifest contract system. More specifically, essential computation and dynamic checking are separated. We believe this investigation is important for modern manifest contract systems because those become more and more complicated and the separation is no longer admissible at a glance.

Future Work. Obvious future work is to lift the restriction we have mentioned in Sect. 1. That aside, the subsumption-free approach is very naive and has an obvious disadvantage, that is, it requires run-time checking even for a cast like $(M : \sigma \wedge \tau \Rightarrow \sigma)$, which should be able to checked and removed at compile time. To address the disadvantage, some manifest contract systems provide the property known as *up-cast elimination* [1]—*a cast from subtype into supertype can be safely removed at compile-time.* An interesting fact is that a well-known up-cast (subtyping) relation for a traditional intersection type system is defined syntactically; while a usual up-cast relation for a manifest contract system depends on semantics. So, focusing on only the traditional subtyping relation, the property might be proven more easily.

Towards a practice language, our cast semantics using strong pairs and non-determinism needs more investigation. For the strong pairs, it will be quite inefficient to evaluate both sides of a strong pair independently since its essence part just computes the same thing. The inefficiency might be reduced by a kind of sharing structures. For the nondeterminism, our theoretical result gives us useful information only for successful evaluation paths; but we have not given a way to pick up a successful one. One obvious way is computing every evaluation path, but of course, it is quite inefficient.

Acknowledgments. We would like to thank Peter Thiemann, John Toman, Yuya Tsuda, and anonymous reviewers for useful comments. This work was supported in part by the JSPS KAKENHI Grant Number JP17H01723.

References

1. Belo, J.F., Greenberg, M., Igarashi, A., Pierce, B.C.: Polymorphic contracts. In: Barthe, G. (ed.) ESOP 2011. LNCS, vol. 6602, pp. 18–37. Springer, Heidelberg (2011). https://doi.org/10.1007/978-3-642-19718-5_2
2. Benzaken, V., Castagna, G., Frisch, A.: CDuce: an XML-centric general-purpose language. In: Proceedings of ICFP, pp. 51–63 (2003)
3. Castagna, G., Lanvin, V.: Gradual typing with union and intersection types. PACMPL 1(ICFP), 41:1–41:28 (2017)
4. Castagna, G., Lanvin, V., Petrucciani, T., Siek, J.G.: Gradual typing: a new perspective. Proc. ACM Program. Lang. 3(POPL), 16:1–16:32 (2019)
5. Charguéraud, A.: The locally nameless representation. J. Autom. Reasoning 49(3), 363–408 (2012)
6. Coppo, M., Dezani-Ciancaglini, M., Venneri, B.: Functional characters of solvable terms. Math. Log. Q. 27(2–6), 45–58 (1981)
7. Dunfield, J.: Refined typechecking with stardust. In: Proceedings of PLPV, pp. 21–32 (2007)
8. Findler, R.B., Felleisen, M.: Contracts for higher-order functions. In: Proceedings of ICFP, pp. 48–59 (2002)
9. Findler, R.B., PLT: DrRacket: programming environment. Technical report, PLT-TR-2010-2, PLT Design Inc. (2010). https://racket-lang.org/tr2/
10. Flanagan, C.: Hybrid type checking. In: Proceedings of POPL, pp. 245–256 (2006)
11. Greenberg, M.: Space-efficient manifest contracts. In: Proceedings of POPL, pp. 181–194 (2015)
12. Greenberg, M., Pierce, B.C., Weirich, S.: Contracts made manifest. In: Proceedings of POPL, pp. 353–364 (2010)
13. Gronski, J., Knowles, K., Tomb, A., Freund, S.N., Flanagan, C.: Sage: hybrid checking for flexible specifications. In: Scheme and Functional Programming Workshop, pp. 93–104 (2006)
14. Keil, M., Thiemann, P.: Blame assignment for higher-order contracts with intersection and union. In: Proceedings of ICFP, pp. 375–386 (2015)
15. Knowles, K., Flanagan, C.: Hybrid type checking. ACM Trans. Program. Lang. Syst. 32(2), 6:1–6:34 (2010)
16. Kobayashi, N., Sato, R., Unno, H.: Predicate abstraction and CEGAR for higher-order model checking. In: Proceedings of PLDI, pp. 222–233 (2011)

17. Liquori, L., Stolze, C.: The Δ-calculus: syntax and types. In: Proceedings of FSCD, pp. 28:1–28:20 (2018)
18. Meyer, B.: Object-Oriented Software Construction, 2nd edn. Prentice-Hall, Upper Saddle River (1997)
19. Nishida, Y., Igarashi, A.: Nondeterministic manifest contracts. In: Proceedings of PPDP, pp. 16:1–16:13 (2018)
20. Plotkin, G.D.: LCF considered as a programming language. Theor. Comput. Sci. **5**(3), 223–255 (1977)
21. Pottinger, G.: A type assignment for the strongly normalizabile λ-terms. In: To H. B. Curry, Essays in Combinatory Logic, Lambda-Calculus and Formalism, pp. 561–577 (1980)
22. Reynolds, J.C.: Preliminary design of the programming language Forsythe. Technical report, CMU-CS-88-159, Carnegie Mellon University (1988)
23. Rondon, P.M., Kawaguchi, M., Jhala, R.: Liquid types. In: Proceedings of PLDI, pp. 159–169 (2008)
24. Sekiyama, T., Igarashi, A.: Stateful manifest contracts. In: Proceedings of POPL, pp. 530–544 (2017)
25. Sekiyama, T., Igarashi, A., Greenberg, M.: Polymorphic manifest contracts, revised and resolved. ACM Trans. Program. Lang. Syst. **39**(1), 3:1–3:36 (2017)
26. Sekiyama, T., Nishida, Y., Igarashi, A.: Manifest contracts for datatypes. In: Proceedings of POPL, pp. 195–207 (2015)
27. Terauchi, T.: Dependent types from counterexamples. In: Proceedings of POPL, pp. 119–130 (2010)
28. Unno, H., Kobayashi, N.: Dependent type inference with interpolants. In: Proceedings of PPDP, pp. 277–288 (2009)
29. Valentini, S.: An elementary proof of strong normalization for intersection types. Arch. Math. Log. **40**(7), 475–488 (2001)
30. Vazou, N., Seidel, E.L., Jhala, R., Vytiniotis, D., Peyton-Jones, S.: Refinement types for Haskell. In: Proceedings of ICFP, pp. 269–282 (2014)
31. Wadler, P., Findler, R.B.: Well-typed programs can't be blamed. In: Proceedings of ESOP, pp. 1–16 (2009)
32. Williams, J., Morris, J.G., Wadler, P.: The root cause of blame: contracts for intersection and union types. Proc. ACM Program. Lang. **2**(OOPSLA), 134:1–134:29 (2018)
33. Zhu, H., Jagannathan, S.: Compositional and lightweight dependent type inference for ML. In: Giacobazzi, R., Berdine, J., Mastroeni, I. (eds.) VMCAI 2013. LNCS, vol. 7737, pp. 295–314. Springer, Heidelberg (2013). https://doi.org/10.1007/978-3-642-35873-9_19

A Dependently Typed Multi-stage Calculus

Akira Kawata$^{(\boxtimes)}$ and Atsushi Igarashi

Graduate School of Informatics, Kyoto University, Kyoto, Japan
akira@fos.kuis.kyoto-u.ac.jp, igarashi@kuis.kyoto-u.ac.jp

Abstract. We study a dependently typed extension of a multi-stage programming language à la MetaOCaml, which supports quasi-quotation and cross-stage persistence for manipulation of code fragments as first-class values and an evaluation construct for execution of programs dynamically generated by this code manipulation. Dependent types are expected to bring to multi-stage programming enforcement of strong invariant—beyond simple type safety—on the behavior of dynamically generated code. An extension is, however, not trivial because such a type system would have to take stages of types—roughly speaking, the number of surrounding quotations—into account.

To rigorously study properties of such an extension, we develop λ^{MD}, which is an extension of Hanada and Igarashi's typed calculus $\lambda^{\triangleright\%}$ with dependent types, and prove its properties including preservation, confluence, strong normalization for full reduction, and progress for staged reduction. Motivated by code generators that generate code whose type depends on a value from outside of the quotations, we argue the significance of cross-stage persistence in dependently typed multi-stage programming and certain type equivalences that are not directly derived from reduction rules.

Keywords: Multi-stage programming · Cross-stage persistence · Dependent types

1 Introduction

1.1 Multi-stage Programming and MetaOCaml

Multi-stage programming makes it easier for programmers to implement generation and execution of code at run time by providing language constructs for composing and running pieces of code as first-class values. A promising application of multi-stage programming is (run-time) code specialization, which generates program code specialized to partial inputs to the program and such applications are studied in the literature [17,20,29].

MetaOCaml [6,18] is an extension of OCaml[1] with special constructs for multi-stage programming, including brackets and escape, which are (hygienic)

---

[1] http://ocaml.org.

© Springer Nature Switzerland AG 2019
A. W. Lin (Ed.): APLAS 2019, LNCS 11893, pp. 53–72, 2019.
https://doi.org/10.1007/978-3-030-34175-6_4

quasi-quotation, and `run`, which is similar to `eval` in Lisp, and cross-stage persistence (CSP) [31]. Programmers can easily write code generators by using these features. Moreover, MetaOCaml is equipped with a powerful type system for safe code generation and execution. The notion of code types is introduced to prevent code values that represent ill-typed expressions from being generated. For example, a quotation of expression `1 + 1` is given type `int code` and a code-generating function, which takes a code value c as an argument and returns $c + c$, is given type `int code -> int code` so that it cannot be applied to, say, a quotation of `"Hello"`, which is given type `string code`. Ensuring safety for `run` is more challenging because code types by themselves do not guarantee that the execution of code values never results in unbound variable errors. Taha and Nielsen [30] introduced the notion of environment classifiers to address the problem, developed a type system to ensure not only type-safe composition but also type-safe execution of code values, and proved a type soundness theorem (for a formal calculus λ^α modeling a pure subset of MetaOCaml).

However, the type system, which is based on the Hindley–Milner polymorphism [23], is not strong enough to guarantee invariant beyond simple types. For example, Kiselyov [17] demonstrates specialization of vector/matrix computation with respect to the sizes of vectors and matrices in MetaOCaml but the type system of MetaOCaml cannot prevent such specialized functions from being applied to vectors and matrices of different sizes.

1.2 Multi-stage Programming with Dependent Types

One natural idea to address this problem is the introduction of dependent types to express the size of data structures in static types [34]. For example, we could declare vector types indexed by the size of vectors as follows.

```
Vector :: Int -> *
```

`Vector` is a type constructor that takes an integer (which represents the length of vectors): for example, `Vector 3` is the type for vectors whose lengths are 3. Then, our hope is to specialize vector/matrix functions with respect to their size and get a piece of function code, whose type respects the given size, *provided at specialization time*. For example, we would like to specialize a function to add two vectors with respect to the size of vectors, that is, to implement a code generator that takes a (nonnegative) integer n as an input and generates a piece of function code of type (`Vector` n `-> Vector` n `-> Vector` n) `code`.

1.3 Our Work

In this paper, we develop a new multi-stage calculus λ^{MD} by extending the existing multi-stage calculus $\lambda^{\triangleright\%}$ [14] with dependent types and study its properties. We base our work on $\lambda^{\triangleright\%}$, in which the four multi-stage constructs are handled slightly differently from MetaOCaml, because its type system and semantics are arguably simpler than λ^α [30], which formalizes the design of MetaOCaml more faithfully. Dependent types are based on λLF [1], which has one of the simplest forms of dependent types. Our technical contributions are summarized as follows:

- We give a formal definition of λ^{MD} with its syntax, type system and two kinds of reduction: full reduction, allowing reduction of any redex, including one under λ-abstraction and quotation, and staged reduction, a small-step call-by-value operational semantics that is closer to the intended multi-stage implementation.
- We show preservation, strong normalization, and confluence for full reduction; and show unique decomposition (and progress as its corollary) for staged reduction.

The combination of multi-stage programming and dependent types has been discussed by Pasalic, Taha, and Sheard [26] and Brady and Hammond [5] but, to our knowledge, our work is a first formal calculus of full-spectrum dependently typed multi-stage programming with all the key constructs mentioned above.

Organization of the Paper. The organization of this paper is as follows. Section 2 gives an informal overview of λ^{MD}. Section 3 defines λ^{MD} and Sect. 4 shows properties of λ^{MD}. Section 5 discusses related work and Sect. 6 concludes the paper with discussion of future work. We omit proofs and (details of) some definitions for brevity; interested readers are referred to a full version of the paper, which is available at https://arxiv.org/abs/1908.02035.

2   Informal Overview of λ^{MD}

We describe our calculus λ^{MD} informally. λ^{MD} is based on $\lambda^{\triangleright\%}$ [14] by Hanada and Igarashi and so we start with a review of $\lambda^{\triangleright\%}$.

2.1 $\lambda^{\triangleright\%}$

In $\lambda^{\triangleright\%}$, brackets (quasi-quotation) and escape (unquote) are written $\blacktriangleright_\alpha M$ and $\blacktriangleleft_\alpha M$, respectively. For example, $\blacktriangleright_\alpha (1+1)$ represents code of expression $1+1$ and thus evaluates to itself. Escape $\blacktriangleleft_\alpha M$ may appear under $\blacktriangleright_\alpha$; it evaluates M to a code value and splices it into the surrounding code fragment. Such splicing is expressed by the following reduction rule:

$$\blacktriangleleft_\alpha(\blacktriangleright_\alpha M) \longrightarrow M.$$

The subscript α in $\blacktriangleright_\alpha$ and $\blacktriangleleft_\alpha$ is a *stage variable*[2] and a sequence of stage variables is called a *stage*. Intuitively, a stage represents the depth of nested brackets. Stage variables can be abstracted by $\Lambda\alpha.M$ and instantiated

---

[2] In Hanada and Igarashi [14], it was called a *transition variable*, which is derived from correspondence to modal logic, studied by Tsukada and Igarashi [32].

by an application M A to stages. For example, $\Lambda\alpha.\blacktriangleright_\alpha((\lambda x : \text{Int}.x + 10)\ 5)$ is a code value, where α is abstracted. If it is applied to $A = \alpha_1 \cdots \alpha_n$, $\blacktriangleright_\alpha$ becomes $\blacktriangleright_{\alpha_1} \cdots \blacktriangleright_{\alpha_n}$; in particular, if $n = 0$, $\blacktriangleright_\alpha$ disappears. So, an application of $\Lambda\alpha.\blacktriangleright_\alpha((\lambda x : \text{Int}.x + 10)\ 5)$ to the empty sequence ε reduces to (unquoted) $(\lambda x : \text{Int}.x + 10)\ 5$ and to 15. In other words, application of a Λ-abstraction to ε corresponds to **run**. This is expressed by the following reduction rule:

$$(\Lambda\alpha.M)\ A \longrightarrow M[\alpha \mapsto A]$$

where stage substitution $[\alpha \mapsto A]$ manipulates the nesting of $\blacktriangleright_\alpha$ and $\blacktriangleleft_\alpha$ (and also $\%_\alpha$ as we see later).

Cross-stage persistence (CSP), which is an important feature of $\lambda^{\triangleright\%}$, is a primitive to embed values (not necessarily code values) into a code value. For example, a $\lambda^{\triangleright\%}$-term

$$M_1 = \lambda x : \text{Int}.\Lambda\alpha.(\blacktriangleright_\alpha((\%_\alpha x) * 2))$$

takes an integer x as an input and returns a code value, into which x is embedded. If M_1 is applied to $38 + 4$ as in

$$M_2 = (\lambda x : \text{Int}.\Lambda\alpha.(\blacktriangleright_\alpha((\%_\alpha x) * 2)))\ (38 + 4),$$

then it evaluates to $M_3 = \Lambda\alpha.(\blacktriangleright_\alpha((\%_\alpha 42) * 2))$. According to the semantics of $\lambda^{\triangleright\%}$, the subterm $\%_\alpha 42$ means that it waits for the surrounding code to be run (by an application to ε) and so it does not reduce further. If M_3 is run by application to ε, substitution of ε for α eliminates $\blacktriangleright_\alpha$ and $\%_\alpha$ and so $42 * 2$, which reduces to 84, is obtained. CSP is practically important because one can call library functions from inside quotations.

The type system of $\lambda^{\triangleright\%}$ uses code types—the type of code of type τ is written $\triangleright_\alpha\tau$—for typing $\blacktriangleright_\alpha$, $\blacktriangleleft_\alpha$ and $\%_\alpha$. It takes stages into account: a variable declaration (written $x : \tau@A$) in a type environment is associated with its declared stage A as well as its type τ and the type judgement of $\lambda^{\triangleright\%}$ is of the form $\Gamma \vdash M : \tau@A$, in which A stands for the stage of term M.[3] For example, $y : \text{Int}@\alpha \vdash (\lambda x : \text{Int}.y) : \text{Int} \to \text{Int}@\alpha$ holds, but $y : \text{Int}@\alpha \vdash (\lambda x : \text{Int}.y) : \text{Int} \to \text{Int}@\varepsilon$ does not because the latter uses y at stage ε but y is declared at α. Quotation $\blacktriangleright_\alpha M$ is given type $\triangleright_\alpha\tau$ at stage A if M is given type τ at stage $A\alpha$; unquote $\blacktriangleleft_\alpha M$ is given type τ at stage $A\alpha$ if M is given type $\triangleright_\alpha\tau$ at stage $A\alpha$; and CSP $\%_\alpha M$ is give type τ at stage $A\alpha$ if M is given type τ at A. These are expressed by the following typing rules.

$$\frac{\Gamma \vdash M : \tau@A\alpha}{\Gamma \vdash \blacktriangleright_\alpha M : \triangleright_\alpha\tau@A} \qquad \frac{\Gamma \vdash M : \triangleright_\alpha\tau@A}{\Gamma \vdash \blacktriangleleft_\alpha M : \tau@A\alpha} \qquad \frac{\Gamma \vdash M : \tau@A}{\Gamma \vdash \%_\alpha M : \tau@A\alpha}$$

2.2   Extending $\lambda^{\triangleright\%}$ with Dependent Types

In this paper, we add a simple form of dependent types—à la Edinburgh LF [15] and λLF [1]—to $\lambda^{\triangleright\%}$. Types can be indexed by terms as in **Vector** in Sect. 1

---

[3] In Hanada and Igarashi [14], it is written $\Gamma \vdash^A M : \tau$.

and λ-abstractions can be given dependent function types of the form $\Pi x : \tau.\sigma$ but we do not consider type operators (such as $\text{list}\,\tau$) or abstraction over type variables. We introduce kinds to classify well-formed types and equivalences for kinds, types, and terms—as in other dependent type systems—but we have to address a question how the notion of stage (should) interact with kinds and types.

On the one hand, base types such as Int should be able to be used at every stage as in $\lambda^{\triangleright\%}$ so that $\lambda x : \text{Int}.\varLambda\alpha.\blacktriangleright_\alpha\lambda y : \text{Int}.M$ is a valid term (here, Int is used at ε and α). Similarly for indexed types such as Vector 4. On the other hand, it is not immediately clear how a type indexed by a variable, which can be used only at a declared stage, can be used. For example, consider

$$\blacktriangleright_\alpha(\lambda x : \text{Int}.(\blacktriangleleft_\alpha(\lambda y : \text{Vector } x.M)N)) \text{ and } \lambda x : \text{Int}.\blacktriangleright_\alpha(\lambda y : \text{Vector } x.M).$$

Is Vector x a legitimate type at ε (and α, resp.) even if x : Int is declared at stage α (and ε, resp.)? We will give our answer to this question in two steps.

First, type-level constants such as Int and Vector can be used at every stage in λ^{MD}. Technically, we introduce a signature that declares kinds of type-level constants and types of constants. For example, a signature for the Boolean type and constants is given as follows $\text{Bool} :: *, \text{true} : \text{Bool}, \text{false} : \text{Bool}$ (where $*$ is the kind of proper types). Declarations in a signature are not associated to particular stages; so they can be used at every stage.

Second, an indexed type such as Vector 3 or Vector x is well formed only at the stage(s) where the index term is well-typed. Since constant 3 is well-typed at every stage (if it is declared in the signature), Vector 3 is a well-formed type at every stage, too. However, Vector M is well-formed only at the stage where index term M is typed. Thus, the kinding judgment of λ^{MD} takes the form $\Gamma \vdash_\Sigma \tau :: K @ A$, where stage A stands for where τ is well-formed. For example, given Vector :: $\text{Int} \to *$ in the signature Σ, $x : \text{Int}@\varepsilon \vdash_\Sigma \text{Vector } x :: *@\varepsilon$ can be derived but neither $x : \text{Int}@\alpha \vdash_\Sigma \text{Vector } x :: *@\varepsilon$ nor $x : \text{Int}@\varepsilon \vdash_\Sigma \text{Vector } x :: *@\alpha$ can be.

Apparently, the restriction above sounds too severe, because a term like $\lambda x : \text{Int}.\blacktriangleright_\alpha(\lambda y : \text{Vector } x.M)$, which models a typical code generator which takes the size x and returns code for vector manipulation specialized to the given size, will be rejected. It seems crucial for y to be given a type indexed by x. We can address this problem by CSP—In fact, Vector x is not well formed at α under $x : \text{Int}@\varepsilon$ but Vector $(\%_\alpha x)$ is! Thus, we can still write $\lambda x : \text{Int}.\blacktriangleright_\alpha(\lambda y : \text{Vector } (\%_\alpha x).M)$ for the typical sort of code generators.

Our decision that well-formedness of types takes stages of index terms into account will lead to the introduction of CSP at the type level and special equivalence rules, as we will see later.

3 Formal Definition of λ^{MD}

In this section, we give a formal definition of λ^{MD}, including the syntax, full reduction, and type system. In addition to the full reduction, in which any redex at any stage can be reduced, we also give staged reduction, which models program execution (at ε-stage).

3.1 Syntax

We assume the denumerable set of *type-level constants*, ranged over by metavariables X, Y, Z, the denumerable set of *variables*, ranged over by x, y, z, the denumerable set of *constants*, ranged over by c, and the denumerable set of *stage variables*, ranged over by α, β, γ. The metavariables A, B, C range over sequences of stage variables; we write ε for the empty sequence. λ^{MD} is defined by the following grammar:

$$
\begin{array}{rl}
\text{kinds} & K, J, I, H, G ::= * \mid \Pi x : \tau.K \\
\text{types} & \tau, \sigma, \rho, \pi, \xi ::= X \mid \Pi x : \tau.\sigma \mid \tau \; M \mid \triangleright_\alpha \tau \mid \forall \alpha.\tau \\
\text{terms} & M, N, L, O, P ::= c \mid x \mid \lambda x : \tau.M \mid M \; N \mid \blacktriangleright_\alpha M \\
& \qquad\qquad \mid \blacktriangleleft_\alpha M \mid \Lambda \alpha.M \mid M \; A \mid \%_\alpha M \\
\text{signatures} & \Sigma ::= \emptyset \mid \Sigma, X :: K \mid \Sigma, c : \tau \\
\text{type env.} & \Gamma ::= \emptyset \mid \Gamma, x : \tau @ A
\end{array}
$$

A kind, which is used to classify types, is either $*$, the kind of proper types (types that terms inhabit), or $\Pi x : \tau.K$, the kind of type operators that takes x as an argument of type τ and returns a type of kind K. A type is a type-level constant X, which is declared in the signature with its kind, a dependent function type $\Pi x : \tau.\sigma$, an application $\tau \; M$ of a type (operator of Π-kind) to a term, a code type $\triangleright_\alpha \tau$, or an α-closed type $\forall \alpha.\tau$. An example of an application of a type (operator) of Π-kind to a term is Vector 10; it is well kinded if, say, the type-level constant Vector has kind $\Pi x : \mathrm{Int}.*$. A code type $\triangleright_\alpha \tau$ is for a code fragment of a term of type τ. An α-closed type, when used with $\triangleright_\alpha$, represents runnable code.

Terms include ordinary (explicitly typed) λ-terms, constants, whose types are declared in signature Σ, and the following five forms related to multi-stage programming: $\blacktriangleright_\alpha M$ represents a code fragment; $\blacktriangleleft_\alpha M$ represents escape; $\Lambda \alpha.M$ is a stage variable abstraction; $M \; A$ is an application of a stage abstraction M to stage A; and $\%_\alpha M$ is an operator for cross-stage persistence.

We adopt the tradition of λLF-like systems, where types of constants and kinds of type-level constants are globally declared in a signature Σ, which is a sequence of declarations of the form $c : \tau$ and $X :: K$. For example, when we use Boolean in λ^{MD}, Σ includes Bool $::$ $*$, true : Bool, false : Bool. Type environments are sequences of triples of a variable, its type, and its stage. We write $dom(\Sigma)$ and $dom(\Gamma)$ for the set of (type-level) constants and variables declared in Σ and Γ, respectively. As in other multi-stage calculi [14,30,32], a variable declaration is associated with a stage so that a variable can be referenced only at the declared stage. On the contrary, constants and type-level constants are *not* associated with stages; so, they can appear at any stage. We define well-formed signatures and well-formed type environments later.

The variable x is bound in M by $\lambda x : \tau.M$ and in σ by $\Pi x : \tau.\sigma$, as usual; the stage variable α is bound in M by $\Lambda\alpha.M$ and τ by $\forall\alpha.\tau$. The notion of free variables is defined in a standard manner. We write $\mathrm{FV}(M)$ and $\mathrm{FSV}(M)$ for the set of free variables and the set of free stage variables in M, respectively. Similarly, $\mathrm{FV}(\tau)$, $\mathrm{FSV}(\tau)$, $\mathrm{FV}(K)$, and $\mathrm{FSV}(K)$ are defined. We sometimes abbreviate $\Pi x : \tau_1.\tau_2$ to $\tau_1 \to \tau_2$ if x is not a free variable of τ_2. We identify α-convertible terms and assume the names of bound variables are pairwise distinct.

The prefix operators $\triangleright_\alpha, \blacktriangleright_\alpha, \blacktriangleleft_\alpha$, and $\%_\alpha$ are given higher precedence over the three forms $\tau\ M$, $M\ N$, $M\ A$ of applications, which are left-associative. The binders Π, $\forall$, and λ extend as far to the right as possible. Thus, $\forall\alpha.\triangleright_\alpha(\Pi x : \mathrm{Int}.\mathrm{Vector}\ 5)$ is interpreted as $\forall\alpha.(\triangleright_\alpha(\Pi x : \mathrm{Int}.(\mathrm{Vector}\ 5)))$; and $\Lambda\alpha.\lambda x : \mathrm{Int}.\blacktriangleright_\alpha x\ y$ means $\Lambda\alpha.(\lambda x : \mathrm{Int}.(\blacktriangleright_\alpha x)\ y)$.

Remark: Basically, we define λ^{MD} to be an extension of $\lambda^{\triangleright\%}$ with dependent types. One notable difference is that λ^{MD} has only one kind of α-closed types, whereas $\lambda^{\triangleright\%}$ has two kinds of α-closed types $\forall\alpha.\tau$ and $\forall^\varepsilon\alpha.\tau$. We have omitted the first kind, for simplicity, and dropped the superscript ε from the second. It would not be difficult to recover the distinction to show properties related to program residualization [14], although they are left as conjectures.

3.2 Reduction

Next, we define full reduction for λ^{MD}. Before giving the definition of reduction, we define two kinds of substitutions. Substitution $M[x \mapsto N], \tau[x \mapsto N]$ and $K[x \mapsto N]$ are ordinary capture-avoiding substitution of term N for x in term M, type τ, and kind K, respectively, and we omit their definitions here. Substitution $M[\alpha \mapsto A], \tau[\alpha \mapsto A], K[\alpha \mapsto A]$ and $B[\alpha \mapsto A]$ are substitutions of stage A for stage variable α in term M, type τ, kind K, and stage B, respectively. We show representative cases below.

$$(\lambda x : \tau.M)[\alpha \mapsto A] = \lambda x : (\tau[\alpha \mapsto A]).(M[\alpha \mapsto A])$$
$$(M\ B)[\alpha \mapsto A] = (M[\alpha \mapsto A])\ B[\alpha \mapsto A]$$
$$(\blacktriangleright_\beta M)[\alpha \mapsto A] = \blacktriangleright_{\beta[\alpha\mapsto A]} M[\alpha \mapsto A]$$
$$(\blacktriangleleft_\beta M)[\alpha \mapsto A] = \blacktriangleleft_{\beta[\alpha\mapsto A]} M[\alpha \mapsto A]$$
$$(\%_\beta M)[\alpha \mapsto A] = \%_{\beta[\alpha\mapsto A]} M[\alpha \mapsto A]$$
$$(\beta B)[\alpha \mapsto A] = \beta(B[\alpha \mapsto A]) \qquad\qquad (\text{if } \alpha \neq \beta)$$
$$(\beta B)[\alpha \mapsto A] = A(B[\alpha \mapsto A]) \qquad\qquad (\text{if } \alpha = \beta)$$

Here, $\blacktriangleright_{\alpha_1\cdots\alpha_n} M$, $\blacktriangleleft_{\alpha_1\cdots\alpha_n} M$, and $\%_{\alpha_1\cdots\alpha_n} M$ $(n \geq 0)$ stand for $\blacktriangleright_{\alpha_1}\cdots\blacktriangleright_{\alpha_n} M$, $\blacktriangleleft_{\alpha_n}\cdots\blacktriangleleft_{\alpha_1} M$, and $\%_{\alpha_n}\cdots\%_{\alpha_1} M$, respectively. In particular, $\blacktriangleright_\varepsilon M = \blacktriangleleft_\varepsilon M = \%_\varepsilon M = M$. Also, it is important that the order of stage variables is reversed for $\blacktriangleleft$ and $\%$. We also define substitutions of a stage or a term for variables in type environment Γ.

Definition 1 (Reduction). *The relations* $M \longrightarrow_\beta N$, $M \longrightarrow_\blacklozenge N$, *and* $M \longrightarrow_\Lambda N$ *are the least compatible relations closed under the rules below.*

$$(\lambda x : \tau.M)N \longrightarrow_\beta M[x \mapsto N]$$
$$\blacktriangleleft_\alpha \blacktriangleright_\alpha M \longrightarrow_\blacklozenge M$$
$$(\Lambda\alpha.M)\ A \longrightarrow_\Lambda M[\alpha \mapsto A]$$

We write $M \longrightarrow M'$ iff $M \longrightarrow_\beta M'$, $M \longrightarrow_\blacklozenge M'$, or $M \longrightarrow_\Lambda M'$ and we call $\longrightarrow_\beta$, $\longrightarrow_\blacklozenge$, and $\longrightarrow_\Lambda$ β-reduction, $\blacklozenge$-reduction, and Λ-reduction, respectively. $M \longrightarrow^* N$ means that there is a sequence of reduction $\longrightarrow$ whose length is greater than or equal to 0.

The relation $\longrightarrow_\beta$ represents ordinary β-reduction in the λ-calculus; the relation $\longrightarrow_\blacklozenge$ represents that quotation $\blacktriangleright_\alpha M$ is canceled by escape and M is spliced into the code fragment surrounding the escape; the relation $\longrightarrow_\Lambda$ means that a stage abstraction applied to stage A reduces to the body of the abstraction where A is substituted for the stage variable. There is no reduction rule for CSP as with Hanada and Igarashi [14]. The CSP operator $\%_\alpha$ disappears when ε is substituted for α. We show an example of a reduction sequence below. Underlines show the redexes.

$$\underline{(\lambda f : \text{Int} \to \text{Int}.(\Lambda\alpha.\blacktriangleright_\alpha(\%_\alpha f\ 1 + (\blacktriangleleft_\alpha \blacktriangleright_\alpha 3))\ \varepsilon))\ (\lambda x : \text{Int}.x)}$$
$$\longrightarrow_\beta (\Lambda\alpha.\blacktriangleright_\alpha(\%_\alpha(\lambda x : \text{Int}.x)\ 1 + (\underline{\blacktriangleleft_\alpha \blacktriangleright_\alpha 3})))\ \varepsilon$$
$$\longrightarrow_\blacklozenge \underline{(\Lambda\alpha.\blacktriangleright_\alpha(\%_\alpha(\lambda x : \text{Int}.x)\ 1 + 3))\ \varepsilon}$$
$$\longrightarrow_\Lambda \underline{(\lambda x : \text{Int}.x)\ 1} + 3$$
$$\longrightarrow_\beta 1 + 3$$
$$\longrightarrow^* 4$$

3.3   Type System

In this section, we define the type system of λ^{MD}. It consists of eight judgment forms for signature well-formedness, type environment well-formedness, kind well-formedness, kinding, typing, kind equivalence, type equivalence, and term equivalence. We list the judgment forms in Fig. 1. They are all defined in a mutual recursive manner. We will discuss each judgment below.

Signature and Type Environment Well-Formedness. The rules for Well-formed signatures and type environments are shown below:

$$\frac{}{\vdash \emptyset} \qquad \frac{\vdash \Sigma \quad \vdash_\Sigma K \text{ kind}@\varepsilon \quad X \notin dom(\Sigma)}{\vdash \Sigma, X :: K} \qquad \frac{\vdash \Sigma \quad \vdash_\Sigma \tau :: *@\varepsilon \quad c \notin dom(\Sigma)}{\vdash \Sigma, c : \tau}$$

$$\frac{}{\vdash_\Sigma \emptyset} \qquad \frac{\vdash_\Sigma \Gamma \quad \Gamma \vdash_\Sigma \tau :: *@A \quad x \notin dom(\Sigma)}{\vdash_\Sigma \Gamma, x : \tau@A}$$

$$\vdash \Sigma \qquad\qquad \text{signature well-formedness}$$
$$\vdash_\Sigma \Gamma \qquad\qquad \text{type environment well-formedness}$$
$$\Gamma \vdash_\Sigma K \text{ kind@}A \qquad\qquad \text{kind well-formedness}$$
$$\Gamma \vdash_\Sigma \tau :: K@A \qquad\qquad \text{kinding}$$
$$\Gamma \vdash_\Sigma M : \tau@A \qquad\qquad \text{typing}$$
$$\Gamma \vdash_\Sigma K \equiv J@A \qquad\qquad \text{kind equivalence}$$
$$\Gamma \vdash_\Sigma \tau \equiv \sigma :: K@A \qquad\qquad \text{type equivalence}$$
$$\Gamma \vdash_\Sigma M \equiv N : \tau@A \qquad\qquad \text{term equivalence}$$

Fig. 1. Eight judgment forms of the type system of λ^{MD}.

To add declarations to a signature, the kind/type of a (type-level) constant has to be well-formed at stage ε so that it is used at any stage. In what follows, well-formedness is not explicitly mentioned but we assume that all signatures and type environments are well-formed.

Kind Well-Formedness and Kinding. The rules for kind well-formedness and kinding are a straightforward adaptation from λLF and $\lambda^{\triangleright\%}$, except for the following rule for type-level CSP.

$$\frac{\Gamma \vdash_\Sigma \tau :: *@A}{\Gamma \vdash_\Sigma \tau :: *@A\alpha} \text{ (K-Csp)}$$

Unlike the term level, type-level CSP is implicit because there is no staged semantics for types.

Typing. The typing rules of λ^{MD} are shown in Fig. 2. The rule T-Const means that a constant can appear at any stage. The rules T-Var, T-Abs, and T-App are almost the same as those in the simply typed lambda calculus or λLF. Additional conditions are that subterms must be typed at the same stage (T-Abs and T-App); the type annotation/declaration on a variable has to be a proper type of kind $*$ (T-Abs) at the stage where it is declared (T-Var and T-Abs).

As in standard dependent type systems, T-Conv allows us to replace the type of a term with an equivalent one. For example, assuming integers and arithmetic, a value of type Vector $(4+1)$ can also have type Vector 5 because of T-Conv.

The rules T-▶, T-◀, T-Gen, T-Ins, and T-Csp are constructs for multi-stage programming. T-▶ and T-◀ are the same as in $\lambda^{\triangleright\%}$, as we explained in Sect. 2. The rule T-Gen for stage abstraction is straightforward. The condition $\alpha \notin \mathrm{FTV}(\Gamma) \cup \mathrm{FTV}(A)$ ensures that the scope of α is in M, and avoids capturing variables elsewhere. The rule T-Ins is for applications of stages to stage abstractions. The rule T-Csp is for CSP, which means that, if term M is of type τ at stage A, then $\%_\alpha M$ is of type τ at stage $A\alpha$. Note that CSP is also applied

$$\frac{c : \tau \in \Sigma}{\Gamma \vdash_\Sigma c : \tau @ A} \ (\text{T-Const}) \qquad\qquad \frac{x : \tau @ A \in \Gamma}{\Gamma \vdash_\Sigma x : \tau @ A} \ (\text{T-Var})$$

$$\frac{\Gamma \vdash_\Sigma \sigma :: {*} @ A \qquad \Gamma, x : \sigma @ A \vdash_\Sigma M : \tau @ A}{\Gamma \vdash_\Sigma (\lambda(x : \sigma).M) : (\Pi(x : \sigma).\tau) @ A} \ (\text{T-Abs})$$

$$\frac{\Gamma \vdash_\Sigma M : (\Pi(x : \sigma).\tau) @ A \qquad \Gamma \vdash_\Sigma N : \sigma @ A}{\Gamma \vdash_\Sigma M \ N : \tau[x \mapsto N] @ A} \ (\text{T-App})$$

$$\frac{\Gamma \vdash_\Sigma M : \tau @ A \qquad \Gamma \vdash_\Sigma \tau \equiv \sigma :: K @ A}{\Gamma \vdash_\Sigma M : \sigma @ A} \ (\text{T-Conv})$$

$$\frac{\Gamma \vdash_\Sigma M : \tau @ A\alpha}{\Gamma \vdash_\Sigma \blacktriangleright_\alpha M : \triangleright_\alpha \tau @ A} \ (\text{T-}\blacktriangleright) \qquad \frac{\Gamma \vdash_\Sigma M : \triangleright_\alpha \tau @ A}{\Gamma \vdash_\Sigma \blacktriangleleft_\alpha M : \tau @ A\alpha} \ (\text{T-}\blacktriangleleft)$$

$$\frac{\Gamma \vdash_\Sigma M : \tau @ A \qquad \alpha \notin \text{FTV}(\Gamma) \cup \text{FTV}(A)}{\Gamma \vdash_\Sigma \Lambda\alpha.M : \forall\alpha.\tau @ A} \ (\text{T-Gen})$$

$$\frac{\Gamma \vdash_\Sigma M : \forall\alpha.\tau @ A}{\Gamma \vdash_\Sigma M \ B : \tau[\alpha \mapsto B] @ A} \ (\text{T-Ins}) \qquad \frac{\Gamma \vdash_\Sigma M : \tau @ A}{\Gamma \vdash_\Sigma \%_\alpha M : \tau @ A\alpha} \ (\text{T-Csp})$$

Fig. 2. Typing Rules.

to the type τ (although it is implicit) in the conclusion. Thanks to implicit CSP, the typing rule is the same as in $\lambda^{\triangleright\%}$.

Kind, Type and Term Equivalence. Since the syntax of kinds, types, and terms is mutually recursive, the corresponding notions of equivalence are also mutually recursive. They are congruences closed under a few axioms for term equivalence. Thus, the rules for kind and type equivalences are not very interesting, except that implicit CSP is allowed. We show a few representative rules below.

$$\frac{\Gamma \vdash_\Sigma K \equiv J @ A}{\Gamma \vdash_\Sigma K \equiv J @ A\alpha} \ (\text{QK-Csp}) \qquad \frac{\Gamma \vdash_\Sigma \tau \equiv \sigma :: {*} @ A}{\Gamma \vdash_\Sigma \tau \equiv \sigma :: {*} @ A\alpha} \ (\text{QT-Csp})$$

$$\frac{\Gamma \vdash_\Sigma \tau \equiv \sigma :: (\Pi x : \rho.K) @ A \qquad \Gamma \vdash_\Sigma M \equiv N : \rho @ A}{\Gamma \vdash_\Sigma \tau \ M \equiv \sigma \ N :: K[x \mapsto M] @ A} \ (\text{QT-App})$$

We show the rules for term equivalence in Fig. 3, omitting straightforward rules for reflexivity, symmetry, transitivity, and compatibility. The rules Q-β, Q-$\blacktriangleleft\blacktriangleright$, and Q-$\Lambda$ correspond to β-reduction, $\blacklozenge$-reduction, and Λ-reduction, respectively.

The only rule that deserves elaboration is the last rule Q-%. Intuitively, it means that the CSP operator applied to term M can be removed if M is also well-typed at the next stage $A\alpha$. For example, constants do not depend on the stage (see T-Const) and so $\Gamma \vdash_\Sigma \%_\alpha c \equiv c : \tau @ A\alpha$ holds but variables do depend on stages and so this rule does not apply.

$$\frac{\Gamma, x : \sigma@A \vdash_\Sigma M : \tau@A \quad \Gamma \vdash_\Sigma N : \sigma@A}{\Gamma \vdash_\Sigma (\lambda x : \sigma.M)\ N \equiv M[x \mapsto N] : \tau[x \mapsto N]@A}\ (\text{Q-}\beta)$$

$$\frac{\Gamma \vdash_\Sigma (\Lambda\alpha.M) : \forall\alpha.\tau@A}{\Gamma \vdash_\Sigma (\Lambda\alpha.M)\ \varepsilon \equiv M[\alpha \mapsto \varepsilon] : \tau[\alpha \mapsto \varepsilon]@A}\ (\text{Q-}\Lambda)$$

$$\frac{\Gamma \vdash_\Sigma M \equiv N : \tau@A}{\Gamma \vdash_\Sigma \blacktriangleleft_\alpha(\blacktriangleright_\alpha M) \equiv N : \tau@A}\ (\text{Q-}\blacktriangleleft\blacktriangleright) \qquad \frac{\Gamma \vdash_\Sigma M : \tau@A\alpha \quad \Gamma \vdash_\Sigma M : \tau@A}{\Gamma \vdash_\Sigma \%_\alpha M \equiv M : \tau@A\alpha}\ (\text{Q-}\%)$$

Fig. 3. Term Equivalence Rules.

Example. We show an example of a dependently typed code generator in a hypothetical language based on $\lambda^{\triangleright\%}$. This language provides definitions by **let**, recursive functions (represented by **fix**), **if**-expressions, and primitives cons, head, and tail to manipulate vectors. We assume that cons is of type $\Pi n :$ Int.Int $\to$ Vector $n \to$ Vector $(n+1)$, head is of type $\Pi n :$ Int.Vector $(n+1) \to$ Int, and tail is of type $\Pi n :$ Int.Vector $(n+1) \to$ (Vector n).

Let's consider an application, for example, in computer graphics, in which we have potentially many pairs of vectors of the fixed (but statically unknown) length and a function—such as vector addition—to be applied to them. This function should be fast because it is applied many times and be safe because just one runtime error may ruin the whole long-running calculation.

Our goal is to define the function vadd of type

$$\Pi n : \text{Int}.\forall\beta.\triangleright_\beta(\text{Vector } (\%_\alpha n) \to \text{Vector } (\%_\alpha n) \to \text{Vector } (\%_\alpha n)).$$

It takes the length n and returns (β-closed) code of a function to add two vectors of length n. The generated code is run by applying it to ε to obtain a function of type Vector $n \to$ Vector $n \to$ Vector n as expected.

We start with the helper function vadd$_1$, which takes a stage, the length n of vectors, and two quoted vectors as arguments and returns code that computes the addition of the given two vectors:

let vadd$_1$: $\forall\alpha.\Pi n :$ Int.$\triangleright_\alpha$Vector $n \to \triangleright_\alpha$Vector $n \to \triangleright_\alpha$Vector n
  = **fix** $f.\Lambda\alpha.\lambda n :$ Int. $\lambda v_1 : \triangleright_\alpha$Vector n. $\lambda v_2 : \triangleright_\alpha$Vector n.
    if $n = 0$ **then** $\blacktriangleright_\alpha$nil
    else $\blacktriangleright_\alpha($ **let** $t_1 = $ tail $(\blacktriangleleft_\alpha v_1)$ **in**
            let $t_2 = $ tail $(\blacktriangleleft_\alpha v_2)$ **in**
            cons (head $(\blacktriangleleft_\alpha v_1)$ + head $(\blacktriangleleft_\alpha v_2)$)
              $\blacktriangleleft_\alpha(f\ (n-1)\ (\blacktriangleright_\alpha t_1)\ (\blacktriangleright_\alpha t_2)))$

Note that the generated code will not contain branching on n or recursion. (Here, we assume that the type system can determine whether $n = 0$ when **then**- and **else**-branches are typechecked so that both branches can be given type $\triangleright_\alpha$Vector n.)

Using vadd$_1$, the main function vadd can be defined as follows:

let vadd : $\varPi n$: Int.$\forall \beta.\triangleright_\beta$(Vector ($\%_\beta n$) $\to$ Vector ($\%_\beta n$) $\to$ Vector ($\%_\beta n$))

$= \lambda n$: Int.$\varLambda\beta.\blacktriangleright_\beta(\lambda v_1$: Vector ($\%_\beta n$). λv_2 : Vector ($\%_\beta n$).

$\blacktriangleleft_\beta(\text{vadd}_1 \ \beta \ n \ (\blacktriangleright_\beta v_1) \ (\blacktriangleright_\beta v_2)))$

The auxiliary function vadd$_1$ generates code to compute addition of the formal arguments v_1 and v_2 without branching on n or recursion. As we mentioned already, if this function is applied to a (nonnegative) integer constant, say 5, it returns function code for adding two vectors of size 5. The type of vadd 5, obtained by substituting 5 for n, is $\forall \beta.\triangleright_\beta$(Vector ($\%_\beta 5$) $\to$ Vector ($\%_\beta 5$) $\to$ Vector ($\%_\beta 5$)). If the obtained code is run by applying to ε, the type of vadd 5 ε is Vector 5 $\to$ Vector 5 $\to$ Vector 5 as expected.

There are other ways to implement the vector addition function: by using tuples instead of lists if the length for all the vectors is statically known or by checking dynamically the lengths of lists for every pair. However, our method is better than these alternatives in two points. First, our function, vadd$_1$ can generate functions for vectors of arbitrary length unlike the one using tuples. Second, vadd$_1$ has an advantage in speed over the one using dynamic checking because it can generate an optimized function for a given length.

We make two technical remarks before proceeding:

1. If the generated function code is composed with another piece of code of type, say, $\triangleright_\gamma$Vector 5, Q-% plays an essential role; that is, Vector 5 and Vector ($\%_\gamma 5$), which would occur by applying the generated code to γ (instead of ε), are syntactically different types but Q-% enables to equate them. Interestingly, Hanada and Igarashi [14] rejected the idea of reduction that removes $\%_\alpha$ when they developed $\lambda^{\triangleright\%}$, as such reduction does not match the operational behavior of the CSP operator in implementations. However, as an equational system for multi-stage programs, the rule Q-% makes sense.

2. By using implicit type-level CSP, the type of vadd could have been written $\varPi n$: Int.$\forall \beta.\triangleright_\beta$(Vector n $\to$ Vector n $\to$ Vector n). In this type, Vector n is given kind at stage ε and type-level CSP implicitly lifts it to stage β. However, if a type-level constant takes two or more arguments from different stages, term-level CSP is necessary. A matrix type (indexed by the numbers of columns and rows) would be such an example.

3.4   Staged Semantics

The reduction given above is full reduction and any redexes—even under $\blacktriangleright_\alpha$—can be reduced in an arbitrary order. Following previous work [14], we introduce (small-step, call-by-value) staged semantics, where only β-reduction or $\varLambda$-reduction at stage ε or the outer-most $\blacklozenge$-reduction are allowed, modeling an implementation.

We start with the definition of values. Since terms under quotations are not executed, the grammar is indexed by stages.

Definition 2 (Values). *The family V^A of sets of values, ranged over by v^A, is defined by the following grammar. In the grammar, $A' \neq \varepsilon$ is assumed.*

$$v^\varepsilon \in V^\varepsilon ::= \lambda x : \tau.M \mid \blacktriangleright_\alpha v^\alpha \mid \Lambda\alpha.v^\varepsilon$$

$$v^{A'} \in V^{A'} ::= x \mid \lambda x : \tau.v^{A'} \mid v^{A'} \ v^{A'} \mid \blacktriangleright_\alpha v^{A'\alpha} \mid \Lambda\alpha.v^{A'} \mid v^{A'} \ B$$

$$\mid \blacktriangleleft_\alpha v^{A''} (if \ A' = A''\alpha \ for \ some \ \alpha, A'' \neq \varepsilon)$$

$$\mid \%_\alpha v^{A''} (if \ A' = A''\alpha)$$

Values at stage ε are λ-abstractions, quoted pieces of code, or Λ-abstractions. The body of a λ-abstraction can be any term but the body of Λ-abstraction has to be a value. It means that the body of Λ-abstraction must be evaluated. The side condition for $\blacktriangleleft_\alpha v^{A'}$ means that escapes in a value can appear only under nested quotations because an escape under a single quotation will splice the code value into the surrounding code. See Hanada and Igarashi [14] for details.

In order to define staged reduction, we define redex and evaluation contexts.

Definition 3 (Redex). *The sets of ε-redexes (ranged over by R^ε) and α-redexes (ranged over by R^α) are defined by the following grammar.*

$$R^\varepsilon ::= (\lambda x : \tau.M) \ v^\varepsilon \mid (\Lambda\alpha.v^\varepsilon) \ \varepsilon$$

$$R^\alpha ::= \blacktriangleleft_\alpha \blacktriangleright_\alpha v^\alpha$$

Definition 4 (Evaluation Context). *Let B be either ε or a stage variable β. The family of sets $ECtx_B^A$ of evaluation contexts, ranged over by E_B^A, is defined by the following grammar (in which A' stands for a non-empty stage).*

$$E_B^\varepsilon \in ECtx_B^\varepsilon ::= \Box \ (if \ B = \varepsilon) \mid E_B^\varepsilon \ M \mid v^\varepsilon \ E_B^\varepsilon \mid \blacktriangleright_\alpha E_B^\alpha \mid \Lambda\alpha.E_B^\varepsilon \mid E_B^\varepsilon \ A$$

$$E_B^{A'} \in ECtx_B^{A'} ::= \Box \ (if \ A' = B) \mid \lambda x : \tau.E_B^{A'} \mid E_B^{A'} \ M \mid v^{A'} \ E_B^{A'}$$

$$\mid \blacktriangleright_\alpha E_B^{A'\alpha} \mid \blacktriangleleft_\alpha E_B^A \ (where \ A\alpha = A')$$

$$\mid \Lambda\alpha.E_B^{A'} \mid E_B^{A'} \ A \mid \%_\alpha \ E_B^A \ (where \ A\alpha = A')$$

The subscripts A and B in E_B^A stand for the stage of the evaluation context and of the hole, respectively. The grammar represents that staged reduction is left-to-right and call-by-value and terms under Λ are reduced. Terms at non-ε stages are not reduced, except redexes of the form $\blacktriangleleft_\alpha \blacktriangleright_\alpha v^\alpha$ at stage α. A few examples of evaluation contexts are shown below:

$$\Box \ (\lambda x : \text{Int}.x) \in ECtx_\varepsilon^\varepsilon$$

$$\Lambda\alpha.\Box \ \varepsilon \in ECtx_\varepsilon^\varepsilon$$

$$\blacktriangleleft_\alpha \blacktriangleright_\alpha \blacktriangleleft_\alpha \Box \in ECtx_\varepsilon^\alpha$$

We write $E_B^A[M]$ for the term obtained by filling the hole $\Box$ in E_B^A by M.

Now we define staged reduction using the redex and evaluation contexts.

Definition 5 (Staged Reduction). *The staged reduction relation, written* $M \longrightarrow_s N$, *is defined by the least relation closed under the rules below.*

$$E_\varepsilon^A[(\lambda x : \tau.M)\ v^\varepsilon] \longrightarrow_s E_\varepsilon^A[M[x \mapsto v^\varepsilon]]$$

$$E_\varepsilon^A[(\Lambda\alpha.v^\varepsilon)\ A] \longrightarrow_s E_\varepsilon^A[v^\varepsilon[\alpha \mapsto A]]$$

$$E_\alpha^A[\blacktriangleleft_\alpha\blacktriangleright_\alpha v^\alpha] \longrightarrow_s E_\alpha^A[v^\alpha]$$

This reduction relation reduces a term in a deterministic, left-to-right, call-by-value manner. An application of an abstraction is executed only at stage ε and only a quotation at stage ε is spliced into the surrounding code—notice that, if $\blacktriangleright_\alpha v^\alpha$ is at stage ε, then the redex $\blacktriangleleft_\alpha\blacktriangleright_\alpha v^\alpha$ is at stage α. In other words, terms in brackets are not evaluated until the terms are run and arguments of a function are evaluated before the application. We show an example of staged reduction. Underlines show the redexes.

$$(\Lambda\alpha.(\blacktriangleright_\alpha\underline{\blacktriangleleft_\alpha\blacktriangleright_\alpha((\lambda x : \text{Int}.x)\ 10)}))\ \varepsilon$$

$$\longrightarrow_s \underline{(\Lambda\alpha.(\blacktriangleright_\alpha((\lambda x : \text{Int}.x)\ 10)))\ \varepsilon}$$

$$\longrightarrow_s \underline{(\lambda x : \text{Int}.x)\ 10}$$

$$\longrightarrow_s 10$$

4   Properties of λ^{MD}

In this section, we show the basic properties of λ^{MD}: preservation, strong normalization, confluence for full reduction, and progress for staged reduction.

The Substitution Lemma in λ^{MD} is a little more complicated than usual because there are eight judgment forms and two kinds of substitution. The Term Substitution Lemma states that term substitution $[z \mapsto M]$ preserves derivability of judgments. The Stage Substitution Lemma states similarly for stage substitution $[\alpha \mapsto A]$.

We let $\mathcal{J}$ stand for the judgments K kind@A, $\tau :: K$@A, $M : \tau$@A, $K \equiv J$@A, $\tau \equiv \sigma$@A, and $M \equiv N : \tau$@A. Substitutions $\mathcal{J}[z \mapsto M]$ and $\mathcal{J}[\alpha \mapsto A]$ are defined in a straightforward manner. Using these notations, the two substitution lemmas are stated as follows:

We proved the next two leammas by simultaneous induction on derivations.

Lemma 1 (Term Substitution). *If* $\Gamma, z : \xi$@$B, \Delta \vdash_\Sigma \mathcal{J}$ *and* $\Gamma \vdash_\Sigma N : \xi$@$B$, *then* $\Gamma, (\Delta[z \mapsto N]) \vdash_\Sigma \mathcal{J}[z \mapsto N]$. *Similarly, if* $\vdash_\Sigma \Gamma, z : \xi$@$B, \Delta$ *and* $\Gamma \vdash_\Sigma N : \xi$@$B$, *then* $\vdash_\Sigma \Gamma, (\Delta[z \mapsto N])$.

Lemma 2 (Stage Substitution). *If* $\Gamma \vdash_\Sigma \mathcal{J}$, *then* $\Gamma[\beta \mapsto B] \vdash_\Sigma \mathcal{J}[\beta \mapsto B]$. *Similarly, if* $\vdash_\Sigma \Gamma$, *then* $\vdash_\Sigma \Gamma[\beta \mapsto B]$.

The following Inversion Lemma is needed to prove the main theorems. As usual [27], the Inversion Lemma enables us to infer the types of subterms of a term from the shape of the term.

Lemma 3 (Inversion).

1. *If $\Gamma \vdash_\Sigma (\lambda x : \sigma.M) : \rho$ then there are σ' and τ' such that $\rho = \Pi x : \sigma'.\tau'$, $\Gamma \vdash_\Sigma \sigma \equiv \sigma'@A$ and $\Gamma, x : \sigma'@A \vdash_\Sigma M : \tau'@A$.*
2. *If $\Gamma \vdash_\Sigma \blacktriangleright_\alpha M : \tau@A$ then there is σ such that $\tau = \triangleright_\alpha \sigma$ and $\Gamma \vdash_\Sigma M : \sigma@A$.*
3. *If $\Gamma \vdash_\Sigma \Lambda\alpha.M : \tau$ then there is σ such that $\sigma = \forall\alpha.\sigma$ and $\Gamma \vdash_\Sigma M : \sigma@A$.*

Proof. Each item is strengthened by statements about type equivalence. For example, the first statement is augmented by

If $\Gamma \vdash_\Sigma \rho \equiv (\Pi x : \sigma.\tau) : K@A$, then there exist σ' and τ' such that $\rho = \Pi x : \sigma'.\tau'$ and $\Gamma \vdash_\Sigma \sigma \equiv \sigma' : K@A$ and $\Gamma, x : \sigma@A \vdash_\Sigma \tau \equiv \tau' : J@A$.

and its symmetric version. Then, they are proved simultaneously by induction on derivations. Similarly for the others. □

Thanks to Term/Stage Substitution and Inversion, we can prove Preservation easily.

Theorem 1 (Preservation). *If $\Gamma \vdash_\Sigma M : \tau@A$ and $M \longrightarrow M'$, then $\Gamma \vdash_\Sigma M' : \tau@A$.*

Proof. First, there are three cases for $M \longrightarrow M'$. They are $M \longrightarrow_\beta M'$, $M \longrightarrow_\Lambda M'$, and $M \longrightarrow_\blacklozenge M'$. For each case, we can use straightforward induction on typing derivations. □

Strong Normalization is also an important property, which guarantees that no typed term has an infinite reduction sequence. Following standard proofs (see, e.g., [15]), we prove this theorem by translating λ^{MD} to the simply typed lambda calculus.

Theorem 2 (Strong Normalization). *If $\Gamma \vdash_\Sigma M_1 : \tau@A$ then there is no infinite sequence $(M_i)_{i \geq 1}$ of terms such that $M_i \longrightarrow M_{i+1}$ for $i \geq 1$.*

Proof. In order to prove this theorem, we define a translation $(\cdot)^\natural$ from λ^{MD} to the simply typed lambda calculus. Second, we prove the $\natural$-translation preserves typing and reduction. Then, we can prove Strong Normalization of λ^{MD} from Strong Normalization of the simply typed lambda calculus. □

Confluence is a property that any reduction sequences from one typed term converge. Since we have proved Strong Normalization, we can use Newman's Lemma [2] to prove Confluence.

Theorem 3 (Confluence). *For any term M, if $M \longrightarrow^* M'$ and $M \longrightarrow^* M''$ then there exists M''' that satisfies $M' \longrightarrow^* M'''$ and $M'' \longrightarrow^* M'''$.*

Proof. We can easily show Weak Church-Rosser. Use Newman's Lemma. □

Now, we turn our attention to staged semantics. First, the staged reduction relation is a subrelation of full reduction, so Subject Reduction holds also for the staged reduction.

Theorem 4. *If $M \longrightarrow_s M'$, then $M \longrightarrow M'$.*

Proof. Easy.   □

The following theorem Unique Decomposition ensures that every typed term is either a value or can be uniquely decomposed to an evaluation context and a redex, ensuring that a well-typed term is not immediately stuck and the staged semantics is deterministic.

Theorem 5 (Unique Decomposition). *If Γ does not have any variable declared at stage ε and $\Gamma \vdash_\Sigma M : \tau @ A$, then either*

1. *$M \in V^A$, or*
2. *M can be uniquely decomposed into an evaluation context and a redex, that is, there uniquely exist B, E_B^A, and R^B such that $M = E_B^A[R^B]$.*

Proof. We can prove by straightforward induction on typing derivations.   □

The type environment Γ in the statement usually has to be empty; in other words, the term has to be closed. The condition is relaxed here because variables at stages higher than ε are considered symbols. In fact, this relaxation is required for proof by induction to work.

Progress is a corollary of Unique Decomposition.

Corollary 1 (Progress). *If Γ does not have any variable declared at stage ε and $\Gamma \vdash_\Sigma M : \tau @ A$, then $M \in V^A$ or there exists M' such that $M \longrightarrow_s M'$.*

5   Related Work

MetaOCaml is a programming language with quoting, unquoting, run, and CSP. Kiselyov [17] describes many applications of MetaOCaml, including filtering in signal processing, matrix-vector product, and a DSL compiler.

Theoretical studies on multi-stage programming owe a lot to seminal work by Davies and Pfenning [11] and Davies [10], who found Curry-Howard correspondence between multi-stage calculi and modal logic. In particular, Davies' λ° [10] has been a basis for several multi-stage calculi with quasi-quotation. λ° did not have operators for run and CSP; a few studies [3,24] enhanced and improved λ° towards the development of a type-safe multi-stage calculus with quasi-quotation, run, and CSP, which were proposed by Taha and Sheard as constructs for multi-stage programming [31]. Finally, Taha and Nielsen invented the concept of environment classifiers [30] and developed a typed calculus λ^α, which was equipped with all the features above in a type sound manner and formed a basis of earlier versions of MetaOCaml. Different approaches to type-safe multi-stage programming with slightly different constructs for composing and running code values have been studied by Kim, Yi, and Calcagno [16] and Nanevski and Pfenning [25].

Later, Tsukada and Igarashi [32] found correspondence between a variant of λ^α called $\lambda^\triangleright$ and modal logic and showed that run could be represented as a special case of application of a transition abstraction $(\Lambda\alpha.M)$ to the empty sequence ε. Hanada and Igarashi [14] developed $\lambda^{\triangleright\%}$ as an extension $\lambda^{\triangleright}$ with CSP.

There is much work on dependent types and most of it is affected by the pioneering work by Martin-Löf [21]. Among many dependent type systems such as λ^{Π} [22], The Calculus of Constructions [9], and Edinburgh LF [15], we base our work on λLF [1] (which is quite close to λ^{Π} and Edinburgh LF) due to its simplicity. It is well known that dependent types are useful to express detailed properties of data structures at the type level such as the size of data structures [34] and typed abstract syntax trees [19,33]. The vector addition discussed in Sect. 3 is also such an example.

The use of dependent types for code generation is studied by Chlipala [8] and Ebner et al. [12]. They use inductive types to guarantee well-formedness of generated code. Aside from the lack of quasi-quotation, their systems are for heterogeneous meta-programming and compile-time code generation and they do not support features for run-time code generation such as run and CSP, as λ^{MD} does.

We discuss earlier attempts at incorporating dependent types into multi-stage programming. Pasalic and Taha [26] designed $\lambda_{H\circ}$ by introducing the concept of stage into an existing dependent type system λ_H [28]. However, $\lambda_{H\circ}$ is equipped with neither run nor CSP. Forgarty, Pasalic, Siek and Taha [13] extended the type system of MetaOCaml with indexed types. With this extension, types can be indexed with a Coq term. Chen and Xi [7] introduced code types augmented with information on types of free variables in code values in order to prevent code with free variables from being evaluated. These systems separate the language of type indices from the term language. As a result, they do not enjoy full-spectrum dependent types but are technically simpler because there is no need to take stage of types into account. Brady and Hammond [5] have discussed a combination of (full-spectrum) dependently typed programming with staging in the style of MetaOCaml to implement a staged interpreter, which is statically guaranteed to generate well-typed code. However, they focused on concrete programming examples and there is no theoretical investigation of the programming language they used.

Berger and Tratt [4] gave program logic for Mini-ML$_e^{\square}$ [11], which would allow fine-grained reasoning about the behavior of code generators. However, it cannot manipulate open code which ours can deal with.

6   Conclusion

We have proposed a new multi-stage calculus λ^{MD} with dependent types, which make it possible for programmers to express finer-grained properties about the behavior of code values. The combination leads to augmentation of almost all judgments in the type system with stage information. CSP and type equivalence (specially tailored for CSP) are keys to expressing dependently typed practical code generators. We have proved basic properties of λ^{MD}, including preservation, confluence, strong normalization for full reduction, and progress for staged reduction.

Developing a typechecking algorithm for λ^{MD} is left for future work. We expect that most of the development is straightforward, except for implicit CSP at the type-level and %-erasing equivalence rules.

Acknowledgments. We would like to thank John Toman, Yuki Nishida, and anonymous reviewers for useful comments.

References

1. Aspinall, D., Hofmann, M.: Dependent types. In: Pierce, B.C. (ed.) Advanced Topics in Types and Programming Languages, chap. 2. MIT press, Cambridge (2005)
2. Baader, F., Nipkow, T.: Term Rewriting and All That. Cambridge University Press, Cambridge (1998)
3. Benaissa, Z.E.A., Moggi, E., Taha, W., Sheard, T.: Logical modalities and multistage programming. In: Federated Logic Conference (FLoC) Satellite Workshop on Intuitionistic Modal Logics and Applications (IMLA) (1999)
4. Berger, M., Tratt, L.: Program logics for homogeneous generative run-time meta-programming. Logical Methods Comput. Sci. **11**(1) (2015). https://lmcs.episciences.org/929
5. Brady, E., Hammond, K.: Dependently typed meta-programming. In: Trends in Functional Programming (2006)
6. Calcagno, C., Taha, W., Huang, L., Leroy, X.: Implementing multi-stage languages using ASTs, gensym, and reflection. In: Pfenning, F., Smaragdakis, Y. (eds.) GPCE 2003. LNCS, vol. 2830, pp. 57–76. Springer, Heidelberg (2003). https://doi.org/10.1007/978-3-540-39815-8_4
7. Chen, C., Xi, H.: Meta-programming through typeful code representation. In: Proceedings of the Eighth ACM SIGPLAN International Conference on Functional Programming ICFP 2003, pp. 275–286. ACM, New York (2003)
8. Chlipala, A.: Ur: statically-typed metaprogramming with type-level record computation. In: Proceedings of the 31st ACM SIGPLAN Conference on Programming Language Design and Implementation PLDI 2010, pp. 122–133. ACM, New York (2010)
9. Coquand, T., Huet, G.: The calculus of constructions. Inf. Comput. **76**(2–3), 95–120 (1988)
10. Davies, R.: A temporal-logic approach to binding-time analysis. In: Proceedings of Eleventh Annual IEEE Symposium on Logic in Computer Science LICS 1996, pp. 184–195. IEEE (1996)
11. Davies, R., Pfenning, F.: A modal analysis of staged computation. J. ACM **48**(3), 555–604 (2001)
12. Ebner, G., Ullrich, S., Roesch, J., Avigad, J., de Moura, L.: A metaprogramming framework for formal verification. PACMPL **1**(ICFP), 34:1–34:29 (2017)
13. Fogarty, S., Pasalic, E., Siek, J., Taha, W.: Concoqtion: indexed types now! In: Proceedings of the 2007 ACM SIGPLAN Symposium on Partial Evaluation and Semantics-based Program Manipulation PEPM 2007, pp. 112–121. ACM, New York (2007)

14. Hanada, Y., Igarashi, A.: On cross-stage persistence in multi-stage programming. In: Codish, M., Sumii, E. (eds.) FLOPS 2014. LNCS, vol. 8475, pp. 103–118. Springer, Cham (2014). https://doi.org/10.1007/978-3-319-07151-0_7

15. Harper, R., Honsell, F., Plotkin, G.: A framework for defining logics. J. ACM **40**(1), 143–184 (1993)

16. Kim, I., Yi, K., Calcagno, C.: A polymorphic modal type system for lisp-like multi-staged languages. In: Proceedings of ACM SIGPLAN-SIGACT Symposium on Principles of Programming Languages (POPL 2003), pp. 257–268 (2006)

17. Kiselyov, O.: Reconciling abstraction with high performance: a MetaOCaml approach. Found. Trends Program. Lang. **5**(1), 1–101 (2018)

18. Kiselyov, O.: The design and implementation of BER MetaOCaml - system description. In: Proceedings of the 12th International Symposium on Functional and Logic Programming, FLOPS 2014, Kanazawa, Japan, 4–6 June 2014, pp. 86–102 (2014)

19. Leijen, D., Meijer, E.: Domain specific embedded compilers. In: Proceedings of the 2nd Conference on Domain-Specific Languages (DSL 1999), pp. 109–122 (1999)

20. Mainland, G.: Explicitly heterogeneous metaprogramming with metahaskell. In: Proceedings of the 17th ACM SIGPLAN International Conference on Functional Programming ICFP 2012, pp. 311–322. ACM, New York (2012)

21. Martin-Löf, P.: An intuitionistic theory of types: predicative part. In: Logic Colloquium, vol. 80, p. 73, January 1973

22. Meyer, A.R., Reinhold, M.B.: "Type" is not a type. In: Proceedings of the 13th ACM SIGACT-SIGPLAN Symposium on Principles of Programming Languages POPL 1986, pp. 287–295. ACM, New York (1986)

23. Milner, R.: A theory of type polymorphism in programming. J. Comput. Syst. Sci. **17**, 348–375 (1978)

24. Moggi, E., Taha, W., Benaissa, Z.E.-A., Sheard, T.: An idealized metaML: simpler, and more expressive. In: Swierstra, S.D. (ed.) ESOP 1999. LNCS, vol. 1576, pp. 193–207. Springer, Heidelberg (1999). https://doi.org/10.1007/3-540-49099-X_13

25. Nanevski, A., Pfenning, F.: Staged computation with names and necessity. J. Funct. Program. **15**(5), 893–939 (2005)

26. Pasalic, E., Taha, W., Sheard, T.: Tagless staged interpreters for typed languages. In: Proceedings of the Seventh ACM SIGPLAN International Conference on Functional Programming ICFP 2002, pp. 218–229. ACM, New York (2002)

27. Pierce, B.C.: Types and Programming Languages. MIT Press, Cambridge (2002)

28. Shao, Z., Saha, B., Trifonov, V., Papaspyrou, N.: A type system for certified binaries. In: Proceedings of the 29th ACM SIGPLAN-SIGACT Symposium on Principles of Programming Languages POPL 2002, pp. 217–232. ACM, New York (2002)

29. Taha, W.: A gentle introduction to multi-stage programming, part II. In: Lämmel, R., Visser, J., Saraiva, J. (eds.) GTTSE 2007. LNCS, vol. 5235, pp. 260–290. Springer, Heidelberg (2008). https://doi.org/10.1007/978-3-540-88643-3_6

30. Taha, W., Nielsen, M.F.: Environment classifiers. In: Proceedings of ACM SIGPLAN-SIGACT Symposium on Principles of Programming Languages (POPL 2003), pp. 26–37. ACM, New York (2003)

31. Taha, W., Sheard, T.: MetaML and multi-stage programming with explicit annotations. Theor. Comput. Sci. **248**(1-2), 211–242 (2000)

32. Tsukada, T., Igarashi, A.: A logical foundation for environment classifiers. Logical Methods Comput. Sci. **6**(4), 1–43 (2010)
33. Xi, H., Chen, C., Chen, G.: Guarded recursive datatype constructors. In: Proceedings of ACM SIGPLAN-SIGACT Symposium on Principles of Programming Languages (POPL 2003), pp. 224–235 (2003)
34. Xi, H., Pfenning, F.: Eliminating array bound checking through dependent types. In: Proceedings of the ACM SIGPLAN Conference on Programming Language Design and Implementation (PLDI 1998), pp. 249–257 (1998)

Existential Types for Relaxed Noninterference

Raimil Cruz[(✉)] and Éric Tanter

PLEIAD Lab, Computer Science Department (DCC), University of Chile,
Santiago, Chile
{racruz,etanter}@dcc.uchile.cl

Abstract. Information-flow security type systems ensure confidentiality by enforcing noninterference: a program cannot leak private data to public channels. However, in practice, programs need to selectively declassify information about private data. Several approaches have provided a notion of *relaxed noninterference* supporting selective and expressive declassification while retaining a formal security property. The *labels-as-functions* approach provides relaxed noninterference by means of declassification policies expressed as functions. The *labels-as-types* approach expresses declassification policies using type abstraction and *faceted types*, a pair of types representing the secret and public facets of values. The original proposal of labels-as-types is formulated in an object-oriented setting where type abstraction is realized by subtyping. The object-oriented approach however suffers from limitations due to its receiver-centric paradigm.

In this work, we consider an alternative approach to labels-as-types, applicable in non-object-oriented languages, which allows us to express advanced declassification policies, such as extrinsic policies, based on a different form of type abstraction: existential types. An existential type exposes abstract types and operations on these; we leverage this abstraction mechanism to express secrets that can be declassified using the provided operations. We formalize the approach in a core functional calculus with existential types, define existential relaxed noninterference, and prove that well-typed programs satisfy this form of type-based relaxed noninterference.

1 Introduction

A sound information-flow security type system ensures confidentiality by means of *noninterference*, a property that states that public values (*e.g.* $\mathsf{String_L}$) do not depend on secret values (*e.g.* $\mathsf{String_H}$). This enables a modular reasoning principle about well-typed programs. For instance, in a pure language, a function

This work is partially funded by CONICYT FONDECYT Regular Projects 1150017 and 1190058. Raimil Cruz is partially funded by CONICYT-PCHA/Doctorado Nacional/2014-63140148.

A. W. Lin (Ed.): APLAS 2019, LNCS 11893, pp. 73–92, 2019.
https://doi.org/10.1007/978-3-030-34175-6_5

$f :$ String$_H \to$ String$_L$ is necessary a constant function because the (public) result cannot leak information about the (private) argument.

However, noninterference is too stringent and real programs need to explicitly *declassify* some information about secret values. A simple mechanism to support explicit declassification is to add a declassify operator from secret to public expressions, as provided for instance in Jif [11]. However, the arbitrary use of this operator breaks formal guarantees about confidentiality. Providing a declassification mechanism while still enforcing a noninterference-like property is an active topic of research [5,6,8,9,13,16].

One interesting mechanism is the *labels-as-functions* approach of Li and Zdancewic [9], which supports *declassification policies* while ensuring *relaxed* noninterference. Instead of using security labels such as L and H that are taken from a security lattice of symbols, security labels are functions. These functions, called declassification policies, denote the intended computations to declassify values. For instance, the function $\lambda x.\lambda y.x == y$ denotes the declassification policy: "the result of the comparison of the secret value x with the public value y can be declassified". The identity function denotes public values, while a constant function denotes secret values. Then, any use of a value that does not follow its declassification policy yields a secret result. The labels-as-functions approach is very expressive, but its main drawback is that label ordering relies on a semantic interpretation of functions and program equivalence, which is hard to realize in practice and rules out recursive declassification policies[1].

An alternative approach to *labels-as-functions* is *labels-as-types*, recently proposed by Cruz et al. [5]. The key idea is to exploit type abstraction to control how much of a value is open to declassification. The approach was originally developed in an object-oriented language, where type abstraction is realized by subtyping. A security type $T \triangleleft U$ is composed of two facets: the safety type T denotes the secret view of the value, and the declassification type U (such that $T <: U$) specifies the public view, *i.e.* the methods that can be used to declassify a secret value. For instance, the type String $\triangleleft$ String denotes a public string value, *i.e.* all the methods of String are available for declassification, while the type String $\triangleleft \top$ (where $\top$ is the empty interface type) denotes a secret String value, *i.e.* there is no method available to declassify information about the secret. Then, the interesting declassification policies are expressed with a type interface between String and $\top$; *e.g.* the type String $\triangleleft$ StringLen exposes the method length of String for declassification. With this type-based approach, label ordering is simplified to standard subtyping, which is a simple syntactic property, and naturally supports recursive declassification. Also, this type-based approach enforces a security property called *type-based relaxed noninterference*, which accounts for type-based declassification and provides a modular reasoning principle similar to standard noninterference.

We observe that developing type-based relaxed noninterference in an object-oriented setting, exploiting subtyping as the type abstraction mechanism,

---

[1] Li and Zdancewic [9] rule out recursive declassification because otherwise the subtyping relation induced by security labels (sets of functions) would be undecidable.

imposes some restrictions on the declassification policies that can be expressed. In particular, because security types are of the form $T \vartriangleleft U$ where the declassification type U is a supertype of the safety type T—a necessary constraint to ensure type safety—means that one cannot declassify properties that are *extrinsic* to (*i.e.* computed externally from) the secret value. For instance, because a typical String type does not feature an encrypt method, it is not possible to express the declassification policy that "the encrypted representation of the password is public".

In this paper, we explore an alternative approach to labels-as-types and relaxed noninterference, exploiting another well-known type abstraction mechanism: existential types. An existential type $\exists X.T$ provides an abstract type X and an interface T to operate with values of the abstract type X. Then instances of the abstract type X are akin to secrets that can be declassified using the operations described by T. For instance, the existential type $\exists X.[\text{get} : X, \text{length} : X \rightarrow \text{Int}]$ makes it possible to obtain a (secret) value of type X with get, that only can be "declassified" with the length function to obtain a (public) integer.

Because existential types are the essence of abstraction mechanisms like abstract data types and modules [10], this work shows how the labels-as-types approach can be applied in non-object-oriented languages. The only required extension is the notion of faceted types, which are necessary to capture the natural separation between *privileged observers* (allowed to observe secret results) and *public observers* (*i.e.* the attacker, which can only observe public values)[2]. Additionally, the existential approach is more expressive than the object-oriented one in that extrinsic declassification policies can naturally be encoded with existential types.

The contributions of this work are:

- We explore an alternative type abstraction mechanism to realize the labels-as-types approach to expressive declassification, retaining the practical aspect of using an existing mechanism (here, existential types), while supporting more expressive declassification policies (Sect. 2).
- We define a new version of type-based relaxed noninterference, called existential relaxed noninterference, which accounts for extrinsic declassification using existential types (Sect. 3).
- We capture the essence of the use of existential types for relaxed noninterference in a core functional language $\lambda_{\mathsf{SEC}}^{\exists}$ (Sect. 4), and prove that its type system soundly enforces existential relaxed noninterference (Sect. 5).

Section 6 explains how the formal definitions apply by revisiting an example from Sect. 3. Section 7 discuses related work and Sect. 8 concludes.

---

[2] To account for $n > 2$ observation levels, faceted types can be extended to have n facets.

2   Overview

We now explain how to use the type abstraction mechanism of existential types to denote secrets that can be selectively declassified. First, we give a quick overview of existential types, with their introduction and elimination forms. Next, we develop the intuitive connection between the type abstraction of standard existential types and security typing. Then, we show that to support computing with secrets, which is natural for information-flow control languages, we need to introduce faceted types.

2.1   Existential Types

An existential type $\exists X.T$ is a pair of an (abstract) type variable X and a type T where X is bound; typically T provides operations to create, transform and observe values of the abstract type X [10].

For instance, the type AccountStore below models a simplified user repository. It provides the password of a user at type X with the function userPass and a function verifyPass to check (observe) whether an arbitrary string value is equal to the password.

$$\text{AccountStore} \triangleq \exists X.[\ \text{userPass} : \text{String} \to X$$
$$\text{verifyPass} : \text{String} \to X \to \text{Bool}]$$

Values of an existential type $\exists X.T$ take the form of a *package* that packs together the *representation* type for the abstract type X with an implementation v of the operations provided by T. One can think of packages as *modules* with signatures.

For instance, the package $p \triangleq \text{pack}(\text{String}, v)$ as AccountStore is a value of type AccountStore, where String is the representation type and v, defined below, is a record implementing functions userPass and verifyPass:

$$v \triangleq [\ \text{userPass} = \lambda x : \text{String}.\ \text{userPassFromDb}(x)$$
$$\text{verifyPass} = \lambda x : \text{String}.\lambda y : \text{String}.\ \text{equal}(x, y)]$$

Note that the implementation, v, directly uses the representation type String, *e.g.* userPass has type String $\to$ String and is implemented using a primitive function userPassFromDb : String $\to$ String to retrieve the user password from a database. Likewise, the implementation of verifyPass uses equality between its arguments of type String.

To use an existential type, we have to *open* the package (*i.e.* import the module) to get access to the implementation v, along with the abstract type that hides the actual representation type. The expression $\text{open}(X, x) = p$ in e' opens the package p above, exposing the representation type abstractly as a type variable X, and the implementation as term variable x, within the scope of the body e'. Crucially, the expression e' has no access to the representation type String, therefore nothing can be done with a value of type X, beyond using it with the operations provided by AccountStore.

2.2   Type-Based Declassification Policies with Existential Types

We can establish an analogy between existential types and selective declassification of secrets: an existential type $\exists X.T$ exposes operations to obtain secret values, at the abstract type X, and the operations of T can be used to declassify theses secrets.

For instance, AccountStore provides a secret string password with the function userPass, and the function verifyPass expresses the declassification policy: "the comparison of a secret password with a public string can be made public". With this point of view, concrete types such as Bool and String represent public values. A fully-secret value, *i.e.* a secret that is not declassified, can be modeled by an existential type without any observation function for the abstract type.

We can use the declassification policy modeled with AccountStore to implement a valid well-typed login functionality. The login function below is defined in a scope where the package p of type AccountStore is opened, providing the type name X for the abstract type and the variable store for the package implementation.

```
open(X, store) = p in
    ...
    String  login (String guess,  String username){
        if ( store . verifyPass (guess, store . userPass(username)))
        ...
    }
```

The login function first obtains the user secret password of type X with store.userPass(username), and then passes the secret password (of type X) to the function verifyPass with the guess public password to obtain the public boolean result. The above code makes a valid use of AccountStore and therefore is well-typed.

The type abstraction provided by AccountStore avoids leaking information accidentally. For instance, directly returning the secret password of type X is a type error, even though internally it is a string. Likewise, the expression length(store.userPass(username)) is ill-typed.

Note that because declassification relies on the abstraction mechanism of existential types, we work under the assumption that the person that writes the security policy—the package implementation and the existential type—is responsible for not leaking the secret due to a bad implementation or specification (*e.g.* exposing the secret password through the identity function of type $X \rightarrow$ String).

Progressive Declassification. The analogy of existential types as a mechanism to express declassification holds when one considers *progressive declassification* [5,9], which refers to the possibility of only declassifying information after a *sequence* of operations is performed. With existential types, we can express progressive declassification by constraining the creation of secrets based on other secrets.

Consider the following refinement of AccountStore, which supports the declassification policy "whether an *authenticated* user's salary is above \$100,000":

$$\mathsf{AccountStore} \triangleq \exists X, Y, Z.[\ \mathsf{userPass} : \mathsf{String} \rightarrow X$$
$$\mathsf{verifyPass} : \mathsf{String} \rightarrow X \rightarrow \mathsf{Option}\,[Y]$$
$$\mathsf{userSalary} : Y \rightarrow Z$$
$$\mathsf{isSixDigit} : Z \rightarrow \mathsf{Bool}]$$

AccountStore provides extra abstract types Y and Z, denoting an authentication token (for a specific user) and a user salary, respectively. The type signatures enforce that, to obtain the user salary, the user must be authenticated: a value of type Y is needed to apply userSalary. Such a value can be obtained only after successful authentication: verifyPass now returns an Option $[Y]$ value, instead of a Bool value. Note that the salary itself is secret, since it has the abstract type Z. Finally, isSixDigit function reveals whether a salary is above \$100,000 by returning a public boolean result.

Observe how the use of abstract type variables allows the existential type to enforce sequencing among operations. Also, we can provide more declassification policies for a user salary Z, and can use the authentication token Y with more operations. An existential type is therefore an expressive means to capture rich declassification policies, including sequencing and alternation.

2.3 Computing with Secrets

As we have seen, with standard existential types, values of an abstract type X must be eliminated with operations provided by the existential type. While so far the analogy between type abstraction with existential types and expressive declassification holds nicely, there are some obstacles.

First, with standard existential types, it is simply forbidden to compute with secrets. For instance, applying the function length: String $\rightarrow$ Int with a (secret) value of type X is a type error. However, information-flow type systems are more flexible: they support computing with secret values, as long as the computation itself is henceforth considered secret, *e.g.* the value it produces is itself secret [18]. Allowing secret computations is useful for privileged observers, which are authorized to see private values.

Faceted types were introduced to support this "dual mode" of information-flow type systems in the labels-as-types approach [5]. While that work is based on objects and subtyping, here we develop the notion of *existential faceted types*: faceted types of the form $T@U$, where T indicates the safety type used for the implementation and U the declassification type used for confidentiality.

Figure 1 shows AccountStore with existential faceted types. Given a public string (T_L denotes $T@T$), userPass returns a value that is a string *for the privileged observer*, and a secret of type X *for the public observer* (*i.e.* the attacker).

When computing with a value of type String@X, there are now two options: either we use a function that expects a value of type String@X as argument, such as verifyPass, or we use a function that goes beyond declassification, such

AccountStore ≜ ∃X, Y, Z.[userPass : String$_L$ → String@X
                              verifyPass : String$_L$ → String@X → Option [Y_L]$_L$
                              userSalary : Y_L → Int@Z
                              isSixDigit : Int@Z → Bool$_L$]

Fig. 1. Account store with faceted types

as length, and should therefore produce a *fully* private result. What type should such private results have? In order to avoid having to introduce a fresh type variable, we assume a fixed (unusable) type ⊤, and write Int$_H$ to denote Int@⊤.

This supports computing with secrets as follows:

```
String_H  login (String_L guess, String_L username){
    if (length (store . userPass(username)) == length(guess ))...;
}
```

Instead of being ill-typed, length(store.userPass(username)) is well-typed at type Int$_H$, so the function login can return a private result, *e.g.* a private string at type String$_H$.

2.4   Public Data as (Declassifiable) Secret

Information-flow type systems allow any value to be considered private. With existential faceted types, this feature is captured by a subtyping relation such that for any T, T@T <: T@⊤, and for any X, T@X <: T@⊤. Value flows that are justified by subtyping are safe from a confidentiality point of view. In particular, if a (declassifiable) value of type String@X is passed at type String$_H$, it is henceforth fully private, disallowing any further declassification.

Additionally, in the presence of declassifiable secrets, of type T@X, one would also expect public values to be "upgraded" to declassifiable secrets. This requires the security subtyping relation to admit that, for any type T and type variable X, we have T_L <: T@X.

Note that admitting such flows means that type variables in a declassification type position are more permissive than when they occur in a safety type position. For instance, isSixDigit can be applied to any public integer (of type Int$_L$), and not only to ones returned by userSalary. In contrast, userSalary can only be applied to a value opaquely obtained as a result of verifyPass. In effect, the representation of authentication tokens is still kept abstract, at type Y_L (*i.e.* Y@Y). This prevents clients from actually knowing how these tokens are implemented, preserving the benefits of standard existential types. Conversely, the salary and password expose their representation types (Int and String respectively), thereby enabling secret computation by clients.

3   Relaxed Noninterference with Existential Types

Existential faceted types support a novel notion of type-based relaxed noninterference called *existential relaxed noninterference* (ERNI) that defines if a program with existential faceted types is secure. ERNI is based on type-based *equivalences* between values at existential faceted types. We formally define the notions of type-based equivalence and ERNI in Sect. 5, but here we provide an intuition for this security criterion and the associated reasoning. Let us first consider simple types, before looking at existential types.

Type-Based Relaxed Noninterference. Two integers are equivalent at type $\mathsf{Int@Int} = \mathsf{Int_L}$ if they are syntactically equal, meaning that a public observer can distinguish between two integers at type $\mathsf{Int_L}$. We can characterize the meaning of the faceted type $\mathsf{Int_L}$ with the partial equivalence relation $Eq_{\mathsf{Int}} = \{(\mathsf{n}, \mathsf{n}) \in \mathsf{Int} \times \mathsf{Int}\}$. Using this, two integers $\mathsf{v_1}$ and $\mathsf{v_2}$ are equivalent at type $\mathsf{Int_L}$ if they are in the relation Eq_{Int}—meaning they are syntactically equal.

Dually, the type $\mathsf{Int@\top} = \mathsf{Int_H}$ characterizes integer values that are indistinguishable for a public observer, therefore *any* two integers are equivalent at type $\mathsf{Int_H}$. Consequently, the meaning of the faceted type $\mathsf{Int_H}$ is the total relation $All_{\mathsf{Int}} = \mathsf{Int} \times \mathsf{Int}$ that relates any two integers $\mathsf{v_1}$ and $\mathsf{v_2}$.

With these base type-based equivalences, one can express the security property of functions, open terms, and programs with inputs as follows: a program p satisfies ERNI at an observation type S_{out} if, given two input values that are equivalent at type S_{in}, the executions of p with each value produce results that are equivalent at type S_{out}. This modular reasoning principle is akin to standard noninterference [18] and type-based relaxed noninterference [5].

Intuitively, S_{in} models the *initial knowledge* of the public observer about the (potentially-secret) input, and S_{out} denotes the *final knowledge* that the public observer has to distinguish results of the executions of the program p. The program p is secure if, given inputs from the same equivalence class of S_{in}, it produces results in the same equivalence class of S_{out}. Consider the program $e = \mathsf{length}(\mathsf{x})$ where x has type $\mathsf{String_H}$. The program e does not satisfy ERNI at type $\mathsf{Int_L}$, because given two strings "a" and "aa" that are equivalent at $\mathsf{String_H}$, *i.e.* ("a", "aa") $\in All_{\mathsf{String}}$, we obtain the results 1 and 2, which are not equivalent at type $\mathsf{Int_L}$, *i.e.* $(1, 2) \notin Eq_{\mathsf{Int}}$. However, e is secure at type $\mathsf{Int_H}$.

Relaxed Noninterference and Existentials. When we introduce faceted types with type variables such as $\mathsf{Int@}X$, we need to answer: what values are equivalent at type $\mathsf{Int@}X$? Without stepping into technical details yet, let us say that the meaning of a type $\mathsf{Int@}X$ is an *arbitrary* partial equivalence relation $R_X \subseteq \mathsf{Int} \times \mathsf{Int}$, and two values $\mathsf{v_1}$ and $\mathsf{v_2}$ are equivalent at $\mathsf{Int@}X$ if they are in R_X. Because X is an existentially-quantified variable, inside the package implementation that exports the type variable X, R_X is known, but outside the package, *i.e.* for clients of a type $\mathsf{Int@}X$, R_X is completely abstract: a public observer that opens a package exporting the type variable X does not know anything about values of type $\mathsf{Int@}X$.

For instance, consider again the program $e = \text{length}(x)$ but assume that x now has type String@Y. Does e satisfy ERNI at type Int_L? Here, we need to know what is the relation R_Y that gives meaning to String@Y. Instead of picking only one relation R_Y, ERNI quantifies over *all* possible relations R_Y. This universal quantification over R_Y corresponds to the standard type abstraction mechanism for abstract types (*i.e.* parametricity [15]). That is, the program e satisfies ERNI at type Int@Int, if it is secure for all relations $R_Y \subseteq \text{String} \times \text{String}$. Then, to show that ERNI at type Int@Int does not hold for e it suffices to exhibit a specific relation for which ERNI is violated. Take the relation $R_Y = \{(\text{``a''}, \text{``aa''})\}$, and observe that $\text{length}(\text{``a''}) \neq \text{length}(\text{``aa''})$.

Illustration. Finally, we give an intuition of how ERNI accounts for extrinsic declassification policies. We reuse the salary operations from AccountStore, simplifying the retrieval of the secret salary. The type SalaryPolicy provides a secret salary and a function isSixDigit to declassify the salary as before.

$$\text{SalaryPolicy} \triangleq \exists Z.[\text{salary} : \text{Int}@Z, \text{isSixDigit} : \text{Int}@Z \to \text{Bool}_L]$$

Intuitively two package values $p_1 \triangleq \text{pack}(\text{Int}, v_1)$ as SalaryPolicy and $p_2 \triangleq \text{pack}(\text{Int}, v_2)$ as SalaryPolicy are equivalent at SalaryPolicy_L if $v_1.\text{salary}$ and $v_2.\text{salary}$ are equivalent at Int@Z and $v_1.\text{isSixDigit}$ and $v_2.\text{isSixDigit}$ are equivalent at Int@$Z \to \text{Bool}_L$, *i.e.* the functions isSixDigit of v_1 and v_2 produce equivalent results at Bool_L when given equivalent arguments at Int@Z.

Consider now the program $e' = x.\text{isSixDigit}(x.\text{salary})$ with input x of type $[\text{salary} : \text{Int}@Z, \text{isSixDigit} : \text{Int}@Z \to \text{Bool}_L]$. Taking into account the above equivalence for SalaryPolicy, the program e' satisfies ERNI at type Bool_L because it adheres to the salary policy. Indeed, given *any* two equivalent packages $p_1 \triangleq \text{pack}(\text{Int}, v_1)$ as SalaryPolicy and $p_2 \triangleq \text{pack}(\text{Int}, v_2)$ as SalaryPolicy, the expressions $v_1.\text{isSixDigit}(v_1.\text{salary})$ and $v_2.\text{isSixDigit}(v_2.\text{salary})$ are *necessarily* equivalent at type Bool_L. However, the program $(x.\text{salary})\%2$ does not satisfy ERNI at Int_L, because given equivalent package implementations $v_1 \triangleq [\text{salary} = 100001, \cdots]$ and $v_2 \triangleq [\text{salary} = 100002, \cdots]$, it yields 1 for v_1 and 0 for v_2, and both values are not equivalent at Int_L, *i.e.* $(1, 0) \notin Eq_{\text{Int}}$.

4 Formal Semantics

We model existential faceted types in $\lambda^{\exists}_{\text{SEC}}$, which is essentially the simply-typed lambda calculus augmented with the unit type, pair types, sum types, existential types, and faceted types. All the examples presented in Sect. 2 can thus be encoded in $\lambda^{\exists}_{\text{SEC}}$ using standard techniques. This section covers the syntax, static and dynamic semantics of $\lambda^{\exists}_{\text{SEC}}$. The formalization of existential relaxed noninterference and the security type soundness of $\lambda^{\exists}_{\text{SEC}}$ are presented in Sect. 5.

$$e ::= \lambda x : S.e \mid e \; e \mid x \mid \mathsf{p} \mid e \oplus e \mid \langle\rangle \mid \langle e, e \rangle \qquad \text{(terms)}$$
$$\mid \mathsf{fst} \; e \mid \mathsf{snd} \; e \mid \mathsf{inl} \; e \mid \mathsf{inr} \; e \mid \mathsf{case} \; t \; \mathsf{of} \; \mathsf{inl} \; x.e \mid \mathsf{inr} \; x.e$$
$$\mid \mathsf{pack}(T, e) \; \mathsf{as} \; T \mid \mathsf{open}(X, x) = e \; \mathsf{in} \; e$$
$$v ::= \lambda x : S.e \mid \mathsf{p} \mid \langle\rangle \mid \langle v, v \rangle \mid \mathsf{inl} \; v \mid \mathsf{inr} \; v \mid \mathsf{pack}(T, v) \; \mathsf{as} \; T \mid \quad \text{(values)}$$
$$T, U ::= S \to S \mid P \mid 1 \mid S + S \mid S \times S \mid \exists X.T \mid X \mid \top \qquad \text{(types)}$$
$$P ::= (e.g. \; \mathsf{Int}, \mathsf{String}) \qquad \text{(primitive types)}$$
$$S ::= T @ U \qquad \text{(security types)}$$
$$T_\mathsf{L} \triangleq T @ T \qquad T_\mathsf{H} \triangleq T @ \top$$

Fig. 2. $\lambda^{\exists}_{\mathsf{SEC}}$: syntax

4.1 Syntax

Figure 2 presents the syntax of $\lambda^{\exists}_{\mathsf{SEC}}$. Expressions e are completely standard [14], including functions, applications, variables, primitive values, binary operations on primitive values, the unit value, pairs with their first and second projections, injections $\mathsf{inl} \; e$ and $\mathsf{inr} \; e$ to introduce sum types, as well as a case construct to eliminate sums; finally, pack and open introduce and eliminate existential packages, respectively. Types T include function types $S \to S$, primitive types P, the unit type 1, sum types $S + S$, pair types $S \times S$, existential types $\exists X.T$, type variables X and the top type $\top$. A security type S is a faceted type $T@U$ where T is the safety type and U is the declassification type.

Well-Formedness of Security Types. We now comment on the rules for valid security types, *i.e.facet-wise* well-formed types. We have three general form of security types T_L and T_H and $T@X$. While there is no constraint on forming types T_L and T_H, such as Int_L, X_L and Int_H, we need two considerations for types such as $\mathsf{Int}@X$.

The first consideration is that *inside* an existential type $\exists X.T$ the type variable X, when used as a declassification type, must be uniquely associated to a concrete safety type. For instance, the existential type $\exists X.(\mathsf{String}@X \to \mathsf{Int}@X)$ is ill-formed, while $\exists X.(\mathsf{Int}@X \to \mathsf{Int}@X)$ and $\exists X.(X@X \to \mathsf{Int}@X)$ are well-formed. For such well-formed types, we use the auxiliary function $\mathsf{sftype}(\exists X.T)$ to obtain the safety type associated to X; for instance $\mathsf{sftype}(\exists X.(X@X \to \mathsf{Int}@X)) = \mathsf{Int}$ (undefined on ill-formed types).

The second consideration is when a client opens a package. The expression $\mathsf{open}(X, x) = e \; \mathsf{in} \; e'$ binds the type variable X in e', therefore the expression e' can declare security types of the form $T'@X$. However, for the declaration of the type $T'@X$ to be valid, the safety type of the declassification type variable X must be T'. For instance, if the safety type of X is Int, the expression e' cannot declare security types such as $\mathsf{String}@X$, otherwise computations over secrets could get stuck. The question is how to determine the safety type T' of X in e'. Crucially, the expression e necessarily has to be of type $(\exists X.T)_\mathsf{L}$, therefore we can obtain the safety type for X with $\mathsf{sftype}(\exists X.T)$. To keep track of the safety type for each type variable X, we use a type variable environment Δ that maps type variables to types T (*i.e.* $\Delta ::= \bullet \mid \Delta, X : T$)

With the previous considerations in mind, the rules for well-formed security types are straightforward. In the rest of the paper, we use the judgment $\Delta \models S$ to mean *well-formed* security types S under type environment Δ. A well formed security type S is both facet-wise well-formed and closed with respect to type variables. We also use $\Delta \models \Gamma$ to indicate that a type environment is well-formed, *i.e.* all types in Γ are well-formed. In the following, we assume well-formed security types and environments.

4.2   Static Semantics

Figure 3 presents the static semantics of $\lambda^{\exists}_{\mathsf{SEC}}$. Security typing relies on a subtyping judgment that validates secure information flows. The left-most rule justifies subtyping by reflexivity. The middle rule justifies subtyping for two security types with the same safety type, when the declassification type of right security type is $\top$. Finally, the right-most rule justifies subtyping between a public type T_{L} and $T@X$.

As usual, the typing judgment $\Delta; \Gamma \vdash e : S$ denotes that "the expression e has type S under the type variable environment Δ and the type environment Γ". The typing rules are mostly standard [14]. Here, we only discuss the special treatment of security types.

Rule (TVar) gives the security type to a type variable from the type environment and rule (TS) is the standard subtyping subsumption rule. Rules (TP), (TFun), (TPair), (TU), (TInl), (TInr) and (TPack) introduce primitive, function, pair, unit, sum and existential types, respectively. In particular, rule (TPack) requires the representation type of the package to be *more precise* than the safety type associated to X in the existential type, *i.e.* $T' \sqsubseteq \mathsf{sftype}(\exists X.T)$. The precision judgment has only two rules: reflexivity $T \sqsubseteq T$, and any type is more precise than a type variable $T \sqsubseteq X$.

Rules (TApp), (TOp), (TFst), (TSnd), (TCase) and (TOpen) are elimination rules for function, primitive, pair, sum and existential types, respectively. When a secret is eliminated, the resulting computation must protect that secret. This is done with $\lceil S' \rceil_S$, which changes the declassification type of S' to $\top$ if the type S is not public:

$$\lceil T_1@U_1 \rceil_{T_2@U_2} = T_1@U_1 \text{ if } T_2 = U_2, \text{ otherwise } T_1@\top$$

Let us illustrate the use of rule (TApp). On the one hand, if the type of the function expression e_1 is $(S_1 \rightarrow S_2)_{\mathsf{L}}$, *i.e.* it represents a public function, then the type of the function application is S_2. On the other hand, if the function expression e_1 has type $(S_1 \rightarrow T_2@U_2)@X$ or $(S_1 \rightarrow T_2@U_2)_{\mathsf{H}}$, *i.e.* it represents a secret, then the function application has type $T_2@\top$.

Rule (TOp) uses an auxiliary function Θ to obtain the signature of a primitive operator and ensures that the resulting type protects both operands with $\lceil \lceil P''@P'' \rceil_{P@U} \rceil_{P'@U'}$. Rules (TFst) and (TSnd) use the same principle to protect the projections of a pair. Rule (TCase) requires the discriminee to be of

$\boxed{S <: S}$

$$T@U <: T@U \qquad T@U <: T@\top \qquad T_{\mathsf{L}} <: T@X$$

$\boxed{\Delta; \Gamma \vdash e : S}$

$$(\text{TVar}) \frac{x \in dom(\Gamma)}{\Delta; \Gamma \vdash x : \Gamma(x)} \qquad (\text{TS}) \frac{\Delta; \Gamma \vdash e : S' \quad S' <: S}{\Delta; \Gamma \vdash e : S} \qquad (\text{TP}) \frac{P = \Theta(\mathsf{p})}{\Delta; \Gamma \vdash \mathsf{p} : P_{\mathsf{L}}}$$

$$(\text{TFun}) \frac{\Delta; \Gamma, x : S \vdash e : S'}{\Delta; \Gamma \vdash \lambda x : S.\, e : (S \to S')_{\mathsf{L}}} \qquad (\text{TPair}) \frac{\Delta; \Gamma \vdash e_1 : S_1 \quad \Delta; \Gamma \vdash e_2 : S_2}{\Delta; \Gamma \vdash \langle e_1, e_2 \rangle : (S_1 \times S_2)_{\mathsf{L}}}$$

$$(\text{TU}) \frac{}{\Delta; \Gamma \vdash \langle \rangle : 1_{\mathsf{L}}} \qquad (\text{TInl}) \frac{\Delta; \Gamma \vdash e : S_1}{\Delta; \Gamma \vdash \mathsf{inl}\ e : (S_1 + S_2)_{\mathsf{L}}} \qquad (\text{TInr}) \frac{\Delta; \Gamma \vdash e : S_2}{\Delta; \Gamma \vdash \mathsf{inr}\ e : (S_1 + S_2)_{\mathsf{L}}}$$

$$(\text{TPack}) \frac{\begin{array}{c} \Delta; \Gamma \vdash e : (T[T'/X])_{\mathsf{L}} \\ T' \sqsubseteq \mathsf{sftype}(\exists X.T) \end{array}}{\Delta; \Gamma \vdash \mathsf{pack}(T', e)\ \mathsf{as}\ \exists X.T : (\exists X.T)_{\mathsf{L}}} \qquad (\text{TApp}) \frac{\begin{array}{c} \Delta; \Gamma \vdash e_1 : S \quad S = (S_1 \to S_2)@U \\ \Delta; \Gamma \vdash e_2 : S_1 \end{array}}{\Delta; \Gamma \vdash e_1\ e_2 : \lceil S_2 \rceil_S}$$

$$(\text{TOp}) \frac{\Theta(\oplus) : P \times P' \to P'' \quad \Delta; \Gamma \vdash e_1 : P@U \quad \Delta; \Gamma \vdash e_2 : P'@U'}{\Delta; \Gamma \vdash e_1 \oplus e_2 : \lceil \lceil P''@P'' \rceil_{P@U} \rceil_{P'@U'}}$$

$$(\text{TFst}) \frac{\begin{array}{c} \Delta; \Gamma \vdash e : S \\ S = (S_1 \times S_2)@U \end{array}}{\Delta; \Gamma \vdash \mathsf{fst}\ e : \lceil S_1 \rceil_S} \qquad (\text{TSnd}) \frac{\begin{array}{c} \Delta; \Gamma \vdash e : S \\ S = (S_1 \times S_2)@U \end{array}}{\Delta; \Gamma \vdash \mathsf{snd}\ e : \lceil S_2 \rceil_S}$$

$$(\text{TCase}) \frac{\begin{array}{c} \Delta; \Gamma \vdash e : S \quad S = (S_1 + S_2)@U \\ \Delta; \Gamma, x_1 : S_1 \vdash e_1 : S' \quad \Delta; \Gamma, x_2 : S_2 \vdash e_2 : S' \end{array}}{\Delta; \Gamma \vdash \mathsf{case}\ e\ \mathsf{of}\ \mathsf{inl}\ x_1.e_1 \mid \mathsf{inr}\ x_2.e_2 : \lceil S' \rceil_S}$$

$$(\text{TOpen}) \frac{\begin{array}{c} \Delta; \Gamma \vdash e : S \quad S = (\exists X.T)@U \quad T' \triangleq \mathsf{sftype}(\exists X.T) \\ \Delta, X : T'; \Gamma, x : T_{\mathsf{L}} \vdash e' : S' \quad \Delta \models S' \end{array}}{\Delta; \Gamma \vdash \mathsf{open}(X, x) = e\ \mathsf{in}\ e' : \lceil S' \rceil_S}$$

Fig. 3. $\lambda^{\exists}_{\mathsf{SEC}}$: static semantics

type $(S_1 + S_2)@U$, and both branches must have the same type S'. Likewise, it protects the resulting computation with $\lceil S' \rceil_S$.

Finally, rule (TOpen) applies to expressions of the form $\mathsf{open}(X, x) = e$ in e', by typing the body expression e' in an extended type variable environment $\Delta, X : T'$ and a type environment $\Gamma, x : T_{\mathsf{L}}$. Two points are worth noticing. First, the association $X : T'$ allows us to verify that security types of the form $T'@X$ defined in the body expression e' are well-formed. Second, we make the well-formedness requirement explicit for the result type $\Delta \models S'$, which implies that S' is facet-wise well-formed and closed under Δ—i.e. the type variable X cannot appear in S'.

4.3   Dynamic Semantics and Type Safety

The execution of $\lambda^{\exists}_{\mathsf{SEC}}$ expressions is defined with a standard call-by-value small-step dynamic semantics based on evaluation contexts (Fig. 4). We abstract over the execution of primitive operators over primitive values using an auxiliary function θ.

$$E ::= [\,] \mid \mathsf{fst}\ E \mid \mathsf{snd}\ E \mid \mathsf{case}\ E\ \text{of}\ \mathsf{inl}\ x_1.e_1 \mid \mathsf{inr}\ x_2.e_2 \quad \text{(evaluation contexts)}$$
$$\mid E\ e \mid v\ E \mid E \oplus e \mid v \oplus E \mid \mathsf{open}(X, x) = E\ \text{in}\ e'$$

$\mathsf{fst}\ \langle v_1, v_2 \rangle \longmapsto v_1$

$\mathsf{snd}\ \langle v_1, v_2 \rangle \longmapsto v_2$

$\mathsf{case}\ \mathsf{inl}\ v\ \text{of}\ \mathsf{inl}\ x_1.e_1 \mid \mathsf{inr}\ x_2.e_2 \longmapsto e_1\ [v/x_1]$

$\mathsf{case}\ \mathsf{inr}\ v\ \text{of}\ \mathsf{inl}\ x_1.e_1 \mid \mathsf{inr}\ x_2.e_2 \longmapsto e_2\ [v/x_2]$

$(\lambda x : S.\ e)\ v \longmapsto e\ [v/x]$

$p_1 \oplus p_2 \longmapsto \theta(\oplus, p_1, p_2)$

$\mathsf{open}(X, x) = (\mathsf{pack}(T', v)\ \text{as}\ \exists X.T)\ \text{in}\ e' \longmapsto e'\ [v/x]\ [T'/X]$

$$\frac{e \longmapsto e'}{E[e] \longmapsto E[e']}$$

Fig. 4. $\lambda^{\exists}_{\mathsf{SEC}}$: Dynamic semantics

We define the predicate $\mathsf{safe}(e)$ to indicate that the evaluation of the expression e does not get stuck.

Definition 1 (Safety). $\mathsf{safe}(e) \iff \forall e'.\ e \longmapsto^* e' \implies e' = v\ \text{or}\ \exists e''.\ e' \longmapsto e''$

Well-typed $\lambda^{\exists}_{\mathsf{SEC}}$ closed terms are safe.

Theorem 1 (Syntactic type safety). $\vdash e : S \implies \mathsf{safe}(e)$

Having formally defined the language $\lambda^{\exists}_{\mathsf{SEC}}$, we move to the main result of this paper, which is to show that the $\lambda^{\exists}_{\mathsf{SEC}}$ is sound from a security standpoint, *i.e.* its type system enforces existential relaxed noninterference.

5   Existential Relaxed Noninterference, Formally

In Sect. 3 we gave an overview of existential relaxed noninterference (ERNI), explaining how it depends on type-based equivalences. To formally capture these type-based equivalences, we define a logical relation, defined by induction on the structure of types. To account for type variables, we build upon prior work on logical relations for parametricity [2,15,17]. Then, we formally define ERNI on top of this logical relation. Finally, we prove that the type system of $\lambda^{\exists}_{\mathsf{SEC}}$ enforces existential relaxed noninterference.

5.1   Logical Relation for Type-Based Equivalence

As explained in Sect. 3, two values v_1 and v_2 are equivalent at type S, if they are in the partial equivalence relation denoted by S. To capture this, the logical relation (Fig. 5) interprets types as set of *atoms*, *i.e.* pairs of closed expressions. We use Atom $[T_1, T_2]$ to characterize the set of atoms with expressions of type T_1 and T_2 respectively. This definition appeals to a simply-typed judgment $\Delta; \Gamma \vdash_1$

$e : T$ that does not consider the declassification type and is therefore completely standard. The use of this simple type system clearly separates the *definition* of secure programs from the *enforcement* mechanism, *i.e.* the security type system of Fig. 3.

In Sect. 3 we explained what it means to be equivalent at type $\text{Int}@X$ appealing to a relation on integers $R_X \subseteq \text{Int} \times \text{Int}$. To formally characterize the set of valid relations R_X for types T_1 and T_2 we use the definition $\text{Rel}[T_1, T_2]$. To keep track of the relation associated to a type variable, most definitions are indexed by an environment ρ that maps type variables X to triplets (T_1, T_2, R), where T_1 and T_2 are two representation types of X and R is a relation on closed values of type T_1 and T_2 (*i.e.* $\rho ::= \emptyset \mid \rho[X \mapsto (T_1, T_2, R)]$). We will explain later where these types T_1 and T_2 come from. We write $\rho_1(U)$ (resp. $\rho_2(U)$) to replace all type variables of ρ in types with the associated type T_1 (resp. T_2), and $\rho_\text{R}(X)$ to retrieve the relation R of a type variable X in ρ.

Figure 5 defines the *value interpretation* of a type T, denoted $\mathcal{V}[\![T]\!]\rho$, then the value interpretation of a security type S, denoted $\mathcal{V}[\![S]\!]\rho$, and finally the *expression interpretation* of a type S, denoted $\mathcal{C}[\![S]\!]\rho$.

Interpreting Concrete Types. We first explain the definitions that do not involve types variables. $\mathcal{V}[\![T@\top]\!]\rho$ (resp. $\mathcal{V}[\![T@T]\!]\rho$) characterizes when values of T are indistinguishable (resp. distinguishable) for the public observer. $\mathcal{V}[\![T@\top]\!]\rho$ is defined as $\text{Atom}[\rho_1(T), \rho_2(T)]$ indicating that any two values of type T are equivalent at type $T@\top$. Note that this also includes values of type $X@\top$.

Two *public* values are equivalent at a security type $T@T$ if they are equivalent at their safety type, *i.e.* $\mathcal{V}[\![T_\text{L}]\!]\rho = \mathcal{V}[\![T]\!]\rho$. The definition $\mathcal{V}[\![P]\!]\rho$ relates syntactically-equal primitive values at type P. Two functions are equivalent at type $S_1 \to S_2$, denoted $\mathcal{V}[\![S_1 \to S_2]\!]\rho$, if given equivalent arguments at type S_1, their applications are equivalent expressions at type S_2. Two pairs are equivalent at type $S_1 \times S_2$ if they are component-wise equivalent. Two values are equivalent at $S_1 + S_2$ if they are either both left-injected values $\text{inl } v_1$ and $\text{inl } v_2$ such as v_1 and v_2 are equivalent at S_1, or both right-injected values $\text{inr } v_1$ and $\text{inr } v_2$ such as v_1 and v_2 are equivalent at S_2.

Finally, two expressions e_1 and e_2 are equivalent at type $T@U$, denoted $\mathcal{C}[\![T@U]\!]\rho$, if they both reduce to values v_1 and v_2 respectively and these values are related at type $T@U$. (Note that all well-typed $\lambda_\text{SEC}^\exists$ expressions terminate.)

Interpreting Existential Types. We now explain the value interpretation of existential types $\exists X.T$, type variables X and security types of the form $T@X$, which all involve type variables.

Two public package expressions $\text{pack}(T_1, v_1)$ as $\exists X.T$ and $\text{pack}(T_2, v_2)$ as $\exists X.T$ are equivalent at type $\exists X.T$, denoted $\mathcal{V}[\![\exists X.T]\!]\rho$, if there exists a relation R on the representation types T_1 and T_2 that makes the package implementations v_1 and v_2 equivalent at type T, denoted $(v_1, v_2) \in \mathcal{V}[\![T]\!]\rho[X \mapsto (T_1, T_2, R)]$. Note that if

$$\text{Atom}\,[T_1, T_2] = \{(e_1, e_2) \mid \bullet; \bullet \vdash_1 e_1 : T_1 \ \wedge \ \bullet; \bullet \vdash_1 e_2 : T_2\}$$
$$\text{Atom}_\rho\,[T] \quad = \text{Atom}\,[\rho_1(T), \rho_2(T)]$$
$$\text{Rel}\,[T_1, T_2] \quad = \{R \subseteq \text{Atom}\,[T_1, T_2]\}$$
$$\mathcal{V}[\![1]\!]\rho \quad = \{(\langle\rangle, \langle\rangle) \in \text{Atom}_\rho\,[1]\}$$
$$\mathcal{V}[\![P]\!]\rho \quad = \{(\mathsf{p}, \mathsf{p}) \in \text{Atom}_\rho\,[P]\}$$
$$\mathcal{V}[\![S_1 \to S_2]\!]\rho = \{(v_1, v_2) \in \text{Atom}_\rho\,[S_1 \to S_2] \mid$$
$$\forall v_1', v_2'. \ (v_1', v_2') \in \mathcal{V}[\![S_1]\!]\rho \implies (v_1 \ v_1', v_2 \ v_2') \in \mathcal{C}[\![S_2]\!]\rho\}$$
$$\mathcal{V}[\![S_1 \times S_2]\!]\rho = \{(\langle v_1, v_1'\rangle, \langle v_2, v_2'\rangle) \in \text{Atom}_\rho\,[S_1 \times S_2] \mid (v_1, v_2) \in \mathcal{V}[\![S_1]\!]\rho \ \wedge \ (v_1', v_2') \in \mathcal{V}[\![S_2]\!]\rho\}$$
$$\mathcal{V}[\![S_1 + S_2]\!]\rho = \{(\mathsf{inl}\ v_1, \mathsf{inl}\ v_2) \in \text{Atom}_\rho\,[S_1 + S_2] \mid (v_1, v_2) \in \mathcal{V}[\![S_1]\!]\rho\}$$
$$\cup \{(\mathsf{inr}\ v_1, \mathsf{inr}\ v_2) \in \text{Atom}_\rho\,[S_1 + S_2] \mid (v_1, v_2) \in \mathcal{V}[\![S_2]\!]\rho\}$$
$$\mathcal{V}[\![\exists X.T]\!]\rho \quad = \{(\mathsf{pack}(T_1, v_1) \text{ as } \exists X.T, \mathsf{pack}(T_2, v_2) \text{ as } \exists X.T) \in \text{Atom}_\rho\,[\exists X.T] \mid$$
$$T_1 \sqsubseteq \mathsf{sftype}(\exists X.T) \ \wedge \ T_2 \sqsubseteq \mathsf{sftype}(\exists X.T) \ \wedge$$
$$\exists R \in \text{Rel}\,[T_1, T_2]. \ (v_1, v_2) \in \mathcal{V}[\![T]\!]\rho\,[X \mapsto (T_1, T_2, R)]\}$$
$$\mathcal{V}[\![X]\!]\rho \quad = \rho_R(X)$$
$$\mathcal{V}[\![T@X]\!]\rho \quad = \rho_R(X) \cup \mathcal{V}[\![T]\!]\rho$$
$$\mathcal{V}[\![T@\top]\!]\rho \quad = \text{Atom}\,[\rho_1(T), \rho_2(T)]$$
$$\mathcal{V}[\![T@\top]\!]\rho \quad = \mathcal{V}[\![T]\!]\rho$$
$$\mathcal{C}[\![T@U]\!]\rho \quad = \{(e_1, e_2) \in \text{Atom}_\rho\,[T] \mid \forall v_1, v_2. \ e_1 \longmapsto^* v_1 \ \wedge \ e_2 \longmapsto^* v_2 \ \wedge \ (v_1, v_2) \in \mathcal{V}[\![T@U]\!]\rho\}$$

Fig. 5. $\lambda^{\exists}_{\mathsf{SEC}}$ Logical relation for type-based equivalence

the existential type $\exists X.T$ has a concrete safety type T' (not a type variable) for X, then both T_1 and T_2 necessarily have to be equal to T'. Otherwise, T_1 and T_2 are arbitrary types. Two values are related at type X, denoted $\mathcal{V}[\![X]\!]\rho$, if they are in the relational interpretation R associated to X (retrieved with $\rho_R(X)$). Two values are related at type $T@X$, denoted $\mathcal{V}[\![T@X]\!]\rho$, if they are in $\rho_R(X)$, or if they are publicly-equivalent values of type T (*i.e.* a package can accept public values of type T where values of $T@X$ are expected).

We illustrate these formal type-based equivalences in Sect. 6, after formally defining existential relaxed noninterference and proving security type soundness.

5.2 Existential Relaxed Noninterference

As illustrated in Sect. 3, ERNI is a modular property that accounts for open expressions over both variables and type variables. To account for open expressions, we first need to define the relational interpretation of a type environment Γ and a type variable environment Δ:

$$\mathcal{G}[\![\cdot]\!]\rho \quad = \{(\emptyset, \emptyset)\}$$
$$\mathcal{G}[\![\Gamma; x : S]\!]\rho = \{(\gamma_1\,[x \mapsto v_1], \gamma_2\,[x \mapsto v_2]) \mid (\gamma_1, \gamma_2) \in \mathcal{G}[\![\Gamma]\!]\rho \ \wedge \ (v_1, v_2) \in \mathcal{V}[\![S]\!]\rho\}$$
$$\mathcal{D}[\![\cdot]\!] \quad = \{\emptyset\}$$
$$\mathcal{D}[\![\Delta; X : T]\!] = \{\rho\,[X \mapsto (T_1, T_2, R)] \mid \rho \in \mathcal{D}[\![\Delta]\!] \ \wedge \ T_1 \sqsubseteq T \ \wedge \ T_2 \sqsubseteq T \ \wedge \ R \in \text{Rel}\,[T_1, T_2]\}$$

The type environment interpretation $\mathcal{G}[\![\Gamma]\!]\rho$ is standard; it characterizes when two value substitutions γ_1 and γ_2 are equivalent. A value substitution γ is a mapping from variables to closed values (*i.e.* $\gamma ::= \emptyset \mid \gamma\,[x \mapsto v]$). Two value substitutions are equivalent if for all associations $x : S$ in Γ, the mapped values to x in γ_1 and γ_2 are equivalent at S. Finally, the interpretation of a type variable environment Δ, denoted $\mathcal{D}[\![\Delta]\!]$, is a set of type substitutions ρ with the same domain as Δ. For each type variable X bound to T in Δ, such a ρ maps X to triples (T_1, T_2, R), where T_1 and T_2 are closed types that are more precise than

T. R must be a valid relation for the types T_1 and T_2. We write $\rho_1(e)$ (resp. $\rho_2(e)$) to replace all type variables of ρ in terms with their associated type T_1 (resp. T_2),

We can now formally define ERNI. An expression e satisfies existential relaxed noninterference for a type variable environment Δ and a type variable Γ at the S, denoted $\mathsf{ERNI}(\Delta, \Gamma, e, S)$ if, given a type substitution ρ satisfying Δ and two values substitutions γ_1 and γ_2 that are equivalent at Γ, applying the substitutions produces equivalent expressions at type S.

Definition 2 (Existential relaxed noninterference)

$$\mathsf{ERNI}(\Delta, \Gamma, e, S) \iff \exists T, U.\ S \triangleq T @ U\ \wedge\ \Delta; \Gamma \vdash_1 e : T\ \wedge\ \Delta \models \Gamma\ \wedge\ \Delta \models S\ \wedge$$
$$\forall \rho, \gamma_1, \gamma_2.\ \rho \in \mathcal{D}[\![\Delta]\!].\ (\gamma_1, \gamma_2) \in \mathcal{G}[\![\Gamma]\!]\rho \implies (\rho_1(\gamma_1(e)), \rho_2(\gamma_2(e))) \in \mathcal{C}[\![S]\!]\rho$$

5.3 Security Type Soundness

Instead of directly proving that the type system of Fig. 3 implies existential relaxed noninterference for all well-typed terms, we prove it through the standard definition of logically-related open terms [5]:

Definition 3 (Logically-related open terms)

$$\Delta; \Gamma \vdash e_1 \approx e_2 : S \iff \Delta; \Gamma \vdash e_i : S\ \wedge\ \Delta \models \Gamma\ \wedge\ \Delta \models S\ \wedge$$
$$\forall \rho, \gamma_1, \gamma_2.\ \rho \in \mathcal{D}[\![\Delta]\!].(\gamma_1, \gamma_2) \in \mathcal{G}[\![\Gamma]\!]\rho \implies (\rho_1(\gamma_1(e_1)), \rho_2(\gamma_2(e_2))) \in \mathcal{C}[\![S]\!]\rho$$

The next lemma captures that if an expression is logically related to itself, then it satisfies ERNI.

Lemma 1 (Self logical relation implies PRNI). $\Delta; \Gamma \vdash e \approx e : S \implies \mathsf{ERNI}(\Delta, \Gamma, e, S)$

The proof of security type soundness relies on the Fundamental Property of the logical relation: a well-typed $\lambda_{\mathsf{SEC}}^{\exists}$ term is related to itself.

Theorem 2 (Fundamental property). $\Delta; \Gamma \vdash e : S \implies \Delta; \Gamma \vdash e \approx e : S$

Security type soundness follows from Lemma 1 and Theorem 2.

Theorem 3 (Security type soundness). $\Delta; \Gamma \vdash e : S \implies \mathsf{ERNI}(\Delta, \Gamma, e, S)$

Proof. By induction on the typing derivation of e. Following Ahmed [2], we define a compatibility lemma for each typing rule; then, each case of the induction directly follows from the corresponding compatibility lemma. □

6   Illustration

With all the formal definitions at hand, we end by revisiting the informal example of Sect. 3. SalaryPolicy can be encoded in $\lambda_{\mathsf{SEC}}^{\exists}$ as follow: $\exists X.\mathsf{Int}@X \times (\mathsf{Int}@X \to \mathsf{Bool_L})$. Let us show that the following two packages are equivalent at type SalaryPolicy$_L$ (gte is a curried comparison function, and we omit the as):

$$p_1 \overset{\triangle}{=} \mathsf{pack}(\mathsf{Int}, \langle 100001, \mathsf{gte}(100000)\rangle) \qquad p_2 \overset{\triangle}{=} \mathsf{pack}(\mathsf{Int}, \langle 100002, \mathsf{gte}(100000)\rangle)$$

The definition of $\mathcal{V}[\![\mathsf{SalaryPolicy}]\!]\emptyset$ requires picking a relation $R \in \mathsf{Rel}\,[\mathsf{Int}, \mathsf{Int}]$. Pick $R = \{(100001, 100002)\}$. Then apply the rest of the definitions to verify that the package implementations are equivalent at $\mathcal{V}[\![\mathsf{Int}@X \times (\mathsf{Int}@X \to \mathsf{Bool_L})]\!]\emptyset\,[X \mapsto (\mathsf{Int}, \mathsf{Int}, R)]$. Use the $\rho_R(X)$ part of the definition of $\mathcal{V}[\![\mathsf{Int}@X]\!]\emptyset\,[X \mapsto (\mathsf{Int}, \mathsf{Int}, R)]$ to show that the first components 100001 and 100002 are equivalent at $\mathsf{Int}@X$, $i.e.$ $(100001, 100002) \in \rho_R(X)$.

First we illustrate the formal reasoning that we obtain from Theorem 3. Let us pose $\Delta = X : \mathsf{Int}$ and $\Gamma = x : (\mathsf{Int}@X \times (\mathsf{Int}@X \to \mathsf{Bool_L}))_L$. The program $e = (\mathsf{snd}\ x)\ (\mathsf{fst}\ x)$ has type $\mathsf{Bool_L}$, therefore, by Theorem 3, $\mathsf{ERNI}(\Delta, \Gamma, e, \mathsf{Bool_L})$ holds—e is secure at $\mathsf{Bool_L}$. We can verify this formally. By Definition 2 we have to assume an arbitrary type substitution $\rho \in \mathcal{D}[\![X : \mathsf{Int}]\!]$ and two values substitutions $(\gamma_1, \gamma_2) \in \mathcal{G}[\![x : (\mathsf{Int}@X \times (\mathsf{Int}@X \to \mathsf{Bool_L}))_L]\!]\rho$ and to show that $(\rho_1(\gamma_1((\mathsf{snd}\ x)\ (\mathsf{fst}\ x))), \rho_2(\gamma_2((\mathsf{snd}\ x)\ (\mathsf{fst}\ x)))) \in \mathcal{C}[\![\mathsf{Bool_L}]\!]\rho$. From $(\gamma_1, \gamma_2) \in \mathcal{G}[\![x : (\mathsf{Int}@X \times (\mathsf{Int}@X \to \mathsf{Bool_L}))_L]\!]\rho$ we know that $\gamma_1 = x \mapsto v_1$ and $\gamma_1 = x \mapsto v_2$, such as $(v_1, v_2) \in \mathcal{V}[\![(\mathsf{Int}@X \times (\mathsf{Int}@X \to \mathsf{Bool_L}))_L]\!]\rho$. Then $(\mathsf{snd}\ v_1)\ (\mathsf{fst}\ v_1) \longmapsto^* v'_{11}\ v'_{12}$ and $(\mathsf{snd}\ v_2)\ (\mathsf{fst}\ v_2) \longmapsto^* v'_{21}\ v'_{22}$, such that $(v'_{11}, v'_{21}) \in \mathcal{V}[\![\mathsf{Int}@X \to \mathsf{Bool_L}]\!]\rho$ and $(v'_{12}, v'_{22}) \in \mathcal{V}[\![\mathsf{Int}@X]\!]\rho$. After the previous reductions we have to verify that $(v'_{11}\ v'_{12}, v'_{21}\ v'_{22}) \in \mathcal{C}[\![\mathsf{Bool_L}]\!]\rho$. At this point, instantiate $(v'_{11}, v'_{21}) \in \mathcal{V}[\![\mathsf{Int}@X \to \mathsf{Bool_L}]\!]\rho$ with $(v'_{12}, v'_{22}) \in \mathcal{V}[\![\mathsf{Int}@X]\!]\rho$ to obtain $(v'_{11}\ v'_{12}, v'_{21}\ v'_{22}) \in \mathcal{C}[\![\mathsf{Bool_L}]\!]\rho$.

Second, we formally show why $\mathsf{ERNI}(\Delta, \Gamma, (\mathsf{fst}\ x)\%2, \mathsf{Int_L})$ does not hold. Instantiate Definition 2 with $\rho = X \mapsto (\mathsf{Int}, \mathsf{Int}, R)$ and $\gamma_1 = x \mapsto \langle 100001, \mathsf{gte}(100000)\rangle$ and $\gamma_2 = x \mapsto \langle 100002, \mathsf{gte}(100000)\rangle$. Note that $\rho = X \mapsto (\mathsf{Int}, \mathsf{Int}, R) \in \mathcal{D}[\![X : \mathsf{Int}]\!]$ and $(\gamma_1, \gamma_2) \in \mathcal{G}[\![\Gamma]\!]\rho$. To show $(\rho_1(\gamma_1((\mathsf{fst}\ x)\%2)), \rho_2(\gamma_2((\mathsf{fst}\ x)\%2))) \in \mathcal{C}[\![\mathsf{Int_L}]\!]\rho$ requires showing $(100001\%2, 100002\%2) \in \mathcal{C}[\![\mathsf{Int_L}]\!]\rho$, which means showing $(1, 0) \in \mathcal{C}[\![\mathsf{Int_L}]\!]\rho$—which is false. Similarly, we can verify that $\mathsf{ERNI}(\Delta, \Gamma, \mathsf{x.salary}, \mathsf{Int_L})$ does not hold, which means that a declassifiable secret cannot be directly observed by a public observer.

7   Related Work

We have already extensively discussed the relation to the original formulation of the labels-as-types approach in an object-oriented setting [5], itself inspired by the work on declassification policies (labels-as-functions) of Li and Zdancewic [9]. Formulating type-based declassification with existential types shows how to exploit another type abstraction mechanism that is found in non-object-oriented languages, with abstract data types and modules. Also, existential types support extrinsic declassification policies, which are not expressible in the receiver-centric approach of objects. For instance, the AccountStore example of Sect. 2 is not supported by design in the object-oriented approach.

The extrinsic declassification policies supported by our approach are closely related to *trusted declassification* [8], where declassification is globally defined, associating principals that own secrets with trusted (external) methods that can declassify these secrets. In our approach, the relation between secrets and declassifiers is not globally defined, but is local to an existential type and its usage. In both approaches the implementations of declassifiers have a privileged view of the secrets.

Bowman and Ahmed [3] present a translation of noninterference into parametricity with a compiler from the Dependency Core Calculus (DCC) [1] to System Fω. In a recent (as yet unpublished) article, Ngo et al. [13] extend this work to support translating declassification policies, inspired by prior work on type-based relaxed noninterference [5]. They first provide a translation into abstract types of the polymorphic lambda calculus [15], and then into signatures of a module calculus [4]. While that work and ours encode declassification policies via existential types (module signatures), we focus on providing a surface language for information flow control with type-based declassification. In particular, their translated programs do not support computing with secrets, which is enabled in both this work and the original work of Cruz et al. [5] thanks to faceted types. Additionally, they only model first-order secrets (integers), while our modular reasoning principle seamlessly accommodates higher-order secrets.

In another very recent piece of work, Cruz and Tanter [6] extend the object-oriented approach to type-based relaxed noninterference with parametric polymorphism, thereby supporting polymorphic declassification policies. Polymorphic declassification for object types is achieved with type variables at the method signature level, which supports the specification of polymorphic policies of the form $T \triangleleft X$. Existential types are closely related to universal types. In particular, the client of a package that exports a type variable X must be polymorphic with respect to X; hence our work supports a form of declassification polymorphism in the client code. It would be interesting to extend $\lambda^{\exists}_{\mathsf{SEC}}$ with universal types in order to study the interaction of both abstraction mechanisms in a standard functional setting. Finally, because of the receiver-centric perspective of objects, they have to resort to ad-hoc polymorphism to properly account for primitive types. Here, primitive types do not require any special treatment for declassification polymorphism, because of our extrinsic approach to declassification.

The idea of using the abstraction mechanism of modules to express a form of declassification can also be found in the work of Nanevski et al. [12] on Relational Hoare Type Theory (RHTT). RHTT is formulated with a monadic security type constructor STsec $A(p, q)$, where p is a pre-condition on the heap, and q is a post-condition relating output values, input heaps and output heaps. Thanks to the expressive power of the underlying dependent type theory, preconditions and postconditions can characterize very precise declassification policies. The price to pay is that proofs of noninterference have to be provided explicitly as proof terms (or discharged via tactics or other means when possible), while our less expressive approach is a simple, non-dependent type system. Finding the right balance between the expressiveness and the complexity of the typing discipline to express security policies is an active subject of research.

8   Conclusion

We present a novel approach to type-based relaxed noninterference, based on existential types as the underlying type abstraction mechanism. In contrast to the object-oriented, subtyping-based approach, the existential approach naturally supports external declassification policies. This work shows that the general approach of faceted security types for expressive declassification can be applied in non-object-oriented languages that support abstract data types or modules. As such, it represents a step towards providing a practical realization of information-flow security typing that accounts for controlled and expressive declassification with a modular reasoning principle about security.

An immediate venue for future work that would be crucial in practice is to develop type inference for declassification types, which should reduce to standard type inference [7]. Finally, a particularly interesting perspective is to study the combination of the existential approach with the object-oriented approach, thereby bridging the gap towards a practical implementation in a full-fledged programming language like Scala that features all these type abstraction mechanisms.

References

1. Abadi, M., Banerjee, A., Heintze, N., Riecke, J.G.: A core calculus of dependency. In: Proceedings of the 26th ACM Symposium on Principles of Programming Languages (POPL 1999), pp. 147–160. ACM Press, San Antonio, January 1999
2. Ahmed, A.: Step-indexed syntactic logical relations for recursive and quantified types. In: Sestoft, P. (ed.) ESOP 2006. LNCS, vol. 3924, pp. 69–83. Springer, Heidelberg (2006). https://doi.org/10.1007/11693024_6
3. Bowman, W.J., Ahmed, A.: Noninterference for free. In: Proceedings of the 20th ACM SIGPLAN Conference on Functional Programming (ICFP 2015), pp. 101–113. ACM Press, Vancouver, August 2015
4. Crary, K.: Modules, abstraction, and parametric polymorphism. In: Proceedings of the 44th ACM SIGPLAN-SIGACT Symposium on Principles of Programming Languages (POPL 2017), pp. 100–113. ACM Press, Paris, January 2017
5. Cruz, R., Rezk, T., Serpette, B., Tanter, É.: Type abstraction for relaxed noninterference. In: Müller, P. (ed.) Proceedings of the 31st European Conference on Object-Oriented Programming (ECOOP 2017). Leibniz International Proceedings in Informatics (LIPIcs), vol. 74, pp. 7:1–7:27. Schloss Dagstuhl-Leibniz-Zentrum fuer Informatik, Barcelona, Spain, June 2017

6. Cruz, R., Tanter, É.: Polymorphic relaxed noninterference. In: Proceedings of the IEEE Secure Development Conference (SecDev 2019). IEEE Computer Society Press, McLean, September 2019 (to appear)

7. Damas, L., Milner, R.: Principal type-schemes for functional programs. In: DeMillo, R.A. (ed.) Proceedings of the 16th ACM Symposium on Principles of Programming Languages (POPL 1989), pp. 207–212. ACM Press, Albuquerque, January 1982

8. Hicks, B., King, D., McDaniel, P., Hicks, M.: Trusted declassification: high-level policy for a security-typed language. In: Proceedings of the workshop on Programming Languages and Analysis for Security (PLAS 2006), pp. 65–74 (2006)

9. Li, P., Zdancewic, S.: Downgrading policies and relaxed noninterference. In: Proceedings of the 32nd ACM SIGPLAN-SIGACT Symposium on Principles of Programming Languages (POPL 2005), pp. 158–170. ACM Press, Long Beach, January 2005

10. Mitchell, J.C., Plotkin, G.D.: Abstract types have existential type. ACM Trans. Program. Lang. Syst. **10**(3), 470–502 (1988)

11. Myers, A.C.: Jif homepage. http://www.cs.cornell.edu/jif/. Accessed Mar 2019

12. Nanevski, A., Banerjee, A., Garg, D.: Verification of information flow and access control policies with dependent types. In: Proceedings of the 32nd IEEE Symposium on Security and Privacy (S&P 2011). pp. 165–179. IEEE Computer Society Press, Berkeley, May 2011

13. Ngo, M., Naumann, D.A., Rezk, T.: Typed-based relaxed noninterference for free. CoRR abs/1905.00922 (2019). https://arxiv.org/abs/1905.00922

14. Pierce, B.C.: Types and Programming Languages. MIT Press, Cambridge (2002)

15. Reynolds, J.C.: Types, abstraction, and parametric polymorphism. In: Mason, R.E.A. (ed.) Information Processing 83, pp. 513–523. Elsevier, Amsterdam (1983)

16. Sabelfeld, A., Sands, D.: Declassification: dimensions and principles. J. Comput. Secur. **17**(5), 517–548 (2009)

17. Wadler, P.: Theorems for free! In: Proceedings of the Fourth International Conference on Functional Programming Languages and Computer Architecture, FPCA 1989, pp. 347–359. ACM, London (1989)

18. Zdancewic, S.: Programming Languages for Information Security. Ph.D. thesis, Cornell University, August 2002

Program Analysis

Dissecting Widening: Separating Termination from Information

Graeme Gange[1], Jorge A. Navas[2(✉)], Peter Schachte[3], Harald Søndergaard[3],
and Peter J. Stuckey[1]

[1] Faculty of Information Technology, Monash University, Melbourne, Australia
[2] SRI International, California, USA
`jorge.navas@sri.com`
[3] Computing and Information Systems, The University of Melbourne,
Melbourne, Australia

Abstract. Widening ensures or accelerates convergence of a program analysis, and sometimes contributes a guarantee of soundness that would otherwise be absent. In this paper we propose a generalised view of widening, in which widening operates on values that are not necessarily elements of the given abstract domain, although they must be in a correspondence, the details of which we spell out. We show that the new view generalizes the traditional view, and that at least three distinct advantages flow from the generalization. First, it gives a handle on "compositional safety", the problem of creating widening operators for product domains. Second, it adds a degree of flexibility, allowing us to define variants of widening, such as delayed widening, without resorting to intrusive surgery on an underlying fixpoint engine. Third, it adds a degree of robustness, by making it difficult for an analysis implementor to make certain subtle (syntactic vs semantic) category mistakes. The paper supports these claims with examples. Our proposal has been implemented in a state-of-the-art abstract interpreter, and we briefly report on the changes that the revised view necessitated.

1 Introduction

A central problem in abstract interpretation is fixpoint finding: designing methods to find fixpoints of functions defined over certain mathematical structures, usually lattices, ideally producing results that are optimal in some sense. Here we shall assume that we are concerned with finding *least* fixpoints, or if that turns out to be difficult, fixpoints that are as small as we can manage.

Least fixpoints are usually found with Kleene's method, through repeated iteration starting from a smallest domain element. However, this iteration may not terminate, or may converge too slowly to be practical. *Widening* operators [8] serve a critical role in this, enforcing termination of Kleene iteration by jumping over infinite ascending chains, or simply accelerating analysis by somehow skipping long chain segments. Since widening may incur a loss of precision, the introduction of widening into an abstract interpretation engine becomes an art.

© Springer Nature Switzerland AG 2019
A. W. Lin (Ed.): APLAS 2019, LNCS 11893, pp. 95–114, 2019.
https://doi.org/10.1007/978-3-030-34175-6_6

The details of when and how to apply widening touch upon delicate trade-offs between the speed and the precision of program analysis.

A classical example is the widening operator often used with interval analysis [8,11]. This analysis determines for each program variable x at each program point, which values x could possibly take, in the form of an interval $[\texttt{lo},\texttt{hi}]$.

For the program in Fig. 1, an interval analysis can determine that, after the loop body has been executed 3 times, x is in the interval [3,6] and y is in [0,3]. Naive interval analysis, however, may not terminate, as it does not track the correspondence between x and y: after 100 iterations, it will see further (spurious) iterates $\{x \in [0, 100], y \in [0, 101]\}$, etc. Note that, as is common, interval analysis over-approximates the set of runtime states. In general, even if the least fixpoint is finitely reachable, it may take intolerably many iterations to reach.

```
x = 0; y = 0;
while(x < 100)
    if(a[x] > 0)
        y++; x++;
    else
        x += 2;
```

Fig. 1. Code snippet

Cousot and Cousot [8] introduced *widening* operations to cope with the problem of naive analysis being slow or non-terminating, and *narrowing* to improve on results (post-fixpoints) obtained after widening. Loosely, the idea behind widening is to introduce means for program analysis to skip long, possibly infinite, chains. For the interval analysis above, we might recognise that y's lower bound seems to remain unchanged in successive iterations, whereas its upper bound changes. Based on this we might move straight to the interval $[0, \infty]$ for y. Alternatively we might look for suggestions for less radical widening, provided by the surrounding program text, for example in the form of constants used in loop conditions. (We later discuss some of the variants of widening that have been proposed.) Narrowing may improve of the result of widening, although it is no panacea [25]. In this paper we are concerned exclusively with widening.

We propose a definition of widening which generalises the original concept in a small but critical way. We do not suggest that there is anything wrong with the original definition(s), and indeed a large number of useful and practical analysis tools have been built based on the standard view. However, *isolating* the termination aspect of widening from the task of finding upper bounds in an abstract domain has advantages, as we hope to show. By not conflating the two aspects, our definition of "isolated" widening covers some common constructions which are not true widenings in the classical sense. At the same time it simplifies certain implementation tasks, enabling compositional design of widening operators, and it eliminates certain pitfalls that surround the implementor.

In Sect. 2 we recapitulate the classical definition, and in Sect. 3 we demonstrate the pitfalls alluded to above. Section 4 defines the notion of *isolated* widening, and in Sect. 5 we demonstrate how isolated widenings resolve some common difficulties. Section 6 reports on our experience with the effort required to incorporate isolated widening in a generic abstract interpretation framework. Section 7 discusses related work and puts our proposal in the context of various forms of widening previously suggested, and Sect. 8 concludes.

2 Kleene Iteration with Widening

At an appropriate level of abstraction, a static analysis problem can be expressed as the search for solutions to an equation system

$$
\begin{pmatrix} x_1 \\ x_2 \\ \vdots \\ x_n \end{pmatrix} = \begin{pmatrix} F_1(x_1, x_2, \ldots, x_n) \\ F_2(x_1, x_2, \ldots, x_n) \\ \vdots \\ F_n(x_1, x_2, \ldots, x_n) \end{pmatrix}
\tag{1}
$$

This assumes a set $\mathsf{Loc} = \{1, \ldots, n\}$ of program *locations* of interest, with $x_i \in \mathcal{C}$ representing (or approximating) the set of program states that may be observed at location i. F_i is the *transfer function* for location i, specifying how information pertaining to that location is computed from the information available at locations feeding into i. The *concrete domain* is assumed to be a partially ordered set $(\mathcal{C}, \subseteq)$, and each $F_i : \mathcal{C}^n \to \mathcal{C}$ is assumed to be monotone, with $\mathcal{C}^n$ ordered component-wise.

We say that x_i *depends* on x_j iff the definition of F_i mentions x_j. The *dependency graph* for (1) is the directed graph with Loc as its set of nodes and an edge from i to j iff x_i depends on x_j.

Working directly with $\mathcal{C}$ is typically impractical, so analysis is performed on some alternate *abstract domain* $(\mathcal{D}, \sqsubseteq)$. $\mathcal{D}$ is related to $\mathcal{C}$ by a monotone *concretisation function* γ.[1] We say abstract state y *abstracts* concrete state x iff $x \subseteq \gamma(y)$. Similarly, we say abstract transfer function $F^\sharp$ *abstracts* transfer function F iff for all $y_1, \ldots, y_n$:

$$
F(\gamma(y_1), \ldots, \gamma(y_n)) \subseteq \gamma(F^\sharp(y_1, \ldots, y_n))
\tag{2}
$$

This ensures that, though $F^\sharp$ may not itself be monotone, it is an upper bound of the image (under γ) of the monotone F. So long as (2) holds, any (post-)fixpoint of $F^\sharp$ is a sound approximation of the sequence $[F(\bot), F^2(\bot), \ldots]$.

Circumstances under which (1) or its abstraction have a solution are well known. For example, $\mathcal{D}$ may be a complete lattice. Even so, simple iteration techniques such as Kleene iteration may fail to find a solution in finite time, if $\mathcal{D}$ has infinite ascending chains. Or, they may just be too slow to be practical, in the context of long ascending chains, even if these are finite. To solve this problem, Cousot and Cousot suggested the use of a *widening* operator.

Definition 1 (Widening [11]). A widening over domain $(\mathcal{D}, \sqsubseteq)$ is a binary operator $\triangledown : \mathcal{D} \times \mathcal{D} \to \mathcal{D}$ such that

- $\forall x, y \in \mathcal{D} : x \sqsubseteq x \triangledown y$
- $\forall x, y \in \mathcal{D} : y \sqsubseteq x \triangledown y$
- For all increasing chains $x_0 \sqsubseteq x_1, \ldots$, the increasing chain defined by $y_0 = x_0, \ldots, y_{i+1} = y_i \triangledown x_{i+1}, \ldots$ is not strictly increasing.

---

[1] Many variants of the concrete/abstract correspondence exist [10]. Here we deliberately adopt a relaxed formalisation which imposes few requirements on the domain.

Some later formulations of $\triangledown$ (e.g., [7]) impose a stricter condition:

For all (a_i), the sequence $(a_i^\triangledown)$ defined as:
$$a_0^\triangledown = a_0, \quad a_{n+1}^\triangledown = a_n^\triangledown \triangledown a_{n+1} \quad \text{is ultimately stationary} \tag{3}$$

The idea is to choose, judiciously, a set $W \subseteq \mathsf{Loc}$ of *widening points*, so that for every cycle C in the dependency graph for (1), $W \cap C \neq \emptyset$. (Such a set W always exists, but the aim is usually to choose a smallest possible set of widening points.) For each location $i \in W$, the equation for x_i in (1) is replaced by

$$x_i = x_i \triangledown F_i(x_1, x_2, \dots, x_n) \tag{4}$$

The impact on Kleene iteration is that the sequence of iterates for location $i \in W$ becomes, using (4),

$$x_i^0 = \bot, \quad x_i^{k+1} = x_i^k \triangledown F_i(x_1^k, x_2^k, \dots, x_n^k) \tag{5}$$

rather than $x_i^0 = \bot, x_i^{k+1} = F_i(x_1^k, x_2^k, \dots, x_n^k)$ using (1). The properties of $\triangledown$ ensure the convergence of (5). Equation (5) also clearly shows the different roles of $\triangledown$'s arguments. The left argument holds "historical" information and we shall refer to it as the *widener*. The right argument holds "current" information, which may be weakened as a result of widening; we shall refer to it as the "widenee".

The widening operator $\triangledown$ lacks a property that is shared by other domain operators: $\triangledown$ is not required to be monotone. Moreover, unlike other upper bound operators used in the context of abstract interpretation, $\triangledown$ is not normally commutative, nor is it intended to be commutative. This is because its role in the system of recurrent equations is very different to other operators: Widening points are the only locations for which x_i is defined in terms of *its own* past values, in the history of iterations. At all other locations, x_i is defined in terms of the values obtained for neighbouring locations.

In spite of these anomalies, the classical formulation of $\triangledown$ leads to a sound analysis framework. There tends, however, to be a distinct mismatch between the formulation and the way widenings are constructed and used in practice. This mismatch manifests in a number of ways, requiring awkward choices in analysis engines. As we shall see, it occasionally causes unexpected non-termination.

Cousot and Cousot [11] demonstrate $\triangledown$'s lack of monotonicity in the context of interval analysis. Consider the complete lattice of intervals $(\mathcal{I}, \sqsubseteq)$ with

$$\mathcal{I} = \{\bot\} \cup \{[\ell, u] \mid \ell \in \mathbb{Z} \cup \{-\infty\}, u \in \mathbb{Z} \cup \{\infty\}, \ell \leq u\}$$

The ordering $\sqsubseteq$ is defined by $z \sqsubseteq z'$ iff $\mathsf{lo}(z') \leq \mathsf{lo}(z) \wedge \mathsf{hi}(z) \leq \mathsf{hi}(z')$, where

$$\mathsf{lo}(z) = \begin{cases} \infty & \text{if } z = \bot \\ x & \text{if } z = [x, y] \end{cases} \qquad \mathsf{hi}(z) = \begin{cases} -\infty & \text{if } z = \bot \\ y & \text{if } z = [x, y] \end{cases}$$

(see Fig. 2, ignoring the dashed lines for now).

For this domain, a natural widening operation is $\triangledown_{\mathcal{I}}$ defined as follows:

$$\bot \triangledown_{\mathcal{I}} Y = Y$$
$$X \triangledown_{\mathcal{I}} \bot = X$$
$$[x_\ell, x_u] \triangledown_{\mathcal{I}} [y_\ell, y_u] = [\text{if } y_\ell < x_\ell \text{ then } -\infty \text{ else } x_\ell, \text{if } x_u < y_u \text{ then } \infty \text{ else } x_u]$$

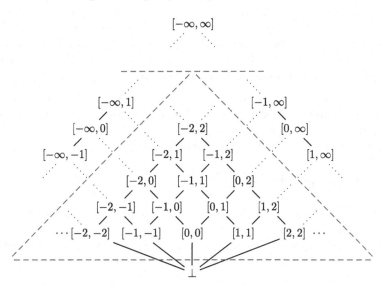

Fig. 2. The integer interval domain as a Hasse diagram. The role of the red dashed lines will be made clear in Sect. 4. (Color figure online)

That is, unstable bounds get extrapolated, lower bounds to $-\infty$ and upper bounds to ∞. To show that $\triangledown$ fails to be monotone in the widener, Cousot and Cousot [11] note that $[0, 1] \sqsubseteq [0, 2]$ but $[0, 1] \triangledown_{\mathcal{I}}[0, 2] = [0, \infty]$ whereas $[0, 2] \triangledown_{\mathcal{I}}[0, 2] = [0, 2]$. While this particular $\triangledown$ happens to be monotone in its widenee, the definition of widening does not enforce such monotonicity.

To see that $\triangledown$ may lack monotonicity in either argument position, consider the complete lattice $(\mathbb{N} \cup \{\infty\}, \sqsubseteq)$, with $\sqsubseteq$ defined $x \sqsubseteq y$ iff $x \le y \lor y = \infty$ (with $\le$ being the usual ordering on $\mathbb{N}$). Define widening on this lattice as follows:

$$x \triangledown y = \begin{cases} \max(x, y) & \text{if } y = 2 \\ \infty & \text{otherwise} \end{cases}$$

Here $1 \sqsubseteq 2$ but $\infty = 0 \triangledown 1 \not\sqsubseteq 0 \triangledown 2 = 2$, so $\triangledown$ is not monotone in the widenee. Yet $\triangledown$ is an upper bound operator, and for every increasing chain $x_0, x_1, \ldots$, the increasing chain $y_0 = x_0, y_{i+1} = y_i \triangledown x_{i+1}$ stabilises, so the classical requirements for a widening operation are satisfied.

It is worth highlighting the impact of (3). Definition 1 only guarantees convergence if the sequence of widenees is increasing. If the abstract transformer $F^\sharp$ relating successive iterations is monotone, this property is ensured. However, the monotonicity of $F^\sharp$ can be easily lost in a number of ways:

- If the abstraction $\mathcal{D}$ is not a join semi-lattice (e.g. [16,17,20]), there is no least-upper bound, thus successive values at control-flow join points may not strictly increase [15].
- If $F^\sharp$ is not the best abstraction of F, but some relaxation (as is common for non-linear operations), the sequence of iterates again may be non-monotone.

- A special case of the above is use of reduction operations to propagate information between multiple domains (discussed in Sect. 3.1). If the operators for channeling information between domains are not idempotent, and are not iterated to a fixpoint, monotonicity is again lost.

In any of these situations, a widening that only satisfies Definition 1 makes no guarantees of termination. Fortunately, the stabilisation-based widenings commonly used for numeric domains all satisfy (3), and for other cases, alternative, stricter, definitions of widening have been proposed.

3 Problems and Pitfalls

To motivate a fresh look at widening, we first discuss some irregular properties of widening: an absence of compositionality, a lack of flexibility, and a certain lack of robustness. In Sect. 5 we return to these aspects, to show how a different view of widening can remove or mitigate some drawbacks.

3.1 Problems of Compositionality

Abstract interpretation makes use of a number of domain product constructions. The reduced product of abstract domains [5,9] is a powerful concept, but difficult to implement in practice. Granger products [21] are a frequent compromise, equipping a pair of domains with 'reduction' operators to propagate information between them. In essence, both approaches take the quotient of $D_1 \times D_2$ under some equivalence relation $\equiv$. However, it is not in general safe to use widenings for D_1 and D_2 directly as a widening for $(D_1 \times D_2)_{/\equiv}$.

Example 1. Consider $D_1 = D_2 = \mathbb{N} \cup \{\infty\}$, with the usual ordering $\leq$, and define:

$$w \triangledown_e x = \begin{cases} w & \textbf{if } x \leq w \\ x & \textbf{if } x > w,\ w \text{ is even, and } x \text{ is odd} \\ x+1 & \textbf{if } x > w,\ w \text{ is even, and } x \text{ is even} \\ \infty & \textbf{otherwise} \end{cases}$$

$$w \triangledown_o x = \begin{cases} w & \textbf{if } x \leq w \\ x & \textbf{if } x > w,\ w \text{ is odd, and } x \text{ is even} \\ x+1 & \textbf{if } x > w,\ w \text{ is odd, and } x \text{ is odd} \\ \infty & \textbf{otherwise} \end{cases}$$

Note that $\triangledown_e$ always converges: if the first value is even, the second iterate will become odd, after which the third increasing step will jump to ∞. $\triangledown_o$ converges by analogous reasoning.

In the reduced product $D_1 \times D_2$, the meaning of (x, y) is simply $\min(x, y)$. Consider what happens to the strictly increasing sequence $0, 1, 2, \ldots$

Sequence to stabilise:	0	1	2	3	4	$\cdots$
Result of $(\triangledown_e, \triangledown_o)$ at iteration i:	$(0,0)$	$(1,\infty)$	$(\infty,2)$	$(3,\infty)$	$(\infty,4)$	$\cdots$
Reduced element at iteration i:	0	1	2	3	4	$\cdots$

When we map the two individual components back onto the quotient class, we regain information that was discarded by the previous widening. As a result, stabilisation is lost.   □

Example 1 shows that traditional widening does not guarantee compositional stabilisation. Each of the widening operators in the example provides stabilisation, one in D_1, the other in D_2, and yet their natural composition does not provide stabilisation in the reduced product of D_1 and D_2. Each has the effect of undermining the other.

The lack of compositionality manifests itself in other ways.

Example 2. Widening with thresholds [24,25] is a common strategy for avoiding precision loss in widening. However, implementing widening with thresholds for a large number of numeric abstract domains is tedious, and it would be preferable to utilise an existing widening operator. Indeed, in Crab [14], a generic version of widening with thresholds was previously implemented as follows:

$$s \nabla_{\mathcal{A}}^T t =$$
$$(s \nabla_{\mathcal{A}} t) \sqcap_{\mathcal{A}} (\text{FROM-INTERVAL}(\text{TO-INTERVAL}(s) \nabla_{\mathcal{I}}^T \text{TO-INTERVAL}(t))) \quad (6)$$

That is, given an arbitrary numerical abstract domain $\mathcal{A}$, extract interval approximations from $s, t \in \mathcal{A}$, using the function TO-INTERVAL that converts from $\mathcal{A}$ to $\mathcal{I}$. Then, apply (non-threshold) widening to the $\mathcal{A}$-operands, apply interval widening with thresholds to the $\mathcal{I}$-operands, convert from $\mathcal{I}$ to $\mathcal{A}$ using the function FROM-INTERVAL, and take the meet of the two results.

This sequence of operations *ought* to be innocuous. With the assumption that widening is applied in an unbroken sequence, and non-widening steps are not allowed after widening, the suggested solution should be safe: $\nabla_{\mathcal{I}}^T$ can be safely interleaved with increasing functions, so the interval component will eventually converge. And since the resulting intervals are stable, adding them back into $s \nabla_{\mathcal{A}} t$ should have no effect. Nevertheless, this widening strategy would—on very rare occasions—cause non-termination.[2]   □

It turns out that the problem in Example 2 is due to the call TO-INTERVAL(s), where we find the interval approximation of a previous iterate. To compute the tightest interval approximation of s, TO-INTERVAL must normalise s, that is, explicate the transitive closure of its representation. Not knowing that s is 'really' a widener, TO-INTERVAL helpfully modifies s in place, inadvertently breaking the termination conditions. There is nothing wrong with (6), read declaratively, and it is hard to blame the implementation of TO-INTERVAL. The root cause is that the termination invariant required by widening relies on invisible properties which are not captured at the semantic (or API) level. What was intended as a syntactic object (a set of constraints) is treated as a semantic object (a set of models). Clearly it would be nice to have a "widening API" that prevents this kind of category confusion.

---

[2] The bug was fixed on July 1st, 2018 in commit https://github.com/seahorn/crab/commit/72ed05690bc2bbee19141f5513cb6a8e8ab3ce9a.

3.2 Flexibility: Handling Variants of Widening

Widenings frequently achieve convergence by retaining only 'stable' information, and discarding everything else. This is excellent for attaining fast termination, but risks throwing away the properties we are attempting to infer.

The threshold widening discussed above is one of many different approaches to avoid excessive information loss in widening. Another common strategy to retain some information is *delayed widening* [3]: perform a bounded number of initial steps using join ($\sqcup$)—in the hope of obtaining stable invariants—before eventually resorting to widening.

These are simple and effective strategies, but implementing variants of widening is surprisingly messy [12]. For example, for delayed widening we need to track how many times each widening point has been processed, but where does this count belong? A common strategy is to remove this decision from the domain entirely, relying on the analysis engine to decide when to switch from "join" mode to "widen" mode. Alternatively, one can place an iteration counter somewhere with shared visibility. In any case, the traditional solutions involve disruptive changes to an underlying fixpoint engine, or a baroque redesign of abstract domains. A cleaner and less intrusive solution would be desirable.

3.3 Problems of Fragility: Termination

Termination problems similar to that of Example 2 are easily provoked. Miné [27,28] observed a related problem with his weakly relational domains: The implementation of these domains rely on transitive closure operations to make implicit binary relations explicit at certain points. For example, a set $\{x \leq y, y \leq z\}$ of constraints may be normalised as $\{x \leq y, y \leq z, x \leq z\}$. However, applying transitive closure to the post-widening state can result in non-termination, *even though the set of models is unchanged*. The root cause of the trouble [27,28] (and in Example 2) is that the domain conflates two views of an abstract state: the lattice operations and abstract transformers see states as *semantic* objects, so two states with identical models are equivalent; closure is, viewed from that angle, a no-op. Widening, however, is non-semantic in its left argument: Once some constraint is discarded as unstable, it must not re-appear in future iterations. If transitive closure is applied between widening steps, we may re-infer relaxed forms of the discarded invariants, which may appear stable in the next iteration, breaking the invariant we need for termination.

Example 3. Miné [27] first identified the problem and gave a concrete example. Consider the sequence of iterates $p_i = \{|y - x| \leq i + 1, |z - x| \leq i + 1, |z - y| \leq 1\}$ for $i = 0, 1, 2, \ldots$. With the standard representation of difference constraints as directed graphs, we can depict the sequence as in the bottom row of Fig. 3. To maintain precision, it is important to apply a transitive closure operation to constraint sets, to detect implied constraints (we say we "normalise" constraints). Now starting a sequence $\omega_0, \omega_1, \ldots$ from $\omega_0 = \{|y - x| \leq 1, |z - y| \leq 1\}$ is fine, except we run into trouble if we normalise the results of widening. Normalising

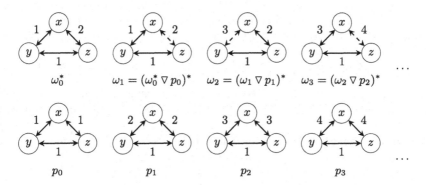

Fig. 3. An example of a divergent sequence of difference constraints, adapted from [27]. At each step, the edges between x and either y or z are discarded, but closure then recreates weaker relations (shown dashed), which are stable during the next iteration.

ω_0 yields $\omega_0^* = \{|y - x| \leq 1, |z - y| \leq 1, |z - y| \leq 2\}$. Under normalisation, the remainder of the widening sequence is shown in the top row of Fig. 3. For example, ω_2 comes about as the closure of $\omega_1 \nabla p_1 = \{|z - y| \leq 1, |z - x| \leq 2\}$, with closure adding the constraint $|y - x| \leq 3$. As can be seen, the widening sequence will not stabilise. The problem arises because closure—which makes no *semantic* difference—restores some constraints discarded by widening, breaking the very property that termination relied on. □

In Sect. 5 we return to the challenges discussed in this section. But first we introduce a different view of widening.

4   Isolated Widening

In the classical treatment of abstract interpretation, the widening iterates inhabit the same type as our abstract domain. But as observed above, this view can mislead the implementor of an abstract domain. For the implementor it is critically important to isolate the effects of a *semantic* widenee from the *non-semantic* widener. As we show in Sect. 5.1, this isolation also aids compositionality.

To make the two aspects of widening transparent, we let the different roles of the widener and widenee be reflected in ∇'s argument types. That is, we relax the requirement that both arguments are of type $\mathcal{D}$ for some abstract domain $\mathcal{D}$. Instead, we take the widener to be an inhabitant of some partially ordered set $(\mathfrak{W}, \preceq)$ (not necessarily a lattice) which has the "ascending chain" property.

Definition 2 (Acc-poset). A partially ordered set $(S, \leq)$ satisfies the ascending chain condition iff, for every sequence $s_0 \leq s_1 \leq s_2 \leq \ldots$ of S, there is some $k \in \mathbb{N}$ such that $s_k = s_{k+1} = s_{k+2} = \ldots$. We refer to such a set as an *acc-poset*.

Example 4. Consider again the interval domain $(\mathcal{I}, \sqsubseteq)$ from Sect. 2. The full and dotted lines in Fig. 2 show the lattice as a Hasse diagram. The natural widening operation $\nabla_{\mathcal{I}}$ defined in Sect. 2 is not monotone. However, consider an alternative ordering $\preceq$, defined by: $\bot \preceq d \preceq d$ for all $d \in \mathcal{I}$, and

$$[a, b] \preceq [c, d] \quad \textbf{iff} \quad (c = -\infty \wedge d \in \{b, \infty\}) \vee (d = \infty \wedge c \in \{-\infty, a\})$$

This results in an order illustrated in Fig. 2 by considering edges that transitively cross a red dashed line. Nodes within one red bordered region are pairwise incomparable. Clearly $\preceq$ is a coarsening of $\sqsubseteq$: we have $i_1 \preceq i_2 \Rightarrow i_1 \sqsubseteq i_2$, but $\preceq$ makes certain elements of $\mathcal{I}$ incomparable which were comparable under $\sqsubseteq$.

Viewed with respect to $\preceq$, $\nabla_{\mathcal{I}}$ satisfies an interesting property:

$$w \preceq w' \wedge x \sqsubseteq x' \Rightarrow w \nabla_{\mathcal{I}} x \preceq w' \nabla_{\mathcal{I}} x'.$$

That is, $\nabla_{\mathcal{I}}$ *is* monotone after all, but with respect to different orderings of its left and right operands. But though $\preceq$ induces a lattice, $\nabla_{\mathcal{I}}$ does not coincide with the join operation over $(\mathcal{I}, \preceq)$, even though that operation does exist. In fact, $\nabla_{\mathcal{I}}$ is not an upper bound operation at all under $\preceq$, only under $\sqsubseteq$. For example, $[-10, 10] \nabla_{\mathcal{I}} [0, 3] = [-10, 10]$, but $[0, 3] \npreceq [-10, 10]$. □

Example 4 provides motivation for the introduction of an isolated widening domain $\mathfrak{W}$, since the key to widening is really an independent acc-poset. The set $\mathfrak{W}$ is related to a given abstract domain $\mathcal{D}$, as specified in Definition 3 below. It is equipped with three operations:

$$reflect : \mathcal{D} \to \mathfrak{W} \qquad reify : \mathfrak{W} \to \mathcal{D} \qquad \mathbb{W} : \mathfrak{W} \times \mathcal{D} \to \mathfrak{W}$$

Here, *reflect* lifts an abstract state to initialize an ascending sequence, $\mathbb{W}$ computes successive (widening) steps in our (finite) ascending chain, and *reify* maps the current iterate back onto the abstract domain, in preparation for computing the next step in the sequence.

Definition 3 (Isolated widening). Let $(\mathcal{D}, \sqsubseteq)$ be an abstraction of poset $(\mathcal{C}, \subseteq)$ given by concretisation γ. The quintuple $\langle \mathfrak{W}, \preceq, reflect, reify, \mathbb{W} \rangle$ is an isolated widening (*I-widening*) for $(\mathcal{D}, \sqsubseteq)$ iff $(\mathfrak{W}, \preceq)$ is an acc-poset and the operators $reflect : \mathcal{D} \to \mathfrak{W}$, $reify : \mathfrak{W} \to \mathcal{D}$, and $\mathbb{W} : \mathfrak{W} \times \mathcal{D} \to \mathfrak{W}$, satisfy:

$$\forall x \in \mathcal{D}. \ \gamma(x) \subseteq \gamma(reify(reflect(x))) \tag{7}$$

$$\forall w \in \mathfrak{W}, \ x \in \mathcal{D}. \ w \preceq (w \ \mathbb{W} \ x) \tag{8}$$

$$\forall w \in \mathfrak{W}, \ x \in \mathcal{D}. \ \gamma(x) \subseteq \gamma(reify(w \ \mathbb{W} \ x)) \tag{9}$$

Equations (7)–(9) generalise the corresponding conditions for classical widenings. Indeed, if $\mathfrak{W} = \mathcal{D}$ and $reflect(x) = reify(x) = x$ then (7) is a tautology, and (8) and (9) ensure $\mathbb{W}$ is an upper bound operator. We do not require the sets $\mathfrak{W}$ and $\mathcal{D}$ to be identical, however. And, importantly, the left argument (the *widener*) and right argument (*widenee*) are generally subject to *different orderings*.

Theorem 1. Consider abstraction $(\mathcal{D}, \sqsubseteq)$ of domain $(\mathcal{C}, \subseteq)$ given by $\gamma : \mathcal{D} \to \mathcal{C}$. Let $\langle \mathfrak{W}, \preceq, reflect, reify, \mathbb{W} \rangle$ be an I-widening for lattice $(\mathcal{D}, \sqsubseteq)$. For every $x \in \mathcal{D}$, monotone function $f : \mathcal{C} \to \mathcal{C}$ and abstraction $f^\sharp : \mathcal{D} \to \mathcal{D}$ of f, the sequence given by

$$w_0 = reflect(x)$$
$$w_i = w_{i-1} \; \mathbb{W} \; f^\sharp(reify(w_{i-1}))$$

stabilises after k steps for some $k \in \mathbb{N}$, and $f^n(\gamma(x)) \sqsubseteq \gamma(reify(w_k))$ for all $n \in \mathbb{N}$.

Proof. Stabilisation follows directly from (8), and $\mathfrak{W}$ having only finite ascending chains. At each iteration, either $w_i = w_{i-1}$ (in which case $w_i \; \mathbb{W} \; f(reify(w_i)) = w_i$, so the sequence has stabilised), or else $w_i \succ w_{i-1}$. The latter may happen only finitely many times, so the sequence stabilises after finitely many steps.

Mathematical induction shows the final result is a post-fixpoint of f. Assume stabilisation happened at iteration k. We wish to show that, for every $i \in \mathbb{N}$, $f^i(\gamma(x)) \subseteq \gamma(reify(w_i))$. From the outset, for $i = 0$, we have $w_i = reflect(x)$, so by (7) we have $\gamma(x) \subseteq \gamma(reify(w_i))$.

Now assume $f^{i-1}(\gamma(x)) \sqsubseteq \gamma(reify(w_{i-1}))$. By (9), we have:

$$\gamma(f^\sharp(reify(w_{i-1}))) \sqsubseteq \gamma(reify(w_{i-1} \; \mathbb{W} \; f(reify(w_{i-1})))) = \gamma(reify(w_i)).$$

As f is monotone, we have $f^i(\gamma(x)) = f(f^{i-1}(\gamma(x))) \subseteq f(\gamma(reify(w_{i-1})))$. And as $f^\sharp$ abstracts f, and γ is monotone, we have:

$$f(\gamma(reify(w_{i-1}))) \subseteq \gamma(f^\sharp(reify(w_{i-1}))) \subseteq \gamma(reify(w_i)).$$

Hence $f^i(\gamma(x)) \subseteq \gamma(reify(w_i))$ for all $i \geq 0$. Thus $\gamma(reify(w_k))$ is a post-fixpoint of f. □

Theorem 2. Consider a widening (in the sense of Definition 1) ∇ on poset $(\mathcal{D}, \sqsubseteq)$ abstracting $(\mathcal{C}, \subseteq)$, which satisfies (3). Let id $: \mathcal{D} \to \mathcal{D}$ be the identity function, and let $\preceq$ be the relation given by:

$$u \preceq v \text{ iff } u = v \lor \exists x. \; u \nabla x = v,$$

with $\preceq^*$ its transitive closure. Then $\langle \mathcal{D}, \preceq^*, \mathsf{id}, \mathsf{id}, \nabla \rangle$ is an I-widening for $(\mathcal{D}, \sqsubseteq)$.

Proof. $\preceq^*$ is reflexive and transitive by construction. Consider $u, v \in \mathcal{D}$ such that $u \preceq^* v$ and $v \preceq^* u$. So either $u = v$, or $\exists x_1, \ldots, x_n. \; v = u \nabla x_1 \nabla \ldots \nabla x_n$, and $\exists y_1 \ldots, y_m. \; u = v \nabla y_1 \nabla \ldots \nabla y_m$. Since ∇ is an upper bound operation in $(\mathcal{D}, \sqsubseteq)$, we have $v \sqsubseteq u$ and $u \sqsubseteq v$. Thus $u = v$. Therefore $(\mathcal{D}, \preceq^*)$ is a partially ordered set.

Assume $(\mathcal{D}, \preceq^*)$ has some infinite ascending chain. Then $(\mathcal{D}, \preceq)$ must similarly have an infinite ascending chain $v_0, v_1, \ldots$. From the definition of $\preceq$, there must then be a sequence $x_1, \ldots \in \mathcal{D}$ such that $v_i = v_{i-1} \nabla x_i$. But (3) guarantees there is no such sequence. Hence $(\mathcal{D}, \preceq^*)$ has no infinite ascending chain, that is, it is an acc-poset.

Finally we show that (7)–(9) hold for $\langle \mathcal{D}, \preceq^*, \mathsf{id}, \mathsf{id}, \nabla \rangle$. Equation (7) follows directly, as $x \sqsubseteq \mathsf{id}(\mathsf{id}(x)) = x$. The relation $\preceq$ is defined such that $w \preceq (w \nabla x)$ for all x, and $\preceq \subseteq \preceq^*$, so (8) also holds. Equation (9) follows from the second condition of Definition 1, which requires $x \sqsubseteq w \nabla x$. As γ is monotone, we have $\gamma(x) \subseteq \gamma(w \nabla x)$.

We conclude that $\langle \mathcal{D}, \preceq^*, \mathsf{id}, \mathsf{id}, \nabla \rangle$ is an I-widening for $\langle \mathcal{D}, \sqsubseteq \rangle$.   □

Theorem 2 states that each classical widening [11] induces an isolated widening. The I-widening derived from an arbitrary classical widening is not necessarily monotone. Indeed, for arbitrary fixed *reflect*, *reify*, and $\preceq$, there may be no *best* widening (though if $(\mathfrak{W}, \preceq)$ has a unique greatest element $\top$, there is always *some* monotone widening, namely $w \, \mathbb{W} \, x = \top$).

5   Properties of Isolated Widening

We now return to the problems and pitfalls identified in Sect. 3. The aim is to show how the separation of concerns that was proposed in Sect. 4 can resolve some of the classical difficulties surrounding widening: *lack of compositionality* (as seen in product widening), *rigidity* (as seen in the difficulty of extending the definition of widening to cover variants such as delayed and threshold widening), and *fragility* (as seen in well-known implementation pitfalls).

5.1   Compositionality: Domain Products and Widening

Example 1 exposed the dangers surrounding synthesis of widening operators for product domains. We now show that I-widening provides compositional stabilisation, also in the presence of reduction. We characterise direct, Granger, and reduced products as quotients of a direct product under a reduction operation.

Definition 4 (Product with reduction). Let $(\mathcal{C}, \subseteq)$ be a meet semi-lattice[3] with abstractions $(\mathcal{D}_1, \sqsubseteq_1)$ and $(\mathcal{D}_2, \sqsubseteq_2)$ given by γ_1 and γ_2. Let $\mathcal{D}_{1 \times 2} = \mathcal{D}_1 \times \mathcal{D}_2$. A function $\rho_i : \mathcal{D}_{1 \times 2} \to \mathcal{D}_i$ is a *reduction operator* if it satisfies:

$$\rho_i(y_1, y_2) \sqsubseteq_i y_i \qquad\qquad i \in \{1, 2\} \qquad (10)$$

$$\gamma_{1 \times 2}(y_1, y_2) \sqsubseteq \gamma_i(\rho_i(y_1, y_2)) \qquad\qquad i \in \{1, 2\} \qquad (11)$$

Equation (10) ensures ρ_i are decreasing, and (11) ensures ρ_i do not discard any sound concrete states.

We use ρ to denote the pointwise application of (ρ_1, ρ_2):

$$\rho \langle y_1, y_2 \rangle = \langle \rho_1 \langle y_1, y_2 \rangle, \rho_2 \langle y_1, y_2 \rangle \rangle.$$

From (10) and (11), we conclude:

$$\gamma_{1 \times 2}(\rho(x)) = \gamma_{1 \times 2}(x) \qquad (12)$$

A *product with reduction* is the quotient class $\mathcal{D}_{1 \times 2 | \rho}$.

---

[3] The requirement for a meet semi-lattice is merely so $\gamma_{1 \times 2}$ is expressible. With a different formalisation (taking γ as a relation $\gamma \subseteq \mathcal{C} \times \mathcal{D}$), we may take $(\mathcal{D}, \sqsubseteq)$ as a poset, and replace (11) by $(y_1, x) \in \gamma_1 \wedge (y_2, x) \in \gamma_2 \Rightarrow (\rho_i(\langle y_1, y_2 \rangle), x) \in \gamma_i$.

In this view, $\rho = \mathrm{id}$ yields the direct product, and the reduced product is obtained with the tightest possible ρ. The continuum of Granger products sit between.

Theorem 3. Consider domain $(\mathcal{C}, \subseteq)$ with abstractions $(\mathcal{D}_1, \sqsubseteq_1)$, $(\mathcal{D}_2, \sqsubseteq_2)$ given by γ_1, γ_2 resp., and reduction operator ρ inducing domain $(\mathcal{D}_{1\times 2|\rho}, \sqsubseteq_{1\times 2|\rho})$.

Let $\langle \mathfrak{W}_1, \preceq_1, \mathit{reflect}_1, \mathit{reify}_1, \mathbb{W}_1 \rangle$ be an I-widening for poset $(D_1, \sqsubseteq_1)$ and let $\langle \mathfrak{W}_2, \preceq_2, \mathit{reflect}_2, \mathit{reify}_2, \mathbb{W}_2 \rangle$ be an I-widening for poset $(D_2, \sqsubseteq_2)$. Define

$$\mathit{reflect}\langle x_1, x_2 \rangle = \langle \mathit{reflect}_1(x_1), \mathit{reflect}_2(x_2) \rangle$$
$$\mathit{reify}_\times \langle w_1, w_2 \rangle = \langle \mathit{reify}_1(w_1), \mathit{reify}_2(w_2) \rangle$$
$$\mathit{reify}\langle w_1, w_2 \rangle = \rho(\mathit{reify}_\times \langle w_1, w_2 \rangle)$$
$$\langle w_1, w_2 \rangle \mathbb{W} \langle x_1, x_2 \rangle = \langle w_1 \mathbb{W}_1 x_1, w_2 \mathbb{W}_2 x_2 \rangle$$

Then $\langle \mathfrak{W}_1 \times \mathfrak{W}_2, \preceq, \mathit{reflect}, \mathit{reify}, \mathbb{W} \rangle$ is an I-widening for domain $(\mathcal{D}_{1\times 2|\rho}, \sqsubseteq_{\sharp 1\times 2|\rho})$ with

$$(x_1, x_2) \sqsubseteq (x_1', x_2') \quad \text{iff} \quad x_1 \sqsubseteq_1 x_1' \wedge x_2 \sqsubseteq_2 x_2'$$
$$(w_1, w_2) \preceq (w_1', w_2') \quad \text{iff} \quad w_1 \preceq_1 w_1' \wedge w_2 \preceq_2 w_2'$$

Proof. The fact that $\langle \mathfrak{W}_1 \times \mathfrak{W}_2, \preceq \rangle$ has no infinite ascending chains follows straightforwardly from this property of $\preceq_1$ and $\preceq_2$.

We now show conditions (7–9) hold. By (7) for $\mathfrak{W}_1$, $\mathfrak{W}_2$ and (12) we have $\gamma_{1\times 2}(x) \sqsubseteq \gamma_{1\times 2}(\mathit{reify}_\times(x)) = \gamma_{1\times 2}(\rho(\mathit{reify}_\times(x))) = \gamma_{1\times 2}(\mathit{reify}(x))$, so (7) holds. Equation (8) follows from the definitions of $\mathbb{W}$ and $\preceq$. For (9), (12) the corresponding condition of $\mathfrak{W}_1$ and $\mathfrak{W}_2$ we have

$$\gamma_{1\times 2}(x) \sqsubseteq \gamma_{1\times 2}(\mathit{reify}_\times(w \triangledown x)) = \gamma_{1\times 2}(\rho(\mathit{reify}_\times(w \triangledown x))) = \gamma_{1\times 2}(\mathit{reify}(w \triangledown x)).$$

Thus (9) holds. We conclude that $\langle \mathfrak{W}_1 \times \mathfrak{W}_2, \preceq, \mathit{reflect}, \mathit{reify}, \mathbb{W} \rangle$ is an I-widening for domain $(\mathcal{D}_{1\times 2|\rho}, \sqsubseteq_{1\times 2|\rho})$. $\square$

As a special case of Theorem 3, we may safely combine multiple widenings for the same domain, in the same manner. Indeed, recall our troublesome construction from Example 2. Using *reflect* and *reify*, this becomes perfectly safe: $\mathfrak{W}$ stores the stable relations and interval properties separately, and they are combined only upon calls to *reify*. The safe replacement for (6) becomes:

$$\mathit{reflect}_{\mathcal{AI}}(s) = \langle \mathit{reflect}_{\mathcal{A}}(s), \mathit{reflect}_{\mathcal{I}}(\text{TO-INTERVAL}(s)) \rangle$$
$$\mathit{reify}_{\mathcal{AI}}(\langle r, i \rangle) = \mathit{reify}_{\mathcal{A}}(r) \sqcap \mathit{reify}_{\mathcal{A}}(\text{FROM-INTERVAL}(\mathit{reify}_{\mathcal{I}}(i)))$$
$$\langle r, i \rangle \mathbb{W}_{\mathcal{AI}} s = \langle r \triangledown_{\mathcal{A}} s, i \triangledown_{\mathcal{I}}^T \text{TO-INTERVAL}(s) \rangle$$

5.2 Flexibility: Variations of Widening

Another advantage of capturing termination aspects of widening via a separate domain $\mathfrak{W}$ is that it becomes possible to define variants of widening without any need for surgery to an underlying fixpoint engine. We now show how delayed widening can be implemented generically.

We simply define a widening combinator, which lifts an isolated widening $\mathfrak{W}$ to a new isolated widening $k\mathfrak{W}$ for some given k, as follows. The values in the widening domain are from a discriminated union with constructors $U : \mathfrak{W} \to k\mathfrak{W}$ and $P : (\mathbb{N} \times \mathcal{D}) \to k\mathfrak{W}$. Let $\sqcup$ be any upper bound operator on $\mathcal{D}$ (for lattices, this will be the least upper bound). The operations are defined by:

$$
\begin{aligned}
reflect_{k\mathfrak{W}}(s) &= P(k,s) & P(0,s) \,\mathbb{W}_{k\mathfrak{W}}\, s' &= U(reflect_{\mathfrak{W}}(s \sqcup s')) \\
reify_{k\mathfrak{W}}(P(l,s)) &= s & P(l,s) \,\mathbb{W}_{k\mathfrak{W}}\, s' &= P(l-1, s \sqcup s'), l > 0 \\
reify_{k\mathfrak{W}}(U(w)) &= reify_{\mathfrak{W}}(w) & U(w) \,\mathbb{W}_{k\mathfrak{W}}\, s' &= U(w \,\mathbb{W}_{\mathfrak{W}}\, s')
\end{aligned}
$$

The ordering $\preceq^-_{k\mathfrak{W}}$ is defined as:

$$
\begin{aligned}
P(l,s) \preceq^-_{k\mathfrak{W}} P(l',s') &\Leftrightarrow (l = l' \wedge s = s') \vee (l > l' \wedge s \sqsubseteq s') \\
P(l,s) \preceq^-_{k\mathfrak{W}} U(w) &\Leftrightarrow \gamma(s) \subseteq \gamma(reify_{\mathfrak{W}}(w)) \\
U(w) \preceq^-_{k\mathfrak{W}} U(w') &\Leftrightarrow w \preceq_{\mathfrak{W}} w' \\
U(w) \preceq^-_{k\mathfrak{W}} P(k,s) &\Leftrightarrow false
\end{aligned}
$$

The ordering of the new domain $\preceq_{k\mathfrak{W}}$ is defined as the transitive closure of $\preceq^-_{k\mathfrak{W}}$.

Proposition 1. Consider domain $(\mathcal{C}, \subseteq)$ with abstraction $(\mathcal{D}, \sqsubseteq)$ equipped with upper bound operator $\sqcup$, and let $\langle \mathfrak{W}, \preceq_{\mathfrak{W}}, reflect_{\mathfrak{W}}, reify_{\mathfrak{W}}, \mathbb{W}_{\mathfrak{W}} \rangle$ be an I-widening for $(\mathcal{D}, \sqsubseteq)$. Then $\langle k\mathfrak{W}, \preceq_{k\mathfrak{W}}, reflect_{k\mathfrak{W}}, reify_{k\mathfrak{W}}, \mathbb{W}_{k\mathfrak{W}} \rangle$ is an I-widening for $(\mathcal{D}, \sqsubseteq)$.

Proof. We show that $\preceq_{k\mathfrak{W}}$ is a partial order. Reflexivity follows immediately from the definition of $\preceq^-_{k\mathfrak{W}}$, specifically the first and third rules.

To see that $\preceq_{k\mathfrak{W}}$ is anti-symmetric, assume $x \preceq_{k\mathfrak{W}} y$ and $y \preceq_{k\mathfrak{W}} x$. Clearly x and y must have the same constructor or one condition cannot hold. If $x = P(l,s)$ and $y = P(l',s')$ then since $x \preceq_{k\mathfrak{W}} y$ there is a finite chain of possibly different values $x = x_0 = P(l_0,s_0), x_1 = P(l_1,s_1), \ldots, x_n = P(l_n,s_n) = y$ where $P(l_i,s_i) \preceq^-_{k\mathfrak{W}} P(l_{i+1},s_{i+1})$ for each $i \in 0..n-1$. The chain is finite since to be different each l value must be different and this is bounded by k. Now $(l_i = l_{i+1} \wedge s_i = s_{i+1}) \vee (l_i > l_{i+1} \wedge s_i \sqsubseteq s_{i+1})$. Similarly since $y \preceq_{k\mathfrak{W}} x$ there is a finite chain of possibly different values $y = y_0 = P(l'_0,s'_0), y_1 = P(l'_1,s'_1), \ldots, y_m = P(l'_m,s'_m) = x$ where $P(l'_i,s'_i) \preceq^-_{k\mathfrak{W}} P(l'_{i+1},s'_{i+1})$ for each $i \in 0..m-1$, and $(l'_i = l'_{i+1} \wedge s'_i = s'_{i+1}) \vee (l'_i > l'_{i+1} \wedge s'_i \sqsubseteq s'_{i+1})$. The only solution to these conditions is that for all $i \in 0..n, j \in 0..m$ we have that $l_i = l'_j \wedge s_i = s'_j$. So $x = y$. If $x = U(w)$ and $u = U(w')$ then $U(w) \preceq_{k\mathfrak{W}} U(w')$ and since $\preceq_{\mathfrak{W}}$ is already transitively closed, equivalently $U(w) \preceq^-_{k\mathfrak{W}} U(w')$ thus $w \preceq_{\mathfrak{W}} w'$. Similarly $w' \preceq_{\mathfrak{W}} w$. Hence $w = w'$. In either case, $x = y$, establishing anti-symmetry.

$\preceq_{k\mathfrak{W}}$ is transitive by construction.

We show the required properties hold for $reflect_{k\mathfrak{W}}$, $reify_{k\mathfrak{W}}$, and $\mathbb{W}_{k\mathfrak{W}}$. Clearly $x = reify_{k\mathfrak{W}}(reflect_{k\mathfrak{W}}(x))$ by definition, guaranteeing (7) holds.

To show (8) $w \preceq_{k\mathfrak{W}} w \,\mathbb{W}\, x$ and (9) $\gamma(x) \subseteq \gamma(reify_{k\mathfrak{W}}(w \,\mathbb{W}_{k\mathfrak{W}}\, x))$ we examine the different cases for w: If $w = P(0,s)$ then $w \,\mathbb{W}_{k\mathfrak{W}}\, x = U(reflect_{\mathfrak{W}}(s \sqcup x))$. From (7), $\gamma(s) \subseteq \gamma(s \sqcup x) \subseteq \gamma(reify_{\mathfrak{W}}(reflect_{\mathfrak{W}}(s \sqcup x))) = \gamma(reify_{k\mathfrak{W}} w \,\mathbb{W}_{k\mathfrak{W}}\, x)$, so we have $P(0, s) \preceq_{k\mathfrak{W}}^- U(w \mathbb{W}_{k\mathfrak{W}} x)$. Similarly we have $reify(w) = s \sqsubseteq s \sqcup x$. By monotonicity of γ, together with (7), we have

$$\gamma(reify(w)) \subseteq \gamma(s \sqcup x) \subseteq \gamma(reify_{\mathfrak{W}}(reflect_{\mathfrak{W}}(s \sqcup x))) = \gamma(reify(w \mathbb{W}_{k\mathfrak{W}} x)).$$

If $w = P(l, s)$ for $l > 0$ then $w \mathbb{W}_{k\mathfrak{W}} x = P(l - 1, s \sqcup x)$. We have $l - 1 < l \wedge s \sqsubseteq s \sqcup x$, so $w \preceq_{k\mathfrak{W}}^- w \mathbb{W}_{k\mathfrak{W}} x$. And γ is monotone, so $\gamma(x) \subseteq \gamma(s \sqcup x) = \gamma(reify(w \mathbb{W}_{k\mathfrak{W}} x))$. Finally, if $w = U(w')$ then $w \mathbb{W}_{k\mathfrak{W}} x = U(w \mathbb{W}_{\mathfrak{W}} x)$. The result follows since $w' \preceq_{\mathfrak{W}} w \mathbb{W}_{\mathfrak{W}} x$ and $\gamma(x) \sqsubset \gamma(reify_{\mathfrak{W}}(w \mathbb{W}_{\mathfrak{W}} x))$.

Equations (8) and (9) hold for all cases, thus all conditions for an I-widening are satisfied.   □

The I-widening framework makes it easy to define delayed widening because it allows the separation of widening control from whatever abstract domain we may be using. Other variations of delayed widening are also simple to encode. For example, we can define $P(l, s) \mathbb{W}_{k\mathfrak{W}} s' = P(l, s)$ when $s \sqcup s' = s$ which may lead to more accurate widening.

5.3   Convergence

Recall the problem of non-convergent DBMs (or octagons), outlined in Sect. 3.3. The underlying problem is a subtle difference in the interpretation of a *state* between the (normal) domain operations and the widening operation.

Viewed in terms of $\sqsubseteq$ and $\preceq$, it is clear where things go astray in Example 3. Computing $\omega_0^* \triangledown p_0$ yields the *set of constraints* $\omega = \{|z - y| \le 1, |y - x| \le 1\}$. This is safe, as $\omega_0^* \preceq \omega$, and $p_0 \sqsubseteq reify(\omega)$. But performing transitive closure on ω yields a result $\omega_1 = \omega \cup \{|z - x| \le 2\}$. And although ω_0^* is still an upper bound of ω_0^* and p_0 with respect to $\sqsubseteq$, $\omega_0^* \npreceq \omega_1$—so the ascending chain of wideners is broken.

The normal lattice operators view Octagons as the *quotient class* of sets of octagon constraints under entailment: two sets of constraints are *equivalent* iff they have the same set of models. The termination argument views Octagon states as sets of constraints: at each iteration, the *number of constraints* decreases, so the iteration process terminates. These are, very subtly, different sets, which are equipped with different partial orders, let us call them $\sqsubseteq_8$ and $\preceq_8$, defined by

$$S \sqsubseteq_8 T \text{ iff } \forall_{c_T \in T}. \; S \Rightarrow c_T$$
$$S \preceq_8 T \text{ iff } \forall_{c_T \in T}. \; c_T \in S$$

Viewing widening through this lens, it becomes clear what goes wrong: The normalization operator (which performs transitive closure) is semantically (that is, with respect to $\sqsubseteq_8$) a no-op—it is merely the identity function. But with respect to $\preceq_8$, closure *moves downwards*. So composing $\triangledown$ and closure is no longer necessarily an upper bound operation with respect to $\preceq_8$.

Formulated as an isolated widening, these sets are kept *distinct*. Let $\equiv_8$ be the equivalence relation induced by $\sqsubseteq_8$ – that is, $S \equiv_8 T \Leftrightarrow S \sqsubseteq_8 T \wedge T \sqsubseteq_8 S$, and let $=_8$ be the equivalence relation similarly induced by $\preceq_8$. Then domain elements occupy the quotient class $O_{/\equiv_8}$, where O is the set of Octagon constraints. In this domain, transitive closure is indeed safe. But widening operands are members of $O_{/=_8}$, which is *simply not equipped* with a closure operator.

With isolated widening, we cannot make this mistake: transitive closure is defined on the domain of abstract states and *cannot be applied* to a widener (which acts on a different set).

6   Implementation

We have implemented isolated widening for Crab [22], a parametric framework for building abstract interpreters. Crab is written in C++ and provides a front-end for analyzing LLVM bitcode. We have used Crab to evaluate the use of isolated widening on a large number of C programs from SV-COMP 2019. Our main aim with the implementation has been to gauge the extent to which isolated widening requires a larger implementation effort than the alternatives.

We modified the Crab fixpoint iterator [1] in order to call *reflect*, *reify*, and $\mathbb{W}$. This required only three new lines of C++ code. Before a new cycle in the weak topological ordering (wto) [4] of the control-flow graph (CFG) is analyzed, the new code calls *reflect*. Then, the cycle is analyzed recursively (i.e., analyzing other nested cycles) until a fixpoint is reached. Before a new fixpoint iteration starts, the new code calls *reify*. Finally, the standard call to Cousot's widening was replaced with a call to $\mathbb{W}$. In addition, we extended each Crab abstract domain $\mathcal{D}$ so as to implement the trivial isolated widening $\langle \mathcal{D}, \preceq^*, \mathrm{id}, \mathrm{id}, \triangledown \rangle$. This required 10 lines of C++ code since all domains share the same implementation.

For proofs of concept, we implemented (a) delayed widening and (b) the reduced product of an arbitrary numerical domain with intervals as I-widening. Recall that the reduction with intervals was motivated by a desire to exploit widening-with-thresholds from the interval domain, so as to implement threshold widening for a number of numerical abstract domains, with less effort. Regarding (a), Crab already implemented delayed widening on top of the fixpoint iterator. We replaced that code with the isolated widening defined in Sect. 5.2. The effort was minimal and it did not add more lines of C++ code. For (b), we needed to add more code although the amount was still relatively small (around 130 lines of C++ code).

Crab provides standard numerical domains such as Interval, Zone, Octagon, and Polyhedra. Since numerical domains are typically insufficient to prove non-trivial properties, Crab allows combining numerical domains as reduced products. Moreover, Crab provides array domains which are implemented as functor domains whose parameters can be arbitrary abstract domains.

With this in mind, we first implemented the I-widening described in Sect. 5.1. The implementation is parametric on the particular numerical domain, and took some 50 lines of code. We also implemented, in 40 lines, an I-widening for the reduced product of two numerical domains and a numerical domain with a finite lattice domain (used to track Boolean variables). Finally, we implemented an I-widening for the array smashing domain, another 40 lines of C++ code.

To test the correctness of the implementation, we compared it against the old implementation, using 2736 programs from the SV-COMP 2019 competition (the categories `ReachSafetyControlFlow`, `ReachSafetyLoops`, and `System_Device-DriversLinux64`). We noted that the new implementation of delayed widening did not affect precision of analysis, nor analysis time.

In conclusion, the implementation of isolated widening in an existing abstract interpreter has been almost effortless.

7   Related Work

The concept of widening in abstract interpretation is almost as old as abstract interpretation itself [8]. Its essential role in both the theory and practice of program analysis was clarified by Cousot and Cousot [11]. While it was initially designed as a tool to ensure or speed up the discovery of fixpoints for *monotone* functions, it has utility beyond that; non-monotone analyses have been proposed that rely on widening to escape iteration sequences that may be looping rather than ascending [15].

We have assumed the definition of (classical) widening given by Cousot and Cousot [11]. Many definitions found in the literature differ in subtle ways, and not all are strictly equivalent. For example, from the earliest work on widening, P. and R. Cousot pointed out that it is not necessary to restrict widening to be a single mechanism; widening could involve the use of a succession of different mechanisms. Cousot [6] thus views a widening operator as having type $\mathbb{N} \to (\mathcal{D} \times \mathcal{D}) \to \mathcal{D}$, to allow for such "dynamic", as well as delayed, widening.

Bourdoncle [4] analysed the use of chaotic iteration with widening and explored how iteration strategy affects both precision and overall efficiency of analysis. A central problem (not discussed in this paper) is how to select a good set W of widening points. Bourdoncle [4] introduced *weak topological orderings* and demonstrated their utility in the choice of W.

Much of the research on widening has been in the context of relational or weakly-relational abstract domains. Widening plays a central role in the seminal work on polyhedral analysis [13]. The implementation problems caused by the non-semantic nature of the left (widener) were previously observed in work on Zones, Octagons and convex polyhedra [2,27,28], although a general solution has not been suggested, to our knowledge.

Delayed widening [3] is an obvious approach to limiting the loss of precision incurred by widening. Widening is delayed for a fixed number k of iterations, so that the widening operator associated with a widening point is treated as a join for k steps. More sophisticated delay can be introduced by taking syntactic aspects of the given program into account. Halbwachs, Proy and Roumanoff [24] proposed such a widening "up to" scheme, which has since been extended and dubbed "widening with thresholds" [25]. Simon and King [29] propose a generalisation ("widening with landmarks") in the context of polyhedral analysis.

Widening/narrowing does not always deal well with complex program structure, including nested loops. Much work has focused on improved precision of analysis, at a reasonable cost of overhead. Our particular perspective on widening (and the implementation discipline it enforces) does not preclude the use of a number of these proposed widening-related techniques. This includes "lookahead widening" and similar "analysis guiding" techniques for loops that exhibit multi-phase behaviour [18,19], widening with landmarks [29], and post-fixpoint improvements such as those suggested by Halbwachs and Henry [23].

A work that is close to ours as far as motivation is concerned, is Mihaila et al.'s recasting of "widening as abstract domain" [26]. The authors also seek a systematic, modular approach to composing abstract domains in the presence of widening, so that ad hoc design or modifications of a fixpoint engine is avoided. They show how different widening strategies can be built into abstract domains, including delayed widening, widening with thresholds, and lookahead widening. The proposed machinery, however, is very different to ours. It assumes that a program location ℓ is a widening point if and only if it is the target of a *back-edge* in a control flow graph, in which case ℓ's join is replaced by a widening operation. Our approach does not restrict the choice of widening points. Rather than force different widening techniques into a given abstract domain, our proposal is to *separate* syntactic and semantic aspects of analysis, by clearly distinguishing the roles of the (syntactic) *widener* and the (semantic) *widenee*.

8   Conclusion

We have proposed an alternative approach to accelerating fixpoint finding in abstract interpretation. The approach, which we have called isolated widening, is a generalisation of the classical widening technique, in that any classical widening can be trivially translated to an I-widening, but the converse does not hold. This generality allows isolated widening to retain any information about the history of widening at a program point, beyond simply the previous and next abstract states, allowing for more flexible widenings than the traditional approach supports, such as delayed widening, all while isolating any added information from the abstract domain itself.

Importantly, this isolation also sidesteps certain pitfalls that arise with classical widenings. For example, it clarifies the distinction between the semantics of an abstract domain, such as Octagons, from the syntactic view of the representation used during widening. Isolated widening makes this distinction explicit, preserving the semantic view in the abstract domain, and transforming the syntactic view into its own view with a distinct semantics in the widening domain. Crucially, this approach keeps the widening information in its own representation rather than immediately transforming it to the abstract domain, avoiding the accidental strengthening of abstract states that Miné and others have observed to undo the effect of widening and cause nontermination of analysis [28]. Additionally, we have shown that I-widenings are compositional, unlike classical widenings, simplifying the implementation of product domains.

We have implemented our approach in the context of the Crab abstract interpretation framework [14], finding that it required minimal effort, and did not affect performance or analysis precision. We conclude that I-widening is a practical generalisation of classical widening.

Acknowledgments. This work was partially supported by the Australian Research Council through Discovery Early Career Researcher Award DE160100568 and US NSF grants 1528153 and 1817204.

References

1. Amato, G., Scozzari, F.: Localizing widening and narrowing. In: Logozzo, F., Fähndrich, M. (eds.) SAS 2013. LNCS, vol. 7935, pp. 25–42. Springer, Heidelberg (2013). https://doi.org/10.1007/978-3-642-38856-9_4
2. Bagnara, R., Hill, P.M., Ricci, E., Zaffanella, E.: Precise widening operators for convex polyhedra. Sci. Comput. Program. **58**, 28–56 (2005)
3. Blanchet, B., et al.: A static analyzer for large safety-critical software. In: ACM Conference on Programming Language Design and Implementation, pp. 196–207 (2003)
4. Bourdoncle, F.: Efficient chaotic iteration strategies with widenings. In: Bjørner, D., Broy, M., Pottosin, I.V. (eds.) Formal Methods in Programming and Their Applications. LNCS, vol. 735, pp. 128–141. Springer, Heidelberg (1993). https://doi.org/10.1007/BFb0039704
5. Cortesi, A., Costantini, G., Ferrara, P.: A survey on product operators in abstract interpretation. In: Banerjee, A., Danvy, O., Doh, K.-G., Hatcliff, J. (eds.) Semantics, Abstract Interpretation, and Reasoning about Programs. Electronic Proceedings in Theoretical Computer Science, vol. 129, pp. 325–336 (2013)
6. Cousot, P.: Semantic foundations of program analysis. In: Muchnick, S.S., Jones, N.D. (eds.) Program Flow Analysis: Theory and Applications, pp. 303–346. Prentice-Hall (1981)
7. Cousot, P.: Forward non-relational infinitary static analysis, 2005. Slide set 18 from MIT Course 16.399, Abstract Interpretation. http://www.mit.edu/afs/athena.mit.edu/course/16/16.399/www/
8. Cousot, P., Cousot, R.: Abstract interpretation: a unified lattice model for static analysis of programs by construction or approximation of fixpoints. In: Proceedings of the Fourth ACM Symposium Principles of Programming Languages, pp. 238–252. ACM Press (1977)
9. Cousot, P., Cousot, R.: Systematic design of program analysis frameworks. In: Proceedings of the Sixth ACM Symposium on Principles of Programming Languages, pp. 269–282. ACM Press (1979)
10. Cousot, P., Cousot, R.: Abstract interpretation frameworks. J. Logic Comput. **2**(4), 511–547 (1992)
11. Cousot, P., Cousot, R.: Comparing the Galois connection and widening/narrowing approaches to abstract interpretation. In: Bruynooghe, M., Wirsing, M. (eds.) PLILP 1992. LNCS, vol. 631, pp. 269–295. Springer, Heidelberg (1992). https://doi.org/10.1007/3-540-55844-6_142
12. Cousot, P., et al.: Combination of abstractions in the ASTRÉE static analyzer. In: Okada, M., Satoh, I. (eds.) ASIAN 2006. LNCS, vol. 4435, pp. 272–300. Springer, Heidelberg (2007). https://doi.org/10.1007/978-3-540-77505-8_23
13. Cousot, P., Halbwachs, N.: Automatic discovery of linear constraints among variables of a program. In: Proceedings of the Fifth ACM Symposium on Principles of Programming Languages, pp. 84–97. ACM Press (1978)

14. Crab: CoRnucopia of ABstractions: A language-agnostic library for abstract interpretation. https://github.com/seahorn/crab
15. Gange, G., Navas, J.A., Schachte, P., Søndergaard, H., Stuckey, P.J.: Abstract interpretation over non-lattice abstract domains. In: Logozzo, F., Fähndrich, M. (eds.) SAS 2013. LNCS, vol. 7935, pp. 6–24. Springer, Heidelberg (2013). https://doi.org/10.1007/978-3-642-38856-9_3
16. Gange, G., Navas, J.A., Schachte, P., Søndergaard, H., Stuckey, P.J.: Interval analysis and machine arithmetic: why signedness ignorance is bliss. ACM Trans. Program. Lang. Syst. **37**(1), 1:1–1:35 (2014)
17. Gange, G., Navas, J.A., Schachte, P., Søndergaard, H., Stuckey, P.J.: An abstract domain of uninterpreted functions. In: Jobstmann, B., Leino, K.R.M. (eds.) VMCAI 2016. LNCS, vol. 9583, pp. 85–103. Springer, Heidelberg (2016). https://doi.org/10.1007/978-3-662-49122-5_4
18. Gopan, D., Reps, T.: Lookahead widening. In: Ball, T., Jones, R.B. (eds.) CAV 2006. LNCS, vol. 4144, pp. 452–466. Springer, Heidelberg (2006). https://doi.org/10.1007/11817963_41
19. Gopan, D., Reps, T.: Guided static analysis. In: Nielson, H.R., Filé, G. (eds.) SAS 2007. LNCS, vol. 4634, pp. 349–365. Springer, Heidelberg (2007). https://doi.org/10.1007/978-3-540-74061-2_22
20. Goubault, E., Gall, T.L., Putot, S.: An accurate join for zonotopes, preserving affine input/output relations. Electr. Notes Theor. Comput. Sci. **287**, 65–76 (2012)
21. Granger, P.: Improving the results of static analyses of programs by local decreasing iterations. In: Shyamasundar, R. (ed.) FSTTCS 1992. LNCS, vol. 652, pp. 68–79. Springer, Heidelberg (1992). https://doi.org/10.1007/3-540-56287-7_95
22. Gurfinkel, A., Kahsai, T., Komuravelli, A., Navas, J.A.: The SeaHorn verification framework. In: Kroening, D., Păsăreanu, C.S. (eds.) CAV 2015. LNCS, vol. 9206, pp. 343–361. Springer, Cham (2015). https://doi.org/10.1007/978-3-319-21690-4_20
23. Halbwachs, N., Henry, J.: When the decreasing sequence fails. In: Miné, A., Schmidt, D. (eds.) SAS 2012. LNCS, vol. 7460, pp. 198–213. Springer, Heidelberg (2012). https://doi.org/10.1007/978-3-642-33125-1_15
24. Halbwachs, N., Proy, Y.-E., Roumanoff, P.: Verification of real-time systems using linear relation analysis. Formal Methods Syst. Des. **11**, 157–185 (1997)
25. Lakhdar-Chaouch, L., Jeannet, B., Girault, A.: Widening with thresholds for programs with complex control graphs. In: Bultan, T., Hsiung, P.-A. (eds.) ATVA 2011. LNCS, vol. 6996, pp. 492–502. Springer, Heidelberg (2011). https://doi.org/10.1007/978-3-642-24372-1_38
26. Mihaila, B., Sepp, A., Simon, A.: Widening as abstract domain. In: Brat, G., Rungta, N., Venet, A. (eds.) NFM 2013. LNCS, vol. 7871, pp. 170–184. Springer, Heidelberg (2013). https://doi.org/10.1007/978-3-642-38088-4_12
27. Miné, A.: A new numerical abstract domain based on difference-bound matrices. In: Danvy, O., Filinski, A. (eds.) PADO 2001. LNCS, vol. 2053, pp. 155–172. Springer, Heidelberg (2001). https://doi.org/10.1007/3-540-44978-7_10
28. Miné, A.: The octagon abstract domain. In: Proceedings of the Workshop in Analysis, Slicing and Transformation, pp. 310–319 (2001)
29. Simon, A., King, A.: Widening polyhedra with landmarks. In: Kobayashi, N. (ed.) APLAS 2006. LNCS, vol. 4279, pp. 166–182. Springer, Heidelberg (2006). https://doi.org/10.1007/11924661_11

Reducing Static Analysis Alarms Based on Non-impacting Control Dependencies

Tukaram Muske[1(✉)], Rohith Talluri[1], and Alexander Serebrenik[2]

[1] TRDDC, TCS Research, Pune, India
{t.muske,rohith.talluri}@tcs.com
[2] Eindhoven University of Technology, Eindhoven, The Netherlands
a.serebrenik@tue.nl

Abstract. Static analysis tools help to detect programming errors but generate a large number of alarms. Repositioning of alarms is recently proposed technique to reduce the number of alarms by replacing a group of similar alarms with a small number of newly created representative alarms. However, the technique fails to replace a group of similar alarms with a fewer representative alarms mainly when the immediately enclosing *conditional statements* of the alarms are different and not nested. This limitation is due to conservative assumption that a conditional statement of an alarm may prevent the alarm from being an error.

To address the limitation above, we introduce the notion of *non-impacting control dependencies* (NCDs). An NCD of an alarm is a transitive control dependency of the alarm's program point, that does not affect whether the alarm is an error. We approximate the computation of NCDs based on the alarms that are similar, and then reposition the similar alarms by considering the effect of their NCDs. The NCD-based repositioning allows to merge more similar alarms together and represent them by a small number of representative alarms than the state-of-the-art repositioning technique. Thus, it can be expected to further reduce the number of alarms.

To measure the reduction obtained, we evaluate the NCD-based repositioning using total 105,546 alarms generated on 16 open source C applications, 11 industry C applications, and 5 industry COBOL applications. The evaluation results indicate that, compared to the state-of-the-art repositioning technique, the NCD-based repositioning reduces the number of alarms respectively by up to 23.57%, 29.77%, and 36.09%. The median reductions are 9.02%, 17.18%, and 28.61%, respectively.

1 Introduction

Static analysis tools help to automatically detect common programming errors like *division by zero* and *array index out of bounds* [2,3,5,33] as well as help in certification of safety-critical systems [6,10,17]. However, these tools report a large number of alarms that are warning messages notifying the tool-user about potential errors [11,15,22,29,31]. Partitioning the alarms into true errors and

© Springer Nature Switzerland AG 2019
A. W. Lin (Ed.): APLAS 2019, LNCS 11893, pp. 115–135, 2019.
https://doi.org/10.1007/978-3-030-34175-6_7

false alarms (false positives) requires manual inspection [11,19,30]. The large number of false alarms generated and effort required to analyze them manually have been identified as primary reasons for underuse of static analysis tools in practice [4,7,15,19].

Clustering is commonly used to reduce the number of alarms reported to the user [14,26]. State-of-the-art clustering techniques [13,20,24,34] group similar alarms[1] together such that (1) there are few dominant and many dominated alarms; and (2) when the dominant alarms of a cluster are false positives, *all the alarms in the cluster* are also false positives. The techniques count only the dominant alarms as the alarms obtained after the clustering.

Repositioning of alarms [27] is recently proposed technique to overcome limitations of the clustering techniques [13,20,24,34]. To achieve the reduction in alarms, the technique repositions a group of similar alarms to a program point where they can be *safely replaced* by a fewer newly created representative alarms (called as *repositioned alarms*). The alarms repositioning is safe and performed only if the following *repositioning criterion* is met—when a repositioned alarm is a false positive, its corresponding *original alarms* are also false positives, and vice versa. Thus, the repositioned alarms act as dominant alarms for the original (similar) alarms that are replaced by them.

Problem. The alarms repositioning technique [27] described above fails to reposition and merge similar alarms when their immediately enclosing conditional statements are different and not nested. As a consequence, in these cases, the repositioning technique does not reduce the number of alarms. We call these cases *repositioning limitation scenarios.* We illustrate this limitation using the alarms (red rectangles) shown in Fig. 1. The code is excerpted from archimedes-0.7.0. The two code examples shown in Figs. 1a and b are independent of each other. Analyzing the code in Fig. 1a (resp. Fig. 1b) using any static analysis tool generates two (resp. four) alarms corresponding to *array index out of bounds* (resp. *division by zero*). Grouping these alarms using the state-of-the-art clustering techniques [13,20,24,34] does not reduce their number.

Among the six alarms shown in Fig. 1, there exist three groups of similar alarms: A_{10} and A_{15}, D_{38} and D_{45}, and D_{42} and D_{48}. The alarms repositioning technique cannot determine whether the control dependencies[2] (i.e. the enclosing conditional statements) of these alarms *can prevent* the alarms from being an error. Thus, the technique conservatively assumes that the control dependencies of these alarms can prevent the alarms from being an error, i.e., the dependencies *can impact* those alarms. For example, the values read for nx at line 33 can be zero due to which two similar alarms D_{38} and D_{45} get generated. However, the technique conservatively assumes that the control dependencies of these alarms can prevent the zero value read for nx from reaching to lines 38 and 45. As a result of the conservative assumption, the repositioning criterion cannot be

---

[1] Broadly, two alarms are said to be *similar* if the property/condition checked in one alarm implies the property/condition checked in the other alarm (Sect. 2).

[2] A control dependency of a program point p is a conditional edge in the control flow graph [1], that decides whether p is to be reached or not (see Sect. 2).

```
1 void HoleHMEPBCs(void){
2 int h2d[309];
3
4 ...
5 fscanf(fp,"%d",&ny);
6
7 //assert(0≤ny≤304);          R7
8
9 if(EDGE[2][i][0]==0){
10   h2d[ny+4]=...;        A10
11 }
12
13 if(EDGE[2][i][0]==1
14  || EDGE[2][i][0]==2){
15   h2d[ny+4]=...;        A15
16 }
17
18}
```

(a) readinputfile.h

```
31 void Read_Input_File(void){
32 ...
33 fscanf(fp,"%d %d",&nx, &ny);
34 fscanf(fp,"%s",pos);
35
36 //assert(nx!=0);              R36
37 if(strcmp(pos,"DOWN")==0)
38   delt=LX/nx;        D38
39
40 //assert(ny!=0);              R40
41 if(strcmp(pos,"RIGHT")==0)
42   delt=LY/ny;        D42
43
44 if(strcmp(pos,"UP")==0)
45   delt=LX/nx;              D45
46
47 if(strcmp(pos,"LEFT")==0)
48   delt=LY/ny;        D48
49 }
```

(b) Hole_bcs.h

Fig. 1. Examples of alarms to illustrate their NCD-based repositioning. (Color figure online)

guaranteed for repositioning of these two similar alarms (D_{38} and D_{45}) to any program point, e.g., to line 36. That is, the resulting repositioned alarm can be an error while none of these two alarms is an error. Thus, the repositioning technique fails to reposition and merge these two similar alarms together. Similarly, the technique also fails to reposition the other two groups of similar alarms shown in Fig. 1. As a result, the repositioning technique does not reduce the number of alarms shown in Fig. 1.

We find that the above assumption about the control dependencies of the alarms' program points limits the reduction achieved by the repositioning technique, because not every control dependency of an alarm's program point can prevent the alarm being an error. For example, the conditions corresponding to the control dependencies of the alarms shown in Fig. 1 are *most likely* to determine whether the program points of those alarms are to be reached and not to prevent the alarms from being an error.

Our pilot study on 16 open source applications indicates that, 38% of the alarms reported after their repositioning are still similar and appear in the repositioning limitation scenarios. These results suggest the scope for improvement.

Our Solution. To overcome the problem above and further reduce the number of alarms, we introduce the notion of *non-impacting control dependencies* (NCDs). An NCD of an alarm is a transitive control dependency of the alarm's program point, that does not affect whether the alarm is an error. As we intend to reposition and merge more similar alarms together for reducing their number, we restrict the scope of NCDs computation to the similar alarms only. Since determining whether a control dependency is an NCD is undecidable, we compute the NCDs of similar alarms approximately (described in Sect. 4.2). The NCDs computed are subsequently used to reposition the similar alarms by considering the effect of their NCDs (*NCD-based repositioning*). Thus, NCD-based repositioning allows to reposition more similar alarms together and replace them by a fewer repositioned (dominant) alarms than the state-of-the-art repositioning technique. For example, our approach to compute NCDs, identifies the control dependencies of the alarms shown in Fig. 1 as NCDs. Repositioning each group of the similar alarms using the NCDs allows to replace the group by a newly created dominant alarm (shown using green circles). Thus, NCD-based repositioning reduces the number of alarms by three.

Although NCD-based repositioning is performed based on approximated NCDs, the repositioned alarms do not miss detection of an error uncovered by the original alarms. Thus, NCD-based repositioning can be expected to further safely reduce the overall number of alarms.

To measure the reduction obtained, we evaluate NCD-based repositioning on total 105,546 alarms generated for the following kinds of applications: (i) 16 open source C applications (ii) 11 industry C applications; and (iii) 5 industry COBOL applications. The alarms are generated by a commercial tool for five safety properties. The evaluation results indicate that, compared to the state-of-the-art repositioning technique, NCD-based repositioning reduces the number of alarms on these applications, respectively by up to 23.57%, 29.77%, and 36.09%. The median reductions are 9.02%, 17.18%, and 28.61%, respectively.

Following are the key contributions of our work.

1. The notion of NCDs of alarms and computing them for similar alarms.
2. An NCD-based repositioning technique to reduce the number of alarms.
3. A large-scale empirical evaluation of the NCD-based repositioning technique using 105,546 alarms on 16 open source and 16 industry applications.

Paper Outline. Sect. 2 presents terms and notations that we use throughout the paper. Section 3 describes the pilot study. Section 4 describes the notion of NCDs and NCD-based repositioning. Section 5 presents a technique/algorithm to implement NCD-based repositioning. Section 6 discusses our empirical evaluation. Section 7 presents related work, and Sect. 8 concludes.

2   Terms and Notations

Control Flow Graph. A control flow graph (CFG) [1] of a program is a directed graph $\langle \mathcal{N}, \mathcal{E} \rangle$, where $\mathcal{N}$ is a set of nodes representing the program statements (e.g., assignments and conditional statements); and $\mathcal{E}$ is a set of edges such that an edge $\langle n, n' \rangle$ represents a possible flow of program control from $n \in \mathcal{N}$ to $n' \in \mathcal{N}$ without any intervening node. We use $n \rightarrow n'$ to denote an edge from

node n to node n'. Depending on whether the program control flows condition-
ally or unconditionally along an edge, the edge is labeled either as conditional
or unconditional. We denote the condition corresponding to a conditional edge
$u \rightarrow v$ as $cond(u \rightarrow v)$. A CFG has two distinguished nodes $Start$ and End,
representing the $entry$ and $exit$ of the corresponding program, respectively. For
a given node n, we use $pred(n)$ to denote predecessors of n in the graph.

Except for the $Start$ and End nodes, we assume that there is a one-to-one
correspondence between the CFG nodes and their corresponding program statements. Thus, we use the terms statement and node interchangeably. Henceforth,
in code examples we use n_m to denote the node of a program statement at
line m. For the sake of simplicity, we assume that the program statements do
not cause side effects and the conditional statements (branching nodes) do not
update values of a variable.

Program Points. We write $entry(n)$ and $exit(n)$ to denote the $entry$ and $exit$ of
a node n, i.e., the program points $just$ $before$ and $immediately$ $after$ the execution
of statement corresponding to the node n, respectively. The entry or exit of a
node is assumed not to be shared with entry or exit of any other node even
though they may indicate the same program point/state. A program point p_1
$dominates$ a program point p_2 if every path from the $program$ $entry$ to p_2 contains
p_1. A program point p_1 $post\text{-}dominates$ a program point p_2 if every path from
p_2 to the $program$ $exit$ contains p_1.

Data Dependencies. A variable v at a program point p is said to be $data$
$dependent$ on a definition d of v, if d is a reaching definition [16,28] of v at
p. Data dependencies of a variable v are the definitions on which v is data
dependent.

Control Dependencies. A node w is said to be $control$ $dependent$ on a conditional edge $u \rightarrow v$ if w post-dominates v; and if $w \neq u$, w does not post-dominate
u [9,12]. Control dependencies of a node n or a program point $entry(n)$ (or
$exit(n)$) are the conditional edges on which the node n is control dependent.
A conditional edge e is called as $transitive$ $control$ $dependency$ of a point p if
e belongs to the transitive closure of control dependencies of p. We use $e \rightsquigarrow p$
to denote that e is a transitive control dependency of a program point p. We
say that the conditions of two conditional edges e_1 and e_2 are $equivalent$ if
$cond(e_1) \Leftrightarrow cond(e_2)$. In the other case, we say that the conditions of the two
dependencies are different. On similar lines, we call two conditional edges $n \rightarrow n'$
and $m \rightarrow m'$ $condition\text{-}wise$ $equivalent$ only if (1) their conditions are equivalent;
and (2) every variable in their conditions has same data dependencies at $exit(n)$
and $exit(m)$.

Static Analysis Alarms. A static analysis tool reports an alarm at the location
where the run-time error corresponding to the alarm is likely to occur. We refer
to the tool generated alarms as the $original$ $alarms$ and to their locations as
the $original$ $locations$. We use $cond(\phi)$ to denote $alarm$ $condition$ of an alarm ϕ,
i.e., the check performed by the analysis tool for detecting an error. The alarm
condition holds iff the corresponding alarm is a false positive. For example,

$nx \neq 0$ is the alarm condition of the alarms D_{38} and D_{45} shown in Fig. 1b. We use *safe values* (resp. *unsafe values*) to refer to the set of values of the variable(s) in $cond(\phi)$ due to which ϕ is a false positive (resp. an error).

We call two alarms ϕ and ϕ' *similar* if $cond(\phi) \Rightarrow cond(\phi')$ or $cond(\phi') \Rightarrow cond(\phi)$. An alarm ϕ is said be a dominant alarm of an alarm ϕ' only if when ϕ is a false positive, ϕ' is also a false positive. We use ϕ_p to denote an alarm ϕ located at a program point p, and thus we say that the transitive control dependencies of ϕ_p are same as the transitive control dependencies of p. We write $e \rightsquigarrow \phi$ to indicate that e is a transitive control dependency of an alarm ϕ. We use tuple $\langle c, p \rangle$ to denote a repositioned alarm at p with c as its alarm condition.

3   Pilot Study

As a sanity check we performed a study to measure (1) what percentage of alarms resulting after the state-of-the-art repositioning [27] are similar; and (2) what percentage of these similar alarms appear in the repositioning limitation scenarios (Sect. 1). The similar alarms appearing in those limitation scenarios are *candidates* for reducing their number through NCD-based repositioning.

We selected 16 open source C applications that were previously used as benchmarks for evaluating the alarms clustering techniques [21,34] and the repositioning technique [27]. We analyzed these applications using our commercial static analysis tool, TCS ECA [32], for five safety properties: division by zero, array index out of bounds (AIOB), arithmetic overflow and underflow, dereference of a null pointer, and uninitialized variables. The generated alarms are postprocessed using the clustering techniques [21,24] and then the resulting *dominant alarms* are repositioned using the state-of-the-art technique [27].   □

We first identified groups of similar alarms from 64779 alarms generated by the setup above. Next we identified similar alarms in each group that have same data dependencies for their variables, and counted those alarms as the similar alarms appearing in the repositioning limitation scenarios. The study indicates that, on an average, 50.89% of the alarms obtained after the state-of-the-art repositioning are similar, and 74% of these similar alarms—38% of the total alarms—appear in the repositioning limitation scenarios. Based on these results we expect postprocessing the alarms using NCD-based repositioning can help to reduce their number. Due to lack of space, the selected applications and the study results are provided in extended version of the paper, available at http://www.win.tue.nl/~aserebre/APLAS2019.pdf.

4   NCDs of Similar Alarms

4.1   The Notion of NCD of an Alarm

Definition 1 (NCD of an alarm). *Let ϕ be an alarm reported in a program P, and $(n \rightarrow n')$ is a transitive control dependency of ϕ. Let P' be obtained from P by replacing the condition of the branching node n with a non-deterministic*

```
1  void f1(int p, int q){              9      if(q == 5){
2     int t, arr[10], i = readInt();  10         arr[i] = 1; │A₁₀│
3                                      11         print(20/i);        │D₁₁│
4     if(p == 1)                       12      }
5        i = 0;                        13
6                                      14      if(q == 5)
7     if(p == 1)                       15         t = arr[i];          │A₁₅│
8        arr[i] = 0;   │A₈│            16  }
```

Fig. 2. Examples to illustrate ICDs and NCDs of alarms.

choice function. We say that the dependency $n \to n'$ is an impacting control dependency *(ICD) of ϕ only if ϕ is a false positive in P but an error in P'. Otherwise, say that the dependency $n \to n'$ is a* non-impacting control dependency *(NCD) of ϕ.* □

We illustrate the notion of NCD/ICD by categorizing the effect of a control dependency $e \rightsquigarrow \phi_p$ on ϕ_p, where $e = n \to n'$. The classification is based on the values that can be assigned to variables in $cond(\phi_p)$.

Class 1. The variables in $cond(\phi_p)$ are assigned with *safe values* by their data dependencies, and thus ϕ_p is a false positive. In this case, e is an NCD of ϕ_p: replacing the condition of the branching node n—the source node of e—by a non-deterministic choice function does not cause ϕ_p to be an error.

Class 2. The variables in $cond(\phi_p)$ are assigned with *unsafe values* by their data dependencies, and ϕ_p is an error if the unsafe values reach the alarm program point p. In this case, the effect of e on ϕ_p is in one of the following two ways depending on whether the unsafe values reach ϕ_p.

Class 2.1: The condition $cond(e)$ prevents the flow of the unsafe values from reaching ϕ_p and thus ϕ_p is a false positive. In this case, if the condition of the source node n of e is replaced by a non-deterministic choice function, the alarm is an error as those unsafe values reach ϕ_p. That is, e affects whether ϕ_p is an error or a false positive. Thus, in this case, we say that e is an ICD of ϕ_p, and $cond(e)$ is a *safety condition* for ϕ_p because e prevents the alarm from being an error. For example, in Fig. 2, the control dependency $n_7 \to n_8$ of A_8 is ICD.

Class 2.2: The condition $cond(e)$ does not prevent the flow of the unsafe values from reaching ϕ_p and thus ϕ_p is an error. In this case, if the condition of the source node n of e is replaced by a non-deterministic choice function, the alarm would still remain as an error. That is, e does not affect whether ϕ_p is an error or a false positive. Thus, we say that e is an NCD of ϕ_p. For example, in Fig. 2, the control dependency $n_9 \to n_{10}$ of D_{11} is NCD.

4.2   Computation of NCDs of Similar Alarms

Computing whether a given dependency e of an alarm ϕ is an ICD or NCD includes determining whether ϕ is a false positive. As determining whether ϕ is a false positive is undecidable in general [11,22], determining whether e is an ICD/NCD of ϕ is also undecidable. Thus, we compute approximation of ICDs/NCDs. As we aim to reposition similar alarms together, we focus on computing NCDs of those similar alarms only. For a given set of similar alarms Φ_S and $\phi \in \Phi_S$, the approximation of NCDs/ICDs of ϕ is described below.

Computation of ICDs. For an alarm ϕ, we compute its transitive control dependency $e \rightsquigarrow \phi$ as ICD, only if every path reaching each alarm $\phi'_p \in \Phi_S$ has a dependency $e' \rightsquigarrow \phi'_p$ on it such that e and e' are *condition-wise equivalent*. For example, the control dependencies of the similar alarms A_{10} and A_{15} in Fig. 2 are ICDs.

Computation of NCDs. For an alarm ϕ, we compute its transitive control dependency $e \rightsquigarrow \phi$ as NCD, if there exists a path reaching at an alarm $\phi'_p \in \Phi_S$ without having a dependency $e' \rightsquigarrow \phi'_p$ on it such that e and e' are *condition-wise equivalent*. For example, in Fig. 1, the control dependencies of the similar alarms D_{38} and D_{45} are NCDs.

In other words, when $\phi \in \Phi_S$, $e \rightsquigarrow \phi$, and a condition equivalent to $cond(e)$ appears on every path to each of the similar alarms Φ_S, then we treat $cond(e)$ as a *potential safety condition* for each alarm in Φ_S, and thus e as an ICD of ϕ. Otherwise, e is an NCD of ϕ.

Intuition Behind the Approximation. The NCDs of similar alarms computed above approximate NCDs as defined in Definition 1. The idea of the approximation is based on the earlier observation by Kumar et al. [18] that removing statements which merely control reachability of an alarm's program point *rarely affects* whether the alarm is false positive or not: removing the non-value impacting control statements of the alarms changed only 2% of the false positive alarms into errors. This suggests that for a given dependency $e \rightsquigarrow \phi$, $cond(e)$ is *rarely* a safety condition for ϕ, i.e., e is *rarely* an ICD of ϕ. Thus, *intuitively, the chance of existing different safety condition for each of the alarms in Φ_S is even lower*: if there exists a safety condition to prevent an alarm from being an error, an *equivalent condition* also should exist for every other similar alarm. For example, in Fig. 1, if the condition $strcmp(pos, \text{``}DOWN\text{''}) == 0$ is a safety condition for D_{38}, the same condition should also have been for its similar alarm D_{45}. Thus, we approximate the control dependencies of those two alarms to be NCDs. On similar lines, the control dependencies of the other alarms in Fig. 1 are NCDs.

In the next section we discuss that, although the above computation of NCDs is observation-based and approximated, the NCDs computed can be *safely* used to reduce the overall number of alarms.

4.3   NCD-Based Repositioning of Similar Alarms

To overcome the limitation of the state-of-the-repositioning (Sect. 1), we reposition a group of similar alarms by considering the effect of their NCDs. We design NCD-based repositioning to satisfy the following constraints, where R is the set of alarms resulting from the repositioning of a set of similar alarms Φ_S.

$C1$: The program points of the repositioned alarms R together dominate the program point of every alarm $\phi \in \Phi_S$, so that when the repositioned alarms R are false positives, the original alarms Φ_S are also false positives.

$C2$: All the paths between the repositioned alarms R and every alarm $\phi \in \Phi_S$ does not have an ICD of ϕ (that is, all the control dependencies of an alarm $\phi \in \Phi_S$ along a path between the repositioned alarms R and ϕ are NCDs).

$C3$: The number of the repositioned alarms R is strictly not greater than the number of original alarms Φ_S.

The constraint $C1$ ensures that when $\phi \in \Phi_S$ is an error, at least one of the repositioned alarms R is also an error. Thus, the repositioning is *safe*, and the repositioned alarms R together act as *dominant alarms* of the original alarms Φ_S. However, as the repositioned alarms are newly created, with $C1$ we cannot guarantee that when a repositioned alarm $r_p \in R$ is an error, at least one of its corresponding original alarms $\Phi' \subseteq \Phi_S$ is an error. That is, r_p may detect an error spuriously. The spurious error detection occurs only when every path between r_p and each $\phi \in \Phi'$ has an ICD of ϕ.

To overcome the problem above—a repositioned alarm detecting a spurious error—we add the second constraint $C2$. The constraint $C1$ together with $C2$ guarantees that when a repositioned alarm is an error, at least one of its corresponding original alarms is also an error, and vice versa. In other words, when the repositioned alarms R are false positives, the original alarms Φ_S are also false positives, and vice versa. Thus, NCD-based repositioning with these two constraints, $C1$ and $C2$, meets the *repositioning criterion* (Sect. 1). As NCD-based repositioning creates new alarms, with the third constraint $C3$, we ensure that the repositioning never results in more alarms than the input for repositioning. Thus, NCD-based repositioning performed with constraints $C1$, $C2$, and $C3$ is safe, without spurious error detection by the repositioned alarms, and without increasing the overall number of alarms.

For example, Fig. 1 also shows NCD-based repositioning of the similar alarms, obtained using the NCDs computed above (Sect. 4.2). The repositioned alarms are shown using green circles. The shown NCD-based repositioning satisfies the three repositioning constraints ($C1$, $C2$, and $C3$).

During the repositioning of a set of similar alarms, when a repositioned alarm can be created at multiple locations satisfying the three repositioning constraints, we choose the location that is closer to its corresponding original alarms. Note that, although NCD-based clustering is performed using approximated NCDs, the repositioning obtained *is still safe* (Constraint $C1$).

When the approximate NCDs computation results in identifying ICDs of a group of similar alarms as NCDs, the obtained repositioned alarm(s) may result in detection of a spurious error. Due to this, (1) educating the tool user about the spurious error detection is required; and (2) we also report traceability links between the repositioned and their corresponding original alarms. The traceability links help user to inspect the corresponding original alarms when when a repositioned alarm is found to be an error. We experimentally evaluate the spurious error detection rate incurred due to computing the NCDs approximately.

Moreover, when the approximate ICDs/NCDs computation results identifying NCDs of a group of similar alarms as ICDs, NCD-based repositioning fails to reposition those alarms.

5   NCD-Based Repositioning Technique: Algorithm

This section presents a technique for NCD-based repositioning of alarms. The technique computes ICDs of the alarms instead of NCDs: ICDs and NCDs of an alarm are mutually exclusive. For efficiency the technique is designed to compute ICDs of alarms while the alarms are repositioned: we do not compute the ICDs separately before the repositioning is performed. We begin describing the technique by defining *live alarm conditions* similarly to the *live variables* [16].

Definition 2 (Live Alarm-condition). *An alarm condition c is said to be* live *at a program point p, if a path from p to the program exit contains an alarm ϕ reported at a program point q with c as its alarm condition, and the path segment from p to q is definition free for any operand of c.*   □

For example, in Fig. 1b, condition $ny \neq 0$ is live at $exit(n_{34})$ due to the alarms D_{42} or D_{48}. However, the same condition is not live at $entry(n_{33})$.

5.1   Live Alarm-Conditions Analysis

Analysis Overview. In this analysis, alarm conditions of *a given set of original alarms Φ* are propagated in the backward direction by computing them as live alarm-conditions (*liveConds*). We use data flow analysis [16,28] to compute liveConds at every program point in the program. The aim of this analysis, that we call *liveConds analysis*, is to compute repositioned alarms for Φ. To this end, for every liveCond ℓ that we compute at a program point p, we also compute the following information.

1. The original alarm(s) due to which ℓ is a liveCond at p. We refer to these alarms as *related original alarms* (relOrigAlarms) of ℓ.
2. The program point(s) that are later used to create repositioned alarms: a (new) repositioned alarm with ℓ as its alarm condition is created at each of these program points. In other words, these program points denote the locations where the relOrigAlarms of ℓ are to be repositioned. Thus, we refer to these program points as *repositioning locations* (reposLocations) of ℓ. A reposLocation of ℓ is either the location of an original alarm due to which ℓ is a liveCond at p, or a program point computed during its backward propagation (the *meet operation* discussed later).

3. The transitive control dependencies of the reposLocations of ℓ such that for every dependency there exists a condition-wise equivalent dependency on all the paths from p to every reposLocation. We refer to these dependencies as *relatedICDs* of ℓ, because their conditions denote at least one safety condition of the alarms that will get created at the reposLocations of ℓ.

To compute traceability links between the repositioned alarms and their corresponding original alarms (and vice versa), we compute the relOrigAlarms of ℓ reposLocation-wise: reposLocations of ℓ are the program points where relOrigAlarms of ℓ are to be repositioned. We refer to the alarms computed corresponding to a reposLocation p as *relOrigAlarms* of p. The relOrigAlarms of ℓ can be obtained by collecting together the relOrigAlarms of reposLocations of ℓ.

Notations. Let $\langle \mathcal{N}, \mathcal{E} \rangle$ be the control flow graph of the program: $\mathcal{N}$ is the set of nodes and $\mathcal{E}$ is the set of edges. Let $\mathcal{P}$ be the set of all program points in the program. Let $\mathcal{E}_c \subset \mathcal{E}$ be the set of all conditional edges in the CFG, i.e., the set of all transitive control dependencies of each $p \in \mathcal{P}$. Let $\mathcal{L}$ be the set of all alarm conditions of a given set of original alarms Φ. Thus, the liveConds computed by the liveConds analysis at a program point are given by a subset of $\mathcal{L}$.

For a liveCond ℓ computed at a program point p, the reposLocations of ℓ and their corresponding relOrigAlarms[3] are given by a subset of $2^{\mathcal{A}}$ where $\mathcal{A} = \mathcal{P} \times 2^{\Phi}$. Thus, the values computed for a liveCond ℓ—its reposLocations (with their corresponding relOrigAlarms) and its relatedICDs—are given by an element of X, where $X = 2^{\mathcal{A}} \times 2^{\mathcal{E}_c}$. We use a function $f : \mathcal{L} \to X$ that maps a liveCond $\ell \in \mathcal{L}$ to a pair of its reposLocations $A \in 2^{\mathcal{A}}$ and relatedICDs $E \in 2^{\mathcal{E}_c}$. We write the liveCond ℓ with the mapped values as tuple $\langle \ell, A, E \rangle$. Thus, at a program point p, the liveConds analysis computes a subset of $\mathcal{L}_b$, where $\mathcal{L}_b = \{ \langle \ell, A, E \rangle \mid \ell \in \mathcal{L}, \; f(\ell) = \langle A, E \rangle \}$.

For a given set $S \subseteq \mathcal{L}_b$ and $A \in 2^{\mathcal{A}}$ we define:

- $condsIn(S) = \{ \ell \mid \langle \ell, A', E' \rangle \in S \}$, the set of all liveConds in S.
- $points(A) = \{ p \mid \langle p, \Phi' \rangle \in A \}$, the set of all reposLocations in A.
- $origAlarms(A) = \cup_{\langle p, \Phi' \rangle \in A} \Phi'$, the set of all relOrigAlarms in A.

Lattice of liveConds Analysis. As liveConds analysis computes subsets of $\mathcal{L}_b$ flow-sensitively at every program point $p \in \mathcal{P}$, we denote the lattice of these values by $\langle \mathcal{B} = 2^{\mathcal{L}_b}, {}^n\sqcap_{\mathcal{B}} \rangle$. We use ${}^n\sqcap_{\mathcal{B}}$ to denote the *meet* of the values flowing in at the *exit* of a branching node n. For simplicity of the equation, we have assumed that the branching node n corresponding to a meet operation is known when the meet is performed. This meet operation is shown using Eq. 1, and it is idempotent, commutative, and associative. The meet operation for a liveCond ℓ is described below.

1. When ℓ flows-in at the meet point through only one branch, its reposLocations and relatedICDs remain unchanged (Eq. 2).

---

[3] Note that the related original alarms (relOrigAlarms) of a liveCond ℓ are computed corresponding to its reposLocations (reposLocation-wise).

2. Following are the updates when (i) ℓ flows-in at the meet point through both the branches, (ii) the reposLocations of ℓ flowing in through both the branches are different; and (iii) the relatedICDs of ℓ flowing in through both the branches does not have a condition-wise equivalent dependency (Eqs. 2 and 5). The reposLocations of ℓ are updated to $entry(n)$, and the relOrigAlarms of this reposLocation are obtained by combining together all the relOrigAlarms of ℓ flowing in through both the branches. Moreover, the relatedICDs of ℓ are updated to $\emptyset$. These updates denote creation of a new reposLocation $entry(n)$: we use $entry(n)$ instead of the meet point $exit(n)$ assuming that the branching nodes do not update values of a variable.

Given $S, S' \in \mathcal{B}$:

$$S \ ^n\sqcap_{\mathcal{B}} \ S' = \bigcup_{\ell \in (condsIn(S) \ \cup \ condsIn \ (S'))} \{ \ meetInfo(\ell, n, S, S') \ \} \tag{1}$$

$$meetInfo(\ell, n, S, S') = \begin{cases} merge(\ell, n, A, E, A', E') & \langle \ell, A, E \rangle \in S, \ \langle \ell, A', E' \rangle \in S' \\ \langle \ell, A, E \rangle & \langle \ell, A, E \rangle \in S, \ \ell \notin condsIn(S') \\ \langle \ell, A', E' \rangle & \langle \ell, A', E' \rangle \in S', \ \ell \notin condsIn(S) \end{cases} \tag{2}$$

$$merge(\ell, n, A, E, A', E') = mergeInfo(\ell, n, A, A', \ meetICDsInfo(E, E')) \tag{3}$$

$$meetICDsInfo(E, E') = \left\{ \ e, e' \ \middle| \ \begin{array}{c} e \in E, \ e' \in E', \\ e \text{ and } e' \text{ are equivalent condition-wise} \end{array} \right\} \tag{4}$$

$$mergeInfo(\ell, n, A, A', E) = \begin{cases} \langle \ell, reposAlarm \ (n, A, A') \ , \emptyset \rangle & points(A) \neq points(A'), \ E = \emptyset \\ \langle \ell, A \cup A', E \rangle & \text{otherwise} \end{cases}$$
$$\tag{5}$$

$$reposAlarm(n, A, A') = \{ \ \langle entry(n), origAlarms(A) \cup origAlarms(A') \rangle \} \tag{6}$$

3. In the cases other than (1) and (2), the reposLocations of ℓ flowing in from both the branches are combined together without updating their respective relOrigAlarms, and the relatedICDs are updated to the control dependencies that are condition-wise equivalent (Eqs. 4 and 5).

Data Flow Equations. Figure 3 shows data flow equations of the liveConds analysis that computes liveConds in intraprocedural setting. Out_n and In_n denote the values computed by the liveConds analysis, respectively, at the *exit* and *entry* of a node n (Eqs. 7 and 9, respectively).

Equation 14 indicates that a liveCond ℓ is generated for every original alarm ϕ reported for a node n, with $\emptyset$ as the relatedICDs of ℓ, and $entry(n)$ as the only reposLocation of ℓ. When the same liveCond l also flows in at $entry(n)$ from a successor of n, (i) the relOrigAlarms of the liveCond flowing in are also added to relOrigAlarms of the reposLocation $entry(n)$ (Eq. 15); and (ii) propagation of the values of l flowing in at $entry(n)$ is stopped (Eq. 16). With this computation and the meet operation (Eq. 1), we ensure that at any program point there exists only one tuple for a liveCond and the values computed for it. Note that the reposLocations of a liveCond are updated only when the liveCond is generated (Eq. 14) or the meet operation is performed (Eq. 1).

Following are the updates to relatedICDs of a liveCond ℓ. (i) When ℓ gets propagated through a transitive control dependency e of its reposLocation, e is added to the relatedICDs of ℓ (Eq. 8). (ii) For a relatedICD e of ℓ, if an

Let $m, n \in \mathcal{N}$; $e \in \mathcal{E}$; $\phi, \phi' \in \Phi$; $\ell, \ell' \in \mathcal{L}$; $S \in B$.

$$Out_n = \begin{cases} \emptyset & n \text{ is } End \text{ node} \\ {}^n\!\!\bigsqcap_{\substack{B \\ m \in pred(n)}} Edge_{e \equiv n \to m}(In_m) & \text{otherwise} \end{cases} \qquad (7)$$

$$Edge_{e = n \to m}(S) = \{\langle \ell, A, E \cup handleCtrlDep(e, A)\rangle \mid \langle \ell, A, E \rangle \in S\} \qquad (8)$$

$$handleCtrlDep(e, A) = \begin{cases} \{e\} & e \text{ is a transitive control dependency of } p \in points(A) \\ \emptyset & \text{otherwise} \end{cases}$$

$$In_n = Gen_n(Survived_n) \ \cup \ (Survived_n \setminus GenRemoved(Survived_n)) \qquad (9)$$

$$Survived_n = processForICDsKill(n, Out_n \setminus Kill_n(Out_n)) \qquad (10)$$

$$Kill_n(S) = \left\{ \langle \ell, A, E \rangle \ \middle| \ \begin{array}{l} \langle \ell, A, E \rangle \in S, \ n \text{ contains a definition} \\ \text{of an operand of } \ell \end{array} \right\} \qquad (11)$$

$$processForICDsKill(n, S) = \{\langle \ell, A, \ E \setminus killICDs(E, n)\rangle \mid \langle \ell, A, E \rangle \in S\} \qquad (12)$$

$$killICDs(E, n) = \left\{ e \ \middle| \ \begin{array}{l} e \in E, \text{ and } n \text{ contains a definition} \\ \text{of an operand of } cond(e) \end{array} \right\} \qquad (13)$$

$$Gen_n(S) = \{ createLiveCond(\phi, n, S) \mid n \text{ has alarm } \phi \in \Phi \text{ reported for it}\} \qquad (14)$$

$$createLiveCond(\phi, n, S) = \begin{cases} createInfo(\phi, n, \{\phi\} \cup origAlarms(R)) & \begin{array}{l} \langle \ell, R, C \rangle \in S, \\ cond(\phi) = \ell \end{array} \\ createInfo(\phi, n, \{\phi\}) & \text{otherwise} \end{cases} \qquad (15)$$

$$createInfo(\phi, n, \Phi') = \langle cond(\phi), \{\langle entry(n), \Phi'\rangle\}, \emptyset \rangle$$

$$GenRemoved_n(S) = \left\{ \langle \ell, A, E \rangle \ \middle| \ \begin{array}{l} n \text{ has alarm } \phi \in \Phi \text{ reported for it,} \\ \langle \ell, A, E \rangle \in S, \ \ell = cond(\phi) \end{array} \right\} \qquad (16)$$

Fig. 3. Data flow equations of the liveConds analysis.

assignment node assigns values to a variable in $cond(\phi)$, then e is removed from the relatedICDs of ℓ (Eq. 12).

For example, in Fig. 1b, $nx \neq 0$ and $ny \neq 0$ are two liveConds computed by the liveConds analysis at entry(n_{34}), i.e. in In_{34}. At this point, the reposLocations (with their relOrigAlarms) and relatedICDs of the first liveCond, $nx \neq 0$, respectively are $\{\langle entry(n_{37}), \{D_{38}, D_{45}\}\rangle\}$ and $\emptyset$. Moreover, the reposLocations (with their relOrigAlarms) and relatedICDs of the second liveCond, $ny \neq 0$, respectively are $\{\langle entry(n_{41}), \{D_{42}, D_{48}\}\rangle\}$ and $\emptyset$.

5.2 NCD-Based Repositioning Using LiveConds Analysis Results

Creation of Repositioned Alarms. As discussed in Sect. 5.1, the liveConds analysis results are used to create repositioned alarms for the original alarms Φ: the repositioned alarms are the results of NCD-based repositioning of Φ. For a liveCond ℓ computed at a program point p, a repositioned alarm $\langle \ell, q \rangle$ is created at each reposLocation q of ℓ (that is, ℓ is the condition of the alarm repositioned at every reposLocation of ℓ). Moreover, the relOrigAlarms of q are identified as the original alarms corresponding to the repositioned alarm $\langle \ell, q \rangle$, and thus use them to report the traceability links between the repositioned alarm $\langle \ell, q \rangle$ and its corresponding original alarms. As a special case, to avoid creating duplicate repositioned alarms, we do not create the repositioned alarm $\langle \ell, q \rangle$ if

```
1 void f1(int p, int q){        21 void f2(int p, int q){
2  int arr[10], i = lib1();     22  int arr[5], i = lib1();
3  if(p < q){                   23   if(p < 5){
4    i = lib();                 24      if(q == 5)
5    arr[i] = 0;    A₅          25        i = lib2();
6  }                            26      arr[i] = 1;    A₂₆
7  //assert(0 ≤ i ≤ 9);         27   }
8  if(p == 5)                   28   else{
9    arr[i] = 3;    A₉          29      if(q == 1)
10                              30        i = lib3();
11 if(q > 2)                    31      arr[i] = 2;    A₃₁
12   arr[i] = 4;    A₁₂         32   }
13}                            33 }
```

(a) Clustering of the repositioned alarms | (b) Applying fallback

Fig. 4. Examples to illustrate postprocessing of the repositioned alarms.

(1) a repositioned alarm $\langle \ell', q \rangle$ that is similar to $\langle \ell, q \rangle$ is already created, or (2) the node n corresponding to q has an original alarm ϕ and $cond(\phi) = \ell$.

At every program point p, we collect the liveConds that are liveConds at p but not at a program point *just prior* to p, and use each of them to create repositioned alarms as described above. The liveConds to be collected are the liveConds that are killed at every node n, given by $Kill_n(Out_n)$. This approach to collect the liveConds removes redundancy in creating the repositioned alarms. As a special case, we collect the liveConds that reach the *procedure entry* (given by In_{Start}), because a liveCond can reach this point (Start node) when all the variables in the liveCond are *local and uninitialized*.

The above approach to collect the liveConds for creating the repositioned alarms ensures the following: each liveCond ℓ that got generated at p due to an original alarm $\phi_p \in \Phi$ gets collected and used to create a repositioned alarm along every path starting at the program entry and ending at p. Thus, along every path reaching p, there exists a repositioned alarm with $\ell = cond(\phi)$ as its alarm condition. As a consequence of this, the repositioned alarms corresponding to the original alarm ϕ_p together dominate ϕ_p. This indicates that the repositioning of Φ thus obtained is *safe*, i.e., the repositioning satisfies the constraint $C1$ (Sect. 4.3). Note that, the Eqs. 1, 8, and 12 together indicate that a repositioned alarm is created only when the constraint $C2$ is satisfied (Sect. 4.3).

Clustering of the Repositioned Alarms. Let R_Φ be the set of all repositioned alarms created using the liveConds analysis results (described above). As a repositioned alarm can be a *dominant alarm* for another repositioned alarm, we postprocess R_Φ for their clustering using the state-of-the-art clustering techniques [20,24,34]. As an example, consider the code in Fig. 4a that has three AIOB alarms reported at lines 5, 9, and 12. The repositioned alarms computed for these alarms are $R_\Phi = \{N_7, A_5\}$, where $N_7 = \langle 0 \le i \le 9, \text{entry}(n_8) \rangle$ with

A_9 and A_{12} as its corresponding original alarms. Observe that N_7 is a dominant alarm of A_5. Thus, to further reduce the number of alarms, we cluster these two alarms. As a result, only one repositioned alarm N_7 gets reported with all the three original alarms as its corresponding original alarms.

Computation of Final Repositioned Alarms. Let R'_Φ be the set of repositioned alarms obtained after their clustering discussed in Sect. 5.2. As a limitation of our technique, in rare cases, repositioning of a given set of original alarms can result into more repositioned alarms than the original alarms. We illustrate this using the two AIOB alarms shown in Fig. 4b. The repositioning of these two alarms results in three repositioned alarms $R_\Phi = \{A_{26}, A_{31}, \langle 0 \leq i \leq 9, \text{entry}(n_{23})\rangle\}$. This limitation case arises because variables in their conditions have different data dependencies. Clustering these repositioned alarms also results in the same set of the repositioned alarms, i.e., $R'_\Phi = R_\Phi$. Thus, we identify the cases where the repositioning of a group of similar alarms $\Phi' \subseteq \Phi$ results in more repositioned alarms than Φ'; and then apply fallback in these cases: we report Φ' instead of reporting their corresponding repositioned alarms. Thus, in this example, finally A_{26} and A_{31} get reported.

Note that the above limitation *may occur* only when the similar alarms being repositioned have different data dependencies. Avoiding such similar alarms in the input to NCD-based repositioning will miss to merge a few similar alarms, e.g., the similar alarms N_7 and A_5 discussed above. Thus, as we intend to reposition more similar alarms together, we accept all the tool-generated alarms as input to NCD-based repositioning and resort to fallback in such limitation cases. Additionally, we apply fallback when the repositioning of a group of similar alarms results in equal number of the repositioned alarms. Applying the fallback ensures that the repositioning obtained using the technique satisfies the constraint $C3$ (Sect. 4.3). Thus, our technique never increases the number of alarms reported to the user than the input original alarms.

Due to lack of space, we provide the overall algorithm of the repositioning technique, theorems and their proofs in extended version of the paper, available at http://www.win.tue.nl/~aserebre/APLAS2019.pdf.

6 Empirical Evaluation

In this section we evaluate the NCD-based repositioning technique (Sect. 5) in terms of the reduction in the number of alarms.

Implementation. We implemented the NCD-based repositioning technique using analysis framework of our commercial static analysis tool, TCS ECA [32]. The analysis framework supports analysis of C and COBOL programs. The framework allows to implement data flow analyses using function summaries. We implemented the liveConds analysis to compute liveConds inter-functionally and by considering transitivity. In the inter-functional implementation, the data flow analysis is solved in bottom-up order only: liveConds are propagated from a called-function to its callers but not from a caller-function to the called functions.

Table 1. Experimental results for NCD-based clustering.

(a) Open source applications

Application	Size (KL OC)	Input Alarms	% Reduction	Time (mins)	% Overhead
archimedes-0.7.0	0.8	2275	10.55	1.9	24.5
polymorph-0.4.0	1.3	25	12.00	0.6	27.5
acpid-1.0.8	1.7	25	8.00	0.4	23.5
spell-1.0	2.0	71	5.63	0.8	18.4
nlkain-1.3	2.5	319	1.57	0.5	15.7
stripcc-0.2.0	2.5	229	8.30	1.0	16.8
ncompress-4.2.4	3.8	92	3.26	0.5	23.6
barcode-0.96	4.2	1064	9.02	2.4	17.7
barcode-0.98	4.9	1310	9.08	2.8	15.7
combine-0.3.3	10.0	819	23.57	4.3	55.3
gnuchess-5.05	10.6	1783	15.09	8.6	95.4
antiword-0.37	27.1	613	9.95	26.7	72.2
sudo-1.8.6	32.1	7433	8.69	133.2	22.5
uucp-1.07	73.7	2068	6.58	21.6	7.5
ffmpeg-0.4.8	83.7	45137	10.41	239.0	11.6
sphinxbase-0.3	121.9	1516	5.67	6.5	17.3

(b) Industry apps. (C & COBOL)

Application	Size (KL OC)	Input Alarms	% Reduction	Time (mins)	% Overhead
C App 1	3.4	383	12.79	1.8	13.3
C App 2	14.6	422	2.37	4.5	15.8
C App 3	18.0	441	22.00	4.0	12.4
C App 4	18.1	1055	20.47	5.6	23.7
C App 5	18.3	535	23.55	4.7	12.5
C App 6	30.5	1001	29.77	5.1	23.4
C App 7	30.9	1379	17.19	42.3	2.8
C App 8	34.6	23404	4.28	186.9	17.8
C App 9	111.0	2241	12.72	7.0	22.2
C App 10	127.8	987	12.97	1.8	21.7
C App 11	187.2	4494	18.09	36.2	36.7
COBOL 1	11.4	341	5.57	1.1	78.3
COBOL 2	11.9	601	28.62	7.1	20.9
COBOL 3	16.7	499	0.40	6.4	179.4
COBOL 4	26.8	1158	32.21	25.7	63.0
COBOL 5	37.8	1826	36.09	3.7	80.0

Selection of Applications and Alarms. To evaluate the applicability and performance of the NCD-based repositioning technique in different contexts, we select in total 32 applications that belonged to the following three categories. (i) 16 open source applications written in C and previously used as benchmarks for evaluating the alarms clustering and repositioning techniques [21,27,34]; (ii) 11 industry C applications from the automotive domain; and (iii) 5 industry COBOL applications from the banking domain.

We analyzed the applications using TCS ECA for five commonly checked categories of run-time errors (safety properties): *array index out of bounds* (AIOB), *division by zero* (DZ), *integer overflow underflow (OFUF)*, *uninitialized variables* (UIV), and *illegal dereference of a pointer* (IDP). The IDP property is not applicable for COBOL applications as COBOL programs do not have pointers. The tool-generated alarms are postprocessed using the alarms clustering techniques [21,24] and then the resulting *dominant alarms* are postprocessed using the state-of-the-art repositioning [27]. The resulting repositioned alarms are provided as input to NCD-based repositioning. All the applications in the three sets were analyzed and the alarms were postprocessed using a machine with i7 2.5 GHz processor and 16 GB RAM.

Results. Table 1 presents the evaluation results as per the categories of the applications (open source and industry). The column *Input Alarms* presents the number of alarms that were given as input to the NCD-based repositioning technique, while the column *% Reduction* presents the percentage reduction achieved in the number of alarms by the technique. The evaluation results indicate that, compared to state-of-the-art repositioning, the NCD-based repositioning technique reduces the number of alarms on the three sets of applications—open source, C industry, and COBOL industry—by up to 23.57%, 29.77%, and 36.09%

respectively. The median reductions are 9.02%, 17.18%, and 28.61%, respectively. Moreover, the average reductions respectively are 10.16%, 8.97%, and 27.68%.

The column *Time* in Table 1 presents the time taken to (i) analyze the applications for those five properties, (ii) postprocess the TCS ECA-generated alarms using the clustering and the state-of-the-art repositioning techniques. The columns *% Overhead* presents the performance overhead incurred due to the extra time taken by the NCD-based repositioning technique. We believe the performance overhead added is acceptable because the alarms reduction can be expected to reduce the users' manual effort which is much more expensive than machine time. Moreover, the reduced alarms may result in performance gain when the alarms are postprocessed for false positives elimination using time-expensive techniques like model checking.

Other Observations: (1) We measured the reduction in the number of alarms generated for each of the properties selected. The median reductions computed property-wise on all the applications, are 25.8% (AIOB), 45.72% (DZ), 6.89% (OFUF), 18.17% (UIV), and 10.3% (IDP). (2) The fallback got applied (Sect. 5.2) in 2592 instances during the NCD-based repositioning of the total 105,546 alarms. (3) Around 43% of the dominant alarms resulting after the NCD-based repositioning on the open source applications are found to be similar alarms, and 64% of these similar alarms appear in the repositioning limitation scenarios. Our manual analysis of 200 alarms appearing in these limitation scenarios showed they are not merged together due to (i) presence of common safety conditions (ICDs), (ii) limitations in our implementation to compute the liveConds inter-functionally, or (iii) the fallback got applied.

Evaluation of Spurious Error Detection by the Repositioned Alarms. As discussed in Sect. 4.3, a repositioned alarm obtained through repositioning based on the approximated NCDs can be a spurious error. A repositioned alarm is a spurious error when a NCD computed with our approach is actually an ICD. To measure the spurious error detection rate, we manually analyzed 150 repositioned alarms that were created due to merging of two or more similar alarms: each repositioned alarm has two or more original alarms corresponding to it. The analyzed alarms are randomly selected from the repositioned alarms generated on the first nine open source applications (Table 1a) and two industry applications (C applications 4 and 7 in Table 1b). These selected 150 repositioned alarms have in total 482 original alarms corresponding to them. In our manual analysis, we checked each of the selected alarms whether it is a spurious error. We found three repositioned alarms to be spurious errors, and thus, the spurious error detection rate to be 2%. This indicates that our approach to compute the NCDs/ICDs of similar alarms is effective, and for the analyzed cases, the NCD-based repositioning technique reduced the number of alarms by 70% but at the cost of detecting a few spurious errors (2%).

7   Related Work

Heckman and Williams [14], and Muske and Serebrenik [26] have recently surveyed literature on postprocessing static analysis alarms. Among the techniques surveyed, our approach to reposition alarms belongs to the category of *clustering of alarms* together with the work of Lee et al. [20], Muske et al. [24,27] and Zhang et al. [34]. However, those techniques are unable to group some of the similar alarms which could be grouped/merged together (discussed in Sect. 1). Among those techniques, as the state-of-the-art repositioning technique [27] overcomes the limitations of the other alarms-clustering techniques [20,24,34], we compared and evaluated our NCD-based repositioning against it.

On the similar lines to alarms repositioning, Cousot et al. [8] have proposed hoisting necessary preconditions for providing the preconditions required by the Design by Contract [23]. Furthermore, Muske et al. [25] have proposed grouping the related/similar alarms based on similarity of modification points. In their approach [24], as the grouped alarms are inspected using values at the modification points of alarm variables, the inspection often finds spurious errors when the alarms are actually false positives solely due to their transitive control dependencies (ICDs). However, none of these techniques [8,24,25] identifies the conditional statements (control dependencies) that are non-impacting to the similar alarms.

Kumar et al. [18] identify the conditional statements that are value-impacting to the alarms. However, the notion of *value-impacting conditional statements* (resp. non value impacting conditional statements) is different from the ICDs (resp. NCDs) of the alarms. That is, a transitive control dependency identified as *non value-impacting* to an alarm can actually be an ICD of the alarm, and a control dependency identified as value-impacting can be an NCD. For example, in Fig. 2, the control dependency $n_7 \rightarrow n_8$ of A_8 is ICD, whereas the technique by Kumar et al. identifies the same dependency is non-value impacting. To the best of our knowledge, no other static analysis technique or alarms postprocessing technique has formally proposed the notion of NCDs/ICDs of alarms or used them in alarms postprocessing.

As the NCD-based clustering of alarms is orthogonal to other alarms postprocessing techniques, it can be applied in conjunction with those. We believe that the combinations will provide more benefits as compared to the benefits obtained by applying them individually.

8   Conclusion

We have proposed the notion of NCDs of alarms, and NCD-based repositioning to reduce the number of alarms. Our approach to compute approximated NCDs of similar alarms is observation-based, and the computation is based on whether conditions in the enclosing conditional statements of a group of similar alarms are equivalent. This approximated approach is required, because the existing alarms clustering and repositioning techniques, being conservative, still report high percentage of similar alarms. The reported large number of alarms increases the cost to postprocess them manually or automatically.

We performed an evaluation of NCD-based repositioning using a large set of alarms on three kinds of applications, 16 open source C applications, 11 industry C applications, and 5 industry COBOL applications. The evaluation results indicate that, compared to the state-of-the-art repositioning technique, NCD-based repositioning reduces the number of alarms respectively by up to 23.57%, 29.77%, and 36.09%. The median reductions are 9.02%, 17.18%, and 28.61%, respectively. Our manual analysis showed that our approach to approximately compute NCDs of similar alarms is effective: the approximation helped to reduce the alarms in the analyzed cases by 70%, however it resulted in 2% of the repositioned alarms detecting a spurious error.

We believe that NCD-based repositioning, being orthogonal to many of the existing approaches to postprocess alarms, can be applied in conjunction with those approaches. We plan to (i) explore a few more techniques to compute NCDs for alarms (similar as well as non-similar alarms); and (ii) use the NCDs to improve the other alarms-postprocessing techniques like automated false positives elimination and version-aware static analysis.

References

1. Allen, F.E.: Control flow analysis. In: Symposium on Compiler Optimization, pp. 1–19. ACM, New York (1970)
2. Ayewah, N., Pugh, W.: The Google FindBugs fixit. In: International Symposium on Software Testing and Analysis, pp. 241–252. ACM, New York (2010)
3. Ayewah, N., Pugh, W., Morgenthaler, J.D., Penix, J., Zhou, Y.: Evaluating static analysis defect warnings on production software. In: Workshop on Program Analysis for Software Tools and Engineering, pp. 1–8. ACM, New York (2007)
4. Beller, M., Bholanath, R., McIntosh, S., Zaidman, A.: Analyzing the state of static analysis: a large-scale evaluation in open source software. In: International Conference on Software Analysis, Evolution, and Reengineering, vol. 1, pp. 470–481 (2016)
5. Bessey, A., et al.: A few billion lines of code later: using static analysis to find bugs in the real world. Commun. ACM **53**(2), 66–75 (2010)
6. Brat, G., Venet, A.: Precise and scalable static program analysis of NASA flight software. In: 2005 IEEE Aerospace Conference, pp. 1–10, March 2005
7. Christakis, M., Bird, C.: What developers want and need from program analysis: an empirical study. In: International Conference on Automated Software Engineering, pp. 332–343. ACM, New York (2016)
8. Cousot, P., Cousot, R., Fähndrich, M., Logozzo, F.: Automatic inference of necessary preconditions. In: Giacobazzi, R., Berdine, J., Mastroeni, I. (eds.) VMCAI 2013. LNCS, vol. 7737, pp. 128–148. Springer, Heidelberg (2013). https://doi.org/10.1007/978-3-642-35873-9_10
9. Cytron, R., Ferrante, J., Rosen, B.K., Wegman, M.N., Zadeck, F.K.: Efficiently computing static single assignment form and the control dependence graph. ACM Trans. Program. Lang. Syst. **13**(4), 451–490 (1991)
10. Denney, E., Trac, S.: A software safety certification tool for automatically generated guidance, navigation and control code. In: 2008 IEEE Aerospace Conference, pp. 1–11, March 2008

11. Dillig, I., Dillig, T., Aiken, A.: Automated error diagnosis using abductive inference. In: Conference on Programming Language Design and Implementation, pp. 181–192. ACM, New York (2012)
12. Ferrante, J., Ottenstein, K.J., Warren, J.D.: The program dependence graph and its use in optimization. ACM Trans. Program. Lang. Syst. **9**(3), 319–349 (1987)
13. Gehrke, M.: Bidirectional Predicate Propagation in Frama-C and its Application to Warning Removal. Master's thesis, Hamburg University of Technology (2014)
14. Heckman, S., Williams, L.: A systematic literature review of actionable alert identification techniques for automated static code analysis. Inf. Softw. Technol. **53**(4), 363–387 (2011)
15. Johnson, B., Song, Y., Murphy-Hill, E., Bowdidge, R.: Why don't software developers use static analysis tools to find bugs? In: International Conference on Software Engineering, pp. 672–681. IEEE Press, Piscataway (2013)
16. Khedker, U., Sanyal, A., Sathe, B.: Data Flow Analysis: Theory and Practice. CRC Press, Boca Raton (2009)
17. Kornecki, A., Zalewski, J.: Certification of software for real-time safety-critical systems: state of the art. Innov. Syst. Softw. Eng. **5**(2), 149–161 (2009)
18. Kumar, S., Sanyal, A., Khedker, U.P.: Value slice: a new slicing concept for scalable property checking. In: Baier, C., Tinelli, C. (eds.) TACAS 2015. LNCS, vol. 9035, pp. 101–115. Springer, Heidelberg (2015). https://doi.org/10.1007/978-3-662-46681-0_7
19. Layman, L., Williams, L., St. Amant, R.: Toward reducing fault fix time: understanding developer behavior for the design of automated fault detection tools. In: International Symposium on Empirical Software Engineering and Measurement, pp. 176–185 (2007)
20. Lee, W., Lee, W., Kang, D., Heo, K., Oh, H., Yi, K.: Sound non-statistical clustering of static analysis alarms. ACM Trans. Program. Lang. Syst. **39**(4), 16:1–16:35 (2017)
21. Lee, W., Lee, W., Yi, K.: Sound non-statistical clustering of static analysis alarms. In: Kuncak, V., Rybalchenko, A. (eds.) VMCAI 2012. LNCS, vol. 7148, pp. 299–314. Springer, Heidelberg (2012). https://doi.org/10.1007/978-3-642-27940-9_20
22. Mangal, R., Zhang, X., Nori, A.V., Naik, M.: A user-guided approach to program analysis. In: Proceedings of the 2015 10th Joint Meeting on Foundations of Software Engineering, ESEC/FSE 2015, pp. 462–473. ACM, New York (2015)
23. Meyer, B.: Design by Contract. Prentice Hall, Upper Saddle River (2002)
24. Muske, T., Baid, A., Sanas, T.: Review efforts reduction by partitioning of static analysis warnings. In: International Working Conference on Source Code Analysis and Manipulation, pp. 106–115 (2013)
25. Muske, T., Khedker, U.P.: Cause points analysis for effective handling of alarms. In: International Symposium on Software Reliability Engineering, pp. 173–184, October 2016
26. Muske, T., Serebrenik, A.: Survey of approaches for handling static analysis alarms. In: International Working Conference on Source Code Analysis and Manipulation, pp. 157–166 (2016)
27. Muske, T., Talluri, R., Serebrenik, A.: Repositioning of static analysis alarms. In: Proceedings of the 27th ACM SIGSOFT International Symposium on Software Testing and Analysis, ISSTA 2018, pp. 187–197. ACM, New York (2018)
28. Nielson, F., Nielson, H.R., Hankin, C.: Principles of Program Analysis. Springer, New York (1999). https://doi.org/10.1007/978-3-662-03811-6

29. Rival, X.: Abstract dependences for alarm diagnosis. In: Yi, K. (ed.) APLAS 2005. LNCS, vol. 3780, pp. 347–363. Springer, Heidelberg (2005). https://doi.org/10. 1007/11575467_23

30. Rival, X.: Understanding the origin of alarms in ASTRÉE. In: Hankin, C., Siveroni, I. (eds.) SAS 2005. LNCS, vol. 3672, pp. 303–319. Springer, Heidelberg (2005). https://doi.org/10.1007/11547662_21

31. Sadowski, C., van Gogh, J., Jaspan, C., Söderberg, E., Winter, C.: Tricorder: building a program analysis ecosystem. In: International Conference on Software Engineering, pp. 598–608. IEEE Press, Piscataway (2015)

32. TCS Embedded Code Analyzer (TCS ECA). https://www.tcs.com/tcs-embedded-code-analyzer. Accessed 30 Aug 2019

33. Venet, A.: A practical approach to formal software verification by static analysis. Ada Lett. XXVII **I**(1), 92–95 (2008)

34. Zhang, D., Jin, D., Gong, Y., Zhang, H.: Diagnosis-oriented alarm correlations. In: Asia-Pacific Software Engineering Conference, vol. 1, pp. 172–179 (2013)

A Type-Based HFL Model Checking Algorithm

Youkichi Hosoi, Naoki Kobayashi$^{(\boxtimes)}$, and Takeshi Tsukada

The University of Tokyo, Tokyo, Japan
{hosoi,tsukada}@kb.is.s.u-tokyo.ac.jp, koba@is.s.u-tokyo.ac.jp

Abstract. Higher-order modal fixpoint logic (HFL) is a higher-order extension of the modal μ-calculus, and strictly more expressive than the modal μ-calculus. It has recently been shown that various program verification problems can naturally be reduced to HFL model checking: the problem of whether a given finite state system satisfies a given HFL formula. In this paper, we propose a novel algorithm for HFL model checking: it is the first practical algorithm in that it runs fast for typical inputs, despite the hyper-exponential worst-case complexity of the HFL model checking problem. Our algorithm is based on Kobayashi et al.'s type-based characterization of HFL model checking, and was inspired by a saturation-based algorithm for HORS model checking, another higher-order extension of model checking. We prove the correctness of the algorithm and report on an implementation and experimental results.

1 Introduction

Higher-order modal fixpoint logic (HFL) has been proposed by Viswanathan and Viswanathan [20]. It is a higher-order extension of the modal μ-calculus and strictly more expressive than the modal μ-calculus; HFL can express non-regular properties of transition systems. There have recently been growing interests in HFL model checking, the problem of deciding whether a given finite state system satisfies a given HFL formula. In fact, Kobayashi et al. [11,21] have shown that various verification problems for higher-order functional programs can naturally be reduced to HFL model checking problems.

Unfortunately, however, the worst-case complexity of HFL model checking is k-EXPTIME complete (where k is a parameter called the *order* of HFL formulas; order-0 HFL corresponds to the modal μ-calculus) [2], and there has been no efficient HFL model checker. Kobayashi et al. [10] have shown that there are mutual translations between HFL model checking and HORS model checking (model checking of the trees generated by higher-order recursion schemes [16]). Since there are practical HORS model checkers available [4,8,9,17,19], one may expect to obtain an efficient HFL model checker by combining the translation from HFL to HORS model checking and a HORS model checker. That approach does not work, however, because the translation of Kobayashi et al. [10] from HFL to HORS model checking involves a complex encoding of natural numbers

A. W. Lin (Ed.): APLAS 2019, LNCS 11893, pp. 136–155, 2019.
https://doi.org/10.1007/978-3-030-34175-6_8

as higher-order functions, which is impractical. Considering that the other translation from HORS to HFL model checking is simpler and more natural, we think that HFL model checking is a more primitive problem than HORS model checking. Also in view of applications to verification of concurrent programs [12,20] (in addition to the above-mentioned applications to higher-order program verification), a direct tool support for HFL model checking is important.

In the present paper, we propose a novel HFL model checking algorithm that is *practical* in the sense that it does not always suffer from the bottleneck of the worst-case complexity, and runs reasonably fast for typical inputs, as confirmed by experiments. To our knowledge, it is the first such algorithm for HFL model checking.

Our algorithm is based on Kobayashi et al.'s type-based characterization [10], which reduces HFL model checking to a typability game (which is an instance of parity games), and was inspired by the saturation-based algorithm for HORS model checking [19]. The detail of the algorithm is, however, different, and its correctness is quite non-trivial. Actually, the correctness proof for our algorithm is simpler and more streamlined than that for their algorithm [19].

We have implemented a prototype HFL model checker based on the proposed algorithm. We confirmed through experiments that the model checker works well for a number of realistic inputs obtained from program verification problems, despite the extremely high worst-case complexity of HFL model checking.

The rest of this paper is structured as follows. Section 2 recalls the definition of HFL model checking, and reviews its type-based characterization. Section 3 formalizes our type-based HFL model checking algorithm, and Sect. 4 gives an outline of its correctness proof. Section 5 is devoted to reporting on implementation and experimental results. Section 6 discusses related work, and Sect. 7 concludes the paper. Omitted details are found in a longer version of the paper [6].

2   Preliminaries

In this section, we review the notion of HFL model checking [20] and its type-based characterization. The latter forms the basis of our HFL model checking algorithm.

2.1   HFL Model Checking

We first review HFL model checking in this section.

A (finite) *labeled transition system* (LTS) $\mathcal{L}$ is a quadruple $(Q, \mathcal{A}, \longrightarrow, q_0)$, where Q is a finite set of states, $\mathcal{A}$ is a finite set of actions, $\longrightarrow \subseteq Q \times \mathcal{A} \times Q$ is a transition relation, and $q_0 \in Q$ is a designated initial state. We use the metavariable a for actions. We write $q \xrightarrow{a} q'$ when $(q, a, q') \in \longrightarrow$.

The *higher-order modal fixpoint logic* (HFL) [20] is a higher-order extension of the modal μ-calculus. The sets of (simple) types and formulas are defined by the following BNF.[1]

---

[1] Following [10], we exclude out negations, without losing the expressive power [14].

$$\varphi \text{ (formulas) } ::= \texttt{true} \mid \texttt{false} \mid X \mid \varphi_1 \vee \varphi_2 \mid \varphi_1 \wedge \varphi_2$$
$$\mid \langle a \rangle \varphi \mid [a]\, \varphi \mid \mu X^\eta . \varphi \mid \nu X^\eta . \varphi$$
$$\mid \lambda X^\eta . \varphi \mid \varphi_1 \, \varphi_2$$
$$\eta \text{ (simple types) } ::= \texttt{o} \mid \eta_1 \to \eta_2$$

The syntax of formulas on the first two lines is identical to that of the modal μ-calculus formulas, except that the variable X can range over *higher-order* predicates, rather than just propositions. Intuitively, $\mu X^\eta . \varphi$ ($\nu X^\eta . \varphi$, resp.) denotes the least (greatest, resp.) predicate of type η such that $X = \varphi$. Higher-order predicates can be manipulated by using λ-abstractions and applications. The type o denotes the type of propositions. A *type environment* $\mathcal{H}$ for simple types is a map from a finite set of variables to the set of simple types. We often treat $\mathcal{H}$ as a set of type bindings of the form $X : \eta$, and write $X : \eta \in \mathcal{H}$ when $\mathcal{H}(X) = \eta$. A *type judgment relation* $\mathcal{H} \vdash \varphi : \eta$ is derived by the typing rules in Fig. 1.

$$\frac{}{\mathcal{H} \vdash \texttt{true} : \texttt{o}} \qquad \frac{}{\mathcal{H} \vdash \texttt{false} : \texttt{o}} \qquad \frac{X : \eta \in \mathcal{H}}{\mathcal{H} \vdash X : \eta}$$

$$\frac{\mathcal{H} \vdash \varphi_1 : \texttt{o} \quad \mathcal{H} \vdash \varphi_2 : \texttt{o}}{\mathcal{H} \vdash \varphi_1 \vee \varphi_2 : \texttt{o}} \quad \frac{\mathcal{H} \vdash \varphi_1 : \texttt{o} \quad \mathcal{H} \vdash \varphi_2 : \texttt{o}}{\mathcal{H} \vdash \varphi_1 \wedge \varphi_2 : \texttt{o}} \quad \frac{\mathcal{H} \vdash \varphi : \texttt{o}}{\mathcal{H} \vdash \langle a \rangle \varphi : \texttt{o}} \quad \frac{\mathcal{H} \vdash \varphi : \texttt{o}}{\mathcal{H} \vdash [a]\, \varphi : \texttt{o}}$$

$$\frac{\mathcal{H} \cup \{X : \eta\} \vdash \varphi : \eta \quad X \notin dom(\mathcal{H})}{\mathcal{H} \vdash \mu X^\eta . \varphi : \eta} \qquad \frac{\mathcal{H} \cup \{X : \eta\} \vdash \varphi : \eta \quad X \notin dom(\mathcal{H})}{\mathcal{H} \vdash \nu X^\eta . \varphi : \eta}$$

$$\frac{\mathcal{H} \cup \{X : \eta_1\} \vdash \varphi : \eta_2 \quad X \notin dom(\mathcal{H})}{\mathcal{H} \vdash \lambda X^{\eta_1} . \varphi : \eta_1 \to \eta_2} \qquad \frac{\mathcal{H} \vdash \varphi_1 : \eta_2 \to \eta \quad \mathcal{H} \vdash \varphi_2 : \eta_2}{\mathcal{H} \vdash \varphi_1 \, \varphi_2 : \eta}$$

Fig. 1. Typing rules for simple types

Note that, for each pair of a type environment $\mathcal{H}$ and an HFL formula φ, there is at most one simple type η such that the type judgment relation $\mathcal{H} \vdash \varphi : \eta$ is derivable. We say an HFL formula φ has type η under a type environment $\mathcal{H}$ if the type judgment relation $\mathcal{H} \vdash \varphi : \eta$ is derivable.

For each simple type η, we define $order(\eta)$ inductively by: $order(\texttt{o}) = 0$, $order(\eta_1 \to \eta_2) = \max(order(\eta_1) + 1, order(\eta_2))$. The order of an HFL formula φ is the highest order of the types of the variables bound by μ or ν in φ. An order-0 HFL formula of type o can be viewed as a modal μ-calculus formula, and vice versa. We write $FV(\varphi)$ for the set of free variables occurring in a formula φ. An HFL formula φ is said to be *closed* if $FV(\varphi) = \emptyset$, and a closed formula is said to be *well-typed* if it has some simple type under the empty type environment.

The Semantics. Let $\mathcal{L} = (Q, \mathcal{A}, \longrightarrow, q_0)$ be an LTS. The semantics of a well-typed HFL formula of type η with respect to $\mathcal{L}$ is given as an element of a complete lattice $(D_{\mathcal{L},\eta}, \sqsubseteq_{\mathcal{L},\eta})$ defined by induction on the structure of η. For the base case, $(D_{\mathcal{L},\texttt{o}}, \sqsubseteq_{\mathcal{L},\texttt{o}})$ is defined by $D_{\mathcal{L},\texttt{o}} = 2^Q$ and $\sqsubseteq_{\mathcal{L},\texttt{o}} = \subseteq$, that is, $(D_{\mathcal{L},\texttt{o}}, \sqsubseteq_{\mathcal{L},\texttt{o}})$ is the powerset lattice of the state set Q. For the step case, $D_{\mathcal{L},\eta_1 \to \eta_2}$ is defined as the set of monotonic functions from $D_{\mathcal{L},\eta_1}$ to $D_{\mathcal{L},\eta_2}$, and $\sqsubseteq_{\mathcal{L},\eta_1 \to \eta_2}$ is defined as the pointwise ordering over it.

For each type environment $\mathcal{H}$, we define $[\![\mathcal{H}]\!]_{\mathcal{L}}$ as the set of functions ρ such that, for each $X \in dom(\mathcal{H})$, the image $\rho(X)$ is in the semantic domain of its type $\mathcal{H}(X)$, that is, $[\![\mathcal{H}]\!]_{\mathcal{L}} = \{\rho : dom(\mathcal{H}) \to \bigcup_\eta D_{\mathcal{L},\eta} \mid \forall X : \eta \in \mathcal{H}. \rho(X) \in D_{\mathcal{L},\eta}\}$. The interpretation of a type judgment relation $\mathcal{H} \vdash \varphi : \eta$ is a function $[\![\mathcal{H} \vdash \varphi : \eta]\!]_{\mathcal{L}} : [\![\mathcal{H}]\!]_{\mathcal{L}} \to D_{\mathcal{L},\eta}$ defined by induction on the derivation of $\mathcal{H} \vdash \varphi : \eta$ by:

$[\![\mathcal{H} \vdash \mathtt{true} : \mathtt{o}]\!]_{\mathcal{L}}(\rho) = Q$

$[\![\mathcal{H} \vdash \mathtt{false} : \mathtt{o}]\!]_{\mathcal{L}}(\rho) = \emptyset$

$[\![\mathcal{H} \vdash X : \eta]\!]_{\mathcal{L}}(\rho) = \rho(X)$

$[\![\mathcal{H} \vdash \varphi_1 \vee \varphi_2 : \mathtt{o}]\!]_{\mathcal{L}}(\rho) = [\![\mathcal{H} \vdash \varphi_1 : \mathtt{o}]\!]_{\mathcal{L}}(\rho) \cup [\![\mathcal{H} \vdash \varphi_2 : \mathtt{o}]\!]_{\mathcal{L}}(\rho)$

$[\![\mathcal{H} \vdash \varphi_1 \wedge \varphi_2 : \mathtt{o}]\!]_{\mathcal{L}}(\rho) = [\![\mathcal{H} \vdash \varphi_1 : \mathtt{o}]\!]_{\mathcal{L}}(\rho) \cap [\![\mathcal{H} \vdash \varphi_2 : \mathtt{o}]\!]_{\mathcal{L}}(\rho)$

$[\![\mathcal{H} \vdash \langle a \rangle \varphi : \mathtt{o}]\!]_{\mathcal{L}}(\rho) = \{q \in Q \mid \exists q' \in [\![\mathcal{H} \vdash \varphi : \mathtt{o}]\!]_{\mathcal{L}}(\rho). q \xrightarrow{a} q'\}$

$[\![\mathcal{H} \vdash [a] \varphi : \mathtt{o}]\!]_{\mathcal{L}}(\rho) = \{q \in Q \mid \forall q' \in Q. q \xrightarrow{a} q' \Rightarrow q' \in [\![\mathcal{H} \vdash \varphi : \mathtt{o}]\!]_{\mathcal{L}}(\rho)\}$

$[\![\mathcal{H} \vdash \mu X^\eta. \varphi : \eta]\!]_{\mathcal{L}}(\rho) = \bigsqcap_{\mathcal{L},\eta} \{d \in D_{\mathcal{L},\eta} \mid [\![\mathcal{H} \vdash \lambda X^\eta. \varphi : \eta \to \eta]\!]_{\mathcal{L}}(\rho)(d) \sqsubseteq_{\mathcal{L},\eta} d\}$

$[\![\mathcal{H} \vdash \nu X^\eta. \varphi : \eta]\!]_{\mathcal{L}}(\rho) = \bigsqcup_{\mathcal{L},\eta} \{d \in D_{\mathcal{L},\eta} \mid d \sqsubseteq_{\mathcal{L},\eta} [\![\mathcal{H} \vdash \lambda X^\eta. \varphi : \eta \to \eta]\!]_{\mathcal{L}}(\rho)(d)\}$

$[\![\mathcal{H} \vdash \lambda X^{\eta_1}. \varphi : \eta_1 \to \eta_2]\!]_{\mathcal{L}}(\rho) = \lambda d \in D_{\mathcal{L},\eta_1}. [\![\mathcal{H} \cup \{X : \eta_1\} \vdash \varphi : \eta_2]\!]_{\mathcal{L}}(\rho[X \mapsto d])$

$[\![\mathcal{H} \vdash \varphi_1 \varphi_2 : \eta]\!]_{\mathcal{L}}(\rho) = [\![\mathcal{H} \vdash \varphi_1 : \eta_2 \to \eta]\!]_{\mathcal{L}}(\rho)([\![\mathcal{H} \vdash \varphi_2 : \eta_2]\!]_{\mathcal{L}}(\rho)).$

Here, $\rho[X \mapsto d]$ denotes the function f such that $f(X) = d$ and $f(Y) = \rho(Y)$ for $Y \neq X$, and the unary operator $\bigsqcup_{\mathcal{L},\eta}$ ($\bigsqcap_{\mathcal{L},\eta}$, resp.) denotes the least upper bound (the greatest lower bound, resp.) with respect to $\sqsubseteq_{\mathcal{L},\eta}$.

Finally, for each closed HFL formula φ of type η, we define the interpretation $[\![\varphi]\!]_{\mathcal{L}}$ by $[\![\varphi]\!]_{\mathcal{L}} = [\![\emptyset \vdash \varphi : \eta]\!]_{\mathcal{L}}(\rho_\emptyset)$, where $\rho_\emptyset$ is the empty map. We say that a closed propositional HFL formula φ is *satisfied* by the state q when $q \in [\![\varphi]\!]_{\mathcal{L}}$.

Example 1. Let φ_1 be $\mu F^{\mathtt{o} \to \mathtt{o}}. \lambda X^\mathtt{o}. X \vee \langle a \rangle (F (\langle b \rangle X))$. The formula $\varphi_1 (\langle c \rangle \mathtt{true})$ can be expanded to:

$$(\lambda X. X \vee \langle a \rangle (\varphi_1 (\langle b \rangle X))) (\langle c \rangle \mathtt{true})$$
$$\equiv \langle c \rangle \mathtt{true} \vee \langle a \rangle (\varphi_1 (\langle b \rangle \langle c \rangle \mathtt{true}))$$
$$\equiv \langle c \rangle \mathtt{true} \vee \langle a \rangle ((\lambda X. X \vee \langle a \rangle (\varphi_1 (\langle b \rangle X))) (\langle b \rangle \langle c \rangle \mathtt{true}))$$
$$\equiv \langle c \rangle \mathtt{true} \vee \langle a \rangle (\langle b \rangle \langle c \rangle \mathtt{true} \vee \langle a \rangle (\varphi_1 (\langle b \rangle \langle b \rangle \langle c \rangle \mathtt{true})))$$
$$\equiv \langle c \rangle \mathtt{true} \vee \langle a \rangle \langle b \rangle \langle c \rangle \mathtt{true} \vee \langle a \rangle \langle a \rangle \langle b \rangle \langle b \rangle \langle c \rangle \mathtt{true} \vee \cdots.$$

Thus, the formula $\varphi_1 (\langle c \rangle \mathtt{true})$ describes the property that there exists a transition sequence of the form $a^n b^n c$ for some $n \geq 0$. As shown by this example, HFL is strictly more expressive than the modal μ-calculus. □

We write $\mathcal{L} \models \varphi$ when the initial state of $\mathcal{L}$ satisfies the property described by φ. The goal of HFL model checking is to decide, given $\mathcal{L}$ and φ as input, whether $\mathcal{L} \models \varphi$ holds.

Example 2. To see how HFL model checking can be applied to program verification, let us consider the following OCaml-like program, which is a variation of the program considered in [11].

```
let rec f x k = if * then (close x; k())
                else (read x; read x; f x k) in
let d = open_in "foo" in f d (fun _ -> ())
```

Here, the asterisk * in the if-condition is a non-deterministic Boolean value. The program first opens the file foo, and then calls the function f with the opened file as an argument. The function f recursively reads the given file even times and closes it upon a non-deterministic condition.

Suppose we wish to check that the file foo is safely accessed as a read-only file. In the reduction methods by Kobayashi et al. [11], a program is transformed to an HFL formula that intuitively says "the behavior of the program conforms to the specification described as an LTS." In this case, the verification problem is reduced to the HFL model checking problem of deciding whether $\mathcal{L}_2 \models \varphi_2$ holds, where $\varphi_2 = (\nu F. \lambda k. \langle close \rangle k \wedge \langle read \rangle \langle read \rangle (F\ k)) (\langle end \rangle \mathbf{true})$ and $\mathcal{L}_2$ is the following LTS, which models the access protocol for read-only files.

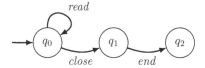

The formula φ_2 can be expanded to $\bigwedge_{n=0}^{\infty} \langle read \rangle^{2n} \langle close \rangle \langle end \rangle \mathbf{true}$, and checking whether $\mathcal{L}_2 \models \varphi_2$ holds is equivalent to checking whether (every prefix of) any sequence of the form $\mathbf{read}^{2n} \cdot \mathbf{close} \cdot \mathbf{end}$ belongs to the prefix-closure of $\mathbf{read}^* \cdot \mathbf{close} \cdot \mathbf{end}$, which is actually true. See [11] for systematic translations from program verification to HFL model checking.   □

2.2   Type-Based Characterization of HFL Model Checking

We now review the type-based characterization of the HFL model checking problem [10], which is going to be used as the basis of our algorithm given in Sect. 3.

To provide the type-based characterization, an HFL formula is represented in the form of a sequence of fixpoint equations $(F_1 : \eta_1 =_{\alpha_1} \varphi_1; \cdots ; F_n : \eta_n =_{\alpha_n} \varphi_n)$, called a *hierarchical equation system* (HES). Here, for each $j \in \{1, \ldots, n\}$, F_j is a distinct variable, α_j is either μ or ν, and φ_j is a fixpoint-free HFL formula that has type η_j under the type environment $\{F_1 : \eta_1, \ldots, F_n : \eta_n\}$. We also require that if $\eta_j = \eta_{j,1} \to \cdots \to \eta_{j,\ell} \to \mathsf{o}$, then φ_j is of the form $\lambda X_1^{\eta_{j,1}} . \cdots \lambda X_\ell^{\eta_{j,\ell}} . \psi_j$, where ψ_j is a propositional formula that does not contain λ-abstractions. For each HES $\mathcal{E}$, we define a closed HFL formula $toHFL(\mathcal{E})$ inductively by:

$$toHFL(F : \eta =_\alpha \varphi) = \alpha F^\eta . \varphi$$
$$toHFL(\mathcal{E}; F : \eta =_\alpha \varphi) = toHFL([\alpha F^\eta . \varphi / F]\,\mathcal{E}),$$

where $[\varphi/X]\,\mathcal{E}$ denotes the HES obtained by replacing all free occurrences of the variable X in $\mathcal{E}$ with the formula φ. Any HFL formula can be transformed to an HES, and vice versa. For example, $\nu X. \mu Y. (\langle a \rangle X \vee \langle b \rangle Y)$ can be expressed as an HES: $X =_\nu Y; Y =_\mu \langle a \rangle X \vee \langle b \rangle Y$. We write $\mathcal{L} \models \mathcal{E}$ when $\mathcal{L} \models toHFL(\mathcal{E})$ holds.

Given an LTS $\mathcal{L} = (Q, \mathcal{A}, \longrightarrow, q_0)$, the set of *(refinement) types* for HFL formulas, ranged over by τ, is defined by:

$$\tau ::= q \mid \sigma \to \tau \qquad \sigma ::= \{\tau_1, \ldots, \tau_k\},$$

where q ranges over Q. Intuitively, q denotes the type of formulas that hold at state q. The type $\{\tau_1, \ldots, \tau_k\} \to \tau$ describes functions that take a value that has type τ_i for every $i \in \{1, \ldots, k\}$ as input, and return a value of type τ (thus, $\{\tau_1, \ldots, \tau_k\}$ is an intersection type). We often write $\top$ for $\emptyset$, and $\tau_1 \wedge \cdots \wedge \tau_k$ for $\{\tau_1, \ldots, \tau_k\}$. Henceforth, we just call τ and σ *types*, and call those ranged over by η *simple types* or *kinds*.

The *refinement relations* $\tau :: \eta$ and $\sigma :: \eta$, read "τ and σ are refinements of η", are inductively defined by:

$$\frac{q \in Q}{q :: \mathrm{o}} \qquad \frac{\forall \tau \in \sigma.\, \tau :: \eta}{\sigma :: \eta} \qquad \frac{\sigma :: \eta_1 \quad \tau :: \eta_2}{\sigma \to \tau :: \eta_1 \to \eta_2}$$

Henceforth, we consider only those that are refinements of simple types, excluding out ill-formed types like $\{q, q \to q\} \to q$.

A *type environment* Γ is a finite set of type bindings of the form $X : \tau$, where X is a variable and τ is a type. Note that Γ may contain more than one type binding for the same variable. We write $dom(\Gamma)$ for the set $\{X \mid \exists \tau.\, X : \tau \in \Gamma\}$ and $\Gamma(X)$ for the set $\{\tau \mid X : \tau \in \Gamma\}$. We also write $\{X : \sigma\}$ for the set $\{X : \tau_1, \ldots, X : \tau_k\}$ when $\sigma = \{\tau_1, \ldots, \tau_k\}$. The *type judgment relation* $\Gamma \vdash_{\mathcal{L}} \varphi : \tau$ for fixpoint-free formulas is defined by the typing rules in Fig. 2.

The typability of an HES $\mathcal{E}$ is defined through the *typability game* $\mathbf{TG}(\mathcal{L}, \mathcal{E})$, which is an instance of parity games [5].

Definition 1 (Typability Game). *Let $\mathcal{L} = (Q, \mathcal{A}, \longrightarrow, q_0)$ be an LTS and $\mathcal{E} = (F_1 : \eta_1 =_{\alpha_1} \varphi_1; \cdots; F_n : \eta_n =_{\alpha_n} \varphi_n)$ be an HES with $\eta_1 = \mathrm{o}$. The typability game $\mathbf{TG}(\mathcal{L}, \mathcal{E})$ is a quintuple $(V_0, V_1, v_0, E_0 \cup E_1, \Omega)$, where:*

- *$V_0 = \{F_j : \tau \mid j \in \{1, \ldots, n\}, \tau :: \eta_j\}$ is the set of all type bindings.*
- *$V_1 = \{\Gamma \mid \Gamma \subseteq V_0\}$ is the set of all type environments.*
- *$v_0 = F_1 : q_0 \in V_0$ is the initial position.*
- *$E_0 = \{(F_j : \tau, \Gamma) \in V_0 \times V_1 \mid \Gamma \vdash_{\mathcal{L}} \varphi_j : \tau\}$.*
- *$E_1 = \{(\Gamma, F_j : \tau) \in V_1 \times V_0 \mid F_j : \tau \in \Gamma\}$.*
- *$\Omega(F_j : \tau) = \Omega_j$ for each $F_j : \tau \in V_0$, where Ω_j is inductively defined by: $\Omega_n = 0$ if $\alpha_n = \nu$, $\Omega_n = 1$ if $\alpha_n = \mu$; and for $i < n$, $\Omega_i = \Omega_{i+1}$ if $\alpha_i = \alpha_{i+1}$, and $\Omega_i = \Omega_{i+1} + 1$ if $\alpha_i \neq \alpha_{i+1}$. In other words, Ω_i ($1 \leq i < n$) is the least even (odd, resp.) number no less than Ω_{i+1} if α_i is ν (μ, resp.).*
- *$\Omega(\Gamma) = 0$ for all $\Gamma \in V_1$.*

A typability game is a two-player game played by player 0 and player 1. The set of positions V_x belongs to player x. A play of a typability game is a sequence of positions $v_1 v_2 \ldots$ such that $(v_i, v_{i+1}) \in E_0 \cup E_1$ holds for each adjacent pair $v_i v_{i+1}$. A maximal finite play $v_1 v_2 \ldots v_k$ is won by player x iff $v_k \in V_{1-x}$, and an infinite play $v_1 v_2 \ldots$ is won by player x iff $\limsup_{i \to \infty} \Omega(v_i) = x \pmod{2}$. We

$$\frac{q \in Q}{\Gamma \vdash_{\mathcal{L}} \mathbf{true} : q} \ \text{(T-TRUE)} \qquad \frac{X : \tau \in \Gamma}{\Gamma \vdash_{\mathcal{L}} X : \tau} \ \text{(T-VAR)}$$

$$\frac{\Gamma \vdash_{\mathcal{L}} \varphi_i : q \ \text{for some} \ i \in \{1,2\}}{\Gamma \vdash_{\mathcal{L}} \varphi_1 \vee \varphi_2 : q} \ \text{(T-OR)} \qquad \frac{\Gamma \vdash_{\mathcal{L}} \varphi_i : q \ \text{for each} \ i \in \{1,2\}}{\Gamma \vdash_{\mathcal{L}} \varphi_1 \wedge \varphi_2 : q} \ \text{(T-AND)}$$

$$\frac{\Gamma \vdash_{\mathcal{L}} \varphi : q' \ \text{for some} \ q' \in Q \ \text{with} \ q \xrightarrow{a} q'}{\Gamma \vdash_{\mathcal{L}} \langle a \rangle \varphi : q} \ \text{(T-SOME)}$$

$$\frac{\Gamma \vdash_{\mathcal{L}} \varphi : q' \ \text{for each} \ q' \in Q \ \text{with} \ q \xrightarrow{a} q'}{\Gamma \vdash_{\mathcal{L}} [a] \varphi : q} \ \text{(T-ALL)}$$

$$\frac{\Gamma \cup \{X : \sigma\} \vdash_{\mathcal{L}} \varphi : \tau \quad X \notin dom(\Gamma) \quad \sigma :: \eta}{\Gamma \vdash_{\mathcal{L}} \lambda X^\eta . \varphi : \sigma \to \tau} \ \text{(T-ABS)}$$

$$\frac{\Gamma \vdash_{\mathcal{L}} \varphi_1 : \sigma \to \tau \quad \Gamma \vdash_{\mathcal{L}} \varphi_2 : \tau' \ \text{for each} \ \tau' \in \sigma}{\Gamma \vdash_{\mathcal{L}} \varphi_1 \, \varphi_2 : \tau} \ \text{(T-APP)}$$

$$\frac{\Gamma \vdash_{\mathcal{L}} \varphi : \tau \quad \tau \leq_{\mathcal{L}} \tau'}{\Gamma \vdash_{\mathcal{L}} \varphi : \tau'} \ \text{(T-SUB)} \qquad \frac{q \in Q}{q \leq_{\mathcal{L}} q} \ \text{(SUBT-BASE)}$$

$$\frac{\forall \tau' \in \sigma' . \exists \tau \in \sigma . \tau \leq_{\mathcal{L}} \tau'}{\sigma \leq_{\mathcal{L}} \sigma'} \ \text{(SUBT-INT)} \qquad \frac{\sigma' \leq_{\mathcal{L}} \sigma \quad \tau \leq_{\mathcal{L}} \tau'}{\sigma \to \tau \leq_{\mathcal{L}} \sigma' \to \tau'} \ \text{(SUBT-FUN)}$$

Fig. 2. Typing rules (where $\mathcal{L} = (Q, \mathcal{A}, \longrightarrow, q_0)$)

say a typability game is winning *if the initial position v_0 is a winning position for player 0, and call a winning strategy for her from v_0 simply a* winning strategy *of the game (such a strategy can be given as a partial function from V_0 to V_1).*

Intuitively, in the position $F_j : \tau$, player 0 is asked to show why F_j has type τ, by providing a type environment Γ under which the body φ_j of F_j has type τ. Player 1 then challenges player 0's assumption Γ, by picking a type binding $F' : \tau' \in \Gamma$ and asking why F' has type τ'. A play may continue indefinitely, in which case player 0 wins if the largest priority visited infinitely often is even.

The following characterization is the basis of our algorithm.

Theorem 1 ([10]). *Let $\mathcal{L}$ be an LTS and $\mathcal{E} = (F_1 : \eta_1 =_{\alpha_1} \varphi_1; \cdots; F_n : \eta_n =_{\alpha_n} \varphi_n)$ be an HES with $\eta_1 = \circ$. Then, $\mathcal{L} \models \mathcal{E}$ if and only if the typability game $\mathbf{TG}(\mathcal{L}, \mathcal{E})$ is winning.*

Example 3. Let $\mathcal{E}_{\mathbf{ex}}$ be the following HES:

$$S =_\nu \langle a \rangle (F (\langle b \rangle S)); \quad F =_\mu \lambda X^\circ . X \vee \langle c \rangle S \vee \langle a \rangle (F (\langle b \rangle X)).$$

It expresses the property that there is an infinite sequence that can be partitioned into chunks of the form $a^k b^k$ or $a^k c$ (where $k \geq 1$), like $a^3 b^3 a^2 c a^2 b^2 a^3 c \cdots$.

Let $\mathcal{L}_{\mathbf{ex}}$ be an LTS shown on the left side of Fig. 3. It satisfies the HES $\mathcal{E}_{\mathbf{ex}}$ as the sequence $abacabac \cdots$ is enabled at the initial state q_0. The corresponding typability game $\mathbf{TG}(\mathcal{L}_{\mathbf{ex}}, \mathcal{E}_{\mathbf{ex}})$ is defined as shown (partially) on the right side of Fig. 3, and a winning strategy (depicted by two-headed arrows) is witnessed by the type judgments $\{S : q_2, F : q_1 \to q_1\} \vdash_{\mathcal{L}_{\mathbf{ex}}} \varphi_S : q_0$, $\{F : \top \to q_0\} \vdash_{\mathcal{L}_{\mathbf{ex}}} \varphi_S : q_2$,

$\emptyset \vdash_{\mathcal{L}_{ex}} \varphi_F : q_1 \to q_1$, and $\{S : q_0\} \vdash_{\mathcal{L}_{ex}} \varphi_F : \top \to q_0$, where φ_S and φ_F denote the right-hand side formulas of the variables S and F, respectively.   □

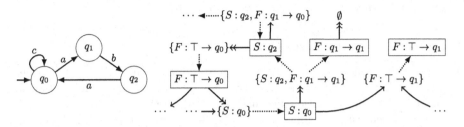

Fig. 3. LTS $\mathcal{L}_{ex}$ (on the left side) and a part of the corresponding typability game **TG**$(\mathcal{L}_{ex}, \mathcal{E}_{ex})$ (on the right side)

3   A Practical Algorithm for HFL Model Checking

We present our algorithm for HFL model checking in this section.

Theorem 1 immediately yields a naive model checking algorithm, which first constructs the typability game **TG**$(\mathcal{L}, \mathcal{E})$ (note that **TG**$(\mathcal{L}, \mathcal{E})$ is finite), and solves it by using an algorithm for parity game solving. Unfortunately, the algorithm does not work in practice, since the size of **TG**$(\mathcal{L}, \mathcal{E})$ is too large; it is k-fold exponential in the size of $\mathcal{L}$ and $\mathcal{E}$, for order-k HES.

The basic idea of our algorithm is to construct a subgame **TG**$'(\mathcal{L}, \mathcal{E})$ of **TG**$(\mathcal{L}, \mathcal{E})$, so that **TG**$'(\mathcal{L}, \mathcal{E})$ is winning if and only if the original game **TG**$(\mathcal{L}, \mathcal{E})$ is winning, and that **TG**$'(\mathcal{L}, \mathcal{E})$ is often significantly smaller than **TG**$(\mathcal{L}, \mathcal{E})$. The main question is of course how to construct such a subgame. Our approach is to consider a series of recursion-free[2] approximations $\mathcal{E}^{(0)}, \mathcal{E}^{(1)}, \mathcal{E}^{(2)}, \ldots$ of $\mathcal{E}$, which are obtained by unfolding fixpoint variables in $\mathcal{E}$ a certain number of times, and are free from fixpoint operators. The key observations are: (i) for sufficiently large m (that may depend on $\mathcal{L}$ and $\mathcal{E}$), $\mathcal{L} \models \mathcal{E}^{(m)}$ if and only if $\mathcal{L} \models \mathcal{E}$, (ii) for such m, a winning strategy for **TG**$(\mathcal{L}, \mathcal{E})$ can be constructed by using only the types used in a winning strategy for **TG**$(\mathcal{L}, \mathcal{E}^{(m)})$, and (iii) (a superset of) the types needed in a winning strategy for **TG**$(\mathcal{L}, \mathcal{E}^{(m)})$ can be computed effectively (and with reasonable efficiency for typical inputs), based on a method similar to saturation-based algorithms for HORS model checking [4,19]. (These observations are not trivial; they will be justified when we discuss the correctness of the algorithm in Sect. 4.)

---

[2] We say an HES is recursion-free if there is no cyclic dependency on fixpoint variables, so that fixpoint variables can be completely eliminated by unfolding them; we omit the formal definition.

In the rest of this section, we first explain more details about the intuitions behind our algorithm in Sect. 3.1.[3] We also introduce some definitions such as $\mathcal{E}^{(m)}$ during the course of explanation. These concepts are not directly used in the actual algorithm, but would help readers understand intuitions behind the algorithm. We then describe the algorithm in Sect. 3.2.

3.1   The Idea of the Algorithm

We first define a non-recursive HES as an approximation of $\mathcal{E}$. By the Kleene fixpoint theorem, we can approximate $\mathcal{E}$ by unfolding fixpoint variables finitely often, and the approximation becomes exact when the depth of unfolding is sufficiently large. Such an approximation can be naturally represented by a non-recursive HES $\mathcal{E}^{(m)}$ defined as follows.

Definition 2 (Non-Recursive HES $\mathcal{E}^{(m)}$). *Let $\mathcal{E} = (F_1 : \eta_1 =_{\alpha_1} \varphi_1; \cdots; F_n : \eta_n =_{\alpha_n} \varphi_n)$ be an HES and m be a positive integer. We define $\mathcal{E}^{(m)} = (F_1^{(m)} : \eta_1 =_{\alpha_1} \varphi_1^{(m)}; \cdots)$ as a non-recursive HES consisting of equations of the form $F_j^\beta : \eta_j =_{\alpha_j} \varphi_j^\beta$.[4] Here, $\beta = (\beta_1, \ldots, \beta_j)$ is a tuple of integers satisfying $0 \leq \beta_k \leq m$ for each $k \in \{1, \ldots, j\}$, and φ_j^β is an HFL formula defined by:*

$$\varphi_j^\beta = \begin{cases} \lambda X_1^{\eta_{j,1}}. \cdots \lambda X_\ell^{\eta_{j,\ell}}. \widehat{\alpha_j} & (\text{if } \beta_j = 0) \\ [F_1^{\beta(1)}/F_1, \ldots, F_n^{\beta(n)}/F_n]\, \varphi_j & (\text{if } \beta_j \neq 0). \end{cases}$$

Here, $\eta_j = \eta_{j,1} \to \cdots \to \eta_{j,\ell} \to \mathsf{o}$, $\widehat{\nu} = \mathtt{true}$, $\widehat{\mu} = \mathtt{false}$, and $\beta(k)$ is defined by:

$$\beta(k) = \begin{cases} (\beta_1, \ldots, \beta_k) & (\text{if } k < j) \\ (\beta_1, \ldots, \beta_j - 1, \underbrace{m, \ldots, m}_{(k-j)\,times}) & (\text{if } j \leq k). \end{cases}$$

We call the superscript β an index. *Intuitively, an index β indicates how many unfoldings are left to be done to obtain the formula represented by $\mathcal{E}^{(m)}$.*

Example 4. Recall the HES $\mathcal{E}_{\mathsf{ex}}$ in Example 3:

$$S =_\nu \langle a \rangle (F (\langle b \rangle S)); \quad F =_\mu \lambda X^\mathsf{o}. X \vee \langle c \rangle S \vee \langle a \rangle (F (\langle b \rangle X)).$$

Then, a finite approximation $\mathcal{E}_{\mathsf{ex}}^{(1)}$ is:

$$S^{(1)} =_\nu \langle a \rangle (F^{(0,1)} (\langle b \rangle S^{(0)})); \; S^{(0)} =_\nu \mathtt{true};$$
$$F^{(0,1)} =_\mu \lambda X^\mathsf{o}. X \vee \langle c \rangle S^{(0)} \vee \langle a \rangle (F^{(0,0)} (\langle b \rangle X)); \; F^{(0,0)} =_\mu \lambda X^\mathsf{o}.\mathtt{false};$$
$$F^{(1,1)} =_\mu \lambda X^\mathsf{o}. X \vee \langle c \rangle S^{(1)} \vee \langle a \rangle (F^{(1,0)} (\langle b \rangle X)); \; F^{(1,0)} =_\mu \lambda X^\mathsf{o}.\mathtt{false}.$$

□

---

[3] Those intuitions may not be clear for non-expert readers. In such a case, readers may safely skip the subsection (except the definitions) and proceed to Sect. 3.2.

[4] Since $\mathcal{E}^{(m)}$ does not contain recursion, the order of equations (other than the first one) does not matter.

For $\mathcal{E}^{(m)}$, its validity can be checked by "unfolding" all the fixpoint variables. The operation of unfolding is formally expressed by the following rewriting relation.

Definition 3 (Rewriting Relation on HFL formulas). *Let* $\mathcal{E} = (F_1 : \eta_1 =_{\alpha_1} \varphi_1; \cdots; F_n : \eta_n =_{\alpha_n} \varphi_n)$ *be an HES. The rewriting relation* $\longrightarrow_{\mathcal{E}}$ *is defined by the rule:*

$$C[F_j \chi_1 \cdots \chi_\ell] \longrightarrow_{\mathcal{E}} C[[\chi_1/X_1, \ldots, \chi_\ell/X_\ell] \psi_j] \text{ if } \varphi_j = \lambda X_1. \cdots \lambda X_\ell. \psi_j.$$

Here, C ranges over the set of contexts defined by:

$$C ::= [\,] \mid C \vee \chi \mid \chi \vee C \mid C \wedge \chi \mid \chi \wedge C \mid \langle a \rangle C \mid [a] C,$$

and $C[\chi]$ denotes the formula obtained from C by replacing $[\,]$ with χ. We write $\longrightarrow_{\mathcal{E}}^*$ for the reflexive transitive closure of the relation $\longrightarrow_{\mathcal{E}}$.

Note that the relation $\longrightarrow_{\mathcal{E}}$ preserves simple types and the semantics of formulas. By the strong normalization property of the simply-typed λ-calculus, if the HES $\mathcal{E}$ does not contain recursion, it is strongly-normalizing. Thus, for $\mathcal{E}^{(m)}$, the initial variable $F_1^{(m)}$ (which is assumed to have type o) can be rewritten to a formula χ without any fixpoint variables, such that an LTS $\mathcal{L}$ satisfies χ if and only if $\mathcal{L}$ satisfies $\mathcal{E}^{(m)}$ (and for sufficiently large m, if and only if $\mathcal{L}$ satisfies $\mathcal{E}$). Furthermore, if the initial state q_0 of $\mathcal{L}$ satisfies χ, then from the reduction sequence:

$$F_1^{(m)} = \chi_0 \longrightarrow_{\mathcal{E}^{(m)}} \chi_1 \longrightarrow_{\mathcal{E}^{(m)}} \cdots \longrightarrow_{\mathcal{E}^{(m)}} \chi_{m'} = \chi,$$

one can compute a series of type environments $\Gamma_{m'} = \emptyset, \Gamma_{m'-1}, \ldots, \Gamma_1, \Gamma_0 = \{F_1^{(m)} : q_0\}$ such that $\Gamma_i \vdash_{\mathcal{L}} \chi_i : q_0$ in a backward manner, by using the standard subject expansion property of intersection type systems (i.e., the property that typing is preserved by backward reductions) [3]. These type environments provide sufficient type information, so that a winning strategy for the typability game $\mathbf{TG}(\mathcal{L}, \mathcal{E}^{(m)})$ can be expressed only by using type bindings in $\Gamma^{(m)} = \Gamma_{m'} \cup \cdots \cup \Gamma_0$. If m is sufficiently large, by using the same type bindings (but ignoring indices), we can also express a winning strategy for $\mathbf{TG}(\mathcal{L}, \mathcal{E})$. Thus, if we can compute (a possible overapproximation of) $\Gamma^{(m)}$ above, we can restrict the game $\mathbf{TG}(\mathcal{L}, \mathcal{E})$ to the subgame $\mathbf{TG}'(\mathcal{L}, \mathcal{E})$ consisting of only types occurring in $\Gamma^{(m)}$, without changing the winner.

The remaining issue is how to compute an overapproximation of $\Gamma^{(m)}$. It is unreasonable to compute it directly based on the definition above, as the "sufficiently large" m is huge in general, and the number m' of reduction steps may also be too large. Instead, we relax the rewriting relation $\longrightarrow_{\mathcal{E}}$ for the original HES $\mathcal{E}$ by adding the following rules:

$$C[F_j \chi_1 \cdots \chi_\ell] \longrightarrow'_{\mathcal{E}} \begin{cases} C[\mathtt{true}] & \text{if } \alpha_j = \nu \\ C[\mathtt{false}] & \text{if } \alpha_j = \mu. \end{cases}$$

The resulting relation $\longrightarrow'_{\mathcal{E}}$ simulates $\longrightarrow_{\mathcal{E}^{(m)}}$ for arbitrary m, in the sense that for any reduction sequence:

$$F_1^{(m)} = \chi_0 \longrightarrow_{\mathcal{E}^{(m)}} \chi_1 \longrightarrow_{\mathcal{E}^{(m)}} \cdots \longrightarrow_{\mathcal{E}^{(m)}} \chi_{m'} = \chi,$$

there exists a corresponding reduction sequence:

$$F_1 = \chi_0' \longrightarrow_{\mathcal{E}}' \chi_1' \longrightarrow_{\mathcal{E}}' \cdots \longrightarrow_{\mathcal{E}}' \chi_{m'}' = \chi,$$

where each χ_i' is the formula obtained by removing indices from χ_i. Thus, to compute $\Gamma^{(m)}$, it suffices to compute type environments for χ_i''s, based on the subject expansion property. We can do so by using the function $\mathcal{F}_{\mathcal{L},\mathcal{E}}$ defined below, without explicitly constructing reduction sequences.

Definition 4 (Backward Expansion Function $\mathcal{F}_{\mathcal{L},\mathcal{E}}$). *Let $\mathcal{L}$ be an LTS, and $\mathcal{E} = (F_1 : \eta_1 =_{\alpha_1} \varphi_1; \cdots; F_n : \eta_n =_{\alpha_n} \varphi_n)$ be an HES. Let $T_{\mathcal{E}}$ denote the set of all type environments for the fixpoint variables of $\mathcal{E}$, that is, $T_{\mathcal{E}} = \{\Gamma \mid dom(\Gamma) \subseteq \{F_1, \ldots, F_n\}, \forall F_j : \tau \in \Gamma . \tau :: \eta_j\}$. The function $\mathcal{F}_{\mathcal{L},\mathcal{E}} : T_{\mathcal{E}} \to T_{\mathcal{E}}$ is a monotonic function defined by:*

$$
\begin{aligned}
\mathcal{F}_{\mathcal{L},\mathcal{E}}(\Gamma) = \Gamma \cup \{\, F_j : \tau \mid\ & \tau :: \eta_j \\
& \varphi_j = \lambda X_1. \cdots \lambda X_\ell. \psi_j, \\
& \tau = \sigma_1 \to \cdots \to \sigma_\ell \to q, \\
& \exists \Delta.\ dom(\Delta) \subseteq FV(\psi_j) \cap \{X_1, \ldots, X_\ell\}, \\
& \Gamma \cup \Delta \vdash_{\mathcal{L}} \psi_j : q,\ \forall k \in \{1, \ldots, \ell\}.\ \sigma_k = \Delta(X_k), \\
& \forall X_i \in dom(\Delta).\ \exists \varphi \in Flow_{\mathcal{E}}(X_i). \forall \tau' \in \Delta(X_i).\ \Gamma \vdash_{\mathcal{L}} \varphi : \tau' \,\}.
\end{aligned}
$$

Here, $Flow_{\mathcal{E}}(X_i)$ denotes the set $\{\, \xi_i \mid F_1 \longrightarrow_{\mathcal{E}}^* C[F\, \xi_1 \cdots \xi_\ell] \,\}$, where X_i is the i-th formal parameter of F (i.e., the equation of F is of the form $F =_\alpha \lambda X_1. \cdots \lambda X_\ell. \psi$).[5]

The following lemma justifies the definition of $\mathcal{F}_{\mathcal{L},\mathcal{E}}$ (see [6] for a proof). It states that the function $\mathcal{F}_{\mathcal{L},\mathcal{E}}$ expands type environments in such a way that we can go backwards through the rewriting relation $\longrightarrow_{\mathcal{E}}$ without losing the typability.

Lemma 1. *If $F_1 \longrightarrow_{\mathcal{E}}^* \varphi \longrightarrow_{\mathcal{E}} \varphi'$ and $\Gamma \vdash_{\mathcal{L}} \varphi' : q$, then $\mathcal{F}_{\mathcal{L},\mathcal{E}}(\Gamma) \vdash_{\mathcal{L}} \varphi : q$.*

Let Γ_0 be the set of strongest type bindings (with respect to subtyping) for the ν-variables of $\mathcal{E}$, that is, $\Gamma_0 = \{F_j : \tau \mid \alpha_j = \nu,\ \tau :: \eta_j,\ \tau = \top \to \cdots \to \top \to q\}$. The following lemma states that, if we are allowed to use the strongest type bindings contained in Γ_0, then we can also go backwards through the relaxed rewriting relation $\longrightarrow_{\mathcal{E}}'$ using the same function $\mathcal{F}_{\mathcal{L},\mathcal{E}}$.

Lemma 2. *If $F_1 \longrightarrow_{\mathcal{E}}'^* \varphi \longrightarrow_{\mathcal{E}}' \varphi'$, $\Gamma \vdash_{\mathcal{L}} \varphi':q$, and $\Gamma \supseteq \Gamma_0$, then $\mathcal{F}_{\mathcal{L},\mathcal{E}}(\Gamma) \vdash_{\mathcal{L}} \varphi:q$.*

Let us write $(\mathcal{F}_{\mathcal{L},\mathcal{E}})^\omega(\Gamma_0)$ for $\bigcup_{i \in \omega}(\mathcal{F}_{\mathcal{L},\mathcal{E}})^i(\Gamma_0)$. As an immediate corollary of Lemma 2, we have: if $F_1 = \chi_0' \longrightarrow_{\mathcal{E}}' \chi_1' \longrightarrow_{\mathcal{E}}' \cdots \longrightarrow_{\mathcal{E}}' \chi_{m'}' = \chi$ and $\emptyset \vdash_{\mathcal{L}} \chi : q_0$, then $(\mathcal{F}_{\mathcal{L},\mathcal{E}})^\omega(\Gamma_0) \vdash_{\mathcal{L}} \chi_i' : q_0$ for every i. Thus, $(\mathcal{F}_{\mathcal{L},\mathcal{E}})^\omega(\Gamma_0)$ serves as an overapproximation of $\Gamma^{(m)}$ mentioned above.

---

[5] Without loss of generality, we assume that $X_1, \ldots, X_\ell$ are distinct from each other and do not occur in the other equations.

Algorithm 1. The proposed HFL model checking algorithm

$\Gamma := \Gamma_0$
while $\Gamma \neq \mathcal{F}'_{\mathcal{L},\mathcal{E}}(\Gamma)$ **do**
$\quad \Gamma := \mathcal{F}'_{\mathcal{L},\mathcal{E}}(\Gamma)$
end while
return whether the subgame $\mathbf{SG}(\mathcal{L}, \mathcal{E}, \Gamma)$ is winning

---

3.2 The Algorithm

Based on the intuitions explained in Sect. 3.1, we propose the algorithm shown in Algorithm 1.

In the algorithm, the function $\mathcal{F}'_{\mathcal{L},\mathcal{E}}$ is an overapproximation of the function $\mathcal{F}_{\mathcal{L},\mathcal{E}}$, obtained by replacing $Flow_{\mathcal{E}}$ in the definition of $\mathcal{F}_{\mathcal{L},\mathcal{E}}$ with an overapproximation $Flow'_{\mathcal{E}}$ satisfying $\forall X.\, Flow_{\mathcal{E}}(X) \subseteq Flow'_{\mathcal{E}}(X)$. This is because it is in general too costly to compute the exact flow set $Flow_{\mathcal{E}}(X)$. The overapproximation $Flow'_{\mathcal{E}}$ can typically be computed by flow analysis algorithms for functional programs, such as 0-CFA [18]. The first four lines compute $\bigcup_{i\in\omega}(\mathcal{F}'_{\mathcal{L},\mathcal{E}})^i(\Gamma_0)$, which is an overapproximation of $\bigcup_{i\in\omega}(\mathcal{F}_{\mathcal{L},\mathcal{E}})^i(\Gamma_0)$ discussed in the previous subsection.

$\mathbf{SG}(\mathcal{L}, \mathcal{E}, \Gamma)$ on the last line denotes the subgame of $\mathbf{TG}(\mathcal{L}, \mathcal{E})$, obtained by restricting the game arena. It is defined as follows.

Definition 5 (Subgame). *Let* $\mathcal{L} = (Q, \mathcal{A}, \longrightarrow, q_0)$ *be an LTS,* $\mathcal{E} = (F_1 : \eta_1 =_{\alpha_1} \varphi_1; \cdots; F_n : \eta_n =_{\alpha_n} \varphi_n)$ *be an HES with* $\eta_1 = \mathsf{o}$, *and* $\Gamma \in \mathcal{T}_{\mathcal{E}}$ *be a type environment for* $\mathcal{E}$. *The subgame* $\mathbf{SG}(\mathcal{L}, \mathcal{E}, \Gamma)$ *is a parity game defined the same as* $\mathbf{TG}(\mathcal{L}, \mathcal{E})$ *except that the set of positions is restricted to the subsets of* Γ. *That is, for* $\mathbf{TG}(\mathcal{L}, \mathcal{E}) = (V'_0, V'_1, v'_0, E'_0 \cup E'_1, \Omega')$, $\mathbf{SG}(\mathcal{L}, \mathcal{E}, \Gamma)$ *is the parity game* $(V_0, V_1, v_0, E_0 \cup E_1, \Omega)$, *where:*

- $V_0 = \Gamma \cup \{v'_0\}$, $V_1 = \{\Gamma' \mid \Gamma' \subseteq \Gamma\}$,
  $v_0 = v'_0$, $E_0 = E'_0 \cap (V_0 \times V_1)$, $E_1 = E'_1 \cap (V_1 \times V_0)$.
- Ω *is the restriction of* Ω' *to* $V_0 \cup V_1$.

The following theorem claims the correctness of the algorithm.

Theorem 2 (Correctness). *Let* $\mathcal{L}$ *be an LTS and* $\mathcal{E} = (F_1 : \eta_1 =_{\alpha_1} \varphi_1; \cdots; F_n : \eta_n =_{\alpha_n} \varphi_n)$ *be an HES with* $\eta_1 = \mathsf{o}$. *Algorithm 1 terminates. Furthermore, it returns "yes" if and only if* $\mathcal{L} \models \mathcal{E}$.

Example 5. Recall the HES $\mathcal{E}_{\mathsf{ex}}$ and the LTS $\mathcal{L}_{\mathsf{ex}}$ in Example 3. The fixpoint computation from the initial type environment $\Gamma_0 = \{S : q_0,\ S : q_1,\ S : q_2\}$ by the function $\mathcal{F}_{\mathcal{L}_{\mathsf{ex}}, \mathcal{E}_{\mathsf{ex}}}$ (with a few simple optimizations)[6] proceeds as shown in Table 1. Note that the flow set $Flow_{\mathcal{E}_{\mathsf{ex}}}(X)$ for the formal parameter X of the fixpoint variable F is calculated as $\{\langle b \rangle S, \langle b \rangle \langle b \rangle S, \ldots\}$, and thus the only candidates for

---

[6] Using subtyping relations, we can refrain from unnecessary type derivations like $\{S : q_0, X : q_1\} \vdash_{\mathcal{L}_{\mathsf{ex}}} \psi_F : q_0$ in this example. See [6] for more details.

the type environment Δ in the algorithm are $\Delta = \emptyset$ and $\Delta = \{X : q_1\}$. The expansion reaches the fixpoint after two iterations,[7] and the algorithm returns "yes" as the resulting type environment contains sufficient type bindings to construct the winning strategy depicted in Fig. 3 of Example 3.   □

Table 1. Fixpoint computation by the function $\mathcal{F}_{\mathcal{L}_{ex}, \mathcal{E}_{ex}}$

Iteration number k	Type environment Γ_k	Newly derivable type judgments
0	$\{S : q_0, \, S : q_1, \, S : q_2\}$	$\{X : q_1\} \vdash_{\mathcal{L}_{ex}} \psi_F : q_1$ $\{S : q_0\} \vdash_{\mathcal{L}_{ex}} \psi_F : q_0$
1	$\Gamma_0 \cup \{F : q_1 \to q_1, \, F : \top \to q_0\}$	$\{F : \top \to q_0\} \vdash_{\mathcal{L}_{ex}} \psi_F : q_2$
2	$\Gamma_1 \cup \{F : \top \to q_2\}$	-

4   Correctness of the Algorithm

We sketch a proof of Theorem 2 in this section. A more detailed proof is found in [6]. We discuss soundness and completeness (Theorems 3 and 4 below) separately, from which Theorem 2 follows.

4.1   Soundness of the Algorithm

The soundness of the algorithm follows immediately from the fact that the replacement of $\mathbf{TG}(\mathcal{L}, \mathcal{E})$ with the subgame $\mathbf{SG}(\mathcal{L}, \mathcal{E}, \Gamma)$ restricts only the moves of player 0, so that the resulting game is harder for her to win.

Theorem 3 (Soundness). *Let $\mathcal{L}$ be an LTS and $\mathcal{E} = (F_1 : \eta_1 =_{\alpha_1} \varphi_1; \cdots; F_n : \eta_n =_{\alpha_n} \varphi_n)$ be an HES with $\eta_1 = \mathsf{o}$. If $\mathcal{L} \nvDash \mathcal{E}$, then the algorithm returns "no", that is, the subgame $\mathbf{SG}(\mathcal{L}, \mathcal{E}, (\mathcal{F}'_{\mathcal{L}, \mathcal{E}})^\omega(\Gamma_0))$ is not winning.*

Proof. We show the contraposition. Suppose that $\mathbf{SG}(\mathcal{L}, \mathcal{E}, (\mathcal{F}'_{\mathcal{L}, \mathcal{E}})^\omega(\Gamma_0))$ is a winning game. Then, there exists a winning strategy ς of player 0 for the node $F_1 : q_0$ in that game. This strategy ς also gives a winning strategy of player 0 for the node $F_1 : q_0$ in the original typability game $\mathbf{TG}(\mathcal{L}, \mathcal{E})$; note that for each position $\Gamma \in V_1$ of $\mathbf{SG}(\mathcal{L}, \mathcal{E}, (\mathcal{F}'_{\mathcal{L}, \mathcal{E}})^\omega(\Gamma_0))$, the set of possible moves of player 1 in $\mathbf{TG}(\mathcal{L}, \mathcal{E})$ is the same as that in $\mathbf{SG}(\mathcal{L}, \mathcal{E}, (\mathcal{F}'_{\mathcal{L}, \mathcal{E}})^\omega(\Gamma_0))$. Therefore, $\mathcal{L} \models \mathcal{E}$ follows from Theorem 1.   □

---

[7] Actually, our prototype model checker reported in Sect. 5 does not derive the type binding $F : \top \to q_2$, and thus the computation terminates in one iteration. This is because it uses information of types in flow analysis, which reveals that it does not affect the result whether formulas of the form $F \varphi$ have type q_2. See [6] for details.

4.2   Completeness of the Algorithm

The completeness of the algorithm is stated as Theorem 4 below.

Theorem 4 (Completeness). *Let $\mathcal{L}$ be an LTS and $\mathcal{E} = (F_1 : \eta_1 =_{\alpha_1} \varphi_1; \cdots;$ $F_n : \eta_n =_{\alpha_n} \varphi_n)$ be an HES with $\eta_1 = \circ$. If $\mathcal{L} \models \mathcal{E}$, then the algorithm returns "yes", that is, the subgame $\mathbf{SG}(\mathcal{L}, \mathcal{E}, (\mathcal{F}'_{\mathcal{L},\mathcal{E}})^\omega(\Gamma_0))$ is winning.*

The proof follows the intuitions provided in Sect. 3.1. Given a type environment Γ for $\mathcal{E}^{(m)}$, we write $Forget(\Gamma)$ for the type environment obtained by removing all the indices from Γ. Theorem 4 follows immediately from Lemmas 3 and 4 below.

Lemma 3. *If the typability game $\mathbf{TG}(\mathcal{L}, \mathcal{E})$ is winning, then for sufficiently large m, the subgame $\mathbf{SG}(\mathcal{L}, \mathcal{E}, Forget((\mathcal{F}_{\mathcal{L},\mathcal{E}^{(m)}})^\omega(\emptyset)))$ is also winning.*

Lemma 4. *$Forget((\mathcal{F}_{\mathcal{L},\mathcal{E}^{(m)}})^\omega(\emptyset))) \subseteq (\mathcal{F}_{\mathcal{L},\mathcal{E}})^\omega(\Gamma_0)$.*

Note that Lemma 4 implies that the game $\mathbf{SG}(\mathcal{L}, \mathcal{E}, (\mathcal{F}'_{\mathcal{L},\mathcal{E}})^\omega(\Gamma_0))$ is more advantageous for player 0 than the game $\mathbf{SG}(\mathcal{L}, \mathcal{E}, Forget((\mathcal{F}_{\mathcal{L},\mathcal{E}^{(m)}})^\omega(\emptyset)))$, which is winning when $\mathcal{L} \models \mathcal{E}$ by Lemma 3.

Lemma 4 should be fairly obvious, based on the intuitions given in Sect. 3.1. Technically, it suffices to show that $F_j^\beta : \tau \in (\mathcal{F}_{\mathcal{L},\mathcal{E}^{(m)}})^i(\emptyset)$ implies $F_j : \tau \in (\mathcal{F}_{\mathcal{L},\mathcal{E}})^i(\Gamma_0)$ by induction on i, with case analysis on β_j. If $\beta_j = 0$, then $\alpha_j = \nu$ and the body of F_j^β is $\lambda \widetilde{X}.\mathtt{true}$. Thus, $F_j : \tau = F_j : \top \rightarrow \cdots \rightarrow \top \rightarrow q \in \Gamma_0 \subseteq (\mathcal{F}_{\mathcal{L},\mathcal{E}})^i(\Gamma_0)$. If $\beta_j > 0$, then the body of F_j^β is the same as that of F_j except indices. Thus, $F_j : \tau \in (\mathcal{F}_{\mathcal{L},\mathcal{E}})^i(\Gamma_0)$ follows from the induction hypothesis and the definition of the function $\mathcal{F}_{\mathcal{L},\mathcal{E}}$. See [6] for details.

To prove Lemma 3, we define another function $Regress$ on type environments. Let $\preceq_k$ be the lexicographic ordering on the first k elements of tuples of integers, and $\prec_k$ be its strict version. We write $\beta_1 =_k \beta_2$ if $\beta_1 \preceq_k \beta_2$ and $\beta_2 \preceq_k \beta_1$. For example, $(1,2) =_0 (1,2,3)$, $(1,2) =_1 (1,2,3)$, $(1,2) =_2 (1,2,3)$, and $(1,2) \prec_3 (1,2,3)$. Note that indices β combined with the order $\preceq_k$ can be used to witness a winning strategy of a parity game through a proper assignment of them (a *parity progress measure* [7]) to positions of the game. The function $Regress$ is defined as follows.

Definition 6 (Function $Regress$). *First, we define Γ_μ^β and Γ_ν^β for a type environment Γ for $\mathcal{E}^{(m)}$ and an index β of length j by:*

$$\Gamma_\mu^\beta = \{F_{j'} : \tau \mid \exists F_{j'}^{\beta'} : \tau \in \Gamma. \beta' \prec_j \beta\}$$
$$\Gamma_\nu^\beta = \{F_{j'} : \tau \mid \exists F_{j'}^{\beta'} : \tau \in \Gamma. \beta' \preceq_{j-1} \beta\},$$

that is, Γ_μ^β is a type environment for the original HES $\mathcal{E}$ consisting of all type bindings in Γ with indices "smaller" than β (the meaning of "smaller" depends on the fixpoint operator α). Using this Γ_α^β, we define $Regress$ as a monotonic function on type environments for $\mathcal{E}^{(m)}$ by:

$$Regress(\Gamma) = \{F_j^\beta : \tau \in \Gamma \mid \Gamma_{\alpha_j}^\beta \vdash_{\mathcal{L}} \varphi_j : \tau\},$$

that is, $Regress(\Gamma)$ consists of all $F_j^\beta : \tau \in \Gamma$ such that the right-hand side formula φ_j of F_j in the original HES $\mathcal{E}$ has type τ under the type environment $\Gamma_{\alpha_j}^\beta$.

Note that *Regress* is a monotonic function on a finite domain. We write $Regress^\omega(\Gamma)$ for $\bigcap_{i \in \omega} Regress^i(\Gamma)$, which is the greatest Γ' such that $\Gamma' \subseteq \Gamma$ and $Regress(\Gamma') = \Gamma'$. Lemma 3 follows immediately from the following two lemmas (Lemmas 5 and 6).

Lemma 5. *If $\Gamma \subseteq (\mathcal{F}_{\mathcal{L},\mathcal{E}^{(m)}})^\omega(\emptyset)$ is a fixpoint of Regress, then $Forget(\Gamma)$ is a subset of the winning region of player 0 for $\mathbf{SG}(\mathcal{L},\mathcal{E},Forget((\mathcal{F}_{\mathcal{L},\mathcal{E}^{(m)}})^\omega(\emptyset)))$.*

This is intuitively because, for each $F_j : \tau \in Forget(\Gamma)$, we can find $F_j^\beta : \tau \in \Gamma$ such that choosing $\Gamma_{\alpha_j}^\beta$ at $F_j : \tau$ gives a winning strategy for player 0. Now it remains to show:

Lemma 6. *If the typability game $\mathbf{TG}(\mathcal{L},\mathcal{E})$ is winning, then for sufficiently large m, $F_1 : q_0 \in Forget(Regress^\omega((\mathcal{F}_{\mathcal{L},\mathcal{E}^{(m)}})^\omega(\emptyset)))$.*

We prepare a few further definitions and lemmas. Let $\Gamma_\omega^{(m)}$ be $(\mathcal{F}_{\mathcal{L},\mathcal{E}^{(m)}})^\omega(\emptyset)$ and $\Gamma_\omega'^{(m)}$ be $Regress^\omega(\Gamma_\omega^{(m)})$. For each $k = 1, 2, \ldots$, we define D_k as the set of type bindings removed by the k-th application of *Regress* to $\Gamma_\omega^{(m)}$, that is, $D_k = Regress^{k-1}(\Gamma_\omega^{(m)}) \backslash Regress^k(\Gamma_\omega^{(m)})$.

Lemma 7. *If $F_j^\beta : \tau \in D_k$ and $\beta_j = 0$, then $\alpha_j = \nu$.*

Lemma 8. *If $F_j^\beta : \tau \in D_k$ and $\beta_j \neq 0$, then there exists k' satisfying $1 \leq k' < k$ such that $F_{j'}^{\beta(j')} : \tau' \in D_{k'}$ holds for some j' and τ'.*

We are now ready to prove Lemma 6.

Proof of Lemma 6. We show the lemma by contradiction. Since the typability game $\mathbf{TG}(\mathcal{L},\mathcal{E})$ is winning, we have $F_1^{(m)} : q_0 \in \Gamma_\omega^{(m)}$ for sufficiently large m (this is intuitively because $\mathbf{TG}(\mathcal{L},\mathcal{E}^{(m)})$ is also winning; see [6] for a formal proof). Suppose it were the case that $F_1^{(m)} : q_0 \notin \Gamma_\omega'^{(m)}$. Then there must be a positive integer k such that $F_1^{(m)} : q_0 \in D_k$. Therefore, by Lemma 8, there exists a sequence of type bindings $F_1^{(m)} : q_0 = F_{j_0}^{\beta_0} : \tau_0, F_{j_1}^{\beta_1} : \tau_1, \ldots, F_{j_\ell}^{\beta_\ell} : \tau_\ell$ such that (i) β_ℓ ends with 0, and (ii) $\beta_i = \beta_{i-1}(j_i)$ and $F_{j_i}^{\beta_i} : \tau_i \in D_{k_i}$ hold for each $i \in \{1, \ldots, \ell\}$, where $k = k_0 > k_1 > \cdots > k_\ell$. Moreover, we have $\alpha_{j_\ell} = \nu$ by Lemma 7. Let $\beta_\ell = (\beta_1, \ldots, \beta_{j_\ell - 1}, 0)$. Then, $(\beta_1, \ldots, \beta_{j_\ell - 1}, m)$, $(\beta_1, \ldots, \beta_{j_\ell - 1}, m - 1)$, $\ldots$, and $(\beta_1, \ldots, \beta_{j_\ell - 1}, 1)$ must exist in the sequence $\beta_0, \beta_1, \ldots, \beta_{\ell-1}$ in this order (see [6] for a proof).

For each $i \in \{0, \ldots, m\}$, let ℓ_i be the integer with $\beta_{\ell_i} = (\beta_1, \ldots, \beta_{j_\ell - 1}, i)$. Since the number of intersection types τ' satisfying $\tau' :: \eta_{j_\ell}$ is finite, there must exist duplicate types in the sequence $\tau_{\ell_0}, \tau_{\ell_1}, \ldots, \tau_{\ell_m}$ for sufficiently large m. Let τ_{ℓ_a} and τ_{ℓ_b} be such a pair with $\ell_a < \ell_b$. Then, we have $F_{j_\ell}^{\beta_{\ell_a}} : \tau_{\ell_a} \in D_{k_{\ell_a}}$ and $F_{j_\ell}^{\beta_{\ell_b}} : \tau_{\ell_b} \in D_{k_{\ell_b}}$. However, since $\alpha_{j_\ell} = \nu$ and $\beta_{\ell_a} =_{j_\ell - 1} \beta_{\ell_b}$, we have

$\Gamma_{\alpha_{j\ell}}^{\beta_{\ell_a}} = \Gamma_{\alpha_{j\ell}}^{\beta_{\ell_b}}$ for any Γ. Therefore, by the definition of the function *Regress* and the assumption $\tau_{\ell_a} = \tau_{\ell_b}$, the type bindings $F_{j\ell}^{\beta_{\ell_a}} : \tau_{\ell_a}$ and $F_{j\ell}^{\beta_{\ell_b}} : \tau_{\ell_b}$ must be removed by *Regress* at the same time. This contradicts the assumption $\ell_a < \ell_b$. Therefore, $F_1^{(m)} : q_0 \in \Gamma_\omega'^{(m)}$ holds for sufficiently large m.   □

5   Implementation and Experiments

We have implemented a prototype HFL model checker HOMUSAT[8] based on the algorithm discussed in Sect. 3. As mentioned in footnotes in Sect. 3, some optimization techniques are used to improve the performance of HOMUSAT. See [6] for an explanation on these optimizations.

We have carried out experiments to evaluate the efficiency of HOMUSAT. As benchmark problems, we used HORS model checking problems used as benchmarks for HORS model checkers TRAVMC2 [15], HORSATP [19], and HORSAT2 [9]. These benchmarks include many typical instances of higher-order model checking, such as the ones obtained from program verification problems. They were converted to HFL model checking problems via the translation by Kobayashi et al. [10]. The resulting set of benchmarks consists of 136 problems of orders up to 8. Whereas the LTS size is moderate (around 10) for most of the instances, there are several instances with large state sets (including those with $|Q| > 100$). HES sizes vary from less than 100 to around 10,000; note that in applications to higher-order program verification [11,21], the size of an HES corresponds to the size of a program to be verified. As to the number of alternations between μ and ν within the HES, over half of the instances (83 out of 136) have no alternation (that is, they are μ-only or ν-only), but there are a certain number of instances that have one or more alternations, up to a maximum of 4. The experiments were conducted on a machine with 2.3 GHz Intel Core i5 processor and 8 GB memory. As a reference, we have compared the result with HORSATP, one of the state-of-the-art HORS model checkers,[9] run for the original problems.

The results are shown in Figs. 4 and 5. Figure 4 compares the running times of HOMUSAT with those of HORSATP. As the figure shows, HOMUSAT often outperforms HORSATP. Although it is not that this result indicates the proposed algorithm is superior as a higher-order model checking algorithm to HORSATP (the two model checkers differ in the degree of optimization),[10] the fact that HOMUSAT works fast for various problems obtained via the mechanical conversion from HORS to HFL, which increases the size of inputs and thus makes

---

[8] The source code and the benchmark problems used in the experiments are available at https://github.com/hopv/homusat.

[9] For the restricted class of properties expressed by trivial automata, HORSAT2 is the state-of-the-art.

[10] Actually, as the two algorithms are both based on type-based saturation algorithm [4], various type-oriented optimization techniques used in HOMUSAT can also be adapted to HORSATP and are expected to improve its performance.

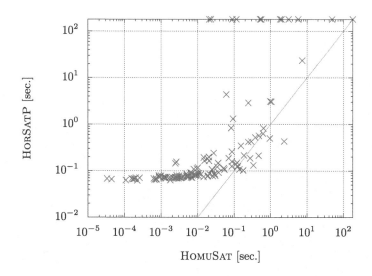

Fig. 4. The experimental results: comparison with HorSatP (timeout = 180 s)

them harder to solve, is promising. Evaluation of the efficiency of the proposed algorithm against a set of problems obtained directly as HFL model checking problems is left for future work.

Figure 5 shows the distribution of the running times of HomuSat with respect to the input HES size. As the figure shows, despite the k-EXPTIME worst-case complexity, the actual running times do not grow so rapidly. This is partially explained by the fact that the time complexity of HFL model checking is fixed-parameter polynomial in the size of HES [10].

6   Related Work

The logic HFL has been introduced by Viswanathan and Viswanathan [20]. Later, Lange and his colleagues studied its various theoretical properties [1,2, 12]. In particular, they have shown that HFL model checking is k-EXPTIME complete for order k HFL formulas. There has been, however, no practical HFL model checker. Lozes has implemented a prototype HFL model checker, but it is restricted to order-1 HFL, and scales only for LTS of size up to 10 or so [13].

Our algorithm is based on the type-based characterization of HFL model checking [10], and type-based saturation algorithms for HORS model checking [4, 19]. In particular, the idea of restricting the arena of the typability game follows that of Suzuki et al. [19]. The detail of the algorithms are however different; in particular, the initial type environment in Suzuki et al. [19] contains $F : \top \to \cdots \to \top \to q$ for any recursive function F, whereas in our algorithm, Γ_0 contains $F : \top \to \cdots \to \top \to q$ only for fixpoint variables bound by ν. The use of a smaller initial type environment may be one of the reasons why our model checker tends to outperform theirs even for HORS model checking problems. Another difference

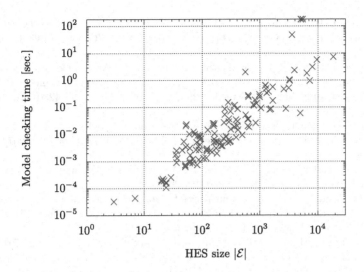

Fig. 5. HES size $|\mathcal{E}|$ versus time required for model checking (timeout = 180 s)

is in the correctness proofs. In our opinion, our proof is significantly simpler and streamlined than theirs. Their proof manipulates infinite derivation trees. In contrast, our proof is a natural generalization of the correctness proof for the restricted fragment of HORS model checking (which corresponds to the μ-only or ν-only fragment of HFL model checking) [4], using the standard concept of parity progress measures.

7   Conclusion

We have proposed the first practical algorithm for HFL model checking, and proved its correctness. We have confirmed through experiments that, despite the huge worst-case complexity, our prototype HFL model checker runs fast for typical instances of higher-order model checking.

Acknowledgments. We would like to thank anonymous referees for useful comments. This work was supported by JSPS KAKENHI Grant Number JP15H05706.

References

1. Axelsson, R., Lange, M.: Model checking the first-order fragment of higher-order fixpoint logic. In: Dershowitz, N., Voronkov, A. (eds.) LPAR 2007. LNCS (LNAI), vol. 4790, pp. 62–76. Springer, Heidelberg (2007). https://doi.org/10.1007/978-3-540-75560-9_7
2. Axelsson, R., Lange, M., Somla, R.: The complexity of model checking higher-order fixpoint logic. Logical Methods Comput. Sci. **3**(2:7), 1–33 (2007). https://doi.org/10.2168/LMCS-3(2:7)2007

3. Barendregt, H., Statman, R., Dekkers, W.: Lambda Calculus with Types. Cambridge University Press (2013). https://doi.org/10.1017/CBO9781139032636

4. Broadbent, C., Kobayashi, N.: Saturation-based model checking of higher-order recursion schemes. In: Proceedings of the 22nd EACSL Annual Conference on Computer Science Logic (CSL 2013). LIPIcs, vol. 23, pp. 129–148. Schloss Dagstuhl-Leibniz-Zentrum fuer Informatik (2013). https://doi.org/10.4230/LIPIcs.CSL.2013.129

5. Grädel, E., Thomas, W., Wilke, T. (eds.): Automata Logics, and Infinite Games. LNCS, vol. 2500. Springer, Heidelberg (2002). https://doi.org/10.1007/3-540-36387-4

6. Hosoi, Y., Kobayashi, N., Tsukada, T.: A type-based HFL model checking algorithm. arXiv e-prints arXiv:1908.10416 (2019)

7. Jurdziński, M.: Small progress measures for solving parity games. In: Reichel, H., Tison, S. (eds.) STACS 2000. LNCS, vol. 1770, pp. 290–301. Springer, Heidelberg (2000). https://doi.org/10.1007/3-540-46541-3_24

8. Kobayashi, N.: Model-checking higher-order functions. In: Proceedings of the 11th ACM SIGPLAN Conference on Principles and Practice of Declarative Programming (PPDP 2009), pp. 25–36. ACM (2009). https://doi.org/10.1145/1599410.1599415

9. Kobayashi, N.: HorSat2: a model checker for HORS based on SATuration (2015). https://github.com/hopv/horsat2

10. Kobayashi, N., Lozes, E., Bruse, F.: On the relationship between higher-order recursion schemes and higher-order fixpoint logic. In: Proceedings of the 44th ACM SIGPLAN Symposium on Principles of Programming Languages (POPL 2017), pp. 246–259. ACM (2017). https://doi.org/10.1145/3009837.3009854

11. Kobayashi, N., Tsukada, T., Watanabe, K.: Higher-order program verification via HFL model checking. In: Ahmed, A. (ed.) ESOP 2018. LNCS, vol. 10801, pp. 711–738. Springer, Cham (2018). https://doi.org/10.1007/978-3-319-89884-1_25

12. Lange, M., Lozes, É., Guzmán, M.V.: Model-checking process equivalences. Theoret. Comput. Sci. **560**, 326–347 (2014). https://doi.org/10.1016/j.tcs.2014.08.020

13. Lozes, É.: Personal communication

14. Lozes, É.: A type-directed negation elimination. In: Proceedings of the 10th International Workshop on Fixed Points in Computer Science (FICS 2015). EPTCS, vol. 191, pp. 132–142 (2015). https://doi.org/10.4204/EPTCS.191.12

15. Neatherway, R.P., Ong, C.H.L.: TravMC2: higher-order model checking for alternating parity tree automata. In: Proceedings of the 2014 International SPIN Symposium on Model Checking of Software (SPIN 2014), pp. 129–132. ACM (2014). https://doi.org/10.1145/2632362.2632381

16. Ong, C.H.L.: On model-checking trees generated by higher-order recursion schemes. In: Proceedings of the 21st Annual IEEE Symposium on Logic in Computer Science (LICS 2006), pp. 81–90. IEEE Computer Society (2006). https://doi.org/10.1109/LICS.2006.38

17. Ramsay, S.J., Neatherway, R.P., Ong, C.H.L.: A type-directed abstraction refinement approach to higher-order model checking. In: Proceedings of the 41st ACM SIGPLAN-SIGACT Symposium on Principles of Programming Languages (POPL 2014), pp. 61–72. ACM (2014). https://doi.org/10.1145/2535838.2535873

18. Shivers, O.: Control-flow analysis of higher-order languages. Ph.D. thesis, Carnegie-Mellon University (1991)

19. Suzuki, R., Fujima, K., Kobayashi, N., Tsukada, T.: Streett automata model checking of higher-order recursion schemes. In: Proceedings of the 2nd International Conference on Formal Structures for Computation and Deduction (FSCD 2017). LIPIcs, vol. 84, pp. 32:1–32:18. Schloss Dagstuhl-Leibniz-Zentrum fuer Informatik (2017). https://doi.org/10.4230/LIPIcs.FSCD.2017.32
20. Viswanathan, M., Viswanathan, R.: A higher order modal fixed point logic. In: Gardner, P., Yoshida, N. (eds.) CONCUR 2004. LNCS, vol. 3170, pp. 512–528. Springer, Heidelberg (2004). https://doi.org/10.1007/978-3-540-28644-8_33
21. Watanabe, K., Tsukada, T., Oshikawa, H., Kobayashi, N.: Reduction from branching-time property verification of higher-order programs to HFL validity checking. In: Proceedings of the 2019 ACM SIGPLAN Workshop on Partial Evaluation and Program Manipulation (PEPM 2019), pp. 22–34. ACM (2019). https://doi.org/10.1145/3294032.3294077

Semantics

Factorization and Normalization, Essentially

Beniamino Accattoli[1], Claudia Faggian[2], and Giulio Guerrieri[3(✉)] ⓘ

[1] Inria & LIX, École Polytechnique, UMR 7161, Palaiseau, France
beniamino.accattoli@inria.fr
[2] Université de Paris, IRIF, CNRS, 75013 Paris, France
faggian@irif.fr
[3] Department of Computer Science, University of Bath, Bath, UK
g.guerrieri@bath.ac.uk

Abstract. λ-calculi come with no fixed evaluation strategy. Different strategies may then be considered, and it is important that they satisfy some abstract rewriting property, such as factorization or normalization theorems. In this paper we provide simple proof techniques for these theorems. Our starting point is a revisitation of Takahashi's technique to prove factorization for head reduction. Our technique is both simpler and more powerful, as it works in cases where Takahashi's does not. We then pair factorization with two other abstract properties, defining *essential systems*, and show that normalization follows. Concretely, we apply the technique to four case studies, two classic ones, head and the leftmost-outermost reductions, and two less classic ones, non-deterministic weak call-by-value and least-level reductions.

1 Introduction

The λ-calculus is the model underlying functional programming languages and proof assistants. The gap between the model and its incarnations is huge. In particular, the λ-calculus does not come with a fixed reduction strategy, while concrete frameworks need one. A desirable property is that the reduction which is implemented terminates on all terms on which β reduction has a reduction sequence to normal form. This is guaranteed by a *normalization theorem*. Two classic examples are the *leftmost-outermost* and *head* normalization theorems (theorems 13.2.2 and 11.4.8 in Barendregt [4]). The former states that if the term has a β-normal form, leftmost-outermost reduction is guaranteed to find it; the latter has a similar but subtler statement, roughly head reduction computes a head normal form, if the term has any.

Another classic theorem for head reduction states that head reduction approximates the β-normal form by computing an essential part of every evaluation sequence. The precise formulation is a *factorization theorem*: a sequence of β steps $t \rightarrow^*_\beta s$ can always be re-arranged as a sequence of head steps ($\rightarrow_h$) followed by a sequence of non-head steps ($\rightarrow_{\neg h}$), that is, $t \rightarrow^*_h u \rightarrow^*_{\neg h} s$. Both head

© Springer Nature Switzerland AG 2019
A. W. Lin (Ed.): APLAS 2019, LNCS 11893, pp. 159–180, 2019.
https://doi.org/10.1007/978-3-030-34175-6_9

and leftmost-outermost reductions play a key role in the theory of the λ-calculus as presented in Barendregt [4] or Krivine [16].

Variants of the λ-calculus abound and are continuously introduced: weak, call-by-value, call-by-need, classical, with pattern matching, sharing, non-determinism, probabilistic choice, quantum features, differentiation, *etc.* So, normalization and factorization theorems need to be studied in many variations. Concepts and techniques to prove these theorems do exist, but they do not have the essential, intuitive structure of other fundamental properties, such as confluence.

This Paper. Here we provide a presentation of factorization and normalization revisiting a simple technique due to Takahashi [28], making it even *simpler* and *more widely applicable.* We separate the abstract reasoning from the concrete details of head reduction, and apply the revisited proof method to several case studies. The presentation is novel and hopefully accessible to anyone familiar with the λ-calculus, without a background in advanced notions of rewriting theory.

We provide four case studies, all following the same method. Two are revisitations of the classic cases of head and leftmost-outermost (shortened to ℓo) reductions. Two are folklore cases. The first is *weak* (*i.e.* out of λ-abstractions) *call-by-value* (shortened to CbV) *reduction* in its non-deterministic presentation. The second is *least-level* (shortened to $\ell\ell$) *reduction*, a reduction coming from the linear logic literature—sometimes called *by levels*—and which is usually presented using proof nets (see de Carvalho, Pagani and Tortora de Falco [6] or Pagani and Tranquilli [24]) or calculi related to proof nets (see Terui [30] or Accattoli [1]), rather than in the ordinary λ-calculus. The ℓo and $\ell\ell$ cases are *full* reductions for β, *i.e.* they have the same normal forms as β. The head and weak CbV cases are not full, as they may not compute β normal forms.

Takahashi. In [28], Takahashi uses the natural inductive notion of *parallel*[1] β reduction (which reduces simultaneously a number of β-redexes; it is also the key concept in Tait and Martin-Löf's classic proof of confluence of the λ-calculus) to introduce a simple proof technique for head factorization, from which head normalization follows. By iterating head factorization, she also obtains leftmost-outermost normalization, via a simple argument on the structure of terms due to Mitschke [19].

Her technique has been employed for various λ-calculi because of its simplicity. Namely, for the λ-calculus with η by Ishii [13], the call-by-value λ-calculus by Ronchi Della Rocca and Paolini [25,27], the resource λ-calculus by Pagani and Tranquilli [23], pattern calculi by Kesner, Lombardi and Ríos [14], the shuffling calculus by Guerrieri, Paolini and Ronchi Della Rocca [8–10], and it has been formalized with proof assistants by McKinna and Pollack [17] and Crary [7].

---

[1] The terminology at work in the literature on λ-calculus and the rewriting terminology often clash: the former calls *parallel β reduction* what the latter calls *multi-step β reduction*—parallel reduction in rewriting is something else.

Takahashi Revisited. Despite its simplicity, Takahashi's proof [28] of factorization relies on substitutivity properties not satisfied by full reductions such as ℓo and $\ell\ell$. Our first contribution is a proof that is independent of the substitutivity properties of the factorizing reductions. It relies on a simpler fact, namely the substitutivity of an *indexed* variant $\overset{n}{\Rightarrow}_\beta$ of parallel β reduction $\Rightarrow_\beta$. The definition of $\overset{n}{\Rightarrow}_\beta$ simply decorates the definition of $\Rightarrow_\beta$ with a natural number n that intuitively corresponds to the number of redexes reduced in parallel by a $\Rightarrow_\beta$ step.

We prove factorization theorems for all our four case studies following this simpler scheme. We also highlight an interesting point: factorization for the two full reductions cannot be obtained directly following Takahashi's method[2].

From Factorization to Essential Normalization. The second main contribution of our paper is the isolation of abstract properties that together with factorization imply normalization. First of all we abstract head reduction into a generic reduction $\to_e$, called *essential*, and non-head reduction $\to_{\neg h}$ into a *non-essential* reduction $\to_{\neg e}$. The first additional property for normalization is *persistence*: steps of the factoring reduction $\to_e$ cannot be erased by the factored out $\to_{\neg e}$. The second one is a relaxed form of determinism for $\to_e$. We show that in such *essential* rewriting systems $\to_e$ has a normalization theorem. The argument is abstract, that is, independent of the specific nature of terms. This is in contrast to how Takahashi [28] obtains normalization from factorization: her proof is based on an induction over the structure of terms, and cannot then be disentangled by the concrete nature of the rewriting system under study.

Normalizing Reductions for β. We apply both our techniques to our case studies of full reduction: ℓo and $\ell\ell$, obtaining simple proofs that they are normalizing reductions for β. Let us point out that ℓo is also—at present—the only known deterministic reduction to β normal form whose number of steps is a reasonable cost model, as shown by Accattoli and Dal Lago [2]. Understanding its normalization is one of the motivations at the inception of this work.

Normalization with Respect to Different Notions of Results. As a further feature, our approach provides for free normalization theorems for reductions that are not full for the rewrite system in which they live. Typical examples are head and weak CbV reductions, which do not compute β and CbV normal forms, respectively. These normalization theorems arise naturally in the theory of the λ-calculus. For instance, functional programming languages implement only weak notions of reduction, and head reduction (rather than ℓo) is the key notion for the λ-definability of computable functions.

We obtain normalization theorems for head and weak CbV reductions. Catching normalization for non-full reductions sets our work apart from the recent studies on normalization by Hirokawa, Middeldorp, and Moser [12] and Van Oostrom and Toyama [22], discussed below among related works.

---

[2] It can be obtained indirectly, as a corollary of standardization, proved by Takahashi [28] using the concrete structure of terms. Thus the proof is not of an abstract nature.

Factorization, Normalization, Standardization. In the literature of the λ-calculus, normalization for ℓo reduction is often obtained as a corollary of the standardization theorem, which roughly states that every reduction sequence can be reorganized as to reduce redexes according to the left-to-right order (Terese [29] following Klop [15] and Barendregt [4], for instance). Standardization is a complex and technical result. Takahashi [28], using Mitschke's argument [19] that iterates head factorization, obtains a simpler proof technique for ℓo normalization—and for standardization as well. Our work refines that approach, abstracts from it and shows that factorization is a general technique for normalization.

Related Work. Factorization is studied in the abstract in [1,18]. Melliès axiomatic approach [18] builds on standardization, and encompasses a wide class of rewriting systems; in particular, like us, he can deal with non-full reductions. Accattoli [1] relies crucially on terminating hypotheses, absent instead here.

Hirokawa, Middeldorp, and Moser [12] and Van Oostrom and Toyama [22] study normalizing strategies via a clean separation between abstract and term rewriting results. Our approach to normalization is similar to the one used in [12] to study ℓo evaluation for first-order term rewriting systems. Our essential systems strictly generalize their conditions: uniform termination replaces determinism (two of the strategies we present here are not deterministic) and—crucially—persistence strictly generalizes the property in their Lemma 7. Conversely, they focus on hyper-normalization and on extending the method to systems in which left-normality is relaxed. We do not deal with these aspects. Van Oostrom and Toyama's study [22] of (hyper-)normalization is based on an elegant and powerful method based on the random descent property and an ordered notion of commutative diagrams. Their method and ours are incomparable: we do not rely on (and do not assume) the random descent property (for its definition and uses see van Oostrom [21])—even if most strategies naturally have that property—and we do focus on factorization (which they explicitly avoid), since we see it as the crucial tool from which normalization can be obtained.

As already pointed out, a fundamental difference with respect to both works is that we consider a more general notion of normalization for reductions that are not full, that is not captured by either of those approaches.

In the literature, normalization is also proved from iterated head factorization (Takahashi [28] for ℓo, and Terui [30] or Accattoli [1] for ℓℓ on proof nets-like calculi, or Pagani and Tranquilli [24] for ℓℓ on differential proof nets), or as a corollary of standardization (Terese [29] following Klop [15] and Barendregt [4] for ℓo), or using semantic principles such as intersection types (Krivine [16] for ℓo and de Carvalho, Pagani and Tortora de Falco [6] for ℓℓ on proof nets). Last, Bonelli *et al.* develop a sophisticated proof of normalization for a λ-calculus with powerful pattern matching in [5]. Our technique differs from them all.

Proofs. Omitted proofs are available online in [3], the long version of this paper.

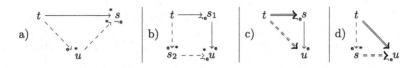

Fig. 1. Diagrams: (a) factorization, (b) weak postponement, (c) merge, (d) split.

2   Factorization and Normalization, Abstractly

In this section, we study factorization and normalization abstractly, that is, independently of the specific structure of the objects to be rewritten.

A *rewriting system* (aka abstract reduction system, see Terese [29, Ch. 1]) S is a pair $(S, \rightarrow)$ consisting of a set S and a binary relation $\rightarrow \subseteq S \times S$ called *reduction*, whose pairs are written $t \rightarrow s$ and called $\rightarrow$-*steps*. A $\rightarrow$-*sequence* from t is a sequence $t \rightarrow s \rightarrow \dots$ of $\rightarrow$-steps; $t \rightarrow^k s$ denotes a sequence of k $\rightarrow$-steps from t to s. As usual, $\rightarrow^*$ (resp. $\rightarrow^=$) denotes the transitive-reflexive (resp. reflexive) closure of $\rightarrow$. Given two reductions $\rightarrow_1$ and $\rightarrow_2$ we use $\rightarrow_1 \cdot \rightarrow_2$ for their composition, defined as $t \rightarrow_1 \cdot \rightarrow_2 s$ if $t \rightarrow_1 u \rightarrow_2 s$ for some u.

In this section we focus on a given sub-reduction $\rightarrow_e$ of $\rightarrow$, called *essential*, for which we study factorization and normalization with respect to $\rightarrow$. It comes with a second sub-reduction $\rightarrow_{\neg e}$, called *inessential*, such that $\rightarrow_e \cup \rightarrow_{\neg e} = \rightarrow$. Despite the notation, $\rightarrow_e$ and $\rightarrow_{\neg e}$ are not required to be disjoint. In general, we write $(S, \{\rightarrow_a, \rightarrow_b\})$ for the rewriting system $(S, \rightarrow)$ where $\rightarrow = \rightarrow_a \cup \rightarrow_b$.

2.1   Factorization

A rewriting system $(S, \{\rightarrow_e, \rightarrow_{\neg e}\})$ satisfies $\rightarrow_e$-*factorization* (also called *postponement of $\rightarrow_{\neg e}$ after $\rightarrow_e$*) if $t \rightarrow^* s$ implies that there exists u such that $t \rightarrow_e^* u \rightarrow_{\neg e}^* s$. Compactly, we write $\rightarrow^* \subseteq \rightarrow_e^* \cdot \rightarrow_{\neg e}^*$. In diagrams, see Fig. 1a.

Proving Factorization. Factorization is a non-trivial rewriting property, because it is *global*, that is, quantified over all reduction sequences from a term. To be able to prove factorization, we would like to reduce it to *local* properties, *i.e.* properties quantified only over one-step reductions from a term. At first sight it may seem that a local diagram such as the one in Fig. 1b would give factorization by a simple induction. Such a diagram however does not allow to infer factorization without further hypotheses—counterexamples can be found in Barendregt [4].

The following abstract property is a special case for which a local condition implies factorization. It was first observed by Hindley [11].

Lemma 1 (Hindley, local postponement). *Let $(S, \{\rightarrow_e, \rightarrow_{\neg e}\})$ be a rewriting system. If $\rightarrow_{\neg e} \cdot \rightarrow_e \subseteq \rightarrow_e^* \cdot \rightarrow_{\neg e}^=$ then $\rightarrow^* \subseteq \rightarrow_e^* \cdot \rightarrow_{\neg e}^*$.*

Proof. The assumption $\to_{\neg e} \cdot \to_e \,\subseteq\, \to_e^* \cdot \to_{\neg e}^=$ implies (#) $\to_{\neg e} \cdot \to_e^* \,\subseteq\, \to_e^* \cdot \to_{\neg e}^=$ (indeed, it is immediate to prove that $\to_{\neg e} \cdot \to_e^k \,\subseteq\, \to_e^* \cdot \to_{\neg e}^=$ by induction on k).

We then prove that $\to^k \,\subseteq\, \to_e^* \cdot \to_{\neg e}^*$, by induction on k. The case $k = 0$ is trivial. Assume $\to \cdot \to^{k-1}$. By *i.h.*, $\to \cdot \to_e^* \cdot \to_{\neg e}^*$. If the first step is $\to_e$, the claim is proved. Otherwise, by (#), from $(\to_{\neg e} \cdot \to_e^*) \cdot \to_{\neg e}^*$ we obtain $(\to_e^* \cdot \to_{\neg e}^=) \cdot \to_{\neg e}^*$. $\qquad\square$

Hindley's local condition is a strong hypothesis for factorization that in general does not hold in λ-calculi—not even in the simple case of head reduction. However, the property can be applied in combination with another standard technique: switching to *macro* steps that compress $\to_e^*$ or $\to_{\neg e}^*$ into just one step, at the price of some light overhead. This idea is the essence of both Tait–Martin-Löf's and Takahashi's techniques, based on *parallel steps*. The role of parallel steps in Takahashi [28] is here captured abstractly by the notion of macro-step system.

Definition 2 (Macro-step system). *A rewriting system $\mathcal{S} = (S, \{\to_e, \to_{\neg e}\})$ is a* macro-step system *if there are two reductions $\Rightarrow$ and $\Rightarrow_{\neg e}$ (called* macro-steps *and* inessential macro-steps, *respectively) such that*

- Macro: $\to_{\neg e} \,\subseteq\, \Rightarrow_{\neg e} \,\subseteq\, \to_{\neg e}^*$.
- Merge: *if $t \Rightarrow_{\neg e} \cdot \to_e u$ then $t \Rightarrow u$. That is, the diagram in Fig. 1c holds.*
- Split: *if $t \Rightarrow u$ then $t \to_e^* \cdot \Rightarrow_{\neg e} u$. That is, the diagram in Fig. 1d holds.*

Note that $\Rightarrow$ just plays the role of a "bridge" between the hypothesis of the merge condition and the conclusion of the split condition—it shall play a crucial role in the concrete proofs in the next sections. In this paper, concrete instances of $\Rightarrow$ and $\Rightarrow_{\neg e}$ shall be parallel β reduction and some of its variants.

Proposition 3 (Factorization). *Every macro-step system $(S, \{\to_e, \to_{\neg e}\})$ satisfies $\to_e$-factorization.*

Proof. By Merge and Split, $\Rightarrow_{\neg e} \cdot \to_e \,\subseteq\, \Rightarrow \,\subseteq\, \to_e^* \cdot \Rightarrow_{\neg e} \,\subseteq\, \to_e^* \cdot \Rightarrow_{\neg e}^=$. By Hindley's lemma (Lemma 1) applied to $\to_e$ and $\Rightarrow_{\neg e}$ (rather than $\to_e$ and $\to_{\neg e}$), we obtain $(\to_e \cup \Rightarrow_{\neg e})^* \,\subseteq\, \to_e^* \cdot \Rightarrow_{\neg e}^*$. Since $\to_{\neg e} \,\subseteq\, \Rightarrow_{\neg e}$, we have $(\to_e \cup \to_{\neg e})^* \,\subseteq\, (\to_e \cup \Rightarrow_{\neg e})^* \,\subseteq\, \to_e^* \cdot \Rightarrow_{\neg e}^*$. As $\Rightarrow_{\neg e} \,\subseteq\, \to_{\neg e}^*$, we have $\to_e^* \cdot \Rightarrow_{\neg e}^* \,\subseteq\, \to_e^* \cdot \to_{\neg e}^*$. Therefore, $\to^* = (\to_e \cup \to_{\neg e})^* \,\subseteq\, \to_e^* \cdot \to_{\neg e}^*$. $\qquad\square$

2.2 Normalization for full reductions

The interest of factorization comes from the fact that the essential reduction $\to_e$ on which factorization pivots has some good properties. Here we pinpoint the abstract properties which make factorization a privileged method to prove normalization; we collect them into the definition of *essential system* (Definition 5).

Normal Forms and Normalization. Let us recall what normalization is about. In general, a term may or may not reduce to a normal form. And if it does, not all reduction sequences necessarily lead to normal form. A term is *weakly* or *strongly normalizing*, depending on if it may or must reduce to normal form. If a term t is strongly normalizing, any choice of steps will eventually lead to a normal form. However, if t is weakly normalizing, how do we compute a normal form? This is the problem tackled by *normalization*: by repeatedly performing *only specific steps*, a normal form will be computed, provided that t can reduce to any.

Recall the statement of the ℓo normalization theorem: if $t \to_\beta^* u$ with u β-normal, then t ℓo-reduces to u. Observe a subtlety: such a formulation relies on the determinism of ℓo reduction. We give a more general formulation of normalizing reduction, valid also for non-deterministic reductions.

Formally, given a rewriting system $(S, \to)$, a term $t \in S$ is:

- $\to$-*normal* (or in $\to$-*normal form*) if $t \not\to$, *i.e.* there are no s such that $t \to s$;
- *weakly* $\to$-*normalizing* if *there exists* a sequence $t \to^* s$ with s $\to$-normal;
- *strongly* $\to$-*normalizing* if there are no infinite $\to$-sequences from t, or equivalently, if *all* maximal $\to$-sequences from t are finite.

We call *reduction for* $\to$ any $\to_e \subseteq \to$. It is *full* if $\to_e$ and $\to$ have the same normal forms.[3]

Definition 4 (Normalizing reduction). *A full reduction $\to_e$ for $\to$ is normalizing (for $\to$) if, for every term t, t is strongly $\to_e$-normalizing whenever it is weakly $\to$-normalizing.*

Note that, since the normalizing reduction $\to_e$ is full, if t is strongly $\to_e$-normalizing then *every* maximal $\to_e$-sequence from t ends in a $\to$-normal form.

Definition 5 (Essential system). *A rewriting system $(S, \{\to_e, \to_{\neg e}\})$ is essential if the following conditions hold:*

1. *Persistence: if $t \to_e s$ and $t \to_{\neg e} u$, then $u \to_e r$ for some r.*
2. *Uniform termination: if t is weakly $\to_e$-normalizing, then it is strongly $\to_e$-normalizing.*
3. *Terminal factorization: if $t \to^* u$ and u is $\to_e$-normal, then $t \to_e^* \cdot \to_{\neg e}^* u$.*

It is moreover full if $\to_e$ is a full reduction for $\to$.

Comments on the definition:

- *Persistence*: it means that essential steps are out of reach for inessential steps, that cannot erase them. The only way of getting rid of essential steps is by reducing them, and so in that sense they are *essential* to normalization.

---

[3] In rewriting theory, a *full reduction for* $\to$ is called a *reduction strategy for* $\to$. We prefer not to use the term strategy because it has different meaning in the λ-calculus, where it is a *deterministic, not necessarily full,* reduction for $\to$.

- *From determinism to uniform termination*: as we already said, in general $\to_e$ is not deterministic. For normalization, then, it is not enough that there is a sequence $t \to_e^* u$ with $u \to$-normal (as in the statement of ℓo-normalization). We need to be sure that there are no infinite $\to_e$-sequences from t. This is exactly what is ensured by the uniform termination property. Note that if $\to_e$ is deterministic (or has the diamond or random descent properties) then it is uniformly terminating.
- *Terminal factorization*: there are two subtleties. First, we need only a weak form of factorization, namely factorization is only required for $\to$-sequences ending in a $\to_e$-normal form[4]. Second, the reader may expect terminal factorization to be required with respect to $\to$-normal rather than $\to_e$-normal forms. The two notions coincide if $\to_e$ is full, and for the time being we only discuss full essential systems. We discuss the more general case in Sect. 2.3.

Example 6. In the λ-calculus with β reduction, head reduction $\to_h$ and its associated $\to_{\neg h}$ reduction (defined in Sect. 4) form an essential system. Similarly, leftmost-outermost $\to_{\ell o}$ reduction and its associated $\to_{\neg \ell o}$ reduction (Sect. 7) form a full essential system. Two more examples are in Sects. 6 and 8.

Theorem 7 (Essential full normalization). *Let $(S, \{\to_e, \to_{\neg e}\})$ be a full essential system. Then $\to_e$ is a normalizing reduction for $\to$.*

Proof. Let t be a weakly $\to$-normalizing term, *i.e.* $t \to^* u$ for some term u in $\to$-normal form (and so in $\to_e$-normal form, since $\to_e \subseteq \to$).

1. *Terminal factorization* implies $t \to_e^* s \to_{\neg e}^* u$ for some s, since u is $\to_e$-normal.
2. Let us show that s is $\to_e$-normal: if not, then $s \to_e r$ for some r, and a straightforward induction on the length of $s \to_{\neg e}^* u$ iterating *persistence* gives that $u \to_e p$ for some p, against the hypothesis that u is $\to_e$-normal. Absurd.
3. By the previous point, t is weakly $\to_e$-normalizing. By *uniform termination*, t is strongly $\to_e$-normalizing. $\qquad\qquad\qquad\qquad\qquad\qquad\qquad\qquad\Box$

2.3 A More General Notion of Normalizing reduction.

Essential systems actually encompass also important notions of normalization for reductions that are *not full*, such as *head normalization*. These cases arise naturally in the λ-calculus literature, where partial notions of result such as head normal forms or values are of common use. Normalization for non-full reductions is instead not so common in the rewriting literature outside the λ-calculus. This is why, to guide the reader, we presented first the natural case of full reductions.

---

[4] The difference between factorization and its terminal case is relevant for normalization: van Oostrom and Toyama [22, footnote 8] give an example of normalizing full reduction for a rewriting system in which factorization fails but terminal factorization holds.

Let us first discuss head reduction: $\rightarrow_h$ is deterministic and not full with respect to $\rightarrow_\beta$, as its normal forms may not be $\rightarrow_\beta$-normal forms. The well-known property of interest is *head normalization* (Cor. 11.4.8 in Barendregt's book [4]):

If $t \rightarrow^*_\beta s$ and s is head normal then $\rightarrow_h$ terminates on t.

The statement has two subtleties[5]. First, t may $\rightarrow_\beta$-reduce to a term in $\rightarrow_h$-normal form in many different ways, possibly without using $\rightarrow_h$, so that the hypotheses may not imply that $\rightarrow_h$ terminates. Second, the conclusion is "$\rightarrow_h$ *terminates on* t" and not $t \rightarrow^*_h s$, because in general the maximal $\rightarrow_h$-sequence from t may end in a term $u \neq s$. For instance, let $I = \lambda y.y$: then $I(x(II)) \rightarrow_\beta I(xI) \rightarrow_\beta xI$ is a $\rightarrow_\beta$-sequence to head normal form, and yet the maximal $\rightarrow_h$-sequence $I(x(II)) \rightarrow_h x(II)$ ends in a different term.

Now, let us abstract from head normalization, taking into account that in general the essential reduction $\rightarrow_e$—unlike head reduction—may not be deterministic, and so we ask for strong $\rightarrow_e$-normalization rather than for $\rightarrow_e$-termination.

Theorem 8 (Essential normalization). *Let $(S, \{\rightarrow_e, \rightarrow_{\neg e}\})$ be an essential system. If $t \rightarrow^* u$ and u is $\rightarrow_e$-normal, then t is strongly $\rightarrow_e$-normalizing.*

Proof. Exactly as for Theorem 7, fullness is not used in that proof.   □

In the next section we shall apply Theorem 8 to head reduction and obtain the head normalization theorem we started with. Another example of a normalization theorem for a non-full reduction is in Sect. 6. Note that the full variant of the theorem (Theorem 7) is in fact an instance of the general one (Theorem 8).

3   The λ-Calculus

This short section recalls basic definitions and properties of the λ-calculus and introduces the indexed variant of parallel β.

The set Λ of *terms* of the λ-calculus is given by the following grammar:

$$\text{TERMS} \quad t, s, u, r ::= x \mid \lambda x.t \mid ts$$

We use the usual notions of free and bound variables, $t\{x \leftarrow s\}$ for the meta-level capture-avoiding substitution of s for the free occurrences of x in t, and $|t|_x$ for the number of free occurrences of x in t. The definition of β reduction $\rightarrow_\beta$ is:

$$\beta \text{ REDUCTION}$$

$$\frac{}{(\lambda x.t)s \rightarrow_\beta t\{x \leftarrow s\}} \qquad \frac{t \rightarrow_\beta t'}{ts \rightarrow_\beta t's} \qquad \frac{t \rightarrow_\beta t'}{\lambda x.t \rightarrow_\beta \lambda x.t'} \qquad \frac{t \rightarrow_\beta t'}{st \rightarrow_\beta st'}$$

Let us recall two basic substitutivity properties of β reduction.

---

[5] "t has a head normal form" is the usual formulation for "$t \rightarrow^*_\beta s$ for some s that is head normal". We prefer the latter to avoid the ambiguity of the former about the reduction leading from t to one of its head normal forms ($\rightarrow^*_\beta$ or $\rightarrow^*_h$?).

1. *Left substitutivity of* $\to_\beta$: if $t \to_\beta t'$ then $t\{x \leftarrow s\} \to_\beta t'\{x \leftarrow s\}$.
2. *Right substitutivity of* $\to_\beta$: if $s \to_\beta s'$ then $t\{x \leftarrow s\} \to_\beta^* t\{x \leftarrow s'\}$. It is possible to spell out the number of $\to_\beta$-steps, which is exactly the number of free occurrences of x in t, that is, $t\{x \leftarrow s\} \to_\beta^{|t|_x} t\{x \leftarrow s'\}$.

Parallel β reduction. Parallel β-reduction $\Rightarrow_\beta$ is defined by:

PARALLEL β REDUCTION

$$\frac{}{x \Rightarrow_\beta x} \qquad \frac{t \Rightarrow_\beta t'}{\lambda x.t \Rightarrow_\beta \lambda x.t'} \qquad \frac{t \Rightarrow_\beta t' \quad s \Rightarrow_\beta s'}{ts \Rightarrow_\beta t's'} \qquad \frac{t \Rightarrow_\beta t' \quad s \Rightarrow_\beta s'}{(\lambda x.t)s \Rightarrow_\beta t'\{x \leftarrow s'\}}$$

Tait–Martin-Löf's proof of the confluence of $\to_\beta$ relies on the diamond property of $\Rightarrow_\beta$[6], in turn based on the following property (see Takahashi [28, p. 1])

$\quad$ *Substitutivity of* $\Rightarrow_\beta$: if $t \Rightarrow_\beta t'$ and $s \Rightarrow_\beta s'$ then $t\{x \leftarrow s\} \Rightarrow_\beta t'\{x \leftarrow s'\}$.

While the diamond property of $\Rightarrow_\beta$ does not play a role for factorization, one of the contributions of this work is a new proof technique for factorization relying on the substitutivity property of an indexed refinement of $\Rightarrow_\beta$.

Indexed parallel β reduction. The new *indexed* version $\overset{n}{\Rightarrow}_\beta$ of parallel β reduction $\Rightarrow_\beta$ is equipped with a natural number n which is, roughly, the number of redexes reduced in parallel by a $\Rightarrow_\beta$; more precisely, n is the length of a particular way of sequentializing the redexes reduced by $\Rightarrow_\beta$. The definition of $\overset{n}{\Rightarrow}_\beta$ is as follows (note that erasing the index one obtains exactly $\Rightarrow_\beta$, so that $\Rightarrow_\beta = \bigcup_{n \in \mathbb{N}} \overset{n}{\Rightarrow}_\beta$):

INDEXED PARALLEL β REDUCTION

$$\frac{}{x \overset{0}{\Rightarrow}_\beta x} \qquad \frac{t \overset{n}{\Rightarrow}_\beta t'}{\lambda x.t \overset{n}{\Rightarrow}_\beta \lambda x.t'} \qquad \frac{t \overset{n}{\Rightarrow}_\beta t' \quad s \overset{m}{\Rightarrow}_\beta s'}{ts \overset{n+m}{\Rightarrow}_\beta t's'} \qquad \frac{t \overset{n}{\Rightarrow}_\beta t' \quad s \overset{m}{\Rightarrow}_\beta s'}{(\lambda x.t)s \overset{n+|t'|_x \cdot m+1}{\Rightarrow}_\beta t'\{x \leftarrow s'\}}$$

$\quad$ The intuition behind the last clause is: $(\lambda x.t)s$ reduces to $t'\{x \leftarrow s'\}$ by

1. first reducing $(\lambda x.t)s$ to $t\{x \leftarrow s\}$ (1 step);
2. then reducing in $t\{x \leftarrow s\}$ the n steps corresponding to the sequence $t \overset{n}{\Rightarrow}_\beta t'$, obtaining $t'\{x \leftarrow s\}$;
3. then reducing s to s' for every occurrence of x in t' replaced by s, that is, m steps $|t'|_x$ times, obtaining $t'\{x \leftarrow s'\}$.

Points 2 and 3 hold because of the substitutivity properties of β reduction.

$\quad$ It is easily seen that $\overset{0}{\Rightarrow}_\beta$ is the identity relation on terms. Moreover, $\to_\beta = \overset{1}{\Rightarrow}_\beta$, and $\overset{n}{\Rightarrow}_\beta \subseteq \to_\beta^n$, as expected. The substitutivity of $\overset{n}{\Rightarrow}_\beta$ is proved by simply indexing the proof of substitutivity of $\Rightarrow_\beta$.

Lemma 9 (Substitutivity of $\overset{n}{\Rightarrow}_\beta$). *If* $t \overset{n}{\Rightarrow}_\beta t'$ *and* $s \overset{m}{\Rightarrow}_\beta s'$, *then* $t\{x \leftarrow s\} \overset{k}{\Rightarrow}_\beta t'\{x \leftarrow s'\}$ *where* $k = n + |t'|_x \cdot m$.

---

[6] Namely, if $s_1 \,_\beta\!\!\Leftarrow t \Rightarrow_\beta s_2$ then there exists u such that $s_1 \Rightarrow_\beta u \,_\beta\!\!\Leftarrow s_2$.

Proof. By induction on the derivation of $t \stackrel{n}{\Rightarrow}_\beta t'$. Consider its last rule. Cases:

- *Variable*: two sub-cases
  - $t = x$: then $t = x \stackrel{0}{\Rightarrow}_\beta x = t'$ then $t\{x \leftarrow s\} = x\{x \leftarrow s\} = s \stackrel{m}{\Rightarrow}_\beta s' = x\{x \leftarrow s'\} = t'\{x \leftarrow s'\}$ that satisfies the statement because $n + |t'|_x \cdot m = 0 + 1 \cdot m = m$.
  - $t = y$: then $t = y \stackrel{0}{\Rightarrow}_\beta y = t'$ and $t\{x \leftarrow s\} = y\{x \leftarrow s\} = y \stackrel{0}{\Rightarrow}_\beta y = y\{x \leftarrow s'\} = t'\{x \leftarrow s'\}$ that satisfies the statement because $n + |t'|_x \cdot m = 0 + 0 \cdot m = 0$.
- *Abstraction*, i.e. $t = \lambda y.u \stackrel{n}{\Rightarrow}_\beta \lambda y.u' = t'$ because $u \stackrel{n}{\Rightarrow}_\beta u'$; we can suppose without loss of generality that $y \neq x$ and y is not free in s (and hence in s'), so $|u'|_x = |t'|_x$ and $t\{x \leftarrow s\} = \lambda y.(u\{x \leftarrow s\})$ and $t'\{x \leftarrow s'\} = \lambda y.(u'\{x \leftarrow s'\})$. By i.h., $u\{x \leftarrow s\} \stackrel{n+|u'|_x \cdot m}{\Rightarrow}_\beta u'\{x \leftarrow s'\}$, thus

$$\frac{u\{x \leftarrow s\} \stackrel{n+|u'|_x \cdot m}{\Rightarrow}_\beta u'\{x \leftarrow s'\}}{t\{x \leftarrow s\} = \lambda y.u\{x \leftarrow s\} \stackrel{n+|t'|_x \cdot m}{\Rightarrow}_\beta \lambda y.u'\{x \leftarrow s'\} = t'\{x \leftarrow s'\}}.$$

- *Application*, i.e. $t = ur \stackrel{n}{\Rightarrow}_\beta u'r' = t'$ with $u \stackrel{n_u}{\Rightarrow}_\beta u'$, $r \stackrel{n_r}{\Rightarrow}_\beta r'$ and $n = n_u + n_r$. By i.h., $u\{x \leftarrow s\} \stackrel{n_u+|u'|_x \cdot m}{\Rightarrow}_\beta u'\{x \leftarrow s'\}$ and $r\{x \leftarrow s\} \stackrel{n_r+|r'|_x \cdot m}{\Rightarrow}_\beta r'\{x \leftarrow s'\}$. Then

$$\frac{u\{x \leftarrow s\} \stackrel{n_u+|u'|_x \cdot m}{\Rightarrow}_\beta u'\{x \leftarrow s'\} \qquad r\{x \leftarrow s\} \stackrel{n_r+|r'|_x \cdot m}{\Rightarrow}_\beta r'\{x \leftarrow s'\}}{t\{x \leftarrow s\} = u\{x \leftarrow s\}r\{x \leftarrow s\} \stackrel{k}{\Rightarrow}_\beta u'\{x \leftarrow s'\}r'\{x \leftarrow s'\} = t'\{x \leftarrow s'\}}$$

  where $k = n_u + |u'|_x \cdot m + n_r + |r'|_x \cdot m = n + (|u'|_x + |r'|_x) \cdot m = n + |t'|_x \cdot m$.
- *β-step*, i.e. $t = (\lambda y.u)r \stackrel{n}{\Rightarrow}_\beta u'\{y \leftarrow r'\} = t'$ with $u \stackrel{n_u}{\Rightarrow}_\beta u'$, $r \stackrel{n_r}{\Rightarrow}_\beta r'$ and $n = n_u + |u'|_y \cdot n_r + 1$. We can assume without loss of generality that $y \neq x$ and y is not free in s (and so in s'), hence $|t'|_x = |u'\{y \leftarrow r'\}|_x = |u'|_x + |u'|_y \cdot |r'|_x$ and $|u'\{x \leftarrow s'\}|_y = |u'|_y$ and $t\{x \leftarrow s\} = (\lambda y.u\{x \leftarrow s\})(r\{x \leftarrow s\})$ and $t'\{x \leftarrow s'\} = u'\{x \leftarrow s'\}\{y \leftarrow r'\{x \leftarrow s'\}\}$. By i.h., $u\{x \leftarrow s\} \stackrel{n_u+|u'|_x \cdot m}{\Rightarrow}_\beta u'\{x \leftarrow s'\}$ and $r\{x \leftarrow s\} \stackrel{n_r+|r'|_x \cdot m}{\Rightarrow}_\beta r'\{x \leftarrow s'\}$. Then

$$\frac{u\{x \leftarrow s\} \stackrel{n_u+|u'|_x \cdot m}{\Rightarrow}_\beta u'\{x \leftarrow s'\} \qquad r\{x \leftarrow s\} \stackrel{n_r+|r'|_x \cdot m}{\Rightarrow}_\beta r'\{x \leftarrow s'\}}{t\{x \leftarrow s\} = (\lambda y.u\{x \leftarrow s\})(r\{x \leftarrow s\}) \stackrel{k}{\Rightarrow}_\beta u'\{x \leftarrow s'\}\{y \leftarrow r'\{x \leftarrow s'\}\} = t'\{x \leftarrow s'\}}$$

  where $k = n_u + |u'|_x \cdot m + |u'|_y \cdot (n_r + |r'|_x \cdot m) + 1 = n_u + |u'|_y \cdot n_r + 1 + |u'|_x \cdot m + |u'|_y \cdot |r'|_x \cdot m = n + |t'|_x \cdot m$. $\qquad\square$

4 Head Reduction, Essentially

We here revisit Takahashi's study [28] of head reduction. We apply the abstract schema for essential reductions developed in Sect. 2, which is the same schema used by Takahashi, but we provide a simpler proof technique for one of the required properties (split). First of all, head reduction $\to_h$ (our essential reduction here) and its associated inessential reduction $\to_{\neg h}$ are defined by:

HEAD REDUCTION

$$\frac{}{(\lambda x.t)s \to_h t\{x \leftarrow s\}} \qquad \frac{t \to_h s \qquad t \neq \lambda x.t'}{tu \to_h su} \qquad \frac{t \to_h s}{\lambda x.t \to_h \lambda x.s}$$

$\neg$HEAD REDUCTION

$$\frac{t \to_\beta t'}{(\lambda x.t)s \to_{\neg h} (\lambda x.t')s} \qquad \frac{t \to_\beta t'}{st \to_{\neg h} st'} \qquad \frac{t \to_{\neg h} t'}{\lambda x.t \to_{\neg h} \lambda x.t'} \qquad \frac{t \to_{\neg h} t'}{ts \to_{\neg h} t's}.$$

Note that $\to_\beta = \to_h \cup \to_{\neg h}$ but $\to_h$ and $\to_{\neg h}$ are not disjoint: $I(II) \to_h II$ and $I(II) \to_{\neg h} II$ with $I = \lambda z.z$. Indeed, $I(II)$ contains two distinct redexes, one is $I(II)$ and is fired by $\to_h$, the other one is II and is fired by $\to_{\neg h}$; coincidentally, the two reductions lead to the same term.

As for Takahashi, a parallel $\neg$head step $t \Rightarrow_{\neg h} s$ is a parallel step $t \Rightarrow_\beta s$ such that $t \to_{\neg h}^* s$. We give explicitly the inference rules for $\Rightarrow_{\neg h}$:

PARALLEL $\neg$HEAD REDUCTION

$$\frac{}{x \Rightarrow_{\neg h} x} \qquad \frac{t \Rightarrow_\beta t' \quad s \Rightarrow_\beta s'}{(\lambda x.t)s \Rightarrow_{\neg h} (\lambda x.t')s'} \qquad \frac{t \Rightarrow_{\neg h} t'}{\lambda x.t \Rightarrow_{\neg h} \lambda x.t'} \qquad \frac{t \Rightarrow_{\neg h} t' \quad s \Rightarrow_\beta s'}{ts \Rightarrow_{\neg h} t's'}$$

Easy inductions show that $\to_{\neg h} \subseteq \Rightarrow_{\neg h} \subseteq \to_{\neg h}^*$. It is immediate that $\to_h$-normal terms are head normal forms in the sense of Barendregt [4, Def. 2.2.11]. We do not describe the shape of head normal forms. Our proofs never use it, unlike Takahashi's ones. This fact stresses the abstract nature of our proof method.

Head Factorization. We show that $\to_h$ induces a macro-step system, with respect to $\to_{\neg h}$, $\Rightarrow_\beta$, and $\Rightarrow_{\neg h}$, to obtain $\to_h$-factorization by Proposition 3.

Therefore, we need to prove merge and split. Merge is easily verified by induction on $t \Rightarrow_{\neg h} s$. The interesting part is the proof of the split property, that in the concrete case of head reduction becomes: if $t \Rightarrow_\beta s$ then $t \to_h^* \cdot \Rightarrow_{\neg h} s$. This is obtained as a consequence of the following easy *indexed split* property based on the indexed variant of parallel β. The original argument of Takahashi [28] is more involved, we discuss it after the new proof.

Proposition 10 (Head macro-step system)

1. Merge: *if* $t \Rightarrow_{\neg h} \cdot \to_h u$ *then* $t \Rightarrow_\beta u$.
2. Indexed split: *if* $t \overset{n}{\Rightarrow}_\beta s$ *then* $t \Rightarrow_{\neg h} s$, *or* $n > 0$ *and* $t \to_h \cdot \overset{n-1}{\Rightarrow}_\beta s$.
3. Split: *if* $t \Rightarrow_\beta s$ *then* $t \to_h^* \cdot \Rightarrow_{\neg h} s$.

That is, $(\Lambda, \{\to_h, \to_{\neg h}\})$ is a macro-step system with respect to $\Rightarrow_\beta$ and $\Rightarrow_{\neg h}$.

Proof. 1. Easy induction on $t \Rightarrow_{\neg h} s$. Details are in [3].

2. By induction on $t \overset{n}{\Rightarrow}_\beta s$. We freely use the fact that if $t \overset{n}{\Rightarrow}_\beta s$ then $t \Rightarrow_\beta s$. Cases:
   - *Variable*: $t = x \overset{0}{\Rightarrow}_\beta x = s$. Then $t = x \Rightarrow_{\neg h} x = s$.
   - *Abstraction*: $t = \lambda x.t' \overset{n}{\Rightarrow}_\beta \lambda x.s' = s$ with $t' \overset{n}{\Rightarrow}_\beta s'$. It follows from the *i.h.*
   - *Application*: $t = rp \overset{n}{\Rightarrow}_\beta r'p' = s$ with $r \overset{n_1}{\Rightarrow}_\beta r'$, $p \overset{n_2}{\Rightarrow}_\beta p'$ and $n = n_1 + n_2$. There are only two subcases:
     - either $rp \Rightarrow_{\neg h} r'p'$, and then the claim holds;
     - or $rp \not\Rightarrow_{\neg h} r'p'$, and then neither $r \Rightarrow_{\neg h} r'$ nor r is an abstraction (otherwise $rp \Rightarrow_{\neg h} r'p'$). By *i.h.* applied to $r \overset{n_1}{\Rightarrow}_\beta r'$, $n_1 > 0$ and there exists r'' such that $r \to_h r'' \overset{n_1-1}{\Rightarrow}_\beta r'$. Thus, $t = rp \to_h r''p$ and

$$\frac{r'' \overset{n_1-1}{\Rightarrow}_\beta r' \qquad p \overset{n_2}{\Rightarrow}_\beta p'}{r''p \overset{n_1-1+n_2}{\Rightarrow}_\beta r'p' = s}.$$

   - *β-step*: $t = (\lambda x.u)r \overset{n}{\Rightarrow}_\beta u\{x \leftarrow r\} = s$ with $u \overset{n_1}{\Rightarrow}_\beta u'$, $r \overset{n_2}{\Rightarrow}_\beta r''$ and $n = n_1 + |u'|_x \cdot n_2 + 1 > 0$. We have $t = (\lambda x.u)r \to_h u\{x \leftarrow r\}$ and by substitutivity of $\overset{n}{\Rightarrow}_\beta$ (Lemma 9) $u\{x \leftarrow r\} \overset{n_1 + |u'|_x \cdot n_2}{\Rightarrow}_\beta u'\{x \leftarrow r'\} = s$.

3. If $t \Rightarrow_\beta s$ then $t \overset{n}{\Rightarrow}_\beta s$ for some n. We prove the statement by induction n. By *indexed split* (Point 2), there are only two cases:
   - $t \Rightarrow_{\neg h} s$. This is an instance of the statement (since $\to_h^*$ is reflexive).
   - $n > 0$ and there exists r such that $t \to_h r \overset{n-1}{\Rightarrow}_\beta s$. By *i.h.* applied to $r \overset{n-1}{\Rightarrow}_\beta s$, there is u such that $r \to_h^* u \Rightarrow_{\neg h} s$, and so $t \to_h^* u \Rightarrow_{\neg h} s$. □

Theorem 11 (Head factorization). *If* $t \to_\beta^* u$ *then* $t \to_h^* \cdot \to_{\neg h}^* u$.

Head Normalization. We show that $(\Lambda, \{\to_h, \to_{\neg h}\})$ is an essential system (Definition 5); thus the essential normalization theorem (Theorem 8) provides normalization. We already proved *factorization* (Theorem 11, hence terminal factorization). We verify persistence and determinism (which implies uniform termination) of $\to_h$.

Proposition 12 (Head essential system)

1. Persistence: *if* $t \to_h s$ *and* $t \to_{\neg h} u$ *then* $u \to_h r$ *for some* r.
2. Determinism: *if* $t \to_h s_1$ *and* $t \to_h s_2$ *then* $s_1 = s_2$.

Then, $(\Lambda, \{\to_h, \to_{\neg h}\})$ *is an essential system.*

Theorem 13 (Head normalization). *If* $t \to_\beta^* s$ *and* s *is a* $\to_h$*-normal form, then* $\to_h$ *terminates on* t.

4.1 Comparison with Takahashi's Proof of the Split Property

Our technique differs from Takahashi's in that it is built on simpler properties: it exploits directly the substitutivity of $\Rightarrow_\beta$, which is instead not used by Takahashi. Takahashi's original argument [28] for the split property (*if* $t \Rightarrow_\beta s$ *then* $t \rightarrow_h^* \cdot \Rightarrow_{\neg h}$, what she calls the *main lemma*) is by induction on the (concrete) definition of $\Rightarrow_\beta$ and relies on two substitutivity properties of $\rightarrow_h$ and $\Rightarrow_{\neg h}$. Looking at them as the reductions $\rightarrow_e$ and $\rightarrow_{\neg e}$ of an essential system, these properties are:

- *Left substitutivity of* $\rightarrow_e$: if $u \rightarrow_e q$ then $u\{x \leftarrow r\} \rightarrow_e q\{x \leftarrow r\}$;
- *Left substitutivity of* $\Rightarrow_{\neg e}$: if $u \Rightarrow_{\neg e} q$ then $u\{x \leftarrow r\} \Rightarrow_{\neg e} q\{x \leftarrow r\}$.

From them, left substitutivity of the composed reduction $\rightarrow_e^* \cdot \Rightarrow_{\neg e}$ easily follows. That is, Takahashi's proof of the split property is by induction on $t \Rightarrow s$ using left substitutivity of $\rightarrow_e^* \cdot \Rightarrow_{\neg e}$ for the inductive case.

We exploit the substitutivity of $\overset{n}{\Rightarrow}$ instead of left substitutivity of $\rightarrow_e$ and $\Rightarrow_{\neg e}$. It holds for a larger number of essential systems because $\overset{n}{\Rightarrow}$ is simply a decoration of $\Rightarrow$, which is substitutive *by design*. There are important systems where Takahashi's hypotheses do not hold. One such case is ℓo reduction (Sect. 7)—*the normalizing reduction of the λ-calculus*—we discuss the failure of left substitutivity for ℓo at the end of Sect. 7; another notable case is $\ell\ell$ reduction (Sect. 8); both are full reductions for β.

Let us point out where the idea behind our approach stems from. In a sense, Takahashi's proof works by chance: the split hypothesis is about a *parallel* step $\Rightarrow_\beta$ but then the key fact used in the proof, left substitutivity of $\rightarrow_h^* \cdot \Rightarrow_{\neg h}$, does no longer stay in the borders of the parallel step, since the prefix $\rightarrow_h^*$ is an arbitrary long sequence that may reduce *created* steps. Our proof scheme instead only focuses on the (expected) substitutivity of $\overset{n}{\Rightarrow}$, independently of creations.

5 The Call-by-Value λ-Calculus

In this short section, we introduce Plotkin's call-by-value λ-calculus [26], where β reduction fires only when the argument is a value. In the next section we define *weak* reduction and prove factorization and normalization theorems using the essential technique, exactly as done in the previous section for head reduction.

The set Λ of terms is the same as in Sect. 3. Values, call-by-value (CbV) β-reduction $\rightarrow_{\beta_v}$, and CbV indexed parallel reduction $\overset{n}{\Rightarrow}_{\beta_v}$ are defined as follows:

$$\text{VALUES} \quad v ::= x \mid \lambda x.t$$

$$\beta_v \text{ REDUCTION}$$

$$\frac{v \text{ value}}{(\lambda x.t)v \rightarrow_{\beta_v} t\{x \leftarrow v\}} \qquad \frac{t \rightarrow_{\beta_v} t'}{\lambda x.t \rightarrow_{\beta_v} \lambda x.t'} \qquad \frac{t \rightarrow_{\beta_v} t'}{ts \rightarrow_{\beta_v} t's} \qquad \frac{t \rightarrow_{\beta_v} t'}{st \rightarrow_{\beta_v} st'}$$

INDEXED PARALLEL β_v REDUCTION

$$\frac{}{x \overset{0}{\Rightarrow}_{\beta_v} x} \qquad \frac{t \overset{n}{\Rightarrow}_{\beta_v} t'}{\lambda x.t \overset{n}{\Rightarrow}_{\beta_v} \lambda x.t'} \qquad \frac{t \overset{n}{\Rightarrow}_{\beta_v} t' \quad s \overset{m}{\Rightarrow}_{\beta_v} s'}{ts \overset{n+m}{\Rightarrow}_{\beta_v} t's'} \qquad \frac{t \overset{n}{\Rightarrow}_{\beta_v} t' \quad v \overset{m}{\Rightarrow}_{\beta_v} v'}{(\lambda x.t)v \overset{n+|t'|_x \cdot m+1}{\Rightarrow}_{\beta_v} t'\{x \leftarrow v'\}}$$

The only difference with the usual parallel β (defined in Sect. 3) is the requirement that the argument is a value in the last rule. As before, the non-indexed parallel reduction $\Rightarrow_{\beta_v}$ is simply obtained by erasing the index, so that $\Rightarrow_{\beta_v} = \bigcup_{n \in \mathbb{N}} \overset{n}{\Rightarrow}_{\beta_v}$. Similarly, it is easily seen that $\overset{0}{\Rightarrow}_{\beta_v}$ is the identity relation on terms, $\to_{\beta_v} = \overset{1}{\Rightarrow}_{\beta_v}$ and $\overset{n}{\Rightarrow}_{\beta_v} \subseteq \to_{\beta_v}^n$. Substitutivity of $\overset{n}{\Rightarrow}_{\beta_v}$ is proved exactly as for $\overset{n}{\Rightarrow}_{\beta}$ (Lemma 9).

Lemma 14 (Substitutivity of $\overset{n}{\Rightarrow}_{\beta_v}$). *If $t \overset{n}{\Rightarrow}_{\beta_v} t'$ and $v \overset{m}{\Rightarrow}_{\beta_v} v'$, then $t\{x \leftarrow v\} \overset{k}{\Rightarrow}_{\beta_v} t'\{x \leftarrow v'\}$ where $k = n + |t'|_x \cdot m$.*

6   Weak Call-by-Value Reduction, Essentially

The essential step we study for the CbV λ-calculus is weak CbV reduction $\to_w$, which does not evaluate function bodies (the scope of λ-abstractions). Weak CbV reduction has practical importance, because it is the base of the ML/CAML family of functional programming languages. We choose it also because it admits the natural and more general *non-deterministic* presentation that follows, even if most of the literature rather presents it in a deterministic way.

WEAK CBV REDUCTION

$$\frac{}{(\lambda x.t)v \to_w t\{x \leftarrow v\}} \qquad \frac{t \to_w t'}{ts \to_w t's} \qquad \frac{t \to_w t'}{st \to_w st'}$$

Note that in the case of an application there is no fixed order in the $\to_w$-reduction of the left and right subterms. Such a non-determinism is harmless as $\to_w$ satisfies a diamond-like property implying confluence, see Proposition 17.2 below. It is well-known that the diamond property implies uniform termination, because it implies that all maximal sequences from a term have the same length. Such a further property is known as *random descent*, a special form of uniform termination already considered by Newman [20] in 1942, see also van Oostrom [21].

The inessential reduction $\to_{\neg w}$ and its parallel version $\Rightarrow_{\neg w}$ are defined by:

¬WEAK REDUCTION

$$\frac{t \to_{\beta_v} s}{\lambda x.t \to_{\neg w} \lambda x.s} \qquad \frac{t \to_{\neg w} t'}{ts \to_{\neg w} t's} \qquad \frac{t \to_{\neg w} t'}{st \to_{\neg w} st'}$$

PARALLEL ¬WEAK REDUCTION

$$\frac{}{x \Rightarrow_{\neg w} x} \qquad \frac{t \Rightarrow_{\beta_v} t'}{\lambda x.t \Rightarrow_{\neg w} \lambda x.t'} \qquad \frac{t \Rightarrow_{\neg w} t' \quad s \Rightarrow_{\neg w} s'}{ts \Rightarrow_{\neg w} t's'}$$

It is immediate to check that $\to_{\beta_v} = \to_w \cup \to_{\neg w}$ and $\to_{\neg w} \subseteq \Rightarrow_{\neg w} \subseteq \to_{\neg w}^*$.

Weak CbV Factorization. We show that $(\Lambda, \{\to_w, \to_{\neg w}\})$ is a macro-step system, with $\Rightarrow_{\beta_v}, \Rightarrow_{\neg w}$ as macro-steps. Merge and split are proved exactly as in Sect. 4.

Proposition 15 (Weak CbV macro-step system)

1. *Merge: if $t \Rightarrow_{\neg w} \cdot \to_w u$ then $t \Rightarrow_{\beta_v} u$.*
2. *Indexed split: if $t \overset{n}{\Rightarrow}_{\beta_v} s$ then $t \Rightarrow_{\neg w} s$, or $n > 0$ and $t \to_w \cdot \overset{n-1}{\Rightarrow}_{\beta_v} s$.*
3. *Split: if $t \Rightarrow_{\beta_v} s$ then $t \to_w^* \cdot \Rightarrow_{\neg w} s$.*

That is, $(\Lambda, \{\to_w, \to_{\neg w}\})$ is a macro-step system with respect to $\Rightarrow_{\beta_v}$ and $\Rightarrow_{\neg w}$.

Theorem 16 (Weak CbV factorization). *If $t \to_{\beta_v}^* s$ then $t \to_w^* \cdot \to_{\neg w}^* s$.*

Plotkin's Left Reduction. The same argument at work in this section adapts easily to factorization with respect to leftmost weak reduction (used by Plotkin [26]), or to rightmost weak reduction, the two natural deterministic variants of $\to_w$.

Weak CbV Normalization. To obtain a normalization theorem for $\to_w$ via the essential normalization theorem (Theorem 8), we need persistence and uniform termination. The latter follows from the well-known diamond property of $\to_w$.

Proposition 17 (Weak CbV essential system)

1. *Persistence: if $t \to_w s$ and $t \to_{\neg w} u$ then $u \to_w r$ for some r.*
2. *Diamond: if $s\ _w{\leftarrow} \cdot \to_w u$ with $s \neq u$ then $s \to_w \cdot _w{\leftarrow} u$.*

Then, $(\Lambda, \{\to_w, \to_{\neg w}\})$ is an essential system.

Theorem 18 (Weak CbV normalization). *If $t \to_{\beta_v}^* s$ and s is a $\to_w$-normal form, then t is strongly $\to_w$-normalizing.*

CbV is often considered with respect to *closed* terms only. In such a case the $\to_w$-normal forms are exactly the (closed) values. Then weak CbV normalization (Theorem 18) implies the following, analogous to Corollary 1 in Plotkin [26] (the result is there obtained from standardization).

Corollary 19. *Let t be a closed term. If $t \to_{\beta_v}^* v$ for some value v, then every maximal $\to_w$-sequence from t is finite and ends in a value.*

7   Leftmost-Outermost Reduction, Essentially

Here we apply our technique to leftmost-outermost (shortened to ℓo) reduction $\to_{\ell o}$, the first example of *full* reduction for $\to_\beta$. The technical development is slightly different from the ones in the previous sections, as factorization relies on persistence. The same shall happen for the full $\ell\ell$ reduction of the next section. It seems to be a feature of full reductions for $\to_\beta$.

ℓo and $\neg \ell o$ reductions. The definition of ℓo reduction relies on two mutually recursive predicates defining normal and neutral terms (neutral = normal and not an abstraction):

Normal and Neutral Terms

$$\frac{}{x \text{ is neutral}} \qquad \frac{t \text{ is neutral} \quad t \text{ is normal}}{ts \text{ is neutral}} \qquad \frac{t \text{ is neutral}}{t \text{ is normal}} \qquad \frac{t \text{ is normal}}{\lambda x.t \text{ is normal}}$$

Dually, a term is not neutral if it is an abstraction or it is not normal. It is standard that these predicates correctly capture β normal forms and neutrality.

The reductions of the ℓo macro-step system are:

ℓo Reduction

$$\frac{}{(\lambda x.t)s \to_{\ell o} t\{x{\leftarrow}s\}} \qquad \frac{t \to_{\ell o} s \quad t \neq \lambda x.t'}{tu \to_{\ell o} su}$$

$$\frac{t \to_{\ell o} s}{\lambda x.t \to_{\ell o} \lambda x.s} \qquad \frac{u \text{ is neutral} \quad t \to_{\ell o} s}{ut \to_{\ell o} us}$$

$\neg\ell o$ Reduction

$$\frac{t \to_\beta t'}{(\lambda x.t)s \to_{\neg\ell o} (\lambda x.t')s} \qquad \frac{t \text{ is not neutral} \quad s \to_\beta s'}{ts \to_{\neg\ell o} ts'}$$

$$\frac{t \to_{\neg\ell o} t'}{ts \to_{\neg\ell o} t's} \qquad \frac{t \to_{\neg\ell o} t'}{st \to_{\neg\ell o} st'} \qquad \frac{t \to_{\neg\ell o} t'}{\lambda x.t \to_{\neg\ell o} \lambda x.t'}$$

Parallel $\neg\ell o$ Reduction

$$\frac{}{x \Rightarrow_{\neg\ell o} x} \qquad \frac{t \text{ is not neutral} \quad t \Rightarrow_{\neg\ell o} t' \quad s \Rightarrow_\beta s'}{ts \Rightarrow_{\neg\ell o} t's'}$$

$$\frac{t \Rightarrow_\beta t' \quad s \Rightarrow_\beta s''}{(\lambda x.t)s \Rightarrow_{\neg\ell o} (\lambda x.t')s'} \qquad \frac{t \Rightarrow_{\neg\ell o} t'}{\lambda x.t \Rightarrow_{\neg\ell o} \lambda x.t'} \qquad \frac{t \text{ neutral} \quad s \Rightarrow_{\neg\ell o} s'}{ts \Rightarrow_{\neg\ell o} ts'}$$

As usual, easy inductions show that $\to_\beta\; =\; \to_{\ell o} \cup \to_{\neg\ell o}$ and $\to_{\neg\ell o}\;\subseteq\;\Rightarrow_{\neg\ell o}\;\subseteq\;\to^*_{\neg\ell o}$.

Factorization depends on persistence, which is why for ℓo reduction most essential properties are proved before factorization. The proofs are easy inductions.

Proposition 20 (ℓo essential properties)

1. *Fullness: if $t \to_\beta s$ then there exists u such that $t \to_{\ell o} u$.*
2. *Determinism: if $t \to_{\ell o} s_1$ and $t \to_{\ell o} s_2$ then $s_1 = s_2$.*
3. *Persistence: if $t \to_{\ell o} s_1$ and $t \to_{\neg\ell o} s_2$ then $s_2 \to_{\ell o} u$ for some u.*

Proposition 21 (ℓo macro-step system)

1. *Merge: if $t \Rightarrow_{\neg\ell o} \cdot \to_{\ell o} u$ then $t \Rightarrow_\beta u$.*
2. *Indexed split: if $t \overset{n}{\Rightarrow}_\beta s$ then $t \Rightarrow_{\neg\ell o} s$, or $n > 0$ and $t \to_{\ell o} \cdot \overset{n-1}{\Rightarrow}_\beta s$.*
3. *Split: if $t \Rightarrow_\beta s$ then $t \to^*_{\ell o} \cdot \Rightarrow_{\neg\ell o} s$.*

That is, $(\Lambda, \{\to_{\ell o}, \to_{\neg\ell o}\})$ is a macro-step system with respect to $\Rightarrow_\beta$ and $\Rightarrow_{\neg\ell o}$.

Proof. We only show the merge property, and only the case that requires persistence—the rest of the proof is in the Appendix of [3]. The proof of the merge property is by induction on $t \Rightarrow_{\neg \ell o} s$. Consider the rule

$$\frac{r \text{ not neutral} \qquad r \Rightarrow_{\neg \ell o} r' \qquad p \Rightarrow_\beta p'}{t = rp \Rightarrow_{\neg \ell o} r'p' = s}.$$

Since r is not neutral, it is an abstraction or it is not normal. If r is an abstraction this case continues as the easy case of $\Rightarrow_{\neg \ell o}$ for β-redexes (see the Appendix of [3]). Otherwise, r is not normal, *i.e.* $r \to_\beta q$. By fullness $r \to_{\ell o} q'$ for some q', and by persistence (Prop. 20.3) $r' \to_{\ell o} r''$ for some r''. The hypothesis becomes $t = rp \Rightarrow_{\neg \ell o} r'p' \to_{\ell o} r''p' = u$ with $r \Rightarrow_{\neg \ell o} r' \to_{\ell o} r''$. By *i.h.*, $r \Rightarrow_\beta r''$. Then,

$$\frac{r \Rightarrow_\beta r'' \qquad p \Rightarrow_\beta p'}{t = rp \Rightarrow_\beta r''p' = u}. \qquad\qquad \square$$

ℓo split. As pointed out in Sect. 4.1, Takahashi's proof [28] of the split property relies on left substitutivity of head reduction, that is, if $t \to_h s$ then $t\{x \leftarrow u\} \to_h s\{x \leftarrow u\}$ for all terms u. Such a property does not hold for ℓo reduction. For instance, $t = x(Iy) \to_{\ell o} xy = t'$ but $t\{x \leftarrow \lambda z.zz\} = (\lambda z.zz)(Iy) \not\to_{\ell o} (\lambda z.zz)y = t'\{x \leftarrow \lambda z.zz\}$. Therefore her proof technique for factorization cannot prove the factorization theorem for ℓo reduction (see also footnote 2).

From Proposition 21 it follows the factorization theorem for ℓo reduction, that together with Proposition 20 proves that $(\Lambda, \{\to_{\ell o}, \to_{\neg \ell o}\})$ is an essential system, giving normalization of $\to_{\ell o}$ for $\to_\beta$.

Theorem 22

1. *ℓo factorization:* if $t \to_\beta^* u$ then $t \to_{\ell o}^* \cdot \to_{\neg \ell o}^* u$.
2. *ℓo normalization:* $\to_{\ell o}$ *is a normalizing reduction for* $\to_\beta$.

8   Least-Level Reduction, Essentially

In this section we study another normalizing full reduction for $\to_\beta$, namely *least-level* (shortened to $\ell\ell$) *reduction* $\to_{\ell\ell}$, which is non-deterministic. The intuition is that $\ell\ell$ reduction fires a β-redex of minimal level, where the *level* of a β-redex is the number of arguments containing it.

The definition of $\to_{\ell\ell}$ relies on an indexed variant $\to_{\beta:k}$ of $\to_\beta$, where $k \in \mathbb{N}$ is the level of the fired β-redex (do not mix it up with the index of $\overset{n}{\Rightarrow}_\beta$). We also define a parallel version $\Rightarrow_{\beta:n}$ (with $n \in \mathbb{N} \cup \{\infty\}$) of $\to_{\beta:k}$, obtained as a decoration of $\Rightarrow_\beta$, where n is the minimal level of the β-redexes fired by a $\Rightarrow_\beta$ step ($\Rightarrow_{\beta:\infty}$ does not reduce any β-redex). From now on, $\mathbb{N} \cup \{\infty\}$ is considered with its usual order and arithmetic, that is, $\infty + 1 = \infty$.

$$\beta \text{ REDUCTION OF LEVEL } k$$

$$\frac{}{(\lambda x.t)s \to_{\beta:0} t\{x \leftarrow s\}} \qquad \frac{t \to_{\beta:k} t'}{\lambda x.t \to_{\beta:k} \lambda x.t'} \qquad \frac{t \to_{\beta:k} t'}{ts \to_{\beta:k} t's} \qquad \frac{t \to_{\beta:k} t'}{st \to_{\beta:k+1} st'}$$

PARALLEL β REDUCTION OF LEAST LEVEL n

$$\frac{t \Rightarrow_{\beta:k} t' \quad s \Rightarrow_{\beta:h} s'}{(\lambda x.t)s \Rightarrow_{\beta:0} t'\{x \leftarrow s'\}} \quad \frac{t \Rightarrow_{\beta:k} t'}{\lambda x.t \Rightarrow_{\beta:k} \lambda x.t'} \quad \frac{t \Rightarrow_{\beta:k} t' \quad s \Rightarrow_{\beta:h} s'}{ts \Rightarrow_{\beta:\min\{k,h+1\}} t's'} \quad \overline{x \Rightarrow_{\beta:\infty} x}$$

Note that $t \to_\beta s$ if and only if $t \to_{\beta:k} s$ for some $k \in \mathbb{N}$.

The *least (reduction) level* $\ell\ell(t) \in \mathbb{N} \cup \{\infty\}$ of a term t is defined as follows:

$$\ell\ell(x) = \infty \quad \ell\ell(\lambda x.t) = \ell\ell(t) \quad \ell\ell(ts) = \begin{cases} 0 & \text{if } t = \lambda x.u \\ \min\{\ell\ell(t), \ell\ell(s)+1\} & \text{otherwise.} \end{cases}$$

The definitions of $\ell\ell$, $\neg\ell\ell$, and *parallel* $\neg\ell\ell$ *reductions* are:

$$\begin{array}{llll} \ell\ell \text{ REDUCTION} & t \to_{\ell\ell} s & \text{if } t \to_{\beta:k} s \text{ with } \ell\ell(t) = k \in \mathbb{N}; \\ \neg\ell\ell \text{ REDUCTION} & t \to_{\neg\ell\ell} s & \text{if } t \to_{\beta:k} s \text{ with } \ell\ell(t) < k \in \mathbb{N}; \\ \text{PARALLEL } \neg\ell\ell \text{ REDUCTION} & t \Rightarrow_{\neg\ell\ell} s & \text{if } t \Rightarrow_{\beta:k} s \text{ with } k = \infty \text{ or } k > \ell\ell(t). \end{array}$$

As usual, easy inductions show that $\to_\beta = \to_{\ell\ell} \cup \to_{\neg\ell\ell}$ and $\to_{\neg\ell\ell} \subseteq \Rightarrow_{\neg\ell\ell} \subseteq \to^*_{\neg\ell\ell}$.

Proposition 23 (Least level properties). *Let t be a term.*

1. *Computational meaning of $\ell\ell$:* $\ell\ell(t) = \inf\{k \in \mathbb{N} \mid t \to_{\beta:k} u \text{ for some term } u\}$.
2. *Monotonicity: if $t \to_\beta s$ then $\ell\ell(s) \geq \ell\ell(t)$.*
3. *Invariance by $\to_{\neg\ell\ell}$: if $t \to_{\neg\ell\ell} s$ then $\ell\ell(s) = \ell\ell(t)$.*

Point 1 captures the meaning of the least level, and gives fullness of $\to_{\ell\ell}$. In particular, $\ell\ell(t) = \infty$ if and only if t is $\to_\beta$-normal, since $\inf \emptyset = \infty$. Monotonicity states that β steps cannot decrease the least level. Invariance by $\to_{\neg\ell\ell}$ says that $\to_{\neg\ell\ell}$ cannot change the least level. Essentially, this is persistence.

Proposition 24 ($\ell\ell$ essential properties)

1. *Fullness: if $t \to_\beta s$ then $t \to_{\ell\ell} u$ for some u.*
2. *Persistence: if $t \to_{\ell\ell} s_1$ and $t \to_{\neg\ell\ell} s_2$ then $s_2 \to_{\ell\ell} u$ for some u.*
3. *Diamond: if $s \,_{\ell\ell}\!\leftarrow \cdot \to_{\ell\ell} u$ with $s \neq u$ then $s \to_{\ell\ell} \cdot \,_{\ell\ell}\!\leftarrow u$.*

As for ℓo, merge needs persistence, or, more precisely, invariance by $\to_{\neg\ell\ell}$.

Proposition 25 ($\ell\ell$ macro-step system)

1. *Merge: if $t \Rightarrow_{\neg\ell\ell} s \to_{\ell\ell} u$, then $t \Rightarrow_\beta u$.*
2. *Indexed split: if $t \overset{n}{\Rightarrow}_\beta s$ then $t \Rightarrow_{\neg\ell\ell} s$, or $n > 0$ and $t \to_{\ell\ell} \cdot \overset{n-1}{\Rightarrow}_\beta s$.*
3. *Split: if $t \Rightarrow_\beta s$ then $t \to^*_{\ell\ell} \cdot \Rightarrow_{\neg\ell\ell} s$.*

That is, $(\Lambda, \{\to_{\ell\ell}, \to_{\neg\ell\ell}\})$ is a macro-step system with respect to $\Rightarrow_\beta$ and $\Rightarrow_{\neg\ell\ell}$.

Theorem 26

1. *$\ell\ell$ factorization: if $t \to^*_\beta u$ then $t \to^*_{\ell\ell} \cdot \to^*_{\neg\ell\ell} u$.*
2. *$\ell\ell$ normalization: $\to_{\ell\ell}$ is a normalizing reduction for $\to_\beta$.*

$\ell\ell$ *split and* ℓo *vs.* $\ell\ell$. As for ℓo reduction, left substitutivity does not hold for $\to_{\ell\ell}$. Consider $t = x(Iy) \to_{\ell\ell} xy = t'$ where the step has level 1, and $t\{x \leftarrow \lambda z.zz\} = (\lambda z.zz)(Iy) \not\to_{\ell\ell} (\lambda z.zz)y = t'\{x \leftarrow \lambda z.zz\}$ since now there also is a step $(\lambda z.zz)(Iy) \to_{\ell\ell} (Iy)(Iy)$ at level 0.

Moreover, $\ell\ell$ and ℓo reductions are incomparable. First, note that $\to_{\ell\ell}$ *but* $\not\to_{\ell o}$: $t = (\lambda x.II)y \to_{\ell\ell} (\lambda x.I)y = s$, because $t \to_{\beta:0} (\lambda x.I)y$ and $\ell\ell(t) = 0$, but $t \not\to_{\ell o} s$, indeed $t \to_{\ell o} II$. This fact also shows that $\to_{\ell\ell}$ is not left–outer in the sense of van Oostrom and Toyama [22]. Second, $\to_{\ell o}$ *but* $\not\to_{\ell\ell}$: $t = x(x(II))(II) \to_{\ell o} x(xI)(II) = s$ but $t \not\to_{\ell\ell} s$, indeed $t \to_{\neg\ell\ell} s$ because $t \to_{\beta:2} s$ and $\ell\ell(t) = 1$, and $t \to_{\ell\ell} x(x(II))I \neq s$.

9   Conclusions

We provide simple proof techniques for factorization and normalization theorems in the λ-calculus, simplifying Takahashi's parallel method [28], extending its scope and making it more abstract at the same time.

About the use of parallel reduction, Takahashi claims: "*once the idea is stated properly, the essential part of the proof is almost over, because the inductive verification of the statement is easy, even mechanical*" [28, p. 122]. Our work reinforces this point of view, as our case studies smoothly follow the abstract schema.

Range of Application. We apply our method for factorization and normalization to two notions of reductions that compute full normal forms:

- the classic example of ℓo reduction, covered also by the recent techniques by Hirokawa, Middeldorp and Moser [12] and van Oostrom and Toyama [22];
- $\ell\ell$ reduction, which is out of the scope of [12,22] because it is neither deterministic (as required by [12]), nor left–outer in the sense of [22] (as pointed out here in Sect. 8).

Our approach naturally covers also reductions that do not compute full normal forms, such as head and weak CbV reductions. These results are out of reach for van Oostrom and Toyama's technique [22], as they clarify in their conclusions.

Because of the minimality of our assumptions, we believe that our method applies to a large variety of other cases and variants of the λ-calculus.

Acknowledgments. This work has been partially funded by the ANR JCJC grant COCA HOLA (ANR-16-CE40-004-01) and by the EPSRC grant EP/R029121/1 "Typed Lambda-Calculi with Sharing and Unsharing".

References

1. Accattoli, B.: An abstract factorization theorem for explicit substitutions. In: 23rd International Conference on Rewriting Techniques and Applications, RTA 2012. LIPIcs, vol. 15, pp. 6–21 (2012). https://doi.org/10.4230/LIPIcs.RTA.2012.6

2. Accattoli, B., Dal Lago, U.: (Leftmost-Outermost) Beta-reduction is invariant, indeed. Logical Methods Comput. Sci. **12**(1) (2016). https://doi.org/10.2168/LMCS-12(1:4)2016
3. Accattoli, B., Faggian, C., Guerrieri, G.: Factorization and normalization, essentially (extended version). CoRR abs/1902.05945 (2019). http://arxiv.org/abs/1908.11289
4. Barendregt, H.P.: The Lambda Calculus - Its Syntax and Semantics. Studies in Logic and the Foundations of Mathematics, vol. 103. North-Holland, Amsterdam (1984)
5. Bonelli, E., Kesner, D., Lombardi, C., Ríos, A.: On abstract normalisation beyond neededness. Theor. Comput. Sci. **672**, 36–63 (2017). https://doi.org/10.1016/j.tcs.2017.01.025
6. de Carvalho, D., Pagani, M., de Falco, L.T.: A semantic measure of the execution time in linear logic. Theor. Comput. Sci. **412**(20), 1884–1902 (2011). https://doi.org/10.1016/j.tcs.2010.12.017
7. Crary, K.: A simple proof of call-by-value standardization. Technical report, CMU-CS-09-137, Carnegie Mellon University (2009)
8. Guerrieri, G.: Head reduction and normalization in a call-by-value lambda-calculus. In: 2nd International Workshop on Rewriting Techniques for Program Transformations and Evaluation, WPTE 2015. OASICS, vol. 46, pp. 3–17 (2015). https://doi.org/10.4230/OASIcs.WPTE.2015.3
9. Guerrieri, G., Paolini, L., Ronchi Della Rocca, S.: Standardization of a Call-By-Value Lambda-Calculus. In: 13th International Conference on Typed Lambda Calculi and Applications, TLCA 2015. LIPIcs, vol. 38, pp. 211–225 (2015). https://doi.org/10.4230/LIPIcs.TLCA.2015.211
10. Guerrieri, G., Paolini, L., Ronchi Della Rocca, S.: Standardization and conservativity of a refined call-by-value lambda-calculus. Logical Methods Comput. Sci. **13**(4) (2017). https://doi.org/10.23638/LMCS-13(4:29)2017
11. Hindley, J.: The Church-Rosser property and a result in combinatory logic. Ph.D. thesis, University of Newcastle-upon-Tyne (1964)
12. Hirokawa, N., Middeldorp, A., Moser, G.: Leftmost outermost revisited. In: 26th International Conference on Rewriting Techniques and Applications, RTA 2015. LIPIcs, vol. 36, pp. 209–222 (2015). https://doi.org/10.4230/LIPIcs.RTA.2015.209
13. Ishii, K.: A proof of the leftmost reduction theorem for $\lambda\beta\eta$-calculus. Theor. Comput. Sci. **747**, 26–32 (2018). https://doi.org/10.1016/j.tcs.2018.06.003
14. Kesner, D., Lombardi, C., Ríos, A.: A standardisation proof for algebraic pattern calculi. In: 5th International Workshop on Higher-Order Rewriting, HOR 2010. EPTCS, vol. 49, pp. 58–72 (2010). https://doi.org/10.4204/EPTCS.49.5
15. Klop, J.W.: Combinatory reduction systems. Ph.D. thesis, Utrecht University (1980)
16. Krivine, J.: Lambda-Calculus. Ellis Horwood Series in Computers and Their Applications. Masson, Types and Models. Ellis Horwood (1993)
17. McKinna, J., Pollack, R.: Some lambda calculus and type theory formalized. J. Autom. Reasoning **23**(3–4), 373–409 (1999). https://doi.org/10.1007/BFb0026981
18. Melliès, P.-A.: A factorisation theorem in rewriting theory. In: Moggi, E., Rosolini, G. (eds.) CTCS 1997. LNCS, vol. 1290, pp. 49–68. Springer, Heidelberg (1997). https://doi.org/10.1007/BFb0026981
19. Mitschke, G.: The standardization theorem for λ-calculus. Math. Logic Q. **25**(1–2), 29–31 (1979). https://doi.org/10.1002/malq.19790250104
20. Newman, M.: On theories with a combinatorial definition of "Equivalence". Ann. Math. **43**(2), 223–243 (1942)

21. Oostrom, V.: Random descent. In: Baader, F. (ed.) RTA 2007. LNCS, vol. 4533, pp. 314–328. Springer, Heidelberg (2007). https://doi.org/10.1007/978-3-540-73449-9_24
22. van Oostrom, V., Toyama, Y.: Normalisation by random descent. In: 1st International Conference on Formal Structures for Computation and Deduction, FSCD 2016. LIPIcs, vol. 52, pp. 32:1–32:18 (2016). https://doi.org/10.4230/LIPIcs.FSCD.2016.32
23. Pagani, M., Tranquilli, P.: Parallel reduction in resource lambda-calculus. In: Hu, Z. (ed.) APLAS 2009. LNCS, vol. 5904, pp. 226–242. Springer, Heidelberg (2009). https://doi.org/10.1007/978-3-642-10672-9_17
24. Pagani, M., Tranquilli, P.: The conservation theorem for differential nets. Math. Struct. Comput. Sci. **27**(6), 939–992 (2017). https://doi.org/10.1017/S0960129515000456
25. Paolini, L., Ronchi Della Rocca, S.: Parametric parameter passing lambda-calculus. Inf. Comput. **189**(1), 87–106 (2004). https://doi.org/10.1016/j.ic.2003.08.003
26. Plotkin, G.D.: Call-by-name, call-by-value and the lambda-calculus. Theor. Comput. Sci. **1**(2), 125–159 (1975). https://doi.org/10.1016/0304-3975(75)90017-1
27. Ronchi Della Rocca, S., Paolini, L.: The Parametric Lambda Calculus - A Metamodel for Computation. TTCS. Springer, Heidelberg (2004). https://doi.org/10.1007/978-3-662-10394-4
28. Takahashi, M.: Parallel reductions in λ-calculus. Inf. Comput. **118**(1), 120–127 (1995). https://doi.org/10.1006/inco.1995.1057
29. Terese: Term Rewriting Systems. Cambridge Tracts in Theoretical Computer Science, vol. 55. Cambridge University Press, Cambridge (2003)
30. Terui, K.: Light affine lambda calculus and polynomial time strong normalization. Arch. Math. Log. **46**(3–4), 253–280 (2007). https://doi.org/10.1007/s00153-007-0042-6

Formal Verifications of Call-by-Need and Call-by-Name Evaluations with Mutual Recursion

Masayuki Mizuno$^{(\boxtimes)}$ and Eijiro Sumii$^{(\boxtimes)}$

Graduate School of Information Sciences, Tohoku University, Sendai, Japan
`mizuno@sf.ecei.tohoku.ac.jp`, `sumii@ecei.tohoku.ac.jp`

Abstract. We present new proofs—formalized in the Coq proof assistant—of the correspondence among call-by-need and (various definitions of) call-by-name evaluations of λ-calculus *with mutually recursive bindings*.

For non-strict languages, the equivalence between high-level specifications (call-by-name) and typical implementations (call-by-need) is of foundational interest. A particular milestone is Launchbury's natural semantics of call-by-need evaluation and proof of its adequacy with respect to call-by-name denotational semantics, which are recently formalized in Isabelle/HOL by Breitner (2018). Equational theory by Ariola et al. is another well-known formalization of call-by-need. *Mutual recursion* is especially challenging for their theory: reduction is complicated by the traversal of dependency (the "need" relation), and the correspondence of call-by-name and call-by-need reductions becomes non-trivial, requiring sophisticated structures such as graphs or infinite trees.

In this paper, we give arguably simpler proofs solely based on (finite) terms and operational semantics, which are easier to handle for proof assistants (Coq in our case). Our proofs can be summarized as follows: (1) we prove the equivalence between Launchbury's call-by-need semantics and heap-based call-by-name natural semantics, where we define a sufficiently (but not too) general correspondence between the two heaps, and (2) we also show the correspondence among three styles of call-by-name semantics: (i) the natural semantics used in (1); (ii) closure-based natural semantics that informally corresponds to Launchbury's denotational semantics; and (iii) conventional substitution-based semantics.

1 Introduction

Church proposed λ-calculus with substitution-based reduction which takes place anywhere, including the inside of λ-abstractions [10, pp. 347–348]. The *call-by-name* evaluation strategy, whose origin dates back to ALGOL 60, has been recognized as a theoretical foundation of non-strict languages [1, 25]. Meanwhile,

We thank the anonymous reviewers for valuable comments and suggestions. This work was partially supported by JSPS KAKENHI Grant Numbers JP19J11926, JP15H02681, JP16K12409 and the Asahi Glass Foundation.

A. W. Lin (Ed.): APLAS 2019, LNCS 11893, pp. 181–201, 2019.
https://doi.org/10.1007/978-3-030-34175-6_10

the *call-by-need* strategy [31], which memoizes values of function arguments, is adopted by typical implementations. Correspondence between the two strategies has thus been of natural interest for non-strict languages. Launchbury's natural semantics [19] and the equational theories of Ariola and Felleisen [3] and Maraist et al. [21] are representative previous research on this topic. The former showed the adequacy of his natural semantics with respect to call-by-name denotational semantics. This proof is recently formalized [7] in Isabelle/HOL. The latter two works proved the correspondence—based on term graphs—between call-by-name and (their definition of) call-by-need reductions. However, mutual recursion was challenging for their formalism [3, section 8].

In this paper, we give new proofs of the correspondence among call-by-need and call-by-name evaluations, and formalize them in the proof assistant Coq. Our proofs are arguably simpler in that they are solely based on syntactic terms and operational semantics. Our proofs consist of the following three correspondences: (1) the correspondence between (a variant of) Launchbury's call-by-need natural semantics and heap-based call-by-name natural semantics, where we define a sufficiently general but simple correspondence between the two heaps without using induction or coinduction; (2) between heap-based and closure-based natural semantics of call-by-name, based on possibly recursive (but still syntactic) environments, which informally corresponds to Launchbury's denotational semantics; and (3) between heap-based and substitution-based semantics of call-by-name, by technical but natural correspondence between terms which distinguishes bindings introduced by function applications and by **let**. We note that, although all of these proofs are based on natural (big-step) semantics, our mechanical formalization partly adopted small-step reductions (with formal correspondence proofs between the two styles of operational semantics) to avoid an ad hoc restriction on coinductive proofs in Coq.

Structure of the Paper. In Sect. 2, we define the syntax of our target language—λ-calculus with mutually recursive bindings—as well as its call-by-need and call-by-name natural semantics. Section 3 outlines our correspondence proofs. Section 4 describes notable points for their mechanical formalization in Coq, Sect. 5 discusses related work, and Sect. 6 concludes with future work.

2   Target Language

2.1   Syntax

The syntax of our λ-calculus with mutual recursion is defined in Fig. 1. Note that unlike Launchbury's definition [19, section 3.1], the syntax is *not* normalized to a restricted form, that is, function arguments are *not* necessarily thunk locations and can be general terms. We use de Bruijn indices [8] for the representation of bindings. The indices introduced by **let**-bindings are deterministically numbered left-to-right. Unlike the locally nameless representation [9], free variables are also indicated by de Bruijn indices (of environments, in Subsect. 2.3). Note that locations (representation of memory addresses; see [27, chapter 13] for example) of thunks are distinguished from variables.

$$x, l \in Nat$$
$$H, \bar{e} \in Term^*$$
$$e \quad \in Term \ ::= \mathbf{var}\ x \mid \mathbf{loc}\ l \mid \mathbf{abs}\ e \mid \mathbf{app}\ e_1\ e_2 \mid \mathbf{let}\ \bar{e}\ \mathbf{in}\ e$$
$$v \quad \in Val \quad ::= \mathbf{abs}\ e$$

Fig. 1. The syntax of λ-calculus with mutually recursive bindings

$$\frac{H_1.l = e \quad \langle H_1 \rangle\, e \Downarrow_d \langle H_2 \rangle\, v}{\langle H_1 \rangle\, \mathbf{loc}\ l \Downarrow_d \langle H_2[l \mapsto v] \rangle\, v} \qquad \frac{}{\langle H \rangle\, \mathbf{abs}\ e \Downarrow_d \langle H \rangle\, \mathbf{abs}\ e}$$

$$\frac{\langle H_1 \rangle\, e_1 \Downarrow_d \langle H_2 \rangle\, \mathbf{abs}\ e_0 \quad \langle H_2,\ e_2 \rangle\, e_0[0 \mapsto \mathbf{loc}\ |H_2|] \Downarrow_d \langle H_3 \rangle\, v}{\langle H_1 \rangle\, \mathbf{app}\ e_1\ e_2 \Downarrow_d \langle H_3 \rangle\, v}$$

$$\frac{\langle H_1,\ \bar{e}[\forall x \mapsto \mathbf{loc}\ (|H_1| + x)] \rangle\, e[\forall x \mapsto \mathbf{loc}\ (|H_1| + x)] \Downarrow_d \langle H_2 \rangle\, v}{\langle H_1 \rangle\, \mathbf{let}\ \bar{e}\ \mathbf{in}\ e \Downarrow_d \langle H_2 \rangle\, v}$$

$$\frac{H.l = e \quad \langle H \rangle\, e \Uparrow_d}{\langle H \rangle\, \mathbf{loc}\ l \Uparrow_d} \qquad \frac{\langle H \rangle\, e_1 \Uparrow_d}{\langle H \rangle\, \mathbf{app}\ e_1\ e_2 \Uparrow_d}$$

$$\frac{\langle H_1 \rangle\, e_1 \Downarrow_d \langle H_2 \rangle\, \mathbf{abs}\ e_0 \quad \langle H_2,\ e_2 \rangle\, e_0[0 \mapsto \mathbf{loc}\ |H_2|] \Uparrow_d}{\langle H_1 \rangle\, \mathbf{app}\ e_1\ e_2 \Uparrow_d}$$

$$\frac{\langle H_1,\ \bar{e}[\forall x \mapsto \mathbf{loc}\ (|H_1| + x)] \rangle\, e[\forall x \mapsto \mathbf{loc}\ (|H_1| + x)] \Uparrow_d}{\langle H_1 \rangle\, \mathbf{let}\ \bar{e}\ \mathbf{in}\ e \Uparrow_d}$$

Fig. 2. Evaluation rules for our variant of Launchbury's natural semantics

2.2 Heap-Based Natural Semantics for Call-by-Need and Call-by-Name

The evaluation rules for our variant of Launchbury's call-by-need natural semantics are shown in Fig. 2. This semantics consist of inductively defined quaternary relation $\langle H \rangle\, e \Downarrow_d \langle H' \rangle\, v$ (the term e under heap H evaluates to v together with the modified heap H') as well as coinductively defined binary relation $\langle H \rangle\, e \Uparrow_d$ (the term e under heap H diverges when evaluated). We use subscripts $_d$ and $_m$ to distinguish call-by-need and call-by-name evaluations. Unlike his original definition [19], we use the latter, coinductive big-step operational semantics [20] to distinguish divergence and stuck state. (Although Sestoft's small-step operational semantics [29] can also separate divergence and stuck state, it is abstract-machine-based rather than structural.)

For simplicity of mechanical formalization (in Coq), we define heaps H by sequences of terms $\bar{e}$. We write $|\bar{e}|$ for the length of $\bar{e}$. The expression $H.l$ denotes the l-th element (numbered from 0) of the sequence H. We write $H[l \mapsto v]$ for H where the l-th item is replaced with v. The sequence $H, \bar{e}$ denotes the concatenation of H and $\bar{e}$, while $e[x \mapsto e']$ denotes capture-avoiding substitution of e' for each free occurrence of x in e. The expression $e[\forall x \mapsto e'_x]$ denotes capture-avoiding parallel substitution of e'_x for each free variable x in e. It is naturally extended for sequences $\bar{e}[\forall x \mapsto e'_x]$.

The evaluation rule for locations (the first rule of Fig. 2) implements the essence of call-by-need: when the content e of the thunk $H_1.l$ assigned to the location l needs to be evaluated, the thunk is updated with the (syntactic) value v of e, that is, the heap H_2 after the evaluation is modified to $H_2[l \mapsto v]$. We omit Launchbury's trick (called "black-hole" [19]) that explicitly detects certain non-terminating evaluations in finite time, since it does not affect the correspondence of call-by-need to call-by-name.

For example, assuming integer arithmetic and using standard notation instead of de Bruijn indices, we have $\langle \rangle$ let $y = (\lambda x. \ x + x) \ (1 + 2)$ in $y + y \Downarrow_d$ $\langle l_1 \mapsto 6, \ l_2 \mapsto 3 \rangle \ 12$ (since the thunk l_1 for y is allocated before the thunk l_2 for x).

We note that syntactic values are obviously normal forms:

Lemma 1. *For any heap H, we have $\langle H \rangle \ v \Downarrow_d \langle H \rangle \ v$, while $\langle H \rangle \ v \Uparrow_d$ does not hold.*

Proof. By case analysis of the value v. □

A similar lemma will also hold for call-by-name.

The call-by-name version of the above natural semantics is obtained from Fig. 2 by replacing $\Downarrow_d$ with $\Downarrow_m$ and the location rule with the following

$$\frac{H_1.l = e \quad \langle H_1 \rangle \ e \Downarrow_m \langle H_2 \rangle \ v}{\langle H_1 \rangle \ \mathbf{loc} \ l \Downarrow_m \langle H_2 \rangle \ v}$$

whereas $\langle H \rangle \ e \Uparrow_m$ is obtained just by replacing $\Uparrow_d$ with $\Uparrow_m$ and $\Downarrow_d$ with $\Downarrow_m$. For instance, the previous example is evaluated like $\langle \rangle$ let $y = (\lambda x. \ x + x) \ (1 + 2)$ in $y + y \Downarrow_m \langle l_1 \mapsto (\lambda x. \ x + x) \ (1 + 2), \ l_2 \mapsto 1 + 2, \ l'_2 \mapsto 1 + 2 \rangle \ 12$, where the subterm $1 + 2$ is computed $2 \times 2 = 4$ times in total.

The above modification leads the following property:

Lemma 2 (monotonic increase of heap). *If $\langle H \rangle \ e \Downarrow_m \langle H' \rangle \ v$ then $H \subseteq H'$ (that is, H is a prefix of H').*

Proof. By straightforward induction on the derivation of $\langle H \rangle \ e \Downarrow_m \langle H' \rangle \ v$. □

Note that, under call-by-need evaluation, the *size* $|H|$ of the heap H increases monotonically as well, but its *contents* may be changed by thunk updates.

We will also use the fact that call-by-name evaluation is deterministic thanks to left-to-right thunk allocation (as in the concatenation $(H_1, \ \overline{e}[\forall x \mapsto \mathbf{loc} \ (|H_1| + x)])$ in the evaluation rule for **let** $\overline{e}$ **in** e):

Lemma 3 (determinacy of heap-based call-by-name evaluation).

1. *If $\langle H \rangle \ e \Downarrow_m \langle H' \rangle \ v$ and $\langle H \rangle \ e \Downarrow_m \langle H'' \rangle \ v'$, then $H' = H''$ and $v = v'$.*
2. *For any H, H', e, and v, we have at most one of $\langle H \rangle \ e \Downarrow_m \langle H' \rangle \ v$ or $\langle H \rangle \ e \Uparrow_m$.*

Proof. By straightforward inductions on the derivation of $\langle H \rangle \ e \Downarrow_m \langle H' \rangle \ v$. □

$$c \in Cls ::= \mathbf{cls}(E, e)$$
$$E \in Env ::= \epsilon \mid c :: E \mid (\mu.\bar{e}) + E$$

Fig. 3. The syntax of environments

Similar lemmas hold for call-by-need and other call-by-name evaluations. Although we could actually do without determinacy, it is convenient for simplifying the correspondence proofs.

We will show in Sect. 3 that the above call-by-need and call-by-name semantics correspond to each other.

2.3   Closure-Based Natural Semantics for Call-by-Name

The previous heap-based natural semantics is just one (not so standard) style of formalization of call-by-name evaluation. We define a higher-level alternative natural semantics, which informally corresponds to Launchbury's denotational semantics [19, section 5.2.1], based on environments and closures. An environment is essentially a partial function associating free variables to their semantic values. Our semantic values are closures [18], that is, pairs of an environment and a (possibly open) term.

We define the syntax of environments as in Fig. 3. The meaning of environment E is given by the following partial function $E(x)$ which returns the x-th (semantic) value of E.

$$\epsilon(x) = \text{undefined}$$
$$(c::E)(x) = \begin{cases} c & (x = 0) \\ E(x-1) & (x > 0) \end{cases}$$
$$((\mu.\bar{e}) + E)(x) = \begin{cases} \mathbf{cls}((\mu.\bar{e}) + E, \bar{e}.x) & (x < |\bar{e}|) \\ E(x - |\bar{e}|) & (x \geq |\bar{e}|) \end{cases}$$

Note that the environment $(\mu.\bar{e}) + E$ informally corresponds to the semantic recursive function $\mu E'. (x_1 \mapsto \llbracket e_1 \rrbracket_{E'} \cdots x_n \mapsto \llbracket e_n \rrbracket_{E'}) \sqcup E$ (cf. [19, section 5.2.1]).

We show the closure-based evaluation rules in Fig. 4. The inductively defined ternary relation $\{E\}e \Downarrow_m c$ means that the term e in the environment E evaluates to closure c, and the coinductively defined binary relation $\{E\}e \Uparrow_m$ that the evaluation does not terminate.

2.4   Substitution-Based Natural Semantics for Call-by-Name

Finally, we define a call-by-name semantics in the most conventional style since Church [10]: substitution. Although conventional substitution-based semantics of λ-calculus are usually small-step, we adopt big-step semantics since its correspondence to previous natural semantics is simpler.

The substitution-based evaluation rules for call-by-name are shown in Fig. 5. This natural semantics is almost straightforward except the rules for **let**-expressions, where we duplicate the mutually recursive bindings when they

$$\frac{\{(\mu.\bar{e}) + E\}e \Downarrow_m c}{\{E\}\textbf{let } \bar{e} \textbf{ in } e \Downarrow_m c} \qquad \overline{\{E\}\textbf{abs } e \Downarrow_m \textbf{cls}(E, \textbf{abs } e)}$$

$$\frac{E(x) = \textbf{cls}(E_0, e) \quad \{E_0\}e \Downarrow_m c}{\{E\}\textbf{var } x \Downarrow_m c}$$

$$\frac{\{E\}e_1 \Downarrow_m \textbf{cls}(E', \textbf{abs } e_0) \quad \{\textbf{cls}(E, e_2) :: E'\}e_0 \Downarrow_m c}{\{E\}\textbf{app } e_1 \ e_2 \Downarrow_m c}$$

$$\frac{\{(\mu.\bar{e}) + E\}e \Uparrow_m}{\{E\}\textbf{let } \bar{e} \textbf{ in } e \Uparrow_m} \qquad \frac{\{E\}e_1 \Uparrow_m}{\{E\}\textbf{app } e_1 \ e_2 \Uparrow_m}$$

$$\frac{E(x) = \textbf{cls}(E_0, e) \quad \{E_0\}e \Uparrow_m}{\{E\}\textbf{var } x \Uparrow_m}$$

$$\frac{\{E\}e_1 \Downarrow_m \textbf{cls}(E', \textbf{abs } e_0) \quad \{\textbf{cls}(E, e_2) :: E'\}e_0 \Uparrow_m}{\{E\}\textbf{app } e_1 \ e_2 \Uparrow_m}$$

Fig. 4. Closure-based natural semantics for call-by-name

$$\frac{e_1 \Downarrow_m \textbf{abs } e_0 \quad e_0[0 \mapsto e_2] \Downarrow_m v}{\textbf{app } e_1 \ e_2 \Downarrow_m v} \qquad \frac{e_1 \Uparrow_m}{\textbf{app } e_1 \ e_2 \Uparrow_m}$$

$$\frac{}{\textbf{abs } e_0 \Downarrow_m \textbf{abs } e_0} \qquad \frac{e_1 \Downarrow_m \textbf{abs } e_0 \quad e_0[0 \mapsto e_2] \Uparrow_m}{\textbf{app } e_1 \ e_2 \Uparrow_m}$$

$$\frac{e[\forall x \mapsto \textbf{let } \bar{e} \textbf{ in } \bar{e}.x] \Downarrow_m v}{\textbf{let } \bar{e} \textbf{ in } e \Downarrow_m v} \qquad \frac{e[\forall x \mapsto \textbf{let } \bar{e} \textbf{ in } \bar{e}.x] \Uparrow_m}{\textbf{let } \bar{e} \textbf{ in } e \Uparrow_m}$$

Fig. 5. Substitution-based natural semantics for call-by-name

are unfolded: for instance, **let var** 1, **var** 0 **in app** (**var** 0) (**var** 1), which is **let** $x = y$, $y = x$ **in** $x \ y$ in usual notation, is expanded to **app** (**let var** 1, **var** 0 **in var** 1) (**let var** 1, **var** 0 **in var** 0), which is (**let** $x = y$, $y = x$ **in** y) (**let** $x = y$, $y = x$ **in** x).

3 Outline of Our Proofs

We now outline our proofs of the correspondence among call-by-need and call-by-name evaluations. The correspondence proofs are threefold: (1) correspondence between heap-based call-by-need and (also heap-based) call-by-name natural semantics, (2) between the heap-based and closure-based call-by-name natural semantics, and (3) between heap-based and substitution-based natural semantics for call-by-name. We recall that (1) the heap-based call-by-name semantics is convenient for proving the correspondence with call-by-need, (2) the closure-based natural semantics informally corresponds to Launchbury's denotational semantics, and (3) the substitution-based semantics is (a big-step version of) traditional evaluation in λ-calculus (in Sect. 4, we also prove the correspondence with small-step substitution-based semantics), thus proving all the three styles of call-by-name semantics.

3.1 Correspondence Between Heap-Based Call-by-Need and Call-by-Name Evaluations

In this subsection, we show the correspondence between heap-based call-by-need and call-by-name evaluations, that is:

> If the heap-based call-by-need evaluation $\Downarrow_d$ of a term e under an empty heap $\langle\rangle$ halts, like $\langle\rangle e \Downarrow_d \langle H_1' \rangle v_1$, then its heap-based call-by-name evaluation $\Downarrow_m$ also halts, like $\langle\rangle e \Downarrow_m \langle H_2' \rangle v_2$, and vice versa. Furthermore, the results $\langle H_1' \rangle v_1$ and $\langle H_2' \rangle v_2$ "correspond" to each other.

We aim to prove the above main theorem by induction on the derivation of the evaluations. As is often the case with any inductive proof, we need to generalize its statement for evaluations $\langle H_1 \rangle e \Downarrow_d$ and $\langle H_2 \rangle e \Downarrow_m$ under non-empty and "corresponding" heaps H_1 and H_2. Moreover, we naturally have to consider evaluations of not necessarily the same, but "corresponding" terms e_1 and e_2, like $\langle H_1 \rangle e_1 \Downarrow_d$ and $\langle H_2 \rangle e_2 \Downarrow_m$. What is then the sufficiently general "correspondence" between the heap-term pairs $\langle H_1 \rangle e_1$ and $\langle H_2 \rangle e_2$?

First Try. Naively, one might consider an overly general correspondence, coinductively defined as a compatibility (context-preserving relation) satisfying:

$$\frac{\langle H_1 \rangle H_1.l_1 \sim \langle H_2 \rangle H_2.l_2}{\langle H_1 \rangle \mathbf{loc}\ l_1 \sim \langle H_2 \rangle \mathbf{loc}\ l_2}$$

$$\frac{\langle H_1 \rangle e_1 \Downarrow_d \langle H_1' \rangle v_1 \quad \langle H_2 \rangle e_2 \Downarrow_m \langle H_2' \rangle v_2 \quad \langle H_1' \rangle v_1 \sim \langle H_2' \rangle v_2}{\langle H_1 \rangle e_1 \sim \langle H_2 \rangle e_2}$$

However, this definition is too inconvenient: for example, monotonicity with respect to heap extension is hard to prove.

Second Try. To find a more specific definition of correspondence, let us consider the call-by-name and call-by-need evaluations of

$$\mathbf{let}\ x = (\mathbf{let}\ y = 1 + 2, z = z\ \mathbf{in}\ y)\ \mathbf{in}\ x + x$$

for instance. Here we use the usual syntax based on variable names rather than de Bruijn indices, as well as arithmetic expressions. To evaluate the above term under an empty heap $\langle\rangle$, we shall evaluate

$$\langle l_1 \mapsto \mathbf{let}\ y = 1 + 2, z = z\ \mathbf{in}\ y \rangle\ l_1 + l_1$$

both in call-by-need and in call-by-name. By substituting the first occurrence of l_1, we obtain

$$\langle l_1 \mapsto \mathbf{let}\ y = 1 + 2, z = z\ \mathbf{in}\ y \rangle\ (\mathbf{let}\ y = 1 + 2, z = z\ \mathbf{in}\ y) + l_1$$

and then:

$$\langle l_1 \mapsto \mathbf{let}\ y = 1 + 2, z = z\ \mathbf{in}\ y, l_2 \mapsto 1 + 2, l_3 \mapsto l_3 \rangle\ l_2 + l_1$$

By substituting l_2, we have

$$\langle l_1 \mapsto \textbf{let } y = 1 + 2, z = z \textbf{ in } y, l_2 \mapsto 1 + 2, l_3 \mapsto l_3 \rangle \ (1 + 2) + l_1$$

and, by evaluating $1 + 2$,

$$\langle l_1 \mapsto \textbf{let } y = 1 + 2, z = z \textbf{ in } y, l_2 \mapsto 1 + 2, l_3 \mapsto l_3 \rangle \ 3 + l_1$$

Now, in call-by-need, the content $1 + 2$ of the location l_2 is updated to its value 3

$$\langle l_1 \mapsto \textbf{let } y = 1 + 2, z = z \textbf{ in } y, l_2 \mapsto 3, l_3 \mapsto l_3 \rangle \ 3 + l_1$$

and similarly for l_1,

$$\langle l_1 \mapsto 3, l_2 \mapsto 3, l_3 \mapsto l_3 \rangle \ 3 + l_1.$$

The value of l_1 is then reused

$$\langle l_1 \mapsto 3, l_2 \mapsto 3, l_3 \mapsto l_3 \rangle \ 3 + 3$$

and thus:

$$\langle l_1 \mapsto 3, l_2 \mapsto 3, l_3 \mapsto l_3 \rangle \ 6$$

On the other hand, in call-by-name, no such updates occur

$$\langle l_1 \mapsto \textbf{let } y = 1 + 2, z = z \textbf{ in } y, l_2 \mapsto 1 + 2, l_3 \mapsto l_3 \rangle \ 3 + l_1$$

and the evaluations of l_1 and l_2 are repeated, like

$$\langle l_1 \mapsto \textbf{let } y = 1 + 2, z = z \textbf{ in } y, l_2 \mapsto 1 + 2, l_3 \mapsto l_3 \rangle \ 3 + (\textbf{let } y = 1 + 2, z = z \textbf{ in } y)$$

and

$$\langle l_1 \mapsto \textbf{let } y = 1 + 2, z = z \textbf{ in } y, l_2 \mapsto 1 + 2, l_3 \mapsto l_3, l'_2 \mapsto 1 + 2, l'_3 \mapsto l'_3 \rangle \ 3 + l'_2$$

for l_1, and

$$\langle l_1 \mapsto \textbf{let } y = 1 + 2, z = z \textbf{ in } y, l_2 \mapsto 1 + 2, l_3 \mapsto l_3, l'_2 \mapsto 1 + 2, l'_3 \mapsto l'_3 \rangle \ 3 + (1 + 2)$$

and

$$\langle l_1 \mapsto \textbf{let } y = 1 + 2, z = z \textbf{ in } y, l_2 \mapsto 1 + 2, l_3 \mapsto l_3, l'_2 \mapsto 1 + 2, l'_3 \mapsto l'_3 \rangle \ 3 + 3$$

for the copy l'_2 of l_2, giving:

$$\langle l_1 \mapsto \textbf{let } y = 1 + 2, z = z \textbf{ in } y, l_2 \mapsto 1 + 2, l_3 \mapsto l_3, l'_2 \mapsto 1 + 2, l'_3 \mapsto l'_3 \rangle \ 6$$

These evaluations lead us to the following three observations: (1) there is *some* correspondence between the call-by-need and call-by-name heaps; (2) the correspondence, however, is not one-to-one but one-to-many, like $\{(l_2, l_2), (l_2, l'_2)\}$ and $\{(l_3, l_3), (l_3, l'_3)\}$; and (3) the contents of the corresponding locations are

$$\frac{(l, l') \in R}{\mathbf{loc}\ l \sim_R \mathbf{loc}\ l'} \qquad \frac{e \sim_R e'}{\mathbf{abs}\ e \sim_R \mathbf{abs}\ e'} \qquad \frac{e_1 \sim_R e'_1 \quad e_2 \sim_R e'_2}{\mathbf{app}\ e_1\ e_2 \sim_R \mathbf{app}\ e'_1\ e'_2}$$

$$\frac{}{\mathbf{var}\ x \sim_R \mathbf{var}\ x} \qquad \frac{|\bar{e}| = |\bar{e}'| \quad \forall i.\ \bar{e}.i \sim_R \bar{e}'.i \quad e \sim_R e'}{(\mathbf{let}\ \bar{e}\ \mathbf{in}\ e) \sim_R (\mathbf{let}\ \bar{e}'\ \mathbf{in}\ e')}$$

Fig. 6. The correspondence of terms for heap-based natural semantics

either the same (up to multiple call-by-name locations corresponding to a call-by-need location, like l_2 and l'_2 to l_2, and l_3 and l'_3 to l_3), or else (re-)evaluating the contents of the call-by-name heap gives the same value as the call-by-need heap.

Based on these observations, we could define the correspondence $H_1 \leq_R H_2$ between the call-by-need heap H_1 and call-by-name H_2 under the one-to-many correspondence R between their locations, by coinduction as follows (where $\sim_R$ is the equality of terms modulo R, in Fig. 6):

$$\frac{\text{For all } (l_1, l_2) \in R, \text{ either } H_1.l_1 \sim_R H_2.l_2 \text{ or}}{\exists R' \supseteq R.\ \exists H'_2, v_2.\ \langle H_2 \rangle\, H_2.l_2 \Downarrow_{\mathsf{m}} \langle H'_2 \rangle\, v_2 \wedge (H_1 \leq_{R'} H'_2) \wedge (H_1.l_1 \sim_{R'} v_2)}{H_1 \leq_R H_2}$$

Here the location correspondence R' is extended from R as the heap H'_2 is extended from H_2 by allocations during the (re-)evaluation of $H_2.l_2$. However again, such a coinductive definition is still inconvenient (when proving that it is preserved by heap updates, for example).

Our Solution. To avoid such a coinductive definition as above, we actually adopt the following definition

Definition 1 (lazy correspondence of heaps). $H_1 \leq_R H_2$ *iff for all* $(l_1, l_2) \in R$, *either* $H_1.l_1 \sim_R H_2.l_2$ *or* $\exists S, H'_2, v_2.\ \langle H_2 \rangle\, H_2.l_2 \Downarrow_{\mathsf{m}} \langle H'_2 \rangle\, v_2 \wedge (H_2 \sim_S H'_2) \wedge (H_1.l_1 \sim_{(R \circ S) \cup R} v_2) \wedge (\forall l'_2.\ (l_1, l'_2) \in R \implies H_2.l_2 \sim_{R^{-1} \circ R} H_2.l'_2)$.

with an auxiliary definition:

Definition 2 (homomorphic heaps). $H \sim_R H'$ *iff* $\forall (l, l') \in R.\ H.l \sim_R H'.l'$.

The fundamental difference from the previous coinductive definition is that, instead of the extended location correspondence R' and the coinductive occurrence of $\leq_{R'}$, we consider only the increased part S of the correspondence, under which the increased heap H'_2 is homomorphic to the original H_2 and the value v_2 recomputed in call-by-name corresponds to the value $H_1.l_1$ already memoized in call-by-need.

Moreover, the condition $\forall l'_2.\ (l_1, l'_2) \in R \implies H_2.l_2 \sim_{R^{-1} \circ R} H_2.l'_2$ in Definition 1 ensures that the contents of "equivalent" call-by-name locations (that is, locations corresponding to a common call-by-need location) are always equivalent (that is, the same if we identify equivalent locations). Indeed, this condition always holds for any call-by-name heap corresponding to a call-by-need heap:

Lemma 4. *If $H_1 \leq_R H_2$ then $H_2 \sim_{R^{-1} \circ R} H_2$.*

Proof. Straightforward by following the definitions of $H_1 \leq_R H_2$ and $H_2 \sim_{R^{-1} \circ R}$ H_2.

The binary relation $R^{-1} \circ R$ means "going back and forth" along R, that is, pairs of call-by-name locations which correspond to a common call-by-need location. Thus $H_2 \sim_{R^{-1} \circ R} H_2$ implies the contents of equivalent locations in the call-by-name heap H are equivalent.

We check the following basic properties of $\sim$ for terms and heaps.

Lemma 5. *1. If $e \sim_R e'$ then $e' \sim_{R^{-1}} e$.*
2. If $e \sim_R e'$ and $e' \sim_S e''$, then $e \sim_{R \circ S} e''$.
3. If $R \subseteq S$ and $e \sim_R e'$, then $e \sim_S e'$.

Proof. By inductions on the derivation of $e \sim_R e'$.   □

Lemma 6. *1. If $H \sim_R H'$ then $H' \sim_{R^{-1}} H$.*
2. If $H \sim_R H'$ and $H' \sim_S H''$, then $H \sim_{R \circ S} H''$.
3. If $H_1 \sim_R H_2$, $H_1 \subseteq H_1'$, and $H_2 \subseteq H_2'$, then $H_1' \sim_R H_2'$.

Proof. Clear from basic properties of the correspondence over terms.   □

Furthermore, call-by-name evaluations are preserved by the correspondence of locations:

Lemma 7 (conversion of call-by-name evaluation).
If $\langle H_1 \rangle\, e_1 \Downarrow_{\mathrm{m}} \langle H_1' \rangle\, v_1$ with $H_1 \sim_R H_2$ and $e_1 \sim_R e_2$, then $\langle H_2 \rangle\, e_2 \Downarrow_{\mathrm{m}} \langle H_2' \rangle\, v_2$ with $H_1' \sim_{R'} H_2'$ and $v_1 \sim_{R'} v_2$ for some $R' \supseteq R$, H_2', and v_2.

Proof. By induction on the derivation of $\langle H_1 \rangle\, e_1 \Downarrow_{\mathrm{m}} \langle H_1' \rangle\, v_1$.   □

The preservation of call-by-name evaluation leads to the following composition property of heap homomorphism and lazy correspondence of heaps.

Lemma 8. *If $H_1 \leq_R H_2$, $H_2 \sim_S H_2'$, and $H_2 \subseteq H_2'$, then $H_1 \leq_{(R \circ S) \cup R} H_2'$.*

Proof. By Lemma 7 and the definition of $H_1 \leq_R H_2$.   □

Note that, by applying this lemma to Definition 1 (with Lemma 2), we obtain the same premise $H_1 \leq_{R'} H_2'$ (with $R' = (R \circ S) \cup R$) as in the previous coinductive definition of $H_1 \leq_R H_2$, allowing the same inversion principle.

Now we are ready to establish the correspondence between heap-based call-by-name and call-by-need evaluations. Our goal is generalized and divided into the following four theorems. The first theorem means that, if call-by-need evaluation converges to a value, call-by-name evaluation of a corresponding (heap and) term also converges and gives a corresponding value.

Theorem 1 (call-by-need $\Rightarrow$ call-by-name convergence). *If $\langle H_1 \rangle\, e_1 \Downarrow_{\mathrm{d}}$ $\langle H_1' \rangle\, v_1$ with $H_1 \leq_R H_2$ and $e_1 \sim_R e_2$, then $\langle H_2 \rangle\, e_2 \Downarrow_{\mathrm{m}} \langle H_2' \rangle\, v_2$ with $H_1' \leq_{R'} H_2'$ and $v_1 \sim_{R'} v_2$ for some $R' \supseteq R$, H_2', and v_2.*

Proof Outline. By induction on the derivation of $\langle H_1 \rangle \, e_1 \, \Downarrow_\mathsf{d} \, \langle H_1' \rangle \, v_1$. The essential case is evaluation of locations, that is, when $e_1 = \mathbf{loc} \ l_1$ and $e_2 = \mathbf{loc} \ l_2$.

$$\frac{\langle H_1 \rangle \, H_1.l_1 \, \Downarrow_\mathsf{d} \, \langle H_1'' \rangle \, v_1}{\langle H_1 \rangle \, \mathbf{loc} \ l_1 \, \Downarrow_\mathsf{d} \, \langle H_1''[l_1 \mapsto v_1] \rangle \, v_1}$$

Here $H_1''[l_1 \mapsto v_1] = H_1'$. From $H_1 \leq_R H_2$, we have two subcases.

Subcase: $H_1.l_1 \sim_R H_2.l_2$. Intuitively, this subcase corresponds to thunk update. We have $\dfrac{\langle H_2 \rangle \, H_2.l_2 \, \Downarrow_\mathsf{m} \, \langle H_2' \rangle \, v_2}{\langle H_2 \rangle \, \mathbf{loc} \ l_2 \, \Downarrow_\mathsf{m} \, \langle H_2' \rangle \, v_2}$. To show $H_1''[l_1 \mapsto v_1] \leq_{R'} H_2'$ by (the latter half of) Definition 1 (lazy correspondence of heaps), we use the induction hypothesis and apply Lemma 7 (conversion of call-by-name evaluation) to $\langle H_2 \rangle \, H_2.l_2 \, \Downarrow_\mathsf{m} \langle H_2' \rangle \, v_2$ with $H_2 \sim_{(R^{-1} \circ R) \circ (R'^{-1} \circ R')} H_2'$ (which follows from $H_1 \leq_R H_2$ and $H_1'' \leq_{R'} H_2'$ with Lemmas 4, 6.2, and 6.3) to obtain $\langle H_2' \rangle \, H_2.l_2' \, \Downarrow_\mathsf{m} \langle H_2'' \rangle \, v_2'$ with $H_2' \sim_S H_2''$ and $v_2 \sim_S v_2'$ for some $S \supseteq (R^{-1} \circ R) \circ (R'^{-1} \circ R')$.

Subcase: $\langle H_2 \rangle \, H_2.l_2 \, \Downarrow_\mathsf{m} \langle H_2' \rangle \, v_2$, $H_2 \sim_S H_2'$, $H_1.l_1 \sim_{(R \circ S) \cup R} v_2$. This corresponds to reevaluation of $H_2.l_2$. From $H_1.l_1 \sim_{R \circ S} v_2$, we know that $H_1.l_1$ is a value. Furthermore, from $\langle H_1 \rangle \, H_1.l_1 \, \Downarrow_\mathsf{d} \, \langle H_1'' \rangle \, v_1$ and the determinacy of call-by-need evaluation, we also know $H_1.l_1 = v_1$. Thus, the thunk update is idempotent, that is, $H_1''[l_1 \mapsto v_1] = H_1''$. The correspondence $H_1 \leq_{(R \circ S) \cup R} H_2'$ is shown by Lemma 8 with $H_1 \leq_R H_2$, $H_2 \sim_S H_2'$, and Lemma 2. $\square$

The second theorem states that, if call-by-need evaluation diverges, then call-by-name evaluation of a corresponding (heap and) term also diverges. Recall that an evaluation either converges to a value, diverges, or neither ("gets stuck").

Theorem 2 (call-by-need $\Rightarrow$ call-by-name divergence). *If $\langle H_1 \rangle \, e_1 \, \Uparrow_\mathsf{d}$ with $H_1 \leq_R H_2$ and $e_1 \sim_R e_2$, then $\langle H_2 \rangle \, e_2 \, \Uparrow_\mathsf{m}$.*

Proof Outline. By straightforward coinduction. We note that Theorem 1 is required in the case $e_1 = \mathbf{app} \ e_{11} \ e_{12}$, $e_2 = \mathbf{app} \ e_{21} \ e_{22}$, and $\langle H_1 \rangle \, e_{11} \, \Downarrow_\mathsf{d} \langle H_1' \rangle \, \mathbf{abs} \ e_{10}$. $\square$

The third theorem is the converse of Theorem 1: if call-by-name evaluation converges to a value, call-by-need evaluation of a corresponding (heap and) term also converges and gives a corresponding value.

Theorem 3 (call-by-name $\Rightarrow$ call-by-need convergence). *If $\langle H_2 \rangle \, e_2 \, \Downarrow_\mathsf{m} \langle H_2' \rangle \, v_2$ with $H_1 \leq_R H_2$ and $e_1 \sim_R e_2$, then $\langle H_1 \rangle \, e_1 \, \Downarrow_\mathsf{d} \langle H_1' \rangle \, v_1$ with $H_1' \leq_{R'} H_2'$ and $v_1 \sim_{R'} v_2$ for some $R' \supseteq R$, H_2', v_2.*

Proof Outline. By induction on the derivation of $\langle H_1 \rangle \, e_1 \, \Downarrow_\mathsf{d} \langle H_1' \rangle \, v_1$. Surprisingly, most cases except reevaluation are the same as in Theorem 1. For the case of reevaluation, let $e_1 = \mathbf{loc} \ l_1$, $e_2 = \mathbf{loc} \ l_2$, $\langle H_2 \rangle \, H_2.l_2 \, \Downarrow_\mathsf{m} \langle H_2' \rangle \, v_2$, $H_2 \sim_S H_2'$, and $H_1.l_1 \sim_{(R \circ S) \cup R} v_2$. Since $H_1.l_1$ is a value (as $H_1.l_1 \sim_{(R \circ S) \cup R} v_2$), we have $\langle H_1 \rangle \, H_1.l_1 \, \Downarrow_\mathsf{d} \langle H_1 \rangle \, H_1.l_1$ by Lemma 1. Similarly to the case of Theorem 1, we obtain $H_1 \leq_{(R \circ S) \cup R} H_2'$ by composing $H_1 \leq_R H_2$ and $H_2 \sim_S H_2'$. $\square$

$$\frac{x < n}{\textbf{var } x \sim_R^n \textbf{var } x} \qquad \frac{e_1 \sim_R^{n+1} e_2}{\textbf{abs } e_1 \sim_R^n \textbf{abs } e_2} \qquad \frac{e_{11} \sim_R^n e_{21} \quad e_{12} \sim_R^n e_{22}}{\textbf{app } e_{11} \, e_{12} \sim_R^n \textbf{app } e_{21} \, e_{22}}$$

$$\frac{x \geq n \quad (l, x - n) \in R}{\textbf{loc } l \sim_R^n \textbf{var } x} \qquad \frac{|\overline{e_{11}}| = |\overline{e_{21}}| \quad \forall i.\ \overline{e_{11}}.i \sim_R^{n+|\overline{e_{11}}|} \overline{e_{21}}.i \quad e_{12} \sim_R^{n+|\overline{e_{11}}|} e_{22}}{(\textbf{let } \overline{e_{11}} \textbf{ in } e_{12}) \sim_R^n (\textbf{let } \overline{e_{21}} \textbf{ in } e_{22})}$$

Fig. 7. The correspondence of terms for closure-based natural semantics

The last theorem in this subsection is the converse of Theorem 2: if call-by-name evaluation diverges, call-by-need evaluation of a corresponding (heap and) term also diverges.

Theorem 4 (call-by-name $\Rightarrow$ call-by-need divergence). *If $\langle H_2 \rangle e_2 \Uparrow_\text{m}$ with $H_1 \leq_R H_2$ and $e_1 \sim_R e_2$, then $\langle H_1 \rangle e_1 \Uparrow_\text{d}$.*

Proof Outline. Similar to Theorem 2 (using Theorem 3) because $\Uparrow_\text{m}$ is defined just by replacing $\Uparrow_\text{d}$ with $\Uparrow_\text{m}$ and $\Downarrow_\text{d}$ with $\Downarrow_\text{m}$ in the second half of Fig. 2. □

3.2   Correspondence Between Heap-Based and Closure-Based Call-by-Name Evaluations

In the previous subsection, we showed the correspondence between heap-based *call-by-need* evaluation and heap-based *call-by-name* evaluation. We now show the correspondence between *heap-based* call-by-name evaluation and *closure-based* call-by-name evaluation, that is:

> *If the heap-based call-by-name evaluation of a term e under an empty heap $\langle \rangle$ halts, like $\langle \rangle\, e \Downarrow_\text{m} \langle H' \rangle\, v$, then its closure-based call-by-name evaluation under an empty environment ϵ also halts, like $\{\epsilon\} e \Downarrow_\text{m} c$, and vice versa. Furthermore, the results $\langle H' \rangle v$ and c correspond to each other.*

Consequently, we obtain the correspondence between heap-based call-by-need and closure-based call-by-name evaluations. Similarly to the previous subsection, we generalize the above statement for evaluations $\langle H \rangle e_1 \Downarrow_\text{m}$ and $\{E\} e_2 \Downarrow_\text{m}$ of corresponding terms e_1 and e_2 under corresponding heap H and environment E.

To find an appropriate definition of correspondence, let us consider the heap-based and closure-based call-by-name evaluations of **let var** $0, \textbf{abs }(\textbf{var } 1)$ **in var** 1 (which is **let** $x = x,\ y = \lambda z.\ x$ **in** y in usual notation). We have the heap-based evaluation

$$\langle \rangle \, \textbf{let var } 0, \textbf{abs }(\textbf{var } 1) \textbf{ in var } 1 \Downarrow_\text{m} \langle l_1 \mapsto \textbf{loc } l_1, l_2 \mapsto \textbf{abs }(\textbf{loc } l_1) \rangle \, \textbf{abs }(\textbf{loc } l_1)$$

and closure-based evaluation

$$\{\epsilon\} \textbf{let var } 0, \textbf{ abs }(\textbf{var } 1) \textbf{ in var } 1 \Downarrow_\text{m} \textbf{cls}((\mu.\ \textbf{var } 0, \textbf{abs }(\textbf{var } 1)) + \!\!\!+\ \epsilon, \textbf{abs }(\textbf{var } 1))$$

where the result of the latter is the closure consisting of the environment

(μ. **var** 0, **abs** (**var** 1)) $+\!\!\!+$ ϵ and the (syntactic) value **abs** (**var** 1). Recall that the closure is recursive (see Subsect. 2.3): let E be (μ. **var** 0, **abs** (**var** 1)) $+\!\!\!+$ ϵ; then $E(0) = \mathbf{cls}(E, \mathbf{var}\ 0)$ and $E(1) = \mathbf{cls}(E, \mathbf{abs}\ (\mathbf{var}\ 1))$. From the above evaluations, we observe that: (1) there is a correspondence between the heap and the recursive environment, requiring some form of coinductive definition; (2) the domain and contents of the corresponding heap and environment are also corresponding.

We thus coinductively define the correspondence $H \leq_R E$ between the heap H and the environment E, under the correspondence R between the locations and variables in the domain of H and E.

$$\frac{\text{For all } (l,x) \in R,\ \exists R', E', e.\ H.l \sim_{R'}^0 e \wedge E(x) = \mathbf{cls}(E', e) \wedge H \leq_{R'} E'}{H \leq_R E}$$

Here $e_1 \sim_R^0 e_2$ is the correspondence of terms e_1 and e_2 under R (Fig. 7).

Intuitively, this rule means that, for any location l and variable x corresponding in R, the contents $H.l$ of the heap H and the term part e of the closure $\mathbf{cls}(E', e)$ obtained from $E(x)$—as well as H and the environment part E' of $E(x)$—are corresponding under some R'. Note that the environment E' (hence resp. R') may be different from E (resp. R). Unlike the correspondence of heaps in the previous subsection, coinduction is not problematic because heaps and environments are immutable in call-by-name evaluations (while call-by-need heaps are destructively updated).

The correspondence $e_1 \sim_R^n e_2$ (Fig. 7) of terms is indexed by an integer $n \geq 0$ to distinguish indices of bound variables ($x < n$, as in the top-left rule) and free variables ($x \geq n$ as in the bottom-left), adjusted in the rules for binders (**abs** and **let**).

Now we prove the correspondence between heap-based and closure-based call-by-name evaluations as four theorems, like the previous subsection.

Theorem 5 (heap-based $\Rightarrow$ closure-based convergence). *If* $\langle H \rangle e_1 \Downarrow_{\mathrm{m}} \langle H' \rangle v_1$ *with* $H \leq_R E$ *and* $e_1 \sim_R^0 e_2$, *then* $\{E\}e_2 \Downarrow_{\mathrm{m}} \mathbf{cls}(E', v_2)$ *with* $H' \leq_{R'} E'$ *and* $v_1 \sim_{R'}^0 v_2$ *for some* R', E', *and* v_2.

Proof Outline. By induction on the derivation of $\langle H \rangle e_1 \Downarrow_{\mathrm{m}} \langle H' \rangle v_1$. The essential case is evaluation of **let**-bindings, that is, when $e_1 = \mathbf{let}\ \overline{e_{11}}\ \mathbf{in}\ e_{12}$ and $e_2 = \mathbf{let}\ \overline{e_{21}}\ \mathbf{in}\ e_{22}$.

$$\frac{\langle H, \overline{e_{11}}[\forall x \mapsto \mathbf{loc}\ (|H| + x)] \rangle\, e_{12}[\forall x \mapsto \mathbf{loc}\ (|H| + x)] \Downarrow_{\mathrm{m}} \langle H' \rangle v_1}{\langle H \rangle\, \mathbf{let}\ \overline{e_{11}}\ \mathbf{in}\ e_{12} \Downarrow_{\mathrm{m}} \langle H' \rangle v_1}$$

We aim to derive $\dfrac{\{(\mu. \overline{e_{21}}) +\!\!\!+ E\}e_{22} \Downarrow_{\mathrm{m}} \mathbf{cls}(E', v_2)}{\{E\}\mathbf{let}\ \overline{e_{21}}\ \mathbf{in}\ e_{22} \Downarrow_{\mathrm{m}} \mathbf{cls}(E', v_2)}$. To apply the induction

hypothesis, we check $(H, \overline{e_{11}}[\forall x \mapsto \mathbf{loc}\ (|H| + x)]) \leq_{\{(l,x+|\overline{e_{11}}|)|(l,x)\in R\}\cup\{(|H|+x,x)|x<|\overline{e_{11}}|\}} (\mu. \overline{e_{21}}) +\!\!\!+ E$, which follows straightforwardly from the above coinductive definition of $\leq$. Note that the original correspondence R is shifted by $|\overline{e_{11}}|$ like

$\{(l, x + |\overline{e_{11}}|)|(l, x) \in R\}$ and extended with the newly introduced correspondence $\{(|H| + x, x)|x < |\overline{e_{11}}|\}$.   □

Theorem 6 (heap-based ⇒ closure-based divergence). *If* $\langle H \rangle e_1 \Uparrow_m$ *with* $H \leq_R E$ *and* $e_1 \sim_R^0 e_2$, *then* $\{E\}e_2 \Uparrow_m$.

Proof Outline. By straightforward coinduction with Theorem 5 when the function part of **app** converges.   □

Theorem 7 (closure-based ⇒ heap-based convergence). *If* $\{E\}e_2 \Downarrow_m$ $\mathbf{cls}(E', v_2)$ *with* $H \leq_R E$ *and* $e_1 \sim_R^0 e_2$, *then* $\langle H \rangle e_1 \Downarrow_m \langle H' \rangle v_1$, $H' \leq_{R'} E'$, *and* $v_1 \sim_{R'}^0 v_2$ *for some* R', H', *and* v.

Proof Outline. By induction on the derivation of $\{E\}e_2 \Downarrow_m \mathbf{cls}(E', v_2)$, similar to Theorem 5.   □

Theorem 8 (closure-based ⇒ heap-based divergence). *If* $\{E\}e_2 \Uparrow_m$, $H \leq_R E$, *and* $e_1 \sim_R^0 e_2$, *then* $\langle H \rangle e_1 \Uparrow_m$.

Proof Outline. By straightforward coinduction similar to Theorem 6.   □

Note that, unlike the correspondence between heap-based call-by-need and call-by-name semantics, these correspondence proofs between heap-based and closure-based call-by-name semantics are more "symmetric" and straightforward since both evaluations are call-by-name and the correspondence between the heap and the environment is "at most one-to-one" rather than one-to-many.

3.3   Substitution-Based and Heap-Based Call-by-Name Evaluations

Our last main theorem is the correspondence between heap-based and substitution-based call-by-name evaluations. This time, we define some correspondence of a pair $\langle H \rangle e_1$ of heap H and term e_1, to a term e_2 after substitution.

To define an appropriate correspondence, let us consider, for example, **let** $x = \lambda w. x$ **in** $(\lambda y. \lambda z. x\, y)$ **true** (assuming the Boolean constant **true**), whose de Bruijn index version e is:

let (abs (var 1)) in app (abs (abs (app (var 2) (var 1)))) true

Its heap-based evaluation gives $\lambda z. l_1\, l_2$ under the heap $\{l_1 \mapsto \lambda w. l_1, l_2 \mapsto \mathbf{true}\}$

$$\langle \rangle\, e \Downarrow_m \langle \mathbf{abs}\ (\mathbf{loc}\ 0), \mathbf{true} \rangle\, \mathbf{abs}\ (\mathbf{app}\ (\mathbf{loc}\ 0)\ (\mathbf{loc}\ 1))$$

while the corresponding substitution-based evaluation is $\lambda z. (\mathbf{let}\ x = \lambda w. x\ \mathbf{in}\ \lambda w. x)\ \mathbf{true}$.

$$e \Downarrow_m \mathbf{abs}\ (\mathbf{app}\ (\mathbf{let}\ (\mathbf{abs}\ (\mathbf{var}\ 1))\ \mathbf{in}\ (\mathbf{abs}\ (\mathbf{var}\ 1)))\ \mathbf{true})$$

Note that the variable x (or **var** 2 in de Bruijn indices) is substituted with **let** $x = \lambda w. x$ **in** $\lambda w. x$ (or **let (abs (var 1)) in abs (var 1)**).

$$\frac{}{\langle H\rangle\,\mathbf{var}\ x \sim_R \mathbf{var}\ x} \qquad \frac{(l, e_2) \in R}{\langle H\rangle\,\mathbf{loc}\ l \sim_R e_2} \qquad \frac{\langle\uparrow^1 H\rangle e_1 \sim_{\uparrow^1 R} e_2}{\langle H\rangle\,\mathbf{abs}\ e_1 \sim_R \mathbf{abs}\ e_2}$$

$$\frac{\langle H\rangle H.l \sim_R e_2}{\langle H\rangle\,\mathbf{loc}\ l \sim_R e_2} \qquad \frac{\langle H\rangle e_{11} \sim_R e_{21} \quad \langle H\rangle e_{12} \sim_R e_{22}}{\langle H\rangle\,\mathbf{app}\ e_{11}\ e_{12} \sim_R \mathbf{app}\ e_{21}\ e_{22}}$$

$$\frac{|\overline{e_{11}}| = |\overline{e_{21}}| \quad \forall i.\ \langle\uparrow^{|\overline{e_{11}}|} H\rangle\overline{e_{11}}.i \sim_{\uparrow^{|\overline{e_{11}}|} R} \overline{e_{21}}.i \quad \langle\uparrow^{|\overline{e_{11}}|} H\rangle e_{12} \sim_{\uparrow^{|\overline{e_{11}}|} R} e_{22}}{\langle H\rangle\,\mathbf{let}\ \overline{e_{11}}\ \mathbf{in}\ e_{12} \sim_R \mathbf{let}\ \overline{e_{21}}\ \mathbf{in}\ e_{22}}$$

Fig. 8. The correspondence of terms for substitution-based natural semantics

Recall that we aim to establish a correspondence between heap-term pairs and after-substitution terms. Thus: (1) there is a mapping R from heap locations to terms substituted for variables corresponding to the locations, for example $R = \{l_1 \mapsto \mathbf{let}\ x = \lambda w.\,x\ \mathbf{in}\ \lambda w.\,x, l_2 \mapsto \mathbf{true}\}$ in the above evaluations; (2) the recursive binding x of $\lambda w.x$ is expanded to $\mathbf{let}\ x = \lambda w.\,x\ \mathbf{in}\ \lambda w.\,x$ in R for l_1; (3) on the other hand, the non-recursive binding of y to $\mathbf{true}$ is put in R for l_2 with no such expansion.

Hence we define the correspondence $e_1 \sim_R e_2$ between terms e_1 and e_2 under the mapping R from locations to terms, and aim to prove theorems as in previous subsections. However, unlike the other semantics, there is no explicit evaluation rule for variable (or location) dereference in the substitution-based semantics (recall Fig. 5). As a result, we face difficulties in proving some of the theorems: specifically, (a) when the heap-based evaluation diverges, we do not immediately get the divergence of substitution-based evaluation, since the former might involve an infinite number of location dereferences while the latter does not; (b) when the substitution-based evaluation converges, we do not immediately know whether the heap-based evaluation converges, for the same reason. A more careful observation leads us to the distinction that (i) bindings introduced by function applications are non-recursive, and therefore their dereferences are finite (intuitively like administrative reductions in CPS transformation [28] are finite), while (ii) **let**-bindings may be recursive and may cause infinite dereferences, but those dereferences always involve **let**-expansions in the substitution-based semantics. We therefore distinguish the two different kinds of bindings in our correspondence $\langle H\rangle e_1 \sim_R e_2$ of heap-based term e_1 to substitution-based e_2, as defined in Fig. 8. Here R only accounts for correspondence between locations and terms substituted for variables introduced by **let**-bindings, while H remembers terms bound by function applications as represented by the rule $\dfrac{\langle H\rangle H.l \sim_R e_2}{\langle H\rangle\,\mathbf{loc}\ l \sim_R e_2}$. Note that the dereference of location l to its contents $H.l$ on the left-hand side is implicit on the right since the corresponding substitution was already applied to e_2 at the time of function application (that introduced l on the left-hand side).

Note also the shift operations $\uparrow^d$ on the codomain (terms) of H and R in the rules for binders (**abs** and **let**) in Fig. 8, which increases by d all the free variables in H and the codomain of R.

$$\frac{}{\langle H\rangle \mathbf{loc}\ l \to_{\mathtt{m}} \langle H\rangle H.l} \qquad \frac{\langle H\rangle e_1 \to_{\mathtt{m}} \langle H'\rangle e_1'}{\langle H\rangle \mathbf{app}\ e_1\ e_2 \to_{\mathtt{m}} \langle H'\rangle \mathbf{app}\ e_1'\ e_2}$$

$$\frac{}{\langle H\rangle \mathbf{app}\ (\mathbf{abs}\ e_0)\ e_2 \to_{\mathtt{m}} \langle H,\ e_2\rangle e_0[0 \mapsto \mathbf{loc}\ |H|]}$$

$$\frac{}{\langle H\rangle \mathbf{let}\ \overline{e}\ \mathbf{in}\ e \to_{\mathtt{m}} \langle H_1,\ \overline{e}[\forall x \mapsto \mathbf{loc}\ (|H_1|+x)]\rangle e[\forall x \mapsto \mathbf{loc}\ (|H_1|+x)]}$$

Fig. 9. Heap-based small-step operational semantics for call-by-name

We now prove the four correspondence theorems with the following auxiliary definition:

Definition 3 (let-only correspondence). *We write* $let_R(H)$ *iff for all* $(l, e_2) \in R,\ \exists \overline{e_{21}}, e_{22}.\ e_2 = \mathbf{let}\ \overline{e_{21}}\ \mathbf{in}\ e_{22} \wedge \langle H\rangle H.l \sim_R e_{22}[\forall i \mapsto \mathbf{let}\ \overline{e_{21}}\ \mathbf{in}\ \overline{e_{21}}.i]$.

Theorem 9 (heap-based $\Rightarrow$ substitution-based convergence). *If* $\langle H\rangle e_1 \Downarrow_{\mathtt{m}}$ $\langle H'\rangle v_1$ *with* $let_R(H)$ *and* $\langle H\rangle e_1 \sim_R e_2$, *then* $e_2 \Downarrow_{\mathtt{m}} v_2$ *with* $let_{R'}(H')$ *and* $\langle H'\rangle v_1 \sim_{R'} v_2$ *for some* $R' \supseteq R$ *and* v_2.

Proof Outline. By straightforward induction on the derivation of $\langle H\rangle e_1 \Downarrow_{\mathtt{m}}$ $\langle H'\rangle v_1$. $\qquad\square$

Theorem 10 (heap-based $\Rightarrow$ substitution-based divergence). *If* $\langle H\rangle e_1 \Uparrow_{\mathtt{m}}$ *with* $let_R(H)$ *and* $\langle H\rangle e_1 \sim_R e_2$, *then* $e_2 \Uparrow_{\mathtt{m}}$.

Proof Outline. By nested induction on the derivation of $\langle H\rangle e_1 \sim_R e_2$ inside coinduction on $\langle H\rangle e_1 \Uparrow_{\mathtt{m}}$. The essential cases are evaluation of applications and locations.

Case: $e_1 = \mathbf{app}\ e_{11}\ e_{12}$, $e_2 = \mathbf{app}\ e_{21}\ e_{22}$.

$$\frac{\langle H\rangle e_{11} \Downarrow_{\mathtt{m}} \langle H'\rangle \mathbf{abs}\ e_{10} \qquad \langle H',\ e_{12}\rangle e_{10}[0 \mapsto \mathbf{loc}\ |H'|] \Uparrow_{\mathtt{m}}}{\langle H\rangle\ \mathbf{app}\ e_{11}\ e_{12} \Uparrow_{\mathtt{d}} H'v}$$

By Theorem 9, we have $e_{21} \Downarrow_{\mathtt{m}} \mathbf{abs}\ e_{20}$ with $let_{R'}(H')$ and $\langle \uparrow^1 H'\rangle e_{10} \sim_{\uparrow^1 R'} e_{20}$. To apply the hypothesis of the outer coinduction, we derive $\langle H',\ e_{12}\rangle e_{10}[0 \mapsto \mathbf{loc}\ |H'|] \sim_{R'} e_{20}[0 \mapsto e_{22}]$, which follows from a kind of "substitution lemma".

Case: $e_1 = \mathbf{loc}\ l$. From $\langle H\rangle e_1 \sim_R e_2$, we have two subcases.

Subcase: $\dfrac{\langle H\rangle H.l \sim_R e_2}{\langle H\rangle \mathbf{loc}\ l \sim_R e_2}$. Immediate from the inner induction hypothesis.

Subcase: $\dfrac{(l, e_2) \in R}{\langle H\rangle \mathbf{loc}\ l \sim_R e_2}$. From $(l, e_2) \in R$, we have $e_2 = \mathbf{let}\ \overline{e_{21}}\ \mathbf{in}\ e_{22}$ with $\langle H\rangle H.l \sim_R e_{22}[\forall i \mapsto \mathbf{let}\ \overline{e_{21}}\ \mathbf{in}\ \overline{e_{21}}.i]$. By the hypothesis of the outer coinduction, we have the divergence of the **let**-expanded term: $\dfrac{e_{22}[\forall i \mapsto \mathbf{let}\ \overline{e_{21}}\ \mathbf{in}\ \overline{e_{21}}.i] \Uparrow_{\mathtt{m}}}{\mathbf{let}\ \overline{e_{21}}\ \mathbf{in}\ e_{22} \Uparrow_{\mathtt{m}}}$ $\square$

$$\frac{e_1 \to_m e_1'}{\mathbf{app}\ e_1\ e_2 \to_m \mathbf{app}\ e_1'\ e_2} \qquad \mathbf{app}\ (\mathbf{abs}\ e_0)\ e_2 \to_m e_0[0 \mapsto e_2]$$

$$\mathbf{let}\ \bar{e}\ \mathbf{in}\ e \to_m e[i \mapsto \mathbf{let}\ \bar{e}\ \mathbf{in}\ \bar{e}.i]$$

Fig. 10. Substitution-based small-step operational semantics for call-by-name

Theorem 11 (substitution-based $\Rightarrow$ heap-based convergence). *If $e_2 \Downarrow_m v_2$ with $let_R(H)$ and $\langle H\rangle e_1 \sim_R e_2$, then $\langle H\rangle e_1 \Downarrow_m \langle H'\rangle v_1$ with $let_{R'}(H')$ and $\langle H\rangle v_1 \sim_R v_2$ for some $R' \supseteq R$, H', and v_2.*

Proof Outline. By nested induction on the derivation of $\langle H\rangle e_1 \sim_R e_2$ inside induction on the derivation of $e' \Downarrow_m v'$. The essential case, that is, evaluation of locations, is similar to Theorem 10. $\qquad\square$

Theorem 12 (substitution-based $\Rightarrow$ heap-based divergence). *If $e_2 \Uparrow_m v_2$ with $let_R(H)$ and $\langle H\rangle e_1 \sim_R e_2$, then $\langle H\rangle e_1 \Uparrow_m$.*

Proof Outline. By straightforward coinduction. $\qquad\square$

4   Formalization in Coq

Our proofs are almost straightforwardly formalized in Coq.[1] However, formalization of Theorem 10 (if heap-based call-by-name evaluation diverges, then substitution-based call-by-name evaluation of the corresponding term also diverges) is subtle because the syntactic guardedness condition [11,13] of coinduction as implemented in Coq—the conclusion must be derived from the coinduction hypothesis only via (possibly other) coinductive definitions—is too restrictive for our proof (mixture of coinduction and induction).

To avoid this problem, we take a "detour" using small-step operational semantics instead of the coinductive definition of divergence. The reduction rules for heap-based and substitution-based small-step semantics are shown in Figs. 9 and 10. Their correspondences with natural semantics required for our proof are stated as follows, where $\to_m^*$ is the reflexive transitive closure of $\to_m$, and $e \to_m$ means that there is a substitution-based reduction $e \to_m e'$ for some term e' ($\langle H\rangle e \to_m$ is similarly defined for heap-based reduction).

Lemma 9 (heap-based big-step $\Rightarrow$ small-step divergence). *If $\langle H\rangle e \Uparrow_m$ and $\langle H\rangle e \to_m^* \langle H'\rangle e'$, then $\langle H'\rangle e' \to_m$.*

Proof. By induction on the number of steps in $\langle H\rangle e \to_m^* \langle H'\rangle e'$. $\qquad\square$

Lemma 10 (substitution-based small-step $\Rightarrow$ big-step divergence). *If $\forall e'.\ e \to_m^* e' \implies e' \to_m$, then $e \Uparrow_m$.*

Proof. By coinduction and case analysis on e. In the case $e = \mathbf{app}\ e_1\ e_2$, we use the law of the excluded middle for $\exists e_1'.\ e_1 \to_{\mathbf{m}}^* e_1' \wedge e_1' \not\to_m$ and its negation (requiring `Classical` in Coq).   □

Note that we also avoid coinductive definition of divergence in the small-step semantics by considering an arbitrary but finite number of reductions instead of an infinite sequence of reductions.

Now Theorem 10 is proved without coinduction:

Alternative Proof Outline of Theorem 10. To apply Lemmas 9 and 10, we aim to derive: if $\forall H', e_1'.\ \langle H \rangle e_1 \to_{\mathbf{m}}^* \langle H' \rangle e_1' \implies \langle H' \rangle e_1' \to_{\mathbf{m}}$ and $e_2 \to_{\mathbf{m}}^* e_2'$ with $\langle H \rangle e_1 \sim_R e_2$ and $let_R(H)$, then $e_2' \to_{\mathbf{m}}$. This property is shown by nested induction on the derivation of $\langle H \rangle e_1 \sim_R e_2$ inside induction on the number of steps in $e_2 \to_{\mathbf{m}}^* e_2'$. Each case is analogous to the original proof of Theorem 10 albeit without coinduction.   □

5   Related Work

While call-by-need is often considered an efficient implementation of call-by-name and has been discussed via abstract machines such as G-machines (e.g. [16, 26]), Launchbury [19] defined big-step natural semantics, followed by small-step reduction semantics of Ariola and Felleisen [2] and Maraist et al. [21]. Correspondence of call-by-need and call-by-name semantics has thus been of natural interest.

In Launchbury [19], applications are restricted to the form $e\ x$, that is, the argument must be a variable. To ensure this convention, preprocessing like K-normalization [5] is required. This syntactic restriction would simplify our proof of the correspondence between substitution-based and heap-based call-by-name evaluations (Subsect. 3.3)—more specifically, bindings by function applications become trivial—but the correspondence proof between the normalized and original terms would anyway require a similar approach to account for administrative reductions [28].

Launchbury also introduced the notion of a "black-hole" to detect cycles in heap dereferences, which we have omitted in the present paper. Our evaluation is probably equivalent to Launchbury's, as his cycle detection does not actually affect the result of an evaluation. Such cycle detection may be useful for an implementation of an interpreter or a compiler to signal an error $\bot$, but his natural semantics cannot anyway distinguish divergence from stuckness (errors) caused by cycle detection. In contrast, we have defined divergence $\Uparrow_{\mathbf{d}}$ (caused by cyclic dereferences such as $\mathbf{let}\ x = x\ \mathbf{in}\ x$, as well as "real" infinite loops such as $(\lambda x.\ x\ x)\ (\lambda x.\ x\ x)$) by coinduction, discriminating it from stuckness.

Finally, Launchbury showed the adequacy of his call-by-need evaluation with respect to call-by-name denotational semantics (via auxiliary, heap-based definition of call-by-name evaluation). Our closure-based natural semantics informally corresponds to his denotational semantics (see Subsect. 2.3). The adequacy proof between his heap-based call-by-name semantics and denotational semantics is, in an informal sense, similar to our correspondence between heap-based and closure-based semantics of call-by-name evaluation. The fixed-point induction in his adequacy proof is replaced by straightforward coinduction in our proof of Theorem 5.

Ariola and Felleisen [3, section 8] introduced elaborate call-by-need reduction for λ-calculus with mutually recursive bindings. Ariola and Blom [2, section 8] defined its non-deterministic variant. The latter also showed the correspondence between their call-by-need and call-by-name reductions. However, their correspondence proof is based on term graphs, which are hard to formalize in proof assistants (like Coq in our case). Maraist et al. [21] also defined small-step reduction for call-by-need λ-calculus, but only without recursive bindings.

Nakata and Hasegawa [23] modified Launchbury's natural semantics [19] and small-step semantics by Ariola et al. [3] to handle black-holes explicitly (and to omit the normalization of terms). In contrast to Launchbury's, their natural semantics can distinguish black-holes from stuckness, thanks to the explicit introduction of • (meaning $\perp$) as a special value. Moreover, they proved the adequacy of their small-step semantics with respect to call-by-name denotational semantics through (the adequacy of) their natural semantics. Their theory of blackholes may also be incorporated into our operational semantics as well.

Stelle and Stefanovic [30] developed a formally verified compiler for a nonstrict language. They adopt call-by-name semantics for the target language, while their actual implementation is call-by-need, and thus their formalization includes the correspondence between call-by-need and call-by-name evaluations. However, their target language does not contain explicit recursion. Although recursion can be encoded by fixed-point combinators such as Curry's $\mathbf{Y}$, such representation destroys sharing. For instance, in the evaluation of $\mathbf{Y}(\lambda x.\mathbf{I}(\lambda y.x))\mathbf{I}\mathbf{I}$ where $\mathbf{I}$ is $\lambda x.x$, the subterm $\mathbf{I}(\lambda y.x)$ is reduced twice, in contrast to the evaluation of $\mathbf{let}\ x = \mathbf{I}(\lambda y.x)\ \mathbf{in}\ x\mathbf{I}\mathbf{I}$.

We [22] mechanically formalized (a variant of) Ariola and Felleisen's call-by-need reduction [3] (in Coq). We also gave an alternative proof of the correspondence between call-by-need and call-by-name evaluations, by using the standardization theorem [12]. However, our target language does not include explicit recursion, either.

More recently, Hackett and Hutton [14] showed their non-deterministic call-by-value evaluation corresponds to Launchbury's call-by-need evaluation. They also discussed how replacing thunk updates with non-determinism simplifies operational reasoning, especially cost analysis. Other recent work on call-by-need evaluation (albeit without explicit recursion) includes Kesner et al. [17]. They proved observational equivalence between call-by-need and (weak-head) needed reduction [4] (another "oracle-based" semantics of non-strict languages) using non-idempotent intersection types [6].

6   Conclusion

We gave arguably simpler proofs, which are easier to formalize in proof assistants such as Coq, of the correspondence among call-by-need and call-by-name evaluations, solely based on operational semantics.

Our approach may also be applicative for proving the correctness of implementations of lazy data structures (such as [24, section 6.3.2] and [15, exercise 2.4.3.6] for example). Correspondence to call-by-name (as in [24, section 5.2]) would be similar to the present work, whereas correspondence to call-by-value (as in [15, section 2.4.3]), assuming convergence, would be somewhat simpler, as divergence and "reevaluation" (like call-by-name) should be omitted.

As future work, we plan to extend our target language with cycle detection (black-holes) like Nakata and Hasewaga [23] as well as with data constructors and pattern matchings (cf. [19, subsection 9.1], [29, section 5]). We conjecture that our simple proofs scale easily to the latter extension since the only fundamental difference between call-by-need and call-by-name in (variants or extensions of) Launchbury's natural semantics is the evaluation rule for variable dereferences even if the target language is extended. Moreover, our techniques may also be applicable for cost analysis of call-by-need evaluations, and verification of compilers (such as GHC) for non-strict languages.

References

1. Abramsky, S.: The lazy lambda calculus. In: Turner, D.A. (ed.) Research Topics in Functional Programming, pp. 65–116. Addison-Wesley Publishing Co., Boston (1990)
2. Ariola, Z.M., Blom, S.: Cyclic lambda calculi. In: Abadi, M., Ito, T. (eds.) TACS 1997. LNCS, vol. 1281, pp. 77–106. Springer, Heidelberg (1997). https://doi.org/10.1007/BFb0014548
3. Ariola, Z.M., Felleisen, M.: The call-by-need lambda calculus. JFP **7**(3), 265–301 (1997)
4. Barendregt, H.P., Kennaway, R., Klop, J.W., Sleep, M.R.: Needed reduction and spine strategies for the lambda calculus. Inf. Comput. **75**(3), 191–231 (1987)
5. Birkedal, L., Tofte, M., Vejlstrup, M.: From region inference to von Neumann machines via region representation inference. In: POPL, pp. 171–183 (1996)
6. Boudol, G., Curien, P., Lavatelli, C.: A semantics for lambda calculi with resources. Math. Struct. Comput. Sci. **9**(4), 437–482 (1999)
7. Breitner, J.: The adequacy of Launchbury's natural semantics for lazy evaluation. JFP **28**, e1 (2018)
8. de Bruijn, N.G.: Lambda calculus notation with nameless dummies, a tool for automatic formula manipulation, with application to the Church-Rosser theorem. Indagationes Mathematicae (Proc.) **75**(5), 381–392 (1972)
9. Charguéraud, A.: The locally nameless representation. J. Autom. Reasoning **49**(3), 363–408 (2012)
10. Church, A.: An unsolvable problem of elementary number theory. Am. J. Math. **58**(2), 345–363 (1936)

11. Coquand, T.: Infinite objects in type theory. In: Barendregt, H., Nipkow, T. (eds.) TYPES 1993. LNCS, vol. 806, pp. 62–78. Springer, Heidelberg (1994). https://doi.org/10.1007/3-540-58085-9_72

12. Curry, H.B., Feys, R.: Combinatory Logic, Studies in Logic and the Foundations of Mathematics, vol. 1. North-Holland, Amsterdam (1958)

13. Giménez, E.: Codifying guarded definitions with recursive schemes. In: Dybjer, P., Nordström, B., Smith, J. (eds.) TYPES 1994. LNCS, vol. 996, pp. 39–59. Springer, Heidelberg (1995). https://doi.org/10.1007/3-540-60579-7_3

14. Hackett, J., Hutton, G.: Call-by-need is clairvoyant call-by-value. In: ICFP (2019, to appear)

15. Halim, S., Halim, F.: Competitive Programming, 3rd edn. Lulu, Morrisville (2013)

16. Johnsson, T.: Efficient compilation of lazy evaluation. In: ACM SIGPLAN Symposium on Compiler Construction, pp. 58–69 (1984)

17. Kesner, D., Ríos, A., Viso, A.: Call-by-need, neededness and all that. In: FOSSACS, pp. 241–257 (2018)

18. Landin, P.J.: The mechanical evaluation of expressions. Comput. J. **6**(4), 308–320 (1964)

19. Launchbury, J.: A natural semantics for lazy evaluation. In: POPL, pp. 144–154 (1993)

20. Leroy, X., Grall, H.: Coinductive big-step operational semantics. Inf. Comput. **207**(2), 284–304 (2009)

21. Maraist, J., Odersky, M., Wadler, P.: The call-by-need lambda calculus. JFP **8**(3), 275–317 (1998)

22. Mizuno, M., Sumii, E.: Formal verification of the correspondence between call-by-need and call-by-name. In: Gallagher, J.P., Sulzmann, M. (eds.) FLOPS 2018. LNCS, vol. 10818, pp. 1–16. Springer, Cham (2018). https://doi.org/10.1007/978-3-319-90686-7_1

23. Nakata, K., Hasegawa, M.: Small-step and big-step semantics for call-by-need. JFP **19**(6), 699–722 (2009)

24. Okasaki, C.: Purely Functional Data Structures. Cambridge University Press, Cambridge (1998)

25. Ong, C.L.: Fully abstract models of the lazy lambda calculus. In: FOCS, pp. 368–376. IEEE Computer Society (1988)

26. Peyton Jones, S.: Implementing lazy functional languages on stock hardware: the spineless tagless G-machine. JFP **2**(2), 127–202 (1992)

27. Pierce, B.C.: Types and Programming Languages, 1st edn. The MIT Press, Cambridge (2002)

28. Plotkin, G.D.: Call-by-name, call-by-value and the λ-calculus. TCS **1**(2), 125–159 (1975)

29. Sestoft, P.: Deriving a lazy abstract machine. JFP **7**(3), 231–264 (1997)

30. Stelle, G., Stefanovic, D.: Verifiably lazy: verified compilation of call-by-need. In: IFL, pp. 49–58 (2018)

31. Wadsworth, C.P.: Semantics and pragmatics of the lambda calculus. Ph.D. thesis, Oxford University (1971)

Recursion Schemes in Coq

Kosuke Murata[✉] and Kento Emoto

Kyushu Institute of Technology, Kitakyushu, Japan
murata@pl.ai.kyutech.ac.jp, emoto@ai.kyutech.ac.jp

Abstract. Program calculation, a programming technique to derive
efficient programs from naive ones by program transformation, is challenging for program optimization. Tesson et al. have shown that Coq,
a popular proof assistant, provides a cost-effective way to implement a
powerful system for verifying correctness of program transformations,
but their applications are limited to list functions in the Theory of Lists.
In this paper, we propose an easy-to-use Coq library to prove more
advanced calculation rules in Coq for various recursion schemes, which
capture recursive programs on an arbitrary algebraic datatype. We prove
all the lemmas and theorems about recursion schemes in Coq including histomorphisms and futumorphisms proposed by Uustalu et al. Our
library can be used to obtain certified runnable programs from their definitions written with recursion schemes in Coq scripts. We demonstrate
a certified runnable program for the Fibonacci numbers and unbounded
knapsack problem from their histomorphic definitions.

Keywords: Program calculation · Functional programming ·
Recursion schemes · Coq

1 Introduction

Naive programs tend to be easy to implement but are often inefficient. In contrast, efficient programs require difficult programming techniques. Achieving
both "program efficiency" and "ease of implementation" is an important challenge in the study of programming.

Program calculation [1,2,11,17,18] is a technique to derive highly technical
and efficient programs from simple and inefficient programs. This technique uses
many transformation rules, such as the map-map fusion law:

$$\mathsf{map}\ g \circ \mathsf{map}\ f = \mathsf{map}\ (g \circ f), \tag{1}$$

where map is the higher-order function that applies a given function to each
element of a given list: $\mathsf{map}\ f\ [a_1, \ldots, a_n] = [f\ a_1, \ldots, f\ a_n]$. Applying the map-
map fusion law to transform a program can make the resulting program faster.

The aim of this study is to verify the "correctness" of program calculations.
This "correctness" consists of both the correctness of the transformation rules

© Springer Nature Switzerland AG 2019
A. W. Lin (Ed.): APLAS 2019, LNCS 11893, pp. 202–221, 2019.
https://doi.org/10.1007/978-3-030-34175-6_11

themselves and their correct application. The ultimate purpose of this study is to establish a method for verifying these aspects.

Coq [16], an interactive theorem prover, is a good choice for certified programs. Coq has the *Gallina* language, which is a typed functional language to write programs. One can write programs in Gallina and prove properties about them.

Tesson et al. [15] designed a tactic library for program calculation in Coq. Their library provides tactic notations for writing Coq scripts in the "chains of equality" style, which is a common notation in program calculation. This tactic library allows users to write Coq proof scripts that are almost the same as handwritten proofs. They also formalized the Theory of Lists [1], which provides a set of calculation rules for list-functions based on the Bird-Meertens Formalism (BMF).

Functional programmers like to use several *algebraic datatypes* (ADTs) such as natural numbers and trees. Tesson et al. focused only on functions on lists, but a novel framework for program calculation has to support several ADTs. Fortunately, several studies have proposed calculation rules for arbitrary ADTs [11,17,18]. In this paper, we call such rules "datatype-generic rules." Datatype-generic rules are stated with terminology of basic category theory: initial algebras and terminal coalgebras for modeling ADTs and *recursion schemes*, such as catamorphism, anamorphism, and paramorphism for modeling programs recursively defined on arbitrary ADTs. For instance, the map-map fusion law is generalized for any ADT by using a bifunctor F with its initial algebra and catamorphism [11,18]: map $f = (\!|\,\mathsf{in}_F \circ F(f, \mathsf{id})\,|\!)$ also satisfies Formula (1).

In this paper, we propose an easy-to-use Coq library for "certified" program calculation. The library is mainly based on that by Tesson et al. [15], and we improved their library for the recursion schemes. The important features of our library can be summarized as follows.

Adopting the shallow embedding approach. This approach enables users to write Gallina programs in terms of recursion schemes; i.e., their programs written with recursion schemes can run in Coq. We call such programs "recursion-scheme-style (RS-style) programs". Users can then verify properties of the RS-style programs in Coq.

Providing notations for concise program definitions and proof scripts. Our library provides concise notations for RS-style programs and the equational proofs. Thanks to these notations, users can write proofs that are almost the same as hand-written proofs in program-calculation papers. We give an example of proof scripts in Sect. 4 and RS-style program definitions in Sect. 5. As we explain in Sect. 5, this conciseness is due to our typeclass-based definitions and the powerful inference of implicit parameters in Coq.

Our contributions are summarized as follows.

1. We provide a novel certified program calculation library, as mentioned above.
2. We prove all the lemmas and theorems proposed by Uustalu et al. [17] in Coq by using our library. This includes advanced recursion schemes and the

set of calculation rules useful for dynamic programming (DP), an important technique for practical programming. An example of the proofs and a list of propositions that we proved are given in Sect. 4.

3. Our library enables users to obtain verified Coq programs and extract runnable programs in various languages. We show that it is possible to obtain programs for the n-th Fibonacci number and for the unbounded knapsack problem (UKP) from their histomorphic definitions. This is explained in Sect. 5.

The remainder of the paper is organized as follows. In Sect. 2, we give an overview of Coq and the tactic library [15] for program calculation and introduce notions of category theory and recursion schemes. In Sect. 3, we explain how to prove equalities of two coinductively defined objects. In Sect. 4, we discuss a method of formalizing ADTs and recursion schemes using typeclasses. In Sect. 5, we explain instantiation of the class of ADTs and give example calculation. In Sect. 6, we describe related work; and we present our conclusions and future work in Sect. 7.

Our Coq scripts are available at the GitHub repository[1].

2   Preliminaries

In this section, we introduce Coq and a tactic library for program calculation proposed by Tesson et al. [15]. We also introduce notions in basic category theory for describing datatype-generic theorems.

2.1   Overview of Coq and a Tactic Library for Program Calculation

A Coq script consists of definitions for datatypes, formulas of propositions that we want to prove, and their proofs. A Coq proof is written with tactics, which are commands for constructing proofs. Coq has a sub-language Ltac for programming user-defined tactics. Ltac provides **Tactic Notation** commands defining various user notation in Coq. For further details, see the Coq reference manual [16].

Tesson et al. [15] designed and implemented a tactic library for program calculation in Coq. Their tactic library provides tactic notations that make it possible to write a Coq script in the "chains of equalities" style, which is a common notation in program calculation.

We re-implemented their library mainly for maintainability. Our library is mainly for equational reasoning and provides the following three tactics:

TACTIC 1. Left = $\langle term \rangle$ TACTIC 2. = $\langle term \rangle$ { $\langle tactic \rangle$ }
TACTIC 3. = Right

These tactics are implemented using **Tactic Notation** commands.

---

[1] https://github.com/muratak17/Recursion-Schemes-in-Coq.

Step	Script buffers	Goal window

0	`intros x y z H0 H1.`
	`Left`
	`= ( x + y ).`
	`= ( x + x )    { rewrite <- H0 }.`
	`= z            { rewrite H1 }.`
	`= Right.`
		`===============================`
		`forall x y z : nat,`
		`x = y -> z = x + x -> x + y = z`

1	`intros x y z H0 H1.`
	`Left`
	`= ( x + y ).`
	`= ( x + x )    { rewrite <- H0 }.`
	`= z            { rewrite H1 }.`
	`= Right.`
		`x, y, z : nat`
		`H0 : x = y`
		`H1 : z = x + x`
		`==============================`
		`x + y = z`

2	`intros x y z H0 H1.`
	`Left`
	`= ( x + y ).`
	`= ( x + x )    { rewrite <- H0 }.`
	`= z            { rewrite H1 }.`
	`= Right.`
		`x, y, z : nat`
		`H0 : x = y`
		`H1 : z = x + x`
		`d := direction Rightwards : Prop`
		`==============================`
		`x + y = z`

3	`intros x y z H0 H1.`
	`Left`
	`= ( x + y ).`
	`= ( x + x )    { rewrite <- H0 }.`
	`= z            { rewrite H1 }.`
	`= Right.`
		`x, y, z : nat`
		`H0 : x = y`
		`H1 : z = x + x`
		`d := direction Rightwards : Prop`
		`==============================`
		`x + x = z`

4	`intros x y z H0 H1.`
	`Left`
	`= ( x + y ).`
	`= ( x + x )    { rewrite <- H0 }.`
	`= z            { rewrite H1 }.`
	`= Right.`
		`x, y, z : nat`
		`H0 : x = y`
		`H1 : z = x + x`
		`d := direction Rightwards : Prop`
		`==============================`
		`z = z`

5	`intros x y z H0 H1.`
	`Left`
	`= ( x + y ).`
	`= ( x + x )    { rewrite <- H0 }.`
	`= z            { rewrite H1 }.`
	`= Right.`	

Fig. 1. Progress of interactive proof in Coq IDE

Figure 1 illustrates an interactive proof with our library to show the proposition $\forall\ (x\ y\ z : \mathtt{nat}),\ (x = y) \to (z = x + x) \to (x + y = z)$. For a goal $t = s$, TACTIC 1 starts the proof by rewriting t to the given *term* by using the tactic `reflexivity`. This can be seen in the first step in Fig. 1. Its specified *term* is the same as the LHS of the goal; thus, the goal remains unchanged. TACTIC 2 advances the chain of the equational reasoning in a similar manner (see the 2nd through 4th steps in Fig. 1). TACTIC 3 finishes the chain; it directly proves the current goal $s = s$ by using `reflexivity`. Note that the term "d := direction Rightwards : Prop" in Fig. 1 is used to memorize the direction of the chain growth.

To make a script shorter and easier to read, we implement short-hands of these tactics. For instance, "= s" is equal to "= s { easy }", and "= s { by t }" is equal to "= s { rewrite t + rewrite <- t }"; the last tactic tries rewriting the current goal using equation t and then rewrites backwards by t if the forward rewriting fails.

Note that our library adopts the textbook style

$$f_1$$
$$= f_2 \ \{\text{the reason why } f_1 = f_2 \text{ holds}\},$$

instead of usual Dijkstra-Feijen style

$$\begin{aligned} & f_1 \\ = \; & \{\text{the reason why } f_1 = f_2 \text{ holds}\} \\ & f_2. \end{aligned}$$

This is because we think this style is better for a short-hand notation such as `Left = t. = s.`, in which reasons are trivial and omitted, than Dijkstra-Feijen style.

To improve readability, we write Coq scripts using roman and sans serif fonts, as used in mathematical expressions, instead of typewriter font.

2.2   Basic Notions of Category Theory

We use the basic notions of category theory for describing datatype-generic theorems. We work the category **Set**, the category of sets and total functions.

We admit the functional extensionality axiom about the equality of functions, i.e., for any two functions $f, g : A \to B$, the equality $f = g$ holds if and only if $\forall \, (x \in A), \; f \, x = g \, x$. Given two sets A, B, we write $A * B$ for the product (just like the Coq standard library), and $A + B$ for the sum. We write $\mathsf{fst} : A * B \to A$ and $\mathsf{snd} : A * B \to B$ for the left and right projection functions, $\mathsf{inl} : A \to A + B$ and $\mathsf{inr} : B \to A + B$ for the constructors of the sum. For $f : A \to B$ and $g : A \to C$, we use $\langle f, g \rangle : A \to B * C$ for the unique morphism h such that $\mathsf{fst} \circ h = f$ and $\mathsf{snd} \circ h = g$. For $f : A \to C$ and $g : B \to C$, we use $[f, g] : A + B \to C$ for the unique morphism h such that $h \circ \mathsf{inl} = f$ and $h \circ \mathsf{inr} = g$. Figure 2 shows the definitions for such morphisms in Coq. These morphisms satisfy the following equalities:

$$\begin{array}{llll} \mathsf{fst} \circ \langle f, g \rangle & = f, & \mathsf{snd} \circ \langle f, g \rangle & = g, \\ [f, g] \circ \mathsf{inl} & = f, & [f, g] \circ \mathsf{inr} & = g, \\ \langle \mathsf{fst} \circ f, \mathsf{snd} \circ f \rangle & = f, & (i \otimes j) \circ \langle f, g \rangle & = \langle i \circ f, j \circ g \rangle, \\ [f \circ \mathsf{inl}, f \circ \mathsf{inr}] & = f, & [f, g] \circ (i \oplus j) & = [f \circ i, g \circ j]. \end{array}$$

These equations are easily proven in Coq by using functional extensionality and are often used implicitly in program calculations.

We define **0** as the initial object, and **1** as the terminal object in **Set**; so **0** is the empty set { }, and **1** is a singleton set {()} with solo element ().

2.3   Modeling Datatypes and Basic Recursion Schemes

We adopt a traditional method of modeling inductively- and coinductively-defined datatypes, namely to use "initial F-algebras" and "terminal F-coalgebras" where $F : \mathbf{Set} \to \mathbf{Set}$ is a polynomial functor. For a polynomial functor $F : \mathbf{Set} \to \mathbf{Set}$, we write $(\mu F, \mathsf{in}_F)$ for the initial F-algebra and $(\nu F, \mathsf{out}_F)$ for the terminal F-coalgebra. Note that the set μF is the least fixed point of F, and the set νF is the greatest fixed point of F. For any polynomial

Definition fprod $\{A \ B \ C : \text{Type}\} \ (f : A \to B) \ (g : A \to C) : A \to B * C :=$
$\boldsymbol{\lambda} \ (x : A) \Rightarrow (f \ x, g \ x).$
Definition fsum $\{A \ B \ C : \text{Type}\} \ (f : A \to C) \ (g : B \to C) : A + B \to C :=$
$\boldsymbol{\lambda} \ (x : A + B) \Rightarrow \textbf{match } x \textbf{ with } \text{inl } x \Rightarrow f \ x \mid \text{inr } x \Rightarrow g \ x \textbf{ end}.$
Notation "$\langle f, g \rangle$" $:= (\text{fprod } f \ g).$ **Notation** "$[f, g]$" $:= (\text{fsum } f \ g).$
Notation "$f \otimes g$" $:= (\langle f \circ \text{fst}, g \circ \text{snd} \rangle).$ **Notation** "$f \oplus g$" $:= ([\text{inl} \circ f, \text{inr} \circ g]).$

Fig. 2. Definitions for product and sum of morphisms in Coq

functor $F : \textbf{Set} \to \textbf{Set}$, there uniquely exists the initial F-algebra and terminal F-coalgebra up to isomorphism. We also use polynomial functors indexed by a constant set A, e.g., $F_A : \textbf{Set} \to \textbf{Set}$ such as $F_A(X) = 1 + A * X$. Indexed functors, such as $F_A(X)$, can be seen as a partial application of bifunctor $F : \textbf{Set} \to \textbf{Set} \to \textbf{Set}$.

Below are examples of initial algebras and terminal coalgebras for modeling finite and infinite datatypes. Note that we use Coq-like notations for lambda abstraction, i.e. we write $\boldsymbol{\lambda} \ x \Rightarrow M$ for the lambda term $\boldsymbol{\lambda} \ x.M$.

Natural numbers. Let $N(X) = 1 + X$. The initial N-algebra $(\mu N, \text{in}_N)$ corresponds to the pair $(\textbf{nat}, [\boldsymbol{\lambda} \ \_ \Rightarrow \text{O}, \text{S}])$, where **nat** is the set of natural numbers and O and S are constructors corresponding to the zero and successor, respectively.

Lists. Let $L_A(X) = 1 + A * X$. The initial L_A-algebra $(\mu L_A, \text{in}_{L_A})$ corresponds to the pair $(\textbf{list } A, [\boldsymbol{\lambda} \ \_ \Rightarrow [\ ], ::])$, where **list** A is the set of finite lists of A and $[\ ]$ and :: are constructors corresponding to 'nil' and 'cons', respectively.

Streams. Let $S_A(X) = A * X$. The terminal S_A-coalgebra $(\nu S_A, \text{out}_{S_A})$ corresponds to the pair $(\textbf{Stream } A, \langle \text{hd}, \text{tl} \rangle)$, where **Stream** A is the set of streams (infinite sequences) of elements in A, hd is the function that returns the head (the first element) of the given stream, and tl is the function that returns the tail (the remainder of the stream except its first element) of the given stream.

Recursion schemes capture the typical patterns of recursively and corecursively defined computations. We introduce some recursion schemes below.

Catamorphism. *Catamorphisms* capture the typical patterns of recursive computations called "fold" that tears down a given tree. Let $(\mu F, \text{in}_F)$ be the initial F-algebra. Given a morphism $\varphi : F(X) \to X$, morphism $(\!|\varphi|\!)_F : \mu F \to X$ is the *catamorphism* for which the equation $\varphi \circ F((\!|\varphi|\!)_F) = (\!|\varphi|\!)_F \circ \text{in}_F$ holds. We write $(\!|\varphi|\!)$ instead of $(\!|\varphi|\!)_F$ when it is obvious what F is. We use the same abbreviations for the other recursion schemes.

Note that in_F is an isomorphism. Its inverse is given by $\text{in}_F^{-1} = (\!|F(\text{in}_F)|\!)$. This result is known as Lambek's lemma; thus $\mu F \cong F(\mu F)$ and indeed μF is a fixed point of F.

Catamorphisms can express many recursive functions on inductively-defined datatypes such as natural numbers and lists. For instance, the addition on the natural numbers *plus* : **nat** $\to$ **nat** $\to$ **nat** can be defined as follows: *plus* $x =$

$(\![\, \lambda \, \_ \, \Rightarrow x, \mathsf{S}]\,)\!)_N$. The 'append' function on lists $append \colon \mathbf{list}\ A \to \mathbf{list}\ A \to$
$\mathbf{list}\ A$ can be defined by $append\ x\ y = (\![\, [\lambda \, \_ \, \Rightarrow y, ::]\,)\!)\ x$.

Let F be a polynomial bifunctor. The mapping $\mathsf{fmap}_F\ f = (\![\, \mathsf{in}_F \circ F(f, \mathrm{id})\,)\!)$
is corresponds to the datatype-generic map function (Vene call it "data
functor" [18]). For instance, L_A has the initial algebra $(\mathbf{list}\ A, [\lambda \, \_ \, \Rightarrow$
$[\ ], ::])$; thus, the mapping fmap_L is defined: it is the map function on lists
$\mathsf{fmap}_L\ f\ [a_1; \ldots; a_n] = [f\ a_1; \ldots; f\ a_n]$ where $[a_1; \ldots; a_n]$ is the abbreviation
of $a_1 :: (\cdots :: (a_n :: [\ ]) \cdots)$. For any F, the data functor satisfies the following property called the *map-map fusion law*: $\mathsf{fmap}_F\ (g \circ f) = \mathsf{fmap}_F\ g \circ \mathsf{fmap}_F\ f$.

Anamorphism. *Anamorphisms* are the dual of catamorphisms and capture
computations of building up trees. Let $(\nu F, \mathsf{out}_F)$ be the terminal F-coalgebra.
Given a morphism $\varphi : X \to F(X)$, morphism $[\![\varphi]\!] : X \to \nu F$ is the *anamorphism*,
for which the equation $F([\![\varphi]\!]) \circ \varphi = \mathsf{out}_F \circ [\![\varphi]\!]$ holds. Similarly to catamorphism, out_F is an isomorphism, and its inverse is given by an isomorphism, and
its inverse is given by $\mathsf{out}_F^{-1} = [\![F(\mathsf{out}_F)]\!]$.

In the case of streams, i.e., $F = S_A$, the anamorphism an isomorphism, and
its inverse is given by $[\![\langle a, f \rangle]\!]_{S_A}$ applied to x generates an infinite sequence: $a\ x$,
$a\ (f\ x)$, $a\ (f^2\ x)$, …. This example shows that the anamorphism corresponds
to the function *unfold*, which is a well-known function in Haskell.

Histomorphism. Let us consider the following definition of Fibonacci numbers,
fibo : $\mathbf{nat} \to \mathbf{nat}$:

$$fibo\ 0 = 1, \quad fibo\ 1 = 1, \quad fibo\ (\mathsf{S}\ (\mathsf{S}\ n)) = fibo\ (\mathsf{S}\ n) + fibo\ n. \qquad (2)$$

This definition is one of the natural characterizations of the function that computes the n-th Fibonacci number, but it is difficult to translate the definition
into one in terms of catamorphisms. Catamorphisms can only use the results of
directly previous computation, but the RHS of the third equation requires the
value of *fibo* n, not a computation on the "direct" substructure of $\mathsf{S}\ (\mathsf{S}\ n)$.

To capture such computation, Uustalu et al. defined a recursion scheme called
histomorphisms [17]. This scheme can remember and use the results of all previous computations (i.e. all the results of computations on substructures). In other
words, it enables us to carry out dynamic programming (DP) algorithms in the
field of functional programming. The key idea of histomorphisms is to introduce
an intermediate data structure for memoizing the results of subcomputations.

First, we define a datatype for the intermediate data structure. Let $F : \mathbf{Set} \to$
$\mathbf{Set}$ be a polynomial functor and A be an object. We define a polynomial functor
$F_A^{\times} : \mathbf{Set} \to \mathbf{Set}$ indexed by A as

$$F_A^{\times}(X) = A * F(X), \qquad F_A^{\times}(f) = \mathrm{id}_A \otimes F(f)$$

and define another functor $\widetilde{F} \colon \mathbf{Set} \to \mathbf{Set}$ as

$$\widetilde{F}(A) = \nu F_A^{\times}, \qquad \widetilde{F}(f) = [\![\langle f \circ \varepsilon_A, \theta_A \rangle]\!]_{F_B^{\times}},$$

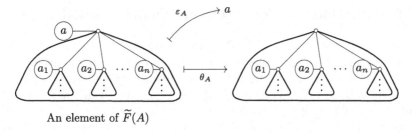

An element of $\widetilde{F}(A)$

Fig. 3. Conceptual diagram for memoization tree that is element of $\widetilde{F}(A)$ and return values of ε_A and θ_A

where $f\colon A \to B$, $\varepsilon_A = \mathsf{fst} \circ \mathsf{out}_{F_A^\times}$, and $\theta_A = \mathsf{snd} \circ \mathsf{out}_{F_A^\times}$. The $\widetilde{F}(A)$ is a datatype for intermediate data structures for memoization. Intuitively, it is the recursive datatype in which every node of νF is annotated by a value of type A. Therefore, $\widetilde{F}(1) \cong \nu F$. Figure 3 is a conceptual drawing for $\widetilde{F}(A)$. The elements $a, a_1, \ldots, a_n$ in this figure are annotation values of type A. The function ε_A returns the annotation value of the root node, which is a for the tree in Fig. 3, and θ_A returns the remainder that is the annotated subtrees without the root.

We now define histomorphisms. Given a morphism $\varphi\colon (F \circ \widetilde{F})(A) \to A$, morphism $\{\!|\varphi|\!\}_F\colon \mu F \to A$ is the *histomorphism* for which the following equation holds:

$$f \circ \mathsf{in}_F = \varphi \circ F(\llbracket\langle f, \mathsf{in}_F^{-1}\rangle\rrbracket) \iff f = \{\!|\varphi|\!\}_F. \tag{3}$$

Intuitively, $\llbracket\langle f, \mathsf{in}_F^{-1}\rangle\rrbracket\colon \mu F \to \widetilde{F}(A)$ builds a memoization tree in which each node holds the partial results, and φ advances the computation by using the memoized results. Note that φ can use values in the memoization tree, which means that it can access all the results of previous computations.

Formula (3) describes one of the characterizations of histomorphisms, but the left side of the iff arrow is a functional equation on f. In fact, Uustalu et al. gave the direct solution described by the following equation: $f = \varepsilon_A \circ (\!|\mathsf{out}_{F_A^\times}^{-1} \circ \langle\varphi, \mathsf{id}\rangle|\!)$. This equation provides a direct definition and a cost-effective way to compute histomorphisms.

Histomorphisms have a powerful expressiveness and can represent *fibo* : **nat** $\to$ **nat**. For $F(X) = 1 + X$, *fibo* can be defined as

$$\textit{fibo} = \{\!|[\textit{onec}, [\textit{onec} \circ \mathsf{snd}, \textit{add} \circ (\mathsf{id} \otimes (\mathsf{fst} \circ \mathsf{out}_{F_{\mathbf{nat}}^\times}))] \circ \textit{distl} \circ \mathsf{out}_{F_{\mathbf{nat}}^\times}]\!\}$$
$$\textbf{where } \textit{onec} = \boldsymbol{\lambda}\,\_ \Rightarrow 1,\ \textit{add}\,(m, n) = m + n, \tag{4}$$
$$\textit{distl}\,(a, \mathsf{inl}\,b) = \mathsf{inl}\,(a, b),\ \textit{distl}\,(a, \mathsf{inr}\,c) = \mathsf{inr}\,(a, c).$$

Note that *distl* in the above definition has the following polymorphic type: $\forall\,\{A\ B\ C : \mathsf{Type}\}, A * (B + C) \to (A * B) + (A * C)$.

Other Recursion Schemes. Uustalu et al. [17] described paramorphisms, apomorphisms, and futumorphisms.

3   Bisimulation for Coinductively Defined Equality

From the perspective of program calculation, equality of coinductively defined objects is important. In particular, anamorphisms generate coinductively defined objects; thus, proving the equation of anamorphisms requires equational reasoning on coinductively defined objects. In this section, we explain how to prove the equality of coinductively defined objects.

Just as equality of inductively-defined objects is proved by induction, that of coinductively-defined object is proved by *coinduction* [13]. To describe the principle of coinduction formally, we begin with defining the F-bisimulation.

Throughout this section, F is a polynomial functor.

Definition 1. *A relation* $\sim \subseteq \nu F \times \nu F$ *is an F-bisimulation if there exists γ such that the two equations $F(\mathsf{fst}) \circ \gamma = \mathsf{out}_F \circ \mathsf{fst}$ and $F(\mathsf{snd}) \circ \gamma = \mathsf{out}_F \circ \mathsf{snd}$ both hold.*

This definition leads to the following coinduction principle.

Theorem 1. *If $\sim \subseteq \nu F \times \nu F$ is F-bisimulation, then $\sim \subseteq \Delta_{\nu F}$ where $\Delta_{\nu F}$ is the diagonal relation on νF.*

Proof. By finality of νF, it follows that $\mathsf{fst} = \mathsf{snd}$ on pairs (x, y) such that $x \sim y$.

The theorem provides a strong principle to prove equalities on coinductively defined objects (for details, see [13]). The following two propositions are examples of bisimilar equalities. The proofs of the propositions are straightforward; thus, omitted.

Proposition 1. *Let $(S_A, \langle \mathsf{hd}, \mathsf{tl} \rangle)$ be the terminal S_A-coalgebra. A relation $\sim \subseteq \nu S_A \times \nu S_A$ is the S_A-bisimulation iff for all $(s, t) \in \sim$,*

$$(\mathsf{hd}\ s = \mathsf{hd}\ t) \wedge (\mathsf{tl}\ s \sim \mathsf{tl}\ t).$$

Proposition 2. *Let $(\widetilde{N}(\mathbf{nat}), \langle \varepsilon, \theta \rangle)$ be the terminal $N_{\mathbf{nat}}^{\times}$-coalgebra. A relation $\sim \subseteq \widetilde{N}(\mathbf{nat}) \times \widetilde{N}(\mathbf{nat})$ is an $N_{\mathbf{nat}}^{\times}$-bisimulation iff for all $(s, t) \in \sim$,*

$$(\varepsilon\ s = \varepsilon\ t) \wedge \left(\begin{matrix} (\theta\ s = \theta\ t = \mathsf{inl}\ ()) \\ \vee\ (\forall s', t'. (\theta\ s = \mathsf{inr}\ s') \to (\theta\ t = \mathsf{inr}\ t') \to (s' \sim t')) \end{matrix} \right).$$

This proposition is used for defining instances of terminal coalgebras in Sect. 5.

4   Recursion Schemes in Coq

In this section, we describe how to model datatypes and recursion schemes in Coq. Types and functions in Coq can be regarded as objects and morphisms in the category **Set**. Thus, what we need is to simply translate the notions used in the category theory into Coq's wording.

One of the key features of our formalization is using notations very similar to those in the original paper in program calculation [17], such as the "chain of equalities" notation introduced in Sect. 2.1. Thanks to this notation, we can easily build the formal proof because we simply write almost the same proof as a hand-written proof in the original paper. We use unicode parentheses, such as ⦇ (U+2987) and 〖 (U+3016), in our Coq scripts to follow the notation used in the original paper, by exploiting Coq's flexibility on characters.

4.1 Polynomial Functor

First, we begin with defining the notion of polynomial functors. Figure 4 shows the definitions and shorthand notation for polynomial functors in Coq. A functor consists of the following two mappings: one from objects to objects and the other from morphisms to morphisms. To define polynomial functors inductively, we first define inductive datatype PolyF to represent the ASTs of polynomial bifunctors and then use it to define the following two mappings for F : PolyF.

- inst F: Type $\to$ Type $\to$ Type and its shorthand $[\![F]\!]$ to map types (objects) to types (objects).
- fmap F: $(A_0 \to A_1) \to (X_0 \to X_1) \to [\![F]\!]\ A_0\ X_0 \to [\![F]\!]\ A_1\ X_1$ and its shorthand $F(-)[-]$ to map morphisms to morphisms.

We can obtain definitions for functors by partial applications: $[\![F]\!]\ A$ and $F(@\mathrm{id}\ A)[-]$ define a functor indexing by type A.

We now give examples for PolyF. Let $L = $ Sum one (Prod arg1 arg2). For A : Type, the type-level function $[\![L]\!]\ A$: Type $\to$ Type means the functor L_A defined in Sect. 2.

Polynomial functors must satisfy the functor laws. We proved the following two lemmas of the functor laws by using simple induction on F.

- **Lemma** functor_comp :

$$\forall\ (F : \mathrm{PolyF})\ \{A_0\ A_1\ A_2\ X_0\ X_1\ X_2 : \mathrm{Type}\}$$
$$(f_0 : A_0 \to A_1)\ (f_1 : A_1 \to A_2)\ (g_0 : X_0 \to X_1)\ (g_1 : X_1 \to X_2),$$
$$F(f_1 \circ f_0)[g_1 \circ g_0] = F(f_1)[g_1] \circ F(f_0)[g_0].$$

- **Lemma** functor_id :

$$\forall\ (F : \mathrm{PolyF})\ \{A\ X : \mathrm{Type}\},\ F(@\mathrm{id}\ A)[@\mathrm{id}\ X] = \mathrm{id}.$$

Note that the occurrences of "@id A" in the above definition are needed for deciding the type indexing F; otherwise, Coq cannot infer the type of $[\![F]\!]$ in "$F[g_1 \circ g_0] = F[g_1] \circ F[g_0]$."

4.2 Initial Algebras and Terminal Coalgebras in Coq

Next, we define notions of the initial algebras and terminal coalgebras in Coq. The basic idea is to write their axioms as typeclasses.

Inductive PolyF : Type :=
  zer : PolyF | one : PolyF | arg1 : PolyF | arg2 : PolyF
 | Sum : PolyF → PolyF → PolyF
 | Prod : PolyF → PolyF → PolyF.

Inductive inst $(F : \text{PolyF})$ $(A \; X : \text{Type})$: Type :=
  match F **with**
    zer ⇒ Empty_set | one ⇒ Unit | arg1 ⇒ A | arg2 ⇒ X
   | Sum $F \; G$ ⇒ $(\text{inst } F \; A \; X) + (\text{inst } G \; A \; X)$
   | Prod $F \; G$ ⇒ $(\text{inst } F \; A \; X) * (\text{inst } G \; A \; X)$
  end.
Notation "$[\![F]\!]$" := $(\text{inst } F)$.

Fixpoint fmap $(F : \text{PolyF})$ $\{A_0 \; A_1 \; X_0 \; X_1 : \text{Type}\}$
    $(f : A_0 \to A_1)$ $(g : X_0 \to X_1)$: $[\![F]\!] \; A_0 \; X_0 \to [\![F]\!] \; A_1 \; X_1$
  := **match** F **with**
        zer ⇒ id | one ⇒ id | arg1 ⇒ f | arg2 ⇒ g
     | Sum $F \; G$ ⇒ $\lambda \; x$ ⇒
         match x **with** inl x ⇒ inl $(\text{fmap } F \; f \; g \; x)$ | inr x ⇒ inr $(\text{fmap } F \; g \; x)$ **end**
     | Prod $F \; G$ ⇒ $\lambda \; x$ ⇒ $(\text{fmap } f \; g \; (\text{fst } x), \text{fmap } G \; f \; g \; x \; (\text{snd } x))$
    end.
Notation "$F(g)[f]$" := $(\text{@fmap } F \; \_ \; \_ \; \_ \; \_ \; g \; f)$ (at level 10).
Notation "$F[f]$" := $(\text{@fmap } F \; \_ \; \_ \; \_ \; \_ \; \text{id } f)$ (at level 10).

Fig. 4. Definitions for polynomial functors in Coq

Initial Algebras and Catamorphisms. We define a typeclass to capture the axiom of initial F-algebras as follows:

  Class initial_algebra $(F : \text{PolyF})$ $(A : \text{Type})$ $(\mu F : \text{Type})$
    := { cata   := $\forall \; (X : \text{Type}), ([\![F]\!] \; A \; X \to X) \to (\mu F \to X)$;
       in_   := $[\![F]\!] \; A \; \mu F \to \mu F$;
     cata_charn : $\forall \; (X : \text{Type}) \; (f : \mu F \to X) \; (\varphi : [\![F]\!] \; A \; X \to X)$,
               $f \circ \text{in}\_ = \varphi \circ F[f] \leftrightarrow f = \text{cata } X \; \varphi$}.
  Notation "$(\!|f|\!)$" := $(\text{cata } \_ \; \_ \; f)$ (at level 5).

For $f : [\![F]\!] \; A \; X \to X$, the term cata $X \; f$ is the catamorphism of f (i.e. $(\!|f|\!)$). The $(\mu F, \text{in}\_)$ is the initial algebra of $[\![F]\!] \; A$. Note that the μF usually depends on A but we not use the variable name $\mu F A$ but use μF, because we do not want to use a type function $\mu F : \text{Type} \to \text{Type}$.

    Next, we prove some properties of initial algebras and catamorphisms. In the type context

      Variable $(F : \text{PolyF})$ $(A \; \mu F : \text{Type})$ $(ia : \text{initial\_algebra } F \; A \; \mu F)$,

we prove that initial algebras and catamorphisms satisfy the following three properties given in Uustalu et al. [17].

- **Proposition** `cata_cancel` :
    $\forall\ (X : \mathsf{Type})\ (\varphi : [\![F]\!]\ A\ X \to X),\ (\!|\varphi|\!) \circ \mathtt{in\_} = \varphi \circ F[(\!|\varphi|\!)].$
- **Proposition** `cata_refl` : $(\!|\mathtt{in\_}|\!) = \mathrm{id}$
- **Proposition** `cata_fusion` :
    $\forall\ (X\ Y : \mathsf{Type})\ (\varphi : [\![F]\!]\ A\ X \to X)\ (\psi : [\![F]\!]\ A\ Y \to Y)\ (f : X \to Y),$
    $f \circ \varphi = \psi \circ F[f] \to f \circ (\!|\varphi|\!) = (\!|\psi|\!).$

These properties are useful for proving the map-map fusion law [18], which is discussed in Sects. 1 and 2.3. Below is the Coq definition of fmap using a catamorphism in the typeclass `initial_algebra`:

$$\textbf{Definition fmap}\ (f : A \to B) := (\!|\,\mathtt{in\_} \circ F(f)\,[\mathrm{id}]\,|\!).$$

Note that this definition is in the following type contexts:

$$\textbf{Variable}\ (F : \mathtt{PolyF})\ (\mu F_A\ \mu F_B\ A\ B : \mathsf{Type})$$
$$(ia_1 : \mathtt{initial\_algebra}\ F\ A\ \mu F_A)$$
$$(ia_2 : \mathtt{initial\_algebra}\ F\ B\ \mu F_B).$$

We prove that this definition satisfies the following map-map fusion law in the appropriate type context:

$$\textbf{Theorem}\ \mathtt{map\_map\_fusion} :$$
$$\forall\ (f : A \to B)\ (g : B \to C),\ (\mathtt{fmap}\ g) \circ (\mathtt{fmap}\ f) = \mathtt{fmap}\ (g \circ f).$$

Example of Proof Scripts. We have already introduced some properties of catamorphisms. These properties are easily proven because we can simply write almost the same proof as the hand-written proof in previous papers [17,18] thanks to the "chain of equalities" notation introduced in Sect. 2.1. For instance, Fig. 5 shows the Coq proof of `map_map_fusion`; the proof script is very similar to that described by Vene (cf. Theorem 2.3 [18]).

Definition and Proposition for Inverse of in. The inverse of `in_` can be defined as

$$\textbf{Definition}\ \mathtt{in\_inv}\ \{F : \mathtt{PolyF}\}\{A\ \mu F : \mathsf{Type}\}$$
$$\{ia : \mathtt{initial\_algebra}\ F\ A\ \mu F\} := (\!|\,F\,(@\mathrm{id}\ A)\,[\mathtt{in\_}]\,|\!).$$

We prove the following proposition for characterization of `in_inv` in the appropriate type context: `in_` $\circ$ `in_inv` $= \mathrm{id} \wedge$ `in_inv` $\circ$ `in_` $= \mathrm{id}$. Proving this proposition in Coq corresponds to formalizing Lambek's lemma.

Terminal Coalgebras and Anamorphisms. Similarly to the definitions of the initial F-algebras and catamorphisms, the terminal F-coalgebras and

Proposition `map_map_fusion` :
$\forall \{A\ B\ C : \mathsf{Type}\}\ (f : A \to B)\ (g : B \to C), (\mathtt{fmap}\ g) \circ (\mathtt{fmap}\ f) = \mathtt{fmap}\ (g \circ f).$

Proof.

intros; unfold fmap.

assert $((\mathtt{fmap}\ g) \circ \mathtt{in\_} \circ F(f)[\mathrm{id}] = \mathtt{in\_} \circ F(g \circ f)[\mathrm{id}] \circ F(\mathrm{id})[\mathtt{fmap}\ g])$ **as** H_0.

{

  Left

  $= ((\!|\ \mathtt{in\_} \circ F(g)[\mathrm{id}]\ |\!) \circ \mathtt{in\_} \circ F(f)[\mathrm{id}]).$

  $= (\mathtt{in\_} \circ (F(g)[\mathrm{id}] \circ F(\mathrm{id})[(\!|\ \mathtt{in\_} \circ F(g)[\mathrm{id}]\ |\!)]) \circ F(f)[\mathrm{id}])$ {**by** `cata_cancel`}.

  $= (\mathtt{in\_} \circ (F(g)[(\!|\ \mathtt{in\_} \circ F(g)[\mathrm{id}]\ |\!)]) \circ F(f)[\mathrm{id}])$ {**by** `functor_comp`}.

  $= (\mathtt{in\_} \circ (F(g \circ f)[(\!|\ \mathtt{in\_} \circ F(g)[\mathrm{id}]\ |\!)]))$ {**by** `functor_comp`}.

  $= (\mathtt{in\_} \circ F(g \circ f)[\mathrm{id}] \circ F(\mathrm{id})[(\!|\ \mathtt{in\_} \circ F(\mathrm{id})[\mathrm{id}]\ |\!)])$ {**by** `functor_comp`}.

  $= $ **Right.**

}

unfold fmap in H_0.

Left

$= ((\!|\ \mathtt{in\_} \circ F(g)[\mathrm{id}]\ |\!) \circ (\!|\ \mathtt{in\_} \circ F(f)[\mathrm{id}]\ |\!)).$

$= ((\!|\ \mathtt{in\_} \circ F(g \circ)[\mathrm{id}]\ |\!))$ {**apply** `cata_fusion`}.

Right.

Qed.

Fig. 5. Coq proof script of `map_map_fusion` written with our tactic library

anamorphisms can be defined as

Class `terminal_coalgebra` $(F : \mathsf{PolyF})\ (A : \mathsf{Type})\ (\nu F : \mathsf{Type})$

$:= \{\,\mathtt{ana}$ $:= \forall\ (X : \mathsf{Type}), (X \to [\![F]\!]\ A\ X) \to (X \to \nu F;$

       $\mathtt{out\_}$ $:= \nu F \to [\![F]\!]\ A\ \nu F;$

     $\mathtt{ana\_charn} :$ $\forall\ (X : \mathsf{Type})\ (f : X \to \nu F)\ (\varphi : X \to [\![F]\!]\ A\ X),$

               $\mathtt{out\_} \circ f = F[f] \circ \varphi \leftrightarrow f = \mathtt{ana}\ X\ \varphi\}.$

Notation $"[\![f]\!]" := (\mathtt{ana}\ \_\ \_\ f)$ (at level 5).

In the appropriate type context, we can prove the theorems about terminal F-coalgebras and anamorphisms listed in Table 1.

4.3 More Advanced Recursion Schemes

We define the more advanced recursion schemes such as paramorphisms and histomorphisms and formalize all the properties listed in Table 1 by chain-style scripts. For instance, histomorphisms can be defined as

Definition `histo` $(F : \mathsf{PolyF})\ (\mu F\ C\ \nu FC : \mathsf{Type})$

                $(ia : \mathtt{initial\_algebra}\ F\ C\ \mu F)$

                $(tc : \mathtt{terminal\_coalgebra}\ (\mathsf{Prod}\ \mathtt{arg1}\ F)\ C\ \nu FC)$

                $(\varphi : [\![F]\!]\ C\ \nu FC \to C)$

                   $:= \mathtt{fst} \circ \mathtt{out\_} \circ (\!|\ \mathtt{out\_inv} \circ \langle \varphi, \mathrm{id} \rangle\ |\!).$

Notation $"\{\!|\varphi|\!\}" := (\mathtt{histo}\ \_\ \_\ \_\ \_\ \_\ \_\ \varphi).$

Table 1. Theorems and some definitions (shaded) for recursion schemes proposed by Uustalu et al.: we omit type contexts due to space limitation

cata_charn	$: f \circ in_\_ = \varphi \circ F[f] \leftrightarrow f = (\!(\varphi)\!)$
cata_cancel	$: (\!(\varphi)\!) \circ in_\_ = \varphi \circ F[(\!(\varphi)\!)]$
cata_refl	$: id = (\!(in_\_)\!)$
cata_fusion	$: f \circ \varphi = \psi \circ F[f] \rightarrow f \circ (\!(\varphi)\!) = (\!(\psi)\!)$
lemma1	$: in_\_ \circ (\!(F[in_\_])\!) = id \wedge (\!(F[in_\_] \circ in_\_)\!) = id$
Def. of in^{-1}	$in\_inv := (\!(F[in_\_])\!)$
in_inv_charn	$: in \circ in\_inv = id \wedge in\_inv \circ in_\_ = id$
ana_charn	$: out_\_ \circ f = F[f] \circ \varphi \leftrightarrow f = [\![\varphi]\!]$
ana_cancel	$: out_\_ \circ [\![\varphi]\!] = F[[\![\varphi]\!]] \circ \varphi$
ana_refl	$: [\![out_\_]\!] = id$
ana_fusion	$: \psi \circ f = F[f] \circ \varphi \rightarrow [\![\psi]\!] \circ f = [\![\varphi]\!]$
Def. of out^{-1}	$out\_inv := [\![F[out_\_]]\!]$
out_inv_charn	$: out\_inv \circ out_\_ = id \wedge out_\_ \circ out\_inv = id$
lemma2	$: f \circ in_\_ = \varphi \circ F[\langle f, id \rangle] \leftrightarrow f = fst \circ (\!(\langle \varphi, in_\_ \circ F[snd]\rangle)\!)$
Def. of para.	$(\![\varphi]\!) := fst \circ (\!(\langle \varphi, in_\_ \circ F[snd]\rangle)\!)$
para_charn	$: f \circ in_\_ = \varphi \circ F[\langle f, id\rangle] \leftrightarrow f = (\![\varphi]\!)$
para_cancel	$: (\![\varphi]\!) \circ in_\_ = \varphi \circ F[\langle (\![\varphi]\!), id\rangle]$
para_refl	$: id = (\![in_\_ \circ F[fst]]\!)$
para_fusion	$: f \circ \varphi = \psi \circ F[f \otimes id] \rightarrow f \circ (\![\varphi]\!) = (\![\psi]\!)$
para_cata	$: (\!(\varphi)\!) = (\![\varphi \circ F[fst]]\!)$
para_any	$: f = (\![f \circ in_\_ \circ F[snd]]\!)$
Def. of apo.	$[\![\varphi]\!] := [\![[\varphi, F[inr] \circ out_\_]]\!] \circ inl$
apo_charn	$: out_\_ \circ f = F[f, id] \circ \varphi \leftrightarrow f = [\![\varphi]\!]$
apo_cancel	$: out_\_ \circ [\![\varphi]\!] = F[[[\![\varphi]\!], id]] \circ \varphi$
apo_refl	$: id = [\![F[inl] \circ out_\_]\!]$
apo_fusion	$: \psi \circ f = F[f \oplus id] \circ \varphi \rightarrow [\![\psi]\!] \circ f = [\![\varphi]\!]$
apo_ana	$: [\![\varphi]\!] = [\![F[inl] \circ \varphi]\!]$
apo_any	$: f = [\![F[inr] \circ out_\_ \circ f]\!]$
lemma3	$: f \circ in_\_ = \varphi \circ F[(\!(\langle f, in\_inv\rangle)\!)]$
	$\leftrightarrow f = fst \circ out_\_ \circ (\!(out\_inv \circ \langle \varphi, id\rangle)\!)$
Def. of histo.	$\{\!\{\varphi\}\!\} := fst \circ out_\_ \circ (\!(out\_inv \circ \langle \varphi, id\rangle)\!)$
histo_charn	$: f \circ in_\_ = \varphi \circ F[(\!(\langle f, in\_inv\rangle)\!)] \leftrightarrow f = \{\!\{\varphi\}\!\}$
histo_cancel	$: \{\!\{\varphi\}\!\} \circ in_\_ = \varphi \circ F[(\!(\langle \{\!\{\varphi\}\!\}, in\_inv\rangle)\!)]$
histo_refl	$: id = \{\!\{in_\_ \circ F[fst \circ out_\_]\}\!\}$
histo_fusion	$: f \circ \varphi = \psi \circ F[(\!(f \otimes id) \circ out_\_)\!] \rightarrow f \circ \{\!\{\varphi\}\!\} = \{\!\{\psi\}\!\}$
histo_cata	$: (\!(\varphi)\!) = \{\!\{\varphi \circ F[(fst \circ out_\_)]\}\!\}$
Def. of futu.	$[\!\{\varphi\}\!] := [\![[\varphi, id] \circ in\_inv]\!] \circ in_\_ \circ inl$
futu_charn	$: out_\_ \circ f = F[[f, out\_inv]] \circ \varphi \leftrightarrow f = [\!\{\varphi\}\!]$
futu_cancel	$: out_\_ \circ [\!\{\varphi\}\!] = F[(\![[\!\{\varphi\}\!], out\_inv]\!)] \circ \varphi$
futu_refl	$: id = [\![F[in_\_ \circ inl] \circ out_\_]\!]$
futu_fusion	$: \psi \circ f = F[(\!(in_\_ \circ (f \oplus id))\!)] \circ \varphi \rightarrow [\![\psi]\!] \circ f = [\!\{\varphi\}\!]$
futu_ana	$: [\![\varphi]\!] = [\![F[(in_\_ \circ inl) \circ \varphi]]\!]$

In this definition, the constructor arg1 is used for the index type C in $F_C^{\times}$. We omit the complete definitions and proofs due to space limitation.

5 Instantiating and Extracting Recursion Schemes

Users can obtain RS-style programs by instantiating the typeclasses. In this section, we discuss obtaining runnable histomorphic programs for the n-th Fibonacci number and the UKP.

Instances of Initial Algebras and Catamorphisms. First, we give an example of capturing nat as an instance of initial_algebra, where nat is the

standard type of the natural numbers in Coq. We can define an instance of
`initial_algebra` as

> **Instance** Nat_ia $(C : \text{Type}) : \text{initial\_algebra} (\text{Sum one arg2})\ C\ \text{nat}$
> := { **cata** $X\ f :=$ **fix** cataf $(n : \text{nat}) :=$
>   **match** n **with**
> $O \Rightarrow f\ (\text{inl }()) \mid Sn' \Rightarrow f\ (\text{inr } (\text{cataf } n'))$ **end**;
>   in_ $:= [\lambda\ \_ \Rightarrow O, S]$ }.

The incomplete proofs of `cata_charn` are easy.

The instance `Nat_IA` make it possible for users to define and evaluate catamorphisms in `nat`. For example, users can define addition on the natural num-
bers in the RS-style as follows: **Definition** plus $x = (\![\ [\lambda\ \_ \Rightarrow y, S]\ ]\!)$. Users can
also evaluate the `plus` by the following command: **Eval** cbv in $(\lambda\ (y : \text{nat}) \Rightarrow$
$(\![\ [\lambda\ \_ \Rightarrow y, S]\ ]\!))$ 100 11. This returns 111.

Such RS-style definitions are possible because of using typeclasses. Consider
the notation of RS-style definition $(\![\varphi]\!)$ of catamorphisms and recall that catamorphisms are indexed by polynomial functors. To use this simple expression
in program calculations, the Coq system needs to determine the following three
items that are arguments of the catamorphisms: (1) a Coq implementation (definition) of the catamorphism associated with the type φ, (2) a Coq datatype of
the initial algebra (object) associated with the type of φ, and (3) a polynomial
functor F that is associated with the type of φ. An instance of the typeclasses
glues these items together and associates them with a polymorphic type of φ,
so that the Coq system can find these items from the type of the given φ (by
using ad-hoc polymorphism). Without using typeclasses, it is difficult for the
Coq system to find these items correctly from the type of a given φ; thus, a user
would need to write more in her/his Coq script to specify the catamorphism.

Instances of Terminal Coalgebras and Anamorphisms. The terminal
F-coalgebras correspond to coinductive datatypes such as streams, and Coq
allows us to define coinductive datatypes by using **CoInductive** commands.
The typeclass `terminal_coalgebra` can be instantiated in the same manner as
`initial_algebra`, but the former has a significant problem that is specific to
coinductive datatypes in Coq: because the default equality `eq` in Coq is defined
inductively, proving the equality of two coinductively-defined objects is very
difficult [5].

We need a new coinductively-defined equality relation for proving an equality
of coinductively-defined objects. Unfortunately, no relation suitable for all coinductive datatypes exists, so we need to define a new relation for each coinductive
datatype. For instance, the Coq standard library `Coq.Lists.Streams` provides
the coinductively-defined equality relation EqSt : $\forall\ \{A : \text{Type}\}$, **Stream** $A \to$
Stream $A \to$ **Prop** for streams. The relation EqSt can be derived from Proposition 1.

Proving the datatype-generic rules in Sect. 4 would need an datatype-generic
equality relation, but there is no such relation; we need to define an equality

relation for each concrete ADT. We need to add the following axioms for each coinductive datatype νF and F-bisimilar relation $\sim$:

$$\textbf{Axiom eq\_ext} : \forall\ (t_1\ t_2 : \nu F), t_1 \sim t_2 \rightarrow t_1 = t_2.$$

This axiom is justified by Theorem 1 introduced in Sect. 3.

Instantiate Terminal $N_{nat}^\times$-Coalgebra. To give an example of instantiating terminal coalgebras, we illustrate instantiation for the terminal $N_{nat}^\times$-coalgebra, which was described in Sect. 3. First, we give the coinductive definition for $\widetilde{N}(\textbf{nat})$ in Coq:

> **CoInductive** mid_tree
> $:=$ Nil : **nat** $\rightarrow$ mid_tree | Cons : **nat** $\rightarrow$ mid_tree $\rightarrow$ mid_tree.

It is named mid_tree because it represents the intermediate (tree) data structure of the computation. We can easily derive the following Coq definition of the equality relation of mid_tree from Proposition 2:

> **CoInductive** EqMidtree $(t_1\ t_2 : $ mid_tree$) : $ Prop $:=$
> | eqmid : $\varepsilon\ t_1 = \varepsilon\ t_2$
> $\rightarrow (\theta\ t_1 = $ inl tt $\wedge \theta\ t_2 = $ inl tt$)$
> $\vee(\forall\ a\ b, \theta\ t_1 = $ inr $a \rightarrow \theta\ t_2 = $ inr $b \rightarrow$ EqMidtree $a\ b)$
> $\rightarrow$ EqMidtree $t_1\ t_2$.

We then add the following axiom because EqMidTree is $N_{nat}^\times$-bisimilar:

$$\textbf{Axiom eq\_ext} : \forall\ (t_1\ t_2 : \text{mid\_tree}), \text{EqMidtree}\ t_1\ t_2 \rightarrow t_1 = t_2.$$

Next, ε and θ are defined as

> **Definition** ε $(t : $ mid_tree$) : $ **nat** $:=$
> **match** t **with** Nil $n \Rightarrow n$ | Cons n _ $\Rightarrow n$ **end**.
> **Definition** θ $(t : $ mid_tree$) : $ **nat** $:=$
> ⸰ **match** t **with** Nil _ $\Rightarrow$ inl () | Cons _ $t' \Rightarrow$ inr t' **end**.

We now show that the pair of the type EqMidtree and function $\langle \varepsilon, \theta \rangle$ is an instance of the typeclass of terminal $N_{nat}^\times$-coalgebras.

Instance Mid_tree_tc : terminal_coalgebra (Prod arg1 (Sum one arg2))
$\qquad\qquad\qquad\qquad\qquad\qquad$ nat mid_tree
$:= \{$ ana $X\ f\ x := $ **match** $(f\ x)$ **with**
$\qquad\qquad\qquad\qquad$ | $(n,\ ux) \Rightarrow$ **match** ux **with**
$\qquad\qquad\qquad\qquad\qquad\qquad$ | inl () $\Rightarrow$ Nil n
$\qquad\qquad\qquad\qquad\qquad\qquad$ | inr $x \Rightarrow$ Cons n (mid_tree_ana $X\ f\ x$)
$\qquad\qquad\qquad\qquad\qquad$ **end**
$\qquad\qquad\qquad$ **end**
$\qquad$ out_ $\qquad := \langle \varepsilon, \theta \rangle \}$.

The axiom eq_ext is needed to prove ana_charn, which is the remaining proof in the above scripts. Proving ana_charn also requires coinduction; it is necessary to pay attention to the guarded condition.

Verifying Histomorphic Definitions and Extracting Histomorphism.
With the above preparations, we can obtain a runnable *fibo* program written as
the following histomorphism:

> **Definition** fibo
> := ⦃[onec, [onec ∘ snd, add ∘ (id ⊗ (fst ∘ out_))] ∘ distl ∘ out_]⦄,

where the functions onec, add, distl correspond to *onec*, *add*, *distl* in Formula (4), respectively.

This histomorphic definition satisfies the property

> **Goal** fibo 0 = 1 ∧ fibo 1 = 1
> ∧ ∀ (n : **nat**), fibo (S (S n)) = fibo (S n) + fibo n,

which corresponds to Formula (2). The property can be proven by a simple script
in Coq. Note that our proof of the third clause uses induction on n. This proof
verifies that this program fibo is definitely the function that computes the n-th
Fibonacci number.

The definition gives a runnable program. The following command makes Coq
evaluate the histomorphism and return 10946 as the result: **Eval** cbv in fibo 20.
This is also extractable: we can obtain OCaml and Haskell programs of fibo
from the above definition.

More Practical Example. A more practical example of a DP algorithm is the
UKP, which is described as follows. For a given list $wvs = [(w_1, v_1), \ldots, (w_n, v_n)]$
of items, each a pair of its weight and value and a fixed weight capacity of the
knapsack c, maximize the total value $\sum_{i=1}^{n} v_i x_i$ subject to $\sum_{i=1}^{n} w_i x_i \leq c$ and
x_i is a natural number. For the sake of clarity, we assume that w_i, v_i and c are
all natural numbers and $w_i > 0$. The following program *knapsack* is a typical
example of a Haskell-like program solving the UKP:

> *knapsack wvs* O   = 0
> *knapsack wvs* (S c) = **maximize** f *wvs*
>   **where** f (w, v) = **if** $w \leq$ S c **then** $v + (knapsack\ wvs\ (S\ c - w))$ **else** 0.

Note that **maximize** f $[a_1, \ldots, a_n]$ returns the maximum value of f $a_1, \ldots, f$ a_n.
We easily obtain the DP program from the above definition by memoizing the
result of recursive calls *knapsack wvs* (S $c - w$). Thus, the above definition is
easy to translate into a histomorphic definition. Figure 6 shows a histomorphic
definition for the UKP.

6   Related Work

Program Calculations and Recursion Schemes. This paper mainly focuses
on the study by Uustalu et al. [15] which proposed *histomorphisms* and *futumorphisms*, but there have been many other studies on program calculations,
and recursion schemes.

Inductive maybe $\{C : \text{Type}\} := \text{Nothing} : \text{maybe} \mid \text{Just} : C \to \text{maybe}.$
Fixpoint midtree_nth_annotation $(t : \text{mid\_tree})$ $(n : \text{nat}) :=$
   match n **with**
   $\mid$ O $\Rightarrow$ Just $(\varepsilon\ t)$
   $\mid$ S $n' \Rightarrow$ **match** t **with**
         $\mid$ Nil _ $\Rightarrow$ Nothing
         $\mid$ Cons _ $t' \Rightarrow$ midtree_nth_annotation $t'\ n'$
         end
   end.
Notation "$t\ !!\ n$" $:= (\text{midtree\_nth\_annotation}\ t\ n)$
Fixpoint maximize $\{A : \text{Type}\}$ $(f : A \to \text{nat})$ $(l : \text{list}\ A) :=$
   match l **with** $[\ ] \Rightarrow 0 \mid a :: l' \Rightarrow max\ (f\ a)\ (\text{maximize}\ f\ l')$ **end**.
Definition knapsack $(wvs : \text{list}\ (\text{nat} * \text{nat})) :=$
   $\{\![\lambda\ \_ \Rightarrow 0, \lambda\ t \Rightarrow \text{maximize}\ (\lambda\ p \Rightarrow \textbf{match}\ p\ \textbf{with}$
                                $\mid (w, v) \Rightarrow \textbf{match}\ t\ !!\ (w - 1)\ \textbf{with}$
                                          $\mid$ Nothing $\Rightarrow 0$
                                          $\mid$ Just a $\Rightarrow v + a$
                                          end
                          end) $wvs]\!\}$

Fig. 6. Histomorphic definition for unbounded knapsack problem

Bird and Meertens proposed a methodology for deriving efficient programs from naive programs by applying various transformation rules. This methodology is mainly for finite list programs [1] and is called BMF. It has been extended for various datatypes by the notions of category theory. Meijer et al. [11] and Meertens [10] proposed a methodology for programming using recursion schemes such as *catamorphism, anamorphism, hylomorphism* and *paramorphism.*

An important recursion scheme that we have not discussed in this paper is hylomorphism. It is useful for modeling computation using intermediate data structures. It first builds up intermediate data structures and then tears down the intermediate data structures. Hylomorphisms are expressive. Hu et al. [8] proposed an algorithm for deriving hylomorphisms from the normal-style recursive definitions. Hylomorphisms also have many useful properties such as the acid-rain theorem [14]. However, hylomorphisms are only defined on a specific category such as **Cpo** (the category of complete partial ordered sets and strict continuous functions) that has the property that for every polynomial functor F its least fixed point μF equals its greatest fixed point νF. Our library is based on shallow embedding approach; thus, we work on the category **Set** because Coq functions always terminate and are total. This approach cannot define hylomorphisms because $\mu F \neq \nu F$ in category **Set**.

Histomorphisms and futumorphisms are good examples of recursion schemes nicely working in **Set**. Another example is *recursive coalgebras* [3]. A recursive coalgebra captures the recursive definitions of the functions that satisfy the *hylo scheme.* An important example captured by recursive coalgebras is the quick sort algorithm.

A recent important issue is the unifying treatment of recursion schemes. Hinze et al. [7] argued that various recursion schemes, such as catamorphism, mutumorphism, and histomorphism, can be uniformly described with adjoint folds.

Certified Program Calculation Rules by Proof Assistant. Our library of program calculation allows users to calculate their programs in a certified manner. Mu et al. [12] built the Agda library, AoPA, for program calculation. Their library enables users to write relational proofs in a style similar to Algebra of Programming [2]. Chiang et al. formalized the derivation of greedy algorithms [4] using AoPA. They use the deep embedding approach and their formalization is based on the relational approach that captures programs as relations. Thus, extracting runnable programs with this approach is not easy.

Another topic of certified program calculation is automatic calculation systems. Loulergue et al. proposed a Coq library for automatic parallelization of sequential programs [9], and Emoto et al. [6] proposed a Coq library that can automatically derive linear programs from exponential programs.

7   Conclusion and Future Work

We formalized all the propositions and theorems proposed by Uustalu et al. [17] and showed that the formal theorems can be applied to Coq programs. We also showed that the programs can be extracted for various languages.

One direction of our future work is to build support systems for defining the initial F-algebras and terminal F-coalgebras. From the perspective of mathematics, the initial F-algebra and terminal F-coalgebra can be automatically derived from F. Due to the limitations of the type theory in Coq, its fully automatic derivation is difficult. As a practical compromise, it is conceivable to leave the definitions of catamorphism and anamorphism to the user and program a tactic for proving the propositions automatically.

Acknowledgements. We thank Jeremy Gibbons for his great shepherding of this paper. We are also grateful to the anonymous reviewers for their valuable feedback. This work was supported by JSPS KAKENHI Grant Number JP19K11903.

References

1. Bird, R.S.: An introduction to the theory of lists. In: Broy, M. (ed.) Logic of Programming and Calculi of Discrete Design. NATO ASI Series (Series F: Computer and Systems Sciences), vol. 36, pp. 5–42. Springer, Heidelberg (1987). https://doi.org/10.1007/978-3-642-87374-4_1
2. Bird, R., de Moor, O.: Algebra of Programming. Prentice-Hall Inc, Upper Saddle River (1997)
3. Capretta, V., Uustalu, T., Vene, V.: Recursive coalgebras from comonads. Inf. Comput. **204**, 437–468 (2006)

4. Chiang, Y.H., Mu, S.C.: Formal derivation of greedy algorithms from relational specifications: a tutorial. J. Logical Algebraic Methods Program. **85**, 879–905 (2016)
5. Chlipala, A.: Certified Programming with Dependent Types: A Pragmatic Introduction to the Coq Proof Assistant. MIT Press, Cambridge (2013)
6. Emoto, K., Loulergue, F., Tesson, J.: A verified generate-test-aggregate Coq library for parallel programs extraction. In: Klein, G., Gamboa, R. (eds.) ITP 2014. LNCS, vol. 8558, pp. 258–274. Springer, Cham (2014). https://doi.org/10.1007/978-3-319-08970-6_17
7. Hinze, R., Wu, N., Gibbons, J.: Unifying structured recursion schemes. In: Proceedings of the 18th ACM SIGPLAN International Conference on Functional Programming ICFP 2013, pp. 209–220. ACM, New York (2013)
8. Hu, Z., Iwasaki, H., Takeichi, M.: Deriving structural hylomorphisms from recursive definitions. In: Proceedings of the 1996 ACM SIGPLAN International Conference on Functional Programming, ICFP 1996, pp. 73–82 (1996)
9. Loulergue, F., Bousdira, W., Tesson, J.: Calculating parallel programs in Coq using list homomorphisms. Int. J. Parallel Program. **45**(2), 300–319 (2017)
10. Meertens, L.: Paramorphism. Formal Aspects Comput. **4**(5), 413–424 (1992)
11. Meijer, E., Fokkinga, M., Paterson, R.: Functional programming with bananas, lenses, envelopes and barbed wire. In: Hughes, J. (ed.) FPCA 1991. LNCS, vol. 523, pp. 124–144. Springer, Heidelberg (1991). https://doi.org/10.1007/3540543961_7
12. Mu, S.C., Ko, H.S., Jansson, P.: Algebra of programming in Agda: dependent types for relational program derivation. J. Funct. Program. **19**(5), 545–579 (2009)
13. Sangiorgi, D.: Introduction to Bisimulation and Coinduction. Cambridge University Press, Cambridge (2011)
14. Takano, A., Meijer, E.: Shortcut deforestation in calculational form. In: Proceedings of the Seventh International Conference on Functional Programming Languages and Computer Architecture FPCA 1995, pp. 306–313. ACM, New York (1995)
15. Tesson, J., Hashimoto, H., Hu, Z., Loulergue, F., Takeichi, M.: Program calculation in Coq. In: Johnson, M., Pavlovic, D. (eds.) AMAST 2010. LNCS, vol. 6486, pp. 163–179. Springer, Heidelberg (2011). https://doi.org/10.1007/978-3-642-17796-5_10
16. The Coq development team: The Coq proof assistant reference manual (2018). https://coq.inria.fr/distrib/current/refman/. version 8.9.0
17. Uustalu, T., Vene, V.: Primitive (co)recursion and course-of-value (co)iteration, categorically. Informatica **10**, 5–26 (1999)
18. Vene, V.: Categorical Programming with inductive and coinductive types. Ph.D. thesis, University of Tartu (2000)

Language Design and Implementation

Lightweight Functional Logic
Meta-Programming

Nada Amin[1(✉)], William E. Byrd[2(✉)], and Tiark Rompf[3(✉)]

[1] Harvard University, Cambridge, MA, USA
namin@seas.harvard.edu
[2] University of Alabama at Birmingham, Birmingham, AL, USA
webyrd@uab.edu
[3] Purdue University, West Lafayette, IN, USA
tiark@purdue.edu

Abstract. Meta-interpreters in Prolog are a powerful and elegant way to implement language extensions and non-standard semantics. But how can we bring the benefits of Prolog-style meta-interpreters to systems that combine functional and logic programming? In Prolog, a program can access its own structure via reflection, and meta-interpreters are simple to implement because the "pure" core language is small. Can we achieve similar elegance and power for larger systems that combine different paradigms?

In this paper, we present a particular kind of functional logic meta-programming, based on embedding a small first-order logic system in an expressive host language. Embedded logic engines are not new, as exemplified by various systems including miniKanren in Scheme and LogicT in Haskell. However, previous embedded systems generally lack meta-programming capabilities in the sense of meta-interpretation. Indeed, shallow embeddings usually do not support reflection.

Instead of relying on reflection for meta-programming, we show how to adapt popular multi-stage programming techniques to a logic programming setting and use the embedded logic to generate reified first-order structures, which are again simple to interpret. Our system has an appealing power-to-weight ratio, based on the simple and general notion of dynamically scoped mutable variables.

We also show how, in many cases, non-standard semantics can be realized without explicit reification and interpretation, but instead by customizing program execution through the host language. As a key example, we extend our system with a tabling/memoization facility. The need to interact with mutable variables renders this a highly nontrivial challenge, and the crucial insight is to extract symbolic representations of their side effects from memoized rules. We demonstrate that multiple independent semantic modifications can be combined successfully in our system, for example tabling and tracing.

© Springer Nature Switzerland AG 2019
A. W. Lin (Ed.): APLAS 2019, LNCS 11893, pp. 225–243, 2019.
https://doi.org/10.1007/978-3-030-34175-6_12

1   Introduction

An appealing aspect of pure logic programming is its declarative nature. For example, it is easy to take a formal system, expressed as inference rules on paper, and turn it into a logic program. If the formal system describes typing rules, the same logic program might be able to perform type checking, type reconstruction, and type inhabitation. Yet, we want more.

First, we would like to leverage abstractions known from functional programming to structure our logic programs. Where logic programming sports search, nondeterminism, and backwards computation, functional programming excels at parameterization, modularity and abstraction. These strengths are complementary, and there is great value in combining them, as evidenced by a large body of ongoing research. Languages such as Curry [17] focus on integrating functional and logic programming into one coherent declarative paradigm.

Second, we would like to customize the execution of logic programs. For example, we want to be able to reason about both failures and successes. In case of success, we may want a proof, i.e., a derivation tree, for why the relation holds. In case of failure, feedback is even more important, and yet, by default, a logic program that fails is one that returns no answers. In Prolog, these tasks can be solved through *meta-programming*, which, in the context of this paper, means to implement a *meta-interpreter* for Prolog clauses. A meta-interpreter for "pure" Prolog clauses, written in Prolog, can customize the search strategy, inspect proof trees or investigate failures [34,35]. However, for non-trivial applications such as abstract interpretation [10], these meta-interpreters do not usually stick to the "pure" Prolog subset themselves. In many cases, for example if we want to extend the execution logic with tabling or memoization, it is necessary to exploit decidedly un-declarative and imperative features of Prolog—in some sense the "dirty little secret" of logic programming.

In this paper, we present a pragmatic solution to combining functional and logic programming on one hand, and declarative logic programming with restricted notions of state on the other hand. We make the case for a particular style of functional logic meta-programming: embedding a simple, first-order logic programming system in an expressive, impure, higher-order functional host language, optionally supported by best-of-breed external constraint solver engines such as Z3 [25] or CVC4 [2], and providing explicit support for dynamically scoped, i.e., "thread-local" state. In the tradition of miniKanren [4–6,13,14], which embeds logic programming in Scheme, we present Scalogno, a logic programming system embedded in Scala, but designed from the ground up with modularity and customization in mind and with explicit support for dynamically scoped mutable variables.

This paper makes the following contributions:

– We introduce our system, Scalogno, and highlight the benefit of *deep linguistic reuse* in logic programming based on examples, e.g., how higher-order functions of the host language can model higher-order relations (e.g., map, flatMap, fold). The logic engine can remain first order, keeping theory and implementation simple. Scalogno can reuse Scala's type classes (e.g., `Ord`), while the logic engine need not be aware of this feature at all. This flexibility goes beyond dedicated functional logic languages like Curry, which do not support type classes for complexity reasons [24] (Sect. 2).

- Tracing, proof trees, etc. are examples of a whole class of use cases where a meta-interpreter augments execution with some state. We introduce dynamically scoped mutable variables to capture this design pattern, enabling modular extensions through the host language as an alternative to explicit interpretation. We discuss the implementation of Scalogno in more detail, and also show how dynamic variables support a generic term reification facility, directly adapting popular multi-stage programming approaches to a logic setting (Sect. 3).
- We show how we can customize the execution order while maintaining the behavior of other extensions that rely on dynamic mutable state. To this end, we extend our logic engine to implement tabling, i.e., memoization. Unlike most existing Prolog implementations (there are exceptions [11]), the implementation directly corresponds to a high-level description of the tabling process, understood in terms of continuations. A key challenge is to interact with mutable variables, which we solve by extracting symbolic representations of their side effects from memoized rules. To the best of our knowledge, ours is the first logic engine that integrates tabling with mutable state in a predictable way (Sect. 4).

Section 5 discusses related work and Sect. 6 offers concluding thoughts. Our code is available at `aplas19.namin.net`.

2 Embedded Logic Programming

When embedding a language into an expressive host, we benefit from *deep linguistic reuse*: we can keep the embedded language simple by directly exploiting features of the host language. In this section, we illustrate deep linguistic reuse with Scalogno in Scala—the embedded logic system is first-order, and re-uses the host language for key features such as naming and structuring logic fragments.

2.1 Relations as Functions

As a running example, we model a graph connecting three nodes a, b, c in a cycle.

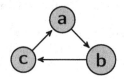

In Prolog (on the left), we can model this graph with a relation, **edge**, listing all the possible edges. In Scalogno (on the right), we can define the same relation as a regular Scala function:

```
edge(a,b).
edge(b,c).
edge(c,a).
```

```
def edge(x: Exp[String],
         y: Exp[String]): Rel =
  (x === "a") && (y === "b") ||
  (x === "b") && (y === "c") ||
  (x === "c") && (y === "a")
```

In Scalogno, infix methods are used for unification (===), conjunction (&&) and disjunction (||). The type Rel represents a relation, while the type Exp[T] represents a term (possibly including unbound logic variables) of type T.

We can now run a query on the just defined relation.

```
| ?- edge(X,Y).
↪ X=a,Y=b; X=b,Y=c; X=c,Y=a.
```

```
run[(String,String)] {
  case Pair(x,y) => edge(x,y) }
↪ pair(a,b); pair(b,c);
  pair(c,a).
```

In Scalogno, we apply the **edge** relation like any ordinary function. The run form serves as an interface between the host and the embedded language, returning an answer list of reified values of the variable it scopes. Here, we directly use pattern matching to introduce the variables x and y as a pair. We can also use the **exists** form to explicitly introduce new logical variables in scope, as in the next example.

In Prolog, we can naturally define relations recursively, and so too in Scalogno. For example, the relation **path** finds all the paths in the graph.

```
path(X,Y) :- edge(X,Y).
path(X,Y) :- edge(X,Z), path(Z,Y).
```

```
def path(x: Exp[T], y: Exp[T]):
  Rel = edge(x,y) ||
  exists[T] { z => edge(x,z) &&
    path(z,y) }
```

```
| ?- path(a,Q).
↪ Q=b; Q=c; ...
```

```
runN[String](10) { q =>
  path("a",q) }
↪ b; c; a; b; c; a; b; c; a; b.
```

Here, asking for all answers (with run instead of runN) would diverge as there are infinitely many paths through the cycle. In Sect. 3, we show how to cope with this divergence by changing the evaluation semantics through meta-programming.

2.2 Higher-Order Relations as Higher-Order Functions

In Scalogno, we can exploit higher-order functions (and hence, relations too), for example parameterizing the relation **path** by the relation **edge** so that it works for any graph:

```
def generic_path(edge: (Exp[T],Exp[T]) => Rel)(x: Exp[T], y: Exp[T]): Rel =
  edge(x,y) || exists[T] { z => edge(x,z) && generic_path(edge)(z,y) }
```

We could also recognize that the `path` relation is really just the reflexive transitive closure of the `edge` relation, and since `generic_path` is already parameterized over an arbitrary binary relation, rename it accordingly as `refl_trans_closure`. This enables defining `path` as:

```
val path = refl_trans_closure(edge)
```

The usual higher-order combinators, such as `map`, `flatMap`, and `fold` also have natural higher-order relational counterparts.

2.3   Object-Oriented Encapsulation

To enable additional abstractions that are not present in typical logic programming settings, we can exploit the object-oriented features of the host language:

```
trait Graph[T] {
  def edge(x: Exp[T], y: Exp[T]): Rel // left abstract
  def path(x: Exp[T], y: Exp[T]): Rel = // defined as before
    edge(x,y) || exists[T] { z => edge(x,z) && path(z,y) }}
val g = new Graph[String] {
  def edge(x:Exp[String],y:Exp[String]) = // defined as before
    (x === "a") && (y === "b") ||
    (x === "b") && (y === "c") ||
    (x === "c") && (y === "a") }
```

The object `g` inherits the definition of `path` from `Graph`.

We can also use the pattern known as 'type classes as objects and implicits' [28], for example to support a relational ordering on polymorphic lists.

3   Dynamic Scope as Meta-Interpreter (Design Pattern)

Here is the recipe for Prolog-style meta-interpreters in Scala: a meta-interpreter (a Scalogno relation itself) is configured with a Scalogno meta-relation to build a reified representation of a Scalogno object-relation (e.g. `path`). In other words, we stay completely in the realm of logic programming.

In this section, we consider a different approach: use the host language to augment the execution of logic programs by customizing the logic engine directly. For this approach to be viable, the logic embedding has to be designed with certain kinds of extensions in mind. Within Scalogno, for example, it is difficult to use mutable state because the execution order uses various flavors of interleaving, as opposed to Prolog's deterministic Selective Linear Definite (SLD) clause resolution. But of course interleaving is desirable, so we would like a model that supports a notion of "thread local" state that is attached to a particular execution path, similar to notions of state in Or-parallel logic programming [16].

```
val Backtrack = new Exception

// dynamically scoped variables
var dvars: immutable.Map[Int, Any] =
    immutable.Map.empty
case class DVar[T](val id: Int,
    val default: T) extends (() => T) {
  dvars += id -> default
  def apply()  = dvars(id).asInstanceOf[T]
  def :=(v: T) = dvars += id -> v }
var dvarCount = 1
def DVar[T](v: T): DVar[T] = {
  val id = dvarCount
  dvarCount += 1
  new DVar[T](id, v) }

// goals and relations
trait Rel {
  def exec(call: Exec)(k: Cont): Unit }
type Exec = Goal => Cont => Unit
type Cont = () => Unit
type Goal = () => Rel

// unconditional ...
val Yes = new Rel { // ... success
  def exec(call: Exec)(k: Cont) = k() }
val No = new Rel { // ... failure
  def exec(call: Exec)(k: Cont) =
      throw Backtrack }

def infix_&&(a: => Rel, b: => Rel): Rel =
  new Rel { def exec(call: Exec)(k: Cont) =
    call(() => a) { () => call(() => b)(k) }}
def infix_||(a: => Rel, b: => Rel): Rel =
  new Rel { def exec(call: Exec)(k: Cont) = {
    call(() => a)(k); call(() => b)(k) }}

// logic terms
case class Exp[T](id: Int)
var varCount: Int = 0
def freshId = { var id = varCount;
  varCount += 1; id }
def fresh[T] = Exp(freshId)
```

```
def exists[T](f: Exp[T] => Rel): Rel =
    f(fresh)
def infix_===[T](a: => Exp[T],
          b: => Exp[T]): Rel = {
  register(IsEqual(a,b)); Yes }
def term[T](key: String, args:
            List[Exp[Any]]): Exp[T] = {
  val e = fresh[T]
  register(IsTerm(e.id, key, args))
  e }

// constraints
abstract class Constraint
case class IsTerm(id: Int, key: String,
          args: List[Exp[Any]])
      extends Constraint
case class IsEqual(x: Exp[Any], y: Exp[Any])
      extends Constraint

var cstore: immutable.Set[Constraint] =
    immutable.Set.empty
def conflict(cs: Set[Constraint],
          c: Constraint): Boolean = ...
def register(c: Constraint): Unit = {
  if (cstore.contains(c)) return
  if (conflict(cstore,c)) throw Backtrack }

// execution (depth-first)
def run[T](f: Exp[T] => Rel): Seq[String] = {
  def call(e: => Rel)(k: Cont): Unit = {
    // save state
    val cstore1 = cstore; val dvars1 = dvars
    try { e.exec(call)(k)
    } catch { case Backtrack => // OK
    } finally { // restore state
      cstore = cstore1; dvars = dvars1 }}
  val q = fresh[T]
  val res = new mutable.ListBuffer[String]()
  call(() => f(q)) { () =>
    res += extractStr(q) }
  res.toList }
def runN[T](max: Int)(f: Exp[T] => Rel):
    Seq[String] = ...
```

Fig. 1. Scalogno engine implementation

3.1   Designing Logic Engines for Meta-Programming

In designing the Scalogno implementation, we have put emphasis on modularity and enabling independent extensions of different parts of the system. An overview of the core Scalogno system is shown in Fig. 1, and we discuss individual aspects step by step below.

Our starting point is an implementation of a Depth-First Search (DFS) engine, where we reuse the host control flow (stack and exception) to manage the pending goals. Nevertheless, Scalogno is modular and supports a range of search strategies, as well as external solvers.

The engine knows generically about goals and their state. A goal is represented as a thunk of a relation. A relation knows how to execute itself via the **exec** method, given an executor engine `call` for solving subgoals and a success continuation **k** for returning satisfied. Failure is achieved through throwing a **Backtrack** exception, to backtrack.

Before showing the engine, it's helpful to see a few primitives and means of combination for relations. Unconditional success, **Yes**, immediately successfully continues. Unconditional failure, **No**, immediately throws. The conjunction of two goals, **&&**, executes the first, and successfully continues with the second. The disjunction of two goals, **||**, executes the first, and thereafter through backtracking as defined by the delimited subcall, the second. These goal combinators make use of call-by-name parameters (denoted by an **=>** after the : and before the parameter type in Scala).

Finally, our DFS engine, in **call**, pushes the current state on to the stack, runs the goal delegating execution to the underlying relation, catches failures and restores the state upon recursive exits.

This engine cannot do much, because we do not have any constraints to solve yet. So let us introduce a domain of terms, and equality constraints between terms.

A term is uniquely identified. A term constraint **IsTerm(id,key,args)** identifies a term **id** as being bound to a value **key(args)**. An unbound term corresponds to a free logic variable. An equality constraint **IsEqual(x,y)** is introduced by unification, enforcing that two terms, **x** and **y**, have the same structure, that is the same keys and, recursively, arguments.

We define new relations using our constraints. The form **exists** takes a query—a goal with a hole—and fills the hole with a fresh variable. The form **===** unifies two terms by registering an equality constraint with the solver. The form **term** introduces a new term also through constraint registration.

This style of "sea of nodes" construction by side effects is reminiscent of multistage programming frameworks like LMS [30]; we will have more to say about this in Sect. 3.4.

We package the core engine in a runnable interface, which takes a pseudo-goal rather than a thunk, but parameterized by a free logic variable, which is the query variable. The interface **runN** caps the number of returned answers to a given maximum, while **run** is intended to return all answers. (We could also have used a streaming interface.)

We simplistically reify answers into strings. Using polytypic typing as discussed in Sect. 2, we could improve the model to reify depending on the type of the query variable.

For conflict detection, we keep track of the transitive closure of the set of constraints registered. One can implement a number of performance improvements, including index structures that enable more efficient lookup and matching of constraints.

If we abstract a solver interface, in particular, how state is pushed and restored in the engine, it becomes easy to interface with external SMT solvers.

We are now ready to run some queries.

```
def e(x: Any) = term(x.toString, Nil)
run[Any]{q => q === e(1) || q === e(2)}
 ↪ List(1,2)
```

As a summary, going back to the basics, what is the essence of a logic programming system? The two main components are (1) search, i.e., nondeterministic execution, and (2) unification and constraints. We implement nondeterministic execution using continuation-passing style (CPS). The class `Rel` comes with implementations for disjunctions and conjunctions, but can be extended for other execution patterns. Method `run` uses an auxiliary `call` to execute individual relations, and the `exec` method of a `Rel` object can invoke its parameter `call` to invoke other relations. The Depth-First Search (DFS) implementation of `call` passes itself to `Rel.exec`. A Breadth-First Search (BFS) implementation would pass a different method that would just collect the calls in a list. This BFS engine just needs to override the `run` method but can share all other code with the DFS implementation.

The handling of constraints and unification is only sketched in Fig. 1. It is a conscious design choice to keep constraints and execution separate as far as possible. The benefit is that both aspects can be extended independently. We model the constraint store `cstore` as a dynamic variable, which keeps its value in a particular execution path (see Sect. 3.2 below). Invoking the infix method `===` on a logic term registers and checks a new constraint on its arguments in the constraint store of the current execution path.

3.2 An Alternative to Reification and Interpretation

Among the usual use cases for meta-interpreters we find tracing, proof trees and similar extensions. What they all have in common is that they augment a vanilla interpreter to thread a piece of state through the execution.

Let us consider how we can implement such functionality without an explicit meta-interpreter, taking tracing as example. Instead of threading state, we can just use mutable state directly. However there is a catch: we cannot directly use a mutable variable in Scala, because we need to keep apart the state from different nondeterministic branches.

In Scalogno, we provide an abstraction for this: mutable variables with dynamic extent (`DVar`). In contrast to meta-interpreters, these variables can exist side by side, so we can have multiple independent extensions at the same time. Intuitively, dynamic variables have the same extent as the substitution map in miniKanren [6] and the constraint store in cKanren [1], and they correspond to certain realizations of mutable state in Or-parallel logic programming [16].

3.3 Tracing with Dynamic Variables

In the simplest case, we can directly modify the relation we are interested in monitoring:

```
val globalTrace = DVar(nil: Exp[List[List[String]]])
def path(x: Exp[T], y: Exp[T]): Rel = {
  globalTrace := cons(term("path",List(x,y)), globalTrace())
  edge(x,y) || exists[T] { z => edge(x,z) && path(y,b) }}
```

But of course this approach is not very modular. Instead, we can introduce a generic abstract operator for named rules:

```
def rule[T,U](s: String)(f: (Exp[T],Exp[U]) => Rel): (Exp[T],Exp[U]) => Rel
```

Now, we modify the `path` relation to explicitly use this `rule` abstraction to indicate that we are indeed defining a named relation, as opposed to just a meta-language abstraction:

```
def path: (Exp[T],Exp[T])=> Rel = rule("path") { (x,y) =>
  edge(x,y) || exists[T] { z => edge(y,z) && path(z,y) }}
```

Instead of modifying the relation directly, we can also build a subclass of `Graph`:

```
trait TracingGraph[T] extends Graph[T] {
  override def path(x:Exp[T],y:Exp[T]) = rule("path")(super.path)(x,y) }
```

In order to implement the actual tracing logic, we define an implementation of the abstract interface as a trait which defines the `rule` method as follows. In Scala, we can mix in this behavior with the otherwise default implementation of the logic engine. We keep the global trace in a variable with dynamic extent.

```
val globalTrace = DVar(nil: Exp[List[List[String]]])
def rule[T,U](s: String)(f: (Exp[T],Exp[U]) => Rel): (Exp[T],Exp[U]) =>
    Rel = { (a,b) =>
  globalTrace := cons(term(s,List(a,b)), globalTrace())
  f(a,b) }
```

We get the same result we would expect:

```
runN[(String,List[String])](5) {
  case Pair(q1,q2) => g.path("a",q1) && globalTrace() === q2 }
↪ pair(b,cons(path(a,b),nil));
    pair(c,cons(path(b,c),cons(path(a,c),nil))); ...
```

We have identified a general design pattern: many meta-interpreters just thread a piece of state. By adding support for this pattern to our engine, we have achieved an alternative implementation approach that removes the need for an entire class of explicit interpreters.

3.4   Clause Reification as Controlled Side Effect

While we have seen that we can often achieve the desired meta-programming effects without explicit meta-interpreters, we may still want explicit interpreters in certain cases. With this goal in mind, we demonstrate another use of dynamic scope: turning logic programs into program generators.

Since we do not want to interpret the meta-language, we need to leverage regular program execution. What can we do? We augment what the program does when run. In an impure language we would use side effects, in a judicious and very controlled way [31]: a `reflect` operation would emit code as side-effect, and a `reify` operation would accumulate code that was produced in its scope. This multi-stage evaluation mechanism is used in program generation frameworks such as LMS [30]. A simple example would be the following:

```
def const(x: Int) = x.toString
def plus(x: String, y: String)  = reflect(s"$x + $y")
def times(x: String, y: String) = reflect(s"$x * $y")
reify { plus(times(const(2), const(3)), times(const(4), const(5))) }
```

↪

```
"val x1 = 2 * 3
 val x2 = 4 * 5
 val x3 = x1 + x2
 x3"
```

Each individual reflected expression generates a val binding, captured by the nearest enclosing reify. The underlying implementation of reify and reflect can be as simple as this:

```
var code: Code
def reify(f: => String) = {
  val temp = code; code = ""
  val res = f
  try (code + res) finally code = temp }
def reflect(rhs: String) = {
  val id = fresh
  code += s"val $id = $rhs\n"
  id }
```

Note how `reify` sets and resets `code` based on the dynamic scope.

How can we adapt this idea to our logic settings? In the place of strings we use a list of goals to accumulate generated terms, based on a dynamic variable to manage scope. The implementation to reflect and reify goals is as follows:

```
val moregoals = DVar(fresh[List[Goal]])
def reifyGoals(goal: => Rel)(goals: Exp[List[Goal]]): Rel = {
  moregoals := goals
  goal && moregoals() === nil }
def reflectGoal(goal: Exp[Goal]): Rel = {
  val hole = moregoals()
  moregoals := fresh
  hole === cons(goal,moregoals()) }
reifyGoals(reflectGoal("path(a,b)") => "cons(path(a,b),nil)"
```

We maintain a global list of clauses, and we can reify clauses given a goal:

```
var allclauses = Map[String,Clause]()
def reifyClause(goal: => Rel)(head: Exp[Goal], body: Exp[List[Goal]]):
  Rel = reifyGoals(goal)(cons(head,nil)) &&
        allclauses(extractKey(head))(head,body)
run[List[Any]] { q =>
  exists[Goal,List[Goal]] { (head,body) =>
    q === cons("to prove", cons(head, cons("prove", cons(body, nil)))) &&
    reifyClause(path(fresh,fresh))(head,body) }}
```

↪

```
cons(to prove,cons(path(a,b),cons(prove,cons(nil,nil)))),
cons(to prove,cons(path(b,c),cons(prove,cons(nil,nil)))),
cons(to prove,cons(path(c,a),cons(prove,cons(nil,nil)))),
cons(to prove,cons(path(a,x0),cons(prove,cons(cons(path(b,x0),nil),nil)))),
cons(to prove,cons(path(b,x0),cons(prove,cons(cons(path(c,x0),nil),nil)))),
cons(to prove,cons(path(c,x0),cons(prove,cons(cons(path(a,x0),nil),nil)))),
```

We use the same rule abstraction as in the previous section to denote named rules. It adds the clause definition to the global table and reflects the goal as a side effect.

```
def rule[A,B](s: String)(f:(Exp[A], Exp[B]) => Rel) = {
  def goalTerm(a: Exp[A], b: Exp[B]) = term[Goal](s,List(a,b))
  allclauses += s -> { (head: Exp[Goal], body: Exp[List[Goal]]) =>
    exists[A,B] { (a,b) =>
      (head === goalTerm(a,b)) && reifyGoals(f(a,b))(body) }}
  (a: Exp[A], b: Exp[B]) => reflectGoal(goalTerm(a,b))}
```

Finally, we adapt a vanilla interpreter to this new model. This interpreter matches the head of the goal against the global clause table, turned into a disjunction.

```
def allclausesRel: Clause = { (head: Exp[Goal], body: Exp[List[Goal]]) =>
  allclauses.values.foldLeft(No:Rel)((r,c) => r || c(head,body)) }
def vanilla(goal: => Rel): Rel =
  exists[List[Goal]] { goals => reifyGoals(goal)(goals) && vanilla(goals) }
def vanilla(goals: Exp[List[Goal]]): Rel =
  goals === nil || exists[Goal,List[Goal],List[Goal]] { (g, gs, body) =>
    (goals === cons(g,gs)) && allclausesRel(g,body) && vanilla(body) &&
      vanilla(gs) }
```

In the same way, we can implement any other meta-interpreter, such as a tracing interpreter.

4   Tabling as an Alternative Execution Strategy

In this section we show how to implement an alternative evaluation strategy. In functional languages, memoization is a well-known way to speed up computations by reusing intermediate results. The logic programming analogue is known as tabling.

We will implement a memo combinator below that can be used as follows to designate particular relations to be tabled:

```
def fib(x:Exp[Int], y:Exp[Int]): Rel = memo(term("fib",List(x,y))) {
  (x === 0) && (y === 1) || (x === 1) && (y === 1) || {
    val x1,x2,y1,y2 = fresh[Int]
    (x === succ(x1)) && (x === (succ(succ(x2)))) &&
    fib(x1,y1) && fib(x2,y2) && add(y1,y2,y) }}
```

The tabled version of fib will only compute a linear number of recursive calls instead of an exponential number.

4.1   Implementation: Meta-Programming via the Host Language

Tabling is one of the cases that can not be implemented by a purely declarative meta-interpreter. Instead, imperative features have to be used. Common Prolog implementations are quite intricate, although the concept is simple. The core is described nicely by Warren [37], which we take as blueprint for our implementation, shown in Fig. 2. The evaluation of a logic program forms a search tree for solutions. We can think of exploring this tree either as a nondeterministic process, or as a set of concurrent deterministic processes. In this latter view, multiple processes are active at the same time. When one process reaches a choice point it forks into two new ones, and when it reaches a failure condition, it terminates.

To add tabling or memoization, the first step is to add a global table `callTable` that keeps track of every call to a memoized rule and all the answers returned for it. In contrast to standard functional memoization, though, there may be any number of answers for each call. An *answer* in this context consists of additional constraints that will be applied to the goal as a side effect of executing the rule (details elided in Fig. 2). For example, the answer to the goal `fib(5,x0)` will be `fib(5,8)` or equivalently the effect of applying constraint `x0=8` to the goal.

When a process is about to call a memoized rule, it checks the global call table to see if the call has already been made. If not, it adds its continuation to the table and continues evaluating the rule body. When the process is about to return from the call—and this may happen multiple times if the process is forked—then it records the answer it has just computed and resumes all continuations registered for this call with this new answer. If the answer is already in the table, then it is a duplicate, and the process terminates.

When a process calls a memoized rule and the call is already in the table, then the current continuation is invoked once for each recorded answer. The continuation is also registered in the table, since we cannot know if computation of answers has already finished. More answers may become available in the future, and will trigger this continuation again.

4.2   Memoization with Symbolic State Transitions

A key question is how our tabling combinator interacts with state. As a first approximation, we make the input and output state of each call explicit by collecting the values of all dynamic variables. We thus represent a call such as `path(a,b)` as `goal(path(a,b),state0(x0..),state1(x1..))`, where `x0..` are the dynamic variables before the call, and `x1..` the dynamic variables after the call. In other words, we make the state transformation explicit.

However, straightforwardly memoizing these augmented goals would not lead to the desired result. State is often used to accumulate extra contextual information, so it changes all the time. It is rare that a rule is called twice in *exactly* the same state and we would like to be sure that adding a piece of state to the program should not change the memoization behavior.

```
// call table data structures and management
type Answer = (Exp[Any] => Unit)
case class Call(key: String, ...) { ... }
def makeCall(goal: Exp[Any], k: Cont): Call = ...
def makeAnswer(goal: Exp[Any]): Answer = ...
val callTable = new mutable.HashMap[String, mutable.HashMap[String,
    Answer]]
val contTable = new mutable.HashMap[String, List[Call]]
// tabling combinator
def memo[A,B](goal: Exp[Any])(a: => Rel): Rel = new Rel {
  override def exec(call: Exec)(k: Cont): Unit = {
    def resume(cont: Call, ans: Answer) = ...
    val cont = makeCall(goal, k)
    callTable.get(cont.key) match {
      case Some(answers) =>         // call key found:
        for (ans <- answers.values) //   continue with stored answers
          resume(cont, ans)
      case None =>                  // call key not found:
        val answers = new mutable.HashMap[String, Answer]
        callTable(cont.key) = answers //   add call table entry
        call { () =>
          cont.updateStateBeforeCall()
          a                         //   execute
        } { () =>
          cont.equateStateAfterCall()
          val ansKey = extractStr(goal)
          if (!answers.contains(ansKey)) {
            val ans = cont.makeAnswer()
            ansMap(ansKey) = ans    //   record new answer and
            for (cont1 <- cont.table) //   resume stored continuations
              resume(cont1, ans)
}}}}}
```

Fig. 2. Tabling combinator implementation. Continuations and answers are memoized in global tables.

For this reason, we memoize not based on the augmented goals but on the call patterns only, ignoring input and output state. But how can we describe a rule's state modification independent of a particular input state? To achieve this, we evaluate rule bodies with a *fresh* input state to obtain a *symbolic representation* of the rule's state modification. Implementation-wise, this is easy to achieve because we already maintain a global table of dynamic variables (dvars in Fig. 1). Before evaluating the body of a memoized rule, we replace all dvars entries with fresh logic variables, which enables us to observe the effects on them when an answer is produced. When resuming a continuation, the symbolic effects need to be unified with the current valuations of the dynamic variables.

With this mechanism in place, we can generate the following answer term for our example of tracing a **path** relation in a graph:

```
goal(path(a,b),state0(x0),state1(cons(path(a,b),x0))),
```

This term makes explicit that the state after the call—that is, the augmented trace—is the state before the call **x0**, with the current head **cons**ed in front.

Using logic variables to abstract over the state before and after the call ensures that we can represent any kind of relation between the two states that can be modelled through matching terms. So dropping an element from the front of a list would be easy (match on cons on the left-hand side), recursive predicates such as removing from the middle of collection would be harder.

4.3 Example: Tabled Graph Evaluation

We first note that, as expected, tabling enables left as well as right recursive relations:

```
def pathL(a: Exp[String], b: Exp[String]): Rel =
    memo(term("path",List(a,b))) {
  edge(a,b) || exists[String] { z => pathL(a,z) && edge(z,b) }
```

Furthermore, we can combine tabling with tracing:

```
val globalTrace = DVar(nil: Exp[List[List[String]]])
def pathLT(a: Exp[String], b: Exp[String]): Rel =
    memo(term("path",List(a,b))) {
  globalTrace := cons(term("path",List(a,b)), globalTrace())
  edge(a,b) || exists[String] { z => pathLT(a,z) && edge(z,b) }}
```

And we can verify that the combination works as we would expect. Here is an example query:

```
run[(String,List[String])] { case Pair(q1,q2) => pathLT("a",q1) &&
    globalTrace() === q2 }
↪
pair(b,cons(path(a,b),nil))
pair(c,cons(path(a,b),cons(path(a,c),nil)))
pair(a,cons(path(a,b),cons(path(a,c),cons(path(a,a),nil))))
```

As we can see, the mutable variable **globalTrace** behaves in the way we would expect, recording paths **ab**, **abc**, and **abca** even though we have drastically changed the evaluation order. Here is the execution trace:

```
    goal(path(a,x0),state0(x1,nil),state1(x2,x3))
⟶  goal(path(a,b),state0(x0,x1),state1(x2,cons(path(a,b),x1)))

    goal(path(a,x0),state0(x1,cons(path(a,x2),x3)),state1(x4,x5))
⟶  goal(path(a,b),state0(x0,x1),state1(x2,cons(path(a,b),x1)))

    goal(path(a,x0),state0(x1,nil),state1(x2,x3))
```

```
⟶ goal(path(a,c),state0(x0,x1),
    state1(x2,cons(path(a,b),cons(path(a,c),x1))))

    goal(path(a,x0),state0(x1,cons(path(a,x2),x3)),state1(x4,x5))
⟶ goal(path(a,c),state0(x0,x1),
    state1(x2,cons(path(a,b),cons(path(a,c),x1))))

    goal(path(a,x0,state0(x1,nil),state1(x2,x3))
⟶ goal(path(a,a),state0(x0,x1),
    state1(x2,cons(path(a,b),cons(path(a,c),cons(path(a,a),x1)))))

    goal(path(a,x0),state0(x1,cons(path(a,x2),x3)),state1(x4,x5))
⟶ goal(path(a,a),state0(x0,x1),
    state1(x2,cons(path(a,b),cons(path(a,c),cons(path(a,a),x1)))))
```

Note how `state1` is expressed in terms of `state0`: the first component of `state0`/`state1` is ignored because dynamic var 0 is used internally—dynamic var 1 is the trace.

4.4   Application: Definite Clause Grammar (DFG)

A well-known application of tabling is to turn parsing in logic programming from naive recursive descent strategies to more efficient strategies, variants of Earley's and chart parsing algorithms. As a case study, we consider an example of parsing an arithmetic expression from prior work on tabling in Prolog [7]:

```
expr(S0, S) :- expr(S0, S1), S1 = [+| S2 ], term(S2, S).
expr(S0, S) :- term(S0, S).
term(S0, S) :- term(S0, S1), S1 = [*| S2 ], fact(S2, S).
term(S0, S) :- fact(S0, S).
fact(S0, S) :- S0 = [ '(' | S1 ], expr(S1, S2), S2 = [ ')' | S ].
fact(S0, S) :- S0 = [ N | S ], integer(N).
```

Notably, the grammar is left-recursive, so we cannot use it as a parser in regular Prolog as the standard depth-first resolution strategy would go into an infinite loop. However, in an implementation that supports tabling, the following works and produces expected results:

```
? - expr ([3 , + , 4 , *] , []). ↪ no
? - expr ([3 , + , 4 , * , 7] , []). ↪ yes
? - expr ([ '(' , 3 , + , 4 , ')' , * , 7] , []). ↪ yes
? - E = [_ ,_ ,_ ,_ ,_ ,_ ,_ , _ ] , expr (E , []). ↪ no
```

The Prolog grammar above translates to Scalogno with tabling as follows:

```
def exp(s0: Exp[List[String]], s: Exp[List[String]]): Rel =
    memo(term("exp", List(s0,s))) {
  { val s1,s2 = fresh[List[String]]
    exp(s0,s1) && (s1 === cons("+",s2)) && trm(s2,s) } ||
  trm(s0, s) }
def trm(s0: Exp[List[String]], s: Exp[List[String]]): Rel =
    memo(term("trm", List(s0,s))) {
```

```
  { val s1,s2 = fresh[List[String]]
    trm(s0,s1) && (s1 === cons("*",s2)) && fct(s2,s) } ||
  fct(s0, s) }
def fct(s0: Exp[List[String]], s: Exp[List[String]]) = memo(term("fct",
    List(s0,s))) {
  { val s1,s2 = fresh[List[String]]
    s0 === cons("(", s1) && exp(s1, s2) && s2 === cons(")", s) } ||
  { val n = fresh[String]
    s0 === cons(n, s) && dgt(n) }
}
def dgt(n: Exp[String]) = memo(term("dgt",List(n))) {
  n === "0" || n === "1" || n === "2" || n === "3" || n === "4" ||
  n === "5" || n === "6" || n === "7" || n === "8" || n === "9"
}
```

We obtain the same behavior as in Prolog: without tabling, search diverges, but with the `memo` call in place, we automatically obtain an Earley-style bottom-up parser from the given left-recursive grammar. The embedded setting of Scalogno has the additional advantage that we can easily combine the parser with normal deterministic Scala code that performs IO and/or tokenization:

```
run[List[String]] { q => exp(tokenize("(3+4)*7"), nil) } ↪ x0
```

The result is a single unbounded logic variable that indicates success, without constraining `q`.

5   Related Work

There is a long tradition of meta-programming in Prolog, going back at least to the early 1980s. Warren [36], O'Keefe [27], and Naish [26] discuss how to express higher-order "meta-predicates" inspired by functional programming, such as `map` and `fold`; O'Keefe uses Prolog's standard `call` operator, while Warren and Naish advocate using an `apply` operator closer in spirit to Lisp. Warren claims that λ-terms are neither necessary nor desirable for higher-order programming in Prolog, arguing that passing the names of top-level predicates to meta-predicates is the best tradeoff between expressivity and keeping the Prolog language simple. Naish believes that `apply` is a more natural construct for higher-order programming than Prolog's traditional `call` operator, and claims that reliance on `call` by the logic languages Mercury [32] and HiLog [8] make higher-order programming in those languages awkward. Our host language Scala supports λ-terms and `apply`—we therefore inherit both the expressivity and the complexity of these language features.

According to Martens [23], interest in Prolog meta-interpreters was spurred by two articles [3,15] from a 1982 collection edited by Clark and Tärnlund. Introductory books on Prolog [27,34] further popularized meta-interpreters, which are now considered a standard approach to Prolog meta-programming. Hill and Lloyd claim that meta-interpreters in Prolog are fatally flawed, since they often use non-declarative features, and since it can be difficult to assign a semantics to untyped, unground logic programs; their strongly statically typed functional-logic-constraint language Gödel [19] (and Lloyd's followup language, Escher [22]) is specifically designed for declarative meta-programming. Martens [23] defends Prolog-style meta-interpreters, arguing that all forms of untyped logic programming have the same issues that Hill and Lloyd point out, but that reasonable semantics can be applied to meta-programming in untyped logic languages. Our perspective is that untyped meta-interpreters are clearly useful, as demonstrated by their long history in Prolog; however, when embedding a system similar to Scalogno in a host language with an expressive static type system (such as Scala, with its type classes), the type system can be put to good use for writing meta-interpreters or achieving similar effects through other means, such as typed variables with dynamic scope. In the spirit of exploiting types but in an orthogonal fashion, OCanren [21] implements an embedding similar to miniKanren while exploiting the type system of OCaml to ensure a well-typed unification from the perspective of the end user.

There is also a long history of trying to combine functional programming and logic programming, once again going back to the early 1980s. There have been many attempts to embed a Prolog-like language in Lisp [12,18,29], and more recently, in Haskell [9,20,33]; to our knowledge, there is no work in the literature on how to best write meta-interpreters for these embedded languages.

6 Conclusion

In this paper, we explored various techniques to meta-program logic programs embedded in a functional host: deep linguistic re-use, reification (of program, and dually, of context), dynamically scoped variables (capturing the common pattern of recording extra information about each run), among others. Like in the Prolog tradition of meta-interpreters, these techniques enable transforming the evaluation of a logic program without complicating its description. In the embedded setting, we have the choice of meta-programming within the embedded language, or stepping out to the host language. By embracing this flexibility, we gain simplicity: the embedded logic language remains "pure" and first-order, tailored for relational programming.

Acknowledgments. Research reported in this publication was supported in part by the National Center For Advancing Translational Sciences of the National Institutes of Health under Award Number OT2TR002517, by DARPA under agreement number AFRLFA8750-15-2-0092, by NSF under Awards 1553471, 1564207, 1918483, by the Department of Energy under Award DE-SC0018050, as well as by gifts from Google, Facebook, and VMware. The views expressed are those of the authors and do not reflect the official policy or position of the National Institutes of Health, Department of Defense, Department of Energy, National Science Foundation, or the U.S. Government. The U.S. Government is authorized to reproduce and distribute reprints for Governmental purposes notwithstanding any copyright notation thereon.

References

1. Alvis, C.E., Willcock, J.J., Carter, K.M., Byrd, W.E., Friedman, D.P.: cKanren: miniKanren with constraints. In: Scheme (2011)
2. Barrett, C., et al.: CVC4. In: Gopalakrishnan, G., Qadeer, S. (eds.) CAV 2011. LNCS, vol. 6806, pp. 171–177. Springer, Heidelberg (2011). https://doi.org/10.1007/978-3-642-22110-1_14
3. Bowen, K.A., Kowalski, R.A.: Amalgamating logic and metalanguage in logic programming. In: Clark, K.L., Tärnlund, S.A. (eds.) Logic Programming, pp. 153–172. Academic Press, Cambridge (1982)
4. Byrd, W.E.: Relational programming in miniKanren: techniques, applications, and implementations. Ph.D. thesis, Indiana University, September 2009
5. Byrd, W.E., Ballantyne, M., Rosenblatt, G., Might, M.: A unified approach to solving seven programming problems (functional pearl). PACML **1**(ICFP), 8 (2017)
6. Byrd, W.E., Holk, E., Friedman, D.P.: miniKanren, live and untagged: quine generation via relational interpreters (programming pearl). In: Scheme (2012)
7. Carro, M., de Guzmàn, P.C.: Tabled logic programming and its applications (2011). http://cliplab.org/~mcarro/Slides/Misc/intro_to_tabling.pdf
8. Chen, W., Kifer, M., Warren, D.S.: HiLog: a foundation for higher-order logic programming. J. Log. Program. **15**(3), 187–230 (1993)
9. Claessen, K., Ljunglöf, P.: Typed logical variables in Haskell. Electr. Notes Theor. Comput. Sci. **41**(1), 37 (2000). Haskell Workshop
10. Codish, M., Søndergaard, H.: Meta-circular abstract interpretation in prolog. In: Mogensen, T.Æ., Schmidt, D.A., Sudborough, I.H. (eds.) The Essence of Computation. LNCS, vol. 2566, pp. 109–134. Springer, Heidelberg (2002). https://doi.org/10.1007/3-540-36377-7_6
11. Desouter, B., Van Dooren, M., Schrijvers, T.: Tabling as a library with delimited control. Theory Pract. Logic Program. **15**(4–5), 419–433 (2015)
12. Felleisen, M.: Transliterating prolog into scheme. Technical report, 182, Indiana University Computer Science Department (1985)
13. Friedman, D.P., Byrd, W.E., Kiselyov, O.: The Reasoned Schemer. MIT Press, Cambridge (2005)
14. Friedman, D.P., Byrd, W.E., Kiselyov, O., Hemann, J.: The Reasoned Schemer, 2nd edn. MIT Press, Cambridge (2018)
15. Gallaire, H., Lasserre, C.: Metalevel control of logic programs. In: Clark, K.L., Tärnlund, S.A. (eds.) Logic Programming, pp. 173–185. Academic Press, Cambridge (1982)
16. Gupta, G., Costa, V.S.: Cuts and side-effects in and-or parallel prolog. J. Logic Program. **27**(1), 45–71 (1996)
17. Hanus, M.: Functional logic programming: from theory to curry. In: Voronkov, A., Weidenbach, C. (eds.) Programming Logics. LNCS, vol. 7797, pp. 123–168. Springer, Heidelberg (2013). https://doi.org/10.1007/978-3-642-37651-1_6
18. Haynes, C.T.: Logic continuations. J. Log. Program. **4**(2), 157–176 (1987)
19. Hill, P.M., Lloyd, J.W.: The Gödel Programming Language. MIT Press, Cambridge (1994)
20. Hinze, R.: Prological features in a functional setting axioms and implementations. In: FLOPS (1998)
21. Kosarev, D., Boulytchev, D.: Typed embedding of relational language in OCaml. In: 2016 ML Family Workshop, September 2016

22. Lloyd, J.W.: Declarative programming in Escher. Technical report, CSTR-95-013, Department of Computer Science, University of Bristol, June 1995
23. Martens, B., Schreye, D.D.: Why untyped nonground metaprogramming is not (much of) a problem. J. Logic Program. **22**(1), 47–99 (1995)
24. Martin-Martin, E.: Type classes in functional logic programming. In: PEPM (2011)
25. de Moura, L., Bjørner, N.: Z3: an efficient SMT solver. In: Ramakrishnan, C.R., Rehof, J. (eds.) TACAS 2008. LNCS, vol. 4963, pp. 337–340. Springer, Heidelberg (2008). https://doi.org/10.1007/978-3-540-78800-3_24
26. Naish, L.: Higher-order logic programming in Prolog. Technical report, 96/2, University of Melbourne (1996)
27. O'Keefe, R.A.: The Craft of Prolog. MIT Press, Cambridge (1990)
28. Oliveira, B.C., Moors, A., Odersky, M.: Type classes as objects and implicits. In: OOPSLA (2010)
29. Robinson, J.A., Sibert, E.E.: LOGLISP: an alternative to PROLOG. In: Hayes, J., Michie, D., Pao, Y.H. (eds.) Machine Intelligence 10, pp. 399–419. Ellis Horwood Ltd., Chichester (1982)
30. Rompf, T.: The essence of multi-stage evaluation in LMS. In: Lindley, S., McBride, C., Trinder, P., Sannella, D. (eds.) A List of Successes That Can Change the World. LNCS, vol. 9600, pp. 318–335. Springer, Cham (2016). https://doi.org/10.1007/978-3-319-30936-1_17
31. Rompf, T., Amin, N., Moors, A., Haller, P., Odersky, M.: Scala-virtualized: linguistic reuse for deep embeddings. Higher-Order Symb. Comput. **25**(1), 165–207 (2013)
32. Somogyi, Z., Henderson, F.J., Conway, T.C.: Mercury, an efficient purely declarative logic programming language. In: Proceedings of the Australian Computer Science Conference, pp. 499–512 (1995)
33. Spivey, J.M., Seres, S.: Embedding prolog in Haskell. In: Meijer, E. (ed.) Proceedings of the 1999 Haskell Workshop. Technical report UU-CS-1999-28, Department of Computer Science, University of Utrecht (1999)
34. Sterling, L., Shapiro, E.: The Art of Prolog, 2nd Edn. Advanced Programming Techniques. MIT Press, Cambridge (1994)
35. Sterling, L., Yalcinalp, L.U.: Explaining prolog based expert systems using a layered meta-interpreter. In: IJCAI 1989, pp. 66–71 (1989)
36. Warren, D.H.D.: Higher-order extensions to Prolog: are they needed? In: Hayes, J., Michie, D., Pao, Y.H. (eds.) Machine Intelligence 10, pp. 441–454. Ellis Horwood Ltd., Chichester (1982)
37. Warren, D.S.: Memoing for logic programs. Commun. ACM **35**(3), 93–111 (1992)

Mimalloc: Free List Sharding in Action

Daan Leijen$^{(\boxtimes)}$, Benjamin Zorn, and Leonardo de Moura

Microsoft Research, Redmond, USA
`{daan,zorn,leonardo}@microsoft.com`

Abstract. Modern memory allocators have to balance many simultaneous demands, including performance, security, the presence of concurrency, and application-specific demands depending on the context of their use. One increasing use-case for allocators is as back-end implementations of languages, such as Swift and Python, that use reference counting to automatically deallocate objects. We present mimalloc, a memory allocator that effectively balances these demands, shows significant performance advantages over existing allocators, and is tailored to support languages that rely on the memory allocator as a backend for reference counting. Mimalloc combines several innovations to achieve this result. First, it uses three page-local sharded free lists to increase locality, avoid contention, and support a highly-tuned allocate and free fast path. These free lists also support *temporal cadence*, which allows the allocator to predictably leave the fast path for regular maintenance tasks such as supporting deferred freeing, handling frees from non-local threads, etc. While influenced by the allocation workload of the reference-counted Lean and Koka programming language, we show that mimalloc has superior performance to modern commercial memory allocators, including tcmalloc and jemalloc, with speed improvements of 7% and 14%, respectively, on redis, and consistently out performs over a wide range of sequential and concurrent benchmarks. Allocators tailored to provide an efficient runtime for reference-counting languages reduce the implementation burden on developers and encourage the creation of innovative new language designs.

1 Introduction

Modern memory allocators have to balance many simultaneous demands, including performance, security, parallelism, and application-specific demands depending on the context of their use. One increasing use-case for allocators is as back-end implementations of languages, such as Swift [34], that use reference counting to automatically deallocate objects, or like Python [29], that typically allocate many small short-lived objects.

When developing a shared runtime system for the Lean [26] and Koka [18,19] languages, these two use cases caused issues with current allocators. First of all, both Lean and Koka are functional languages that perform many small short-lived allocations. In Lean, using a custom allocator for such small allocations outperformed even highly optimized allocators like jemalloc [8]. Secondly, just

© Springer Nature Switzerland AG 2019
A. W. Lin (Ed.): APLAS 2019, LNCS 11893, pp. 244–265, 2019.
https://doi.org/10.1007/978-3-030-34175-6_13

like Swift and Python, the runtime system uses reference counting [32] to manage memory. In order to limit pauses when deallocating large data structures, we also need to support deferred decrementing of reference counts. To do this well, cooperation from the allocator is required – as the best time to resume a deferred decrement is when there is memory pressure.

To address these issues, we implemented a new allocator that uses various novel ideas to achieve excellent performance:

- The main idea is to use extreme *free list sharding*: instead of one large free list per size class, we instead have a free list per mimalloc *page* (usually 64KiB). This keeps locality of allocation as `malloc` allocates inside one page until that page is full, regardless of where other objects are freed in the heap.
- Moreover, we use separate *thread-free* lists for frees by other threads to avoid atomic operations in the fast path of `malloc`. These thread-free lists are also sharded per page to minimize contention among them. Such list is moved to the local free list atomically every once in a while which effectively *batches* the remote frees [24].
- Finally, we use a third *local-free* list per page for thread-local frees. When the allocation free list becomes empty, the local-free list becomes the new free list. This design ensures that the generic allocation path is always taken after a fixed number of allocations, establishing a *temporal cadence*. This routine can now be used to amortize more expensive operations: (1) do free-ing for deferred reference count decrements, (2) maintain a deterministic heartbeat, and (3) collect the concurrent thread-free lists. Using the separate local-free list thus enables us to have a single check in the fast allocation path to handle all the above scenarios through the generic "collection" routine.
- We highly optimize the common allocation and free code paths and defer to the generic routine in other cases. This means that the data structures need to be very regular in order to minimize conditionals in the fast path. This consistent design also reduces special cases and increases code reuse – leading to more regular and simpler code. The core library is less than 3500 LOC, much smaller than the core of other industrial strength allocators like tcmalloc (~20k LOC) and jemalloc (~25k LOC).
- The allocator is completely lock free, and all thread interaction is done using atomic operations. It has bounded worst-case allocation times, and meta-data overhead is about 0.2% with at most 12.5% ($\frac{1}{8}$th) waste in allocation size classes.

We tested mimalloc against many other leading allocators over a wide range of benchmarks and mimalloc consistently outperforms all others (Section). Moreover, we succeeded to outperform our own custom allocators for small objects in Lean. Our results show that mimalloc has superior performance to modern commercial memory allocators, including tcmalloc and jemalloc, with speed improvements of with speed improvements of 7% and 14%, respectively, on redis, and consistently out performs over a wide range of sequential and concurrent benchmarks with similar peak memory usage.

Historically, allocator design has focused on performance issues such as reducing the time in the allocator, reducing memory usage, or scaling to many concurrent threads. Less often, allocator design is primarily motivated by improving the reference locality of the application. For example VAM [9] and early versions of PHKmalloc also use free list sharding to ensure that sequential allocations often come from the same page. mimalloc also improves application memory reference locality and improves on VAM by implementing multi-threading and adding additional sharded free lists to reduce contention and support amortizing maintenance tasks. Our design demonstrates that allocators focused on improving application memory locality can also provide high allocator performance and concurrent scalability.

In the rest of this paper, we present the design of mimalloc, including motivating the three free lists, consider issues such as security and portability, and evaluate its performance against many state of the art allocator implementations. mimalloc is implemented in C, and runs on Linux, FreeBSD, MacOSX, and Windows, and is freely available on github [20], and with its simplified and regular code base, is particularly amenable to being integrated into other language runtimes.

2   Free List Sharding

We start with an overview of the specifics of free list sharding, the local free list, and the thread free list. After this, Sect. 3 goes into the details of the full heap layout (Fig. 1) and the implementation of `malloc` and `free`, followed by the benchmark results in Sect. 4.

2.1   The Allocation Free List

The allocation pattern for functional style programming is to allocate and free many small objects. Many allocators use a single free list per size class which can lead to bad spatial locality where objects belonging to a single structure can be spread out over the entire heap. Consider for example the following heap state (A) where the free list spans a large part of the heap:

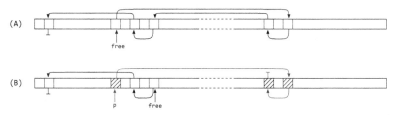

When allocating a list p of three elements, we end up in state (B) where the newly allocated list is also spread out over a large part of the heap with bad spatial locality. This is not an uncommon situation. On the contrary, most functional style programs will converge to this form of heap state. This happens in particular when folding over older data structures and building new data structures of a different size class where the interleaved allocation leads to these spread-out free lists.

To improve the spatial locality of allocation, mimalloc use *free list sharding* where the heap is divided into *pages* (per size-class) with a free list per page (where pages[1] are usually 64KiB for small objects). The previous heap state will now look like following situation (A), where each page has a small free list:

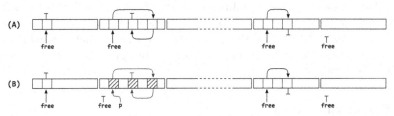

After allocating the three element p list, we end up in state (B) where the list is now fully allocated within the page with much better spatial locality. We believe that the good performance of mimalloc comes in a large part from the improved allocation locality.

To test this, we did an experiment in the Lean compiler [26]. Version 3 of the compiler had a custom allocator for allocating small objects where it used a single free list. We replaced this implementation with just a sharded free list per slab (page) and on some benchmarks with large data structures in a 1GiB heap, we saw performance improvements of over 25% with this single change! Early work by Feng and Berger [9] on the locality improving VAM allocator also used a sharded free list design and they measured a significant reduction in the L2 cache misses.

2.2   No Bump Pointer

The allocation path for allocating inside a page can now simply pop from the page local list:

```
void* malloc_in_page( page_t* page, size_t size ) {
    block_t* block = page->free;              // page-local free list
    if (block==NULL) return malloc_generic(size); // slow path
    page->free = block->next;
    page->used++;
    return block;
}
```

where

```
struct block_t { struct block_t* next; }
```

---

[1] Do not confuse the word *page* with OS pages. A mimalloc page is larger and corresponds more closely to a *superblock* [4] or *subslab* [24] in other allocators.

There is just a single conditional and a pop in the fast path now. The used increment is needed to be able to efficiently determine when all objects in a page are freed. Many allocators use a *reap* design where a bump pointer is used initially when the page is empty [6,9,24]. We tested a variant of mimalloc with bump pointer allocation but across our benchmarks it was consistently about 2% worse. One reason might be that adding bump pointer allocation means there are now 2 conditionals in the fast path: either use the bump pointer, or use the free list. Moreover, these conditionals cannot be predicted well as each one depends on the page where one happens to allocate in. Moreover, for security reasons it is not good to allocate predictably in a sequential way which rules out bump pointers too. As shown in Sect. 3.5, we initialize the free list in a fresh page in a randomized way.

2.3   The Local Free List

For the Koka and Lean runtimes, we wanted to bound the worst-case allocation and free times. In particular, when freeing large data structures, the number of recursive free calls need to be limited. Koka and Lean use reference counting in the runtime (similar to Swift and Python), but the problem occurs in any language with large data structures. Limiting the number of free calls with reference counting can be done with a simple limit counter and pushing the remaining pointers on a *deferred decrement* list.

The question is when to free again from this deferred decrement list? Here cooperation from allocator is necessary since the best time to do this is when the allocator is under pressure and needs to find more free space. The mimalloc allocator calls a user defined `deferred_free` callback when that happens. This is called from the slow path in mimalloc in the `malloc_generic` routine exactly when the page local free list is empty. This nicely combines with the single conditional in the fast path. We will see that we reuse this technique again, and put any more expensive operations into the generic routine guarded by the single conditional.

However, this does not quite work yet as there is no guarantee that the generic routine is called regularly: a user may free and allocate repeatedly within one page with the free list in the page never becoming empty. What we want instead is to ensure the generic routine is called after some fixed number of allocations.

Therefore, we shard the free list once more: we add a sharded *local free list* to each page and while we allocate from the regular free list, we put any freed objects on the *local* free list instead. This guarantees that the free list becomes empty after a fixed number of allocations. In the generic routine we can now simply move the local free list to the free list and keep allocating:

```
page->free = page->local_free;  // move the list
page->local_free = NULL;        // and the local list is empty again
```

Note again that we did not need to add a conditional in the fast path for this situation and put the work into the slow path. Now that `deferred_free` is guaranteed to be called regularly after a bounded number of allocations, we can also use it as a deterministic *heartbeat*. This is used in Lean as a form of portable timer to time-out threads if they take too long (for proofs). In that case we cannot use wall-clock time since that would not be deterministic across machines while the heartbeat is.

2.4   The Thread Free List

In mimalloc, pages belong to a thread-local heap and allocation is always done in the local heap. This way no locks are needed for thread local allocations. Nevertheless, any thread can free an object. To avoid locks for thread local frees as well, we shard the free list one more final time and add a sharded *thread free list* per page, where other threads push freed objects in that page.

If a non-local free happens, we use atomic operations to push the freed object p atomically on the thread free list:

```
atomic_push( &page->thread_free, p );
```

where

```
void atomic_push( block_t** list, block_t* block ) {
   do { block->next = *list; }
   while (!atomic_cas(list, block /*new*/, block->next /*compare*/));
}
```

The beauty of the sharded thread free list is that it also reduces contention among threads since threads freeing in different pages do not contend with each other. On current architectures, uncontended atomic operations are very efficient and usually implemented as part of the cache consistency protocol [30].

Again, we use the generic routine to collect the thread free list and add it to the free list, just as we did with the local free list:

```
tfree = atomic_swap( &page->thread_free, NULL );
append( page->free, tfree );
```

Since the entire thread free list is moved at once, this effectively batches non-local free calls as well. This is especially important for asymmetric concurrent work loads where some threads predominantly free objects and others predominantly allocate. The snmalloc allocator [24] was especially created to handle this situation well and also uses a batching technique to reduce expensive synchronization. This workload is tested by the xmallocN benchmark in Sect. 4.

3   Implementation

Given the sharded free lists, we can now understand the full design of the allocator, where Fig. 1 shows a detailed overview of the layout of the heap. Except for the sharded lists, the overall design is otherwise quite similar to other size-segregated thread-caching allocators.

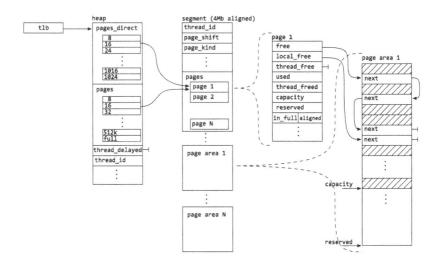

Fig. 1. Heap layout

3.1   Malloc

To allocate an object, mimalloc first gets a pointer to the thread local heap (tlb). From there it needs to find a page of the right size class. For small objects under 1Kb the heap contains a direct array of pointers to the first available page in that size class. For small object allocation, the code becomes:

```
void* malloc_small( size_t n ) {                         // 0 < n <= 1024
  heap_t*  heap  = tlb;
  page_t*  page  = heap->pages_direct[(n+7)>>3];  // divide up by 8
  block_t* block = page->free;
  if (block==NULL) return malloc_generic(heap,n); // slow path
  page->free = block->next;
  page->used++;
  return block;
}
```

which expands to efficient assembly with only one conditional.

As seen in Fig. 1, the pages and the page meta-data all live in large *segments* (sometimes called *slab* or *arena* in other allocators). These segments are 4MiB (or larger for huge objects that are over 512KiB), and start with the segment- and page meta data, followed by the actual pages where the first page is shortened by the size of the meta data plus a guard page. There are three page sizes: for small objects under 8KiB the pages are 64KiB and there are 64 in a segment; for large objects under 512KiB there is one page that spans the whole segment, and finally huge objects over 512KiB have one page of the required size. The reason to still use a segment and single page for large and huge objects is to simplify the data structures and reduce the code size and complexity by having a consistent interface and code with few special cases. This pays off in practice and the code size of mimalloc is far smaller than most other allocators.

3.2 Free

Pages and their meta data are allocated in a segment mostly to reduce expensive allocation calls to the underlying OS, but there is another important reason: when freeing a pointer, we need to be able to find the page meta data belonging to that pointer. The way this is done in mimalloc is to align the segments to a 4MiB boundary. Finding the segment holding a pointer p can then be done by masking the lower bits. The code for `free` becomes:

```
void free( void* p ) {
  segment_t* segment = (segment_t*)((uintptr_t)p & ~(4*MB));
  if (segment==NULL) return;
  page_t*  page  = &segment->pages[(p-segment) >> segment->page_shift];
  block_t* block = (block_t*)p;
  if (thread_id() == segment->thread_id) {  // local free
    block->next = page->local_free;
    page->local_free = block;
    page->used-;
    if (page->used - page->thread_freed == 0) page_free(page);
  }
  else {                                    // non-local free
    atomic_push( &page->thread_free, block);
    atomic_incr( &page->thread_freed );
  }
}
```

The free function first gets the segment pointer by masking the lower bits of the freed pointer p. When the pointer is NULL, the segment will be NULL too and we check for that. In the generated assembly this removes an explicit comparison operation as the bitwise *and* sets the zero-flag if the result is zero. From there we can calculate the page index by taking the difference and shifting by the segment `page_shift`: for small pages this is 16 (= 64KiB), while for large and huge pages it is 22 (= 4MiB) such that the index is always zero in those cases (as there is just one page). Again, by using a uniform representation we avoid special cases and conditionals in the fast path.

The main conditional tests whether this is a thread local free, or a free by another thread. Here mimalloc relies on an efficient `thread_id()` call to get the id of the current thread and comparing that to the `thread_id` field of the segment. On most operating systems this can be done very efficiently by loading the thread id from a fixed address of the thread local data (for example, on Linux on 64-bit Intel/AMD chips this at offset 0 relative to the `fs` register).

If the free is done by another thread, the object is pushed atomically on the `thread_free` list. Otherwise, the free is local and we simply push the object on the `local_free` list. We also test here if all objects are freed in that page and free the page in that case. We could skip this and instead only collect full free pages when looking for a fresh page in the slow path, but for certain work loads it turns out to be more efficient to try to make such pages available as early as possible.

Note that we read the thread shared `thread_freed` count without a read-barrier meaning there is tiny probability that we miss that all objects in the page were just all freed. However, that is okay – since we are guaranteed to call the generic allocation routine sometimes, we can collect any such pages later on (and indeed – on asymmetric workloads where some threads only allocate and others only free, the collection in the generic routine is the *only* way such pages get freed).

3.3   Generic Allocation

The generic allocation routine, `malloc_generic`, is our "slow path" which is guaranteed to be called every once in a while. This routine gives us the opportunity to do more expensive operations whose cost is amortized over many allocations, and can almost be seen as a form of garbage collector. In pseudo code:

```
void* malloc_generic( heap_t* heap, size_t size ) {
  deferred_free();
  foreach( page in heap->pages[size_class(size)] ) {
    page_collect(page);
    if (page->used - page->thread_freed == 0) {
      page_free(page);
    }
    else if (page->free != NULL) {
      return malloc(size);
    }
  }
  .... // allocate a fresh page and malloc from there
}

void page_collect(page) {
  page->free = page->local_free;  // move the local free list
  page->local_free = NULL;
  ... // move the thread free list atomically
}
```

The generic routine linearly walks through the pages of a size class and frees any pages that contain no more objects. It stops when it finds the first page that has free objects. In the actual implementation not all pages are immediately freed but some are retained a bit in a cache for possible future use; also, the maximum number of freed pages is bounded to limit the worst-case allocation time. When a page is found with free space, the page list is also rotated at that point so that a next search starts from that point.

3.4   The Full List

The implementation as described already performs very well on almost all of our wide range of benchmarks – except some. In particular, on the SpecMark gcc benchmark we observed a 30% slowdown compared to some other allocators. This anecdote shows that there is no silver bullet and an industrial strength memory allocator needs to address many corner cases that might show up only for particular workloads.

In the case of the gcc benchmark it happens to use its own custom allocators and allocate many large objects initially that than stay live for a long time. For mimalloc this leads to many (over 18000) *full* pages that are now traversed linearly every time in the generic allocation routine.

The solution that we implemented is to have a separate *full list* that holds all the pages that are full, and move those back to the regular page lists when an object is freed in such page. This fixes the gcc benchmark but unfortunately this seemingly small change introduces significant complexity for the multi-threaded case.

In particular, on a non-local free of an object in a full page, we need to somehow signal the owning heap that the page is no longer full, and if possible without taking an expensive lock. We are going to do this through a heap-owned list of *thread delayed free* blocks. In the generic routine, we first atomically take over this list and free all the blocks in the delayed free list normally – possibly moving pages from the full list back to the regular lists.

But how does a non-local free know whether to push on the page local *thread free* list, or whether do push on the owning heap *thread delayed free* list? For this we use the 2 least significant bits in the thread free list pointer to atomically encode 3 states: NORMAL, DELAYED, and DELAYING. Usually, the state is NORMAL and we push on the local thread free list. When a page is moved to the full list, we set the DELAYED state – signifying that non-local free operations should push on the owning heap delayed free list. While doing that, the DELAYING state is temporarily set to ensure the owning heap structure itself stays valid in case the owning thread terminates in the mean time. After a delayed free, the state is always set to NORMAL again since we only need one delayed free per page to check if the page is no longer full. This turns out to be an important optimization: again, with asymmetric concurrent workloads the freeing thread may free many objects and we should ensure the more expensive initial delayed free is only done once. Without this optimization, the xmalloc-test benchmark is 30% slower.

3.5   Security

The design of mimalloc lends itself well to implement various security mitigations that one would consider required in browser environments for example. For a good overview we refer to Novark and Berger [27] and Berger and Zorn [5]. We implemented a secure variant of mimalloc (called smimalloc) that implements various security mitigations:

- It puts OS guard pages in-between every mimalloc page such that heap over-flow attacks are always limited to one mimalloc page and can never overflow into the heap meta data.
- The initial free list in a page is initialized randomly such that there is no predictable allocation pattern (to protect against *heap feng shui* [31]). Also, on a full list, the secure allocator will sometimes extend instead of using the local free list to increase randomness further.
- To guard against heap block-overflow attacks that overwrite the free list, we *xor*-encode the free list in each page. This prevents overwriting with known values but also allows efficient detection of such attack.
- Already, mimalloc efficiently supports multiple heaps. This can further increase security by allocating internal objects like virtual method tables etc. in a separate heap from other application allocated objects.

As we see in Sect. 4, the secure version of mimalloc is on average about 3% slower plain mimalloc. This was quite surprising to us as we initially expected much larger slowdowns due to the above mitigations.

4   Evaluation

We tested mimalloc against many other top allocators over a wide range of bench-marks, ranging from various real world programs to synthetic benchmarks that see how the allocator behaves under more extreme circumstances. The bench-mark suite is fully scripted and available on Github [21].

Allocators are interesting as there exists no algorithm that is generally opti-mal – for a given allocator one can usually construct a workload where it does not do so well. The goal is thus to find an allocation strategy that performs well over a wide range of benchmarks without suffering from underperformance in less common situations (which is what the second half of our benchmark set tests for).

In our benchmarks, mimalloc always outperforms all other leading allocators (jemalloc, tcmalloc, Hoard, etc), and usually uses less memory (up to 25% more in the worst case). A nice property is that it does *consistently* well over the wide range of benchmarks: only snmalloc shares this property while all other allocators exhibit sudden (severe) underperformance in certain situations. We try to highlight and explain these situations in the text and hope these insights can lead to improvements in other allocator designs as well.

4.1   Allocators

We tested mimalloc with 7 leading allocators over 12 benchmarks and the Spec-Mark benchmarks. The tested allocators are:

- **mi**: The mimalloc allocator [20], using version tag v1.0.0. We also test a secure version of mimalloc as **smi** which uses the techniques described in Sect. 3.5.

- **tc**: The tcmalloc allocator [10] which comes as part of the Google performance tools and is used in the Chrome browser. Installed as package `libgoogle-perftools-dev` version 2.5-2.2ubuntu3.
- **je**: The jemalloc allocator by Evans [8] is developed at Facebook and widely used in practice, for example in FreeBSD and Firefox. Using version tag 5.2.0.
- **sn**: The snmalloc allocator is a recent concurrent message passing allocator by Liétar et al. [24], using `git-0b64536b`. We would like to remark that since these results, the authors have improved performance considerably where it performs close to mimalloc now (2019-08). Many improvements, like the addition of free-list sharding, were directly inspired by the initial technical report on mimalloc.
- **rp**: The rpmalloc allocator uses 32-byte aligned allocations and is developed by Jansson [14] at Rampant Pixels. Using version tag 1.3.1.
- **hd**: The Hoard allocator by Berger et al. [4]. This is one of the first multi-thread scalable allocators. Using version tag 3.13.
- **glibc**: The system allocator. Here we use the glibc allocator (which is originally based on Ptmalloc2), using version 2.27.0. Note that version 2.26 significantly improved scalability over earlier versions.
- **tbb**: The Intel TBB allocator that comes with the Thread Building Blocks (TBB) library [12,13,15]. Installed as package `libtbb-dev`, version 2017~U7-8.

All allocators run exactly the same benchmark programs on Ubuntu 18.04.1 and use `LD_PRELOAD` to override the default allocator. The wall-clock elapsed time and peak resident memory (rss) are measured with the `time` program. The average scores over 5 runs are used. Performance is reported relative to mimalloc, e.g. a time of 1.5× means that the program took 1.5× longer than mimalloc.

4.2 Benchmarks

The first set of benchmarks are real world programs and consist of:

- **cfrac**: by Dave Barrett, implementation of continued fraction factorization which uses many small short-lived allocations – exactly the workload we are targeting for Koka and Lean.
- **espresso**: a programmable logic array analyzer, described by Grunwald, Zorn, and Henderson [11] in the context of cache aware memory allocation.
- **barnes**: a hierarchical n-body particle solver [3] which uses relatively few allocations compared to `cfrac` and `espresso`. Simulates the gravitational forces between 163840 particles.
- **leanN**: The Lean compiler by de Moura et al. [26], version 3.4.1, compiling its own standard library concurrently using N threads (`./lean -make -j N`). Big real-world workload with intensive allocation.
- **redis**: running the redis 5.0.3 server on 1 million requests pushing 10 new list elements and then requesting the head 10 elements. Measures the requests handled per second.

- **larsonN**: by Larson and Krishnan [17]. Simulates a server workload using 100 separate threads which each allocate and free many objects but leave some objects to be freed by other threads. Larson and Krishnan observe this behavior (which they call bleeding) in actual server applications, and the benchmark simulates this.

The second set of benchmarks are stress tests and consist of:

- **alloc-test**: a modern allocator test developed by OLogN Technologies AG (ITHare.com) [28]. Simulates intensive allocation workloads with a Pareto size distribution. The alloc-testN benchmark runs on N cores doing $100 \cdot 10^6$ allocations per thread with objects up to 1KiB in size. Using commit 94f6cb (master, 2018-07-04)
- **sh6bench**: by MicroQuill [25] as part of SmartHeap. Stress test where some of the objects are freed in a usual last-allocated, first-freed (LIFO) order, but others are freed in reverse order. Using the public source (retrieved 2019-01-02)
- **sh8benchN**: by MicroQuill [25] as part of SmartHeap. Stress test for multi-threaded allocation (with N threads) where, just as in larson, some objects are freed by other threads, and some objects freed in reverse (as in sh6bench). Using the public source (retrieved 2019-01-02)
- **xmallocN**: by Lever and Boreham [22] and Christian Eder. We use the updated version from the SuperMalloc repository [16]. This is a more extreme version of the larson benchmark with 100 purely allocating threads, and 100 purely deallocating threads with objects of various sizes migrating between them. This asymmetric producer/consumer pattern is usually difficult to handle by allocators with thread-local caches.
- **cscratch**: by Berger et al. [4]. Introduced with the Hoard allocator to test for passive-false sharing of cache lines: first some small objects are allocated and given to each thread; the threads free that object and allocate immediately another one, and access that repeatedly. If an allocator allocates objects from different threads close to each other this will lead to cache-line contention.

4.3   On a 16-Core AMD EPYC

Figure 2 (and Fig. 6 for memory in the Appendix) shows the benchmark results on a r5a.4xlarge [2] instance consisting of a 16-core AMD EPYC 7000 at 2.5 GHz with 128 GB ECC memory, running Ubuntu 18.04.1 with LibC 2.27 and GCC 7.3.0.

In the first five benchmarks we can see mimalloc outperforms the other allocators moderately, but we also see that all these modern allocators perform well – the times of large performance differences in regular workloads are over. In cfrac and espresso, mimalloc is a tad faster than tcmalloc and jemalloc, but a solid 10% faster than all other allocators on espresso. The tbb allocator does not do so well here and lags more than 20% behind mimalloc. The cfrac and espresso programs do not use much memory (~1.5 MB) so it does not matter too much, but still mimalloc uses about half the resident memory of tcmalloc.

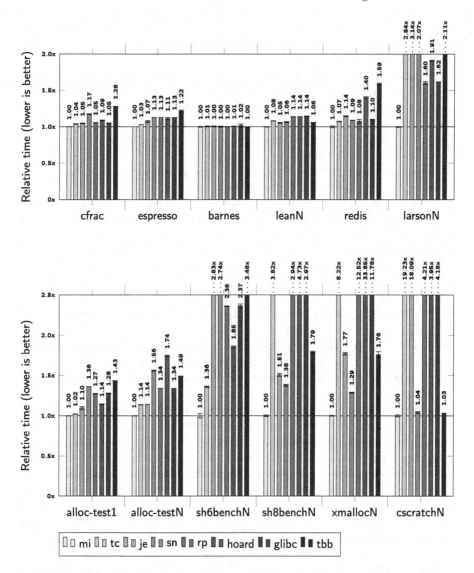

Fig. 2. Time benchmark on a 16-core AMD Epyc r5a-4xlarge instance. Benchmarks ending with "N" run in parallel on all cores.

The leanN program is most interesting as a large realistic and concurrent workload and there is a 8% speedup over tcmalloc. This is quite significant: if Lean spends 20% of its time in the allocator that means that mimalloc is 1.3× faster than tcmalloc here. This is surprising as that is *not* measured in a pure allocation benchmark like alloc-test. We conjecture that we see this outsized improvement here because mimalloc has better locality in the allocation which improves performance for the *other* computations in a program as well.

The redis benchmark shows more differences between the allocators where mimalloc is 14% faster than jemalloc. On this benchmark tbb (and Hoard) do not do well and are over 40% slower.

The larson server workload which allocates and frees objects between many threads shows even larger differences, where mimalloc is more than 2.5× faster than tcmalloc and jemalloc which is quite surprising for these battle tested allocators – probably due to the object migration between different threads. This is a difficult benchmark for other allocators too where mimalloc is still 48% faster than the next fastest (snmalloc).

The second benchmark set tests specific aspects of the allocators and shows even more extreme differences between them.

The alloc-test is very allocation intensive doing millions of allocations in various size classes. The test is scaled such that when an allocator performs almost identically on alloc-test1 as alloc-testN it means that it scales linearly. Here, tcmalloc, snmalloc, and Hoard seem to scale less well and do more than 10% worse on the multi-core version. Even the best allocators (tcmalloc and jemalloc) are more than 10% slower as mimalloc here.

Also in sh6bench mimalloc does much better than the others (more than 2× faster than jemalloc). We cannot explain this well but believe it is caused in part by the "reverse" free-ing pattern in sh6bench.

Again in sh8bench the mimalloc allocator handles object migration between threads much better and is over 36% faster than the next best allocator, snmalloc. Whereas tcmalloc did well on sh6bench, the addition of object migration caused it to be almost 3 times slower than before.

The xmallocN benchmark simulates an asymmetric workload where some threads only allocate, and others only free. The snmalloc allocator was especially developed to handle this case well as it often occurs in concurrent message passing systems. Here we see that the mimalloc technique of having non-contended sharded thread free lists pays off and it even outperforms snmalloc. Only jemalloc also handles this reasonably well, while the others underperform by a large margin. The optimization on mimalloc to do a *delayed free* only once for full pages is quite important – without it mimalloc is almost twice as slow (as then all frees contend again on the single heap delayed free list).

The cscratch benchmark also demonstrates the different architectures of the allocators nicely. With a single thread they all perform the same, but when running with multiple threads the allocator induced false sharing of the cache lines causes large run-time differences, where mimalloc is more than 18× faster than jemalloc and tcmalloc! Crundal [7] describes in detail why the false cache line sharing occurs in the tcmalloc design, and also discusses how this can be avoided with some small implementation changes. Only snmalloc and tbb also avoid the cache line sharing like mimalloc. Kukanov and Voss [15] describe in detail how the design of tbb avoids the false cache line sharing.

4.4   On a 4-Core Intel Xeon Workstation

Figure 3 shows the benchmark results on an HP Z4-G4 workstation with a 4-core Intel® Xeon® W2123 at 3.6 GHz with 16 GB ECC memory, running Ubuntu 18.04.1 with LibC 2.27 and GCC 7.3.0. This time we added the secure version of mimalloc as **smi**.

Overall, the relative results are quite similar as before. Most allocators fare better on the larsonN benchmark now – either due to architectural changes (AMD vs. Intel) or because there is just less concurrency.

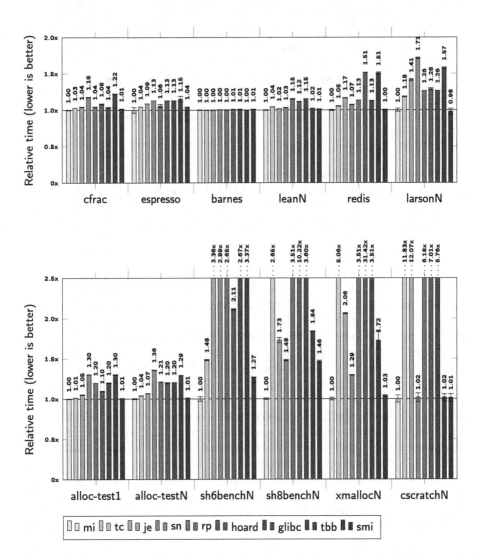

Fig. 3. Time benchmark on a 4-core Intel Xeon workstation. Benchmarks ending with "N" run in parallel on all cores.

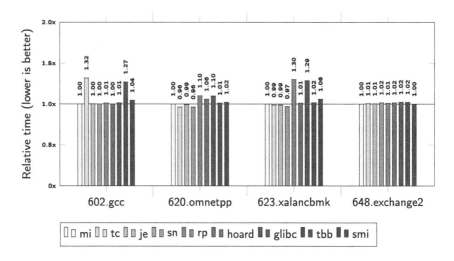

Fig. 4. Time benchmark on a 4-core Intel Xeon workstation for selected SpecMark 2019 benchmarks.

The secure mimalloc version uses guard pages around each (mimalloc) page, encodes the free lists and uses randomized initial free lists, and we expected it would perform quite a bit worse – but on the first benchmark set it performed only about 3% slower on average, and is second best overall.

4.5 SpecMark 2019

We also ran SpecMark 2019 benchmarks. Most benchmarks there do not allocate a lot and all the modern allocators perform mostly identical for most of them. There are only 4 of them that show larger differences, which we show in Figs. 4 and 5: 602.gcc, 620.omnetpp, 623.xalancbmk, and 648.exchange2.

On these benchmarks mimalloc does well but is slightly slower than tcmalloc, jemalloc, and snmalloc, on omnetpp and xalancbmk. As discussed in Sect. 3.4, the gcc benchmarks allocates a lot of initial long lived data and we needed the *full* list to avoid long searches. We conjecture this is happening in tcmalloc and tbb as well, as both have a similar underperformance of about 30% (just like mimalloc before the optimization). We see something similar happen in the xalancbmk benchmark for rp and glibc but we are not sure what is the cause of that.

In Fig. 5 the relative peak memory usage is shown. Interestingly, the gcc benchmark shows two outliers too, but this time Hoard and tbb underperform by 30%. On the exchange2 benchmark it is surprising to see that both tcmalloc and jemalloc use significantly more memory than mimalloc even though especially jemalloc is optimized to reduce the resident memory usage for long running server programs.

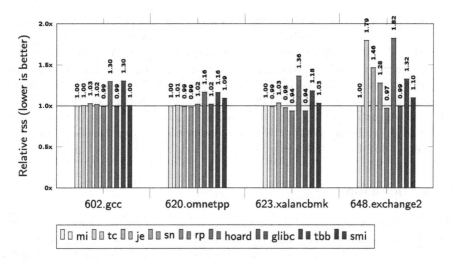

Fig. 5. Peak memory usage on a 4-core Intel Xeon workstation for selected SpecMark 2019 benchmarks.

5   Related Work

Feng and Berger's VAM [9] is the allocator design most closely related to mimalloc. VAM pioneered the idea of prioritizing application reference locality over reducing memory fragmentation and our sharded free list design improves on VAM's original design. VAM maintained free lists per 4k hardware page and supported bump-pointer allocations (which we considered but rejected). As many allocators contemporaneous with VAM did, VAM treated large and medium-sized objects differently than small objects by incorporating inline meta data with each object to support a best-fit allocation strategy. VAM was not a multi-threaded allocator design, as mimalloc is, and its implementation is not currently available for measuring.

Grunwald et al. [11] highlight the impact of allocator design on overall application reference locality and argue that a segregated size-class approach, as implemented in QuickFit [33] would provide better reference locality. While Grunwald argues that QuickFit is only part of a more general allocator solution, unlike Grunwald or VAM, mimalloc demonstrates that a uniform approach to object representation across all sizes leads to significant benefits in reduced complexity and improved performance.

The Intel TBB (Thread Building Block) multi-threaded allocator [12,15] has elements in common with mimalloc. It uses size-segregated bins, has thread-local free lists, allocates from a private free list and and has a public free list per bin that foreign threads return local objects to. Unlike mimalloc, TBB does not have a separate private free list that local objects are returned on, choosing instead to immediately reuse freed objects instead of deferring reuse.

We recently learned of the scalloc allocator [1] which provide scalable multi-core allocation through global sharing of spans (segments) which is possible through scalable lock-free pools and queue data structures. Another recent allocator is snmalloc which focuses on improving the performance of multi-threaded producer/consumer workloads [23], as exemplified by the xmallocN benchmark. snmalloc uses a novel radix-tree structure to avoid potential bottlenecks with different consumer threads contending with each other on returning an object to the same producer. mimalloc handles contention between threads performing frees of non-local objects by sharding the thread free list in every page.

6   Conclusion

We present mimalloc, an allocator motivated by the need to support deferred reference decrements in language runtimes and focused on improving the overall reference locality of an application. mimalloc provides three sharded free lists per software page (64KiB), increasing overall locality, reducing multi-threaded contention, and supporting temporal cadence, where slow-path operations are deferred but guaranteed to happen with regularity. To avoid costly branches on the fast path, mimalloc simplifies object representation and eliminates complexities such as doing bump-pointer allocation, representing medium-objects differently, etc. Comparing against state-of-the-art commercial allocator implementations, we show that mimalloc consistently outperforms other allocators in their default configuration including on both single-threaded workloads, such as redis, as well as on multi-threaded stress tests. mimalloc is implemented in C, is freely available on github [20] and with its simple and small code base is particularly amenable to being integrated into other language runtimes.

Acknowledgements. We would like to thank Matthew Parkison, and the other authors of snmalloc, for the valuable feedback, and encouragement to include the xmallocN benchmark.

A   Evaluation of Peak Working Memory

Figure 6 shows the peak working memory (RSS) relative to mimalloc. These figures correspond to the earlier performance Figs. 2 and 3 respectively. Note that the memory usage of xmallocN should be disregarded as the faster the benchmark runs, the more memory it uses. Also the cfrac, espresso, and cscratchN benchmarks use just little active memory and the differences in RSS are not very important here.

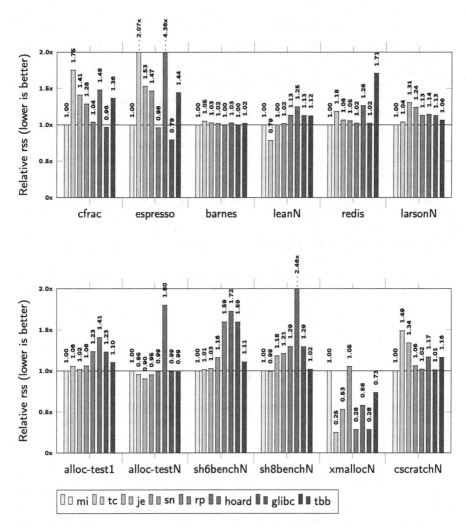

Fig. 6. Peak memory usage on a 16-core AMD Epyc r5a-4xlarge instance. (xmallocN is not normalized and should be disregarded)

References

1. Aigner, M., Kirsch, C.M., Lippautz, M., Sokolova, A.: Fast, multicore-scalable, low-fragmentation memory allocation through large virtual memory and global data structures. CoRR abs/1503.09006 (2015). http://arxiv.org/abs/1503.09006
2. Amazon EC2. Cloud Instance Types (2019). https://aws.amazon.com/ec2/instance-types/
3. Barnes, J., Hut, P.: A hierarchical O(N Log N) force-calculation algorithm. Nature **324**, 446–449 (1986). https://doi.org/10.1038/324446a0

4. Berger, E.D., McKinley, K.S., Blumofe, R.D., Wilson, P.R.: Hoard: a scalable memory allocator for multithreaded applications. In: Proceedings of the Ninth International Conference on Architectural Support for Programming Languages and Operating Systems, ASPLOS IX, Cambridge, Massachusetts, USA, pp. 117–128. ACM (2000). https://doi.org/10.1145/378993.379232

5. Berger, E.D., Zorn, B.G.: DieHard: probabilistic memory safety for unsafe languages. In: Proceedings of the 27th ACM SIGPLAN Conference on Programming Language Design and Implementation, PLDI 2006, Ottawa, Ontario, Canada, pp. 158–168 (2006). https://doi.org/10.1145/1133981.1134000

6. Berger, E.D., Zorn, B.G., McKinley, K.S.: Reconsidering Custom Memory Allocation, vol. 37, no. 11. ACM (2002)

7. Crundal, T.: Reducing Active-False Sharing in TCMalloc (2016). http://courses.cecs.anu.edu.au/courses/CSPROJECTS/16S1/Reports/Timothy*Crundal*Report.pdf. CS16S1 project at the Australian National University

8. Evans, J.: Jemalloc. In: Proceedings of the 2006 BSDCan Conference, BSDCan 2006, Ottowa, CA, May 2006. http://people.freebsd.org/~jasone/jemalloc/bsdcan2006/jemalloc.pdf

9. Feng, Y., Berger, E.D.: A locality-improving dynamic memory allocator. In: Proceedings of the 2005 Workshop on Memory System Performance, Chicago, Illinois, USA, pp. 68–77, January 2005. https://doi.org/10.1145/1111583.1111594

10. Google. Tcmalloc (2014). https://github.com/gperftools/gperftools.

11. Grunwald, D., Zorn, B., Henderson, R.: Improving the cache locality of memory allocation. ACM SIGPLAN Not. **28**(6), 177–186 (1993). https://doi.org/10.1145/173262.155107

12. Hudson, R.L., Saha, B., Adl-Tabatabai, A.R., Hertzberg, B.C.: McRT-Malloc: a scalable transactional memory allocator. In: Proceedings of the 5th International Symposium on Memory Management, pp. 74–83. ACM (2006)

13. Intel. Thread Building Blocks (TBB) (2017). https://www.threadingbuildingblocks.org/

14. Jansson, M.: Rpmalloc (2017). https://github.com/rampantpixels/rpmalloc

15. Kukanov, A., Voss, M.J.: The foundations for scalable multi-core software in Intel threading building blocks. Intel Technol. J. **11**(4), 309–322 (2007)

16. Kuszmaul, B.C.: SuperMalloc: a super fast multithreaded malloc for 64-bit machines. In: Proceedings of the 2015 International Symposium on Memory Management, ISMM 2015, Portland, OR, USA, pp. 41–55. ACM (2015). https://doi.org/10.1145/2754169.2754178

17. Larson, P.-Å., Krishnan, M.: Memory allocation for long-running server applications. In: Proceedings of the 1998 International Symposium on Memory Management, ISMM 1998, pp. 176–185 (1998)

18. Leijen, D.: Koka: programming with row polymorphic effect types. In: MSFP 2014, 5th Workshop on Mathematically Structured Functional Programming (2014). https://doi.org/10.4204/EPTCS.153.8

19. Leijen, D.: Type directed compilation of row-typed algebraic effects. In: Proceedings of the 44th ACM SIGPLAN Symposium on Principles of Programming Languages (POPL 2017), Paris, France, pp. 486–499, January 2017. https://doi.org/10.1145/3009837.3009872

20. Leijen, D.: Mimalloc Repository, June 2019. https://github.com/microsoft/mimalloc

21. Leijen, D.: Mimalloc Benchmark Repository, June 2019. https://github.com/daanx/mimalloc-bench

22. Lever, C., Boreham, D.: Malloc() performance in a multithreaded Linux environment. In: USENIX Annual Technical Conference, Freenix Session, San Diego, CA, June 2000. Malloc-test available from https://github.com/kuszmaul/SuperMalloc/tree/master/tests

23. Liétar, P., et al.: Snmalloc: a message passing allocator. In: Proceedings of the 2019 ACM SIGPLAN International Symposium on Memory Management, pp. 122–135. ACM (2019)

24. Liétar, P., et al.: Snmalloc: a message passing allocator. In: Proceedings of the 2019 International Symposium on Memory Management, ISMM 2019, Phoenix, AZ (2019). https://github.com/Microsoft/snmalloc

25. MicroQuill. SmartHeap (2006). http://www.microquill.com. sh6bench available at http://www.microquill.com/smartheap/shbench/bench.zip. sh8benc available at http://www.microquill.com/smartheap/SH8BENCH.zip

26. de Moura, L., Kong, S., Avigad, J., van Doorn, F., von Raumer, J.: The lean theorem prover (system description). In: Felty, A.P., Middeldorp, A. (eds.) CADE 2015. LNCS (LNAI), vol. 9195, pp. 378–388. Springer, Cham (2015). https://doi.org/10.1007/978-3-319-21401-6_26

27. Novark, G., Berger, E.D.: DieHarder: securing the heap. In: Proceedings of the 17th ACM Conference on Computer and Communications Security, CCS 2010, Chicago, Illinois, USA, pp. 573–584 (2010). https://doi.org/10.1145/1866307.1866371

28. OLogN Technologies AG (ITHare.com). Testing Memory Allocators: ptmalloc2 vs Tcmalloc vs Hoard vs Jemalloc, While Trying to Simulate Real-World Loads, July 2018. http://ithare.com/testing-memory-allocators-ptmalloc2-tcmalloc-hoard-jemalloc-while-trying-to-simulate-real-world-loads/. Test available at https://github.com/node-dot-cpp/alloc-test

29. Sanner, M.F., et al.: Python: a programming language for software integration and development. J. Mol. Graph. Model. **17**(1), 57–61 (1999)

30. Schweizer, H., Besta, M., Hoefler, T.: Evaluating the cost of atomic operations on modern architectures. In: 2015 International Conference on Parallel Architecture and Compilation (PACT), pp. 445–456, October 2015. https://doi.org/10.1109/PACT.2015.24

31. Sotirov, A.: Heap Feng Shui in JavaScript (2007). https://www.blackhat.com/presentations/bh-europe-07/FSotirov/Presentation/bh-eu-07-sotirov-apr19.pdf. Blackhat Europe

32. Ullrich, S., de Moura, L.: Counting immutable beans - reference counting optimized for purely functional programming. In: Proceedings of the 31st Symposium on Implementation and Application of Functional Languages (IFL 2019), Singapore, September 2019

33. Weinstock, C.B., Wulf, W.A.: An efficient algorithm for heap storage allocation. ACM SIGPLAN Not. **23**(10), 141–148 (1988)

34. Wilde, M., Hategan, M., Wozniak, J.M., Clifford, B., Katz, D.S., Foster, I.: Swift: a language for distributed parallel scripting. Parallel Comput. **37**(9), 633–652 (2011)

LiFtEr: Language to Encode Induction Heuristics for Isabelle/HOL

Yutaka Nagashima[1,2(✉)] ⓘ

[1] Czech Technical University in Prague, Prague, Czech Republic
Yutaka.Nagashima@cvut.cz
[2] University of Innsbruck, Innsbruck, Austria

Abstract. Proof assistants, such as Isabelle/HOL, offer tools to facilitate inductive theorem proving. Isabelle experts know how to use these tools effectively; however, there is a little tool support for transferring this expert knowledge to a wider user audience. To address this problem, we present our domain-specific language, `LiFtEr`. `LiFtEr` allows experienced Isabelle users to encode their induction heuristics in a style independent of any problem domain. `LiFtEr`'s interpreter mechanically checks if a given application of induction tool matches the heuristics, thus automating the knowledge transfer loop.

Keywords: Induction · Isabelle/HOL · Domain-specific language

1 Introduction

Consider the following reverse functions, `rev` and `itrev`, presented in a tutorial of Isabelle/HOL [26]:

```
primrec rev::"'a list =>'a list" where
  "rev  []      = []"
| "rev (x # xs) = rev xs @ [x]"
```

```
fun itrev::"'a list =>'a list =>'a list" where
  "itrev  []     ys = ys"
| "itrev (x#xs) ys = itrev xs (x#ys)"
```

where `#` is the list constructor, and `@` appends two lists. How do you prove the following lemma?

```
lemma "itrev xs ys = rev xs @ ys"
```

We thank Ekaterina Komendantskaya, Josef Urban, and anonymous reviewers for APLAS2019 for their valuable comments on an early draft of this paper. This work was supported by the European Regional Development Fund under the project AI & Reasoning (reg. no.CZ.02.1.01/0.0/0.0/15_003/0000466).

© Springer Nature Switzerland AG 2019
A. W. Lin (Ed.): APLAS 2019, LNCS 11893, pp. 266–287, 2019.
https://doi.org/10.1007/978-3-030-34175-6_14

Since both `rev` and `itrev` are defined recursively, it is natural to imagine that we can handle this problem by applying induction. But how do you apply induction and why? What induction heuristics do you use? In which language do you describe those heuristics?

Modern proof assistants (PAs), such as Isabelle/HOL [26], are forming the basis of trustworthy software. Klein *et al.*, for example, verified the correctness of the seL4 micro-kernel in Isabelle/HOL [11], whereas Leroy developed a certifying C compiler, CompCert, using Coq [15]. Despite the growing number of such complete formal verification projects, the limited progress in proof automation still keeps the cost of proof development high, thus preventing the wide spread adoption of complete formal verification.

A noteworthy approach in proof automation for proof assistants is hammer tools [1]. Sledgehammer, for example, exports proof goals in Isabelle/HOL to various external automated theorem provers (ATPs) to exploit the state-of-the-art proof automation of these backend provers; however, the discrepancies between the polymorphic higher-order logic of Isabelle/HOL and the monomorphic first-order logic of the backend provers severely impair Sledgehammer's performance when it comes to inductive theorem proving (ITP).

This is unfortunate for two reasons. Firstly, many Isabelle users chose Isabelle/HOL precisely because its higher-order logic is expressive enough to specify mathematical objects and procedures involving recursion without introducing new axioms. Secondly, induction lies at the heart of mathematics and computer science. For instance, induction is often necessary for reasoning about natural numbers, recursive data-structures, such as lists and trees, computer programs containing recursion and iteration [3].

This is why ITP remains as a long-standing challenge in computer science, and its automation is much needed. Facing the limited automation in ITP, Gramlich surveyed the problems in ITP and presented the following prediction in 2005 [6]:

> in the near future, ITP will only be successful for very specialized domains for very restricted classes of conjectures. ITP will continue to be a very challenging engineering process.

We address this conundrum with our domain-specific language, `LiFtEr`. `LiFtEr` allows experienced Isabelle users to encode their induction heuristics in a style independent of problem domains. `LiFtEr`'s interpreter mechanically checks if a given application of induction is compatible with the induction heuristics written by experienced users. Our research hypothesis is that:

> *it is possible to encode valuable induction heuristics for Isabelle/HOL in LiFtEr and these heuristics can be valid across diverse problem domains, because LiFtEr allows for meta-reasoning on applications of induction methods, without relying on concrete proof goals, their underlying proof states, nor concrete applications of induction methods.*

We developed `LiFtEr` as an Isabelle theory and integrated `LiFtEr` into Isabelle's proof language, Isabelle/Isar, and its proof editor, Isabelle/jEdit. This allows for an easy installation process: to use `LiFtEr`, users only have to import the relevant theory files into their theory files, using Isabelle's `import` keyword. Our working prototype is available at GitHub [20].

The important difference of `LiFtEr` from other tactic languages, such as Eisbach [16] and Ltac [4], is that `LiFtEr` itself is not a tactic language but a language to write how one should use Isabelle's existing proof method for induction. To the best of our knowledge, `LiFtEr` is the first language in which one can write how to use a tactic by mechanically analyzing the structures of proof goals in a style independent of any problem domain.

2   Induction in Isabelle/HOL

To handle inductive problems, modern proof assistants offer tools to apply induction. For example, Isabelle comes with the `induct` proof method and the `induction` method[1]. Nipkow *et al.* proved our ongoing example as follows [25]:

```
lemma model_prf:"itrev xs ys = rev xs @ ys"
  apply(induct xs arbitrary: ys) by auto
```

Namely, they applied structural induction on `xs` while generalizing `ys` before applying induction by passing the string `ys` to the `arbitrary` field. The resulting sub-goals are:

```
1. !!ys. itrev [] ys = rev [] @ ys
2. !!a xs ys. (!!ys. itrev xs ys = rev xs @ ys) ==>
              itrev (a # xs) ys = rev (a # xs) @ ys
```

where `!!` is the universal quantifier and `==>` is the implication in Isabelle's meta-logic. Due to the generalization, the `ys` in the induction hypothesis is quantified within the hypothesis, and it is differentiated from the `ys` that appears in the conclusion. Had Nipkow *et al.* omitted `arbitrary: ys`, the first sub-goal would be the same, but the second sub-goal would have been:

```
2. !!a xs. itrev xs ys = rev xs @ ys ==>
           itrev (a # xs) ys = rev (a # xs) @ ys
```

Since the same `ys` is shared by the induction hypothesis and the conclusion, the subsequent application of `auto` fails to discharge this sub-goal.

It is worth noting that in general there are multiple equivalently appropriate combinations of arguments to prove a given inductive problem. For instance, the following proof snippet shows an alternative proof script for our example:

```
lemma alt_prf:"itrev xs ys = rev xs @ ys"
  apply(induct xs ys rule:itrev.induct) by auto
```

---

[1] Proof methods are the Isar syntactic layer of LCF-style tactics.

Here we passed the `itrev.induct` rule to the `rule` field of the `induct` method
and proved the lemma by recursion induction[2] over `itrev`. This rule was derived
by Isabelle automatically when we defined `itrev`, and it states the following:

```
(!!ys. P [] ys) ==>
(!!x xs ys. P xs (x # ys) ==> P (x # xs) ys) ==>
P a0 a1
```

Essentially, this rule states that to prove a property `P` of `a0` and `a1` we have to
prove it for two cases where `a0` is the empty list and the list with at least two
elements. When the `induct` method takes this rule and `xs` and `ys` as induction
variables, Isabelle produces the following sub-goals:

```
1. !!ys. itrev [] ys = rev [] @ ys
2. !!x xs ys. itrev xs (x # ys) = rev xs @ x # ys ==>
              itrev (x # xs) ys = rev (x # xs) @ ys
```

where the two sub-goals correspond to the two clauses in the definition of `itrev`.

There are other lesser-known techniques to handle difficult inductive problems using the `induct` method, and sometimes users have to develop useful auxiliary lemmas manually; however, for most cases the problem of how to apply
induction boils down to the following three questions:

- On which terms do we apply induction?
- Which variables do we generalize?
- Which rule do we use for recursion induction?

Isabelle experts resort to induction heuristics to answer such questions and decide
what arguments to pass to the `induct` method; however, such reasoning still
requires human engineers to carefully investigate the inductive problem at hand.
Moreover, Isabelle experts' induction heuristics are sparsely documented across
various documents, and there was no way to encode their heuristics as programs.
For the wide spread adoption of complete formal verification, we need a program
language to encode such heuristics and the system to check if an invocation of
the `induct` method written by an Isabelle novice complies with such heuristics.
We developed `LiFtEr`, taking these three groups of questions as a design space.

3 Overview and Syntax of LiFtEr

We designed `LiFtEr` to encode induction heuristics as assertions on invocations
of the `induct` method in Isabelle/HOL. An assertion written in `LiFtEr` takes
the pair of a proof goal with its underlying proof state and arguments passed to
the `induct` method. When one applies a `LiFtEr` assertion to an invocation of
the `induct` method, `LiFtEr`'s interpreter returns a boolean value as the result
of the assertion applied to the proof goals and their underlying proof state.

---

[2] Recursion induction is also known as functional induction or computation induction.

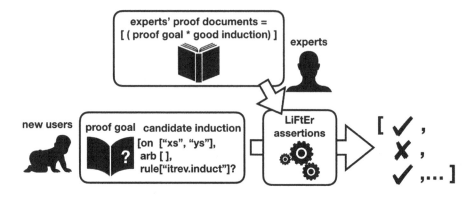

Fig. 1. The workflow of LiFtEr.

The goal of a LiFtEr programmer is to write assertions that implement reliable heuristics. A heuristic encoded as a LiFtEr assertion is reliable when it satisfies the following two properties:

1. The LiFtEr interpreter is likely to evaluate the assertion to True when the arguments of the induct method are appropriate for the given proof goal.
2. The LiFtEr interpreter is likely to evaluate the assertion to False when the arguments are inappropriate for the goal.

Figure 1 illustrates the workflow of LiFtEr. Firstly, Isabelle experts encode the gist of promising applications of induction based on experts' proofs. Note that the heuristics encoded in LiFtEr become applicable to problem domains that the experts users have not even encountered at the time of writing the assertions.

When new Isabelle users are facing an inductive problem and are unsure if their application of induction is a valid approach or not, they can apply LiFtEr assertions written by experts using the assert_LiFtEr keyword to their proof goal and their candidate arguments.

LiFtEr's interpreter checks if the pair of new users' proof goal and candidate arguments to the induct method is compatible with the experts' heuristics. If the interpreter evaluates the pair to True, Isabelle prints "Assertion succeeded." in the Output panel of Isabelle/jEdit [28]. If the interpreter evaluates the pair to False, Isabelle highlights the assert_LiFtEr in red and prints "Assertion failed." in the Output panel.

Program 1 shows the essential part of LiFtEr's abstract syntax. LiFtEr has four types of variables: number, rule, term, and term_occurrence. A value of type number is a natural number from 0 to the maximum of the following two numbers: the number of terms appearing in the proof goals at hand, and the maximum arity of constants appearing in the proof goals. A value of type rule corresponds to a name of an auxiliary lemma passed to the induct method as an argument in the arbitrary field.

Program 1 The Abstract Syntax of LiFtEr.

---

assertion := *atomic* | *connective* | *quantifier* | (*assertion*)
type := `term` | `term_occurrence` | `rule` | `number`
modifier_term := `induction_term` | `arbitrary_term`
quantifier := ∃x : *type*. *assertion*
          | ∀x : *type*. *assertion*
          | ∃x : `term` ∈ *modifier_term* . *assertion*
          | ∀x : `term` ∈ *modifier_term* . *assertion*
          | ∃x : `rule` . *assertion*
          | ∃x : `term_occurrence` ∈ y : `term` . *assertion*
          | ∀x : `term_occurrence` ∈ y : `term` . *assertion*
connective := `True` | `False` | *assertion* ∨ *assertion* | *assertion* ∧ *assertion*
          assertion → *assertion* | ¬ *assertion*
pattern := `all_only_var` | `all_constructor` | `mixed`
atomic :=
     rule `is_rule_of` *term_occurrence*
   | *term_occurrence* `term_occurrence_is_of_term` *term*
   | `are_same_term` (*term_occurrence* , *term_occurrence*)
   | *term_occurrence* `is_in_term_occurrence` *term_occurrence*
   | `is_atomic` *term_occurrence*
   | `is_constant` *term_occurrence*
   | `is_recursive_constant` *term_occurrence*
   | `is_variable` *term_occurrence*
   | `is_free_variable` *term_occurrence*
   | `is_bound_variable` *term_occurrence*
   | `is_lambda` *term_occurrence*
   | `is_application` *term_occurrence*
   | *term_occurrence* `is_an_argument_of` *term_occurrence*
   | *term_occurrence* `is_nth_argument_of` *term_occurrence*
   | *term* `is_nth_induction_term` *number*
   | *term* `is_nth_arbitrary_term` *number*
   | `pattern_is` (*number* , *term_occurrence* , *pattern*)
   | `is_at_deepest` *term_occurrence*
   | ...

The difference between `term` and `term_occurrence` is crucial: a value of `term` is a term appearing in proof goals, whereas a value of `term_occurrence` is an *occurrence* of such terms. It is important to distinguish terms and term occurrences because the `induct` method in Isabelle/HOL only allows its users to specify induction terms but it does not allow us to specify on which occurrences of such terms we intend to apply induction.

The connectives, ∧, ∨, ¬, and → correspond to conjunction, disjunction, negation, and implication in the classical logic, respectively; and → admits the principle of explosion.

LiFtEr has four essential quantifiers and two quantifiers as syntactic sugar. As is often the case, ∀ quantifies over variables universally, and ∃ stands for the existence of a variable it binds. Again, it is important to notice the difference between the quantifiers over `term` and the ones over `term_occurrence`. For example, $\forall\_. \in$ `term` quantifies all sub-terms appearing in the proof goals, whereas $\forall\_. \in$ `term_occurrence` quantifies all *occurrences* of such sub-terms. Quantified variables restricted to `induction_term` by the membership function $\in$ are quantified over all terms passed to the `induct` method as induction terms, while quantified variables restricted to `arbitrary_term` are quantified over all terms passed to the `induct` method as arguments in the `arbitrary` field.

Some atomic assertions judge properties of term occurrences, and some judge the syntactic structure of proof goals with respect to certain terms, their occurrences, or certain numbers. While most atomic assertions work on the syntactic structures of proof goals, `Pattern` provides a means to describe a limited amount of semantic information of proof goals since it checks how terms are defined. Section 4 explains the meaning of important atomic assertions through `LiFtEr`'s standard heuristics.

Attentive readers may have noticed that `LiFtEr`'s syntax does not cover any user-defined types or constants. This absence of specific types and constants is our intentional choice to promote induction heuristics that are valid across various problem domains: it encourages `LiFtEr` users to write heuristics that are not specific to particular data-types or functions. And `LiFtEr`'s interpreter can check if an application of the `induct` method is compatible with a given `LiFtEr` heuristic even if the proof goal involves user-defined data-types and functions even though such types and functions are unknown to the `LiFtEr` developer or the author of the heuristic but come into existence in the future only after developing `LiFtEr` and such heuristic.

4   LiFtEr's Standard Heuristics

This section presents `LiFtEr`'s standard heuristics and illustrates how to use those atomic assertions and quantifiers to encode induction heuristics.

4.1   Heuristic 1: Induction Terms Should Not Be Constants

Let us revise the first example lemma about the equivalence of two reverse functions, `itrev` and `rev`. One naive induction heuristic would be *"any induction term should not be a constant"*[3] In `LiFtEr`, we can encode this heuristic as the following assertion[4]:

$\forall$ $t1$: term $\in$ induction_term.
    $\exists$ $to1$: term_occurrence.

---

[3] This *naive heuristic* is not very reliable: there are cases where the `induct` method takes terms involving constants and apply induction appropriately by automatically introducing induction variables. See Concrete Semantics [25] for more details.

[4] For better readability we omit parentheses where the binding of terms is obvious from indentation.

($to1$ term_occurrence_is_of_term $t1$)

$\wedge$

$\neg$ (is_constant $to1$)

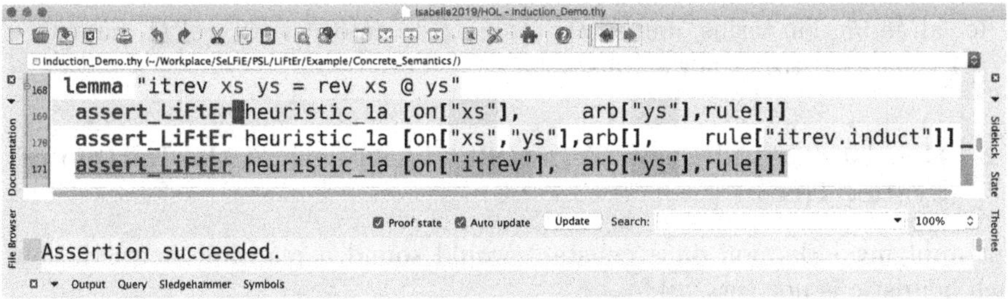

Fig. 2. The user interface of LiFtEr.

Note the use of quantifiers over induction_terms and term_occurrences: when LiFtEr handles induction terms, LiFtEr treats them as terms, but it is often necessary to analyze the *occurrences* of these terms in the proof goal to decide how to apply induction. In our example lemma, xs is a variable, which appears twice: once as the first argument of itrev, and once as the first argument of rev. With this in mind, the above assertion reads as follows:

for all induction terms, named $t1$, there exists a term occurrence, named $to1$, such that $to1$ is an occurrence of $t1$ and $to1$ is not a constant.

Now we compare this heuristic with the model proof by Nipkow *et al.*

The only induction term, xs, has two occurrences in the proof goal both as variables. Therefore, if we apply this LiFtEr assertion to the model proof, LiFtEr's interpreter acknowledges that the model proof complies with the induction heuristic defined above.

Figure 2 shows the user interface of LiFtEr. In the second line where the cursor is staying, LiFtEr's interpreter executes the aforementioned reasoning and concludes that the model proof by Nipkow *et al.* is compatible with this heuristic, printing "Assertion succeeded." in the Output panel. On the contrary, the fourth line applies the same heuristic to another possible combination of arguments to the induct method (induct itrev arbitrary: ys) and concludes that this candidate induction is not compatible with our heuristic because itrev is a constant. LiFtEr also highlights this line in red to warn the user.

It is a common practice to analyze occurrences of specific terms when describing induction heuristics. Therefore, we introduced two pieces of syntactic sugar to avoid boilerplate code: $\exists_-$: term_occurrence $\in$ _ : term and $\forall_-$: term_occurrence $\in$ _ : term. Both of these quantify over term occurrences of a particular term rather than all term occurrences in the proof goal at hand. Using $\exists_-$: term_occurrence $\in$ _ : term, we can shrink the above assertion from 5 lines to 3 lines as follows:

```
∀ t1 : induction_term.
  ∃ to1 : term_occurrence ∈ t1 : term.
     ¬ ( is_constant  to1 )
```

In English, this reads as follows:

> for all induction terms, named $t1$, there exists an occurrence of $t1$, named $to1$, such that $to1$ is not a constant.

4.2   Heuristic 2. Induction Terms Should Appear at the Bottom of Syntax Trees

Not applying induction on a constant would sound a plausible heuristic, but such heuristic is not very useful.

In this sub-section, we encode an induction heuristic that analyzes not only the properties of the induction terms but also the location of their occurrences within the proof goal at hand. When attacking inductive problems with many variables, it is sometimes a good attempt to apply induction on variables that appear at the bottom of the syntax tree representing the proof goal. We encode such heuristic using is_at_deepest as the following LiFtEr assertion:

```
∀ t1 : induction_term.
  ∃ to1 : term_occurrence ∈ t1 : term.
     is_atomic to1   →   is_at_deepest to1
```

In English, this assertion reads as follows:

> for all induction terms, named $t1$, there exists an occurrence of $t1$, named $to1$, such that if $to1$ is an atomic term then $to1$ lies at the deepest layer in the syntax tree that represents the proof goal.

We used the infix operator, →, to add the condition that we consider only the induction terms that are atomic terms. An atomic term is either a constant, free variable, schematic variable, or variable bound by a lambda abstraction. We added this condition because it makes little sense to check if the induction term resides at the bottom of the syntax tree when an induction term is a compound term: such compound terms have sub-terms at lower layers.

LiFtEr's interpreter acknowledges that the model solution provided by Nipkow *et al.* complies with this heuristic when applied to this lemma: there is only one induction term, xs, and xs appears as an argument of rev on the right-hand side of the equation in the lemma at the lowest layer of this syntax tree.

4.3   Heuristic 3. All Induction Terms Should Be Arguments of the Same Occurrence of a Recursively Defined Function

Probably, it is more meaningful to analyze where induction terms reside in the proof goal with respect to other terms in the goal. More specifically, one heuristic for promising application of induction would be *"apply induction on terms that appear as arguments of the same occurrence of a recursively defined function"*. We encode this heuristic using LiFtEr's atomic assertions, is_recursive_constant and is_an_argument_of, as follows:

```
∃ t1 : term.
  ∃ to1 : term_occurrence ∈ t1 : term.
    ∀ t2: term ∈ induction_term.
      ∃ to2 : term_occurrence ∈ t2 : term.
        is_recursive_constant to2  ∧  to2 is_an_argument_of to1
```

where is_recursive_constant checks if a constant is defined recursively or not, and is_an_argument_of takes two term occurrences and checks if the first one is an argument of the second one.

Note that using is_recursive_constant this assertion checks not only the syntactic information of the proof goal at hand, but it also extracts an essential part of the semantic information of constants appearing in the goal, by investigating how these constants are defined in the underlying proof context. As a whole, this assertion reads as follows:

> there exists a term, named $t1$, such that there exists an occurrence of $t1$, named $to1$, such that for all induction terms, named $t2$, there exists an occurrence of $t2$, named $to2$, such that $to1$ is defined recursively and $to2$ appears as an argument of $to1$.

Attentive readers may have noticed that we quantified over induction terms within the quantification over $to1$, so that this induction heuristic checks if all induction terms occur as arguments of the same constant.

The LiFtEr interpreter confirms that the model proof is compatible with this heuristic as well: the constant, itrev, is defined recursively and has an occurrence that takes the only induction variable xs as the first argument.

4.4 Heuristic 4. One Should Apply Induction on the nth Argument of a Function where the nth Parameter in the Definition of the Function Always Involves a Data-Constructor

The previous heuristic checks if all induction terms are arguments of the same occurrence of a recursively defined function. Sometimes we can even estimate on which arguments of such function we should apply induction by inspecting the definition of the function more carefully.

We introduce two constructs to support this style of reasoning: is_nth_argument_of and pattern_is. is_nth_argument_of takes a term occurrence, a number, and another term occurrence, and it checks if the first term occurrence is the nth argument of the second term occurrence where counting starts at 0. pattern_is takes a number, a term occurrence, one of three *pattern*s: all_only_var, all_constructor, and mixed. Each of such patterns describes how the term is defined.

For example, `pattern_is` (n, `to`, `all_only_var`) denotes that the nth parameter is always a variable on the left-hand side of the definition of the term that has the term occurrence, `to`. Likewise, `all_constant` denotes the case where the corresponding parameter of the definition of a particular constant always involves a data-constructor, whereas `mixed` denotes that the corresponding parameter is a variable in some clauses but involves a data-constructor in other clauses. With these atomic assertions in mind, we write the following LiFtEr assertion:

```
¬ (∃ r1 : rule. True)
→
  ∃ t1 : term.
    ∃ to1 : term_occurrence ∈ t1 : term.
       is_recursive_constant to1
     ∧
        ∀ t2 : term ∈  induction_term.
          ∃ to2 : term_occurrence ∈ t2 : term.
             ∃ n : number.
                pattern_is (n, to1, all_constant)
             ∧
                is_nth_argument_of (to2, n, to1)
```

This roughly translates to the following English sentence:

> if there is no argument in the **rule** field in the **induct** method, then there exists a recursively defined constant, $t1$, with an occurrence, $to1$, such that for all induction terms $t2$, there exists an occurrence, $to2$, of $t2$, such that there exists a number, n, such that the nth parameter involves a data-constructor in all the clauses of the definition of $t1$, and $to2$ appears as the nth argument of $to1$ in the proof goal.

Note that we added ¬ (∃$r1$: **rule**. **True**) to focus on the case where the **induct** method does not take any auxiliary lemma in the **rule** field since this heuristic is known to be less reliable if there is an auxiliary lemma passed to the **induct** method.

LiFtEr's interpreter confirms that Nipkow's proof about **itrev** and **rev** conforms to this heuristic: there exists an occurrence of **itrev**, such that **itrev** is recursively defined and for the only induction term, **xs**, there is an occurrence of **xs** on the left-hand side of the proof goal, such that **itrev**'s first parameter involves data-constructor in all clauses of its definition, and this occurrence of **xs** appears as the first argument of the occurrence of **itrev** in the goal[5].

---

[5] Note that in reality the counting starts at 0 internally. Therefore, "the first argument" in this English sentence is processed as the 0th argument within LiFtEr.

4.5 Heuristic 5. Induction Terms Should Appear as Arguments of a Function that Has a Related .induct Rule in the rule Field

When the induct method takes an auxiliary lemma in the rule field that Isabelle automatically derives from the definition of a constant, it is often true that we should apply induction on terms that appear as arguments of an occurrence of such constant.

See, for example, our alternative proof, alt_prf, for our ongoing example theorem. When Nipkow *et al.* defined the itrev function with the fun keyword, Isabelle automatically derived the auxiliary lemma itrev.induct, and the occurrence of itrev on the left-hand side of the equation takes xs and ys as its arguments. Furthermore, the alternative proof passes xs and ys to the rule field in the same order they appear as the arguments of the occurrence of itrev in the proof goal.

We introduce is_rule_of to relate a term occurrence with an auxiliary lemma passed to the rule field. is_rule_of takes a term occurrence and an auxiliary lemma in the rule field of the induct method, and it checks if the rule was derived by Isabelle at the time of defining the term. Moreover, we introduce is_nth_induction_term, which allows us to specify the order of induction terms passed to the induct method: is_nth_induction_term takes a term and a number, and it checks if the term is passed to the induct method as the nth induction term. Using these constructs, we can encode the aforementioned heuristic as follows:

```
∃ r1 : rule. True
→
∃ r1 : rule.
   ∃ t1 : term.
      ∃ to1 : term_occurrence ∈ t1 : term.
         r1 is_rule_of to1
      ∧
         ∀ t2 : term ∈ induction_term.
            ∃ to2 : term_occurrence ∈ t2 : term.
               ∃ n : number.
                  is_nth_argument_of (to2, n, to1)
               ∧
                  t2 is_nth_induction_term n
```

As a whole this LiFtEr assertion checks if the following holds:

if there exists a rule, $r1$, in the rule field of the induct method, then there exists a term $t1$ with an occurrence $to1$, such that $r1$ is derived by Isabelle when defining $t1$, and for all induction terms $t2$, there exists an occurrence $to2$ of $t2$ such that, there exists a number n, such that $to2$ is the nth argument of $to1$ and that $t2$ is the nth induction terms passed to the induct method.

Our alternative proof is compatible with this heuristic: there is an argument, `itrev.induct`, in the `rule` field, and the occurrence of its related term, `itrev`, in the proof goal takes all the induction terms, `xs` and `ys`, as its arguments in the same order.

4.6   Heuristic 6. Generalize Variables in Induction Terms

Isabelle's `induct` method offers the `arbitrary` field, so that users can specify which terms to be generalized in induction steps; however, it is known to be a hard problem to decide which terms to generalize.

Of course `LiFtEr` cannot provide you with a decision procedure to determine which terms to generalize, but it allows us to describe heuristics to identify variables that are likely to be generalized by experienced Isabelle users. For example, experienced users know that it is usually a bad idea to pass induction terms themselves to the `arbitrary` field. We also know that it is often a good idea to generalize variables appearing within induction terms if induction terms are compound terms.

We can encode the former heuristic using `are_same_term`, which checks if two terms are the same term or not. For instance, we can write the following:

$\forall$ $t1$: term $\in$ arbitrary_term.
  $\neg$ ($\exists$ $t2$: term $\in$ induction_term. are_same_term ($t1$, $t2$))

By now, it should be easy to see that this assertion checks if the following holds:

> for all terms in the **arbitrary** field, there is no induction term of the same term in the **induct** method.

The latter heuristic involves the description of the term structure constituting the proof goal. For this purpose we use `is_in_term_occurrence` to check if a term occurrence resides within another term occurrence. With this construct, we can encode the latter heuristic as follows:

$\exists$ $t1$: term $\in$ induction_term.
  $\exists$ $to1$: term_occurrence $\in$ $t1$: term.
    $\forall$ $t2$: term.
      $\exists$ $to2$: term_occurrence $\in$ $t2$: term.
        ($to2$ is_in_term_occurrence $to1$ $\wedge$ is_free_variable $to2$)
        $\rightarrow$
          $\exists$ $t3$: term $\in$: arbitrary_term. are_same_term ($t2$, $t3$)

Again, we used the implication (_ $\rightarrow$ _) to avoid applying this generalization heuristics to the cases without compound induction terms.

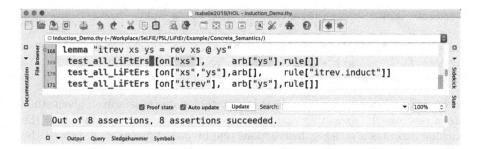

Fig. 3. The `test_all_LiFtErs` command.

4.7 Apply All Assertions Using the `test_all_LiFtErs` Command

In this section we have written eight assertions (two assertions from each of Sects. 4.1 and 4.6). To exploit all the available LiFtEr assertions, we developed the `test_all_LiFtErs` command. The `test_all_LiFtErs` command first takes a combination of induction arguments to the `induct` method. Then, it applies all the available LiFtEr assertions to the pair of the combination of arguments and the proof goal at hand. Finally, it counts how many assertions return `True`. For example, the second line in Fig. 3 executed the eight available assertions to the combination of arguments (`[on["xs"], arb["ys"], rule[]]`) and the proof goal. The output panel shows the result: `Out of 8 assertions, 8 assertions succeeded`. This indicates that the model proof by Nipkow is indeed a good solution in terms of all the heuristics we discussed in this section.

5 Induction Heuristics Across Problem Domains

In Sect. 4 we wrote eight assertions in LiFtEr. When writing these eight assertions, we emphasized that none of them is specific to the data structure `list` or the function `itrev` appearing in the proof goal. In this section we demonstrate that the LiFtEr assertions written in Sect. 4 are applicable across domains, taking an inductive problem from a completely different domain as an example. The following code is the formalization of a simple stack machine from Concrete Semantics [25]:

```
type_synonym vname = string
type_synonym val   = int
type_synonym state = "vname => val"
datatype instr     = LOADI val | LOAD vname | ADD
type_synonym stack = "val list"

fun exec1 :: "instr => state => stack => stack" where
  "exec1 (LOADI n) _ stk      =  n      # stk"
| "exec1 (LOAD x) s stk       =  s(x)   # stk"
```

```
| "exec1  ADD      _ (j#i#stk)  =  (i + j) # stk"

fun exec :: "instr list => state => stack => stack" where
  "exec []      _ stk = stk"
| "exec (i#is) s stk = exec is s (exec1 i s stk)"
```

exec1 defines how the stack machine in a certain state transforms a given stack into a new one by executing one instruction, whereas exec specifies how the machine executes a series of instructions one by one. Nipkow *et al.* proved the following lemma using structural induction.

```
lemma exec_append_model_prf [simp]:
  "exec (is1 @ is2) s stk = exec is2 s (exec is1 s stk)"
  apply(induct is1 arbitrary: stk) by auto
```

This lemma states that executing a concatenation of two lists of instructions in a state to a stack produces the same stack as executing the first list of the instructions first in the same state to the same stack and executing the second list again in the same state again but to the resulting new stack. As in the case with the equivalence of two reverse functions, there is also an alternative proof based on recursion induction:

```
lemma exec_append_alt_prf:
  "exec (is1 @ is2) s stk = exec is2 s (exec is1 s stk)"
  apply(induct is1 s stk rule:exec.induct) by auto
```

where exec.induct is automatically derived by Isabelle when defining exec. Now we check if the heuristics from Sect. 4 correctly recommend these proofs.

Heuristic 1. Both exec_append_model_prf and exec_append_alt_prf comply with this heuristic. For example, is1 is the only induction term in exec_append_model_prf, and it has occurrences in the proof goal, where it occurs as a variable.

Heuristic 2. exec_append_model_prf complies with the second heuristic: its only induction term, is1, occurs at the bottom of the syntax tree as a variable, which is an atomic term. exec_append_alt_prf also complies with this heuristic: is1, s, and stk as the arguments of the inner exec on the right-hand side of the equation are all atomic terms at the deepest layer of the syntax tree.

Heuristic 3. Both proof scripts comply with this heuristic. For example, the inner occurrence of exec on the right-hand side of the equation takes all the induction terms of the alternative proof (namely, is1, s, and stk) as its arguments.

Heuristic 4. This heuristic works for both proof scripts, but it explains the model answer particularly well: it has a recursively defined constant, exec, and the inner occurrence of exec on the right-hand side of the equation has an occurrence that takes the only induction term is1 as its first argument, and the first parameter of exec always involve a data-constructor in the definition of exec.

Heuristic 5. This heuristic also works for both proof scripts, but it fits particularly well with the alternative answer: the rule exec.induct is derived by Isabelle when defining exec, while exec has an occurrence as part of the third argument of another exec on the right-hand side of the equation, and this inner occurrence of exec takes all the induction terms (is1, s, and stk) in the same order.

Heuristic 6. None of our proofs involve induction on a compound term, making the second assertion in Sect. 4.6 rather irrelevant, whereas the first assertion in Sect. 4.6 explains the model answer well: the only generalized term, stk, does not appear as an induction term.

6   Real World Example

In Sects. 4 and 5, we introduced simple LiFtEr assertions applied to smaller problems. For example, all induction terms in the examples were variables, even though Isabelle's induct method can induct on non-atomic terms.

Program 2 is a more challenging proof about a formalization of an imperative language, IMP2 [14], from the Archive of Formal Proofs [12]. Due to the space constraints, we refrain ourselves from presenting the complete formalization of IMP2 but focus on the essential part of the proof document.

In this project, Lammich *et al.* proved the equivalence between IMP2's big-step semantics and small-step semantics. smalls_seq in Program 2 is an auxiliary lemma useful to prove the equivalence. The proof of smalls_seq appears to be somewhat similar to that of alt_prf in Sect. 2 and exec_append_alt_prf in Sect. 5: smalls_seq's proof uses the auxiliary lemma small_steps.induct, which Isabelle derived automatically when Lammich *et al.* defined small_steps. Furthermore, the three induction terms, π, (c, s), and Some (c', s'), are the arguments of one occurrence of small_steps.

The difference from the preceding examples is the generalization of four free variables appearing in induction terms: in Program 2, c and s appear within (c, s), while c' and s' appear within Some (c', s'). As we discussed in Sect. 4.6, when applying induction on non-atomic terms in Isabelle/HOL it is often a good idea to generalize free variables appearing within such non-atomic induction terms.

To encode such heuristic, we strengthened Example 5 in Sect. 4 using the is_in_term_occurrence assertion. Program 3 checks if any induction term is non-atomic and contains a free variable, all such free variables are generalized in the arbitrary field. Note that LiFtEr's interpreter evaluates the universal quantifier over *to3* to True when all induction terms are atomic, since *to3* term_occurrence_is_of_term *t3* is guarded by ¬ (is_atomic *to2*), making this assertion valid even for the cases where induction terms are atomic variables.

Program 2 A Proof about the Semantics of an Imperative Language, IMP2.

```
datatype com =
  SKIP                        (*No-op*)
(*Assignment*)
| AssignIdx vname aexp aexp   (*Assign to index in array*)
| ArrayCpy vname vname        (*Copy whole array*)
| ArrayClear vname            (*Clear array*)
| Assign_Locals "vname => val"  (*Assign all local variables*)
(*Block*)
| Seq    com  com             (*Sequential composition*)
| ...

fun small_step :: "program => com × state => (com × state) option" where
  "small_step π ((AssignIdx x i a, s) =
    Some (SKIP, s(x := (s x)(aval i s := aval a s)))"
| "small_step π (ArrayCpy x y, s)    = Some (SKIP, s(x := s y))"
| "small_step π (ArrayClear x, s)    = Some (SKIP, s(x := (λ_. 0)))"
| "small_step π (Assign_Locals l, s) = Some (SKIP, <l|s>)"
| "small_step π (SKIP ;; c, s)       = Some (c, s)"
| "small_step π (c1 ;; c2, s)        = (case small_step π (c1, s) of
    Some (c1', s') => Some (c1' ;; c2, s') | _ => None)"
| ...

inductive small_steps ::
  "program => com × state => (com × state) option => bool" where
  "small_steps π cs (Some cs)"
| "small_step π cs = None ──→ small_steps π cs None"
| "small_step π cs = Some cs1 ──→
   small_steps π cs1 cs2 ──→ small_steps π cs cs2"

lemma smalls_seq:
  "small_steps π (c, s) (Some (c', s')) ⟹
   small_steps π (c ;; cx, s) (Some (c';; cx, s'))"
  apply (induct π "(c, s)" "Some (c', s')"
         arbitrary: c s c' s' rule: small_steps.induct)
  apply (auto dest: small_seq intro: small_steps.intros)
  by (metis option.simps(1) prod.simps(1)
            small_seq small_step.simps(31) small_steps.intros(3))
```

Program 3 An Assertion for the Generalization of Variables in Induction Terms.

```
∃ r1 : rule. True
→
  ∃ r1 : rule.
    ∃ t1 : term.
      ∃ to1 : term ∈ t1 : term.
          r1 is_rule_of to1
        ∧
          ∀ t2 : term ∈ induction_term.
            ∃ to2 : term_occurrence ∈ t2 : term.
              ∃ n1 : number.
                  is_nth_argument_of (to2, n1, to1)
                ∧
                  t2 is_nth_induction_term n1
            ∧
              ∀ to3 : term_occurrence.
                  ¬ ( is_atomic to2 )
                ∧
                  is_free_variable to3
                ∧
                  to3 is_in_term_occurrence to2
                →
                  ∃ t3 : arbitrary_term.
                  to3 term_occurrence_is_of_term t3
```

7   Conclusions, Related and Future Work

ITP has been considered as a very challenging task. To address this issue, we presented LiFtEr. LiFtEr is a domain-specific language in the sense that we developed LiFtEr to encode induction heuristics; however, heuristics written in LiFtEr are often not specific to any problem domains. To the best of our knowledge, LiFtEr is the first programming language developed to capture induction heuristics across problem domains, and its interpreter is the first system that executes meta-reasoning on interactive inductive theorem proving.

The recent development in proof automation for higher-order logic takes the meta-tool approach. Gauthier *et al.*, for example, developed an automated tactic prover, TacticToe, on top of HOL4 [5]. TacticToe learns how human engineers used tactics and applies the knowledge to execute a tactic based Monte Carlo tree search. To automate proofs in Coq [27], Komendantskaya *et al.* developed ML4PG [13]. ML4PG uses recurrent clustering to mine a proof database and attempts to find a tactic-based proof for a given proof goal. Both of them try to identify useful lemmas or hypotheses as arguments of a tactic; however, they do not identify promising terms as arguments of a tactic even though identifying such terms is crucial to apply induction effectively.

The most well-known approach for ITP is called the Boyer-Moore waterfall model [17]. This approach was invented for a first-order logic on Common Lisp. Most waterfall provers attempt to apply six proof techniques (simplification, destructor elimination, cross-fertilization, generalization, elimination of irrelevance, and induction) in a fixed order, store the resulting sub-goals in a pool, and keep applying these techniques until the pool becomes empty.

ACL2 [18] is the most commonly used waterfall model based prover, which has achieved industrial-scale proofs [10]. When deciding how to apply induction, ACL2 computes a score, called *hitting ratio*, to estimate how good each induction scheme is for the term which it accounts for and proceeds with the induction scheme with the highest hitting ratio [2, 19].

Compared to the hitting ratio used in the waterfall model, LiFtEr's atomic assertions let us analyze the structures of proof goals directly while LiFtEr's quantifiers let us keep LiFtEr assertions non-specific to any problem. While ACL2 produces many induction schemes and computes their hitting ratios, LiFtEr assertions do not directly produce induction schemes but analyze the given proof goal and the arguments passed to the induct method, re-using Isabelle's existing tool to (implicitly) produce induction principles. We consider LiFtEr's approach to be a reasonable choice, since it extends the usability of the already well-developed proof assistant, Isabelle/HOL, while avoiding to reinvent the mechanism to produce induction principle.

Furthermore, the choice of Isabelle/HOL as the host system of LiFtEr allowed us to take advantage of human interaction more aggressively both from Isabelle experts and new Isabelle users: Isabelle experts can encode their own heuristics since LiFtEr is a language, and new Isabelle users can inspect the results of LiFtEr assertions and decide how to attack their proof goals instead of following the fixed order of six proof techniques as in the waterfall model.

Heras *et al.* used ML4PG learning method to find patterns to generalize and transfer inductive proofs from one domain to another in ACL2 [8]. Jiang *et al.* followed the waterfall model and ran multiple waterfalls [9] to automate ITP in HOL light [7]. However, when deciding induction variables, they naively picked the first free variable with recursive type and left the selection of appropriate induction variables as future work.

To determine induction variables automatically, we developed a proof strategy language PSL and its default proof strategy, try_hard for Isabelle/HOL [23]. PSL tries to identify useful arguments for the induct method by conducting a depth-first search. Sometimes it is not enough to pass arguments to the induct method, but users have to specify necessary auxiliary lemmas before applying induction. To automate such labor-intensive work, PGT [24], a new extension to PSL, produces many lemmas by transforming the given proof goal while trying to identify a useful one in a goal-oriented manner.

The drawback of PSL and PGT is that they cannot produce recommendations if they fail to complete a proof search: when the search space becomes enormous, neither PSL and PGT gives any advice to Isabelle users.

PaMpeR [22], on the other hand, recommends which proof method is likely to be useful to a given proof goal, using a supervised learning applied to the Archive of Formal Proofs [12]. The key of PaMpeR was its feature extractor: PaMpeR first applies 108 assertions to each invocation of proof methods and converts each pair of a proof goal with its context and the name of proof method applied to that goal into an array of boolean values of length 108 because this simpler format is amenable for machine learning algorithms to analyze. The limitation of PaMpeR is, unlike PSL, it cannot recommend which arguments in the induct method to tackle a given proof goal.

Taking the same approach as PaMpeR, we attempted to build a recommendation tool, MeLoId [21], to automatically suggest promising arguments for the induct method without completing a proof: we wrote many assertions in Isabelle/ML. Unfortunately, encoding induction heuristics as assertions directly in Isabelle/ML caused an immense amount of code-clutter, and we could not encode even the human-friendly notion of depth in syntax tree since multi-arity functions are represented as curried functions in Isabelle. Therefore, we developed LiFtEr, expecting that LiFtEr serves as a language for feature extraction.

We hope that when combined into the supervised learning framework of MeLoId, assertions written in LiFtEr extract the essence of induction in Isabelle/HOL in a cross-domain style and produce a useful database for machine learning algorithms, so that new Isabelle users can have the recommendation of promising arguments for the induct method in a fully automatic way.

References

1. Blanchette, J., Kaliszyk, C., Paulson, L., Urban, J.: Hammering towards QED. J. Formalized Reasoning **9**(1), 101–148 (2016). https://doi.org/10.6092/issn.1972-5787/4593
2. Boyer, R.S., Moore, J.S.: A Computational Logic Handbook, Perspectives in Computing, vol. 23. Academic Press, Boston (1979)
3. Bundy, A.: The automation of proof by mathematical induction. In: Robinson, J.A., Voronkov, A. (eds.) Handbook of Automated Reasoning (in 2 volumes), pp. 845–911. Elsevier and MIT Press (2001)
4. Delahaye, D.: A tactic language for the system Coq. In: Parigot, M., Voronkov, A. (eds.) LPAR 2000. LNAI, vol. 1955, pp. 85–95. Springer, Heidelberg (2000). https://doi.org/10.1007/3-540-44404-1_7
5. Torra, V., Karlsson, A., Steinhauer, H.J., Berglund, S.: Artificial intelligence. In: Said, A., Torra, V. (eds.) Data Science in Practice. SBD, vol. 46, pp. 9–26. Springer, Cham (2019). https://doi.org/10.1007/978-3-319-97556-6_2
6. Gramlich, B.: Strategic issues, problems and challenges in inductive theorem proving. Electr. Notes Theor. Comput. Sci. **125**(2), 5–43 (2005). https://doi.org/10.1016/j.entcs.2005.01.006
7. Harrison, J.: HOL light: a tutorial introduction. In: Srivas, M., Camilleri, A. (eds.) FMCAD 1996. LNCS, vol. 1166, pp. 265–269. Springer, Heidelberg (1996). https://doi.org/10.1007/BFb0031814

8. Heras, J., Komendantskaya, E., Johansson, M., Maclean, E.: Proof-pattern recognition and lemma discovery in ACL2. In: McMillan, K., Middeldorp, A., Voronkov, A. (eds.) LPAR 2013. LNCS, vol. 8312, pp. 389–406. Springer, Heidelberg (2013). https://doi.org/10.1007/978-3-642-45221-5_27

9. Jiang, Y., Papapanagiotou, P., Fleuriot, J.: Machine learning for inductive theorem proving. In: Fleuriot, J., Wang, D., Calmet, J. (eds.) AISC 2018. LNCS (LNAI), vol. 11110, pp. 87–103. Springer, Cham (2018). https://doi.org/10.1007/978-3-319-99957-9_6

10. Kaufmann, M., Moore, J.S.: An industrial strength theorem prover for a logic based on Common Lisp. IEEE Trans. Software Eng. **23**(4), 203–213 (1997). https://doi.org/10.1109/32.588534

11. Klein, G., et al.: seL4: formal verification of an operating-system kernel. Commun. ACM **53**(6), 107–115 (2010). https://doi.org/10.1145/1743546.1743574

12. Klein, G., Nipkow, T., Paulson, L., Thiemann, R.: The Archive of Formal Proofs (2004). https://www.isa-afp.org/

13. Komendantskaya, E., Heras, J.: Proof mining with dependent types. In: Geuvers, H., England, M., Hasan, O., Rabe, F., Teschke, O. (eds.) CICM 2017. LNCS (LNAI), vol. 10383, pp. 303–318. Springer, Cham (2017). https://doi.org/10.1007/978-3-319-62075-6_21

14. Lammich, P., Wimmer, S.: IMP2 - simple program verification in Isabelle/HOL. Arch. Formal Proofs **2019** (2019). https://www.isa-afp.org/entries/IMP2.html

15. Leroy, X.: Formal verification of a realistic compiler. Commun. ACM **52**(7), 107–115 (2009). https://doi.org/10.1145/1538788.1538814

16. Matichuk, D., Murray, T.C., Wenzel, M.: Eisbach: a proof method language for Isabelle. J. Autom. Reasoning **56**(3), 261–282 (2016). https://doi.org/10.1007/s10817-015-9360-2

17. Moore, J.S.: Computational logic: structure sharing and proof of program properties. Ph.D. thesis, University of Edinburgh, UK (1973). http://hdl.handle.net/1842/2245

18. Moore, J.S.: Symbolic simulation: an ACL2 approach. In: Formal Methods in Computer-Aided Design, Second International Conference, FMCAD 1998, Palo Alto, California, USA, 4–6 November 1998, Proceedings, pp. 334–350 (1998). https://doi.org/10.1007/3-540-49519-3_22

19. Moore, J.S., Wirth, C.: Automation of mathematical induction as part of the history of logic. CoRR abs/1309.6226 (2013). http://arxiv.org/abs/1309.6226

20. Nagashima, Y.: data61/PSL. https://github.com/data61/PSL/releases/tag/v0.1.4-alpha

21. Nagashima, Y.: Towards machine learning mathematical induction. CoRR abs/1812.04088 (2018). http://arxiv.org/abs/1812.04088

22. Nagashima, Y., He, Y.: PaMpeR: proof method recommendation system for Isabelle/HOL. In: Proceedings of the 33rd ACM/IEEE International Conference on Automated Software Engineering, ASE 2018, Montpellier, France, 3–7 September 2018, pp. 362–372 (2018). https://doi.org/10.1145/3238147.3238210

23. Nagashima, Y., Kumar, R.: A proof strategy language and proof script generation for Isabelle/HOL. In: de Moura, L. (ed.) CADE 2017. LNCS (LNAI), vol. 10395, pp. 528–545. Springer, Cham (2017). https://doi.org/10.1007/978-3-319-63046-5_32

24. Nagashima, Y., Parsert, J.: Goal-oriented conjecturing for Isabelle/HOL. In: Rabe, F., Farmer, W.M., Passmore, G.O., Youssef, A. (eds.) CICM 2018. LNCS (LNAI), vol. 11006, pp. 225–231. Springer, Cham (2018). https://doi.org/10.1007/978-3-319-96812-4_19

25. Nipkow, T., Klein, G.: Concrete Semantics - With Isabelle/HOL. Springer, Cham (2014). https://doi.org/10.1007/978-3-319-10542-0
26. Nipkow, T., Wenzel, M., Paulson, L.C. (eds.): Isabelle/HOL - A Proof Assistant for Higher-Order Logic. LNCS, vol. 2283. Springer, Heidelberg (2002). https://doi.org/10.1007/3-540-45949-9
27. The Coq development team: The Coq proof assistant. https://coq.inria.fr
28. Wenzel, M.: Isabelle/jEdit – a prover IDE within the PIDE framework. In: Jeuring, J., et al. (eds.) CICM 2012. LNCS (LNAI), vol. 7362, pp. 468–471. Springer, Heidelberg (2012). https://doi.org/10.1007/978-3-642-31374-5_38

Concurrency

Android Multitasking Mechanism: Formal Semantics and Static Analysis of Apps

Jinlong He[1,3], Taolue Chen[2,4], Ping Wang[1,3], Zhilin Wu[1,5(✉)], and Jun Yan[1,3]

[1] State Key Laboratory of Computer Science, Institute of Software,
Chinese Academy of Sciences, Beijing, China
wuzi@ios.ac.cn
[2] Birkbeck, University of London, London, UK
[3] University of Chinese Academy of Sciences, Beijing, China
[4] State Key Laboratory for Novel Software Technology, Nanjing University,
Nanjing, China
[5] Shanghai Key Laboratory of Trustworthy Computing,
East China Normal University, Shanghai, China

Abstract. In this paper we formalize the semantics of the Android multitasking mechanism and develop efficient static analysis methods with automated tool supports. For the formalization, we propose an extension of the existing Android Stack Machine model to capture all the core elements of the mechanism, in particular, the intent flags used in inter-component communication. For the static analysis, we consider the configuration reachability and stack boundedness problem, designing new algorithms and developing a prototype tool TaskDroid to fully support automated model construction and analysis of Android apps. The experimental results show that TaskDroid is effective and efficient in analyzing Android apps in practice.

1 Introduction

Android, a mobile operating system developed by Google, features over 2 billion monthly active users and over 80% of the share of the global mobile operating system market.[1] The Google Play store, Google's official pre-installed app store on Android devices, has supplied 2 million apps since 2016.[2] Multitasking is a fundamental mechanism of the Android operating system. Its unique design, via activities, back stacks and task stacks, greatly facilitates organizing user sessions through tasks, and provides rich features such as handy application switching, background app state maintenance, and smooth task history navigation (using the "back" button) [13]. Although the Android multitasking mechanism has substantially enhanced user experiences of the Android system and promoted personalized features in app design, it is notoriously complex and

---

[1] https://expandedramblings.com/index.php/android-statistics/.
[2] https://www.statista.com/statistics/266210/number-of-available-applications-in-the-google-play-store/.

© Springer Nature Switzerland AG 2019
A. W. Lin (Ed.): APLAS 2019, LNCS 11893, pp. 291–312, 2019.
https://doi.org/10.1007/978-3-030-34175-6_15

difficult to understand. As a witness, it constantly baffles app developers and has become a common topic of question-and-answer websites.[3] In addition, such a complex mechanism is plagued by serious security concerns, e.g., GUI phishing and hijacking attacks, denial of service attacks, and privilege leakage [3,13,15].

The Android multi-tasking mechanism, despite its importance, had not been systematically studied until very recently. Lee *et al.* formalized the operational semantics of the Android multitasking mechanism [7,8]. Independently, we introduced a formal model, i.e., Android Stack Machine (ASM), to capture the fundamental aspects of the multitasking mechanism [5], where the first step was made towards static analysis of Android apps based on the ASM model. It appears that, despite these initiatives, much more studies are needed to understand the multitasking mechanism, and to utilize it to design, analyse, test and verify Android apps. For instance, the operational semantics [8] is lengthy and hard to grip, while the ASM model [5], being more succinct and accessible, is incomplete, as intent flags, an important and pervasive feature of the multitasking mechanism, were not taken into account. More importantly, static analysis of the multitasking behavior of apps and its supporting tools, which is the focus of the current paper, are largely missing (with the exception that a static analysis tool was developed in [7], but was specialised for detecting activity injection attacks while did not fit for general-purpose analysis). This is in contrast to the large body of work on the static analysis of the other aspects of Android apps.

Contributions. The current paper aims to deepen the understanding of the Android multitasking mechanism via formalization of its semantics, and to develop effective and efficient approaches to the general-purpose static analysis of the multitasking behavior of Android apps.

For the formal semantics of the multitasking mechanism (Sect. 3), we significantly extend the ASM model [5]. The most pronounced extension lies in the introduction of intent flags which are pervasive for Android inter-component communication but which were ignored by the original ASM model. Our improvements over the operational semantics [8] are as follows: (1) We formalize the semantics for Android 7.0/8.0, which is—interestingly and perhaps surprisingly—different from that of Android 6.0. (The semantics for Android 7.0 and 8.0 also have slight differences.) In particular, we identify the notion of *real activity* which plays an essential role in allocating newly launched activities into respective tasks (referred to as the task allocation mechanism). In contrast, the semantics given before [7,8] is for Android 6.0 and uses a different and simpler tasking allocation mechanism. To the best of our knowledge, this is the first time that the discrepancies of the multitasking mechanism for different Android versions are thoroughly studied and formalized. (2) The semantics we give is more succinct and structured. Instead of an explicit enumeration which takes tens of pages [8], we organize and group different cases, leading to a much shorter and more accessible description with underlying principles identified which greatly facilitate the understanding. (3) We validate the semantics against the actual behavior of the Android system by designing a diagnosis app and conducting

---

[3] For instance, https://stackoverflow.com/questions/3219726/.

exhaustive experiments. All the experimental data are made publicly available to encourage reproductivity (cf. the full version [6]).

For static analysis (Sect. 4), we consider some of the most fundamental problems based on the extended ASM model. In particular, we consider configuration reachability analysis, which is arguably the cornerstone of any automated analysis of this kind. By this analysis, one can determine whether a particular configuration of the app can be reached by interacting with the mobile phone users and/or possible interaction with other (potentially malicious) apps. It is not very difficult to envisage that most existing security vulnerabilities related to the multitasking mechanism can be reduced to such an analysis. We also consider the stack boundedness analysis. In general, app developers may be interested in checking whether there is a sequence of user actions which can force the height of some task(s) to grow unboundedly. If this were the case, there would be a security risk that the app may crash or even lead to rebooting of mobile devices, if a user or a malicious app interacts with the app by following the sequence. The stack boundedness analysis is used to detect such a vulnerability.

To carry out such analysis, we build ASM models from Android apps by first constructing the call graphs and control flow graphs based on the soot tool [14], then applying control and data flow analysis (Sect. 4.1). We give new, practical algorithms to solve the configuration reachability and stack boundedness problems (Sect. 4.2). For the configuration reachability problem, we reduce the problem to the reachability problem of finite state machines, by imposing a (specified) constant bound on the height of tasks. The latter problem can be solved by off-the-shelf symbolic model checkers (e.g., nuXmv [4]) efficiently. For the stack boundedness problem, the algorithm searches witness cycles of transitions for each task along which its back stack may run unbounded with the involvement of other tasks.

To evaluate our approaches, we implement a prototype tool TaskDroid and carry out extensive experiments on over 4, 000 apps, which are either open-source apps from F-Droid or apps downloaded from app markets, e.g., Google Play (Sect. 5). The experimental results show that our approaches are effective and efficient in analysing the apps in practice. Remarkably, TaskDroid enables us to detect that 29 apps from F-Droid are stack unbounded, and our experiments confirm that the stack unboundedness poses a real threat (Sect. 5.2): The 29 stack-unbounded F-Droid apps, when being fed into the Monkey tool to simulate the detected witness cycles for hundreds or thousands of times, exhibit black screen, app crash, or even rebooting of mobile devices.

Related Work. We discuss the related work from the following three perspectives.

Android GUI Models. Some models addressing GUI activities of Android apps have been proposed. *Activity transition graphs* [2] were probably the first model to represent Android GUI activity transitions, but they are essentially a syntactic model without addressing the semantics sufficiently. *Window transition graphs* [17] can represent the possible GUI activity (window) sequences and their associated events and callbacks, and thus can capture how the events and callbacks modify the task stack. However, this model addresses neither the launch modes other than "standard" nor task affinities. Labeled transition graphs with stack and widget (LATTE [16]) consider the effects of launch modes on the task stack, but not those of task affinities. Essentially, it provides a finite-state abstraction of the behavior of the task stack. The ASM model [5] is the basis of the current work, but its was oversimplified for the purpose of formalizing the semantics of Android multi-tasking mechanism.

Static Analysis. Static analysis for Android apps has been thoroughly studied, and we refer the readers to [9], which provides a systematic literature review involving 124 research papers published during the period for 2011–2015. More recently, [12] investigated the problem of composite constant propagation, which was able to infer Android inter-component communication values, and developed a tool called IC3. Our model construction may use IC3 but we choose not to do mainly because: (1) IC3 is unable to discover the *indirect* activation between activities in general. (For instance, if the activity A calls a function of the non-activity class C in which the activity B is started, then IC3 does not conclude that B can be started by A, since it will ignore the function call from A to C.) (2) IC3 analyses more information than what the ASM model needs making it less efficient for the purpose of ASM model generation. Finally, we mention recent work which exploits neural networks or probabilistic models to improve the precision and scalability of static analysis [11,19]. On a different matter, [18] introduced a launch-mode aware context-sensitive activity transition analysis, but did not consider task affinities or intent flags.

Security Related to Multi-tasking Mechanism. Various work has identified potential security vulnerabilities related to the android multitasking mechanism, which has become one of the strong motivations to provide a complete formalization. [13] firstly reported task hijacking attacks, which means "malware reside side by side with the victim apps in the same task and hijack the user sessions of the victim apps." [7] analyzed the activity injection vulnerability referring to "inject malicious activities into a victim app's activity stack to hijack user interaction flows." As discussed in the introduction, our formalization provides several improvements over this work. Static analysis was also considered there, but was restricted to the detection of activity injection vulnerabilities. [15] recognized that the multitasking mechanism could give additional privilege to apps, which can be exploited by attackers. The authors analyzed the system/app conditions that can enable privilege leakage and identified new end-to-end attacks where attackers can actively interfere with victim apps to steal sensitive information. [10] introduced TDroid, an approach to detecting app switching attacks, which combines both static and dynamic analysis.

2   Android Multitasking Mechanism

This section provides an overview of the Android system mainly from an UI perspective focusing on the multitasking mechanism. For the purpose of this paper, an Android app can be considered as a collection of activities.[4] An activity is an instance of the android.content.Activity class, and provides GUI on screen [1]. A *task*, as a logical notion, is a collection of activities that users interact with when performing a certain job. The running activities of a task are managed by Android as a stack in the order that each activity is opened. Such a stack is usually referred to as a *back stack*. (Unfortunately the terminologies in literature are not necessarily consistent, for instance, [5] use back stack differently.) In the sequel, we will usually identify a back stack and the task it belongs to. In a task there are two distinguished activities, i.e., the "root activity" which is the one sitting at the bottom, and the "top activity" which is the topmost activity. Note that in Android, activities from different apps can stay in the same task, and activities from the same app can enter different tasks.

The Android system may have multiple tasks: one *foreground* task and possibly several *background* tasks. They are organized as a stack as well, which is referred to as a *task stack* [7] (aka. activity stack [13]). The foreground task, as expected, sits on the top of the task stack. When a task comes to the *foreground*, its top activity is displayed on the device screen. When an activity finishes, it is popped from the back stack. If the back stack is not empty, the new top activity is displayed on the screen. Otherwise, the task itself finishes in which case it is popped from the task stack. We mention that, the Home screen comes to the foreground when a user presses the Home button (in this case the task stack will be emptied) or when the task stack becomes empty. The task stack is the central data structure for Android multi-tasking mechanism, and we are mostly interested in its evolution in response to activity activation. When an activity is started, there are three basic attributes which determine the resulting task stack: *launch mode, task affinity,* and *intent flags*. All the activities of an app, as well as their launch modes and task affinities, are defined in the *manifest file* (Android-Manifest.xml). Differently, intent flags are set by caller activities to declare how to activate target activities by calling startActivity() or startActivityForResult() with the intent flags as its arguments. The launch mode attribute specifies one of four modes to launch an activity: standard, singleTop, singleTask, and single-Instance, with standard being the default. The task affinity attribute specifies to which task the activity prefers to belong. By default, all the activities from the same app have the same affinity (i.e., all activities in the same app prefer to be in the same task). However, one can modify the default affinity of the activity. Android allows a great degree of flexibility: activities defined in different apps can share a task affinity whilst activities defined in the same app can be assigned with different task affinities.

Android supports inter-component communication via *intents*. An intent is an asynchronous message that activates activities. Android provides 21 intent flags related to activities, but only part of them may govern activity activation.

---

[4] In this paper, activities as viewed as atomic objects, and thus sub-components (e.g., fragments, https://developer.android.com/guide/components/fragments) contained in activities are simply ignored.

Intent flags are set by caller activities to declare how to activate target activities and are passed to startActivity() or startActivityForResult() as their arguments.

3   Formalization

In this section, we provide a formalization of the semantics of the Android multitasking mechanism. We focus on the evolution of the task stack when an activity is launched. For this purpose we adapt and extend the ASM model [5]. For $k \in \mathbb{N}$, let $[k] = \{1, \cdots, k\}$.

Following the overview of Sect. 2, we shall concentrate on the launch mode, the task affinity, and the intent flags when an activity is launched. There are four launch modes in Android: "standard" (STD), "singleTop" (STP), "singleTask" (STK) and "singleInstance" (SIT). For the task affinity, we note that its default value is the package name of the app (i.e., when it is not specified explicitly). However, we find that Android system exhibits unexpected behavior when it is an empty string. Our formal semantics takes special care of this which has not been addressed before, to the best of our knowledge. Furthermore, Android provides 21 intent flags related to activities[5], namely, the flags whose names start with FLAG_ACTIVITY. Among these 21 intent flags, we consider the following seven that are commonly used in Android apps,

- FLAG_ACTIVITY_NEW_TASK (NTK),
- FLAG_ACTIVITY_CLEAR_TOP (CTP),
- FLAG_ACTIVITY_SINGLE_TOP (STP),
- FLAG_ACTIVITY_CLEAR_TASK (CTK),
- FLAG_ACTIVITY_MULTIPLE_TASK (MTK),
- FLAG_ACTIVITY_REORDER_TO_FRONT (RTF),
- FLAG_ACTIVITY_TASK_ON_HOME (TOH).

The rest will not be addressed in this paper. We remark that some flags, i.e., NTK, CTP, STP, can be modeled by launch modes, as mentioned in [5]. However, CTK, MTK, RTF, and TOH cannot be captured.

3.1   The Extended ASM Model

Let $\mathcal{F} = \{\text{NTK}, \text{CTP}, \text{STP}, \text{CTK}, \text{MTK}, \text{RTF}, \text{TOH}\}$ denote the set of intent flags, $\mathcal{B}(\mathcal{F})$ denote the set of formulae $\phi = \bigwedge_{F \in \mathcal{F}} \theta_F$, where $\theta_F = F$ or $\neg F$.

Definition 1 (Android stack machine). *An* Android stack machine *(ASM)* *is a tuple* $\mathcal{A} = (\text{Sig}, \Delta)$, *where*

- Sig $= (\text{Act}, \text{Lmd}, \text{Aft}, A_0)$ *is the* activity signature, *where*
  - Act *is a finite set of activities,*
  - Lmd : Act $\rightarrow \{\text{STD}, \text{STP}, \text{STK}, \text{SIT}\}$ *is the launch-mode function,*

---

[5] https://developer.android.com/reference/android/content/Intent#flags.

- Aft : Act $\rightarrow [m] \cup \{0\}$ *is the task-affinity function, where* $m = |\text{Act}|$,
- $A_0 \in \text{Act}$ *is the* main *activity*,

- $\Delta \subseteq (\text{Act} \cup \{\triangleright\}) \times \text{Inst}$ *is the transition relation, where* $\text{Inst} = \{\text{back}\} \cup \{\alpha(A, \phi) \mid \alpha \in \{\text{start}, \text{finishStart}\}, A \in \text{Act}, \phi \in \mathscr{B}(\mathcal{F})\}$ *such that* $(A, \text{back}) \in \Delta$ *for each* $A \in \text{Act}$. *(Intuitively, the* back *button can be pressed in any time) and for each transition* $(\triangleright, inst) \in \Delta$, *it holds that* $inst = \text{start}(A_0, \bigwedge_{F \in \mathcal{F}} \neg F)$.

Intuitively, $\triangleright$ denotes an empty task stack, $\text{Aft}(A) = 0$ denotes the task affinity of A being the empty string, back denotes the pop action, $(A, \text{start}(B, \phi))$ denotes the action that the activity B is started with some intent flags satisfying ϕ, and $(A, \text{finishStart}(B, \phi))$ is the same as $(A, \text{start}(B, \phi))$, except that the activity A is popped after starting B. For convenience, we usually write $(A, \alpha(B, \phi)) \in \Delta$ as $A \xrightarrow{\alpha(\phi)} B$, where A is the *caller* activity, and B is the *callee* activity.

Remark 1. The main differences wrt [5] are: introducing intent flags, removing control states, and assuming that back actions are always enabled.

3.2   Semantics of ASM

We first discuss briefly how the core concepts such as tasks, task stack, and configurations are formalized. In general, a *task* is encoded as a word $S = [A_1, \cdots, A_n] \in \text{Act}^+$ which denotes the content of its back stack, where n is called the *height* of S. A *task stack* is encoded as a non-empty sequence $\rho = ((S_1, A_1), \cdots, (S_n, A_n))$, where for each $i \in [n]$, S_i is a task and A_i is the real activity of S_i. The *real activity*[6] of a task is the activity which was pushed into the task—as the bottom activity—when the task is created. For any activity A, we refer to an A-task as a task whose real activity is A. The tasks S_1 and S_n are called the top and the bottom task respectively. (Intuitively, S_1 is the foreground task.) The symbol ε is used to denote the empty task stack. The *affinity of a task* is defined as the affinity of its real activity.

A task is called the *main task* of the task stack if it is the first task that was created when launching the app. Note that the current task stack may *not* contain the main task, since it may have been popped out from the task stack. This notion is introduced since the semantics of ASM is also dependent on whether the task stack contains the main task or not.

A *configuration* of $\mathcal{A}$ is a pair $= (\rho, \ell)$, where $\rho = ((S_1, A_1), \cdots, (S_n, A_n))$ with $S_i = [B_{i,1}, \cdots, B_{i,m_i}]$ for each $i \in [n]$ and $B_{i,j} \in \text{Act}$ for $j \in [m_i]$, moreover, $\ell \in [n] \cup \{0\}$. We require (ρ, ℓ) to satisfy that if $\ell \in [n]$, then $A_\ell = A_0$. Intuitively, ℓ is the index of the main task. (If $\ell = 0$, then ρ contains no main task.) Let $\text{Conf}_{\mathcal{A}}$ denote the set of configurations of $\mathcal{A}$. The *initial* configuration of $\mathcal{A}$ is $(\varepsilon, 0)$. The *height* of ρ is defined as $\max_{i \in [m]} |S_i|$, where $|S_i|$ is the height of S_i. By convention, the height of ε is defined as 0.

---

[6] The name is inherited from the Android system.

We use the relation $\xrightarrow{\mathcal{A}}$ which comprises the quadruples

$$((\rho, \ell), \tau, i, (\rho', \ell')) \in \mathsf{Conf}_{\mathcal{A}} \times \Delta \times \{0, 1, 2\} \times \mathsf{Conf}_{\mathcal{A}}$$

to formalize the semantics of $\mathcal{A}$.

Auxiliary Functions and Predicates. To specify the transition relation precisely and concisely, we define the following functions and predicates. Here (ρ, ℓ) is a configuration with $\rho = ((S_1, A_1), \cdots, (S_n, A_n))$ and $B \in \mathsf{Act}$.

- Let $S = [B_1, \cdots, B_{m'}]$ be a task, then $\mathsf{Top}(S) = B_1$ and $\mathsf{Btm}(S) = B_{m'}$.
- $\mathsf{TopTsk}(\rho) = S_1$, $\mathsf{TopAct}(\rho) = \mathsf{Top}(\mathsf{TopTsk}(\rho))$.
- $\mathsf{Push}((\rho, \ell), B) = (((([B] \cdot S_1), A_1), (S_2, A_2), \cdots, (S_n, A_n)), \ell)$.
- $\mathsf{MvAct2Top}((\rho, \ell), B) = ((([B] \cdot S_1' \cdot S_1''), (S_2, A_2), \cdots, (S_n, A_n)), \ell)$, if $S_1 = S_1' \cdot [B] \cdot S_1''$ with $S_1' \in (\mathsf{Act} \setminus \{B\})^*$.
- $\mathsf{ClrTop}((\rho, \ell), B) = (((S_1'', A_1), (S_2, A_2), \cdots, (S_n, A_n)), \ell)$ if $S_1 = S_1' \cdot S_1''$ with $S_1' \in (\mathsf{Act} \setminus \{B\})^* B$.
- $\mathsf{ClrTsk}((\rho, \ell)) = ((([], A_1), (S_2, A_2), \cdots, (S_n, A_n)), \ell)$.
- Let $i \in [n]$, then $\mathsf{MvTsk2Top}((\rho, \ell), S_i) = (((S_i, A_i), (S_1, A_1), \cdots, (S_{i-1}, A_{i-1}), (S_{i+1}, A_{i+1}), \cdots, (S_n, A_n)), \ell')$, where ℓ' is defined as follows: if $\ell = 0$, then $\ell' = 0$; if $\ell = i$, then $\ell' = 1$; if $i + 1 \leq \ell \leq n$, then $\ell' = \ell$; if $1 \leq \ell \leq i - 1$, then $\ell' = \ell + 1$.
  [Note that ℓ' is the simply the new position of the main task.]
- $\mathsf{NewTsk}((\rho, \ell), B) = ((([B], B), (S_1, A_1), \cdots, (S_n, A_n)), \ell')$, where $\ell' = 0$ if $\ell = 0$, and $\ell' = \ell + 1$ otherwise.
- $\mathsf{GetRealTsk}(\rho, B) = S_i$ such that $i \in [n]$ is the *minimum* index satisfying $A_i = B$ if such an index i exists; $\mathsf{GetRealTsk}(\rho, B) = *$ otherwise.
- $\mathsf{GetTsk}(\rho, B) = S_i$ such that $i \in [n]$ is the *minimum* index satisfying $\mathsf{Aft}(A_i) = \mathsf{Aft}(B)$, if such an index i exists; $\mathsf{GetTsk}(\rho, B) = *$ otherwise.
- Let $i \in \{1, 2\}$ and $S_i = [B_1, \cdots, B_{m'}]$. Then

$$\mathsf{RmAct}((\rho, \ell), i) = \begin{cases} (0, (((S_1, A_1), \cdots, (S_{i-1}, A_{i-1}), \\ \quad (S_{i+1}, A_{i+1}), \cdots, (S_n, A_n)), 0)) & \text{if } m' = 1 \text{ and } \ell = 0 \text{ or } i, \\ (0, (((S_1, A_1), \cdots, (S_{i-1}, A_{i-1}), \\ \quad (S_{i+1}, A_{i+1}), \cdots, (S_n, A_n)), \ell)) & \text{if } m' = 1 \text{ and } 1 \leq \ell \leq i - 1, \\ (0, (((S_1, A_1), \cdots, (S_{i-1}, A_{i-1}), \\ \quad (S_{i+1}, A_{i+1}), \cdots, (S_n, A_n)), \ell - 1)) & \text{if } m' = 1 \text{ and } i + 1 \leq \ell \leq n, \\ (i, (((S_1, A_1), \cdots, (S_{i-1}, A_{i-1}), ([B_2, \cdots, B_{m'}], A_i), \\ \quad (S_{i+1}, A_{i+1}), \cdots, (S_n, A_n)), \ell)) & \text{if } m' > 1. \end{cases}$$

Intuitively, $\mathsf{RmAct}((\rho, \ell), i) = (i', (\rho', \ell'))$, where (ρ', ℓ') is obtained from (ρ, ℓ) by removing the top activity of S_i from ρ, and $i' = 0, 1, 2$ denotes the position of the task S_i in ρ'. (In particular, $i' = 0$ denotes that the task S_i disappears in ρ'.)

Transition Relation. For readability, we write $((\rho, \ell), \tau, i, (\rho', \ell')) \in \xrightarrow{A}$ as $(\rho, \ell) \xrightarrow[\tau, i]{A} (\rho', \ell')$. Intuitively, (ρ, ℓ) is the current configuration, (ρ', ℓ') is the configuration obtained after executing the transition rule τ, and $i = 0, 1, 2$ corresponds to the cases that the top task of ρ is absent in ρ', remains to be the top task of ρ', or becomes the task immediately below the top task of ρ', respectively.

For $\tau = (A, \mathsf{back})$ such that $\mathsf{TopAct}(S_1) = A$,

- if S_1 contains at least two activities, then $(\rho, \ell) \xrightarrow[\tau, 1]{A} (\rho', \ell')$ with $\rho' = ((S_1', A_1), (S_2, A_2), \cdots, (S_n, A_n))$, where S_1' is obtained from S_1 by removing the top activity A from S_1;
- otherwise, we have $(\rho, \ell) \xrightarrow[\tau, 0]{A} (\rho', \ell')$ with $\rho' = ((S_2, A_2), \cdots, (S_n, A_n))$ and $\ell' = \ell - 1$ if $\ell > 1$ and 0 otherwise.

For $\tau = \rhd \to \mathsf{start}(A_0, \bigwedge_{F \in \mathcal{F}} \neg F)$, if (ρ, ℓ) is the initial configuration $(\varepsilon, 0)$, we have $(\rho, \ell) \xrightarrow[\tau, 0]{A} (([A_0], A_0), 1)$. (Here 0 is used because there is no top task in ρ.)

In the sequel, we first present the semantics for $\tau = A \xrightarrow{\mathsf{start}(\phi)} B$, which will be followed by the semantics for $\tau = A \xrightarrow{\mathsf{finishStart}(\phi)} B$.

Suppose $\rho = ((S_1, A_1), \cdots, (S_n, A_n))$ for some $n \geq 1$. Let $A = \mathsf{TopAct}(\rho)$.

Transition rules for $\tau = A \xrightarrow{\mathsf{start}(\phi)} B$

We distinguish two cases, i.e., $\phi \models \neg\mathsf{TOH}$ or $\phi \models \mathsf{TOH}$.

Case $\phi \models \neg\mathsf{TOH}$

$\boxed{\text{CASE } \mathsf{Lmd}(B) = \mathsf{SIT}}$

- if $\mathsf{GetRealTsk}(\rho, B) = S_j$ for some $j \in [n]$, then
  - if $j = 1$, then $i = 1$ and $(\rho', \ell') = (\rho, \ell)$,
  - if $j \neq 1$, then $i = 2$ and $(\rho', \ell') = \mathsf{MvTsk2Top}((\rho, \ell), S_j)$,
- if $\mathsf{GetRealTsk}(\rho, B) = *$, then $i = 2$ and $(\rho', \ell') = \mathsf{NewTsk}((\rho, \ell), B)$.

$\boxed{\text{CASE } \mathsf{Lmd}(B) = \mathsf{STK}}$

- if $\mathsf{GetRealTsk}(\rho, B) = S_j$ or $\mathsf{GetRealTsk}(\rho, B) = * \wedge \mathsf{GetTsk}(\rho, B) = S_j$, then $i = 1$ if $j = 1$, and $i = 2$ otherwise. Moreover,
  - if $\phi \models \neg\mathsf{CTK}$, then
    * if $B \notin S_j$, then $(\rho', \ell') = \mathsf{Push}(\mathsf{MvTsk2Top}((\rho, \ell), S_j), B)$,
    * if $B \in S_j$, then $(\rho', \ell') = \mathsf{Push}(\mathsf{ClrTop}(\mathsf{MvTsk2Top}((\rho, \ell), S_j), B), B)$,
  - if $\phi \models \mathsf{CTK}$, then $(\rho', \ell') = \mathsf{Push}(\mathsf{ClrTsk}(\mathsf{MvTsk2Top}((\rho, \ell), S_j)), B)$,
- if $\mathsf{GetTsk}(\rho, B) = *$, then $i = 2$ and $(\rho', \ell') = \mathsf{NewTsk}((\rho, \ell), B)$.

$\boxed{\text{CASE } \mathsf{Lmd}(B) = \mathsf{STD}}$

- if $\mathsf{Lmd}(A) \neq \mathsf{SIT}$ and $\phi \models \neg\mathsf{NTK}$, then $i = 1$ and
  - if $\phi \models \mathsf{STP} \vee \mathsf{RTF} \vee \mathsf{CTP}$ and $\mathsf{TopAct}(\rho) = B$, then $(\rho', \ell') = (\rho, \ell)$,

- if $\phi \models \neg\mathsf{STP}\wedge\neg\mathsf{RTF}\wedge\neg\mathsf{CTP}$, or $\phi \models \mathsf{STP}\wedge\neg\mathsf{RTF}\wedge\neg\mathsf{CTP}$ and $\mathsf{TopAct}(\rho) \neq B$,

  or $\phi \models \mathsf{RTF} \vee \mathsf{CTP}$ and $B \notin \mathsf{TopTsk}(\rho)$, then $(\rho', \ell') = \mathsf{Push}((\rho, \ell), B)$,
  - if $\phi \models \mathsf{RTF} \wedge \neg\mathsf{CTP}$ and $B \in \mathsf{TopTsk}(\rho)$, then $(\rho', \ell') = \mathsf{MvAct2Top}((\rho, \ell), B)$,
  - if $\phi \models \mathsf{CTP}$ and $B \in \mathsf{TopTsk}(\rho)$, then $(\rho', \ell') = \mathsf{Push}(\mathsf{ClrTop}((\rho, \ell), B), B)$,
- if $\phi \models \mathsf{NTK} \wedge \mathsf{MTK}$, or $\mathsf{Lmd}(A) = \mathsf{SIT}$ and $\phi \models \mathsf{MTK}$, then $i = 2$ and $(\rho', \ell') = \mathsf{NewTsk}((\rho, \ell), B)$,
- if $\phi \models \mathsf{NTK} \wedge \neg\mathsf{MTK}$, or $\mathsf{Lmd}(A) = \mathsf{SIT}$ and $\phi \models \neg\mathsf{MTK}$, then
  - if $\mathsf{GetRealTsk}(\rho, B) = S_j$, then $i = 1$ if $j = 1$, and $i = 2$ otherwise. Moreover,
    * if $\phi \models \neg\mathsf{CTP} \wedge \neg\mathsf{CTK}$, then
      · if $j \neq \ell$, or $\phi \models \mathsf{STP}$ and $\mathsf{Top}(S_j) = B$, then

      $$(\rho', \ell') = \mathsf{MvTsk2Top}((\rho, \ell), S_j),$$

      · otherwise, $(\rho', \ell') = \mathsf{Push}(\mathsf{MvTsk2Top}((\rho, \ell), S_j), B)$,
    * if $\phi \models \mathsf{CTP} \wedge \neg\mathsf{CTK}$, then
      · if $B \notin S_j$, then $(\rho', \ell') = \mathsf{Push}(\mathsf{MvTsk2Top}((\rho, \ell), S_j), B)$,
      · otherwise,$(\rho', \ell') = \mathsf{Push}(\mathsf{ClrTop}(\mathsf{MvTsk2Top}((\rho, \ell), S_j), B), B)$,
    * if $\phi \models \mathsf{CTK}$, then $(\rho', \ell') = \mathsf{Push}(\mathsf{ClrTsk}(\mathsf{MvTsk2Top}((\rho, \ell), S_j)), B)$,
  - if $\mathsf{GetRealTsk}(\rho, B) = *$ and $\mathsf{GetTsk}(\rho, B) = S_j$, then $i = 1$ if $j = 1$, and $i = 2$ otherwise. Moreover,
    * if $\phi \models \neg\mathsf{STP} \wedge \neg\mathsf{CTP} \wedge \neg\mathsf{CTK}$, or $\phi \models \mathsf{STP} \wedge \neg\mathsf{CTP} \wedge \neg\mathsf{CTK}$ and $\mathsf{Top}(S_j) \neq B$, then $(\rho', \ell') = \mathsf{Push}(\mathsf{MvTsk2Top}((\rho, \ell), S_j), B)$,
    * if $\phi \models \mathsf{STP} \wedge \neg\mathsf{CTP} \wedge \neg\mathsf{CTK}$ and $\mathsf{Top}(S_j) = B$, then $(\rho', \ell') = \mathsf{MvTsk2Top}((\rho, \ell), S_j)$,
    * if $\phi \models \mathsf{CTP} \wedge \neg\mathsf{CTK}$, then
      · if $B \notin S_j$, then $(\rho', \ell') = \mathsf{Push}(\mathsf{MvTsk2Top}((\rho, \ell), S_j), B)$,
      · otherwise, $(\rho', \ell') = \mathsf{Push}(\mathsf{ClrTop}(\mathsf{MvTsk2Top}((\rho, \ell), S_j), B), B)$,
    * if $\phi \models \mathsf{CTK}$, then $(\rho', \ell') = \mathsf{Push}(\mathsf{ClrTsk}(\mathsf{MvTsk2Top}((\rho, \ell), S_j)), B)$,
  - if $\mathsf{GetTsk}(\rho, B) = *$, then $i = 2$ and $(\rho', \ell') = \mathsf{NewTsk}((\rho, \ell), B)$.

CASE $\mathsf{Lmd}(B) = \mathsf{STP}$

The semantics is adapted from the case $\mathsf{Lmd}(B) = \mathsf{STD}$ by assuming $\phi \models \mathsf{STP}$ (cf. the full version [6] for details).

Case $\phi \models \mathsf{TOH}$

We then consider the transition rules $\tau = A \xrightarrow{\mathsf{start}(\phi)} B$ with $\phi \models \mathsf{TOH}$. It turns out that we can largely reuse the semantic definitions of the case that $\phi \models \neg\mathsf{TOH}$. Namely, let $\tau' = A \xrightarrow{\mathsf{start}(\phi')} B$ where ϕ' is obtained from ϕ by replacing TOH with $\neg\mathsf{TOH}$. (The behavior of τ' is fully prescribed before, viz, $(\rho, \ell) \xrightarrow[\tau', i]{\mathcal{A}} (\rho', \ell')$ where $\rho' = ((S_1', A_1'), \cdots, (S_{n'}', A_{n'}'))$.) Then we have that

- if $i = 1$, then $(\rho, \ell) \xrightarrow[\tau, i]{\mathcal{A}} (\rho', \ell')$,

– if $i = 2$, then $(\rho, \ell) \xrightarrow[\tau,0]{\mathcal{A}} (((S_1', A_1')), \ell'')$, and $\ell'' = 1$ if $\ell' = 1$; 0 otherwise.

Note that if $i = 2$, then due to the effect of TOH, all the tasks in ρ', except the top one, will be removed.

Transition rules for $\tau = A \xrightarrow{\text{finishStart}(\phi)} B$

We now consider $\tau = A \xrightarrow{\text{finishStart}(\phi)} B$. Intuitively, $A \xrightarrow{\text{finishStart}(\phi)} B$ specifies that B is started with the intent flags ϕ followed by the termination of A. Let $\tau' = A \xrightarrow{\text{start}(\phi)} B$ and $(\rho, \ell) \xrightarrow[\tau',i]{\mathcal{A}} (\rho', \ell')$, with $\rho' = ((S_1', A_1'), \cdots, (S_{n'}', A_{n'}'))$. Then the semantics of $\tau = A \xrightarrow{\text{finishStart}(\phi)} B$ is defined as follows.

– If $i = 0$ (this may happen when $\phi \models$ TOH), then $(\rho, \ell) \xrightarrow[\tau,0]{\mathcal{A}} (\rho', \ell')$.

– If $i = 2$, then $(\rho, \ell) \xrightarrow[\tau,i']{\mathcal{A}} (\rho'', \ell'')$, where $(i', (\rho'', \ell'')) = \mathsf{RmAct}((\rho', \ell'), 2)$.

– If $i = 1$, then
  - if $|S_1'| = |S_1| + 1$ (in this case, the top activity of S_1' is B, and the top second is A), then let S_1'' obtained from S_1' by removing the second activity from the top, and ρ'' obtained from ρ' by replacing S_1' with S_1'', then we have $(\rho, \ell) \xrightarrow[\tau,1]{\mathcal{A}} (\rho'', \ell')$,
  - if $|S_1'| = |S_1|$, then $(\rho, \ell) \xrightarrow[\tau,i']{\mathcal{A}} (\rho'', \ell'')$, where if $\mathsf{Top}(S_1') = A$, then $(i', (\rho'', \ell'')) = \mathsf{RmAct}((\rho', \ell'), 1)$, otherwise (in this case, $\phi \models$ RTF, $\mathsf{Top}(S_1') = B$, and the top second activity of S_1' is A), $i' = 1$, $\ell'' = \ell'$, and ρ'' is obtained from ρ' by removing from S_1' the top second activity,
  - if $|S_1'| < |S_1|$, then $(\rho, \ell) \xrightarrow[\tau,1]{\mathcal{A}} (\rho', \ell')$.

3.3   High-Level Descriptions

We now present some high-level description which would facilitate the understanding of the semantics.

Task Allocation Mechanism. One of the main elements of the semantics of ASM is the *task allocation mechanism*, namely, to specify, when an activity is launched, to which task will it be allocated. Via extensive experiments, we identify a crucial notion, i.e., real activity of tasks, in Android 7.0 and 8.0, which plays a pivotal role in such a mechanism.

Generally speaking, for an activity B which is not to land on the top task, the following three steps will apply: (1) If there is any task whose real activity is B, then B will be put on the task; (2) Otherwise, if there is any task whose real activity has the same task affinity as B, then B will be put on the task (3) Otherwise, a new task is created to hold B. In the first two cases, if there are multiple instances, the first occurrence starting from the top task will be selected. Note that, due to the CTK flag, the bottom activity of a task may *not* be the real activity of the task.

Dependencies Between Launch Modes and Intent Flags. For transitions $A \xrightarrow{\alpha(\phi)} B$, the launch modes of A, B and the intent flags in ϕ may depend on each other. The dependency can exhibit in the following three forms: n *subsumes* n', i.e., n' is ignored if n co-occurs with n', (2) n *enables* n', i.e., n' takes effect if n co-occurs with n', (3) n *implies* n', i.e., if n' subsumes (resp. enables) n'', then n subsumes (resp. enables) n'' as well. We summarize these dependencies in Fig. 1, where the solid lines represent the "subsume" relation, the dashed lines represent the "enable" relation, the dotted lines represent the "implies" relation.

The following properties hold for these relations: (1) the "subsume" and "imply" relations are transitive, (2) the composition of the "imply" relation and the "subsume" (resp. "enable") relation is a subset of the "subsume" (resp. "enable") relation. Moreover, we remark that the two "enable" edges to TOH in Fig. 1 are "incomplete" for TOH, in the sense that the two edges do not fully cover the situations where TOH takes effect, viz. the situations where *the launched activity B is not to land on the original top task.*

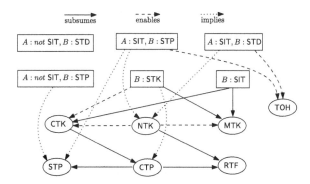

Fig. 1. Dependency graph for launch modes and intent flags in transitions $A \xrightarrow{\alpha(\phi)} B$. The launch modes (resp. the intent flags) are in boxes (resp. circles)

The Empty-String Task Affinity. Intuitively, if the task affinity of some activity A is the empty string, then *the transition rules involving A are the same as if the task affinity of A were different from those of all the other activities.* Formally, suppose $A_1, \cdots, A_{m'}$ are an enumeration of all the activities with the empty-string task affinity, then the semantics of $\mathcal{A}$ is defined as that of $\mathcal{A}'$, where $\mathcal{A}'$ is obtained from $\mathcal{A}$ by setting $\mathsf{Aft}(A_j) = m + j$ for each $j \in [m']$ (recall that $m = |\mathsf{Act}|$).

The Differences of the Semantics for Android 6.0, 7.0, and 8.0. The semantics of ASM for Android 7.0 and Android 8.0 are almost the same except that: In Android 7.0, in case that $\mathsf{Lmd}(A) \neq \mathsf{SIT}$, $\mathsf{Lmd}(B) = \mathsf{STD}/\mathsf{STP}$, B occurs on the top task of ρ, and $\phi \models \neg\mathsf{NTK} \wedge \mathsf{RTF} \wedge \neg\mathsf{CTP}$, the successor configuration (ρ', ℓ') is obtained from (ρ, ℓ) by first clearing the top task, then pushing B into it. Note that here, RTF acts like CTK,[7] although CTK is not enabled and takes no effect (see Fig. 1).

The task allocation mechanism of Android 6.0 is considerably different, which is irrelevant to the real activities of tasks and only uses the affinities of tasks. Its semantics can be adapted from that of Android 8.0 and is given in the full version [6]. We remark that the semantics of ASM for Android 6.0 formalized here is essentially the same as that in [7,8] modulo some minor differences. Indeed, we have found that some of transition rules given in [8] are inconsistent to our semantics. For instance, in case $A \xrightarrow{\text{start}(\phi)} B$ where $\mathsf{Lmd}(A) = \mathsf{SIT}$, $\mathsf{Lmd}(B) = \mathsf{STD}$, $\phi \models \mathsf{MTK} \wedge \mathsf{STP}$, and there exists some task with the same affinity as B in the current task stack: according to the 6th rule on page 22 of [8], the task whose affinity is $\mathsf{Aft}(B)$ and which is closest to the top task will be moved to top and no new task will be created, whereas in our semantics, a new task $S' = [B]$ will be created and become the top of the task stack.

Validation of the Formal Semantics. To validate that the formal semantics of ASM conforms to the actual behavior of the respective Android versions, we have conducted exhaustive experiments by designing a diagnosis app and comparing, for each case in the definition of the formal semantics, the exhibited behavior of the app against the formal semantics. The details of the experiments can be found in the full version [6].

4   Static Analysis of Apps

In this section, we consider static analysis of Android apps. At first, we show how to build the ASM model out of Android apps. Then, we illustrate how to solve the reachability and boundedness problems of ASM.

4.1   From Apps to ASM

We show how to construct an ASM model for an Android app. Recall that an ASM model comprises a signature of activities and a transition relation.

We take the input as either an Android PacKage (apk) file or simply the source code. We extract the manifest file from the source code or by decompiling the apk file. From the manifest file, we can obtain the signature of activities, namely, a list of activities of the app with their launch modes and task affinities, as well as the main activity. In addition, the intent filters, which include actions, categories and data, are also extracted from the manifest file to facilitate the construction of the transition relation.

In a nutshell, we construct the transition relation by the static analysis of the control- and data-flow of Android apps. Recall that a transition $A \xrightarrow{\alpha(\phi)} B$ contains a caller activity A, a callee activity B, an action α, and intent flags

---

[7] It is a confirmed bug of the multitasking mechanism affecting Android 4.4, 7.0 and 7.1.1; see https://issuetracker.google.com/issues/36986021 for the discussions.

ϕ. It is noteworthy that a caller activity can start a callee activity, and finish itself at the same time by invoking the function finish(). In terms of modeling by an ASM, the action is finishStart if finish() is invoked, and start otherwise. As mentioned before, Android may use intents and the functions startActivity() and startActivityForResult() to activate activities. There are two types of intents: explicit intents and implicit intents. The former sets the name of the callee activity directly, while the latter declares the desired values of actions, categories and data fields. Activities that can be activated by implicit intents will declare intent filters in the manifest file. Android starts the activity that an implicit intent intends to run by matching the parameters of the intent with all the intent filters. If an implicit intent matches several intent filters of different activities, users can pick up which activity to launch.

We locate all the methods invoking functions startActivity() or startActivity-ForResult(), and all the activities accessing these methods, which are the caller activities in these transitions. We then exploit data-flow analysis to identify the sets of possible values of the parameters of the intents. From these values, we then obtain the intent flags directly. For explicit intents, we also obtain the callee activities whereas for implicit intents, we compute the set of callee activities by matching the values of these parameters with the intent filters obtained from the manifest file.[8]

Remark that, in this work, we focus on activities and ignore the other Android application components (e.g., services). Therefore, during the construction of the ASM model, we ignore all the occurrences of startActivity() and startActivityForResult() in the functions related to these components, e.g., "onServiceConnected()".

4.2   Static Analysis of ASM

We perform static analysis for Android apps based on the ASM model. We shall focus on two types of analysis, i.e., configuration reachability and stack boundedness analysis, with applications. For simplicity, we restrict our attention to ASMs where the intent flag MTK is absent. This is *not* a severe restriction as the proportion of benchmarks containing the MTK flag is approximately 1% (37/3,245). However, it could tremendously facilitate our analysis because in each configuration of the ASM, the affinities of non-SIT tasks would be distinct.

Configuration Reachability. The configuration reachability problem is formally defined as follows: Given an ASM $\mathcal{A}$ and a configuration ρ, decide whether $([A_0], 1) \overset{\mathcal{A}}{\Rightarrow} (\rho, \ell)$ for some ℓ, where $\overset{\mathcal{A}}{\Rightarrow}$ is the reflexive and transitive closure of $\overset{\mathcal{A}}{\longrightarrow}$. Note here we ignore the components (τ, i) in tuples $(\rho, \ell) \overset{\mathcal{A}}{\underset{\tau,i}{\longrightarrow}} (\rho', \ell')$ and take $\overset{\mathcal{A}}{\longrightarrow}$ as a binary relation over $\mathsf{Conf}_{\mathcal{A}} \times \mathbb{N}$.

In the sequel, we assume that there is a given constant bound $\hbar$ on the heights of tasks in the configurations, and the resulting reachability relation is called $\hbar$-*reachable*. (Evidently, $\hbar$-reachable implies reachable but not vice versa.) This

---

[8] cf. https://developer.android.com/guide/components/intentsfilters.

assumption yields a finite, though exponential, state space, and the evolution of configurations can be captured by a finite state machine (FSM). To tackle the exponential state space we resort to the well-known symbolic model checker nuXmv [4] to provide an efficient and scalable analysis.

Our general approach is to translate an ASM $\mathcal{A}$ with a constant bound $\hbar$ (over heights of tasks) to an FSM $\mathcal{M}_{\mathcal{A}}$, the size of which is polynomial in the size of $\mathcal{A}$. Intuitively, the states of $\mathcal{M}_{\mathcal{A}}$ represent the configurations of $\mathcal{A}$ whose heights are bounded by $\hbar$, and the transitions of $\mathcal{M}_{\mathcal{A}}$ simulate the transition rules of $\mathcal{A}$. More technically, since each configuration ρ contains at most $m = |\mathsf{Aft}(\mathsf{Act} \setminus \mathsf{Act}_{\mathsf{SIT}})| + |\mathsf{Act}_{\mathsf{SIT}}|$ tasks and the height of each back stack is bounded by $\hbar$, ρ can be represented by a word of length exactly $m(\hbar + 1)$. In particular, each task is represented by a word of length $\hbar + 1$, where the last letter specifies the real activity of the task. (Dummy symbols $\perp \notin \mathsf{Act}$ are to be appended if the number of tasks in ρ is less than m or the height of a task is less than $\hbar$.)

As per the semantics of ASM, after some transition, a task may emerge to become the top task, which means that in the corresponding simulation, a subword of length $\hbar + 1$ will become the prefix of the new configuration representation. It turns out that, for the translation purpose, this is cumbersome to define, so we adapt the word representation of configurations as follows: an extra "pointer" word v of length m is introduced where each letter of v refers to a task currently in the configuration via its real activity. The order of the tasks can then be captured by permutations of v. (Note that if the number of tasks is less than m, then the dummy symbol $\perp$ is also used in v.) Generally, the "pointer" word is a word of real activities, possibly followed by multiple $\perp$'s, with a total length m. The detailed encoding is technical and is given in the full version [6].

The configuration reachability problem is fundamental to static program analysis and has various applications. Below we present an example; A further application is given in the stack boundedness section.

Back Pattern Analysis. The back pattern analysis computes, for a given activity A in $\mathcal{A}$, the set of activities B such that when pressing the back button, the foreground activity can switch from A to B. We shall denote this set by $\mathsf{Act}_{\mathsf{back}}(A)$. Such information is valuable for developers of Android apps, for instance, to validate the multitasking design of the app and to detect unexpected behaviors.

For a given $A \in \mathsf{Act}$, it is not hard to see that we can compute the desired set of activities B by solving for each $B \in \mathsf{Act}$, a slightly more general version of the configuration reachability problem, namely, whether a configuration matching the regular expression $e = A\perp^* B$ is reachable. The nuXmv tool facilitates handling this generalized version of the reachability problem. Furthermore, for each A and $B \in \mathsf{Act}_{\mathsf{back}}(A)$, a path can be generated by nuXmv to witness an occurrence of (some word matching) e.

Stack Boundedness. Formally, an ASM $\mathcal{A}$ is said to be *stack-unbounded*, if for every $n \in \mathbb{N}$ there is a configuration (ρ, ℓ) of $\mathcal{A}$ such that $(\epsilon, 0) \overset{\mathcal{A}}{\Rightarrow} (\rho, \ell)$ and the height of ρ is at least n. We will consider a relaxation of stack-unboundedness, i.e., *k-stack unbounded* where k is a (purported small) natural number. Intuitively, an ASM $\mathcal{A}$ is k-stack unbounded if $\mathcal{A}$ is stack-unbounded and the unboundedness is caused by a particular task such that the height of the task is unbounded during the evolution which involves the interplay with at most k other tasks.

We are interested in the *stack boundedness problem* which is to decide whether a given ASM is stack unbounded. While this turns out to be difficult, we hypothesize that, most stack unbounded ASMs are actually k-stack unbounded for a small number k (normally, $k \leq 2$). As a result, as a practical solution, we can appeal to checking k-stack unboundedness for a small k. (See the full version [6] for justification.)

We start with some notations. Let $\mathsf{Act_{real}}$ be the set of activities $A \in \mathsf{Act}$ such that one of the following conditions holds: (1) $\mathsf{Lmd}(A) = \mathsf{SIT}$, (2) $\mathsf{Lmd}(A) = \mathsf{STK}$, (3) $\mathsf{Lmd}(A) = \mathsf{STD}$ or STP, and A occurs in some transition $B \xrightarrow{\alpha(\phi)} A$ such that $\mathsf{Lmd}(B) = \mathsf{SIT}$ or $\phi \models \mathsf{NTK}$. Intuitively, $\mathsf{Act_{real}}$ is the set of activities that may occur as a real activity of tasks.

Two activities $A, B \in \mathsf{Act_{real}}$ are said to *represent different tasks* if one of the following conditions holds: (1) $\mathsf{Lmd}(A) = \mathsf{Lmd}(B) = \mathsf{SIT}$ and $A \neq B$, (2) $\mathsf{Lmd}(A) = \mathsf{SIT}$ and $\mathsf{Lmd}(B) \neq \mathsf{SIT}$, (3) $\mathsf{Lmd}(A) \neq \mathsf{SIT}$ and $\mathsf{Lmd}(B) = \mathsf{SIT}$, (4) $\mathsf{Lmd}(A) \neq \mathsf{SIT}$, $\mathsf{Lmd}(B) \neq \mathsf{SIT}$, and $\mathsf{Aft}(A) \neq \mathsf{Aft}(B)$. For each activity $A \in \mathsf{Act_{real}}$ such that $\mathsf{Lmd}(A) \neq \mathsf{SIT}$, let $\mathsf{Reach}(\Delta, A)$ denote the least subset $\Theta \subseteq \Delta$ satisfying that $B \xrightarrow{\alpha(\phi)} C \in \Theta$ (where $\alpha = \mathsf{start}$ or $\mathsf{finishStart}$) whenever the following two constraints are satisfied:

- $B = A$ or there exists a transition $A' \xrightarrow{\alpha'(\phi')} B \in \Theta$ (where $\alpha' = \mathsf{start}$ or $\mathsf{finishStart}$),
- $\mathsf{Lmd}(C) \neq \mathsf{SIT}$, and if $\mathsf{Lmd}(C) = \mathsf{STK}$ or $\phi \models \mathsf{NTK}$, then $\mathsf{Aft}(C) = \mathsf{Aft}(A)$.

Intuitively, $\mathsf{Reach}(\Delta, A)$ comprises all the transition rules that can be applied and once applied would retain an A-task as the top task. By abusing the notation slightly, $\mathsf{Reach}(\Delta, A)$ also denotes the graph whose edge set is $\mathsf{Reach}(\Delta, A)$.

$\mathsf{Reach}(\Delta, A)$ can be generalized to the case that $A \in \mathsf{Act_{real}}$ and $\mathsf{Lmd}(A) = \mathsf{SIT}$, where $\mathsf{Reach}(\Delta, A)$ is regarded as the graph that contains a single node A without edges.

In the rest of this section, we will sketch a procedure to check stack unboundedness for $k = 0$. The underpinning idea is to search, for each $A \in \mathsf{Act_{real}}$, a *witness cycle*, i.e., a sequence of transitions from $\mathsf{Reach}(\Delta, A)$, the execution of which would force the stack to grow indefinitely.

Formally, a witness cycle is a simple cycle in $\mathsf{Reach}(\Delta, A)$ of the form

$$\mathcal{C} = A_1 \xrightarrow{\alpha_1(\phi_1)} A_2 \cdots A_{n-1} \xrightarrow{\alpha_{n-1}(\phi_{n-1})} A_n$$

where $n \geq 2$ and $\alpha_i = \mathsf{start}$ or $\mathsf{finishStart}$ for each $i \in [n]$ satisfying the following two constraints:

[Non-clearing.] The content of an A-task is *not* cleared when $\mathcal{C}$ is executed. Namely, for each $i \in [n-1]$, $\phi_i \models \neg\mathsf{CTP}$, moreover, either $\phi_i \models \neg\mathsf{CTK}$, or

$\phi_i \models \neg\mathsf{NTK}$ and $\mathsf{Lmd}(A_{i+1}) \neq \mathsf{STK}$ (intuitively, this means that CTK is not enabled, cf. Fig. 1).

[Height-increasing.] The height of the task content is increasing after C is executed. Namely, it is required that $\sum_{i\in[n-1]} weight_C(\tau_i) > 0$, where for each $i \in [n-1]$, $\tau_i = A_i \xrightarrow{\alpha_i(\phi_i)} A_{i+1}$ and $weight_C(\tau_i)$ is defined as follows.

- If $\alpha_i = \mathsf{start}$, then
  - if $\phi_i \models \mathsf{RTF}$, then $weight_C(\tau_i) = 0$,
  - if $\phi_i \models \neg\mathsf{RTF}$, $A_i = A_{i+1}$, and either $\phi_i \models \mathsf{STP}$ or $\mathsf{Lmd}(A_{i+1}) = \mathsf{STP}$, then $weight_C(\tau_i) = 0$,
  - otherwise, $weight_C(\tau_i) = 1$.
- If $\alpha_i = \mathsf{finishStart}$, then
  - if $\phi_i \models \mathsf{RTF}$, then $weight_C(\tau_i) = -1$,
  - if $\phi_i \models \neg\mathsf{RTF}$, $A_i = A_{i+1}$, and either $\phi_i \models \mathsf{STP}$ or $\mathsf{Lmd}(A_{i+1}) = \mathsf{STP}$, then $weight_C(\tau_i) = -1$,
  - otherwise, $weight_C(\tau_i) = 0$.

If a witness cycle exists for some $A \in \mathsf{Act_{real}}$, the algorithm returns "stack unbounded". Otherwise, if Δ is a directed acyclic graph, then the algorithm returns "stack bounded". Otherwise, the procedure reports "unknown".

The more general cases for $k \geq 1$ are much more technical and involved. We introduce the concept of "virtual transitions" for tasks to capture the situation that the content of a task can be indirectly modified by first jumping off the task and returning to the task later on. When this happens, the procedure adds virtual transitions for each task before checking the existence of witness cycles. The details of the procedure can be found in the full version [6].

As mentioned before, stack unboundedness suggests a potential security vulnerability. As a result, when this is spotted, it is desirable to synthesize a concrete transition sequence so that the developers can, for instance, follow this sequence to test and improve their apps. It turns out that the synthesis can be reduced to the more general version of the configuration reachability problem mentioned in the back pattern analysis. This can be easily incorporated and has been implemented in the tool.

5   Evaluation

We implement the procedures in Sect. 4 and develop a tool TaskDroid which comprises two modules, APP2ASM and ASMAnalyzer.

The former module builds ASM models from Android apps. The inputs of APP2ASM are either Android PacKage (apk) files or simply source codes. APP2ASM is based on the widely adopted Java bytecode analysis framework soot [14]. APP2ASM uses soot to create call graphs (CG) to represent the calling relationship between functions, and the control flow graphs (CFG) of functions to represent the control flow of the function bodies. APP2ASM includes two sub-modules, i.e., *Manifest Analyzer* and *Transition Extractor* which generate the signature Sig and the transition relation Δ of the ASM model respectively (cf. Definition 1). Manifest Analyzer extracts the manifest file from the source code or by decompiling the apk file. It then obtains the signature Sig from the manifest file. Moreover, it also gets the intent filters from the manifest file and passes them to the Transition Extractor for further analysis. Transition Extractor constructs the transition relation Δ from the call graph and the control flow graphs of functions (cf. Sect. 4.1). In order to make the model-building process more efficient, Transition Extractor applies the program slicing technique to extract those statements that are related to the attributes of intent objects corresponding to callee activity classes, intent flags, as well as actions, categories, and data of intent filters.

ASMAnalyzer carries out the static analysis on ASM models. ASMAnalyzer includes two submodules for *Reachability analysis* and *Boundedness analysis* respectively which implement the procedures given in Sect. 4.2. Note that the Reachability submodule can generate witness paths for reachability. The Boundedness submodule utilises the Reachability module to generate a path starting from the main activity when the ASM is found to be stack unbounded.

Benchmarks. The benchmarks comprise 4,496 apps (apk files) collected from three sources, i.e., the open-source F-Droid repository (https://f-droid.org/), the Google Play market, and app market Wandoujia (https://www.wandoujia.com/). The statistics of these apps can be found in Table 1. For F-Droid, we use a web crawler to download all the available apps. For Google Play (resp. the app market X), we download the first 500 apps of each of the 32 categories (resp. 14 categories) according to the displaying order. (Note that Google Play disallows direct app-downloading, so we use a third-party website APKLeecher http://apkleecher.com/.) Note that we have removed the apps that use fragment components which are not considered in this paper.

Table 1. Statistics of the benchmarks

Source	F-Droid	Google play	Market Wandoujia
Num. of apps	674(15.0%)	2,068(46.0%)	1,754(39.0%)
Avg. Size	3.1 MB	15 MB	18 MB
Max. Size	158.0 MB	103.9 MB	428.7 MB
Total num. of apps	4,496		

We carry out all experiments on a Linux server with a CPU of Intel® Xeon® Processor E5-2680 v4 at 2.40 GHz and 64 GB memory.

5.1   Scalability of Our Approaches

APP2ASM. We evaluate the scalability of APP2ASM on the 4,496 apps, where the timeout is set to 600 s. The experimental results are shown in Table 2. Out of these 4,496 apps, there are 1,251 apps that the soot tool fails to handle. The average/maximum time of APP2ASM on these apps is 33.7/599.2 s. In the end, APP2ASM outputs 3,245 ASM models to the ASMAnalyzer module.

Table 2. Scalability: APP2ASM

Total num. of apps	Num. of soot-failing apps	Avg. time	Max. time
4,496	1,251	33.7 s	599.2 s
Num. of ASMs output by APP2ASM			
3,245			

Reachability Analysis. We evaluate the performance of the Reachability analysis submodule by carrying out the back pattern analysis on the 3,245 ASMs (generated by the APP2ASM module), where the stack height bound $\hbar$ is set to 4 and the timeout period is set to 60 s. The experimental results are shown in Table 3. Only 9 (0.3%) ASMs out of the 3,245 ASMs time out. Furthermore, relatively large ASM models (e.g., with 50 activities and 128 transitions, or 72 activities and 72 transitions) can be handled successfully. The average (resp. maximum) running time is only 0.1 s (resp. 3.3 s).

Boundedness Analysis. We evaluate the performance of the Boundedness submodule based on the same 3,245 ASM models. The parameter k (i..e., the number of interplaying tasks, cf. Sect. 4.2) is set to 2 and the timeout is set to 60 s. The experimental results are shown in Table 4. On this occasion, no timeout happened and the average (resp. maximum) running time is only 0.01 (resp. 0.4) s.

It is noteworthy that, for the reachability analysis, we hypothesize that the heights of involved tasks are bounded by a small number (i.e., $\hbar \leq 4$). Likewise, for the stack-boundedness analysis, we hypothesize that only a small number of tasks are involved ($k \leq 2$). In the full version [6] we empirically justify these hypotheses which give sufficiently precise results for the $\hbar$ and k we have set.

Table 3. Scalability: reachability (Back pattern)

Avg. size ($|\mathsf{Act}|, |\Delta|$) of ASMs	(6.7, 12.0)
Max. size ($|\mathsf{Act}|, |\Delta|$) of ASMs	(130, 292)/(63, 677)
Num. of T.O. ASMs	9(0.3%)
Max. size of non-T.O. ASMs	(50, 128)/(72, 72)
Avg. time	0.1 s
Max. time	3.3 s
Avg. of $|\mathsf{Act}_{\mathsf{back}}(A)|$	1.7
Max. of $|\mathsf{Act}_{\mathsf{back}}(A)|$	18

Table 4. Scalability: boundedness

Total num. of ASMs	3,245
Avg. size ($|\mathsf{Act}|, |\Delta|$) of ASMs	(6.7, 12.0)
Max. size ($|\mathsf{Act}|, |\Delta|$) of ASMs	(130, 292)/(63, 677)
Num. of T.O. ASMs	0
Num. of stack-unbounded ASMs	989
Avg. time	0.01 s
Max. time	0.4 s

The experimental results demonstrate efficiency and scalability of the model construction and static analysis when applied to real-world Android apps.

5.2 Threat of Stack Unboundedness

As shown in the preceding section, TaskDroid has discovered that 989 ASMs out of 3,245 ASMs are stack unbounded (cf. Table 4). We investigate whether the stack unboundedness pose genuine threats in practice. Out of those 989 stack-unbounded ASMs, we select apps from F-Droid as examples to evaluate the threat of the stack-unboundedness.[9] We carry out the experiments using Android Emulator[10] to create a virtual device for Nexus 6 (RAM size 512 MB, heap size 16 MB, and Android version 7.1.1). Moreover, we use Monkey[11] and ADB (Android Debug Bridge[12]) tools. The experiments proceed in the following steps: (1) Generate a witness cycle as well as a reachability path for stack unboundedness. (Note that the witness cycle is a segment of the reachability path.) (2) For each activity A in the reachability path, locate the UI widget corresponding to A by reading the source code and locating the occurrence of the intent object corresponding to the activation of A. (3) Find the coordinates of the UI widgets which are used to generate a Monkey script, specifically, a sequence of click operations, to simulate the witness cycle. (4) Install the app in the virtual device, simulate the sequence of click operations manually until reaching the witness cycle, then use Monkey to repeatedly run the script (corresponding to the witness cycle). We use ADB to obtain the number of activities in tasks and calculate the number of repetitions of the witness cycle.

The results of the experiments are reported in Table 5. Out of the analysed 101 F-Droid apps, the witness cycles synthesized by TaskDroid can be successfully simulated in 29 apps. After hundreds or thousands of repetitions of the

---

[9] The experiments need considerable manual work and are very time-consuming, we choose to conduct experiments on the F-Droid apps only as they are relatively small in size. We plan to carry out more extensive experiments in the near future.

[10] https://developer.android.com/studio/run/emulator.

[11] http://developer.android.com/tools/help/monkey.html.

[12] https://developer.android.com/studio/command-line/adb.

witness cycle, the 29 apps end up with either app crash, or black screen, or even rebooting of device. These suggest that stack-unbounded apps can be potentially harmful to, and thus a vulnerability of, the Android system, highlighting the importance of such an analysis. For the other 72 apps, we were unable to simulate the witness cycles, due to the following reasons: login is required (23 apps), apps crash immediately after launching (14 apps), ASM models are imprecise (35 apps) so the potential threat returned by TaskDroid may be spurious.

Table 5. Threat of stack unboundedness

Abnormal behavior	Num. of apps	Num. of repetitions of the witness cycle		
		Avg.	Min.	Max
App crash	21	709	66	1418
Black screen	6	1002	228	1213
Device reboot	2	2451	406	4495

6   Conclusion

We have provided a rigorous formalization of the Android multitasking mechanism, which gives a considerably more complete and concise account of the evolution of the Android task stack in relation to activity activation, and highlights the discrepancy between the semantics of different Android versions. Based on the formalized Android stack machine model and its semantics, we have provided new modeling and static analysis methods for Android apps, which have been implemented in a prototype tool TaskDroid. Experiments on large-scale benchmarks confirmed the efficacy and efficiency of our approaches.

Future work includes further improving the precision of the ASM modeling and analysis, more extensive experiments on Android app markets, and in-depth investigations of the decidability and complexity of static analysis.

Acknowledgements. This work is partially supported by the NSFC grants (No. 61672505, 61872340, 61572478), Key Research Program of Frontier Sciences, Chinese Academy of Sciences (No. QYZDJ-SSW-JSC036), Guangdong Science and Technology Department grant (No. 2018B010107004), the Open Project of Shanghai Key Laboratory of Trustworthy Computing (No. 07dz22304201601), and the INRIA-CAS joint research project VIP. Taolue Chen is also partially supported by Birkbeck BEI School Project (ARTEFACT) and an oversea grant from the State Key Laboratory of Novel Software Technology, Nanjing University (KFKT2018A16).

References

1. Android documentation. https://developer.android.com/guide/components/activities/tasks-and-back-stack.html

2. Azim, T., Neamtiu, I.: Targeted and depth-first exploration for systematic testing of android apps. In: OOPSLA, pp. 641–660 (2013)
3. Bianchi, A., Corbetta, J., Invernizzi, L., Fratantonio, Y., Kruegel, C., Vigna, G.: What the app is that? deception and countermeasures in the android user interface. In: SP 2015, pp. 931–948 (2015)
4. Cavada, R., et al.: The NUXMV symbolic model checker. In: Biere, A., Bloem, R. (eds.) CAV 2014. LNCS, vol. 8559, pp. 334–342. Springer, Cham (2014). https://doi.org/10.1007/978-3-319-08867-9_22
5. Chen, T., He, J., Song, F., Wang, G., Wu, Z., Yan, J.: Android stack machine. In: Chockler, H., Weissenbacher, G. (eds.) CAV 2018. LNCS, vol. 10982, pp. 487–504. Springer, Cham (2018). https://doi.org/10.1007/978-3-319-96142-2_29
6. He, J., Chen, T., Wang, P., Wu, Z., Yan, J.: Android multitasking mechanism: Formal semantics and static analysis of apps (Full version) (2019). https://github.com/LoringHe/TaskDroid
7. Lee, S., Hwang, S., Ryu, S.: All about activity injection: threats, semantics, and detection. In: ASE 2017, pp. 252–262 (2017)
8. Lee, S., Hwang, S., Ryu, S.: Operational semantics for the android activity activation mechanism. Technical report (2017)
9. Li, L., et al.: Static analysis of android apps: a systematic literature review. Inform. Softw. Technol. 88, 67–95 (2017)
10. Liu, J., Wu, D., Xue, J.: TDroid: exposing app switching attacks in android with control flow specialization. In: ASE 2018, pp. 236–247 (2018)
11. Octeau, D., et al.: Combining static analysis with probabilistic models to enable market-scale android inter-component analysis. In: POPL 2016, pp. 469–484 (2016)
12. Octeau, D., Luchaup, D., Jha, S., McDaniel, P.D.: Composite constant propagation and its application to android program analysis. IEEE Trans. Software Eng. 42(11), 999–1014 (2016)
13. Ren, C., Zhang, Y., Xue, H., Wei, T., Liu, P.: Towards discovering and understanding task hijacking in android. In: USENIX Security, pp. 945–959 (2015)
14. Vallée-Rai, R., Co, P., Gagnon, E., Hendren, L.J., Lam, P., Sundaresan, V.: Soot – a Java bytecode optimization framework. In: Proceedings of the 1999 conference of the Centre for Advanced Studies on Collaborative Research (1999)
15. Xiao, Y., Bai, G., Mao, J., Liang, Z., Cheng, W.: Privilege leakage and information stealing through the android task mechanism. In: PAC 2017, pp. 152–163 (2017)
16. Yan, J., Wu, T., Yan, J., Zhang, J.: Widget-sensitive and back-stack-aware GUI exploration for testing android apps. In: QRS 2017, pp. 42–53 (2017)
17. Yang, S., Zhang, H., Wu, H., Wang, Y., Yan, D., Rountev, A.: Static window transition graphs for android. In: ASE 2015, pp. 658–668 (2015)
18. Zhang, Y., Sui, Y., Xue, J.: Launch-mode-aware context-sensitive activity transition analysis. In: ICSE 2018, pp. 598–608 (2018)
19. Zhao, J., Albarghouthi, A., Rastogi, V., Jha, S., Octeau, D.: Neural-augmented static analysis of android communication. In: FSE 2018, pp. 342–353 (2018)

Conflict Abstractions and Shadow Speculation for Optimistic Transactional Objects

Thomas Dickerson[1], Eric Koskinen[2(✉)], Paul Gazzillo[3], and Maurice Herlihy[1]

[1] Brown University, Providence, USA
thomas_dickerson@alumni.brown.edu
[2] Stevens Institute of Technology, Hoboken, USA
eric.koskinen@stevens.edu
[3] University of Central Florida, Orlando, USA

Abstract. Concurrent data structures implemented with software transactional memory (STM) perform poorly when operations which do not conflict in the definition of the abstract data type nonetheless incur conflicts in the concrete state of an implementation. Several works addressed various aspects of this problem, yet we still lack efficient, general-purpose mechanisms that allow one to readily integrate black-box concurrent data-structures into existing STM frameworks.

In this paper we take a step further toward this goal, by focusing on the challenge of how to use black-box concurrent data structures in an *optimistic* transactional manner, while exploiting an off-the-shelf STM for transaction-level conflict detection. To this end, we introduce two new enabling concepts. First, we define data-structure conflict in terms of commutativity but, unlike prior work, we introduce a new format called *conflict abstractions*, which is kept separate from the object implementation and is fit for optimistic conflict detection. Second, we describe *shadow speculation* for wrapping off-the-shelf concurrent objects so that updates can be speculatively and opaquely applied—and even return values observed—but then later dropped (on abort) or else atomically applied (on commit). We have realized these concepts in a new open-source transactional system called ScalaPROUST, built on top of ScalaSTM and report encouraging experimental results.

Further detail and experimental results can be found in the extended version of this paper [8].

1 Introduction

Modern software transactional memory (STM) systems typically perform synchronization on the basis of *read-write* conflicts: two transactions conflict if they access the same memory location, and at least one access is a write. It is well

E. Koskinen—Partially supported by NSF Award #1618542.
P. Gazzillo—Partially supported by NSF Awards #1618542 and #1840934.
Brown University—Partially supported by NSF Awards #1561807 and #1908806.

understood that this technique works poorly for contended data objects because operations that could have correctly executed concurrently are deemed to conflict, causing unnecessary rollbacks and serialization.

Some prior works were aimed at this problem and found solutions to some cases. Transactional Boosting [17] centers around constructing a transactional "wrapper" for legacy thread-safe concurrent data structures. Designing a boosting wrapper requires identifying which operations commute, as well as providing operation inverses. Boosting can take advantage of existing thread-safe libraries, so there is no need to re-invent the wheel, but is limited to pessimistic treatment of object operations. Hassan *et al.* [14] provide an optimistic strategy, but requires white-box access to the data-structure. Transactional Predication [4] maps semantic conflicts onto read-write conflicts handled by an underlying STM. Predication can exploit highly-optimized mechanisms provided by off-the-shelf STM systems, but applies only to sets and maps. Software Transactional Objects (STO) [18] is an STM design that provides built-in primitives to track conflicts among arbitrary operations, not just read-write conflicts. Similarly, Transactional Data Structure Libraries [30] describes techniques for building libraries of transaction-aware data structures. The latter two works do not readily support existing concurrent ADT implementations (*e.g.* `java.util.concurrent`), which would be appealing because these implementations are highly optimized.

Despite the advances noted above, we still lack general approaches to building transactional systems that exploit both the conflict resolution of state-of-the-art STM systems, as well as the high performance of off-the-shelf concurrent abstract data type (ADT) implementations. Here is an example: imagine we wanted to use an off-the-shelf concurrent priority queue that supported efficient (copy-on-write) snapshots, but had no efficient inverse for `insert`. These seemingly simple requirements escape all prior techniques. Predication [4] doesn't quite fit the bill because it is limited to sets/maps. Optimistic boosting [14] requires white-box access to the data-structure. Boosting [17] could be made to work with an inefficient synthetic inverse; however, it would still require pessimistic synchronization, which isn't a good fit for most STMs. Thus, new abstractions must be developed to support efficient use of ADTs with STM systems.

This paper takes a step further toward this goal: we address the challenge of how to allow updates to black-box highly concurrent objects to be performed optimistically, while exploiting off-the-shelf STMs. To this end, we introduce two new key concepts—*conflict abstractions* and *shadow speculation*—which, together, enable programmers to build such transactional systems.

We first consider the challenge of defining and detecting conflict. Conflict between ADT operations is typically understood in terms of commutativity specifications [2,17,23,31] which are implementation-independent, but aren't easily translated into code. To resolve this tension, we introduce an approximation of commutativity, called *conflict abstractions* specifically fit for *optimistic* synchronization. We build upon the idea that commutativity-based conflict specifications can be kept separate from object itself, by extending the concept to keep *implementations* of commutativity-based conflict detection separate from the implementation of the data structure. In fact, we can even use the STM itself to detect non-commutativity, even when the data structure implementation doesn't use the STM at all. The principal advantage is that a programmer can readily integrate an off-the-shelf concurrent object into a transactional setting, without knowing the complex implementation details of the object. Instead, the programmer simply needs to understand the abstract type.

Conflict abstractions can be used with optimistic STMs (such as ScalaSTM) to enable optimistic commutativity-based conflict detection. But now how do we cope with operations being speculatively applied to the objects themselves? One could potentially delay the application of operations to commit time, but what about operations that involve return values that are needed by the transaction to continue? This requires the ability to predict the effects of operations which have not yet been applied. To this end, we introduce the idea of *shadow speculation*, allowing a transaction to speculatively apply ADT operations to an object while ensuring the updates cannot be viewed by concurrent transactions. These updates can be atomically applied at commit time or else discarded in the case of an abort. This is achieved by first tracking operation replay logs. We then describe two strategies (based on *snapshots* and *memoization*) that each allow transactions to maintain their own shadow of a shared data structure and observe return values of their speculative operations. By combining these shadow copies with commutativity-based conflict abstractions, we enable non-commutative operations to be applied speculatively to off-the-shelf ADTs and in a way that is opaque to concurrent transactions.

We have incorporated these ideas into a new transactional object system called ScalaPROUST[1], built on top of ScalaSTM. ScalaPROUST, unlike predication, goes beyond sets/maps and can support objects of arbitrary abstract type such as priority queues and non-zero indicators. Meanwhile, unlike boosting, ScalaPROUST allows optimistic synchronization and integrates with the underlying STM, to take advantage of well-engineered STM conflict-detection mechanisms. While the ScalaPROUST tool also supports pessimistic updates, this paper focuses on contributions pertaining to optimistic updates.

In summary, we make the following contributions:

1. *Conflict abstractions* provide a novel way to concretely realize an abstract data type's semantic notions of conflict so it can efficiently cooperate with a generic software transactional memory run-time (Sect. 3).
2. *Shadow speculation* allows individual transactions to make private speculative updates to highly-concurrent black-box objects (Sect. 4).
3. *The* ScalaPROUST *transactional system*,[2] built on top of ScalaSTM and combines off-the-shelf ADTs with existing STMs (Sect. 5).
4. *An experimental evaluation* demonstrates scalability competitive with existing specialized approaches such as transactional predication, but with a wider range of applicability (Sect. 6).

---

[1] This name is a portmanteau of *predication* and *boosting*, both influential prior works. The name is also an *hommage* to Marcel Proust, an author famous for his exploration of the complexities of memory.

[2] www.github.com/ScalaProust/ScalaProust/.

Limitations. The mechanisms described in this paper are designed for transactional objects and currently don't support mixtures between transactional objects and STM-managed read/write operations. We leave this to future work. This paper makes conceptual contributions and experimental demonstrates their impact. A proof of opacity could perhaps be achieved by adapting existing theoretical models (*e.g.* [22]), another important step for future work.

2   Overview

We now highlight the key ideas of this paper with two example concurrent ADTs—a priority queue and a non-zero indicator (NZI)—and describe how *conflict abstractions* and *shadow speculation* allow black box implementations of the ADTs to be used optimistically with an off-the-shelf STM.

2.1   From Commutativity to Conflict Abstractions

Let us first consider the priority queue ADT, supporting the three operations min()/x, removeMin()/x, and insert(x). We assume that the programmer already has a concurrent implementation (*e.g.* from java.util.concurrent). Moreover, like in transactional boosting [17], we will first require the programmer to be aware which operations commute under which circumstances. (Recent work has shown that commutativity can be synthesized from the ADT's specification [1].) We say that two ADT operations *commute* provided that they lead to the same final state and return the same values, regardless of the order in which they are applied. As a reminder, the table to the right summarizes sound commutativity conditions for pairs of priority queue

	min()/x	removeMin()/x	insert(x)
min()/y	true	false	$y \leq x$
removeMin()/y	false	$x = y$	$y \leq x$
insert(y)	$y \geq x$	$y \geq x$	true

operations. For a more complete collection of commutativity conditions of ADTs, see [1,19]. In the above example, insert(42) always commutes with removeMin()/1 because the value inserted (42) was greater than the minimum value (1) in the priority queue. Also, insertions always commute because the internal order of the inserted elements will be dictated by their values.

   While commutativity specifications benefit from being independent of the implementation, they are difficult to translate into program source code. In the pessimistic setting, transactional boosting [17] uses so-called abstract locking and, for priority queues, gives an example of a single read/write lock to approximate commutativity. The challenge remains: how can we use commutativity specifications as the basis for *optimistic* conflict detection and, moreover, can we exploit black-box optimistic STMs to perform this abstract conflict detection?

   Toward this challenge, we begin by introducing *conflict abstractions*. The idea is to approximate commutativity-based conflict detection by using the STM itself, keeping the implementation of conflict detection separate from the implementation of the ADT (which may not even use the STM at all). Let's say thread T_1 would like to perform min() and thread T_2 would like to perform `removeMin()`. The (logical) commutativity of these operations tells us that we should assume these operations conflict. The idea of a conflict abstraction is to represent this logical notion of conflict by introducing *concrete* STM-managed variables and rules for when those variables should be read/written so that the STM will detect a conflict when these two transactions try to proceed with non-commutative operations. As a trivial example, we could create a new variable v, and require T_1 to read v and T_2 to write (some random fresh value) to v. In this way, the $read(v)$ summarizes the logical "read-only" nature of `min`, while the $write(v)$ summarizes the logical update made by `removeMin()`. Notice that we have now (in a limited way) tricked the STM to perform commutativity-based conflict detection and have not had to touch the internals of the priority queue. Note that, in some cases, this new variable v could potentially be removed by a compiler, and so we must protect v with an annotation such as `volatile`.

Let's now generalize beyond this single-variable example. The idea is that threads summarize the ADT operations they plan to perform—a sort of *digest*—through a few read/write operations on some freshly-introduced STM-managed variables. The primitives in this digest are chosen to reflect various conceptual aspects of the object's abstract state (*e.g.* a priority queue's minimum value, size, and multiset). This digest, if written correctly, is such that whenever the ADT operations being performed by two threads do not commute, operations on the digest primitives will be found to conflict. This mapping of abstract state to STM variables, and the rules for which to read and which to write—as a function of the ADT operation being performed—is what we call a *conflict abstraction*. Here is a conflict abstraction for the priority queue ADT:

Conflict Abstraction for Priority Queue
CA STM vars: $v_{min}, v_{incr}, v_{decr}$, with CA operation rules:

`min()/x` $: rd(v_{min})$
`removeMin()/x` $: wr(v_{decr}); wr(v_{min})$
`insert(x)` $: wr(v_{incr}); \text{if } (x < \text{min()})) \ wr(v_{min}) \text{ else } rd(v_{min})$
`size()/n` $: rd(v_{decr}); rd(v_{incr})$

In this conflict abstraction (CA), we use STM-managed variables v_{min}, v_{incr}, and v_{decr}. Intuitively, v_{min} summarizes whether operations are somehow dependent upon the minimum element. Writing to variable v_{incr} summarizes whether the operation increases the size of the queue, while reading from v_{incr} indicates that the operation is sensitive to whether the size will increase. v_{decr} is similar. Notice that if we take *any* initial state, and consider *any* pair of ADT operations, if the CA operation rules are followed, then the STM will detect some kind of conflict on at least one of the memory locations v_{min}, v_{incr} or v_{decr}.

As an example, let's say that we have operations T_1 : `removeMin()/42` and T_2 : `insert(1)`. In general these operations do not commute because the element being inserted is less than the current minimum value so, depending on the order of the operations, T_1 will observe different values (and the final state of the ADT will be different). Following the CA operation rules, T_1 will write v_{decr} and write v_{min}. Meanwhile, T_2 will write v_{incr} and either read or write v_{min}, depending on the ADT's current `min`. (Here `min` is a another ADT method, which will itself perform a read on v_{min}.) Off-the-shelf STMs will detect some kind of conflict, e.g., a write/read or write/write conflict on v_{min}, effectively doing the work of non-commutativity detection. On the other hand, let's assume that initially 33 is the minimal element of the priority queue and consider two commutative operations: T_1 : `insert`(42) and T_2 : `min`/33. In this case T_1 will write v_{incr} and read v_{min}, while T_2 will read v_{min}. An off-the-self STM won't detect any conflicts (two reads on v_{min} don't conflict), correctly reflecting that these abstract ADT operations commute.

This approach is not limited to priority queues. Let's consider a second example: a Counter that is capable of non-zero indication (NZI), as inspired by Ellen *et al.* [10]. Like the priority queue, this is a standard ADT, but not a map/set-like structure required by predication [4]. NZI provides three operations: `inc()`, `dec()`/p, `zero()`/p, where `dec()` returns a flag indicating if the operation failed because the NZI was already zero. The commutativity is to the right. Two `inc()` operations are independent, as are two `zero()` operations.

	`inc()`	`dec()`/p	`zero()`/p
`inc()`	true	$\neg p$	$\neg p$
`dec()`/q	$\neg q$	$q = p$	$q = p$
`zero()`/q	$\neg q$	$q = p$	true

Naturally, an `inc()` may alter the return value of `zero()` and `dec()` which further complicates matters. In these cases, commutativity depends on the return values of `dec()` and `zero()`. Once again, we cannot directly use this commutativity specification, because it is not in a format readily understood by STMs. The following corresponding conflict abstraction can be:

Conflict Abstraction for Non-Zero Indicator (NZI)
CA STM vars: v_{zero}, with CA operation rules:

> `inc()`   : if (`zero()`) $wr(v_{zero})$ else $rd(v_{zero})$
> `dec()`/q : if (`willBeZero()`) $wr(v_{zero})$ else $rd(v_{zero})$
> `zero()`/q : $read(v_{zero})$

For NZI, one can use a *single* STM memory location v_{zero} to summarize the abstract conflict. As we discuss in Sect. 3, one can construct a CA differently, depending on the ADT and how finely grained one would like to characterize conflict. Taking an example of T_1 : `inc()` and T_2 : `zero()`, it is easy to see that an STM will detect conflict on v_{zero}, depending on whether the NZI is zero. Notice that we have used `zero()` which, itself is an operation. The ScalaPROUST system, outlined in Sect. 5, is able to support CAs that, themselves contain other method calls, by collecting transitive dependencies. Our conflict abstraction above also used another helper method `willBeZero()`. This function depends not only the NZI ADT's current state, but also on potential future states, to characterize its commutativity. In the Sect. 4 we will describe how we support such helper functions to examine aspects of the state (and even predicted state) and enable more precise conflict abstractions.

While this paper focuses on optimism, as a side node, conflict abstractions can also be used for pessimistic conflict detection, by defining boosting-like abstract locks. Each CA variable can instead be a lock and the conflict abstraction indicates whether the lock should be acquired in read or write mode.

2.2 Support for Shadow Speculation

While conflict abstractions provide a route to optimistic, commutativity-based conflict detection, the question remains: is it safe to perform the ADT operations optimistically? The answer is, of course, no. Optimistic transactions may abort and, to ensure opacity, their uncommitted effects must not be observed by concurrent transactions. The next idea of this paper—called *shadow speculation*—allow one to take an off-the-shelf ADT implementation and perform speculative updates on it, and even view return values. Our strategy makes these speculative updates invisible to concurrent transactions and permits them to be either discarded (on abort) or atomically applied (on commit). In Sect. 4 we describe how to achieve shadow speculation using a combination of wrappers, operation replay logs, and one of two techniques to predict values: *fast snapshots* and *memoization*.

2.3 The ScalaPROUST Transactional System

With conflict abstractions and shadow speculation, we now have a path to use black-box ADTs in an optimistic setting, with black-box optimistic STMs. In Sect. 5 we discuss ScalaPROUST, built on top of ScalaSTM [5].

In Sect. 6 we conclude with an evaluation, demonstrating that black-box ADT implementations can be used on top of high-performance STMs with optimistic read/write conflict detection. Moreover, we can obtain performance that is on the order of transactional predication, yet permits a more expressive class of objects (beyond map/set-like structures).

2.4 Related Work

In Sect. 1, we noted prior works including transactional boosting [17], transactional predication [4], optimistic boosting [14], software transactional objects [18], and transactional data structure libraries [30]. While these prior works were sources of inspiration, each of them tackled slightly different problems. The concepts of conflict abstractions and shadow speculation described here are novel, as well as our new ScalaPROUST transactional system.

Two aforementioned recent works aimed at developing data-structure *implementations* from the ground-up so that they are amenable to a transactional setting. Herman *et al.* [18] build on top of a core infrastructure that provides operations on version numbers and abstract tracking sets that can be used to make object-specific decisions at commit time. Spiegelman *et al.* [30] describe how to build data-structure libraries using traditional STM read/write tracking primitives. In this way, the implementation can exploit these STM internals. Unlike these prior works, our aim is to reuse existing linearizable objects and exploit the decades of hard-work and ingenuity that went into their implementations.

In recent years, it has been shown the commutativity can be verified [19] or even synthesized [1] from ADT specifications. Early work on exploiting commutativity for concurrency control includes Korth [20], Weihl [32], CRDTs [29], and Galois [24]. Some false conflicts in STMs can be alleviated by other escape mechanisms such as open nesting [25], elastic transactions [11], and transactional collection classes [6]. Other mechanisms that exploit commutativity include automatic semantic locking [13] and dynamic race detection [9].

3   Conflict Abstractions

The principal challenge for any type-specific transactional object implementation is how to map type-specific notions of conflict into a low-level synchronization framework. Like others [4,17,21,22], we identify type-specific synchronization conflicts with a *failure to commute*: two operations commute if applying them in either order yields the same return values and the same final object state. In this section, we describe *conflict abstractions* which permit optimistic transactional conflict detection, without exposing the internals of a black-box object. Our approach symbolically represents aspects of the object's abstract state as STM-managed memory locations, kept separate from the ADT implementation itself.

We will use the following definitions. $\mathcal{M}$ are the set of object *methods* $o.m, o.n$, etc. A method *signature* is denoted $o.m(\bar{x})$ where $\bar{x}$ represents the vector of arguments to method m. $\mathcal{A}$ are method argument *values*. We denote a vector of argument values as $\bar{\alpha}$ where each element α is the value for the corresponding element in $\bar{x}$ (as denoted earlier in this paper). An *invocation* is an application of a method to a vector of arguments, $o.m(\bar{\alpha}), o.n(\bar{\beta})$, etc. Σ_o is the *abstract* state space for object o; we do not need to model the implementation of o. We also assume that the object provides (or can be extended to provide) various read-only methods that permit a transaction to query aspects of the object's abstract state, such as $o.\texttt{size}()$, etc. Finally, we write $P : \Sigma \to \mathbb{B}$ to be the type of a state predicate.

As discussed in Sect. 2.1, a conflict abstraction (CA) is a way of approximating commutativity by summarizing the effects of black-box object methods using a series of memory operations. More precisely,

Definition 1 (Conflict abstraction). *A conflict abstraction is a pair* (X, f) *where X is a finite set of variables and* $f : \mathcal{M} \to \mathcal{A} \to \Sigma \to (P \times X \times \{\textsf{rd}, \textsf{wr}\})$ *list.*

Intuitively, a conflict abstraction first has a set of abstract locations X, representing STM-managed memory (or locks if used pessimistically). For a given object method $o.m(\bar{\alpha})$ with arguments $\bar{\alpha}$ and object state σ_o, the conflict abstraction function f returns a list of $(p, x, mode)$ tuples. Each tuple consists of a condition p, a location x and a mode (read or write). For each tuple, if the condition p holds, then the thread is instructed to access location x with the given read-vs-write mode. Recall from Sect. 2.1 the priority queue example. We can now define the conflict abstraction so that $f(o.insert, [1], \sigma_{pq}) = \{(\textsf{true}, v_{incr}, \textsf{wr}), (1 < o.\texttt{min}(),$

$v_{min}, \mathsf{wr}), (1 \geq o.\mathsf{min}(), v_{min}, \mathsf{rd})\}$. That is, the transaction is instructed to write to v_{incr} and then read or write to v_{min} depending on whether 1 is less than the current minimum value. (Note $o.\mathsf{min}()$ appears in the CA of $o.\mathsf{insert}()$, so $o.\mathsf{insert}()$'s CA depends on $o.\mathsf{min}()$'s.) Similarly, we let $f(o.min, [], \sigma_{pq}) = \{(true, v_{min}, \mathsf{rd})\}$. In Sect. 5 we describe how these conflict abstractions are used inside "wrappers" so that transactions perform these STM read/write operations just before the corresponding operation and again before commit.

The impact of conflict abstractions is that we can leverage an STM to perform transactional conflict detection, even though the ADT is treated as black-box. In the above example, the STM will detect a read/write conflict on v_{min} and we have enabled efficient STMs to do the work of conflict detection.

Conflict abstractions have several benefits over conflict strategies based on abstract locks [17] or commutativity alone. The format of a conflict abstraction is more algorithmic and less declarative than prior strategies. A programmer will already have at least an intuitive understanding of the black-box object's abstract state, and it is easier to translate this into a series of STM locations and read/write operations. This avoids the need to think about pair-wise reasoning (as in commutativity or abstract locks) upfront: one instead simply considers the effects of each operation independently. Later, one can verify the correctness of their conflict abstraction through pair-wise reasoning (see discussion below).

Notice that a conflict abstraction can be more fine-grained or more coarse-grained with respect to how it represents the object's abstract state. A trivial coarse-grained conflict abstraction would have cardinality 1 and use a single STM location x, and map all read-oriented object methods to read x and map all object mutator methods to write x. While simple and correct, the downside is of course that concurrency may be lost. The choice of granularity (cardinality) is often specific to the data structure and the workload. Regardless, it is important that the conflict abstraction be correct:

Definition 2 (Correctness). *A conflict abstraction (X, f) is correct provided that for every $m(\bar{\alpha})$ and $n(\bar{\beta})$ that do not commute, and every σ_o, there exists some $(p, v, m_1) \in f(o.m, \bar{\alpha}, \sigma_o)$ and $(q, v, m_2) \in f(o.n, \bar{\beta}, \sigma_o)$ such that $p(\sigma_o)$ and $q(\sigma_o)$ and either $m_1 = \mathsf{wr}$ or $m_2 = \mathsf{wr}$.*

A CA is correct if, for any pair of non-commutative method invocations, there will be some location with either a read/write or write/write conflict.

Verifying Conflict Abstractions. Existing software verification tools can verify the correctness of a conflict abstraction. Specifically, the question of correctness can be reduced to satisfiability, fit for reasoning with SAT/SMT tools. We do not need the ADT's implementation; instead, it is sufficient to work with a model (or sequential implementation) of the abstract data type. As done previously [1], it is easy to model a variety of ADTs in SMT.

Once we have modeled object methods m and n, we further model conflict abstractions. SMT reasoning then proceeds by asserting the following series of constraints: (1) Method m performs its conflict abstraction reads/writes. (2) Method m performs its data-structure operation. (3) Method n performs its conflict abstraction reads/writes. (4) No read/write or write/write conflict occurs. (5) Method n performs its data-structure operation. We now need to ensure that the resulting state is the same as it would have been if the operations executed in the opposite order. Using different variable names for the intermediate states, we then assert the other order (n before m). Finally, we assert that the results (return values and final state) were different and check whether this is satisfiable. If it is not satisfiable, then the conflict abstraction is correct.

Other ADTs. To highlight the generality of our approach, we now describe conflict abstractions for some other ADTs.

– *Stack.* Since stack operations are typically focused only on the top element, most operations conflict. A suitable conflict abstraction can consist of a single variable v, where both **push** and **pop** write to v. If the stack supports a **peek** operation (*i.e.* inspecting the top element without removing it), then **peek** can simply perform a read of v, enabling concurrent **peek** operations. A more sophisticated conflict abstraction could take into account the *values* on the stack.

– *Sets and Map.* A conflict abstraction for a Set or Map can use a strategy similar to boosting [17]. Since the number of elements/keys could be large, one may not want a CA that separately tracks each element or key. Instead, some smaller number N of CA locations can be used and, when an element e is accessed, the CA can instead read or write location $v_{e\%N}$. The choice of N can depend on the workload. Naturally, **put(k,v)**, for example, would write to location $v_{k\%N}$, while **get(k)** would read.

– *Directed Graph.* Consider a directed graph with methods **addNode(nid)**, **addEdge(nid,nid')**, and **getNext(nid)/nids**. As with Sets and Hashtables, the number of nodes n may be large so we may want to only have some $N << n$ CA locations. We can thus define a conflict abstraction (X, f) where $X = \{v_0, \ldots, v_N\}$ and

$$
\begin{aligned}
f(\texttt{addNode}, [\texttt{nid}], \sigma) &= \{(\texttt{true}, v_{\texttt{nid}\%N}, \texttt{wr})\} \\
f(\texttt{getNext}, [\texttt{nid}], \sigma) &= \{(\texttt{true}, v_{\texttt{nid}\%N}, \texttt{rd})\} \\
f(\texttt{addEdge}, [\texttt{nid},\texttt{nid'}], \sigma) &= \{(\texttt{true}, v_{\texttt{nid}\%N}, \texttt{wr})\}
\end{aligned}
$$

The idea is to approximate conflict by focusing on the *nodes*. This node-based notion of conflict is one approach but one could imagine an alternative CA that uses edges as a basis for conflict. Each strategy is an approximation of conflict and the choice of strategy may depend on the specific semantics of the graph, methods, and/or workload. Indeed, one could even use edges *and* nodes as a basis for a CA, if a very fine-grained notion of conflict is needed. Notice that this CA places no restrictions on how the directed graph is actually implemented.

4   Shadow Speculation

Transactional Boosting [17] performed ADT operations *eagerly* and used inverse operations to apply an *operation undo log* to cleanup an aborted transaction.

Unfortunately, this approach was coupled with pessimistic conflict resolution, where execution blocks when a conflict is detected. In an optimistic setting, transactions execute as if they will not encounter conflicts, and abort/retry if conflicts are detected. The key challenge is that a transaction must be able to observe the results of its own speculative updates to shared objects, without those updates becoming visible to other transactions until a successful commit occurs.

This is where *shadow speculation* helps. Shadow speculation is a technique for transactional objects, where updates are made on a separate local copy of a data-structure and then later merged with the master copy at commit time, similar to version control. This is conceptually similar to the thread-local copies used by lock-free and wait-free universal constructions [15,16]; however, conflict abstractions allow our approach to support finer grained concurrency, and we describe several techniques which allow our shadow copies to incur a lower memory overhead.

Replay Logs. We begin by creating wrappers around a black-box ADT implementation so that we can replace the default behavior of a method invocation (*i.e.* immediately applying it to the object) with a more speculative strategy.

To support commit, we maintain an *operation replay log*, tracking the method names and arguments of all operations performed by a transaction rather than applying operations directly on the object (as seen in Boosting). Then, at commit, we can use a single data-structure lock to atomically replay the log of operations onto the shared object.

Unfortunately, this is insufficient for most applications as once an active transaction enqueues an operation to the log, it may need to know the return value in order to continue.

Speculative Wrapper. Conceptually, the natural next step is for active transactions to be able to operate on their own local or *shadow* copy of the shared data-structure. This allows those transactions to perform operations that are invisible to concurrent transactions, and in particular, it also allows transactions to view the return values of these uncommitted operations. Our shadow copies are implemented inside the wrapper and designed so that when client code (speculatively) calls ADT operations, it predicts the result of each operation, intuitively reaching forward in time to see what return value would be generated if the transaction were to commit. The predicted values for a transaction T is calculated based on the committed state of the (black-box) object, combined with the uncommitted operations performed thus far by T. When a transaction aborts, a wrapper of this variety has no further work, because the underlying data structure has not been altered, and the shadow copy can be discarded. On the other hand, when a transaction commits, the wrapper must use the operation replay log to ensure that every speculative operation is finally applied to the underlying object.

While shadow copies are conceptually simple, they are not practical if implemented naïvely. Therefore, we must consider how to efficiently implement shadow copies for a variety of data structures.

Efficient Shadow Copies. Here we describe two approaches for efficient shadow copies.

1. *Memoization.* For some data-structures, the results of an operation (even an update) can be computed purely from the initial state of the wrapped data-structure, or from the arguments of other pending operations. In these cases, we may implement shadow copies by memoization. Repeated operations to the same key can be cached in a transaction-local table, and queried, to determine the results of the next operation on that key. If the key is not present, it's state can be determined by reading the unmodified backing data structure. Then, when the transaction commits, we can replay a single synthetic operation for each key in the table, to capture its final state.

   Memoization works particularly well for ADTs such as maps and sets: the result of `m.set(a,x)` followed by `m.get(a)` (a read-only operation) is `x`. We implemented this approach in our LazyHashMap, using Java's ConcurrentHashMap as the underlying data-structure.

2. *Snapshots.* For many data structures, memoization will be insufficient. A more general approach uses the fast-snapshot semantics provided by many concurrent data structures [3, 26–28] to support shadow speculation. Such snapshots typically employ a lazy copy-on-write strategy to allow snapshots to initially share their internal structure with the original, and only copy as much data as is needed to perform each subsequent modification.

   Using snapshots for our shadow copies, the first time a transaction attempts to perform an update, a snapshot is made, and all further updates are performed on that snapshot. Whenever a transaction commits, any changes to the snapshot are replayed onto the shared copy.

   Snapshot implementations of shadow copies are also helpful in providing the "peek" methods such as `min` (priority queue) and `zero/willBeZero` (NZI) discussed above. For example, shadow copies let us determine ahead of time if the operation in question will change the result of `zero()` before and after the invocation.

   We implemented two data-structures this way: LazyTrieMap (based on Scala'a TrieMap) and LazyPriorityQueue (based on a concurrent Braun heap [7]).

5   The ScalaPROUST Transactional System

In this section we describe our implementation ScalaPROUST, an open source transactional system, available at the following URL:

www.github.com/ScalaProust/ScalaProust/

Our implementation includes support for both *pessimistic* operations on black-box highly concurrent ADTs (similar to boosting) as well as *optimistic* operations, as discussed in this paper. In this way the tool generalizes both boosting and predication. In this paper, however, we focus on how ScalaPROUST is used for optimistic operations, based on conflict abstractions (Sect. 3) and shadow speculation (Sect. 4).

We first define a conflict abstraction (X, f) for the ADT, as discussed in Sect. 3. Next, we create a ScalaProust wrapper and decide whether the wrapper will manage shadow speculation via snapshots or via a memoization table, as discussed in Sect. 4. The wrapper can then be constructed, as defined to the right, to invoke each supported operation. proust_apply must execute in the context of a transaction T in order to register onCommit events.

The wrapper proceeds as follows. First, the conflict abstraction f is consulted for the given method m and arguments $\bar{\alpha}$, returning the list of $(p, v, mode)$ tuples (Line 2). Next, the wrapper follows the instructions of each tuple of the conflict abstraction: if $p(\bar{\alpha}, \sigma_o)$ holds, then location v is either read or written (Line 3). The shadow speculation facility is used next (Line 8) to speculatively apply the

```
1  let proust_apply(T, o.m, ᾱ) =
2      let locs = f(o.m, ᾱ, σₒ) in
3      foreach (fun (p, v, mode) →
4          if p(ᾱ, σₒ) then match mode with
5          | rd → stm_read(v)
6          | wr → stm_write(v)
7      ) locs
8      let rv = Predict(o.m, ᾱ) in
9      T.onCommit(fun () → { o.m(ᾱ);
10         foreach (fun (_,v,_) → stm_read(v) )
11         locs });
12     return rv
```

method and obtain a return value rv. Finally, the wrapper registers an onCommit handler (Line 9) which will invoke the method on the shared object and once again read all of the conflict abstraction memory locations to guard against opacity violations.

ScalaProust includes a library API implementing conflict abstractions, as well as replay logs for both shadow speculation techniques. ScalaProust also provides a number of wrapped data structures out of the box, including both transactional maps and transactional priority queues, which can be used as-is, or serve as example code for developers to create their own wrappers.

6   Evaluation

Our goal in this section is to evaluate whether our optimistic treatment of black-box ADTs is efficient. Notably, our evaluation includes experiments to determine whether ScalaProust is competitive with the state-of-the-art specialized optimistic treatment of set/map-like structures found in predication [4]. Note that, for lack of space, we summarize the experimental results here. In the extended version of this paper [8], we have included additional experimental results and a discussion of how ScalaProust can be used pessimistically.

We focus our evaluation on time-efficiency rather than memory-efficiency for several reasons. First, it is difficult to reproducibly measure memory usage on the JVM due to its weak guarantees concerning garbage collection. Second, the memory usage is likely to be dependent on the specific implementation of the shadow copy, as well as the workload. However, we expect that for tree-like data-structures which exploit structural sharing for fast snapshots, the first

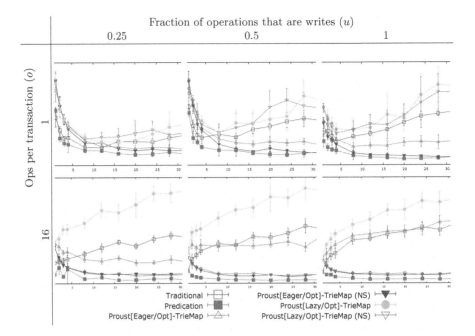

Fig. 1. Time to process 10^6 operations on concurrent maps (*smaller is better*), varying %-updates and #ops/txn. For each chart, the x-axis is the number of threads from 0 to 32 and the y-axis is the average time in milliseconds from 0 to 250. The (NS) variants disabled `size()`.

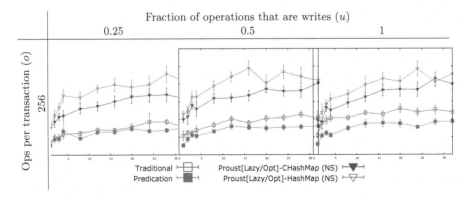

Fig. 2. Memoizing shadow copies allow updates of the same entry to be combined, providing a substantial decrease in execution time. *Smaller is better.*

modification will introduce $O(\log(n))$ memory overhead, and gradually saturate towards $O(n)$.

We classify data structure wrappers based on conflict abstractions along two axes: their choice of synchronization strategy (optimistic or pessimistic), and

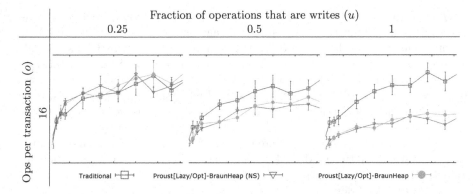

Fig. 3. Time to process 10^6 operations on concurrent priority queues (*smaller is better*), varying %-updates. For each chart, the x-axis is the number of threads from 0 to 32 and the y-axis is the average time in milliseconds from 0 to 2400. The (NS) variants disabled `size()`.

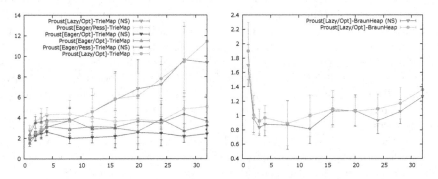

Fig. 4. Overhead of the transactional wrapper (relative to the base data structure) for different configurations of ScalaPROUST (vertical axis) vs thread count (horizontal axis), with $o = 1$. On the left are transactional maps and on the right are transactional priority queues. *Smaller is better.*

their choice of update strategy (lazy or eager). Optimistic synchronization has been the primary focus of this work; however, pessimistic synchronization has been used in transactional boosting [17]. Similarly, lazy updates based on shadow copies and replay logs have been the primary focus this work; however, the conflict abstraction methodology can also be applied to eager updates based on inverses and undo logs à la boosting. We present results for three of the four possible quadrants: lazy/optimistic, eager/optimistic, and eager/pessimistic. Lazy/pessimistic wrappers are possible, but it seems unlikely that the extra memory overhead for lazy updates will pay off when pessimistic synchronization already ensures exclusive access to the relevant portions of the shared state.

Maps. We benchmarked several ScalaPROUST map wrappers (including variants with and without a `size()` operation) against both predication and a traditional pure-STM hash map, with a setup similar to that used by Bronson, et al. for predication [4]. We ran our experiments on an Amazon EC2 `m4.10xlarge` instance,[3] which has 40 vCPUs and 160 GB of RAM. For each experiment, we performed 10^6 random operations on a shared map, split across t threads, with o operations per transaction. A fraction u of the operations were writes (evenly split between `put` and `remove`), and the remaining $(1 - u)$ were `get` operations. We varied t, o, and u to achieve different levels of contention[4]. For each configuration, we warmed up the JVM for 10 executions, then timed each of the following 10 executions, garbage collecting in between to reduce jitter, and reported the mean and standard deviation.

Notes on Experimental Setup. First, our implementation was limited in its communication with the CCSTM contention manager. ScalaPROUST can communicate conflicts with CCSTM but currently does not provide the reason for the conflict. Consequently, CCSTM is limited in its ability to intelligently schedule retries. In particular, we found that under the artificially high contention seen in these experiments, longer transaction times could lead to live-lock, as the STM lacked required information about the instigating (non-STM) memory accesses. For this reason, we only show the pessimistic results in the initial $o = 1$ experiments. Second, though the Eager/Optimistic configuration does not satisfy opacity under the CCSTM backend for ScalaSTM, we benchmarked it anyway, and did not observe any instances where this violated correctness (notably our benchmark makes no explicit control flow decisions based on the results of map accesses, and ScalaSTM performs an abort and retry if it ever observes an unchecked exception). It seems likely that a performance penalty was paid for late detection of inconsistent memory accesses, and we believe this speaks well to the potential performance of Eager/Optimistic wrappers on STMs where they satisfy opacity. Third, substantial performance differences between the standard and (NS) wrapper variants illustrate the previously discussed impedance mismatch between "pure" writes in a conflict abstraction and "impure" writes provided by STMs. We note that disabling the `size` operation for the (NS) variants did not require modifications to the underlying data structure, merely that we control which operations of the underlying data structure are exposed through the wrapper.

Results. The experimental results depicted in Fig. 1 display the effects of several competing trends. Intuitively, ScalaPROUST's performance scales much better than the traditional STM implementation as contention increases, due to varying t and u (though we are consistently outperformed by the highly engineered

---

[3] https://aws.amazon.com/blogs/aws/the-new-m4-instance-type-bonus-price-reduction-on-m3-c4/.

[4] We did not vary key range as in the predication paper, as garbage collection was not a focus of this implementation.

predication implementation[5]); however, increasing values of o have a negative influence on the relative performance of the ScalaPROUST wrappers. Intuitively, this is to be expected, as our log sizes (either to undo or replay) are proportional to the number of updates performed, whereas predication and traditional implementations replay with time proportional to the number of unique memory locations updated, and as o increases, so does the probability that multiple writes will alter the same location. An optimization for memoization-, rather than snapshot-, based shadow speculation is to apply only the final state of each abstract state element; resulting in Fig. 2. The overhead of the wrapper, relative to the base data structure can be seen in Fig. 4.

Priority Queues. We used a nearly identical experimental setup to compare the runtimes of two priority queues based on Braun heaps (one traditional STM implementation and one wrapper around the snapshot-able concurrent implementation referenced earlier [7]). The writes were split evenly between `insert` and `removeMin` operations.

The experimental results in Fig. 3 show that across a variety of conditions, the queue was competitive with, or outperformed, the traditional implementation. In general, run times were substantially longer than for the map throughput test, as the min-element is subject to heavy contention; however, unlike for map, the effects of additional operations per transaction were less pronounced, as most contention is discovered early in the transaction. The overhead of the wrapper, relative to the base data structure is shown in Fig. 4.

7   Conclusions and Future Work

We introduced conflict abstractions and shadow speculation, permitting us to use existing highly-concurrent objects in an optimistic transactional manner, separately using off-the-shelf STMs for performing commutativity-based conflict detection. Benchmarks show we outperform, or are competitive with fine-tuned STM techniques (*i.e.* predication), while we are able to leverage existing ADT libraries and avoid implementing them from scratch. While we are outperformed by predication on the map throughput tests, we believe that our utility as a tool for wrapping arbitrary data structures will encourage use beyond sets and maps.

One important direction forward is to integrate pessimistic and optimistic treatment of black-box ADTs with standard STM memory operations. This brings with it some opacity challenges. To further improve performance, one could also explore an extension of our log-combining optimization from memoized replays to snapshot replays and undo logs. Alternatively, shadow copies based on confluently persistent data structures could even be merged without an explicit log [12]. In another direction, the use of conflict abstractions to describe commutativity and synchronization reveals a use-case for STMs to support "pure

---

[5] Predication as a technique is specialized to maps and sets, in essence embedding their conflict abstraction as the member elements of the backing collection and allowing frequent updates to the same element to avoid updating the concrete state of the backing data structure.

writes", allowing them to match the expressivity of handcrafted locks. Finally, automatic verification techniques (such as those mentioned in Sect. 3) might be used as a building-block for an automatic synthesis technique, perhaps along the lines of recent techniques for synthesizing commutativity conditions [1].

References

1. Bansal, K., Koskinen, E., Tripp, O.: Automatic generation of precise and useful commutativity conditions. In: Beyer, D., Huisman, M. (eds.) TACAS 2018. LNCS, vol. 10805, pp. 115–132. Springer, Cham (2018). https://doi.org/10.1007/978-3-319-89960-2_7
2. Bernstein, A.: Analysis of programs for parallel processing. IEEE Trans. Electron. Comput. **15**(5), 757–763 (1966)
3. Bronson, N.G., Casper, J., Chafi, H., Olukotun, K.: A practical concurrent binary search tree. In: Proceedings of the 15th ACM SIGPLAN Symposium on Principles and Practice of Parallel Programming, PPoPP 2010, pp. 257–268. ACM, New York (2010)
4. Bronson, N.G., Casper, J., Chafi, H., Olukotun, K.: Transactional predication: high-performance concurrent sets and maps for STM. In: Proceedings of the 29th ACM SIGACT-SIGOPS Symposium on Principles of Distributed Computing, PODC 2010, pp. 6–15. ACM, New York (2010)
5. Bronson, N.G., Chafi, H., Olukotun, K.: CCSTM: a library-based STM for scala. def 9 (2010). 10
6. Carlstrom, B.D., McDonald, A., Carbin, M., Kozyrakis, C., Olukotun, K.: Transactional collection classes. In: Proceedings of the 12th ACM SIGPLAN Symposium on Principles and Practice of Parallel Programming, PPoPP 2007, pp. 56–67. ACM, New York (2007)
7. Dickerson, T.D.: Fast snapshottable concurrent braun heaps. arXiv preprint arXiv:1705.06271 (2017)
8. Dickerson, T.D., Gazzillo, P., Koskinen, E., Herlihy, M.: Proust: a design space for highly-concurrent transactional data structures. CoRR abs/1702.04866 (2017)
9. Dimitrov, D., Raychev, V., Vechev, M., Koskinen, E.: Commutativity race detection. In: Proceedings of the 35th ACM SIGPLAN Conference on Programming Language Design and Implementation, PLDI 2014, pp. 305–315. ACM (2014)
10. Ellen, F., Lev, Y., Luchangco, V., Moir, M.: SNZI: scalable nonzero indicators. In: Proceedings of the Twenty-Sixth Annual ACM Symposium on Principles of Distributed Computing, PODC 2007, pp. 13–22. ACM (2007)
11. Felber, P., Gramoli, V., Guerraoui, R.: Elastic transactions. In: Keidar, I. (ed.) DISC 2009. LNCS, vol. 5805, pp. 93–107. Springer, Heidelberg (2009). https://doi.org/10.1007/978-3-642-04355-0_12
12. Fiat, A., Kaplan, H.: Making data structures confluently persistent. J. Algorithms **48**, 1 (2003). 12th ACM-SIAM Symposium on Discrete Algorithms
13. Golan-Gueta, G., Ramalingam, G., Sagiv, M., Yahav, E.: Automatic semantic locking. SIGPLAN Not. **49**(8), 385–386 (2014)
14. Hassan, A., Palmieri, R., Ravindran, B.: Optimistic transactional boosting. In: Proceedings of the 19th ACM SIGPLAN Symposium on Principles and Practice of Parallel Programming, PPoPP 2014, pp. 387–388. ACM (2014)
15. Herlihy, M.: Wait-free synchronization. ACM Trans. Program. Lang. Syst. **13**(1), 124–149 (1991)

16. Herlihy, M.: A methodology for implementing highly concurrent data objects. ACM Trans. Program. Lang. Syst. (TOPLAS) **15**(5), 745–770 (1993)
17. Herlihy, M., Koskinen, E.: Transactional boosting: a methodology for highly-concurrent transactional objects. In: Proceedings of the 13th ACM SIGPLAN Symposium Principles and Practice of parallel Programming, PPoPP 2008. ACM (2008)
18. Herman, N., et al.: Type-aware transactions for faster concurrent code. In: Proceedings of the Eleventh European Conference on Computer Systems, EuroSys 2016, pp. 31:1–31:16. ACM, New York (2016)
19. Kim, D., Rinard, M.C.: Verification of semantic commutativity conditions and inverse operations on linked data structures. In: Proceedings of the 32nd ACM SIGPLAN Conference on Programming Language Design and Implementation, PLDI 2011, San Jose, CA, USA, 4–8 June, pp. 528–541 (2011)
20. Korth, H.F.: Locking primitives in a database system. J. ACM **30**, 1 (1983)
21. Koskinen, E., Parkinson, M., Herlihy, M.: Coarse-grained transactions. In: Proceedings of the 37th Annual ACM SIGPLAN-SIGACT Symposium on Principles of Programming Languages (2010), POPL 2010, pp. 19–30. ACM (2010)
22. Koskinen, E., Parkinson, M.J.: The push/pull model of transactions. In: Proceedings of the 36th ACM SIGPLAN Conference on Programming Language Design and Implementation (PLDI 2015). ACM, Portland (2015)
23. Kulkarni, M., Pingali, K., Walter, B., Ramanarayanan, G., Bala, K., Chew, L.P.: Optimistic parallelism requires abstractions. In: Proceedings of the ACM SIGPLAN 2007 Conference on Programming Language Design and Implementation (PLDI 2007), pp. 211–222 (2007)
24. Kulkarni, M., Pingali, K., Walter, B., Ramanarayanan, G., Bala, K., Chew, L.P.: Optimistic parallelism requires abstractions. Commun. ACM **52**(9), 89–97 (2009)
25. Ni, Y., et al.: Open nesting in software transactional memory. In: Proceedings of the 12th ACM SIGPLAN Symposium on Principles and Practice of Parallel Programming (2007), PPoPP 2007, pp. 68–78. ACM (2007)
26. Petrank, E., Timnat, S.: Lock-free data-structure iterators. In: Afek, Y. (ed.) DISC 2013. LNCS, vol. 8205, pp. 224–238. Springer, Heidelberg (2013). https://doi.org/10.1007/978-3-642-41527-2_16
27. Prokopec, A.: SnapQueue: lock-free queue with constant time snapshots. In: Proceedings of the 6th ACM SIGPLAN Symposium on Scala, SCALA 2015, pp. 1–12. ACM, New York (2015)
28. Prokopec, A., Bronson, N.G., Bagwell, P., Odersky, M.: Concurrent tries with efficient non-blocking snapshots, pp. 151–160
29. Shapiro, M., Preguiça, N., Baquero, C., Zawirski, M.: Conflict-free replicated data types. In: Défago, X., Petit, F., Villain, V. (eds.) SSS 2011. LNCS, vol. 6976, pp. 386–400. Springer, Heidelberg (2011). https://doi.org/10.1007/978-3-642-24550-3_29
30. Spiegelman, A., Golan-Gueta, G., Keidar, I.: Transactional data structure libraries. In: Proceedings of the 37th ACM SIGPLAN Conference on Programming Language Design and Implementation, pp. 682–696. ACM (2016)
31. Steele, Jr., G.L.: Making asynchronous parallelism safe for the world. In: Proceedings of the 17th ACM SIGPLAN-SIGACT Symposium on Principles of Programming Languages (POPL 1990), pp. 218–231. ACM Press, New York (1990)
32. Weihl, W.: Commutativity-based concurrency control for abstract data types. IEEE Trans. Comput. **37**(12), 1488–1505 (1988)

TxForest: A DSL for Concurrent Filestores

Jonathan DiLorenzo[1(✉)], Katie Mancini[1], Kathleen Fisher[2], and Nate Foster[1]

[1] Cornell University, Ithaca, NY 14850, USA
dilorenzo@cs.cornell.edu
[2] Tufts University, Medford, MA 02155, USA

Abstract. Many systems use ad hoc collections of files and directories to store persistent data. For consumers of this data, the process of properly parsing, using, and updating these *filestores* using conventional APIs is cumbersome and error-prone. Making matters worse, most filestores are too big to fit in memory, so applications must process the data incrementally while managing concurrent accesses by multiple users. This paper presents Transactional Forest (TxForest), which builds on earlier work on Forest to provide a simpler, more powerful API for managing filestores, including a mechanism for managing concurrent accesses using serializable transactions. Under the hood, TxForest implements an optimistic concurrency control scheme using Huet's *zippers* to track the data associated with filestores. We formalize TxForest in a core calculus, develop a proof of serializability, and describe our OCaml prototype, which we have used to build several practical applications.

Keywords: Data description languages · File systems · Ad hoc data · Concurrency · Transactions · Zippers

1 Introduction

Modern database systems offer numerous benefits to programmers, including rich query languages and impressive performance. However, programmers in many areas including finance, telecommunications, and the sciences, rely on *ad hoc* data formats to store persistent data—e.g., flat files organized into structured directories. This approach avoids some of the initial costs of using a database such as writing schemas, creating user accounts, and importing data, but it also means that programmers must build custom tools for correctly processing the data—a cumbersome and error-prone task.

In many applications, multiple users must read and write the data stored on the file system concurrently, and even in settings where there is only a single user, parallelism can often be used to improve performance. For example, many instructors in large computer science courses rely on filestores to manage student data, encoding assignments, rosters, and grades as ad hoc collections of directories, CSVs, and ASCII files respectively. During grading, instructors use

© Springer Nature Switzerland AG 2019
A. W. Lin (Ed.): APLAS 2019, LNCS 11893, pp. 332–354, 2019.
https://doi.org/10.1007/978-3-030-34175-6_17

various scripts to manipulate the data—e.g., computing statistics, normalizing raw scores, and uploading grades to the registrar. However, these scripts are written against low-level file system APIs and rarely handle multiple concurrent users. This can easily lead to incorrect results or even data corruption in courses that use large numbers of TAs to help with grading.

The PADS/Forest family of languages offers a promising approach for managing ad hoc data. In these languages, the programmer specifies the structure of an ad hoc data format using a simple, declarative specification, and the compiler generates an in-memory representation for the data, load and store functions for mapping between in-memory and on-disk representations, as well as tools for analyzing, transforming, and visualizing the data. PADS focused on ad hoc data stored in individual files [6], while Forest handles ad hoc data in *filestores*— i.e., structured collections of files, directories, and links [5]. Unfortunately, the languages that have been proposed to date lack support for concurrency.

To address this challenge, this paper proposes Transactional Forest (TxForest), a declarative domain-specific language for correctly processing ad hoc data in the presence of concurrency. Like its predecessors, TxForest uses a type-based abstraction to specify the structure of the data and its invariants. From a TxForest description, the compiler generates a typed representation of the data as well as a high-level programming interface that abstracts away direct interactions with the file system and provides operations for automatically loading and storing data, while gracefully handling errors. TxForest also offers serializable transactions to help implement concurrent applications.

The central abstraction that facilitates TxForest's serializable semantics, as well as several other desired properties, is based on Huet's *zippers* [10]. Rather than representing a filestore in terms of the root node and its children, a zipper encodes the current node, the path traversed to get there, and the nodes encountered along the way. Importantly, local changes to the current node as well as common navigation operations involving adjacent nodes can be implemented in constant time. Additionally, by replacing the current node with a new value and then 'zipping' the tree back up to the root, modifications can be implemented in a purely functional way.

As others have also observed [11], zippers are a natural abstraction for filestores, for several reasons: (1) the concept of the working path is cleanly captured by the current node; (2) most operations are applied close to the current working path; (3) the zipper naturally captures incrementality by loading data as it is encountered in the zipper traversal; and (4) a traversal (along with annotations about possible modification) provides all of the information necessary to provide rich semantics, such as copy-on-write, as well as a simple optimistic concurrency control scheme that guarantees serializability.

In this paper, we first formalize the syntax and semantics of TxForest assuming a single thread of execution, and we establish various correctness properties, including roundtripping laws in the style of lenses [8]. Next, we extend the semantics to handle multiple concurrent threads, and introduce a transaction manager that implements a standard optimistic concurrency scheme. We prove that all

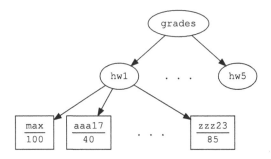

Fig. 1. Example: file system fragment used to store course data.

transactions that sucessfully commit are serializable with respect to one another. Finally, we present a prototype implementation of TxForest as an embedded language in OCaml, illustrating the feasibility of the design, and use it to implement several realistic applications.

Overall, the contributions of this paper are as follows:

- We present Transactional Forest, a declarative domain-specific language for processing ad hoc data in concurrent settings (Sects. 3 and 4).
- We describe a prototype implementation of Transactional Forest as an embedded domain-specific language in OCaml (Sect. 5).
- We prove that our design satisfies several formal properties including round-tripping laws and serializability.

The rest of this paper is structured as follows: Sect. 2 introduces a simple example to motivate TxForest. Section 3 presents the syntax and single-threaded semantics of TxForest. Section 4 adds the multi-threaded semantics and the serializability theorem. Section 5 discusses the OCaml implementation of TxForest and an application. We review related work in Sect. 6 and conclude in Sect. 7. The proofs of formal properties are in the technical report [2].

2   Example: Course Management System

This section introduces an example of an idealized course management system to motivate the design of TxForest. Figure 1 shows a fragment of a filestore used in tracking student grades. The top-level directory (**grades**) contains a set of sub-directories, one for each homework assignment (**hw1–hw5**). Each assignment directory has a file for each student containing their grade on the assignment (e.g., **aaa17**), as well as a special file (**max**) containing the maximum score for that homework. Although this structure is simple, it closely resembles filestores that have actually been used to keep track of grades at several universities.

There are various operations that one might want to perform on this filestore, but to illustrate the challenges related to concurrency, we will focus on normalization. Normalization might be used to ensure that the grades for a particular homework fall between some specified limits or match a given distribution. We assume an idempotent operation f that takes assignment statistics and the current score as arguments and computes a normalized score.

OCaml Implementation. To start, let us see how we might write a renormalization procedure for this filestore in a general-purpose language—e.g., OCaml. For simplicity, the code relies on helper functions, which are explained below.

```
let renormalize f hw gmin =
  let hwDir = sprintf "grades/hw%d" hw in
  let gmax = get_score (hwDir ^/ "max") in
  let studentFiles = get_students hwDir in
  let (cmin, cmax) = get_min_and_max studentFiles in
  map_scores (f cmin cmax gmin gmax) studentFiles
```

The renormalize function takes as input a function to normalize individual scores (f), the identifier of a homework assignment (hw), and the minimum score to use when scaling scores (gmin). It retrieves the value from the max file, using the get_score helper, which reads the file and parses it into a score. Next, it retrieves the paths to every student file (studentFiles) and computes the minimum (cmin) and maximum (cmax) score over all students using a helper function (get_min_and_max), which again accesses data in the underlying file system. Finally, it maps the function f over each score (using the aggregate statistics), and writes the new score back to the file, again using a helper function to perform the necessary iteration (map_scores) and file writes.

Although this procedure is simple, there are several potential pitfalls that could arise because of its use of low-level file system APIs. For example, one of the files or directories might not exist or there might be extra files in the file system. The structure of the filestore might be malformed, or might change over time. Any of these mistakes could lead to run-time errors, or worse they might silently succeed but produce incorrect results. This implementation also suffers from a more insidious set of problems related to concurrency. Consider what happens if multiple members of the course staff execute the renormalization procedure concurrently. If the stage that computes the minimum and maximum scores is interleaved with the stage that invokes f and writes the normalized values back to the file system, we could easily be left with a mangled filestore and incorrect results—something that would likely be difficult to detect, diagnose, and fix.

Classic Forest Implementation. Next, let us consider an implementation in Forest [5]. We start by specifying the structure of the filestore as follows:

```
grades = [h :: hws | h <- matches RE "hw[0-9]+"]
students = file
hws = directory {
  max is "max" :: file;
  students is [s :: students | s <- matches RE "[a-z]+[0-9]+"];
}
```

The `grades` specification describes the structure of the top-level directory: a list of homework directories, each containing a file named *max* and a list of `students` (each represented as a `file`[1]).

Given this specification, the Forest compiler generates an in-memory representation for the data, as well as associated functions for loading data from and storing data to the file system:

```
type students_rep = string
type hws_rep = { max : string; students : students_rep list}
type grades_rep = hws_rep list
type grades_md = hws_md list md
val grades_load : filepath -> grades_rep * grades_md
val grades_store : filepath -> grades_rep * grades_md -> unit
```

The `md` types store metadata including permissions and information about whether errors were encountered during loading. The `load` and `store` functions map between the on-disk and in-memory representations, and automatically check for errors and inconsistencies in the data. Using these functions, we can write the `renormalize` procedure as follows:

```
let renormalize f hw gmin : unit =
 let (gr,gmd) = grades_load (baseDir ^/ "grades") in
 if gmd.num_errors = 0 then
   let (hwr,hwmd) = find (sprintf "hw%d" hw) (gr,gmd) in
   let gmax = get_score hwr.max in
   let (cmin, cmax) = get_min_max hwr in
   map_scores (f cmin cmax gmin gmax) hwr hwmd
 else
   failwith (String.concat "\n" gmd.error_msg)
```

This code is similar to the OCaml implementation, but there are a few key differences. It first loads the entire `grades` directory and checks that it has no errors. This makes the auxilliary functions, like `get_score` (which now just turns a string into an integer) and `set_score` simpler and more robust, since they no longer need to worry about such issues. It then locates the representation and metadata for the assignment, computes aggregate statistics, and invokes `f` to renormalize and update the scores. The `get_min_max` and `map_scores` helpers are similar to the direct versions discussed previously.

The Forest implementation offers several important benefits over the OCaml code: (1) the structure of the filestore is explicit in the specification and the code; (2) the use of types makes certain programming mistakes impossible, such as attempting to read a file at a missing path; and (3) any part of the filestore not conforming to the specification is automatically detected.

---

[1] By integrating with PADS [6], we could go a step further and specify the contents of the file as well—i.e. a single line containing an integer.

However, the Forest code still suffers from the same concurrency issues discussed above. Further, it is unnecessary (and often infeasible) to load the entire filestore into memory—e.g., suppose we only need to manipulate data for a single homework or an individual student.

Transactional Forest Implementation. TxForest offers the same advantages as Forest, while dealing with issues related to concurrency and incrementality. The only cost is a small shift in programming style—i.e., navigating using a zipper.

The TxForest specification for our running example is identical to the Forest version. However, this surface-level specification is then translated to a core language (Sect. 3) that uses Huet's zipper internally and also provides transactional guarantees. The TxForest code for the **renormalize** function is different than the Forest version. Here is one possible implementation:

```
let renormalize f hw gmin zipper : (unit,string) Result.t =
  let%bind hwZ = goto_name_p (sprintf "hw%d" hw) zipper in
  let%bind gmax = goto_name_p "max" hwZ >>= get_score in
  let%bind studentZ = goto "students" hwZ in
  let%bind (cmin, cmax) = get_min_and_max studentZ in
  map_scores (f cmin cmax gmin gmax) studentZ
```

Note that the type of the function has changed so that it takes a zipper as an argument and returns a value in the result monad:

```
type ('a,'b) Result.t = Ok of 'a | Error of 'b
```

Intuitively, this monad tracks the same sorts of errors seen in the Forest code—e.g. from malformed filestores, but not from concurrency issues.

The goto_name_p function traverses the zipper—e.g., goto_name_p "hw1" zipper navigates to the comprehension node named *hw1* and then down to the corresponding file system path, ending up at a **hws** node. The *bind* operator (>>=) threads the resulting zipper through the monad. The let%bind $x = e_1$ in e_2 syntax is shorthand for e_1 >>= fun x -> e_2 . The goto function is similar to goto_name_p, but is limited to directories and does not walk down the last path operator. Finally, the helper functions, map_scores and get_min_max, use TxForest library functions to map and fold over the zipper respectively.

To use the **renormalize** function, users need some way to construct a zipper. The TxForest library provides functions called run_txn and loop_txn:

```
type txError = TxError | OpError of string
val run_txn : spec -> path -> (zipper -> ('a,string) Result.t) ->
                (unit -> ('a,txError) Result.t)
val loop_txn : spec -> path -> (zipper -> ('a,string) Result.t) ->
                (unit -> ('a,string) Result.t)
```

which might be used as follows:

```
match run_txn grades_spec "grades" (renormalize 1 60) () with
| Error TxError -> printf "Transaction aborted due to conflict"
| Error(OpError err) -> printf "Transaction aborted with error: %s" err
| Ok _ -> printf "Renormalization successful"
```

The run_txn function takes a specification, an initial path, and a function from zippers to results and produces a thunk. When the thunk is forced, it constructs a zipper focused on the given path and runs the function. If this execution results in an error, the outer computation produces an OpError. Otherwise, it attempts to commit the modifications produced during the computation. If the commit succeeds, it returns the result of the function, otherwise it discards the results and returns a TxError. The loop_txn function is similar, but retries the transaction until there is no conflict or the input function produces an error.

TxForest guarantees that transactions will be serializable with respect to other transactions—i.e., the final file system will be equivalent to one produced by executing the committed transactions in some serial order. See Sect. 4 for the formal concurrent semantics and the serializability theorem. In our example, this means that no errors can occur due to running multiple renormalization transactions simultaneously. Furthermore, TxForest automatically provides incrementality by only loading the data needed to traverse the zipper—an important property in larger filestores. Incremental Forest [3] provides a similar facility, but requires explicit user annotations. Overall, TxForest provides incremental support for filestore applications in the presence of concurrency. The next two sections present the language in detail, develop an operational model, and establish its main formal properties.

3   Transactional Forest

This section presents TxForest in terms of a core calculus. We discuss the goals and high level design decisions for the language before formalizing the syntax and semantics as well as several properties including round-tripping laws, equational identities, and consistency relations. Finally, we give a taste of the core calculus by using it to encode functions that would be useful for the course management example above. This section deals primarily with the single-threaded semantics, while the next section presents a concurrent model.

The main goals of this language are to allow practical processing of filestores for non-expert users. This leads to several requirements: (1) an intuitive way of specifying filestores [5]; (2) automatic, incremental processing, as filestores are typically large; (3) automatic concurrency control, as concurrency is both common and difficult to get right; and (4) transparency, as filestore interaction can be expensive and should therefore be explicit.

The zipper abstraction that our language is based on helps us achieve our second and fourth requirement. Both of these requirements and concurrency are then further addressed by our locality-centered language design: The semantics of every command and expression only considers the locale around the focus node of the zipper. This means that every command can restrict its attention to a small part of the filestore, which, along with the fact that data can be loaded as-required while traversing the zipper, gives us incrementality. We believe that the combination of locality and explicit zipper traversal commands also gives us transparency. In particular, the footprint of any command is largely predictable based on the filestore specification and current state. Predictability also simplifies tasks such as logging reads and writes, which is useful for concurrency control.

3.1   Syntax

Strings	$u \in \Sigma^*$	
Integers	$i \in \mathbb{Z}$	
Variables	$x \in Var$	
Values	$v \in Val$	
Environments	$E \in Env$:	$Var \mapsto Val$
Paths	$p ::= /$ $\mid$ p/u	
Contents	$T ::= \mathtt{Dir}\ \{\overline{u}\}$ $\mid$ $\mathtt{File}\ u$	
File Systems	fs :	$Path \mapsto Content$
Contexts	$ctxt$:	$Env \times Path \times 2^{Path} \times Zipper$

Fig. 2. Preliminaries

In our formal model, we view a file system as a map from paths to file system contents, which are either directories (a set of their children's names) or files (strings). For a path and file system, p and fs, we define $p \in fs \triangleq p \in \mathrm{dom}(fs)$. See Fig. 2 for the metavariable conventions used in our formalization. We assume that all file systems are well formed—i.e., that they encode a tree, where each node is either a directory or a file with no children:

Definition 1 (Well-Formedness). *A file system fs is well-formed iff:*

1. $fs(/) = Dir$ _ *(where $/$ is the root node)*
2. $p/u \in fs \iff fs(p) = Dir\ \{u; \dots\}$

In this definition, the notation _ indicates an irrelevant hole which may be filled by any well-typed term. We use this convention throughout the paper.

In the previous section, we gave a flavor of the specifications one might write in TxForest. We wrote these specifications in our surface language, which compiles down to a core calculus, whose syntax is given in Fig. 3. The core specifications are described fully below, but first, we will provide the translation of the hws specification from Sect. 2 to provide an intuition:

```
directory {
    max is "max" :: file;
    students is [s :: students | s <- matches RE "[a-z]+[0-9]+"]
}
```
becomes
$$\langle max : "max" :: File, \langle dir : Dir, [s :: students \mid s \in e]\rangle\rangle$$
```
where e = filter (Run Fetch_Dir dir) "[a-z]+[0-9]+"
```

Specifications	$s \in spec ::= File \mid Dir \mid e :: s \mid \langle x : s_1, s_2 \rangle$
	$\mid [s \mid x \in e] \mid s? \mid P(e)$
Zippers	$z ::= \{\text{ancestor} : Zipper \text{ option};$
	$\text{left} : (Env \times spec) \text{ list};$
	$\text{current} : (Env \times spec);$
	$\text{right} : (Env \times spec) \text{ list}\}$
Commands	$c ::= fc \mid \text{Skip} \mid c_1; c_2 \mid x := e$
	$\mid \text{If } b \text{ Then } c_1 \text{ Else } c_2 \mid \text{While } b \text{ Do } c$
Forest Commands	$fc ::= fn \mid fu$
Forest Navigations	$fn ::= \text{Down} \mid \text{Up} \mid \text{Next} \mid \text{Prev}$
	$\mid \text{Into\_Pair} \mid \text{Into\_Comp} \mid \text{Into\_Opt} \mid \text{Out}$
Forest Updates	$fu ::= \text{Store\_File } e \mid \text{Store\_Dir } e \mid \text{Create\_Path}$
Expressions	$e, b ::= fe \mid v \mid x \mid e_1\ e_2 \mid \ldots$
Forest Expressions	$fe ::= \text{Fetch\_File} \mid \text{Fetch\_Dir} \mid \text{Fetch\_Path}$
	$\mid \text{Fetch\_Comp} \mid \text{Fetch\_Opt} \mid \text{Fetch\_Pred}$
	$\mid \text{Run } fn\ e \mid \text{Run } fe\ e \mid \text{Verify}$
Log Entries	$le ::= \text{Write\_file } T_1\ T_2\ p \mid \text{Read } T\ p$
	$\mid \text{Write\_dir } T_1\ T_2\ p$
Logs	$\sigma : LogEntry \text{ list}$
Programs	$g ::= (p, s, c)$

Fig. 3. Main syntax

Directories become dependent pairs, allowing earlier parts of directories to be referenced by later parts. Comprehensions, which use regular expressions to query the file system, also turn into dependent pairs: The first component of the pair is a *Dir*. The second component fetches from and filters the first component using a regular expression. Section 3.4 gives examples of functions written against this specification using the command language described below. We proceed by describing the syntax shown in Fig. 3 in-depth.

Formally, a TxForest specification s describes the shape and contents of a *filestore*, which is a structured subtree of a file system. Such specifications are almost identical to those in Classic Forest [5]. To a first approximation, they can be understood as follows:

– *Files and Directories.* The *File* and *Dir* specifications describe filestores with a file and directory, respectively, at the current path.
– *Paths.* The $e :: s$ specification describes a filestore modeled by s at the extension of the current path denoted by e.
– *Dependent Pairs.* The $\langle x : s_1, s_2 \rangle$ specification describes a filestore modeled by both s_1 and s_2. Additionally, s_2 may use the variable x to refer to the portion of the filestore matched by s_1.
– *Comprehensions.* The $[s \mid x \in e]$ specification describes a filestore modeled by s when x is bound to any element in the set e.

- *Options.* The s? specification describes a filestore that is either modeled by s or where the current path does not exist.
- *Predicates.* The $P(e)$ specification describes a filestore where the boolean e is **true**. This construct is typically used with dependent pairs.

Most specifications can be thought of as trees with as many children as they have sub-specifications. Comprehensions are the exception; we think of them as having as many children as there are elements in the set e.

To enable incremental and transactional manipulation of data contained in filestores, TxForest uses a *zipper* which is constructed from a specification. The zipper traverses the specification tree while keeping track of an environment that binds variables from dependent pairs and comprehensions. The zipper can be thought of as representing a tree along with the particular node of the tree that is in focus. We use the symbol **current** to represents the focus node, while **left** and **right** represent its siblings to the left and right respectively. The symbol **ancestor** tracks the focus node's ancestors by containing the zipper we came from before moving down to this depth of the tree. Key principles to keep in mind regarding zippers are that (1) the tree can be unfolded as it is traversed and (2) operations near the current node are fast, thus optimizing for locality.

To express navigation on the zipper, we use standard imperative (IMP) commands, c, as well as special-purpose Forest Commands, fc, which are divided into Forest Navigations, fn, and Forest Updates, fu. Navigation commands are those that traverse the zipper, while Update commands modify the file system. Expressions are mostly standard and pure: they never modify the file system and only Forest Expressions query it. Forest Commands and Expressions will be described in greater detail in Sect. 3.2. To ensure serializability among multiple TxForest threads executing concurrently, we will maintain a log. An entry **Read** T p indicates that we have read T at path p while **Write_file** T_1 T_2 p (respectively **Write_dir** T_1 T_2 p) indicates that we have written the file (respectively directory) T_2 to path p, where T_1 was before.

3.2 Semantics

Having defined the syntax, we now present the denotational semantics of TxForest. The semantics of IMP commands are standard and thus elided. We start by defining the semantics of a program:

$$[\![(p, s, c)]\!]_g \; fs \; \triangleq \; \texttt{project\_fs} \; ([\![c]\!]_c \; (\{\}, p, \{\}, \wr\{\}, s\wr) \; fs)$$

The denotation of a TxForest program is a function on file systems. We use the specification s to construct a new zipper, seen in the figure using our zipper notation defined after this paragraph. Then we execute the command c using the denotation of commands $[\![\cdot]\!]_c$. The denotation function takes a context, which we construct using the zipper and the path p, and a file system fs as arguments. The denotation function then produces a new context and file system, from which we project out the file system with **project_fs**.

Definition 2 (Zipper Notation). *We define notation for constructing and deconstructing zippers. To construct a zipper we write*

$$left \leftharpoondown \{\!current\}^z \rightharpoonup right \triangleq \{ancestor = Some(z); left; current; right\},$$

where any of ancestor, *left, and* right *can be omitted to denote a zipper with* ancestor = None, *left* = [], *and* right = [] *respectively. For example:*

$$\{\!current\} \triangleq \{ancestor = None; left = []; current; right = []\}$$

Likewise, to destruct a zipper we write left $\leftharpoondown$ (current)^z $\rightharpoonup$ right *where any part can be omitted to ignore that portion of the zipper, but any included part must exist. For example,* $z = (\_)^{z'} :\Longleftrightarrow z.ancestor = Some(z').$

The two key invariants that hold during the execution of any command are (1) that the file system remains well-formed (Definition 1) and (2) that if $[\![fc]\!]_c \ (\_, p/u, \_, \_) \ fs = ((\_, p'/u', \_, \_), fs', \_)$ and $p \in fs$, then $p' \in fs'$. The first property states that no command can make a well-formed file system ill-formed. The second states that, as we traverse the zipper, we maintain a connection to the real file system. It is important that only the parent of the current file system node is required to exist as this allows us to construct new portions of the filestore and handle the option specification. A central design choice that underpins the semantics is that each command acts *locally* on the current zipper and does not require further context. This makes the cost of the operation apparent and, as in Incremental Forest [3], facilitates partial loading and storing. These properties can be seen from Fig. 4 which defines the semantics of Forest Commands.

As illustrated in the top row of the table, each row should be interpreted as defining the meaning of evaluating a command in a given context, (E, p, ps, z), and file system, fs, provided the conditions hold. The denotation function is partial, being undefined if none of the rows apply. Intuitively, a command is undefined when it is used on a malformed filestore with respect to its specification, or when it is ill-typed—i.e. used on an unexpected zipper state. Operationally, the semantics of each command can be understood as follows:

- Down and Up are duals: the first traverses the zipper into a path expression, simultaneously moving us down in the file system, while the other does the reverse. Additionally, Down queries the file system, producing a Read.
- Into and Out are duals: the first traverses the zipper into its respective type of specification, while the second moves back out to the parent node. Additionally, their subexpressions may produce logs.

  For dependent pairs, we update the environment of the second child with a context constructed from the first specification.

  For comprehensions, the traversal requires the set denoted by e to be non-empty, and maps it to a list of children with the same specification, but environments with different mappings for x, before moving to the first child.

Command: fc	Conditions: Φ	Def. of $[\![fc]\!]_c\ (E, p, ps, z)\ fs$ when Φ
Down	$z = (\!E_L, e :: s\!)$ $(u, \sigma) = [\![e]\!]_e\ (E_L, p, ps, z)\ fs$ $\text{Dir } \ell = fs(p)$	$\sigma' = \sigma \cdot (\text{Read } (\text{Dir } \ell)\ p)$ $((E, p/u, ps \cup (p/u), (\!E_L, s\!)^z), fs, \sigma')$
Up	$z = (\!\_\!)^{z'}$ $z' = (\!\_, e :: s\!)$	$((E, \text{pop } p, ps, z'), fs, \epsilon)$
Into_Opt	$z = (\!E_L, s?\!)$	$((E, p, ps, (\!E_L, s\!)^z), fs, \epsilon)$
Into_Pair	$z = (\!E_L, \langle x : s_1, s_2 \rangle\!)$	$ctxt = (\!E_L, p, ps, (\!E_L, s_1\!)\!)$ $z' = (\!E_L, s_1\!)^z \rightharpoonup [(\!E_L[x \mapsto ctxt], s_2)]$ $((E, p, ps, z'), fs, \epsilon)$
Into_Comp	$z = (\!E_L, [s \mid x \in e]\!)$ $(h \cdot t, \sigma) = [\![e]\!]_e\ (E_L, p, ps, z)\ fs$	$r = \text{map } (\lambda u.\ (E_L[x \mapsto u], s))\ t$ $z' = (\!E_L[x \mapsto h], s\!)^z \rightharpoonup r$ $((E, p, ps, z'), fs, \sigma)$
Out	$z = (\!\_\!)^{z'}$ $z' \neq (\!\_, e :: s\!)$	$((E, p, ps, z'), fs, \epsilon)$
Next	$z = l \leftharpoonup (\!c'\!)^{z'} \rightharpoonup (c \cdot r)$	$z'' = (c' \cdot l) \leftharpoonup (\!c\!)^{z'} \rightharpoonup r$ $((E, p, ps, z''), fs, \epsilon)$
Prev	$z = (c \cdot l) \leftharpoonup (\!c'\!)^{z'} \rightharpoonup r$	$z'' = l \leftharpoonup (\!c\!)^{z'} \rightharpoonup (c' \cdot r)$ $((E, p, ps, z''), fs, \epsilon)$
Store_File e	$z = (\!\_, File\!)$ $(u, \sigma) = [\![e]\!]_e\ (E, p, ps, z)\ fs$	$(fs', \sigma') = \text{make\_file } fs\ p\ u$ $((E, p, ps, z), fs', \sigma \cdot \sigma')$
Store_Dir e	$z = (\!\_, Dir\!)$ $(\ell, \sigma) = [\![e]\!]_e\ (E, p, ps, z)\ fs$	$(fs', \sigma') = \text{make\_directory } fs\ p\ \ell$ $((E, p, ps, z), fs', \sigma \cdot \sigma')$
Create_Path	$z = (\!E_L, e :: s\!)$ $(u, \sigma) = [\![e]\!]_e\ (E_L, p, ps, z)\ fs$	$(fs', \sigma') = \text{create } fs\ p/u$ $\sigma'' = \sigma \cdot (\text{Read } fs(p)\ p) \cdot \sigma'$ $((E, p, ps, z), fs', \sigma'')$

Fig. 4. fc command semantics

- **Next** and **Prev** are duals: the first traverses the zipper to the right sibling and the second to the left sibling.
- **Store_File** e, **Store_Dir** e, and **Create_Path** all update the file system, leaving the zipper untouched. All of the functions they call out to close the file system to remain well-formed and their definitions can be found in the technical report [2]. These functions produce logs recording their effects.

  For **Store_File** e, e must evaluate to a string, u, after which the command turns the current file system node into a file containing u.

  For **Store_Dir** e, e must evaluate to a string set, ℓ, after which the command turns the current file system node into a directory containing that set. If the node is already a directory containing ℓ', then any children in $\ell' \setminus \ell$ are removed, any children in $\ell \setminus \ell'$ are added (as empty files) and any children in $\ell \cap \ell'$ are untouched.

  For **Create_Path**, the current node is turned into a directory containing the

Expression: fe	Conditions: Φ	Def. of $[\![fe]\!]_e \ (E, p, ps, z) \ fs$ when Φ
Fetch_File	$z = (\!\!|\_, File|\!\!)$ File $u = fs(p)$	$(u, [\text{Read } (\text{File } u) \ p])$
Fetch_Dir	$z = (\!\!|\_, Dir|\!\!)$ Dir $\ell = fs(p)$	$(\ell, [\text{Read } (\text{Dir } \ell) \ p])$
Fetch_Path	$z = (\!\!|E_L, e :: s|\!\!)$	$[\![e]\!]_e \ (E_L, p, ps, z) \ fs$
Fetch_Comp	$z = (\!\!|E_L, [s \mid x \in e]|\!\!)$	$[\![e]\!]_e \ (E_L, p, ps, z) \ fs$
Fetch_Opt	$z = (\!\!|\_, s?|\!\!)$	$(p \in fs, [\text{Read } fs(p) \ p])$
Fetch_Pred	$z = (\!\!|E_L, P(e)|\!\!)$	$[\![e]\!]_e \ (E_L, p, ps, z) \ fs$
Run fn e	$(ctxt', \sigma') = [\![e]\!]_e \ (E, p, ps, z) \ fs$ $(ctxt, fs, \sigma) = [\![fn]\!]_c \ ctxt' \ fs$	$(ctxt, \sigma' \cdot \sigma)$
Run fe e	$(ctxt', \sigma') = [\![e]\!]_e \ (E, p, ps, z) \ fs$ $(v, \sigma) = [\![fe]\!]_e \ ctxt \ fs$	$(v, \sigma' \cdot \sigma)$
Verify	true	$(p', z') = \text{goto\_root } (E, p, ps, z) \ fs$ PConsistent $(p', ps, z') \ fs$

Fig. 5. Expression semantics

path that the path expression points to. The operation is idempotent and does the minimal work required: If the current node is already a directory, then the path is added. If the path was already there, then Create_Path is a no-op, otherwise it will map to an empty file.

With that, we have covered the semantics of all of the Forest Commands, but their subexpressions remain. The semantics of non-standard expressions is given in Fig. 5. The interpretation of each row is the same as for commands. There is one Fetch expression per specification except for pairs, which have no useful information available locally. Since a pair is defined in terms of its sub-specifications, we must navigate to them before fetching information from them. This design avoids incurring the cost of eagerly loading a large filestore.

Fetching a file returns the string contained by the file at the current path. For a directory, we get the names of its children. Both of these log Reads since they inspect the file system. For a path specification, the only locally available information is the actual path. For a comprehension, we return the set e. For an option, we determine whether the current path is in the file system and log a Read regardless. Finally, for a predicate, we determine if its condition holds.

There are two Run expressions. The subexpression, e, must evaluate to a context. These can only come from a dependent pair, which means that Runs can only occur as subexpressions of specifications. We utilize them by performing traversals (Run fn e) and evaluating Forest expressions (Run fe e) in the input context. For example, a filestore defined by a file index.txt and a set of files listed in that index could be described as follows:

$\langle index : "index.txt" :: File, [x :: File \mid x \in e] \rangle$
where e = lines_of (Run Fetch_File (Run Down $index$))

where lines_of maps a string to a string set by splitting it by lines.

Finally, Verify checks the partial consistency of the traversed part of the filestore—i.e. whether it conforms to our specification. Unfortunately, checking the entire filestore, even incrementally can be very expensive and, often, we have only performed some local changes and thus do not need the full check. Partial consistency is a compromise wherein we only check the portions of the filestore that we have traversed, as denoted by the path set. This ensures that the cost of the check is proportional to the cost of the operations we have already run. Partial consistency is formally defined in the next subsection, which among other properties, details the connection between partial and full consistency.

3.3 Properties

This section establishes properties of the TxForest core calculus: consistency and partial consistency, equational identities on commands, and round-tripping laws.

The formal definition of partial consistency is given in Fig. 6. Intuitively, full consistency (Consistent) captures whether a filestore conforms to its specification. For example, the file system, fs, at p conforms to $File$ if and only if $fs(p) = \text{File}$ _ and to $e :: s$ if e evaluates to u and fs at p/u conforms to s. Partial consistency (PConsistent) then checks partial conformance (i.e. does the filestore conform to part of its specification). PConsistent returns two booleans (and a log), the first describing whether the input filestore is consistent with the input specification and the second detailing whether that consistency is total or partial. The definition of full consistency is very similar to partial, except that there are no conditions and the path set is ignored. The properties below describe the relationship between partial consistency and full consistency. Their proofs can be found in the technical report [2].

Theorem 1. *Consistency implies partial consistency:*
$\forall ps.\ consistent?\ (Consistent\ (p, ps, z)\ fs) \implies$
$\quad consistent?\ (PConsistent\ (p, ps, z)\ fs)$

Theorem 2. *Partial Consistency is monotonic w.r.t. the path set:*
$\forall ps_1, ps_2.\ ps_2 \subseteq ps_1 \implies$
$\quad consistent?\ (PConsistent\ (p, ps_1, z)\ fs) \implies$
$\quad consistent?\ (PConsistent\ (p, ps_2, z)\ fs)$
$\quad \wedge\ complete?\ (PConsistent\ (p, ps_2, z)\ fs) \implies$
$\quad complete?\ (PConsistent\ (p, ps_1, z)\ fs)$

This theorem says that if ps_1 is partially consistent, then any path set, ps_2, that is a subset of ps_1 will also be partially consistent. Conversely, if the consistency of ps_2 is total, or complete, then ps_1 will also be totally consistent.

Theorem 3. *Given a specification s and a path set ps that covers the entirety of s, partial consistency is exactly full consistency:*
$\forall ps.\ \exists ps'.\ Cover\ (p, ps', z)\ fs\ \wedge\ ps' \subseteq ps \implies$
$\quad consistent?\ (Consistent\ (p, ps, z)\ fs) \iff$
$\quad consistent?\ (PConsistent\ (p, ps, z)\ fs)$

Spec: s	Conditions: Φ	Def. of PConsistent $(p, ps, \langle\!\langle(E, s)\rangle\!\rangle$ as $z)$ fs when Φ
$\_$	$p \notin ps$	$((\mathtt{true}, \mathtt{false}), \epsilon)$
$File$	$p \in ps$	$((fs(p) = \mathtt{File}\ \_, \mathtt{true}), [\mathtt{Read}\ fs(p)\ p])$
Dir	$p \in ps$	$((fs(p) = \mathtt{Dir}\ \_, \mathtt{true}), [\mathtt{Read}\ fs(p)\ p])$
$e :: s$	$p \in ps$	$(u, \sigma) = [\![e]\!]_e\ (E, p, ps, z)\ fs$ $((fs(p) = \mathtt{Dir}\ \_, \mathtt{true}), \sigma \cdot (\mathtt{Read}\ fs(p)\ p))\ \wedge_\sigma$ PConsistent $(p/u, ps, \langle\!(E, s)\rangle\!\rangle^z)\ fs$
$\langle x : s_1, s_2 \rangle$	$p \in ps$	$ctxt = (E, p, ps, \langle\!(E, s_1)\rangle\!\rangle)$ $E' = E[x \mapsto ctxt]$ PConsistent $(p, ps, \langle\!(E, s_1)\rangle\!\rangle^z \rightharpoonup [(E', s_2)])\ fs\ \wedge_\sigma$ PConsistent $(p, ps, [(E, s_1)] \leftharpoonup \langle\!(E', s_2)\rangle\!\rangle^z)\ fs$
$[s \mid x \in e]$	$p \in ps$	$(\ell, \sigma') = [\![e]\!]_e\ (E, p, ps, z)\ fs$ $((b_1, b_2), \sigma) = \bigwedge\limits_{v \in \ell} \mathtt{PConsistent}\ (p, ps, \langle\!(E[x \mapsto v], s)\rangle\!\rangle^z)\ fs$ $((b_1, b_2), \sigma' \cdot \sigma)$
$s?$	$p \in ps$	$((p \notin fs, \mathtt{true}), [\mathtt{Read}\ fs(p)\ p])\ \vee_\sigma$ PConsistent $(p, ps, \langle\!(E, s)\rangle\!\rangle^z)\ fs$
$P(e)$	$p \in ps$	$(b, \sigma) = [\![e]\!]_e\ (E, p, ps, z)\ fs$ $((b, \mathtt{true}), \sigma)$

$$((\mathtt{false}, \_), \sigma)\ \wedge_\sigma\ \_ \quad \triangleq \quad ((\mathtt{false}, \mathtt{false}), \sigma)$$
$$((b_1, b_2), \sigma)\ \wedge_\sigma\ ((b_1', b_2'), \sigma') \quad \triangleq \quad ((b_1 \wedge b_1', b_2 \wedge b_2'), \sigma \cdot \sigma')$$
$$((\mathtt{true}, \mathtt{true}), \sigma)\ \vee_\sigma\ \_ \quad \triangleq \quad ((\mathtt{true}, \mathtt{true}), \sigma)$$
$$((b_1, b_2), \sigma)\ \vee_\sigma\ ((b_1', b_2'), \sigma') \quad \triangleq \quad ((b_1 \vee b_1', b_2 \vee b_2'), \sigma \cdot \sigma')$$

$$\mathtt{complete?}\ ((\_, b), \_) \quad \triangleq \quad b$$
$$\mathtt{consistent?}\ ((b, \_), \_) \quad \triangleq \quad b$$

$$\mathtt{Cover}\ (p, ps, z)\ fs \quad :\Longleftrightarrow\ \mathtt{complete?}\ (\mathtt{PConsistent}\ (p, ps, z)\ fs)$$

Fig. 6. Partial consistency and cover

This theorem says that if the path set, ps is a superset of one that covers the entirety of the filestore, ps', as defined in Fig. 6, then the filestore is totally consistent exactly when it is partially consistent. Intuitively, if a path set covers a filestore then we can never encounter a path outside of the path set while traversing the zipper.

Other properties of the language include identities of the form $[\![\mathtt{Down}; \mathtt{Up}]\!]_c \equiv [\![\mathtt{Skip}]\!]_c$ where $\equiv$ denotes equivalence modulo log when defined. That is, either $[\![\mathtt{Down}; \mathtt{Up}]\!]_c$ is undefined, or it has the same action as $[\![\mathtt{Skip}]\!]_c$, barring logging. Additionally, we have proven round-tripping laws in the style of lenses [8] stating, for example, that storing just loaded data is equivalent to $\mathtt{Skip}$. Further identities and formal statements of these laws can be found in the technical report [2].

3.4   Examples

This subsection details the core calculus encodings of a few useful functions for interfacing with the course management system introduced in Sect. 2. The goal is to build an intuition for the language and how programming against the zipper abstraction might look. In practice, one would compile a higher-level language down to this core calculus for ease of use.

For the purposes of these examples, we will assume that in variables contain our input arguments at the start of each function and that out should contain the output of the function, if any, at the end. Additionally, all of our examples will be written against the same single-homework specification that we saw earlier in both our higher-level description language and in the core calculus:

```
directory {
    max is "max" :: file;
    students is [s :: students | s <- matches RE "[a-z]+[0-9]+"]
}
```

that is,

$$\langle max : "max" :: File, \langle dir : Dir, [s :: students \mid s \in e] \rangle \rangle$$
where e = filter (Run Fetch_Dir dir) "[a-z]+[0-9]+"

With that said, we will proceed to encode simple primitive functions for getting and setting the score of a single student and adding a student, a fold function over path comprehensions and finally a function for getting the average score of all students for a single homework.

```
getScore := λ(). to_int Fetch_File
setScore ≜ Store_File (of_int in)
```

In getScore and setScore, we assume that the zipper is already at a student. getScore, which we can define as an expression in the language, takes a unit input and fetches the current file, converting the string to an integer. setScore, like the rest of our examples, is instead a metavariable representing a particular command. This command converts *in* to a string before storing it as a file.

```
addStudent ≜
    Into_Pair; Next; Into_Pair;      # Go to dir
    Store_Dir (Fetch_Dir ∪ {in});   # Add in to the directory
    Out; Prev; Out                    # Return
```

In addStudent, we start from the root of the filestore and navigate to the first component of the internal pair. We then fetch the names of the current files in the directory before adding *in* and storing it back. Finally, we return to the root.

$$\vdots$$

$$
\begin{array}{lll}
ts \in Timestamp & \text{Timestamps} \\
GL \in TSLog & \text{Timestamped Logs} \\
td \in Thread & \triangleq Context \times Filesystem \times Command \\
TxS \in TxState & \triangleq Command \times Timestamp \times Log \\
t \in Transaction & \triangleq Thread \times TxState \\
T \in Thread\ Pool & \triangleq Transaction\ Bag
\end{array}
$$

Fig. 7. Global semantics additional syntax

```
fold ≜
  num := length Fetch_Comp; Into_Comp;
  While num > 0 Do
    Down;                     # Enter path
    inAcc := inF inAcc;       # Execute function and update accumulator
    Up; Next; num := num − 1  # Go to next element
  Out;
  out := inAcc
```

In `fold`, the zipper should start at a comprehension whose subspecification is a path expression. We take two inputs: $inAcc$, which is the initial accumulator value, and inF, which is a function that produces a new accumulator from the old one. The code for `fold` starts by getting the number of elements in the comprehension, before traversing the elements one by one and calling inF to update the accumulator at each element.

Finally, `getAvg` computes the average score across all students:

```
getAvg ≜
  Into_Pair; Next; Into_Pair; Next;
  number := length Fetch_Comp;
  inAcc := 0;
  inF := λx. getScore () + x;
  fold;
  Prev; Out; Prev; Out;
  out := out / number
```

It starts at the root of the filestore and navigates to the comprehension. Next, it stores the number of students in $number$, sets $inAcc$ to 0 and constructs inF, which gets the score of the current student and adds it to its argument. Then it folds, returns to the root of the filestore and divides the result of the fold (out) by the number of students to obtain the final result.

4 Concurrency Control

This section introduces the global semantics of Transactional Forest, using both a denotational semantics to concisely capture a serial semantics, and an operational semantics to capture thread interleavings and concurrency. We also state a serializability theorem that relates the two semantics.

$$\frac{\langle td\rangle \xrightarrow{\sigma'}_L \langle td'\rangle}{\langle FS, GL, \{(td, (cs, ts, \sigma))\} \uplus T\rangle \rightarrow_G \langle FS, GL, \{(td', (cs, ts, \sigma \cdot \sigma'))\} \uplus T\rangle}$$

$$\frac{\text{is\_Done? } td \quad \text{check\_log } GL \ \sigma \ ts}{FS' = \text{merge } FS \ \sigma \quad GL' = GL \cdot (\text{add\_ts fresh\_ts } \sigma)}{\langle FS, GL, \{(td, (cs, ts, \sigma))\} \uplus T\rangle \rightarrow_G \langle FS', GL', T\rangle}$$

$$\frac{\text{is\_Done? } td \quad \neg(\text{check\_log } GL \ \sigma \ ts) \quad ts' = \text{fresh\_ts}}{(z', p') = \text{goto\_root } (E, p, ps, z) \ fs \quad td' = ((\{\}, p', \{\}, z'), FS, cs)}{\langle FS, GL, \{(td, (cs, ts, \sigma))\} \uplus T\rangle \rightarrow_G \langle FS, GL, \{(td', (cs, ts', []))\} \uplus T\rangle}$$

Fig. 8. Global operational semantics

Figure 7 lists the additional syntax used in this section. Timestamped logs are the logs of the global semantics. They are identical to local logs except that each entry also contains a timestamp signifying when it was written to the log.

Each *Thread* is captured by its local context, which, along with its transactional state, *TxState*, denotes a *Transaction*. The transactional state has 3 parts: (1) the command the transaction is executing; (2) the time when the transaction started; and (3) the transaction-local log recorded so far.

Our global denotational semantics is defined as follows:

$$[\![((ctxt, \_, c), \_)]\!]_G \ fs \triangleq \text{project\_fs } ([\![c]\!]_c \ ctxt \ fs)$$
$$[\![\ell]\!]_G \ fs \triangleq \text{fold } fs \ \ell \ [\![\cdot]\!]_G$$

The denotation of one or more transactions is a function on file systems. For a single transaction, it is the denotation of the command with the encapsulated context except for the file system which is replaced by the input. For a list of transactions, it is the result of applying the local denotation function in serial order. Note that the denotation of a transaction is precisely the denotation of a program, $[\![\cdot]\!]_g$, which can be lifted to multiple programs by folding. The key point to note about this semantics is that there is no interleaving of transactions. By definition, the transactions are run sequentially. While this ensures serializability, it also does not allow for any concurrency.

We will instead use an operational semantics that more easily models thread interleaving and prove that it is equivalent to the denotational semantics. First, we introduce an operational semantics for local commands. This semantics is standard for IMP commands, but for Forest Commands, it uses the denotational semantics, considering each a single atomic step, as seen below:

$$\frac{((E', p', ps', z'), fs', \sigma) = [\![fc]\!]_c \ (E, p, ps, z) \ fs}{\langle (E, p, ps, z), fs, fc\rangle \xrightarrow{\sigma}_L \langle (E', p', ps', z'), fs', \text{Skip}\rangle}$$

Next, we can construct the global operational semantics, as seen in Fig. 8. The global stepping relation is between two global contexts which have three parts: A global file system, a global log, and a thread pool, or bag of transactions.

$$\text{merge } FS \ \sigma \triangleq \text{fold } FS \ \sigma \text{ update}$$

$$\text{update } fs \ (\text{Read } T \ p) \triangleq fs$$
$$\text{update } fs \ (\text{Write\_file } \_ \ T \ p) \triangleq \text{close\_fs } (fs[p \mapsto T])$$
$$\text{update } fs \ (\text{Write\_dir } \_ \ T \ p) \triangleq \text{close\_fs } (fs[p \mapsto T])$$

$$\text{check\_log } GL \ \sigma \ ts \triangleq \forall p' \in \text{extract\_paths } \sigma. \ \forall (ts', le) \in GL.$$
$$ts > ts' \ \lor \ \neg(\text{conflict\_path } p' \ le)$$
$$\text{conflict\_path } p' \ (\text{Read } \_ \ p) \triangleq \text{false}$$
$$\text{conflict\_path } p' \ (\text{Write\_file } \_ \_ \ p) \triangleq \text{subpath } p' \ p$$
$$\text{conflict\_path } p' \ (\text{Write\_dir } \_ \_ \ p) \triangleq \text{subpath } p' \ p$$

$$\text{extract\_paths } [] \triangleq \{\}$$
$$\text{extract\_paths } ((\text{Read } \_ \ p) \cdot tl) \triangleq \{p\} \cup (\text{extract\_paths } tl)$$
$$\text{extract\_paths } ((\text{Write\_file } \_ \_ \ p) \cdot tl) \triangleq \{p\} \cup (\text{extract\_paths } tl)$$
$$\text{extract\_paths } ((\text{Write\_dir } \_ \_ \ p) \cdot tl) \triangleq \{p\} \cup (\text{extract\_paths } tl)$$

Fig. 9. merge and check_log

There are only three actions that the global semantics can take:

1. A transaction can step in the local semantics and append the resulting log.
2. A transaction that is done, and does not conflict with previously committed transactions, can commit. It must check that none of its operations conflicted with those committed since its start. Conflicts occur when the transaction read stale data. Then, it will update the global file system according to any writes performed. Finally, the transaction will leave the thread pool. The definitions of check_log and merge can be found in Fig. 9.
3. A transaction that is done, but conflicts with previously committed transactions, cannot commit and instead has to restart. It does this by getting a fresh timestamp and resetting its log and local context.

In the operational semantics, thread steps can be interleaved arbitrarily, but changes will get rolled back in case of a conflict. Furthermore, while Forest Commands are treated as atomic for simplicity they could also be modeled at finer granularity without affecting our results.

With a global semantics where transactions are run concurrently, we now aim to prove that our semantics guarantees serializability. The theorem below captures this property by connecting the operational and denotational semantics:

Theorem 4 (Serializability). *Let* FS, FS' *be file systems,* GL, GL' *be global logs, and* T *a thread pool such that* $\forall t \in T.$ *initial* $FS \ t$, *then:*

$$\langle FS, GL, T \rangle \rightarrow_G^* \langle FS', GL', \{\} \rangle \implies \exists \ell \in Perm(T). \ [\![\ell]\!]_G \ FS = FS'$$

where $\rightarrow_G^*$ *is the reflexive, transitive closure of* $\rightarrow_G$.

The serializability theorem states that given a starting file system and a thread pool of starting threads, if the global operational semantics commits them all, then there is some ordering of these threads for which the global denotational semantics will produce the same resulting file system. Note that although it is not required by the theorem, the commit order is one such ordering. Additionally, though not explicitly stated, it is easy to see that any serial schedule that is in the domain of the denotation function is realizable by the operational semantics. See the technical report [2] for the proof.

The prototype system described in the next section implements the local semantics from the previous section along with this global semantics, reducing the burden of writing correct concurrent applications.

5   Implementation

This section describes our prototype implementation of Transactional Forest as an embedded domain-specific language in OCaml. Our prototype comprises 6089 lines of code (excluding blank lines and comments) and encodes Forest's features as a PPX syntax extension.

We have implemented a simple course management system similar to the running example from Sect. 2. It has several additional facilities beyond renormalization, including computing various statistics about students or homeworks and changing rubrics while automatically updating student grades accordingly. The most interesting piece of the example is based on our experience with a professional grading system which uses a queue from which graders can get new problems to grade. Unfortunately, this system did not adequately employ concurrency control, resulting in duplicated work. Using TxForest, we implemented a simple grading queue where graders can add and retrieve problems, which does not suffer from such concurrency issues.

The embedded language in our prototype implementation implements almost precisely the language seen in Sect. 3. Additionally, we provide a surface syntax (as seen in Sect. 2 and papers on the earlier versions of Forest [3,5]) for specifications that compiles down to the core calculus seen in Sect. 3. This specification can then be turned into a zipper by initiating a transaction. The majority of the commands and expressions seen in the core semantics are then exposed as functions in a library. Additionally, there is a more ad hoc surface command language that resembles the surface syntax and parallels the behavior of the core language. Finally, the global semantics looks slightly different compared to in Sect. 4, though this should not affect users and the minor variant has been proven correct. We provide a simple shell for interacting with filestores, which makes it significantly easier to force conflicts and test the concurrent semantics.

6   Related Work

We discuss four families of related work: languages for ad hoc data processing, zippers, transaction semantics, and transactional file systems.

Ad hoc Data Processing. Transactional Forest builds on a long line of work in ad hoc data processing. PADS [6,7] (Processing Ad hoc Data Streams) is a declarative domain-specific language designed to deal with ad hoc data. It allows users to write declarative specifications describing the structure of a file and uses such descriptions to generate types, transformations between on-disk and in-memory representations with robust error handling, and various statistical analysis tools.

Forest [5] extends the concept of PADS to full filestores and additionally provides formal guarantees about the generated transformations in the form of bidirectional lens laws. The original version of Forest was implemented in Haskell and relied on its host language's laziness to load only required data. Unfortunately, it was not always clear what actions might trigger loading the entire filestore. For example, checking if there were errors at any level would load everything below that level. Incremental Forest [3] addressed this issue by introducing *delays* to make explicit the amount of loading corresponding to any action. It also supported a cost semantics that precisely characterized the cost of any such action for varied, user-defined notions of cost. It did not address concurrent access to Incremental Forest-described filestores, however.

A bit farther afield, Microsoft's LINQ [12] and F#'s Type Providers [16] share the Forest family's goal of making data-oriented programming easier. While they lack support for declarative specifications of filestores, LINQ and Type Providers both include nice interfaces for interacting with data. In contrast, languages like XFiles [1] do allow declarative filestore specifications, but do not directly interoperate with general purpose programming languages.

Zippers. Huet [10] introduced Zippers as an elegant data structure for traversing and updating a functional tree. There has been much work studying zippers since, though the closest to our work is Kiselyov's Zipper file system [11]. Kiselyov builds a small functional file system with a zipper as its core abstraction. This file system offers a simple transaction mechanism by providing each thread its own view of the file system. The system lacks formal guarantees and is generic: it does not support an application-specific view of the file system as a filestore. In contrast, Transactional Forest uses type-based specifications to describe the structure and invariants of filestores. Further, we present a formal syntax and semantics for our core language, a model of concurrency, and a proof of serializability.

Transaction Semantics. Moore and Grossman [14] present a family of languages with software transactions, investigating how these languages support parallelism and what restrictions are necessary to ensure correctness in the presence of weak isolation. Additionally, they provide a type-and-effect system which ensures the serializability of well-typed programs. At a high level, they describe what the core of a language used to write concurrent programs might look and act like, including constructs like spawning threads or atomic sections. Our transactional semantics is higher-level and specific to our domain, describing a transaction manager designed simply to ensure serializability among TxForest threads.

Transactional File Systems. General support for transactional file systems has been well studied [4,9,13,15]. All of this work starts at a lower level than Transactional Forest, providing transaction support for file system commands. We, instead, provide transactions from the perspective of the higher-level application, easily allowing an arbitrary high-level computation to be aborted or restarted if there is a conflict at the file system level.

7 Conclusion

We have presented the design, syntax, and semantics of Transactional Forest, a domain-specific language for incrementally processing ad hoc data in concurrent applications. TxForest aims to provide an easier and less error-prone approach to modeling and interacting with a structured subset of a file system, which we call a *filestore*. We achieve this by leveraging Huet's Zippers [10] as our core abstraction. Their traversal-based structure naturally lends itself to incrementality and a simple, efficient logging scheme that we use for our optimistic concurrency control. We provide a core language with a formal syntax and semantics based on zipper traversal, both for local, single-threaded applications, and for a global view with arbitrarily many Forest processes. We prove that this global view enforces serializability between threads, that is, the resulting effect on the file system of any set of concurrent threads is the same as if they had run in some serial order. Our OCaml prototype provides a surface language mirroring Classic Forest [5] and a library of functions for manipulating the filestore.

Acknowledgments. The authors wish to thank the anonymous APLAS reviewers for helpful comments on an earlier draft of this paper. Our work is supported in part by the National Science Foundation under grant CNS-1413972 and by the Defense Advanced Research Projects Agency.

References

1. Buraga, S.C.: An XML-based semantic description of distributed file systems. In: RoEduNet (2003)
2. DiLorenzo, J., Mancini, K., Fisher, K., Foster, N.: TxForest: A DSL for Concurrent Filestores. Technical report (2019). https://arxiv.org/abs/1908.10273
3. DiLorenzo, J., Zhang, R., Menzies, E., Fisher, K., Foster, N.: Incremental forest: a DSL for efficiently managing filestores. In: ACM SIGPLAN Notices, OOPSLA 2016, vol. 51, pp. 252–271 (2016)
4. Escriva, R., Sirer, E.G.: The design and implementation of the warp transactional filesystem. In: Proceedings of the 13th Usenix Conference on Networked Systems Design and Implementation, NSDI 2016, pp. 469–483. USENIX Association, Berkeley (2016)
5. Fisher, K., Foster, N., Walker, D., Zhu, K.Q.: Forest: a language and toolkit for programming with filestores. In: Proceedings of the 16th ACM SIGPLAN International Conference on Functional Programming, ICFP 2011, pp. 292–306. ACM, New York (2011). https://doi.org/10.1145/2034773.2034814

6. Fisher, K., Gruber, R.: PADS: a domain-specific language for processing ad hoc data. In: Proceedings of the 2005 ACM SIGPLAN Conference on Programming Language Design and Implementation, PLDI 2005, pp. 295–304. ACM, New York (2005). https://doi.org/10.1145/1065010.1065046

7. Fisher, K., Walker, D.: The PADS project: an overview. In: Proceedings of the 14th International Conference on Database Theory, ICDT 2011, ACM, New York (2011). https://doi.org/10.1145/1938551.1938556

8. Foster, J.N., Greenwald, M.B., Moore, J.T., Pierce, B.C., Schmitt, A.: Combinators for bidirectional tree transformations: a linguistic approach to the view update problem. ACM Trans. Program. Lang. Syst. (TOPLAS) **29**(3) (2007). Short version in POPL 2005

9. Garcia, J., Ferreira, P., Guedes, P.: The PerDiS FS: a transactional file system for a distributed persistent store. In: Proceedings of the 8th ACM SIGOPS European Workshop on Support for Composing Distributed Applications, EW 8, pp. 189–194. ACM, New York (1998). https://doi.org/10.1145/319195.319224

10. Huet, G.: The Zipper. J. Funct. Program. **7**(5), 549–554 (1997). https://doi.org/10.1017/S0956796897002864

11. Kiselyov, O.: Tool demonstration: a zipper based file/operating system. In: Proceedings of the 2005 ACM SIGPLAN Workshop on Haskell, Haskell 2005 (2005). http://okmij.org/ftp/continuations/ZFS/zfs-talk.pdf

12. LINQ: NET language-integrated query, February 2007. http://msdn.microsoft.com/library/bb308959.aspx

13. Liskov, B., Rodrigues, R.: Transactional file systems can be fast. In: Proceedings of the 11th Workshop on ACM SIGOPS European Workshop, EW 2004, ACM, New York (2004). https://doi.org/10.1145/1133572.1133592

14. Moore, K.F., Grossman, D.: High-level small-step operational semantics for transactions. In: Proceedings of the 35th Annual ACM SIGPLAN-SIGACT Symposium on Principles of Programming Languages, POPL 2008, pp. 51–62. ACM, New York (2008). https://doi.org/10.1145/1328438.1328448

15. Schmuck, F., Wylie, J.: Experience with transactions in QuickSilver. In: Proceedings of the Thirteenth ACM Symposium on Operating Systems Principles, SOSP 1991, pp. 239–253. ACM, New York (1991). https://doi.org/10.1145/121132.121171

16. Syme, D.: Looking ahead with F#: taming the data deluge. Presentation at the Workshop on F# in Education, November 2010

Verification

J-ReCoVer: Java Reducer Commutativity Verifier

Yu-Fang Chen[1,2], Chang-Yi Chiang[2], Lukáš Holík[3], Wei-Tsung Kao[1],
Hsin-Hung Lin[1(✉)], Tomáš Vojnar[3], Yean-Fu Wen[2], and Wei-Cheng Wu[1]

[1] Institute of Information Science, Academia Sinica, Taipei, Taiwan
{yfc,hlin}@iis.sinica.edu.tw,b05901009@ntu.edu.tw,spencerwu85@gmail.com
[2] Graduate Institute of Information Management, National Taipei University,
Taipei, Taiwan
a2235486@gmail.com,yeanfu@mail.ntpu.edu.tw
[3] FIT, IT4I Centre of Excellence, Brno University of Technology, Brno, Czechia
{holik,vojnar}@fit.vutbr.cz

Abstract. The MapReduce framework for data-parallel computation
was first proposed by Google [10] and later implemented in the Apache
Hadoop project. Under the MapReduce framework, a reducer computes
output values from a sequence of input values transmitted over the network. Due to non-determinism in data transmission, the order in which
input values arrive at the reducer is not fixed. In relation to this, the
commutativity problem of reducers asks if the output of a reducer is
independent of the order of its inputs. Indeed, there are several advantages for a reducer to be commutative, e.g., the verification problem
of a MapReduce program can be reduced to the problem of verifying
a sequential program. We present the tool J-ReCoVer (Java Reducer
Commutativity Verifier) that implements effective heuristics for reducer
commutativity analysis. J-ReCoVer is the first tool that is specialized
in checking reducer commutativity. Our experimental results over 118
benchmark examples collected from open repositories are very positive;
J-ReCoVer correctly handles over 97% of them.

1 Introduction

MapReduce belongs among the most popular frameworks for data parallel computation. A MapReduce program [10] consists of several pairs of *mappers* and
reducers running on a machine cluster for handling big data in parallel. Usually,
mappers and reducers are the only components in a MapReduce program that
involve concurrency. Mappers read data from a distributed database and output a sequence of *key-value* pairs. The elements of the sequence (i.e., key-value
pairs) with the same key are sent to the same reducer for further processing.
Due to scheduling policies and network latency, the same inputs may arrive at
a reducer in different orders in different executions. Therefore, reducers are typically required to be *commutative*, that is, the output of a reducer is required to

The work was supported by the Minister of Science and Technology of Taiwan project
106-2221-E-001-009-MY3 and the Czech Science Foundation project 17-12465S.

© Springer Nature Switzerland AG 2019
A. W. Lin (Ed.): APLAS 2019, LNCS 11893, pp. 357–366, 2019.
https://doi.org/10.1007/978-3-030-34175-6_18

be independent of the order of its inputs. The problem of checking whether this is indeed the case is known as the *commutativity problem* of reducers [6,8,9,17].

If a reducer is commutative, it will have the same external behaviour under all possible schedules, and one then suffices with considering any chosen interleaving of input values when examining its behaviour instead of having to consider all of them. By fixing a schedule, the verification problem of a MapReduce program reduces to the verification problem of a sequential program, which is known to be much easier than the verification problem of concurrent programs.

On the other hand, the non-commutative behaviour of a reducer is often the source of very tricky bugs. A study conducted by Microsoft investigated the commutativity problem of 508 reducers running on their MapReduce server [17]. These reducers were carefully checked using all traditional means such as code review, testing, and experiments with real data for months. Still, five of these programs contained very subtle bugs caused by non-commutativity (which was confirmed by the programmers).

However, checking reducer commutativity is a difficult problem on its own right [6–8]. Even for a simple case in which all values are mathematical integers, it is proved undecidable in [6]. For the case when all values are machine integers (e.g., 64-bits integers), the problem is decidable, but the only available algorithm, which was proposed in [6] too, is of very high complexity and hence of theoretical interest only.

In this paper, we present the J-ReCoVer tool (Java Reducer Commutativity Verifier), which is available at http://www.jrecover.tk/. The tool implements a heuristic approach for checking the commutativity problem that—despite its simplicity—works very efficiently on a large set of practical integer reducer programs as shown by our experiments. The main ingredient of the approach is a reduction from the commutativity problem to an SMT problem. The reduction is incomplete but sound. It is accompanied with several heuristics which enable the approach to scale to real-world examples. For the case when the reducer is not proven commutative, we complement the approach by using testing to find concrete counterexamples.

We collected benchmarks from open repositories such as GitHub and Bitbucket to evaluate J-ReCoVer. With the help of a search engine *searchcode.com* over those repositories, we collected 118 programs. We provide this collection of programs to other interested researchers as a side contribution of the paper. Our tool J-ReCoVer is able to correctly analyse all but three of the programs.

Related Work. The reducer commutativity problem can be reduced to a *program equivalence* problem. One creates another program R' that first non-deterministically swaps two consecutive input values and then executes the code of R. If R' and R are equivalent, using the fact that all permutations of a list can be obtained by swapping consecutive list elements finitely many times[1], R can be proved to be commutative. A series of research works address program equivalence checking (or closely related topics such as regression verification and translation validation), cf. [3,11,13,15] to name a few.

From a high-level view, checking equivalence of two programs P and P' can be reduced to a sequential verification problem by executing P' after P, followed by checking whether the two programs always produce the same outputs. The approach can be made more efficient by finding the right *synchronization points* and combining the code of P and P' in an interleaved manner. A lot of research effort have been invested into finding good synchronization points. In this work, we propose the *head of the top-level reducer loop* as the synchronization point suitable for reducer commutativity analysis. According to our experience, discussed later on, the reducers usually contain just a single such loop. Moreover, for the case when there are more top-level loops in a reducer, we propose a way of breaking the reducer into several ones to be checked independently.

However, we observe that if one naively reduces the commutativity problem to an equivalence problem and checks it in a precise manner, many reducers cannot be verified. Therefore, J-ReCoVer uses an over-approximation of the reducer's behaviour. This approximation allows for a much more efficient, yet—according to our experiments—precise enough commutativity analysis.

Our approach can be seen as using some form of *sequentialisation* of the concurrent behaviour. Sequentialisation is the key approach behind many current successful approaches for verifying multithreaded programs [12,14]. However, our sequentialisation approach is specialised for the case of reducers and quite different from what is used in sequentialisation of multithreaded programs: indeed, in MapReduce programs there is no notion of threads nor context switches.

Various forms of sequentialisation are also used in works dealing with the concept of *robustness* of event-driven asynchronous programs [5] or works dealing with programs running under some *relaxed memory models* [1,2,4]. However, their computation models are again quite different from that of reducers, and their results cannot be directly applied. Besides verification, another interesting research direction, using commutativity analysis as a component, is *synthesis* of MapReduce programs [16].

2   Notations and Definitions

We use $[n, m]$ to denote the set of integers $\{k \mid n \leq k \leq m\}$ and lift the equality predicate $=$ to tuples in the standard, component-wise, way.

---

[1] Here is an example to produce [3;2;5;1;4] from [1;2;3;4;5] by swapping consecutive elements: [**1**;**2**;3;4;5] → [2;**1**;**3**;4;5] → [2;3;**1**;**4**;5] → [2;3;**1**;**5**;4] → [**2**;**3**;5;1;4] → [3;2;5;1;4].

To present our approach, we introduce a highly simplified language for describing reducers. Let Var be a set of *integer variables*. An *integer expression* in Exp can either be a variable from Var, a constant value, a call to the *cur*() function that reads and consumes an input value of the reducer, a non-deterministically chosen integer value $*$, or a combination of integer expressions over basic arithmetic operations. A *command* in Cmd can be an assignment, a branch statement, a sequence of commands, or an *out*(v) statement that outputs the value of $v \in$ Var. A *reducer program* is defined as s_1; **Loop**$\{s_2\}$; s_3 where $s_1, s_2, s_3 \in$ Cmd.

$s := 0; c := 0;$
Loop$\{$
   $s := s + cur();$
   $c := c + 1$
$\}$
$; o := s/c;$
out(o)

Fig. 1. A reducer that computes the average value.

According to our observation over hundreds of reducer programs in open repositories, reducer programs are almost always in this form. The **Loop**$\{s_2\}$ statement enters the loop body to execute s_2 repeatedly for each input element until the entire input list is consumed. An example of a reducer is shown in Fig. 1. In the paper, to simplify the presentation, we assume that a reducer does never produce any output in the loop body s_2. J-ReCoVer implements an algorithm to deal with an output inside the loop (as briefly mentioned at the end of Sect. 4.2).

Some reducers use two (or more) top-level loops to compute the output, possibly interleaved with some non-looping code. These loops are executed sequentially, repeatedly iterating over the input list from its beginning. For example, for calculating the standard deviation, one first computes the average of inputs and then uses it to compute the final result (using two passes over the input list). In that case, we suggest to verify the reducer by first partitioning it into two (or more) reducers, each containing a single top-level loop, and then verifying these reducers separately.[2] The top-level loops communicate through shared variables. After the transformation, reducers corresponding to the second top-level loop (and possibly further such loops) will work with random initial values of the shared variable, which over-approximates the original behaviour. In our experience, the second (or further) top-level loop are usually commutative even with arbitrary initial shared variable values, and so J-ReCoVer can be used to handle such reducers.

3   Overview of the J-ReCoVer tool

The input of J-ReCoVer is a reducer program written in Java, which is the most popular programming language used in the Hadoop MapReduce framework. The J-ReCoVer tool has three main components, *Preprocessor*, *Prover*, and *BugFinder*. As the name suggests, Preprocessor reads as input a reducer program and performs the required preprocessing. The goal of Prover is to show that a given reducer is commutative, and the goal of BugFinder is the opposite. The architecture of J-ReCoVer can be found in Fig. 2. The user can input a

---

[2] Nested loops can be removed by adding additional branch statements since both the inner and outer loop are over the same input list. In fact, such a program construct has never occurred in the examples we have seen.

reducer program to J-ReCoVer either through our web-interface or use a binary application installed on his/her own machine.

The *Preprocessor component* first compiles a reducer program to bytecode and uses the tool Soot[3] to further convert it to the so-called "Jimple" format, which is an intermediate language designed to simplify the analysis of Java programs. Under the Hadoop MapReduce framework, the permutation of the input is handled by the scheduler/shuffler component and is affected by issues like network latency, which are not controllable by programmers. In order to deal with such

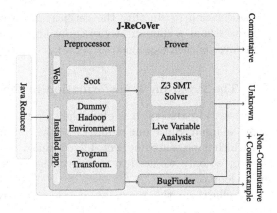

Fig. 2. Overview of the J-ReCoVer tool.

issues, we wrote our own dummy Hadoop environment for the reducer as a part of the Preprocessor component so that the input order of the reducer is now controlled by J-ReCoVer. Finally, the Preprocessor performs a program transformation to simplify the analysis.

The *BugFinder component* generates random pairs of lists, with the list of each pair being permutations of each other. A concrete counterexample is reported if the reducer outputs different results for the two lists of a generated pair. Our procedure for generating random pairs is quite naive. We use five different input list of lengths 5, 7, 9, 11, and 13. For each length, we generate 100 lists and pick uniformly at random one of its permutations. Although the approach is simple; in practice, it finds counterexamples in all of our non-commutative benchmarks in few seconds.

The *Prover component* reduces the commutativity problem to an SMT problem. From a high-level point of view, we are checking equivalence between a reducer program and its variant that has two consecutive inputs swapped. We show that this equivalence check can be reduced to a first-order formula and give it to the SMT solver Z3 for solving. In case that Z3 proves the formula unsatisfiable, we know that swapping any two consecutive inputs of the reducer will not change its output. Since all permutations of a list can be obtained by swapping consecutive elements finitely many times, it follows that the reducer outputs the same value for all permutations of the same list of inputs. In this case, J-ReCoVer stops and reports that the reducer is commutative.

---

[3] https://github.com/Sable/soot.

4   The Preprocessor and the Prover

Before entering the Prover component, the Preprocessor first performs a program transformation to simplify the verification task (Sect. 4.1). The output of the preprocessor is a commutativity-equivalent reducer program. The algorithm of the Prover is then explained in Sect. 4.2.

4.1   The Program Transformation in the Preprocessor

In real-world reducers, it is often the case that the s_1 part of the reducer reads from the input. Since our reduction of the commutativity problem to SMT solving, which is presented in Sect. 4.2, concentrates on the influence of the input on the loop s_2 only, we need to transform the reducer such that any input happens in the loop only.

To illustrate the issue, we consider the reducer shown in Fig. 3. The reducer presented in the figure remembers the first input value in the variable m, increases its value by 10, and then updates its value to bigger ones if any occur in the loop. The main loop of the reducer is commutative in this case, but the reducer is not commutative. A counterexample can be easily found. With the list $[1, 2, 3, 4, 5]$ and its permutation $[5, 4, 3, 2, 1]$ as the inputs, the reducer outputs 11 and 15, respectively.

$$m := cur() + 10;$$
$$\textbf{Loop}\{$$
$$\quad t := cur()$$
$$\quad \textbf{if } t > m \textbf{ then}$$
$$\quad\quad m := t$$
$$\}$$
$$; out(m)$$

Fig. 3.   The max^+ reducer with input before the main loop.

Our transformation will handle the example from Fig. 3 as follows. We move the prefix s_1 into the loop body and use a new variable s to force that the execution of s_1 is always before the original loop body. The result after the transformation is demonstrated in Fig. 4. The new reducer program has the same inputs/outputs as the original one. Therefore, if the new reducer is commutative, the original one is also commutative.

In general, the problem with the input before the loop can be handled as follows, including the case where $cur()$ occurs multiple times in s_1. Assume that the s_1 part of the reducer $s_1; \textbf{Loop}\{s_2\}; s_3$ has the form $c_0; x_1 := cur(); c_1; \ldots; x_m := cur(); c_m$ where $cur()$ does not occur in $c_0, c_1, \ldots, c_m$. In the transformed reducer, the part before the loop will be $c_0; s := 1$, and the loop body will contain several new branch statements. In particular, for all $j \in [1, m]$, we add the branch statement **if** $s = j$ **then** $x_j := cur(); c_j; s := s + 1$. Moreover, we transform the original loop body into the branch **if** $s = m + 1$ **then** s_2.

$$s := 1;$$
$$\textbf{Loop}\{$$
$$\quad \textbf{if } s = 1 \textbf{ then}$$
$$\quad\quad m := cur() + 10; s := 2$$
$$\quad \textbf{else}$$
$$\quad\quad t := cur()$$
$$\quad\quad \textbf{if } t > m \textbf{ then}$$
$$\quad\quad\quad m := t$$
$$\}$$
$$; out(m)$$

Fig. 4. The max^{+fix} reducer.

4.2   The Prover: Reduce Commutativity Checking to SMT Solving

After the transformation described above, the reducer $s_1; \mathbf{Loop}\{s_2\}; s_3$ never calls the $cur()$ function in the s_1 part before entering the loop. Further, we assume w.l.o.g. that the reducer reads exactly one input in one loop iteration. When multiple reads from the input occur in a single execution path from the begin to the end of the loop body, we can use additional variables and branch statements to break the path into several auxiliary ones, each reading just once.

The command s_2 can be viewed as a function F that reads the values of all variables and the current input before executing s_2 and outputs the values of all variables after s_2. Note that s_2 contains no nested loop structure. Hence, a bounded summary in quantifier-free linear integer arithmetic is sufficient for describing F.

Formally, the function $F(n, x_1, x_2, \ldots, x_k) : \mathbb{Z}^{k+1} \rightarrow \mathbb{Z}^k$ returns a tuple of values $x'_1, x'_2, \ldots, x'_k$ where n is the current input value of the reducer, x_i and x'_i are the values of the variables before and after the execution of s_2, respectively, for $i \in [1, k]$. The construction of F from s_2 can be done in the standard way.

We reduce the reducer commutativity verification to checking validity of the following formula for all possible values of $n_1, n_2, x_1, x_2, \ldots, x_k$:

$$F(n_1, F(n_2, x_1, x_2, \ldots, x_k)) = F(n_2, F(n_1, x_1, x_2, \ldots, x_k)). \tag{1}$$

Intuitively, the formula says that starting from the same initial valuations of variables and with two different input orders, $[n_1; n_2]$ and $[n_2; n_1]$, the values of all program variables are the same after we execute the loop body twice. The first execution reads n_1 and then reads n_2. The other execution reads the two inputs in the reverse order. Since any permutation of the input can be obtained by a sequence of permutations of neighbouring inputs, the validity of Formula 1 implies that the permutations will not change the final variable valuation and hence the output in s_3.

Consider the reducer computing the average value (Fig. 1) as an example. The reducer has two variables s and c. We get that $F_{average}(n, s, c) = (s + n, c + 1)$. In this case, Formula 1 is valid since $F_{average}(n_1, F_{average}(n_2, s, c)) = F_{average}(n_1, s + n_2, c + 1) = (s + n_1 + n_2, c + 2) = F_{average}(n_2, s + n_1, c + 1) = F_{average}(n_2, F_{average}(n_1, s, c))$. This implies that the reducer is commutative.

A Note on Dealing with Output in the Main Loop. So far we have assumed that there was no output in the main loop and mentioned that this restriction is lifted in J-ReCoVer. Due to space restrictions, a proper explanation of the way of handling this issue is beyond the scope of this paper, but we give at least a brief sketch of the solution. In particular, the Preprocessor performs one more transformation which adds an assignment $v := e$ for every $out(e)$ statement in the main loop where v is a fresh variable assigned just once in the loop body. This makes the output visible for our analysis since v appears in Formula 1. The Prover then makes an additional check whether the value of $F(n, x_1, x_2, \ldots, x_k)$ projected on v stays the same for any input value n and any initial values of the variables x_i.

4.3   An Optimisation by Live Variable Analysis

We now explain how a simple live variable analysis is used in J-ReCoVer to significantly improve the precision of commutativity checking.

In our initial experiments, we realised that Formula 1 is too strong, too often violated by reducers that are commutative. To illustrate the issue, we present a simple example. In the loop body, the input is first stored in a variable t and this is then assigned to s, i.e., $t := cur()$; $s := s+t$. After the loop, the value of s is output. In this case, the function F returns the updated values of both s and t after the execution of the loop body. Observe that $F(c_1, F(c_2, s, t)) = (s + c_1 + c_2, c_1)$ and $F(c_2, F(c_1, s, t)) = (s + c_1 + c_2, c_2)$. It follows that Formula 1 is invalid. The second component of the returned tuples, which causes the invalidity, corresponds to the value of t after executing the loop body twice. Their values are c_1 and c_2, respectively, in $F(c_1, F(c_2, s, t))$ and $F(c_2, F(c_1, s, t))$. However, in this case, the value of t will not affect the output of the reducer.

To handle the above issue, we perform a simple backward live variable analysis to collect all variables whose value may propagate to the output command after the loop execution. Only these variables are then required to be equivalent. For the example above, the variable t will be ignored in the equivalence checking and hence the program can be proven commutative. In our evaluation, the ratio of reducers that our approach can successfully analyse is significantly increased—in particular, from 6.8% to 97.5%—by using this optimisation.

5   Evaluation

J-ReCoVer is implemented in Java and built on top of Soot 2.5.0 and Z3 4.7.1. We ran J-ReCoVer on a virtual machine with 4 GB of memory running Ubuntu 16.04.5 LTS on a server with AMD Opteron 6376 CPU.

Benchmark Collection. In order to properly evaluate the performance of J-ReCoVer, we used the search engine *searchcode.com* to collect Java programs containing the key strings "public void reduce" or "protected void reduce". Since there is an upper bound on the number of results

Table 1. Size of the reducers.

	Line	Variable	Branch
Min.	5	4	0
Avg.	20.5	14.7	1.2
Max.	58	37	5

returned from the search engine, we added different search filters in order to get more data. We tried all 12 combinations of six filters on the code length $\{< 50, 50–250, 250–450, 450–650, 650–850, 850–1050, 1050–1250\}$ and two filters for data sources $\{$github.com, bitbuckect.com$\}$. In total, we got 11,346 Java programs. We excluded cases that were not Hadoop MapReduce reducer programs (those do not import the Hadoop library, do not extend or implement the reducer interface) and obtained 1,273 examples. We further removed duplicates, those that could not be compiled, and those with non-numerical data types (e.g., strings). We obtained 118 reducers as the final benchmarks. Table 1 contains more details of the considered reducer functions.

Results. J-ReCoVer successfully handled 115 cases (97.5%) out of the considered ones. Among them, 106 cases are commutative, while 9 are not. The analysis time ranged between 9.8 and 8.6 s. On average, 72% of the execution time was spent in compiling Java source code to bytecode, which is the input of the Soot tool. Further, 27% of the execution time was spent in the Preprocessor, in which Soot is used to transform Java bytecode to Jimple and perform the program transformation. The time spent in Solver is quite limited ($<1\%$) since the real-world integer reducer programs are usually not that big.

There is no other tool that could handle the reducers as they are. Perhaps some other tools could be applied on the transformed programs, but the transformation would still be needed, and our SMT-based back-end verifier (the Solver) turned out to work efficiently. Hence, we did not feel a need to replace it by another verification tool. Of course, in the future, this can be done if need be.

J-ReCoVer failed in three cases out of the considered ones because the three reducers use more complicated control structures than what J-ReCoVer currently supports. Namely, they use a branch statement before entering the loop, i.e., they have the form of **if** g **then** $(s_1; \mathbf{Loop}\{s_2\}; s_3)$ **else** $(s_1'; \mathbf{Loop}\{s_2'\}; s_3')$. In theory, such a program can be handled by more sophisticated program transformation. For example, we can merge the two loops and push the outer branch condition into the merged loop. Extensions of J-ReCoVer to be able to handle such constructions, together with a support for more data types, is among our future directions.

References

1. Abdulla, P.A., Atig, M.F., Chen, Y.-F., Leonardsson, C., Rezine, A.: Counter-example guided fence insertion under TSO. In: Flanagan, C., König, B. (eds.) TACAS 2012. LNCS, vol. 7214, pp. 204–219. Springer, Heidelberg (2012). https://doi.org/10.1007/978-3-642-28756-5_15
2. Abdulla, P.A., Atig, M.F., Chen, Y.-F., Leonardsson, C., Rezine, A.: MEMORAX, a precise and sound tool for automatic fence insertion under TSO. In: Piterman, N., Smolka, S.A. (eds.) TACAS 2013. LNCS, vol. 7795, pp. 530–536. Springer, Heidelberg (2013). https://doi.org/10.1007/978-3-642-36742-7_37
3. Barthe, G., Crespo, J.M., Kunz, C.: Relational verification using product programs. In: Butler, M., Schulte, W. (eds.) FM 2011. LNCS, vol. 6664, pp. 200–214. Springer, Heidelberg (2011). https://doi.org/10.1007/978-3-642-21437-0_17
4. Bouajjani, A., Derevenetc, E., Meyer, R.: Checking and enforcing robustness against TSO. In: Felleisen, M., Gardner, P. (eds.) ESOP 2013. LNCS, vol. 7792, pp. 533–553. Springer, Heidelberg (2013). https://doi.org/10.1007/978-3-642-37036-6_29
5. Bouajjani, A., Emmi, M., Enea, C., Ozkan, B.K., Tasiran, S.: Verifying robustness of event-driven asynchronous programs against concurrency. In: Yang, H. (ed.) ESOP 2017. LNCS, vol. 10201, pp. 170–200. Springer, Heidelberg (2017). https://doi.org/10.1007/978-3-662-54434-1_7
6. Chen, Y.-F., Hong, C.-D., Sinha, N., Wang, B.-Y.: Commutativity of reducers. In: Baier, C., Tinelli, C. (eds.) TACAS 2015. LNCS, vol. 9035, pp. 131–146. Springer, Heidelberg (2015). https://doi.org/10.1007/978-3-662-46681-0_9

7. Chen, Y.F., Lengál, O., Tan, T., Wu, Z.: Register automata with linear arithmetic. In: LICS, pp. 1–12 (2017)
8. Chen, Y.-F., Song, L., Wu, Z.: The commutativity problem of the mapreduce framework: a transducer-based approach. In: Chaudhuri, S., Farzan, A. (eds.) CAV 2016. LNCS, vol. 9780, pp. 91–111. Springer, Cham (2016). https://doi.org/10.1007/978-3-319-41540-6_6
9. Csallner, C., Fegaras, L., Li, C.: New ideas track: testing mapreduce-style programs. In: FSE, pp. 504–507 (2011)
10. Dean, J., Ghemawat, S.: MapReduce: simplified data processing on large clusters. In: OSDI (2004)
11. Fedyukovich, G., Gurfinkel, A., Sharygina, N.: Automated discovery of simulation between programs. In: Davis, M., Fehnker, A., McIver, A., Voronkov, A. (eds.) LPAR 2015. LNCS, vol. 9450, pp. 606–621. Springer, Heidelberg (2015). https://doi.org/10.1007/978-3-662-48899-7_42
12. Inverso, O., Tomasco, E., Fischer, B., La Torre, S., Parlato, G.: Bounded model checking of multi-threaded C programs via lazy sequentialization. In: Biere, A., Bloem, R. (eds.) CAV 2014. LNCS, vol. 8559, pp. 585–602. Springer, Cham (2014). https://doi.org/10.1007/978-3-319-08867-9_39
13. Klebanov, V., Rümmer, P., Ulbrich, M.: Automating regression verification of pointer programs by predicate abstraction. Formal Methods Syst. Des. **52**(3), 229–259 (2018)
14. Lal, A., Reps, T.: Reducing concurrent analysis under a context bound to sequential analysis. In: Gupta, A., Malik, S. (eds.) CAV 2008. LNCS, vol. 5123, pp. 37–51. Springer, Heidelberg (2008). https://doi.org/10.1007/978-3-540-70545-1_7
15. Pnueli, A., Siegel, M., Singerman, E.: Translation validation. In: Steffen, B. (ed.) TACAS 1998. LNCS, vol. 1384, pp. 151–166. Springer, Heidelberg (1998). https://doi.org/10.1007/BFb0054170
16. Smith, C., Albarghouthi, A.: MapReduce program synthesis. In: PLDI, pp. 326–340 (2016)
17. Xiao, T., et al.: Nondeterminism in MapReduce considered harmful? In: ICSE, pp. 44–53 (2014)

Completeness of Cyclic Proofs
for Symbolic Heaps with Inductive
Definitions

Makoto Tatsuta[1]([⊠]), Koji Nakazawa[2], and Daisuke Kimura[3]

[1] National Institute of Informatics/Sokendai, Hayama, Japan
tatsuta@nii.ac.jp
[2] Nagoya University, Nagoya, Japan
knak@is.nagoya-u.ac.jp
[3] Toho University, Tokyo, Japan
kmr@is.sci.toho-u.ac.jp

Abstract. Separation logic is successful for software verification in both theory and practice. Decision procedure for symbolic heaps is one of the key issues. This paper proposes a cyclic proof system for symbolic heaps with general form of inductive definitions called cone inductive definitions, and shows its soundness and completeness. Cone inductive definitions are obtained from bounded-treewidth inductive definitions by imposing some restrictions for existentials, but they still include a wide class of recursive data structures. The completeness is proved by using a proof search algorithm and it also gives us a decision procedure for entailments of symbolic heaps with cone inductive definitions. The time complexity of the algorithm is nondeterministic double exponential. A prototype system for the algorithm has been implemented and experimental results are also presented.

1 Introduction

Separation logic is successful for software verification [6,7,25]. Several systems based on this idea have been actively investigated and implemented. One of the keys of these systems is the entailment checker that decides the validity of a given entailment of symbolic heaps, which are restricted forms of separation logic formulas.

Inductive predicates are used to describe recursive data structures such as lists and trees. In order to verify programs with recursive data structures, symbolic heaps with inductive predicates are useful. Our purpose is to obtain a decision procedure for entailments of symbolic heaps with general inductive definitions.

The validity of entailments for symbolic heaps with inductive definitions is known to be undecidable [1]. Hence it is important to find an expressive class of inductive definitions such that we have efficient decision procedure. Iosif et al. [19] proposed the system SLRD$_{btw}$, which is the first decidable system for entailments of symbolic heaps with general inductive definitions. The condition on inductive definitions imposed in [19] is called the *bounded-treewidth condition*, which is one of the most flexible conditions for decidability.

© Springer Nature Switzerland AG 2019
A. W. Lin (Ed.): APLAS 2019, LNCS 11893, pp. 367–387, 2019.
https://doi.org/10.1007/978-3-030-34175-6_19

In [19], the decision procedure is given by model theoretic engine. On the other hand, proof theoretic engine, namely proof search based on some proof theory, has several advantages. (1) We can extend it by adding new inference rules. (2) It provides reasons for the output. (3) It may be fast when the input entailment is valid. (4) We can easily change it into a semi-decision procedure by adding some heuristics for proof search. There are some decision procedure based on proof systems for separation logic [6,7]. However, they have only hard-coded predicates such as only lists and trees. Therefore, it is important to find an expressive class of inductive definitions such that we can present decision procedure based on a proof system.

Many proof systems with inductive definitions use Martin-Löf style introduction and elimination rules to describe inductive predicates. On the other hand, cyclic-proof systems [10,11] may give us a better system for our purpose. In cyclic proof systems, the induction is represented as a cyclic structure, where some open assumptions are allowed as induction hypotheses. This mechanism gives us more efficient proof search, since we need not fix an induction formula in advance. In fact, some systems (explicitly or implicitly) based on cyclic-proof systems have been proposed for the entailment checking problem for separation logic [10,11,15,29,30]. However it is not well studied on complete cyclic-proof systems for separation logic.

Our contributions are: (1) We propose a new class of inductive definitions, called the *cone inductive definitions*. This class is useful since it is sufficiently large, and we can present a proof system with the following nice properties. (2) We propose a new cyclic proof system for entailment with symbolic heaps and cone inductive definitions. (3) We will show that our proof system is complete. (4) We present a proof search algorithm for the proof system, which decides the validity of entailment. (5) In order to make these possible, we develop new ideas: (a) a new rule for *spatial factorization*, called the *factor rule*, to divide a spatial atomic formula, (b) a new rule for the split rule that can handle disjunction in the succedent, and (c) an auxiliary extension of the language for explicit case analysis. Furthermore, in order to confirm that our results are useful, we implemented a prototype system based on our proof-search algorithm and present some experimental results.

The class of the *cone inductive definitions* is obtained from the class of the bounded-treewidth by imposing an additional condition that the definition body itself guarantees existentials to be allocated. The cone inductive definition requires that every definition clause of the inductive predicate $P(x, \overrightarrow{y})$ contains $x \mapsto (t)$ for some t. We call the first argument x a *root* of $P(x, \overrightarrow{y})$, since it is the root of a tree-like structure described by the predicate. An example of cone inductive definitions is the following singly-linked list: $\mathrm{ls}(x, y) =_{\mathrm{def}} x \mapsto y \vee \exists z(x \mapsto (z) * \mathrm{ls}(z, y))$, where it is a bounded tree-width inductive definition and the existential z is guaranteed to be allocated by $\mathrm{ls}(z, y)$ in the definition clause. The cone inductive definitions are still quite expressive, since this class contains doubly-linked lists, skip lists, nested lists, and so on.

Based on the Unfold-Match strategy to the cone inductive definitions and the cyclic proofs, our algorithm will use the following *Unfold-Match-Remove-Split* strategy (written as U-M-R-S). First, unfold predicates of the same root x

in both antecedent and succedent. Next, the existentials of the antecedent are replaced by fresh variables and instantiate the existentials of the succedent by matching. Then, remove the same $x \mapsto (t)$ in both antecedent and succedent. Finally we split $F_1 * F_2 \vdash G_1 * G_2$ into $F_1 \vdash G_1$ and $F_2 \vdash G_2$ by the split rule of separation logic. We repeat these steps for each subgoal.

However the U-M-R-S strategy may get stuck when we cannot find predicates which have a common root on both sides. In order to solve this problem, we propose a new inference rule called the factor rule, which uses *inductive wands*. The inductive wand $P\text{---}*^{ind}Q$ represents a subheap of Q which is obtained by removing a heap which satisfies P. The inductive wands are also predicates defined by cone inductive definitions. By the inductive wand, we can divide a predicate $P(x)$ in into two predicates $Q(y)\text{---}*^{ind}P(x)$ and $Q(y)$, where we can find the root y in $Q(y)$ which occurs as a root on both sides. The definition clauses of the inductive wand $Q(y)\text{---}*^{ind}P(x)$ are automatically generated from the definitions of $P(x)$ and $Q(y)$, and they satisfy the condition of the cone inductive definition. We will also use the factor rule in order to make the allocated variables of the antecedent and each disjunct of the succedent coincide when we apply the split rule.

A similar idea to the inductive wand has been proposed as the inductive segment in [5], where they used it for software verification by abstract interpretation. By the inductive segment, they can unfold inductive predicates in the reverse direction to find some fixed points in shape analysis. On the other hand, we will use inductive wands for a different purpose, namely, deciding entailments of symbolic heaps.

We will show the class of cone inductive predicates is closed under inductive wands. It is not easy to obtain a useful class of inductive definition that is closed under inductive wands. For example, the class of inductive definitions with bounded treewidth is not closed under inductive wands. Magic wands often causes undecidability [4]. By this closure property, it is not necessary to add any special clauses to the definition of semantics for inductive wands.

The split rule is new since it handles disjunctions in the succedent. The ideas for the split rule will be fully explained in Sect. 4.

For completeness, we extend the succedent to disjunctions and introduce predicates $t \downarrow$ and $t \Uparrow$, where $t \downarrow$ means that t is in the domain of the heap, and $t \Uparrow$ means that t is not related to the heap. They will be defined in Sect. 3 and explained in Sect. 4.

Many entailment checkers for symbolic heaps with inductive definitions have been discussed. Several of them do not have general inductive definitions and have only hard-coded inductive predicates [6,7,16,22,23]. The entailment checkers for general inductive definitions are studied in [10,11,14,15,17–21,24,29–31]. The systems in [17–21,24,31] are all model theoretic. The algorithm in [21] has better time complexity than ours. The system in [20] does not have disequality. The systems in [10,11,15,29,30] use cyclic proofs, but neither of them is complete. The system in [14] is based on ordinary sequent calculus and is not complete.

The cyclic proofs have been intensively investigated for the first-order predicate logic [2,3,9,11,26], a bunched implication system [8], and a symbolic heap system [10,11].

Section 2 defines separation logic with inductive definitions. In Sect. 3 we extend our language. In Sect. 4, we explain main ideas. Section 5 defines the system CSLID$^\omega$ and proves its soundness. In Sect. 6 we give the proof search algorithm, and show its partial correctness and termination. Section 7 proves the completeness of CSLID$^\omega$. Section 8 presents experimental results. We conclude in Sect. 9.

2   Symbolic Heaps with Inductive Definitions

This section defines symbolic heaps, inductive definitions, and their semantics.

We will use vector notation $\overrightarrow{x}$ to denote a sequence $x_1, \ldots, x_k$ for simplicity. $|\overrightarrow{x}|$ denotes the length of the sequence. Sometimes we will also use a notation of a sequence to denote a set for simplicity. Then we will write $\overrightarrow{p} + \overrightarrow{q}$ for the disjoint union set of the sets $\overrightarrow{p}$ and $\overrightarrow{q}$. We write $\equiv$ for the syntactical equivalence.

2.1   Language

Our language is a first order language with a new connective $*$ and inductive predicates, and defined as follows.

First-order variables $x, y, z, w, v, \ldots$.

Terms $t, u, p, q, r:: = x \mid$ nil.   Inductive Predicate Symbols $P, Q, \ldots$.

We define formulas F, G of separation logic as those of the first-order language generated by these terms, the propositional constant emp, predicate symbols $=$, $\mapsto$, $P, Q, \ldots$, and an additional logical connective $*$. We write $t \neq u$ for $\neg t = u$. We assume some number n_{cell} for the number of elements in a cell. Next we define symbolic heaps.

Pure formulas $\Pi:: = t = t \mid t \neq t \mid \Pi \wedge \Pi$.

Spatial formulas $\Sigma:: = \mathrm{emp} \mid t \mapsto (t_1, \ldots, t_{n_{\mathrm{cell}}}) \mid P(\overrightarrow{t}) \mid \Sigma * \Sigma$.

We suppose $*$ binds more tightly than $\wedge$. We will sometimes write $P(t)$ for $P(t, \overrightarrow{t})$. We write $*_{i \in [1,n]} P_i(x_i)$ for $P_1(x_1) * \ldots * P_n(x_n)$. Similarly we write $*_{i \in I} P_i(x_i)$. We write $\Pi \subseteq \Pi'$ when all the conjuncts of Π are contained in those of Π'.

qf-Symbolic Heaps $A, B:: = \Pi \wedge \Sigma \mid \Sigma$. Symbolic Heaps $\phi:: = \exists \overrightarrow{x} A$.

Entailments $A \vdash B_1, \ldots, B_n$ where the succedent is a set $\{\Phi_1, \ldots, \Phi_n\}$.

The language has inductive definitions of inductive predicates.

Inductive Definitions $P(x, \overrightarrow{y}) =_{\mathrm{def}} \bigvee_i \phi_i(x, \overrightarrow{y})$ where ϕ_i is a definition clause.

Definition Clauses $\phi(x, \overrightarrow{y}) \equiv \exists \overrightarrow{z} (\Pi \wedge x \mapsto (\overrightarrow{u}) * *_{i \in I} P_i(z_i, \overrightarrow{t}_i))$, where

- $\{z_i \mid i \in I\} \subseteq \overrightarrow{u}$ (connectivity).
- $\overrightarrow{z} = \{z_i \mid i \in I\}$ (strong establishment).

We call the first argument x of a spatial atomic formula $P(x, \overrightarrow{t})$ a *root*.

The strong establishment implies the establishment condition required by the bounded-treewidth condition. These conditions guarantee that the cell at address x decides the content of every existential variable. It is similar to the constructively valued condition in [13].

We give some examples of the inductive definitions in the following.

The list segment: $\mathrm{ls}(x, y) =_{\mathrm{def}} x \mapsto y \vee \exists z (x \mapsto (z) * \mathrm{ls}(z, y))$.

The doubly-linked list: $\mathrm{dll}(h, p, n, t) =_{\mathrm{def}} h = t \wedge h \mapsto (p, n) \vee \exists z (h \mapsto (p, z) * \mathrm{dll}(z, h, n, t))$.

The nested list: $\mathrm{listnest}(x) =_{\mathrm{def}} \exists z (x \mapsto (z, \mathrm{nil}) * \mathrm{ls}(z, \mathrm{nil})) \vee \exists z_1 z_2 (x \mapsto (z_1, z_2) * \mathrm{ls}(z_1, \mathrm{nil}) * \mathrm{listnest}(z_2))$.

The nested list segment: $\mathrm{lsnest}(x, y) =_{\mathrm{def}} \exists z (x \mapsto (z, \mathrm{nil}) * \mathrm{ls}(z, y)) \vee \exists z_1 z_2 (x \mapsto (z_1, z_2) * \mathrm{ls}(z_1, y) * \mathrm{lsnest}(z_2, y))$.

The skip list: $\mathrm{skl1}(x, y) =_{\mathrm{def}} x \mapsto (\mathrm{nil}, y) \vee \exists z (x \mapsto (\mathrm{nil}, z) * \mathrm{skl1}(z, y))$, $\mathrm{skl2}(x, y) =_{\mathrm{def}} \exists z (x \mapsto (y, z) * \mathrm{skl1}(z, y)) \vee \exists z_1 z_2 (x \mapsto (z_1, z_2) * \mathrm{skl1}(z_2, z_1) * \mathrm{skl2}(z_1, y))$.

Many examples in [10] are definable in our system as follows: List, ListE, ListO are definable, RList is not definable. DLL, PeList, SLL, BSLL, BinTree, BinTreeSeg, BinListFirst, BinListSecond, BinPath are not definable but will be definable in a straightforward extension of our system by handling emp in the base cases.

We prepare some notions. We define $P^{(m)}$ by

$$P^{(0)}(\overrightarrow{x}) \equiv (\mathrm{nil} \neq \mathrm{nil}),$$
$$P^{(m+1)}(\overrightarrow{x}) \equiv \bigvee_i \phi_i[P := P^{(m)}],$$

where $P(\overrightarrow{x}) =_{\mathrm{def}} \bigvee_i \phi_i$. $P^{(m)}$ is m-time unfold of P. We define $F^{(m)}$ as obtained from F by replacing every inductive predicate P by $P^{(m)}$.

We write T for a finite set of terms. We define $(\neq (T_1, T_2))$ as $\bigwedge_{t_1 \in T_1, t_2 \in T_2, t_1 \not\equiv t_2} t_1 \neq t_2$. We write $y \neq \overrightarrow{t}$ for $(\neq (\{y\}, \overrightarrow{t}))$. We define $(\neq (T))$ as $(\neq (T \cup \{\mathrm{nil}\}, T))$.

2.2 Semantics

This subsection gives semantics of the language.

We define the following structure: Vars is the set of variables, Val $= N$, Locs $= \{x \in N | x > 0\}$, Heaps $=$ Locs $\rightarrow_{fin}$ Val$^{n_{\mathrm{cell}}}$, Stores $=$ Vars $\rightarrow$ Val. Each $s \in$ Stores is called a *store*. Each $h \in$ Heaps is called a *heap*, Dom(h) is the domain of h, and Range(h) is the range of h. We write $h = h_1 + h_2$ when Dom(h_1) and Dom(h_2) are disjoint and the graph of h is the union of those of h_1 and h_2. A pair (s, h) is called a *heap model*, which means a memory state. The value $s(x)$ means the value of the variable x in the model (s, h). Each value $a \in$ Dom(h)

means an address, and the value of $h(a)$ is the content of the memory cell at address a in the heap h. We suppose each memory cell has n_{cell} elements as its content.

The interpretation $s(t)$ for any term t is defined as 0 for nil and $s(x)$ for the variable x. For a formula F we define the interpretation $s, h \models F$ as follows.

$s, h \models t_1 = t_2$ if $s(t_1) = s(t_2)$,

$s, h \models F_1 \wedge F_2$ if $s, h \models F_1$ and $s, h \models F_2$,

$s, h \models \neg F$ if $s, h \not\models F$,

$s, h \models \text{emp}$ if $\text{Dom}(h) = \emptyset$,

$s, h \models t \mapsto (t_1, \ldots, t_{n_{\text{cell}}})$ if $\text{Dom}(h) = \{s(t)\}$ and $h(s(t)) = (s(t_1), \ldots, s(t_{n_{\text{cell}}}))$,

$s, h \models F_1 * F_2$ if $s, h_1 \models F_1$ and $s, h_2 \models F_2$ for some $h_1 + h_2 = h$,

$s, h \models P(\overrightarrow{t})$ if $s, h \models P^{(m)}(\overrightarrow{t})$ for some m,

$s, h \models \exists z F$ if $s[z := b], h \models F$ for some $b \in \text{Val}$.

We write $A \models B_1, \ldots, B_n$ for $\forall s h (s, h \models A \rightarrow ((s, h \models B_1) \vee \ldots \vee (s, h \models B_n)))$. The entailment $A \vdash B_1, \ldots, B_n$ is said to be valid if $A \models B_1, \ldots, B_n$ holds. Our goal in this paper is to decide the validity of a given entailment.

For saving space, we identify some syntactical objects that have the same meaning, namely, we use implicit transformation of formulas by using the following properties: $\wedge$ is commutative, associative, and idempotent; $*$ is commutative, associative, and has the unit emp; $=$ is symmetric; $\exists x G \leftrightarrow G$, $\exists x(F \wedge G) \leftrightarrow \exists x F \wedge G$, and $\exists x(F * G) \leftrightarrow \exists x F * G$, when F, G are formulas and $x \notin \text{FV}(G)$; $\Pi \wedge (F * G) \leftrightarrow (\Pi \wedge F) * G$.

3   Language Extension

3.1   Extended Language

In this section, we extend our language from symbolic heaps by $\downarrow$, $\Uparrow$ and $\mathrel{-\!\!*}^{\text{ind}}$, since they are necessary to show the completeness.

We extend inductive predicate symbols with $Q_1 \mathrel{-\!\!*}^{\text{ind}} \ldots \mathrel{-\!\!*}^{\text{ind}} Q_m \mathrel{-\!\!*}^{\text{ind}} P$ where $Q_1, \ldots, Q_m, P$ are original inductive predicate symbols. We call m the *depth of wands*. We write $Q_1(\overrightarrow{t}_1) \mathrel{-\!\!*}^{\text{ind}} \ldots \mathrel{-\!\!*}^{\text{ind}} Q_m(\overrightarrow{t}_m) \mathrel{-\!\!*}^{\text{ind}} P(\overrightarrow{t})$ for $(Q_1 \mathrel{-\!\!*}^{\text{ind}} \ldots \mathrel{-\!\!*}^{\text{ind}} Q_m \mathrel{-\!\!*}^{\text{ind}} P)(\overrightarrow{t}, \overrightarrow{t}_1, \ldots, \overrightarrow{t}_m)$.

We extend our first-order language with the extended inductive predicate symbols and unary predicate symbols $\downarrow$ and $\Uparrow$. $t \downarrow$ means that t is in $\text{Dom}(h)$ and $t \Uparrow$ means that t is unrelated to the heap. We write $t \uparrow$ for $\neg t \downarrow$. Then $t \uparrow$ means that t is not in the domain of the heap.

We write F, G, Σ, A, B, ϕ for the same syntactical objects with the extended inductive predicate symbols. We also extend definition clauses with the extended inductive predicate symbols. We use X, Y for a finite set of variables and write $X \uparrow$ for $\bigwedge \{t \uparrow \mid t \in X\}$. $X \downarrow$ and $X \Uparrow$ are similarly defined. We write $\exists \overrightarrow{x} \downarrow$ for $\exists \overrightarrow{x}(\overrightarrow{x} \downarrow \wedge \ldots)$. Similarly we write $\exists \overrightarrow{x} \Uparrow$.

We define: $\mathcal{P} :: = \mapsto \mid P$ where P varies in inductive predicate symbols,

Cones $\Delta :: = \mathcal{P}(\overrightarrow{t}) \wedge X \downarrow$, and $\Gamma :: = \Delta \mid \Gamma * \Gamma$, and $\psi :: = Y \uparrow \wedge \Pi \wedge \Gamma$, and $\Phi :: = \exists \overrightarrow{x} \exists \overrightarrow{y} \Uparrow (\Pi \wedge \Gamma)$.

A cone $\mathcal{P}(\overrightarrow{t}) \wedge X \downarrow$ is a unit of our spatial formula. It means that the atomic formula $\mathcal{P}(\overrightarrow{t})$ specifies the heap as well as the variables X are allocated in the heap. Γ is a separating conjunction of cones. ψ will be used as an antecedent of our extended entailment and has more information that the variables Y are not allocated in the heap. Φ will be used in a succedent of our extended entailment and it existentially quantifies variables $\overrightarrow{x}\,\overrightarrow{y}$ with information that the variables $\overrightarrow{y}$ are not related to the heap.

We define entailments as $\psi \vdash \Phi_1, \ldots, \Phi_n$.

We write J for an entailment. In ψ, Φ, we call Γ a *spatial part* and Π a *pure part*.

We define $\mathrm{Roots}(X \Uparrow \wedge Y \uparrow \wedge \Pi \wedge *_{i \in I}(\mathcal{P}_i(x_i, \overrightarrow{t}_i) \wedge X_i \downarrow)) = \{x_i | i \in I\}$. Then we define $\mathrm{Roots}(\exists x \Phi) = \mathrm{Roots}(\Phi)$ if $x \notin \mathrm{Roots}(\Phi)$, and undefined otherwise. We define $\mathrm{Cells}(X \Uparrow \wedge Y \uparrow \wedge \Pi \wedge *_{i \in I}(X_i \downarrow \wedge \mathcal{P}_i(x_i))) = \bigcup_{i \in I} X_i$. Then we define $\mathrm{Cells}(\exists x \Phi) = \mathrm{Cells}(\Phi) - \{x\}$. We write $\mathrm{Alloc}(F)$ for $\mathrm{Roots}(F) \cup \mathrm{Cells}(F)$ and call them *allocated variables* of F. $\mathrm{Alloc}(F)$ means the set of variables allocated in the heap.

We define a substitution as a map from the set of variables to the set of terms. For a substitution θ, we define $\mathrm{Dom}(\theta) = \{x | \theta(x) \neq x\}$ and $\mathrm{Range}(\theta) = \{\theta(x) | x \in \mathrm{Dom}(\theta)\}$. We define a *variable renaming* as a substitution that is a bijection among variables with a finite domain.

We define semantics of the extended language.

Definition 3.1. $s, h \models t \downarrow$ if $s(t) \in \mathrm{Dom}(h)$.
$s, h \models t \Uparrow$ if $s(t) \notin \mathrm{Range}(h) \cup \mathrm{Dom}(h)$.
We say $\psi \vdash \Phi_1, \ldots, \Phi_n$ is valid when for all s, h, if $s, h \models \psi$ then there is some i such that $s, h \models \Phi_i$. We write $\psi \models \Phi_1, \ldots, \Phi_n$ when $\psi \vdash \Phi_1, \ldots, \Phi_n$ is valid.

For saving space, we identify some syntactical objects that have the same meaning, namely, we use implicit transformation of formulas by using the following property: $(F * G) \wedge X \Uparrow \leftrightarrow (F \wedge X \Uparrow) * (G \wedge X \Uparrow)$.

3.2 Inductive Wand

This section gives the definition clauses for inductive predicates that contain the inductive wand.

Definition 3.2. The definition clauses of $Q(y, \overrightarrow{w}) \mathbin{-\!*^{\mathrm{ind}}} P(x, \overrightarrow{y})$ are as follows:

Case 1. $\exists(\overrightarrow{z} - z_i)((\overrightarrow{w} = \overrightarrow{t}_i \wedge \Pi \wedge x \mapsto (\overrightarrow{u}) * *_{l \neq i} P_l(z_l, \overrightarrow{t}_l))[z_i := y])$ where $Q = P_i$ and $\exists \overrightarrow{z}(\Pi \wedge x \mapsto (\overrightarrow{u}) * *_l P_l(z_l, \overrightarrow{t}_l))$ is a definition clause of $P(x, \overrightarrow{y})$.

Case 2. $\exists \overrightarrow{z}(\Pi \wedge x \mapsto (\overrightarrow{u}) * *_{l \neq i, l \in L} P_l(z_l, \overrightarrow{t}_l) * (Q(y, \overrightarrow{w}) \mathbin{-\!*^{\mathrm{ind}}} P_i(z_i, \overrightarrow{t}_i)))$ where $i \in L$ and $\exists \overrightarrow{z}(\Pi \wedge x \mapsto (\overrightarrow{u}) * *_{l \in L} P_l(z_l, \overrightarrow{t}_l))$ is a definition clause of $P(x, \overrightarrow{y})$.

$Q(y) \mathbin{-\!*^{\mathrm{ind}}} P(x)$ is inductively defined by the definition clauses obtained by removing $Q(y)$ from the definition clauses of $P(x)$. The inductive wand

$Q(y)\mathbin{-\!\!*}^{\mathrm{ind}}P(x)$ plays a similar role to the ordinary magic wand $Q(y)\mathbin{-\!\!*}P(x)$, but it is stronger than the ordinary magic wand and it is defined syntactically. Roughly speaking, it is defined to be false if it cannot be defined syntactically.

Example 3.3. $\mathrm{ls}(y,v)\mathbin{-\!\!*}^{\mathrm{ind}}\mathrm{ls}(x,w) =_{\mathrm{def}} w = v \wedge x \mapsto (y) \vee \exists z(x \mapsto (z) * (\mathrm{ls}(y,v)\mathbin{-\!\!*}^{\mathrm{ind}}\mathrm{ls}(z,w)))$.

We can show $P(x)\mathbin{-\!\!*}^{\mathrm{ind}}Q(y)\mathbin{-\!\!*}^{\mathrm{ind}}R(z)$ and $Q(y)\mathbin{-\!\!*}^{\mathrm{ind}}P(x)\mathbin{-\!\!*}^{\mathrm{ind}}R(z)$ are equivalent.

Lemma 3.4. *If $\overrightarrow{R}$ is $P_1(\overrightarrow{t}_1),\ldots,P_n(\overrightarrow{t}_n)$ and $\overrightarrow{R}'$ is its permutation, then $\overrightarrow{R}'\mathbin{-\!\!*}^{\mathrm{ind}}P(\overrightarrow{t})$ is equivalent to $\overrightarrow{R}\mathbin{-\!\!*}^{\mathrm{ind}}P(\overrightarrow{t})$.*

We have an elimination rule for inductive wands.

Lemma 3.5 (Strong Wand Elimination). $(Q(y,\overrightarrow{w})\mathbin{-\!\!*}^{\mathrm{ind}}P(x,\overrightarrow{z})) * \overline{(R(v,\overrightarrow{u})}\mathbin{-\!\!*}^{\mathrm{ind}}Q(y,\overrightarrow{w})) \models \overline{R(v,\overrightarrow{u})}\mathbin{-\!\!*}^{\mathrm{ind}}P(x,\overrightarrow{z})$.

We define $\mathrm{Dep}(P)$ as the set of inductive predicate symbols that appear in the unfolding of P.

We have an introduction rule for inductive wands.

Lemma 3.6 (Strong Wand Introduction). $x \neq y \wedge y \downarrow \wedge \overline{(R(v,\overrightarrow{u})}\mathbin{-\!\!*}^{\mathrm{ind}}$
$P(x,\overrightarrow{z})) \models \{\exists \overrightarrow{w}((Q(y,\overrightarrow{w}),\overline{R_1(v_1,\overrightarrow{u}_1)}\mathbin{-\!\!*}^{\mathrm{ind}}P(x,\overrightarrow{z})) * \overline{(R_2(v_2,\overrightarrow{u}_2)}\mathbin{-\!\!*}^{\mathrm{ind}}Q(y,$
$\overrightarrow{w})) \mid R(v,\overrightarrow{u}) = (R_1(v_1,\overrightarrow{u}_1) + R_2(v_2,\overrightarrow{u}_2)), Q \in \mathrm{Dep}(P), \overrightarrow{R}_2 \subseteq \mathrm{Dep}(Q)\}$.

4   Main Ideas

We explain our main ideas of our contributions. They are for the language extension and the proof search algorithm.

A rule is defined to be *locally complete* if all its assumptions are valid when its conclusion is valid.

(1) We extend our language to $t \downarrow$ and $t \uparrow$ and disjunction in a succedent. We use them to case analysis. One of advantages by this case analysis is to guide how to use the split rule. For a formula F, by case analysis, we can assume every variable x is in $\mathrm{Alloc}(F)$ or has $x \uparrow$ in F. Then we can impose the condition $\mathrm{Alloc}(F_1) = \mathrm{Alloc}(G_1)$ and $\mathrm{Alloc}(F_2) = \mathrm{Alloc}(G_2)$ to use the split rule

$$\frac{F_1 \vdash G_1 \quad F_2 \vdash G_2}{F_1 * F_2 \vdash G_1 * G_2}$$

without loss of generality in proof search, since a valid subgoal has the same allocated variables on both sides.

Disjunction of a succedent is necessary for completeness. If we unfold $P(x)$ in the succedent of $A \vdash P(x) * B$ and $P(x)$ has two definition clauses $R_1(x)$ and $R_2(x)$, we need $A \vdash ((R_1(x) * B) \vee (R_2(x) * B))$ to preserve the validity of the entailment by unfolding. We will write $A \vdash R_1(x) * B, R_2(x) * B$ for it.

(2) Our new inference rules are the factor rule and the split rule. The factor rule transforms $P(x)$ into $(Q(y) \mathbin{-\!\!*^{\mathrm{ind}}} P(x)) * Q(y)$, where $Q(y) \mathbin{-\!\!*^{\mathrm{ind}}} P(x)$ is an atomic formula with another inductive predicate $Q(-) \mathbin{-\!\!*^{\mathrm{ind}}} P(-)$, which is called an *inductive wand*. The factor rule exposes a hidden y as the root of the inductive predicate Q, and this will be used for the unfolding step in our proof search algorithm. Since the factor rule divides a single atomic formula $P(x)$ into two atomic formulas $Q(y) \mathbin{-\!\!*^{\mathrm{ind}}} P(x)$ and $Q(y)$ where x is allocated in one formula and y is allocated in the other formula, this will also enable us to split separating conjunction according to allocated variables in our proof search algorithm.

We may consider a nested inductive wand like $R(-) \mathbin{-\!\!*^{\mathrm{ind}}} (Q(-) \mathbin{-\!\!*^{\mathrm{ind}}} P(-))$. We will show that the depth of necessary inductive wands for our proof search algorithm has a fixed upper bound.

(3) The split rule is new since it handles disjunctions in the succedent.

For our proof search algorithm, we need the split rule that keeps validity. A naive split rule does not keep validity. For example, consider $F_1 * F_2 \vdash G_1^1 * G_2^1, G_1^2 * G_2^2$ where $\mathrm{Alloc}(F_1) = \mathrm{Alloc}(G_1^i)$ and $\mathrm{Alloc}(F_2) = \mathrm{Alloc}(G_2^i)$ for $i = 1, 2$. Then, if $s, h_1 \models F_1$ and $s, h_2 \models F_2$, and $s, h_1 + h_2 \models G_1^i * G_2^i$, then $s, h_1 \models G_1^i$ and $s, h_2 \models G_2^i$ because of the shape of a heap for a cone. Then we have $F_1 \vdash G_1^1, G_1^2$ and $F_2 \vdash G_2^1, G_2^2$. If we transform it into $F_1 \vdash G_1^1, G_1^2$ and $F_2 \vdash G_2^1, G_2^2$, this transformation does not keep validity, namely, the naive split rule

$$\frac{F_1 \vdash G_1^1, G_1^2 \quad F_2 \vdash G_2^1, G_2^2}{F_1 * F_2 \vdash G_1^1 * G_2^1, G_1^2 * G_2^2}$$

is locally complete but may not be sound, since there is a case when G_1^1 and G_2^2 are true but G_2^1 and G_1^2 are false. We will propose a new split rule for disjunction. We do not transform the goal into a single subgoal set that keeps validity, but instead we will transform the goal into a set of subgoal sets such that at least one subgoal set keeps validity. We will say these rules are *selectively local complete*. For example, by our split rule, $F_1 * F_2 \vdash G_1^1 * G_2^1, G_1^2 * G_2^2$ will be transformed into four subgoal sets:

(A) $F_1 \vdash G_1^1$ and $F_1 \vdash G_1^2$ and $F_2 \vdash G_2^1, G_2^2$,

or (B) $F_1 \vdash G_1^2$ and $F_2 \vdash G_2^2$,

or (C) $F_1 \vdash G_1^1$ and $F_2 \vdash G_2^1$,

or (D) $F_1 \vdash G_1^1, G_1^2$ and $F_2 \vdash G_2^1$ and $F_2 \vdash G_2^2$.

Then we can show that at least one of these four cases is valid when $F_1 * F_2 \models G_1^1 * G_2^1, G_1^2 * G_2^2$.

(4) We explain an outline of our proof search algorithm.

Our proof search algorithm is based on the U-M-R-S strategy illustrated in the introduction. Given a goal entailment J, we start with a singleton subgoal set $\{J\}$. We repeatedly apply the following steps to a subgoal set to transform a goal entailment into subgoal entailments keeping validity. When the subgoal set becomes empty, we return Yes. If a new subgoal entailment is the same as that appeared already during computation, we finish this subgoal, since we can discharge this subgoal by the bud-companion relation in cyclic proofs. This algorithm is nondeterministic because of choice of the split rules at the step 6.

Step 1. Choose a subgoal entailment J from a subgoal set.

Step 2. Unfold atomic formulas of the root x in both antecedent and succedent of J, for some common root x in the antecedent and each disjunct of the succedent. If necessary, we use the factor rule to find a common root.

Step 3. Match the atomic formula $x \mapsto (\overrightarrow{t})$ of root x in both antecedent and succedent.

Step 4. Remove the same $x \mapsto (\overrightarrow{t})$ in both the antecedent and the succedent.

Step 5. If the antecedent has emp, do the following. If the succedent also has emp, then we finish this subgoal (this subgoal is valid) and remove it from the subgoal set. Otherwise we return No (this subgoal is invalid).

Step 6. Apply the split rule repeatedly until the spatial part of the antecedent in every entailment becomes atomic. According to our split rule, we will split it so that the allocated variables of the antecedent and each disjunct of the succedent coincide. If necessary, use the factor rule to divide an atomic formula so that the split rule is applicable.

This algorithm terminates since the set of entailments whose antecedent spatial part is atomic is finite up to variable renaming after some normalization. If the algorithm were not terminating, by executing the step 6 infinitely many time, we would have infinitely many such entailments, which leads to contradiction.

5   Logical System CSLID$^\omega$

This section defines our logical system CSLID$^\omega$ and shows its soundness.

5.1   Inference Rules

This subsection gives the set of inference rules.

We write $F[F']$ to explicitly display the subformula F' at a positive position in F. We say Φ is *equality-full* when Π contains $(\neq (\overrightarrow{y}, V \cup \overrightarrow{y} \cup \{nil\}))$ where Φ is $\exists \overrightarrow{x} \exists \overrightarrow{y} \Uparrow (\Pi \wedge \Gamma)$ and $V = \mathrm{FV}(\Phi)$.

Standard or easy inference rules are given in Fig. 1. The other inference rules are given in Fig. 2. A set of rules is defined to be *selectively locally complete* if there is some locally complete rule in the set.

The rule (Factor) is sound, since $P(t)$ from $(Q(y) \mathbin{-\!\!*^{ind}} P(t)) * Q(y)$ is true by the definition of $\mathbin{-\!\!*^{ind}}$. For local completeness, the rule (Factor) lists up all possible cases for $Q(y)$ in the disjunction.

The rules ($\exists$ Amalg1, 2) amalgamate $\exists x$'s under some condition, which guarantees that existentials have the same values. The soundness and local completeness of these rules can be shown by using the definition of $t \downarrow$ and $t \Uparrow$.

The rule ($*$) is a new split rule since it handles disjunction in the succedent. We explain the idea of our split rule. Consider $F_1 * F_2 \models G_1^1 * G_2^1, G_1^2 *$ $G_2^2, G_1^3 * G_2^3, G_1^4 * G_2^4$ where $\mathrm{Alloc}(F_1) = \mathrm{Alloc}(G_1^i)$ and $\mathrm{Alloc}(F_2) = \mathrm{Alloc}(G_2^i)$ for $i = 1, 2, 3, 4$. Let I be $\{1, 2, 3, 4\}$. Then for any $I' \subseteq I$ we have $F_1 \models \{G_1^i \mid i \in I'\}$

$$\frac{F \vdash \vec{G}}{F\theta \vdash \vec{G}\theta} \text{ (Subst)} \qquad \frac{}{\text{emp} \vdash \text{emp}} \text{ (emp)} \qquad \frac{}{F \vdash \vec{G}} \text{ (Unsat)} \quad (F \text{ unsatisfiable})$$

$$\frac{F \vdash \vec{G}}{F' \wedge F \vdash \vec{G}} \text{ ($\wedge$L)} \qquad \frac{F \vdash \vec{G}, \exists \vec{z}(G \wedge G')}{F \vdash \vec{G}, \exists \vec{z}G} \text{ ($\wedge$Elim)} \qquad \frac{F \vdash \vec{G}, \exists \vec{z}(G \wedge \neg G)}{F \vdash \vec{G}} \text{ ($\vee$Elim)}$$

$$\frac{F \wedge F' \vdash \vec{G}, G}{F \wedge F' \vdash \vec{G}, G \wedge F'} \text{ ($\wedge$R)} \qquad \frac{(x \uparrow \wedge F_1) * F_2 \vdash \vec{G}}{F_1 * F_2 \vdash \vec{G}} \text{ ($\uparrow$ Elim)} \quad (x \in \text{Alloc}(F_2))$$

$$\frac{F \vdash \vec{G}}{F \vdash \vec{G}, G} \text{ ($\vee$R)} \quad \frac{F \vdash \vec{G}, G[w := t]}{F \vdash \vec{G}, \exists w G} \text{ ($\exists$R)} \quad \frac{F[x := t] \vdash \vec{G}[x := t]}{x = t \wedge F \vdash \vec{G}} \text{ (= L)} \quad \frac{F \vdash \vec{G}, G}{F \vdash \vec{G}, G \wedge t = t} \text{ (= R)}$$

$$\frac{F * (F_1 \wedge x \downarrow) * F_2 \vdash \vec{G} \quad F * F_1 * (F_2 \wedge x \downarrow) \vdash \vec{G}}{F * ((F_1 * F_2) \wedge x \downarrow) \vdash \vec{G}} \text{ ($\downarrow$ Case L)} \qquad \frac{F \vdash \vec{G}, G}{F \vdash \vec{G}, \exists y \uparrow (y \neq t \wedge G)} \text{ ($\uparrow$ R)} \quad (y \notin \text{FV}(G))$$

$$\frac{F \vdash \vec{G}, \exists \vec{z}(G * (G_1 \wedge t \downarrow) * G_2), \exists \vec{z}(G * G_1 * (G_2 \wedge t \downarrow))}{F \vdash \vec{G}, \exists \vec{z}(G * ((G_1 * G_2) \wedge t \downarrow))} \text{ ($\downarrow$ Case R)} \qquad \frac{F * P(t, \vec{t}) \vdash \vec{G}, G}{F * P(t, \vec{t}) \vdash \vec{G}, G \wedge t \downarrow} \text{ ($\downarrow$ R)}$$

$$\frac{F \wedge F' \vdash \vec{G} \quad F \wedge \neg F' \vdash \vec{G}}{F \vdash \vec{G}} \text{ (Case L)}$$

$$\frac{A(x, \vec{t}, \vec{z}) * F \vdash \vec{G} \quad \text{(for every definition clause } \exists \vec{z} A(x, \vec{t}, \vec{z}) \text{ of } P(x, \vec{t}))}{P(x, \vec{t}) * F \vdash \vec{G}} \text{ (Pred L)}$$

$$\frac{F \vdash \vec{G}, \{G[\phi] \mid \phi \text{ is a definition clause of } P(x, \vec{t})\}}{F \vdash \vec{G}, G[P(x, \vec{t})]} \text{ (Pred R)} \quad (G[\ ] \text{ $\forall$-free})$$

$$\frac{x \uparrow \wedge F \vdash \{G_i \mid i \in I\}}{F * x \mapsto (\vec{t}) \vdash \{G_i * x \mapsto (\vec{t}) \mid i \in I\}} \text{ ($* \mapsto$)}$$

Fig. 1. Inference rules 1

or $F_2 \models \{G_2^i \mid i \in I - I'\}$. It is because $F_1 \not\models \{G_1^i \mid i \in I'\}$ and $F_2 \not\models \{G_2^i \mid i \in I - I'\}$ imply $F_1 * F_2 \not\models G_1^1 * G_2^1, G_1^2 * G_2^2, G_1^3 * G_2^3, G_1^4 * G_2^4$. For example, by taking I' to be $\{1, 2\}$, we have $F_1 \models G_1^1, G_1^2$ or $F_2 \models G_2^3, G_2^4$. The split rule is defined by picking up either of $F_1 \vdash \{G_1^i \mid i \in I'\}$ or $F_2 \vdash \{G_2^i \mid i \in I - I'\}$ for each $I' \subseteq I$ and taking them to be the assumptions. Then each of these rules becomes sound, by some property of propositional logic. Moreover at least one of these rule becomes locally complete, since either of $F_1 \models \{G_1^i \mid i \in I'\}$ or $F_2 \models \{G_2^i \mid i \in I - I'\}$ for all $I' \subseteq I$.

5.2   Proofs in CSLID$^\omega$

We define a proof in CSLID$^\omega$. It is the same as that in [9] except we use a slightly different form of global trace condition.

Definition 5.1. For CSLID$^\omega$, we define a *preproof* to be an ordinary proof figure by the inference rules with open assumptions. For a preproof, we consider a map (called a *bud-companion relation*) from the set of occurrences of open assumptions (called a *bud*) to the set of inner occurrences of sequents (called a *companion*). For CSLID$^\omega$, We define a *cyclic proof* to be a preproof with a bud-companion relation where each bud has a companion below it and there is some rule $(* \mapsto)$ between them.

$$\frac{F \vdash \overrightarrow{G}, \{G[\exists \overrightarrow{w}((\overrightarrow{Q_1(\overrightarrow{t}_1)}, Q(y, \overrightarrow{w}) \mathbin{-\!\!*^{\mathrm{ind}}} P(\overrightarrow{t})) * (\overrightarrow{Q_2(\overrightarrow{t}_2)} \mathbin{-\!\!*^{\mathrm{ind}}} Q(y, \overrightarrow{w})))] \mid}{\overline{R(\overrightarrow{u})} = (Q_1(\overrightarrow{t}_1) + Q_2(\overrightarrow{t}_2)), Q \in \mathrm{Dep}(P), \overrightarrow{Q}_2 \subseteq \mathrm{Dep}(Q), \overrightarrow{w} \text{ fresh}}{F \vdash \overrightarrow{G}, G[\overline{R(\overrightarrow{u})} \mathbin{-\!\!*^{\mathrm{ind}}} P(\overrightarrow{t})]} \quad \text{(Factor)} \qquad (G[\,] \;\forall\text{-free})$$

$$\frac{F \vdash \overrightarrow{G}, G[\exists x \Uparrow \Phi_1 * \exists x \Uparrow \Phi_2]}{F \vdash \overrightarrow{G}, G[\exists x \Uparrow (\Phi_1 * \Phi_2)]} \;(\exists\,\text{Amalg1}) \;\; (\exists x \Uparrow \Phi_1, \exists x \Uparrow \Phi_2 \text{ equality-full})$$

$$\frac{F \vdash \overrightarrow{G}, G[\exists x \Phi_1 * \exists x \Uparrow \Phi_2]}{F \vdash \overrightarrow{G}, G[\exists x (\Phi_1 * (x \Uparrow \wedge \Phi_2))]} \;(\exists\,\text{Amalg2}) \left(\begin{array}{l} x \in \mathrm{Cells}(\Phi_1), \, (x \neq \mathrm{FV}(\exists x \Uparrow \Phi_2)) \subseteq \Phi_1, \\ \exists x \Uparrow \Phi_2 \text{ equality-full} \end{array}\right)$$

$$\frac{F_1 \vdash \{G_1^i \mid i \in I'\} \text{ or } F_2 \vdash \{G_2^i \mid i \in I - I'\} \quad (\forall I' \subseteq I)}{F_1 * F_2 \vdash \{G_1^i * G_2^i \mid i \in I\}} \;(*)$$

Fig. 2. Inference rules 2

Instead of the global trace condition in ordinary cyclic proof systems [9], CSLID^ω requires some $(* \mapsto)$ rule between a bud and its companion.

We can show the soundness theorem of CSLID^ω by using the fact that $|\mathrm{Dom}(h)|$ decreases upwardly by the rule $(* \mapsto)$.

Theorem 5.2 (Soundness). *If J is provable in CSLID^ω, then J is valid.*

6   Proof Search Algorithm

This section gives the proof search algorithm to decide the provability of a given entailment. It will also be shown to decide the validity of a given entailment. First we define normal form, next define the algorithm, then we will show the partial correctness, and finally the termination of the algorithm by using normal form.

6.1   Normal Form

This section defines normal form.

In our proof search algorithm, a normal form appears as a bud in cyclic proofs. A normal form is obtained from an entailment such that the spatial part of its antecedent is a single cone, by transforming it into a simpler form keeping validity. The set of normal forms with d can be shown to be finite up to renaming. Since there is some d such that we can show that extended inductive predicates of depth $\leq d$ are sufficient for the algorithm, the termination of the algorithm will be proved by counting normal forms.

Definition 6.1 (Normal Form). For a given number d, an entailment J is called *normal* with d if J is of the form $Y \uparrow \wedge \Pi \wedge \Gamma \vdash \{\Phi_i \mid i \in I\}$ and Φ_i is of the form $\exists \overrightarrow{x}_i \exists \overrightarrow{y}_i \Uparrow (\Pi_i \wedge \Gamma_i)$ and by letting V be $\mathrm{FV}(J)$,

1. Γ is a single cone (single cone condition),
2. $Y + \mathrm{Alloc}(\Gamma) = V$ (variable condition),

3. Roots(Φ_i) is defined (disjunct root condition),
4. Alloc(Γ) = Alloc(Φ_i) for every $i \in I$ (allocation condition),
5. $\overrightarrow{x}_i \subseteq$ Cells(Γ_i) (disjunct existential condition),
6. Π is ($\neq V$) (equality condition),
7. Π_i is ($\neq (\overrightarrow{x}_i \overrightarrow{y}_i, V + \{\overrightarrow{x}_i \overrightarrow{y}_i, \text{nil}\})$) (disjunct equality condition),
8. if $i \neq j$, then $\Phi_i \not\equiv \Phi_j \theta$ for all variable renaming θ such that Dom(θ) $\cap$ FV(Γ) = $\emptyset$ (disjunct renaming condition),
9. FV(Y, Π) $\subseteq$ FV($\Gamma, (\Phi_i)_i$) (antecedent variable condition),
10. $|\overrightarrow{Q}| \leq d$ for every predicate symbol $\overrightarrow{Q}$—$*^{\text{ind}} P$ in J (wand condition).

For example, the following is a normal form:

$$\{y, z\} \uparrow \wedge \neq (\{x, y, z\}) \wedge \text{ls}(x, y) \vdash \exists w \Uparrow (w \neq \{x, y, z, \text{nil}\} \wedge \text{ls}(y, w)—*^{\text{ind}} \text{ls}(x, z)).$$

6.2   Definition of Proof Search Algorithm

For a given entailment $A \vdash \overrightarrow{B}$ of quantifier-free symbolic heaps, our proof search algorithm returns Yes or No according to whether $A \vdash \overrightarrow{B}$ is valid or not.

The function MainLoop is called in the main function of the algorithm. Mainloop repeatedly executes the unfold-match-remove-split steps, to produce subgoals from a subgoal. When the same subgoal is generated as that generated already, by cyclic proof mechanism, this subgoal is discharged immediately. Because of a choice of the split rules, MainLoop is executed nondeterministically.

Let $k_{\max}$ be the maximum arity for predicate symbols in the original language.

We assume a satisfiability checking procedure for ψ by extending that for symbolic heaps given in [12]. This procedure is given in [32].

In our algorithm, we do the following trivial steps at several places and we omit their description for simplicity: (1) case analysis by $x = t \vee x \neq t$ for each variable x and term t, (2) case analysis by $x \downarrow \vee x \uparrow$, (3) transformation into the form of entailment $\psi \vdash \overrightarrow{\Phi}$, (4) removing unsatisfiable disjuncts, (5) removing a subgoal when its antecedent is unsatisfiable. For (1), the case analysis by $x = t \vee x \neq t$ in the antecedent means to transform $F \vdash \overrightarrow{G}$ into two subgoals $x = t, F \vdash \overrightarrow{G}$ and $x \neq t, F \vdash \overrightarrow{G}$. The case analysis by $x = t \vee x \neq t$ in the succedent means to transform $F \vdash (G_i)_i$ into a subgoal $F \vdash (G_i \wedge x = t, G_i \wedge x \neq t)_i$. For (2), the case analysis in the antecedent and the succedent is similarly defined to (1).

The proof search algorithm is defined in Algorithm 1.

The input for the proof search algorithm is an entailment of quantifier-free symbolic heaps. First we do case analysis of $=, \neq$ and $\downarrow, \uparrow$ to produce subgoals $\overrightarrow{J}$. For example,

$$\text{ls}(x, y) * \text{ls}(y, z) \vdash \text{ls}(x, z)$$

is transformed into subgoals, one subgoal of which is equivalent to

$$z \uparrow \wedge z = x \wedge z \neq y \wedge z \neq \text{nil} \wedge \text{ls}(x, y) * \text{ls}(y, z) \vdash \text{ls}(x, z) \wedge y \downarrow.$$

Algorithm 1: Proof Search Algorithm

---

input: quantifier-free symbolic heap $A \vdash \vec{B}$
output: Yes or No
Do case analysis of $=, \neq$ and $\downarrow, \uparrow$ on $A \vdash \vec{B}$ to obtain subgoal entailments $\vec{J}$.
for each J in $\vec{J}$ **do**
    $d_{\text{wand}} := k_{\max} + |\text{Alloc}(\text{antecedent of } J)|$.
    Call MainLoop(J, d_{wand}).
    if some nondeterministic computation of MainLoop returns Yes **then**
        continue
    else return No
    end if
end for
return Yes.

MainLoop is nondeterministically executed. When some nondeterministic computation returns Yes, J is valid and we go to the next subgoal. If every nondeterministic computation returns No, J is invalid and we return No. When all the subgoals are solved, we return Yes.

The function MainLoop is defined in Algorithm 2.

The input J of MainLoop is a goal entailment J and the input d is the depth for the factor procedure. First we set S to be $\{(J, \emptyset)\}$. S is a set of pairs of a subgoal and a history (a set of entailments that appear already). In the while loop, we take a subgoal J and a history H from the set S. If J appears already, we can discharge J by cyclic proof mechanism, and go to the next subgoal. We add J to the history H. If J does not have common roots on both sides, then we call the factor procedure with depth d. The factor procedure applies the factor rule with the condition $|\overrightarrow{Q_1(\vec{t}_1), Q(y, \vec{w})}| \leq d$ and $|\overrightarrow{Q_2(\vec{t}_2)}| \leq d$. Then we do the unfold-match-remove steps, namely, we unfold predicates with the common root x in the antecedent and each disjunction of the succedent, and we match $x \mapsto (\vec{t})$ on both sides of the antecedent and the succedent, and we remove the same $x \mapsto (\vec{t})$ from the antecedent and the succedent. Then we check termination condition as follows when the spatial part of the antecedent is emp: if the spatial part of some disjunct in the succedent is emp, we discharge this subgoal (J is valid), and otherwise we return No (J is invalid). Then we apply the split procedure. In the split procedure, first we apply the factor rule to divide an atomic formula if necessary, next we apply ($\exists$Amalg1) and ($\exists$Amalg2) for dividing existential scopes if necessary, and then we apply the split rule under the condition $\text{Alloc}(F_j) = \text{Alloc}(G_j^i)$ for $j = 1, 2$ and $i \in I$. Since the split rules at this step are selectively locally complete, we try all the split rules and we produce a set G of subgoal sets instead of a single subgoal set. We repeat until subgoals become those with a single cone. At least one subgoal set in G keeps validity. Hence we nondeterministically continue computation for each subgoal set R in G. Then we transform each subgoal in R into normal form and put it into the subgoal set S.

Algorithm 2: Function MainLoop

---

input: goal entailment J, maximum inductive wand depth d
output: Yes or No
$S := \{J\}$. $H := \emptyset$.
while $S \neq \emptyset$ **do**
    Choose $J \in S$.
    $S := S - \{J\}$.
    if there are some $J' \in H$ and θ such that $J'\theta \equiv J$ **then continue**
    $H := H + \{J\}$
    if J does not have common roots **then**
        apply the factor procedure with depth d to J.
    end if
    Do unfold-match-remove steps to J.
    if antecedent of J has emp **then**
        if succedent of J has emp **then continue**
        else return No
    end if
    Apply the split procedure repeatedly to J to obtain a set G of subgoal sets
    with a single cone.
    Nondeterministically choose a subgoal set $R \in G$. ·
    for each J in R **do**
        Normalize J.
        $S := S \cup \{J\}$.
    end for
end while
return Yes

We can show the partial correctness of the algorithm with Yes, by checking each step consists of application of inference rules. We will discuss the case with No in the completeness proof later. Note that we can transform a cyclic proof produced by the algorithm such that the companion may not be below some bud into a cyclic proof such that the companion is below any bud, by expanding each bud by the companion some times and finding a repetition on each path.

Lemma 6.2 (Partial Correctness). *If the algorithm returns Yes, then the input entailment is provable.*

6.3 Termination

This subsection shows the termination of the algorithm.

Since a normal form during the loop has the maximum depth of inductive wands, the number of normal forms up to variable renaming is proved to be finite.

Lemma 6.3. *The set of normal forms with d up to variable renaming is finite.*

We can show the termination by using the finiteness.

Lemma 6.4 (Termination). *(1) Every nondeterministic computation of MainLoop terminates.*

(2) The proof search procedure terminates.

The proof of the previous lemma evaluates the length of the history H used in the algorithm. By using it, we can show time complexity of the algorithm.

Proposition 6.5. *The time complexity of the proof search algorithm is nondeterministic double exponential time.*

7   Completeness of CSLID$^\omega$

This section shows the completeness of CSLID$^\omega$ by using the algorithm.

By using the properties of each step in the algorithm, we can show that for a valid input, some nondeterministic computation does not return No.

Lemma 7.1. *(1) Each step in the proof search algorithm except the application of the split rule and the factor rule transforms a valid entailment into valid entailments.*

(2) In the proof search algorithm there is some nondeterministic computation in which every application of the split rule and the factor rule is locally complete.

(3) If a valid entailment is given to MainLoop, some nondeterministic computation does not return No.

Finally we can prove the completeness of CSLID$^\omega$.

Theorem 7.2 (Completeness). *(1) The system CSLID$^\omega$ is complete. Namely, if a given entailment J is valid, then it is provable in CSLID$^\omega$.*

(2) The proof search algorithm decides the validity of a given entailment. Namely, For a given input J, the proof search algorithm returns Yes when the input is valid, and it returns No when the input is invalid.

Proof. (1) Assume J is valid in order to show J is provable in CSLID$^\omega$. When we input J to the algorithm, by Lemma 7.1 (3), in each case of calling MainLoop, some nondeterministic computation does not return No. By Lemma 6.4 (1), the nondeterministic computation returns Yes. Hence the algorithm returns Yes. By Lemma 6.2, J is provable.

(2) Assume J is valid, in order to show the algorithm with input J returns Yes. In the same way as (1), the algorithm is shown to return Yes.

Assume J is invalid, in order to show the algorithm with input J returns No. By Lemma 6.4 (2), the algorithm terminates. Assume that it returns Yes, in order to show contradiction. By Lemma 6.2, J is provable. By Theorem 5.2, J is valid, which leads to contradiction.   □

8   Implementation and Experiments

This section explains our entailment checker Cycomp, which is an implementation of our proof search algorithm. Cycomp is implemented in OCaml with about 7600 lines of codes (including the internally-called satisfiability checker and some optimization). The core part is an implementation of the pseudocode given in a detailed version of this paper [32]. The test problems for evaluating Cycomp and the definitions of inductive predicates used in the problems are presented in Tables 1 and 2, respectively.

The table also compares Cycomp with the other two state-of-the-art entailment solvers for separation logic with general inductively defined predicates: Songbird and Cyclist. Songbird searches structural induction proofs synthesizing lemmas which would be induction hypotheses. We used the latest version of Songbird (called SLS [28]), which can solve most of the valid entailments from SL-COMP [27]. Cyclist [33] is based on a proof search procedure with the Unfold-Match strategy on cyclic proofs. Our test was done with the option of Cyclist that enables lemma synthesis. OutScope in the Songbird column about

Table 1. Experimental results

No	Problem	Status	Cycomp	Cyclist	Songbird
1	$ls(x, y) * list(y) \vdash list(x)$	Valid	0.020	0.072	0.098
2	$ls(x1, x2) * ls(x2, x3) \vdash ls(x1, x3)$	Valid	0.121	0.075	0.071
3	$ls(x1, x2) * ls(x2, x3) * ls(x3, x4) \vdash ls(x1, x4)$	Valid	0.446	0.546	0.102
4	$ls(x, y) \vdash ls0(x, y), lsE(x, y)$	Valid	0.258	Timeout	OutScope
5	$ls(x, y) \vdash ls0(x, y)$	Invalid	0.122	Timeout	(UN)6.345
6	$ls0(x, y) * lsE(y, z) \vdash ls(x, z)$	Valid	1.953	1.534	0.056
7	$ls(x, y) \vdash lsa(x, y, y)$	Invalid	0.239	Timeout	(IC)6.251
8	$ls(x, z) * ls(z, x) \vdash lsa(x, x, z)$	Valid	0.187	14.241	0.158
9	$lsa(x, x, y) \vdash lsa(y, y, x)$	Valid	0.819	Timeout	(IC)0.040
10	$h \mapsto (p, z) * dll(z, h, n, t) \vdash dll(h, p, n, t)$	Valid	15.157	0.019	0.031
11	$dll(h, nil, nil, t) \vdash dllr(t, nil, nil, h)$	Valid	0.342	Timeout	13.320
12	$dll(h, p, n, t) \vdash dllr(t, n, p, h)$	Valid	225.930	0.257	0.099
13	$x \mapsto (y, a) * slk1(a, y) * slk2(y, z) \vdash slk2(x, z)$	Valid	1.167	0.016	0.212
14	$x \mapsto (y, a) * slk1(a, b) * slk1(b, y) * slk2(y, nil) \vdash slk2(x, nil)$	Valid	2.154	4.421	0.136
15	$bpath(x, y) * bpath(y, z) \vdash bpath(x, z)$	Valid	0.422	0.169	0.057
16	$bpath(x, y) \vdash bts(x, y)$	Valid	1.309	0.124	0.081
17	$bts(x, nil) \vdash bt(x)$	Valid	0.117	0.280	0.591
18	$bt(x) \vdash bts(x, nil)$	Valid	0.086	0.256	0.630
19	$bts(x, y) * bt(y) \vdash bt(x)$	Valid	2.457	0.398	1.060
20	$bpath(x, y) * bts(y, nil) \vdash bt(x)$	Valid	1.016	20.046	0.959
21	$dll(h, p, z, w) * dlist(z, w, t) \vdash dlist(h, p, t)$	Valid	Timeout	0.066	0.051
22	$dll(h, nil, z, u) * dll(z, u, nil, t) \vdash dll(h, nil, nil, t)$	Valid	Timeout	2.457	0.071
23	$slk2(x, y) * slk2(y, nil) \vdash slk2(x, nil)$	Valid	Timeout	0.182	0.117
24	$bts(x, y) * bts(y, nil) \vdash bts(x, nil)$	Valid	Timeout	0.749	0.299
25	$bpath(x, y) * y \mapsto (l, r) * bt(l) * bts(r, nil) \vdash bts(x, nil)$	Valid	Timeout	1.394	0.585
26	$ls(x, x) * list(y) \vdash list(x)$	Invalid	0.018	Timeout	(UN)0.342
27	$ls(x1, x2) * ls(x2, x3) \vdash ls(x1, x1)$	Invalid	0.038	Timeout	(UN)0.041
28	$ls0(x, y) * lsE(y, z) \vdash ls(x, x)$	Invalid	0.333	Timeout	(UN)7.461
29	$dll(h, nil, nil, t) \vdash h \mapsto (nil, nil)$	Invalid	0.029	Timeout	(UN)0.039
30	$dll(h, nil, nil, t) \vdash dllr(h, nil, nil, t)$	Invalid	0.055	Timeout	(UN)8.863

the problem 4 means that the format of the problem is out of the syntactic restriction of Songbird, namely the problem contains multiple conclusions. Times with (UN) and (IC) in that column mean that Songbird answered "Unknown" and an incorrect answer with that time, respectively.

The test was done on a laptop PC with a 1.60 GHz Intel(R) Core(TM) i5-8250U CPU, 8 GB memory, and Linux Mint 19. The inputs were executed with 600 seconds timeout setting.

In general, for valid problems, the performance of Cycomp strongly depends on the numbers of inductive predicates and variables that appear in an input entailment. These numbers cause increasing of the number of succedents after applying the factor rule, then the number of the case analysis for (∗)-rule drastically increases, since it requires 2^n cases for an subgoal entailment with n-succedents. Our implementation contains some simple optimization processes to reduce this increase as much as possible. With this optimization, Cycomp quickly shows problems with small numbers, such as the problems 1, 2, and 3. The problem 11 is obtained from the problem 12 by substituting nil for the variables p and n. Cycomp can show the problem 11 faster than the problem 12, since the number of variables are decreased by the substitution. (Interestingly, Cyclist and Songbird have the opposite results.) However, for more complicated valid problems such as the problems from 21 to 25, Cycomp causes time out. In order to obtain a more efficient procedure, it would be important to introduce suitable heuristics to handle numbers of succedents. Supporting the lemma synthesis mechanism would be a possible direction.

For invalid problems, Cycomp explores all branches including back-tracking of the (∗)-split rule and finally answers "Invalid" when all the branches are finished with failure. Although this mechanism may potentially take time depending on problems, Cycomp can finish quickly if it finds a contradiction of each

Table 2. Definitions of inductive predicates

Singly-linked list	$\texttt{list}(x) := x \mapsto (\text{nil}) \vee \exists z(x \mapsto (z) * \texttt{list}(z))$
Lseg with odd length	$\texttt{lsO}(x, y) := x \mapsto (y) \vee \exists z(x \mapsto (z) * \texttt{lsE}(z, y))$
Lseg with even length	$\texttt{lsE}(x, y) := \exists z(x \mapsto (z) * \texttt{lsO}(z, y))$
Lseg with allocated cell	$\texttt{lsa}(x, y, z) := x = z \wedge x \mapsto (y) \vee \exists w(x = z \wedge x \mapsto (w) * \texttt{lsa}(w, y, w))$
	$\vee \exists w(x \mapsto (w) * \texttt{lsa}(w, y, z))$
Doubly-linked list	$\texttt{dlist}(h, p, t) := h = t \wedge h \mapsto (p, \text{nil}) \vee \exists z(h \mapsto (p, z) * \texttt{dlist}(z, h, t))$
Reversed dll	$\texttt{dllr}(h, p, n, t) := h = t \wedge h \mapsto (n, p) \vee \exists z(h \mapsto (z, p) * \texttt{dllr}(z, h, n, t))$
Skip list (1st level)	$\texttt{slk1}(a, b) := a \mapsto (\text{nil}, b) \vee \exists c(a \mapsto (\text{nil}, c) * \texttt{slk1}(c, b))$
Skip list (2nd level)	$\texttt{slk2}(x, y) := x \mapsto (y, y) \vee \exists z, a(x \mapsto (z, z) * \texttt{slk2}(z, y))$
	$\vee \exists z, a(x \mapsto (z, a) * \texttt{slk1}(a, z) * \texttt{slk2}(z, y))$
Binary tree	$\texttt{bt}(x) := x \mapsto (\text{nil}, \text{nil}) \vee \exists l(x \mapsto (l, \text{nil}) * \texttt{bt}(l)) \vee \exists r(x \mapsto (\text{nil}, r) * \texttt{bt}(r))$
	$\vee \exists l, r(x \mapsto (l, r) * \texttt{bt}(l) * \texttt{bt}(r))$
Binary tree segment	$\texttt{bts}(x, y) := x \mapsto (y, \text{nil}) \vee x \mapsto (\text{nil}, y) \vee \exists l(x \mapsto (l, \text{nil}) * \texttt{bts}(l, y))$
	$\vee \exists r(x \mapsto (\text{nil}, r) * \texttt{bts}(r, y)) \vee \exists l, r(x \mapsto (l, r) * \texttt{bt}(l) * \texttt{bts}(r, y))$
	$\vee \exists l, r(x \mapsto (l, r) * \texttt{bts}(l, y) * \texttt{bt}(r))$
Path in binary-tree	$\texttt{bpath}(x, y) := x \mapsto (\text{nil}, y) \vee x \mapsto (y, \text{nil}) \vee \exists z(x \mapsto (z, \text{nil}) * \texttt{bpath}(z, y))$
	$\vee \exists z(x \mapsto (\text{nil}, z) * \texttt{bpath}(z, y))$

branch at an earlier stage, as our experimental results of the problems 5, 7, and 26–30 show. For these invalid problems, Cyclist timed out and Songbird almost answered "Unknown", since they are not decision procedures. It would be an advantage of Cycomp against these existing solvers.

9   Conclusion

We have proposed the cyclic proof system CSLID$^\omega$ for symbolic heaps with cone inductive definitions, and have proved its soundness theorem and its completeness theorem, and have given the proof search algorithm that decides the validity of a given entailment. Furthermore we have implemented a prototype system for the algorithm and have presented experimental results.

Future work would be to extend ideas in this paper to other systems, in particular, a system with arrays.

Acknowledgments. We would like to thank Prof. Kazushige Terui for valuable discussions. This is partially supported by Core-to-Core Program (A. Advanced Research Networks) of the Japan Society for the Promotion of Science.

References

1. Antonopoulos, T., Gorogiannis, N., Haase, C., Kanovich, M., Ouaknine, J.: Foundations for decision problems in separation logic with general inductive predicates. In: Muscholl, A. (ed.) FoSSaCS 2014. LNCS, vol. 8412, pp. 411–425. Springer, Heidelberg (2014). https://doi.org/10.1007/978-3-642-54830-7_27

2. Berardi, S., Tatsuta, M.: Classical system of Martin-Löf's inductive definitions is not equivalent to cyclic proof system. In: Esparza, J., Murawski, A.S. (eds.) FoSSaCS 2017. LNCS, vol. 10203, pp. 301–317. Springer, Heidelberg (2017). https://doi.org/10.1007/978-3-662-54458-7_18

3. Berardi, S., Tatsuta, M.: Equivalence of inductive definitions and cyclic proofs under arithmetic. In: Proceedings of LICS 2017, pp. 1–12 (2017)

4. Brochenin, R., Demri, S., Lozes, E.: On the almighty wand. In: Kaminski, M., Martini, S. (eds.) CSL 2008. LNCS, vol. 5213, pp. 323–338. Springer, Heidelberg (2008). https://doi.org/10.1007/978-3-540-87531-4_24

5. Chang, B.-Y.E., Rival, X.: Relational inductive shape analysis. In: Proceedings of POPL 2008, pp. 247–260 (2008)

6. Berdine, J., Calcagno, C., O'Hearn, P.W.: A decidable fragment of separation logic. In: Lodaya, K., Mahajan, M. (eds.) FSTTCS 2004. LNCS, vol. 3328, pp. 97–109. Springer, Heidelberg (2004). https://doi.org/10.1007/978-3-540-30538-5_9

7. Berdine, J., Calcagno, C., O'Hearn, P.W.: Symbolic execution with separation logic. In: Yi, K. (ed.) APLAS 2005. LNCS, vol. 3780, pp. 52–68. Springer, Heidelberg (2005). https://doi.org/10.1007/11575467_5

8. Brotherston, J.: Formalised inductive reasoning in the logic of bunched implications. In: Nielson, H.R., Filé, G. (eds.) SAS 2007. LNCS, vol. 4634, pp. 87–103. Springer, Heidelberg (2007). https://doi.org/10.1007/978-3-540-74061-2_6

9. Brotherston, J., Simpson, A.: Sequent calculi for induction and infinite descent. J. Logic Comput. **21**(6), 1177–1216 (2011)

10. Brotherston, J., Distefano, D., Petersen, R.L.: Automated cyclic entailment proofs in separation logic. In: Bjørner, N., Sofronie-Stokkermans, V. (eds.) CADE 2011. LNCS (LNAI), vol. 6803, pp. 131–146. Springer, Heidelberg (2011). https://doi.org/10.1007/978-3-642-22438-6_12

11. Brotherston, J., Gorogiannis, N., Petersen, R.L.: A generic cyclic theorem prover. In: Jhala, R., Igarashi, A. (eds.) APLAS 2012. LNCS, vol. 7705, pp. 350–367. Springer, Heidelberg (2012). https://doi.org/10.1007/978-3-642-35182-2_25

12. Brotherston, J., Fuhs, C., Gorogiannis, N., Navarro Pérez, J.: A decision procedure for satisfiability in separation logic with inductive predicates. In: Proceedings of CSL-LICS 2014, Article 25 (2014)

13. Brotherston, J., Gorogiannis, N., Kanovich, M., Rowe, R.: Model checking for symbolic-heap separation logic with inductive predicates. In: Proceedings of POPL 2016, pp. 84–96 (2016)

14. Chin, W., David, C., Nguyen, H., Qin, S.: Automated verification of shape, size and bag properties via user-defined predicates in separation logic. Sci. Comput. Program. **77**(9), 1006–1036 (2012)

15. Chu, D., Jaffar, J., Trinh, M.: Automatic induction proofs of data-structures in imperative programs. In: Proceedings of PLDI 2015, pp. 457–466 (2015)

16. Cook, B., Haase, C., Ouaknine, J., Parkinson, M., Worrell, J.: Tractable reasoning in a fragment of separation logic. In: Katoen, J.-P., König, B. (eds.) CONCUR 2011. LNCS, vol. 6901, pp. 235–249. Springer, Heidelberg (2011). https://doi.org/10.1007/978-3-642-23217-6_16

17. Enea, C., Saveluc, V., Sighireanu, M.: Compositional invariant checking for overlaid and nested linked lists. In: Felleisen, M., Gardner, P. (eds.) ESOP 2013. LNCS, vol. 7792, pp. 129–148. Springer, Heidelberg (2013). https://doi.org/10.1007/978-3-642-37036-6_9

18. Enea, C., Lengál, O., Sighireanu, M., Vojnar, T.: Compositional entailment checking for a fragment of separation logic. In: Garrigue, J. (ed.) APLAS 2014. LNCS, vol. 8858, pp. 314–333. Springer, Cham (2014). https://doi.org/10.1007/978-3-319-12736-1_17

19. Iosif, R., Rogalewicz, A., Simacek, J.: The tree width of separation logic with recursive definitions. In: Bonacina, M.P. (ed.) CADE 2013. LNCS (LNAI), vol. 7898, pp. 21–38. Springer, Heidelberg (2013). https://doi.org/10.1007/978-3-642-38574-2_2

20. Iosif, R., Rogalewicz, A., Vojnar, T.: Deciding entailments in inductive separation logic with tree automata. In: Cassez, F., Raskin, J.-F. (eds.) ATVA 2014. LNCS, vol. 8837, pp. 201–218. Springer, Cham (2014). https://doi.org/10.1007/978-3-319-11936-6_15

21. Katelaan, J., Matheja, C., Zuleger, F.: Effective entailment checking for separation logic with inductive definitions. In: Vojnar, T., Zhang, L. (eds.) TACAS 2019. LNCS, vol. 11428, pp. 319–336. Springer, Cham (2019). https://doi.org/10.1007/978-3-030-17465-1_18

22. Navarro Pérez, J.A., Rybalchenko, A.: Separation logic modulo theories. In: Shan, C. (ed.) APLAS 2013. LNCS, vol. 8301, pp. 90–106. Springer, Cham (2013). https://doi.org/10.1007/978-3-319-03542-0_7

23. Piskac, R., Wies, T., Zufferey, D.: Automating separation logic using SMT. In: Sharygina, N., Veith, H. (eds.) CAV 2013. LNCS, vol. 8044, pp. 773–789. Springer, Heidelberg (2013). https://doi.org/10.1007/978-3-642-39799-8_54

24. Piskac, R., Wies, T., Zufferey, D.: Automating separation logic with trees and data. In: Biere, A., Bloem, R. (eds.) CAV 2014. LNCS, vol. 8559, pp. 711–728. Springer, Cham (2014). https://doi.org/10.1007/978-3-319-08867-9_47

25. Reynolds, J.C.: Separation logic: a logic for shared mutable data structures. In: Proceedings of Seventeenth Annual IEEE Symposium on Logic in Computer Science (LICS 2002), pp. 55–74 (2002)

26. Simpson, A.: Cyclic arithmetic is equivalent to Peano arithmetic. In: Esparza, J., Murawski, A.S. (eds.) FoSSaCS 2017. LNCS, vol. 10203, pp. 283–300. Springer, Heidelberg (2017). https://doi.org/10.1007/978-3-662-54458-7_17

27. SL-COMP2014. https://www.irif.fr/~sighirea/slcomp14/

28. SLS: Songbird+Lemma Synthesis. https://songbird-prover.github.io/lemma-synthesis/

29. Ta, Q.-T., Le, T.C., Khoo, S.-C., Chin, W.-N.: Automated mutual explicit induction proof in separation logic. In: Fitzgerald, J., Heitmeyer, C., Gnesi, S., Philippou, A. (eds.) FM 2016. LNCS, vol. 9995, pp. 659–676. Springer, Cham (2016). https://doi.org/10.1007/978-3-319-48989-6_40

30. Ta, Q., Le, T., Khoo, S., Chin, W.: Automated lemma synthesis in symbolic-heap separation logic. In: Proceedings of POPL 2018 (2018)

31. Tatsuta, M., Kimura, D.: Separation logic with monadic inductive definitions and implicit existentials. In: Feng, X., Park, S. (eds.) APLAS 2015. LNCS, vol. 9458, pp. 69–89. Springer, Cham (2015). https://doi.org/10.1007/978-3-319-26529-2_5

32. Tatsuta, M., Nakazawa, K., Kimura, D.: Completeness of Cyclic Proofs for Symbolic Heaps (2018). https://arxiv.org/abs/1804.03938

33. The Cyclist Framework and Provers. http://www.cyclist-prover.org/

Uniform Random Process Model Revisited

Wenbo Zhang[1](✉) ⓘ, Huan Long[1](✉) ⓘ, and Xian Xu[2](✉) ⓘ

[1] BASICS, Shanghai Jiao Tong University, Shanghai, China
{wbzhang,longhuan}@sjtu.edu.cn
[2] East China University of Science and Technology, Shanghai, China
xuxian@ecust.edu.cn

Abstract. Recently, a proper bisimulation equivalence relation for random process model has been defined in a model independent approach. Model independence clarifies the difference between nondeterministic and probabilistic actions in concurrency and makes the new equivalence relation to be congruent. In this paper, we focus on the finite state randomized CCS model and deepen the previous work in two aspects. First, we show that the equivalence relation can be decided in polynomial time. Second, we give a sound and complete axiomatization system for this model. The algorithm and axiomatization system also have the merit of model independency as they can be easily generalized to the randomized extension of any finite state concurrent model.

1 Introduction

Probabilistic processes have been studied for many years as an important extension of classical concurrency theory. Representative work includes the probabilistic extensions of CCS [9,14], the probabilistic CSP [20], the probabilistic ACP [1], and the probabilistic asynchronous π calculus [15].

As being summarized in [8], there are mainly two kinds of channel randomness used in these works. One is generative models [9,17] which bind probabilistic choice to external actions, and the other is reactive models [5,11,19] which interleave nondeterministic choice with probabilistic distributions (i.e., probabilistic choice). The former setup could lead to difficulties in the interleaving of process operations such as composition and restriction. The latter one, however, forces an alternation between nondeterministic choice and probabilistic distribution which brings unnecessary complexity to the system. A different approach is proposed to tackle these problems, by taking a fundamental separation between nondeterministic interaction and probabilistic choice [8]. More specifically, the only probabilistic choice (or random choice) allowed in this new setup is defined as

$$\bigoplus_{i \in I} p_i \tau.T_i \tag{1}$$

where the size of the index set I is at least 2 and $\sum_{i \in I} p_i = 1$. For any (non-probabilistic) process model $\mathbb{M}$, τ is an abstraction for its internal actions. As

© Springer Nature Switzerland AG 2019
A. W. Lin (Ed.): APLAS 2019, LNCS 11893, pp. 388–404, 2019.
https://doi.org/10.1007/978-3-030-34175-6_20

probabilistic choice only happens via τ, (1) ensures the probabilistic choice to be independent of the settings of the original model $\mathbb{M}$. Thus we can uniformly extend $\mathbb{M}$ into its randomized version. In addition to the syntax conciseness, using this extension the probabilistic model will have some elegant algebraic properties. In [8], the author has proposed two examples (processes A, C) to show that (1) helps to overcome the possible confusing caused by traditional syntax, especially under process combinators such as summation, composition, and restriction. At the same time, the corresponding branching bisimilarity relation is shown to be congruent.

Apart from the nice properties brought by this model independent approach, there are still a few issues which require re-investigation, such as equivalence checking and axiomatization. Equivalence checking is one of the important problems in the area of automatic verification. Given two processes E and F of a model, equivalence checking decides whether E and F can be related by a specific equivalence relation. There has been a lot of work on equivalence checking since 1980s [18]. At the same time, axiomatization aims at understanding a language through a set of axioms and inference rules that help to reason about the properties of programs [5]. It is worthwhile to work out a complete axiomatization system for the branching bisimilarity defined in [8].

In this paper we focus on these two problems for randomized model. As a case study, we consider the randomized CCS (Milner's Calculus of Communicating Systems [21]) model. As CCS model is Turing complete the general equivalence checking problem is undecidable, it is standard to consider the finite state submodel [10,22]. Studies on these problems can shed light on the study of other probabilistic process models, such as probabilistic π et al.

The rest of the paper is structured as follows. Section 2 gives preliminary definitions, notational conventions, the random process model and the equivalence congruence; Sect. 3 gives the polynomial equivalence checking algorithm; Sect. 4 axiomatizes the relation of Sect. 2 and shows the soundness and completeness of the axiomatic system; Sect. 5 contains some concluding remarks.

2   Preliminary

Let $Chan$ be the set of channels, ranged over by lowercase letters. The set of nondeterministic actions is denoted as $Act_d = Chan \cup \{\tau\}$, ranged over by small Greek letters. The set of probabilistic actions is $Act_p = \{q\tau \mid 0 < q < 1\}$. $Act = Act_d \cup Act_p$. For a natural number $k \in \mathbb{N}$, we use $[k]$ to denote the set $\{1, 2, \ldots, k\}$.

2.1   Finite State Random Process Model

It is well known that Milner's CCS [21] is Turing complete, which means that RCCS (Randomized CCS) in [8] is also Turing complete as it is an extension of CCS. In order to get any meaningful algorithmic results, as well as what is more suitable for modeling the reality, we will concentrate on the finite state fragment of the full model, denoted as $RCCS_{fs}$. The grammar of $RCCS_{fs}$, is as follows:

$$T := X \ \Big| \ \sum_{i \in I} \alpha_i.T_i \ \Big| \ \mu X.T \ \Big| \ \bigoplus_{i \in I} p_i\tau.T_i \tag{2}$$

In (2), X is a variable. $\sum_{i \in I} \alpha_i.T_i$ means nondeterministic choice term. $\bigoplus_{i \in I} p_i\tau.T_i$ means probabilistic choice term. $\mu X.T$ means fixpoint term. The indexing set I is finite and $\sum_{i \in I} p_i = 1$. We write $\mathbf{0}$ for the nondeterministic term $\sum_{i \in \emptyset} \alpha_i.T_i$ in which $\emptyset$ is the empty set. A trailing $\mathbf{0}$ is often omitted. Particularly, sometimes instead of the standard form $T = \sum_{i \in I} \alpha_i.T_i$ we use $T = T' + \alpha.T''$ to specify one of the summand terms $\alpha.T''$.

A process variable X that appears in $\sum_{i \in I} \alpha_i.T_i$ or $\bigoplus_{i \in I} p_i\tau.T_i$ is guarded, X appears in $a.T_i$ for some visible action a is strongly guarded. We use $fv(T)$ to stand for the set of variables occurring free (i.e., not bound by μ) in T. A term is a *process* if it contains no free variables. We will use X, Y, Z for process variables and $A, B, C, D, E, F, G, H, L$ for processes. The set of all $RCCS_{fs}$ processes (terms resp.) will be represented by $\mathcal{P}_{RCCS_{fs}}$ ($\mathcal{T}_{RCCS_{fs}}$ resp.). Comparing to the definition in [8], we drop the composition operation for its combination with fixpoint operator could lead to processes with infinite state. A simple counterexample is $\mu X.(s + t|\tau.X)$.

The transition semantics of $RCCS_{fs}$ is generated by the following labelled transition rules, where $\lambda \in Act$:

$$\overline{X \xrightarrow{X} \mathbf{0}} \qquad \overline{\sum_{i \in I} \alpha_i.T_i \xrightarrow{\alpha_i} T_i} \qquad \overline{\bigoplus_{i \in I} p_i\tau.T_i \xrightarrow{p_i\tau} T_i}$$

$$\frac{T\{\mu X.T/X\} \xrightarrow{\lambda} T'}{\mu X.T \xrightarrow{\lambda} T'} \tag{3}$$

Follow the convention used in [8], for an equivalence relation $\mathcal{E}$ on $\mathcal{P}_{RCCS_{fs}}$, we write $A\mathcal{E}B$ for $(A, B) \in \mathcal{E}$. The notation $\mathcal{P}_{RCCS_{fs}}/\mathcal{E}$ stands for the set of equivalence classes defined by $\mathcal{E}$. The equivalence class containing A is denoted by $[A]_{\mathcal{E}}$. For $\mathcal{C} \in \mathcal{P}_{RCCS_{fs}}/\mathcal{E}$ we write $A \xrightarrow{l} \mathcal{C}$ for the fact that $A \xrightarrow{l} A' \in \mathcal{C}$ for some A'.

We use $\mathcal{T}_v$ to stand for terms that are actually a variable (the one in the first rule). Terms that can immediately do a nondeterministic choice (as in the second rule) are called *nondeterministic terms*, denoted as $\mathcal{T}_d$. Terms that can immediately do a probabilistic action are called *probabilistic terms*, denoted as $\mathcal{T}_p$ (as in the last rule). It is obvious that $\mathcal{T}_{RCCS_{fs}} = \mathcal{T}_d \cup \mathcal{T}_p \cup \mathcal{T}_v$.

For terms S and T, if S can be transformed into T via one or a sequence of rules in (3), we say that S can *reach* T, or equivalently, T is *reachable* from S.

Given $S \in \mathcal{P}_{RCCS_{fs}}$, we use R_S to stand for the set of process expressions reachable from S. The following proposition justifies the finite state property of the model defined in (2).

Proposition 1. *Given $S \in \mathcal{P}_{RCCS_{fs}}$, R_S is finite.*

The proposition can be proved by induction on the grammar depth which is standard. We omit the details here.

2.2   Branching Bisimulation Congruence

Here we give the bisimulation relation for which we will study the equivalence checking algorithm and axiomatization. For self-containment, we include relating definitions in this section.

The collective silent transition is firstly introduce in [8]:

$$\bigoplus_{i \in I} p_i \tau.T_i \xrightarrow{\amalg_{i \in I} p_i \tau} \coprod_{i \in I} T_i$$

Definition 1 (ϵ-tree [8]). *Let $A \in \mathcal{P}_{RCCS_{fs}}$ be a process and $\mathcal{E}$ be an equivalence relation on $\mathcal{P}_{RCCS_{fs}}$ An ϵ-tree $t_{\mathcal{E}}^A$ of A with regard to $\mathcal{E}$ is a labeled-tree such that the following statements hold true.*

- *Every node of $t_{\mathcal{E}}^A$ is labeled by elements of $[A]_{\mathcal{E}}$. The root is labeled by A.*
- *The edges are labeled by elements of $(0, 1]$.*
- *If an edge from a node B to a node B' is labeled p for some $p \in (0,1)$, then some collective silent transition $B \xrightarrow{\amalg_{i \in [k]} p_i \tau} \coprod_{i \in [k]} B_i$ exists such that for every $i \in [k]$, there exists an edge from B to B_i labeled p_i, and $B_1, \ldots, B_k$ are the only children of B.*
- *If an edge from a node B to a node B' is labeled 1, then $B \xrightarrow{\tau} B'$ and B' is the only child of B.*

Intuitively epsilon-tree is a random version of a sequence of state-preserving internal actions. Sometimes we will use t instead of $t_{\mathcal{E}}^A$ for simplicity when A and $\mathcal{E}$ are unstressed in the context.

A *branch* in an ϵ-tree t is either a finite path going from the root to a leaf or an infinite path. The length $|\pi|$ of a branch π is the number of edges in π if π is finite; it is ω otherwise. For $i \leq |\pi|$ let $\pi(i)$ be the label of the i-th edge. The probability $\mathbb{P}(\pi)$ of a finite branch π is $\prod_{i \leq |\pi|} \pi(i)$. A branch of length zero is a single node, and its probability is 1. The probability of an infinite path $A \xrightarrow{p_1} \xrightarrow{p_2} \ldots \xrightarrow{p_k} \ldots$ is $\lim_{k \to \infty} \prod_{i < k} p_i$.

Given an ϵ-tree t, the probability of the finite branches of t is defined by $\mathbb{P}^f(t) = \lim_{k \to \infty} \mathbb{P}^k(t)$, where

$$\mathbb{P}^k(t) = \sum \{ \mathbb{P}(\pi) \mid \pi \text{ is a finite branch in } t \text{ such that } |\pi| \leq k \}.$$

An ϵ-tree $t_{\mathcal{E}}^A$ is *regular* if $\mathbb{P}^f(t_{\mathcal{E}}^A) = 1$.

Definition 2 (l-transition [8]). *For $l \in Act_d$ and $\mathcal{B} \in \mathcal{P}_{RCCS_{fs}}/\mathcal{E}$, suppose $l \neq \tau \vee \mathcal{B} \neq [A]_{\mathcal{E}}$. An l-transition from A to $\mathcal{B}$ with regard to $\mathcal{E}$ consists of a regular ϵ-tree $t_{\mathcal{E}}^A$ of A with regard to $\mathcal{E}$ and a transition $L \xrightarrow{l} L' \in \mathcal{B}$ for every leaf L of $t_{\mathcal{E}}^A$. We will write $A \rightsquigarrow_{\mathcal{E}} \xrightarrow{l} \mathcal{B}$ if there is an l-transition from A to $\mathcal{B}$ with regard to $\mathcal{E}$.*

Intuitively l-transition characterizes that after some state-preserving silent transitions, an l-action is performed and the resulting processes should be in the same equivalence class.

Suppose $L \xrightarrow{\amalg_{i \in [k]} p_i \tau} \amalg_{i \in [k]} L_i$ such that $\exists i \in [k]$, $L_i \in \mathcal{B} \neq [L]_{\mathcal{E}}$. We define

$$\mathbb{P}(L \xrightarrow{\amalg_{i \in [k]} p_i \tau} \mathcal{B}) = \sum \{p_i | L \xrightarrow{p_i \tau} L_i \in \mathcal{B} \land i \in [k]\}$$

Define the weighted probability

$$\mathbb{P}_{\mathcal{E}}(L \xrightarrow{\amalg_{i \in [k]} p_i \tau} \mathcal{B}) = \mathbb{P}(L \xrightarrow{\amalg_{i \in [k]} p_i \tau} \mathcal{B})/(1 - \mathbb{P}(L \xrightarrow{\amalg_{i \in [k]} p_i \tau} [L]_{\mathcal{E}}))$$

Definition 3 (q-transition [8]). *A q-transition from A to $\mathcal{B}$ with regard to $\mathcal{E}$ consists of a regular ϵ-tree $t_{\mathcal{E}}^A$ of A with regard to $\mathcal{E}$ and for every leaf L of $t_{\mathcal{E}}^A$, a collective silent transition $L \xrightarrow{\amalg_{i \in [k]} p_i \tau} \amalg_{i \in [k]} L_i$ such that $\mathbb{P}_{\mathcal{E}}(L \xrightarrow{\amalg_{i \in [k]} p_i \tau} \mathcal{B}) = q$. We use $A \rightsquigarrow_{\mathcal{E}} \xrightarrow{q} \mathcal{B}$ to mean there is a q-transition from A to $\mathcal{B}$ with regard to the relation $\mathcal{E}$.*

Intuitively q-transition characterizes that after some state-preserving silent transitions, random choices with total conditional probability q are performed and the resulting processes should be in the same equivalence class.

Definition 4. *[8] An equivalence $\mathcal{E}$ on $\mathcal{P}$ is a branching bisimulation if $(1,2)$ are valid.*

1. *If $\mathcal{B} \mathcal{E} A \rightsquigarrow_{\mathcal{E}} \xrightarrow{l} \mathcal{C} \in \mathcal{P}/\mathcal{E}$ such that $l \neq \tau \lor \mathcal{C} \neq [A]_{\mathcal{E}}$, then $\mathcal{B} \rightsquigarrow_{\mathcal{E}} \xrightarrow{l} \mathcal{C}$.*
2. *If $\mathcal{B} \mathcal{E} A \rightsquigarrow_{\mathcal{E}} \xrightarrow{q} \mathcal{C} \in \mathcal{P}/\mathcal{E}$ such that $\mathcal{C} \neq [A]_{\mathcal{E}}$, then $\mathcal{B} \rightsquigarrow_{\mathcal{E}} \xrightarrow{q} \mathcal{C}$.*

Finally we can define the equality on $\mathcal{P}_{\mathrm{RCCS}_{fs}}$. It is the largest branching bisimulation on $\mathcal{P}_{\mathrm{RCCS}_{fs}}$, denoted by $\simeq_{\mathrm{RCCS}_{fs}}$. Sometimes we will use $\simeq$ instead of $\simeq_{\mathrm{RCCS}_{fs}}$ for simplicity when its meaning is clear from the context.

The following proposition is a special case of the Theorem 17 in [8]. Here we present it without proof.

Proposition 2. *The equality $\simeq_{RCCS_{fs}}$ is a congruence.*

3   Equivalence Checking Algorithm

Equivalence checking is one of the key problems in verification. It gives the answer whether two systems are related by a given equivalent relation. As far as branching bisimulation is concerned, some representative includes [7,16]. Meanwhile, to the probabilistic process calculus model, there are also some interesting work such as [3,23].

Here we develop an algorithm to decide the equivalence relation $\simeq_{\mathrm{RCCS}_{fs}}$ for RCCS_{fs} processes. Recall that for a given random process A, we use R_A to denote the set of all processes reachable from A. In Proposition 1, we have already known that this set is finite, here we will further show that it can be constructed in polynomial time with respect to the length of the given process. Pseudocode of our algorithm is given in Algorithm 1.

Algorithm 1. Compute R_A

Input: $A \in \mathcal{P}_{\mathrm{RCCS}_{f_s}}$
Output: R_A
1: $R_A := \emptyset$, $R' := \{A\}$
2: **while** $R' \neq \emptyset$ **do**
3:    Choose a process B from R', $R' := R' - \{B\}$, $R_A := R_A \cup \{B\}$
4:    **if** $B = \sum_{i \in I} \alpha_i.T_i$ **then**
5:       $R' := R' \cup \{T_i : i \in I\} \setminus R_A$
6:    **else if** $B = \bigoplus_{i \in I} p_i\tau.T_i$ **then**
7:       $R' := R' \cup \{T_i : i \in I\} \setminus R_A$
8:    **else if** $B = \mu X.T$ **then**
9:       $R' := R' \cup \{T\{\mu X.T/X\}\} \setminus R_A$
10: **return** R_A

For a better understanding of the algorithm, we give one simple example here.

Example 1. Let $H = \mu X.(\frac{1}{2}\tau.(a + \tau.X) \oplus \frac{1}{2}\tau.(b + \tau.X))$, then Algorithm 1 will return

$$R_H = \left\{H, \frac{1}{2}\tau.(a + \tau.H) \oplus \frac{1}{2}\tau.(b + \tau.H), a + \tau.H, b + \tau.H, \mathbf{0}\right\}.$$

As usual, a *partition* of process set $\mathcal{P}$ is a collection of $\mathcal{X}$ containing pairwise disjoint subsets of $\mathcal{P}$ such that each element $A \in \mathcal{P}$ is contained in some $\mathcal{C} \in \mathcal{X}$. The equivalence class containing A is denoted by $[A]_\mathcal{X}$. Let $\mathcal{E}_\mathcal{X}$ be the equivalence relation induced by the partition $\mathcal{X}$. Given two partitions $\mathcal{X}_1$ and $\mathcal{X}_2$ of the same set. We say $\mathcal{X}_1$ is coarser than $\mathcal{X}_2$ (or equivalently $\mathcal{X}_2$ is finer than $\mathcal{X}_1$) if every element in $\mathcal{X}_2$ is a subset of some element in $\mathcal{X}_1$.

Next we propose a technical definition which is closely related to the conception of ϵ-tree given in Definition 1.

Definition 5. *The ϵ-graph of A with regard to an equivalence relation $\mathcal{E}$ is a weighted directed graph, denoted by $G_\mathcal{E}^A$. $G_\mathcal{E}^A$ is defined by merging nodes of the same name from an ϵ-tree $t_\mathcal{E}^A$ into one node. A vertex in $G_\mathcal{E}^A$ is called a sink node if its out degree is 0. Let $sn(G_\mathcal{E}^A)$ be the set of all sink nodes of $G_\mathcal{E}^A$.*

For given process A and $\mathcal{E}$, though there could be infinitely many different ϵ-trees, the number of all possible ϵ-graphs of A with regard to $\mathcal{E}$ is finite.

Proposition 3. *Let $\mathcal{P}$ be a process set and $\mathcal{E}$ be an equivalence relation. For a process $A \in \mathcal{P}$, and a process set $\mathcal{P}' \subseteq \mathcal{P}$, there exists a regular ϵ-tree $t_\mathcal{E}^A$ with leaf nodes set $\mathcal{P}'$ (all of the same name) if and only if there exists an ϵ-graph $G_\mathcal{E}^A$ with a sink node named $\mathcal{P}'$.*

By Proposition 3, the transformation from ϵ-tree to ϵ-graph will not affect the bisimilarity relation. Yet ϵ-graph is technically more convenient for presenting our equivalence checking algorithm.

We put an example here to explain the difference between ϵ-tree and ϵ-graph.

Example 2. For the process H in Example 1, a branching bisimulation for $\mathcal{P}_H$ is the equivalence $\mathcal{E}$ rendering the truth that $[H]_\mathcal{E} = [a + \tau.H]_\mathcal{E} = [b + \tau.H]_\mathcal{E}$. For the ϵ-tree in Fig. 1(a), the corresponding ϵ-graph has a sink node $b + \tau.H$. For the second one in Fig. 1(b) the sink node is $a + \tau.H$. For the ϵ-tree in Fig. 1(c), there does not exist a visible action that all leaves can immediately do, and there does not exist a sink node for the ϵ-graph.

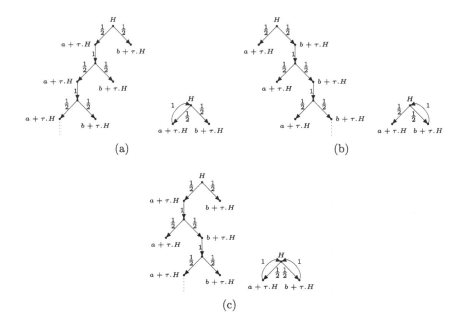

Fig. 1. ϵ-trees and corresponding ϵ-graphs

Here we will introduce one more convention for the description of our algorithm. We use the symbol $\hat{\wp}\tau$ to represent *any* $p\tau$ where $p \in (0, 1]$. In other words, using $\hat{\wp}\tau$ means we are talking about a probabilistic action without specifying the concrete probability value.

Definition 6. *Let $\mathcal{X}$ be a partition of process set $\mathcal{P}$. A* splitter *of a partition $\mathcal{X}$ is a triple $(\mathcal{C}_1, l, \mathcal{C}_2)$ consisting of $\mathcal{C}_1, \mathcal{C}_2 \in \mathcal{X}$ and an action $l \in Act_d \cup \{\hat{\wp}\tau\}$. One of the following statements is valid:*

1. *If $l \in Act_d$, and $\mathcal{C}_1 \neq \mathcal{C}_2$ when $l = \tau$, then there exist some $A, A' \in \mathcal{C}_1$, such that for exactly one of A, A', there is an ϵ-graph $G_\mathcal{X}^A$ ($G_\mathcal{X}^{A'}$ resp.), all of $sn(G_\mathcal{X}^A)$ ($sn(G_\mathcal{X}^{A'})$ resp.) can do an immediate l action to $\mathcal{C}_2$.*

2. If $l = \hat{\wp}\tau$, and $\mathcal{C}_1 \neq \mathcal{C}_2$, then there exist $A, A' \in \mathcal{C}_1$ and $q \in (0,1]$, such that for exactly one of A, A', there is an ϵ-graph $G_{\mathcal{X}}^A$ ($G_{\mathcal{X}}^{A'}$ resp.), for any $T \in sn(G_{\mathcal{X}}^A)$ ($sn(G_{\mathcal{X}}^{A'})$ resp.), $\mathbb{P}_{\mathcal{E}_{\mathcal{X}}}(T \xrightarrow{\amalg_{i \in [k]} p_i \tau} \mathcal{C}_2) = q$.

Intuitively speaking, our equivalence checking strategy starts with a finite set which contains all reachable states for a pair of processes (the coarsest partition). Keep refining the current sets into finer ones according to their one-step difference until no further refinement is possible (the finest partition), where states of the same set are equivalent to each other.

In detail, to refine the partition $\mathcal{X}$, according to Definition 6, there are two cases to be considered:

1. If $\mathcal{X}$ has a splitter $(\mathcal{C}_1, \hat{\wp}\tau, \mathcal{C}_2)$.

   Let $tn(\mathcal{P}, \mathcal{X}) \subseteq \mathcal{P}$ be the set composed of all processes that can perform probabilistic τ step into a different class with nonzero probability. Firstly, we split $\mathcal{C}_1 \cap tn(\mathcal{P}, \mathcal{X})$ into $\mathcal{C}_1 \cap tn(\mathcal{P}, \mathcal{X})/ =_p$, where $A =_p A'$ iff $\mathbb{P}_{\mathcal{X}}(A \xrightarrow{\amalg_{i \in [k]} p_i \tau} \mathcal{C}_2) = \mathbb{P}_{\mathcal{X}}(A' \xrightarrow{\amalg_{i \in [k]} p_i \tau} \mathcal{C}_2)$. Then, an equivalent class $\mathcal{B} \in \mathcal{C}_1 \cap tn(\mathcal{P}, \mathcal{X})/ =_p$ is enriched with process $B \in \mathcal{C}_1 \setminus tn(\mathcal{P}, \mathcal{X})$ which satisfies (denoted as Δ) :

   (a) There exists an ϵ-graph $G_{\mathcal{X}}^B$ with $sn(G_{\mathcal{X}}^B) \subseteq \mathcal{B}$.

   (b) For any other $\mathcal{B}' \in \mathcal{C}_1 \cap tn(\mathcal{P}, \mathcal{X})/ =_p$, there does not exist an ϵ-graph $G_{\mathcal{X}}^B$ with $sn(G_{\mathcal{X}}^B) \subseteq \mathcal{B}'$.

   Let $\overline{\mathcal{B}} \stackrel{\text{def}}{=} \mathcal{B} \cup \{B : B \in \mathcal{C}_1, B \text{ satisfies } \Delta\}$ be the closure of $\mathcal{B}$. We put the remaining processes into

   $Res(\mathcal{C}_1) \stackrel{\text{def}}{=} \{C \in \mathcal{C}_1 : C \text{ does not satisfies } \Delta \text{ for any } \mathcal{B} \in \mathcal{C}_1 \cap tn(\mathcal{P}, \mathcal{X})/ =_p\}$.
   Formally, the strategy we used for refining $\mathcal{X}$ via a splitter $(\mathcal{C}_1, p\tau, \mathcal{C}_2)$ is:

   $$\mathbf{Refine}(\mathcal{X}, (\mathcal{C}_1, \tau, \mathcal{C}_2)) \stackrel{\text{def}}{=} (\mathcal{X} \setminus \{\mathcal{C}_1\}) \cup \{\overline{\mathcal{B}} : \mathcal{B} \in \mathcal{C}_1 \cap tn(\mathcal{P}, \mathcal{X})/ =_p\}$$
   $$\cup (\{Res(\mathcal{C}_1)\} \setminus \{\emptyset\}).$$

2. If $\mathcal{X}$ has a splitter $(\mathcal{C}_1, \alpha, \mathcal{C}_2)$, $\alpha \in Act_d$, and $\mathcal{C}_1 \neq \mathcal{C}_2$ when $\alpha = \tau$.

   Let $\mathcal{D} \stackrel{\text{def}}{=} \{B \in \mathcal{C}_1 : \text{there exists an } \epsilon\text{-graph } G_{\mathcal{X}}^B, \text{ all of } sn(G_{\mathcal{X}}^B) \text{ can do an immediate } \alpha \text{ action to } \mathcal{C}_2\}$. We can define the method for refining $\mathcal{X}$ via a splitter $(\mathcal{C}_1, \alpha, \mathcal{C}_2)$:

   $$\mathbf{Refine}(\mathcal{X}, (\mathcal{C}_1, \alpha, \mathcal{C}_2)) \stackrel{\text{def}}{=} (\mathcal{X} \setminus \{\mathcal{C}_1\}) \cup \mathcal{D} \cup (\mathcal{C}_1 \setminus \mathcal{D}).$$

Note that for every partition $\mathcal{X}$ which is coarser than $\mathcal{P}/ \simeq$ and every nonempty splitter $(\mathcal{C}_1, l, \mathcal{C}_2)$ of $\mathcal{X}$, the partition $\mathbf{Refine}(\mathcal{X}, (\mathcal{C}_1, l, \mathcal{C}_2))$ is no finer than $\mathcal{P}/ \simeq$ while strictly finer than $\mathcal{X}$. If there is no splitter for $\mathcal{X}$ (i.e., if neither of the above two cases applies), then through proof by contradiction, it can be easily concluded that $\mathcal{X} = \mathcal{P}/ \simeq$. This analysis turns out to be the proof of the following proposition.

Proposition 4. *Let $\mathcal{X}$ be a partition of process set $\mathcal{P}$. If $\mathcal{X}$ cannot be refined anymore, then $\mathcal{X} = \mathcal{P}/ \simeq$.*

This justifies the correctness of Algorithm 2.

Algorithm 2. Equivalence Checking Algorithm

Input: Process A , B
Output: Is $A \simeq B$?
 1: Compute $R := R_A \cup R_B$
 2: $\mathcal{X} := \{R\}$
 3: **while** $\mathcal{X}$ contains a splitter $(\mathcal{C}_1, l, \mathcal{C}_2)$ **do**
 4:     $\mathcal{X} := \mathbf{Refine}(\mathcal{X}, (\mathcal{C}_1, l, \mathcal{C}_2))$
 5: **if** $[A]_{\mathcal{X}} = [B]_{\mathcal{X}}$ **then**
 6:     **return** true
 7: **else**
 8:     **return** false

Theorem 1. $\simeq_{RCCS_{fs}}$ *can be decided in polynomial time.*

Proof. There exists a constant c, such that the numbers of elements in R is bounded by $c \cdot (|A| + |B|)$ and for process $E \in R$, $|E| < c \cdot (|A| + |B|)$. The **while** loop of line 3–4 can be repeated at most $c \cdot (|A| + |B|)$ times. For each l and $\mathcal{C}_2$, we can construct the process set $S = \{A \mid A \in \mathcal{C}_1, A \xrightarrow{l} \mathcal{C}_2\}$ in $\mathcal{O}((|A| + |B|)^3)$ time and then decide the condition in line 3 by searching for an ϵ-graph with sink nodes in S. It can be done by depth first search in $\mathcal{O}((|A| + |B|)^3)$ time. Overall the algorithm will terminate in $\mathcal{O}((|A| + |B|)^4)$ time.

4   Axiomatizations

4.1   Discussion of the Axioms

In the original CCS model, a complete axiomatization for branching bisimulation congruence of finite process will first convert any expression into a strongly guarded one. If two strongly guarded expressions are branching bisimilar, they can be proved to be equal in axiomatic system [10]. However, in probabilistic model, there exist some expressions that cannot be transformed to a strongly guarded one, e.g., $\mu X(\tau.(\frac{1}{2}\tau.X \oplus \frac{1}{2}\tau.b) + a)$. It means that a τ-loop containing probabilistic τ may be not state-preserving under $\simeq$. We will define *probabilistically guarded*. Intuitively X is probabilistically guarded in T if T can not do some τ actions to X with probability 1.

Definition 7. *The variable X is probabilistically guarded in T if at least one of the following statements is true:*

- *There is no free occurrence of X in T, or every free occurrence of X in T occurs within some subexpression $a.F$.*
- *If $T \in \mathcal{T}_d$, then for any term T' such that $T \xrightarrow{\tau} T'$, X is probabilistically guarded in T'.*

– *If $T \in \mathcal{T}_p$, then there exists a term T' such that $T \xrightarrow{p\tau} T'$, X is probabilistically guarded in T'.*

Otherwise X is probabilistically unguarded in T.

Example 3. X is probabilistically guarded in $\frac{1}{2}\tau.(\frac{1}{2}\tau.a \oplus \frac{1}{2}\tau.X) \oplus \frac{1}{2}\tau.(\frac{1}{2}\tau.X \oplus \frac{1}{2}\tau.X)$. X is probabilistically unguarded in $a.X + \tau.X$.

If for every occurrence of $\mu X.T$ in E, X is probabilistically guarded in T, we call process E is probabilistically guarded. Let $\mathcal{P}^g_{\mathrm{RCCS}_{fs}}$ be the set of probabilistically guarded processes.

The axioms that characterize the equivalence relation given in Sect. 2.2 are listed below. We will prove that this set of axioms is sound and complete for the relation $\simeq_{\mathrm{RCCS}_{fs}}$.

E1 $T = T$
E2 if $S = T$ then $T = S$
E3 if $S = T$ and $T = R$ then $S = R$
E4 if $S_i = T_i$ for each $i \in I$ then $\sum_{i \in I} \alpha_i.S_i = \sum_{i \in I} \alpha_i.T_i$
E5 if $S_i = T_i$ for each $i \in I$ and $\sum_{i \in I} p_i = 1$, then $\bigoplus_{i \in I} p_i\tau.S_i = \bigoplus_{i \in I} p_i\tau_i.T_i$
E6 if $S = T$ then $\mu X.S = \mu X.T$

A1 $\bigoplus_{i \in I} p_i\tau.S_i \oplus p\tau.S \oplus q\tau.S = \bigoplus_{i \in I} p_i\tau.S_i \oplus (p+q)\tau.S$, $p + q < 1$
A2 $p\tau.S \oplus q\tau.S = \tau.S$

B1 $\left(\sum_{i \in I' \subseteq I} \alpha_i.S_i\right) + \tau.(\sum_{i \in I} \alpha_i.S_i) = \sum_{i \in I} \alpha_i.S_i$
B2 if $\frac{p_1}{q_1} = \cdots = \frac{p_i}{q_i} < 1$ and $\sum_{i \in I} q_i = 1$,
  then $\bigoplus_{i \in I} p_i\tau.S_i \oplus p\tau.(\bigoplus_{i \in I} q_i\tau.S_i) = \bigoplus_{i \in I} q_i\tau.S_i$, $p = 1 - \sum_{i \in I} p_i$

R1 $\mu X.T = T\{\mu X.T/X\}$
R2 if $S = T\{S/X\}$ then $S = \mu X.T$, provided X is probabilistically guarded in T
R3 $\mu X.(\tau.X + \sum_{i \in I} \alpha_i.T_i) = \mu X.(\sum_{i \in I} \alpha_i.T_i)$
R4 $\mu X.(\tau.(\tau.S + \sum_{i \in I} \alpha_i.T_i) + \sum_{j \in J} \beta_j.R_j) = \mu X.(\tau.S + \sum_{i \in I} \alpha_i.T_i + \sum_{j \in J} \beta_j.R_j)$,
  provided X is probabilistically unguarded in S

One writes $\mathcal{A} \vdash E = F$, with $\mathcal{A}$ a list of axiom names, if the equation $E = F$ is derivable from the axioms in $\mathcal{A}$. In this paper, we take the convention that $E1-6$ and $A1-2$ are always in $\mathcal{A}$.

Comparing to the earlier work on axiomatization for probabilistic bisimulation [2,4,6,13,17,24], $B2$ highlights the nucleus of the model independent approach for random process model. That is, instead of the absolute probability value (or probability distribution), we use the *weighted* probability in [8], which basically characterizes the conditional probability of transferring from one state to another.

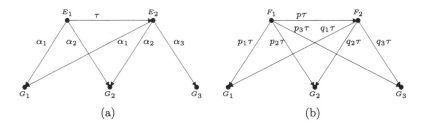

Fig. 2. State-preserving τ and $p\tau$ actions

Axioms $B1$, $B2$ are both motivated by the axiom B in [10]. $B1$ modifies B in two aspects: Firstly, it does not use the heading external action, as the grammar ensures the terms are weak guarded; Secondly, it uses summation of a set of terms rather than binary summation. The intuition of axiom $B1$ is showed in Fig. 2(a) [12]. The τ action $E_1 \xrightarrow{\tau} E_2$ is state-preserving if process E_2 can do any actions E_1 can do. $B2$ is a random extension of $B1$. The intuition of axiom $B2$ is showed in Fig. 2(b). The probabilistic τ action $F_1 \xrightarrow{p\tau} F_2$ is state-preserving if process F_2 can do exactly F_1 can do with the same *weighted* probability($\frac{p_i}{q_i}$ is a constant value for $i \in \{1, 2, 3\}$).

The presentation of our work on soundness and completeness follows a similar strategy as in [10]. One can refer to van Glabbeek's paper for a comparison.

4.2   Soundness

The soundness of $E1 - 6$ has been validated by Proposition 2. The soundness of $A1 - 2$, $B1$ and $R3$ can be easily shown by the definition of the equivalence relation. The soundness of $R1$ follows from the fact that $\mu X.T \xrightarrow{\alpha} F \iff T\{\mu X.T/X\} \xrightarrow{\alpha} F$. The soundness of the remaining axioms are given below.

Proposition 5 (Soundness of $B2$). *If* $\frac{p_1}{q_1} = \cdots = \frac{p_i}{q_i} < 1$ *and* $\sum_{i \in I} q_i = 1$, *then* $\bigoplus_{i \in I} p_i \tau.E_i \oplus p\tau.(\bigoplus_{i \in I} q_i \tau.E_i) \simeq \bigoplus_{i \in I} q_i \tau.E_i$, $p = 1 - \sum_{i \in I} p_i$.

Proof. Let $F_1 = \bigoplus_{i \in I} q_i \tau.E_i$ and $F_2 = \bigoplus_{i \in I} p_i \tau.E_i \oplus p\tau.(\bigoplus_{i \in I} q_i \tau.E_i)$. We consider the following two cases:

- $\forall i \in I, E_i \simeq F_1$.
  For every ϵ-tree $t_{\simeq}^{F_j}$, $j \in \{1, 2\}$, we can construct an ϵ-tree $t_{\simeq}^{F_{3-j}}$ with the same set of leaf nodes of $t_{\simeq}^{F_j}$. Thus $F_1 \simeq F_2$.
- $\exists i \in I, E_i \not\simeq F_1$.
  Let $I' \subseteq I$ be the set of indices satisfying $E_{i'} \not\simeq F_1$, $i' \in I'$. Let $r_{i'} = \frac{q_{i'}}{\sum_{i' \in I'} q_{i'}}$, then $F_j \rightsquigarrow_{\varepsilon} \xrightarrow{r_{i'}} [E_{i'}]_{\simeq}$ for $j \in \{1, 2\}$.

Definition 8. *A branching bisimulation up to* $\simeq$ *is a symmetric relation* $\mathcal{R} \subseteq$ $\mathcal{P}_{RCCS_{fs}} \times \mathcal{P}_{RCCS_{fs}}$ *such that*

- *if* $E\mathcal{R}F$ *and* $E \rightsquigarrow_{\simeq} \overset{l}{\rightarrow} \mathcal{B}_1$ *such that* $l \neq \tau \vee \mathcal{B}_1 \neq [E]_{\simeq}$, *then there exists* E', F' *such that* $E' \in \mathcal{B}_1 \wedge F' \in \mathcal{B}_2 \wedge F \rightsquigarrow_{\simeq} \overset{l}{\rightarrow} \mathcal{B}_2 \wedge (E', F') \in \mathcal{R}$.
- *if* $E\mathcal{R}F$ *and* $E \rightsquigarrow_{\simeq} \overset{q}{\rightarrow} \mathcal{B}_1$ *such that* $\mathcal{B}_1 \neq [E]_{\simeq}$, *then there exists* E', F' *such that* $E' \in \mathcal{B}_1 \wedge F' \in \mathcal{B}_2 \wedge F \rightsquigarrow_{\simeq} \overset{q}{\rightarrow} \mathcal{B}_2 \wedge (E', F') \in \mathcal{R}$.

Proposition 6. *If* $\mathcal{R}$ *is a branching bisimulation up to* $\simeq$ *and* $E\mathcal{R}F$, *then* $E \simeq F$.

Proposition 7. *Variable* X *is probabilistically guarded in a term* $T \in \mathcal{T}_{RCCS_{fs}}$. *If there is an* l-*transition or* q-*transition from* $T\{F/X\}$ *to* $\mathcal{B}$, *then there is a process* $T'\{F/X\} \in \mathcal{B}$ *such that* T' *is reachable from* T.

Proof. Induction on the structure of T.

Proposition 8 (Soundness of R2**).** *If* $F \simeq S\{F/X\}$, *then* $F \simeq \mu X.S$, *provided* X *is probabilistically guarded in* S.

Proof. Consider the following relation

$$\mathcal{R} = \Big\{ (T\{F/Y\}, T\{\mu X.S/Y\}) \mid \text{fv}(T) = \{Y\} \Big\}.$$

Then $(F, \mu X.S) \in \mathcal{R}$. By Proposition 6, it suffices to prove that the symmetric closure of $\mathcal{R}$ is a branching bisimulation up to $\simeq$.

- If $T\{F/Y\} \rightsquigarrow_{\simeq} \overset{l}{\rightarrow} \mathcal{B}_1$ such that $l \neq \tau \vee \mathcal{B}_1 \neq [T\{F/Y\}]_{\simeq}$.
  Consider the ϵ-tree $t_{\simeq}^{T\{F/Y\}}$, we can construct an ϵ-tree $t_{\simeq}^{T\{\mu X.S/Y\}}$ from $t_{\simeq}^{T\{F/Y\}}$ by recursively replace the subtree from node F with an ϵ-tree $t_{\simeq}^{S\{F/X\}}$.
  If there is a process $E' = T'\{F/Y\} \in \mathcal{B}_1$ such that T' is reachable from T, then $E'\mathcal{R}F' = T'\{\mu X.S/Y\} \in \mathcal{B}_2$ and $T\{\mu X.S/Y\} \rightsquigarrow_{\simeq} \overset{l}{\rightarrow} \mathcal{B}_2$.
  Otherwise, every branch of $t_{\simeq}^{T\{F/Y\}}$ steps into F. Let $E' \in \mathcal{B}_1$, E' is reachable from F. Since $F \simeq S\{F/X\}$, and X is probabilistically guarded in S, by Proposition 7, there is a process $E''\{F/X\} \simeq E'$ where E'' is reachable from S. What's more, there is a process $F' = E''\{\mu X.S/X\} \in \mathcal{B}_2$ and $T\{\mu X.S/Y\} \rightsquigarrow_{\simeq} \overset{l}{\rightarrow} \mathcal{B}_2$. Then we have

  $$(E''\{F/X\}, F') = (E''\{Y/X\}\{F/Y\}, E''\{\mu X.Y/X\}\{\mu X.S/Y\}) \in \mathcal{R}$$

- If $T\{F/Y\} \rightsquigarrow_{\simeq} \overset{q}{\rightarrow} \mathcal{B}_1$ such that $\mathcal{B}_1 \neq [T\{F/Y\}]_{\simeq}$.
  Similar with the case of l-transition.

Proposition 9 (Soundness of $R4$**).** $\mu X.(\tau.(\tau.S + \sum_{i \in I} \alpha_i.T_i) + \sum_{j \in J} \beta_j.R_j)$ $\simeq \mu X(\tau.S + \sum_{i \in I} \alpha_i.T_i + \sum_{j \in J} \beta_j.R_j)$, *provided* X *is probabilistically unguarded in term* E.

Proof. Let

$$A_1 = \mu X.(\tau.(\tau.S + \sum_{i \in I} \alpha_i.T_i) + \sum_{j \in J} \beta_j.R_j)$$

$$A_2 = \tau.S\{A_1/X\} + \sum_{i \in I} \alpha_i.T_i\{A_1/X\}$$

$$B_1 = \mu X(\tau.S + \sum_{i \in I} \alpha_i.T_i + \sum_{j \in J} \beta_j.R_j)$$

First, we show that $A_1 \simeq A_2$. It is obvious that A_1 can simulate A_2. For the other direction, since X is probabilistically unguarded in S, actions $l_i \in \{\tau\} \cup \{p\tau \mid 0 < p < 1\}$ in $A_2 \xrightarrow{\tau} S\{A_1/X\} \xrightarrow{l_1} S_1\{A_1/X\} \xrightarrow{l_2} \dots \xrightarrow{l_m} A_1$, can be proved state-preserving. We can construct an ϵ-tree $t_{\simeq}^{A_2}$ with every branch stepping into A_1. Thus for every $t_{\simeq}^{A_1}$, there is an ϵ-tree $t_{\simeq}^{A_2}$ with the same set of leaf nodes.

With the fact $A_1 \xrightarrow{\tau} A_2$ is state-preserving, A_1 can simulate B_1. For the other direction, we will construct an ϵ-tree $t_{\simeq}^{B_1}$ by a given $t_{\simeq}^{A_1}$. $t_{\simeq}^{B_1}$ does nothing if $A_1 \xrightarrow{\tau} A_2$ in $t_{\simeq}^{A_1}$, and follows $t_{\simeq}^{A_1}$ in other cases. It can be seen that $t_{\simeq}^{A_1}$ and $t_{\simeq}^{B_1}$ have the same set of leaf nodes.

Corollary 1 (Soundness). *For* E, $F \in \mathcal{P}_{RCCS_{fs}}$, *if* $B1-2$, $R1-4 \vdash E = F$, *then* $E \simeq F$.

4.3   Completeness

By induction on the structure of $\mathcal{T}_{\mathrm{RCCS}_{fs}}$, we can prove that:

Lemma 1. *For a term* $T \in \mathcal{T}_{\mathrm{RCCS}_{fs}}$,

- *if* $T \xrightarrow{X} 0$, *then* $\vdash T = X$;
- *if* $T \in \mathcal{T}_d$, *then* $\vdash T = \sum_{i \in I} \{\alpha_i.T_i \mid T \xrightarrow{\alpha_i} T_i\}$;
- *if* $T \in \mathcal{T}_p$, *then* $\vdash T = \bigoplus_{i \in I} \{p_i\tau.T_i \mid T \xrightarrow{p_i\tau} T_i\}$.

Definition 9. *A recursive specification* $\mathbb{S}$ *is a set of equations* $\{X = S_X \mid X \in V_{\mathbb{S}}\}$ *with* $V_{\mathbb{S}}$ *being a variable set. Process* E $\mathcal{A}$-*provably satisfies the recursive specification* $\mathbb{S}$ *in the variable* $X_0 \in V_{\mathbb{S}}$ *if there are processes* E_X *for* $X \in V_{\mathbb{S}}$ *with* $E = E_{X_0}$, *such that for* $X \in V_{\mathbb{S}}$

$$\mathcal{A} \vdash E_X = S_X\{E_Y/Y\}_{Y \in V_{\mathbb{S}}}$$

Let $\mathbb{S}$ be a specification, and $X, Y \in V_{\mathbb{S}}$ define $X >_u Y$ if Y occurs free and probabilistically unguarded in E_X. $\mathbb{S}$ is called guarded if $>_u$ is well-founded on $V_{\mathbb{S}}$.

Proposition 10 (Unique Solutions). *If $\mathbb{S}$ is a finite guarded recursive specification and $X_0 \in V_{\mathbb{S}}$, then there is a process E which R1-provably satisfies $\mathbb{S}$ in X_0. Moreover if there are two such processes E and F, then $R2 \vdash E = F$.*

Proof. By induction on the number of equations of $\mathbb{S}$ as in [22].

Proposition 11. *Let $E_0, F_0 \in \mathcal{P}_{RCCS_{fs}}^g$. If $E_0 \simeq F_0$, then there is a finite guarded recursive specification $\mathbb{S}$ provably satisfied in the same variable X_0 by both E_0 and F_0.*

Proof. Take a fresh set of variables $V_{\mathbb{S}} = \{X_{EF} | E \in \mathcal{P}_{E_0}, F \in \mathcal{P}_{F_0}, E \simeq F\}$. $X_0 = X_{E_0 F_0}$. Now for $X_{EF} \in V_{\mathbb{S}}$, $\mathbb{S}$ contains the following equations:

1. If $E \in \mathcal{T}_p$, and for every E' such that $E \xrightarrow{p\tau} E'$, $E' \simeq E$, then $X_{EF} = \bigoplus\{p\tau.X_{E'F} | E \xrightarrow{p\tau} E'\}$.
2. If condition in case 1 is not satisfied, $F \in \mathcal{T}_p$, and for every F' such that $F \xrightarrow{p\tau} F'$, $F' \simeq F$, then $X_{EF} = \bigoplus\{p\tau.X_{EF'} | F \xrightarrow{p\tau} F'\}$.
3. If conditions in case 1 and 2 are not satisfied, and $E \in \mathcal{T}_p, F \in \mathcal{T}_p$, then for every $\mathcal{B}_i$ such that $E \rightsquigarrow_\sim \xrightarrow{q} \mathcal{B}_i$, $F \rightsquigarrow_\sim \xrightarrow{q} \mathcal{B}_i$, choose a pair of processes $E_i, F_i \in \mathcal{B}_i$, $X_{EF} = \bigoplus_{\mathcal{B}_i}\{q\tau.X_{E_i F_i}\}$.
4. If $E \in \mathcal{T}_d, F \in \mathcal{T}_d$ then $X_{EF} = \sum\{\alpha.X_{E'F'} | E \xrightarrow{\alpha} E', F \xrightarrow{\alpha} F', E' \simeq F'\} + \sum\{\tau.X_{E'F} | E \xrightarrow{\tau} E', E' \simeq F\} + \sum\{\tau.X_{EF'} | F \xrightarrow{\tau} F', E \simeq F'\}$.
5. Otherwise, $X_{EF} = \sum\{\tau.X_{E'F} | E \xrightarrow{\tau} E', E' \simeq F\} + \sum\{\tau.X_{EF'} | F \xrightarrow{\tau} F', E \simeq F'\}$.

The corresponding process of variable X_{EF} is E. We will prove $B1-2, R1-2 \vdash E = S_{X_{EF}}\{E'/X_{E'F'}\}_{X_{E'F'} \in V_{\mathbb{S}}}$. Then E_0 is $B1-2, R1-2$ provably satisfying S in X_0. The same statement for F_0 then follows by symmetry.

The case 1, 2, 5 can be proved directly by Lemma 1.

Case 3 is the different part with the proof in [10]. In case 3, $E \in \mathcal{T}_p, F \in \mathcal{T}_p$, and both of E and F can directly do some probabilistic τ action to a different equivalence class. It will be sufficient to prove the following claim:

Claim. For $G \in \mathcal{P}_{RCCS_{fs}}^g$, if $G \rightsquigarrow_\sim \xrightarrow{q_i} E_i$ for $i \in I$, then $B1-2, R1-2 \vdash G = \bigoplus_{i \in I} q_i \tau.E_i$.

Proof. Define the lexicographic ordering $(m, n) < (m', n')$ as $m < m'$ or $(m = m'$ and $n < n')$. We also define $(m_1, n_1) + (m_2, n_2) = (m_1 + m_2, n_1 + n_2)$ and $(m, n)_1 = m, (m, n)_2 = n$.

Define the following rank function $r : \mathcal{P}_{RCCS_{fs}}^g \to \mathbb{N} \times \mathbb{N}$:

$$r(\mathbf{0}) = (0, 0)$$

$$r(\bigoplus_{i \in I} p_i \tau.E_i) = (0, 1) + \max_{i \in I}\{r(E_i)\}$$

$$r(\sum_{i \in I} \alpha_i.E_i) = \max\left\{\{(0, 1) + r(E_i) | \alpha_i = \tau\} \cup \{(0, 1) | \alpha_i \neq \tau\}\right\}$$

$$r(\mu X.T) = (1 + r(T\{\mathbf{0}/X\})_1, 0)$$

By induction on $r(G)$, we can formally prove case 3:

- If $r(G) = (0,1)$, and $G \leadsto_{\simeq} \xrightarrow{q_i} E_i$ for $i \in I$.
  Then G must be of the form $\bigoplus_{i \in I}\{\bigoplus_{j \in J_i} p_j\tau.E_i | \sum_{j \in J_i} p_j = q_i\}$. Then $(A1) \vdash G = \bigoplus_{i \in I} q_i\tau.E_i$.
- If $r(G) = (m,n) > (0,1)$, and $G \leadsto_{\simeq} \xrightarrow{q_i} E_i$ for $i \in I$.
  - $G = \sum_{j \in J} \alpha_j.G_j$. For every $j \in J$, $\alpha_j = \tau$ and $G \simeq G_j \leadsto_{\simeq} \xrightarrow{q_i} E_i$. And $r(G_j) < r(G)$.
    By induction hypothesis, $B1-2, R1-2 \vdash G_j = \bigoplus_{i \in I} q_i\tau.E_i$ for every $j \in J$. We can conclude that $B1-2, R1-2 \vdash G = \bigoplus_{i \in I} q_i\tau.E_i$ for every $j \in J$.
  - $G = \bigoplus_{j \in J} p_j\tau.G_j$. If there exists some $j \in J$, $G_j \not\simeq G$, by Lemma 1,
    $\vdash G = \bigoplus_{i \in I}\{p_i\tau.E_i | \frac{p_i}{q_i} = c < 1, G \xrightarrow{p_i\tau} E_i \not\simeq G\} \oplus \bigoplus_{j \in J-I}\{p_j\tau.G_j :$
    $G \xrightarrow{p_j\tau} G_j \simeq G\}$. For every $j \in J - I$, $r(G_j) < r(G)$. By induction hypothesis, $B1, B2, R2 \vdash G_j = \bigoplus_{i \in I} q_i\tau.E_i$ for every $j \in J - I$, then $B2(A1) \vdash G = \bigoplus_{i \in I} q_i\tau.E_i$.
    If for every $j \in J$, $G_j \simeq G$. Then for every $j \in J$, $G_j \leadsto_{\simeq} \xrightarrow{q_i} E_i$ and $r(G_j) < r(G)$. By induction hypothesis, $B1-2, R1-2 \vdash G_j = \bigoplus_{i \in I} q_i\tau.E_i$, then $(A1) \vdash G = \bigoplus_{i \in I} q_i\tau.E_i$.
  - $G = \mu X.T$
    $T\{\mu X.T/X\} \leadsto_{\simeq} \xrightarrow{q_i} E_i$, then $T\{\bigoplus_{i \in I} q_i\tau.E_i/X\} \leadsto_{\simeq} \xrightarrow{q_i} E_i$. Since $r(\mu X.T)_1 = 1 + r(T\{\bigoplus_{i \in I} q_i\tau.E_i/X\})_1$, $r(\mu X.T) > r(T\{\bigoplus_{i \in I} q_i\tau.E_i/X\})$.
    By induction hypothesis, $\vdash T\{\bigoplus_{i \in I} q_i\tau.E_i/X\} = \bigoplus_{i \in I} q_i\tau.E_i$, $R2 \vdash \mu X.T = \bigoplus_{i \in I} q_i\tau.E_i$.

In case 4, $E \in \mathcal{T}_d$ and $F \in \mathcal{T}_d$. We need to prove

$$B1 \vdash E = \sum\{\alpha.E' | E \xrightarrow{\alpha} E', F \xrightarrow{\alpha} F', E' \simeq F'\} \\ + \sum\{\tau.E' | E \xrightarrow{\tau} E', E' \simeq F\} + \sum\{\tau.E | F \xrightarrow{\tau} F', E \simeq F'\} \tag{4}$$

By Lemma 1, $\vdash E = \sum_{i \in I}\{\alpha_i.E_i : E \xrightarrow{\alpha_i} E_i\}$, then

$$B1 \vdash E = \sum\{\alpha.E' | E \xrightarrow{\alpha} E', F \xrightarrow{\alpha} F', E' \simeq F'\} \\ + \sum\{\tau.E' | E \xrightarrow{\tau} E', E' \simeq F\} + \tau.E \tag{5}$$

If there exists a process F' with $F \xrightarrow{\tau} F' \simeq E$, (4) and (5) are equal directly. Otherwise, every action from E should be bisimulated by F directly, which means the set $\{\alpha_i.E_i : E \xrightarrow{\alpha_i} E_i\}$ equals to the set $\{\alpha.E' | E \xrightarrow{\alpha} E', F \xrightarrow{\alpha} F', E' \simeq F'\} \cup \{\tau.E' | E \xrightarrow{\tau} E', E' \simeq F\}$.

Corollary 2 (Completeness for probabilistically guarded processes). For $E, F \in \mathcal{P}^g_{RCCS_{fs}}$, if $E \simeq F$ then $B1-2, R1-2 \vdash E = F$.

Proposition 12. *For $E \in \mathcal{P}_{RCCS_{fs}}$, there exists a probabilistically guarded process E' with $R1, 3, 4 \vdash E = E'$.*

Proof. Induction on the depth of nesting of recursions in $\mu X.T$ [10].

Corollary 3 (Completeness for all processes). *For $E, F \in \mathcal{P}_{RCCS_{fs}}$, if $E \simeq F$ then $B1-2$, $R1-4 \vdash E = F$.*

5 Concluding Remarks

We have studied algorithm and axiomatization of the branching bisimulation relations for randomized CCS model. We give a polynomial time algorithm for equivalence checking and show that our axiom system is sound and complete. These two results, besides their value to the randomized CCS model itself, can be generalized to other randomized finite state models. The reason is that the essence of our work is dealing with probabilistic actions, which however, is model independent.

We are currently planning to extend our axiomatization to the divergence-sensing branching bisimulation and other equivalences such as testing equivalence. Another interesting topic is to implement the ϵ-tree technique on other classical probabilistic process calculi. We believe this is an expecting topic as it can be regarded as an extension and application of the philosophy of the model independent method.

Acknowledgement. We are grateful to Prof. Yuxi Fu for his instructive discussions and feedbacks. We thank Dr. Mingzhang Huang, Dr. Qiang Yin and other members of BASICS for offering helps in the revision stage. We also thank the anonymous referees for their questions and detailed comments. The support from the National Science Foundation of China (61772336, 61872142, 61572318) is acknowledged.

References

1. Andova, S.: Process algebra with probabilistic choice. In: Katoen, J.-P. (ed.) ARTS 1999. LNCS, vol. 1601, pp. 111–129. Springer, Heidelberg (1999). https://doi.org/10.1007/3-540-48778-6_7
2. Baeten, J.C.M., Bergstra, J.A., Smolka, S.A.: Axiomatizing probabilistic processes: Acp with generative probabilities. Inf. Comput. **121**(2), 234–255 (1995)
3. Baier, C., Hermanns, H.: Weak bisimulation for fully probabilistic processes. In: Grumberg, O. (ed.) CAV 1997. LNCS, vol. 1254, pp. 119–130. Springer, Heidelberg (1997). https://doi.org/10.1007/3-540-63166-6_14
4. Bandini, E., Segala, R.: Axiomatizations for probabilistic bisimulation. In: Orejas, F., Spirakis, P.G., van Leeuwen, J. (eds.) ICALP 2001. LNCS, vol. 2076, pp. 370–381. Springer, Heidelberg (2001). https://doi.org/10.1007/3-540-48224-5_31
5. Deng, Y.: Semantics of Probabilistic Processes: An Operational Approach. Springer, Heidelberg (2015). https://doi.org/10.1007/978-3-662-45198-4
6. Deng, Y., Palamidessi, C.: Axiomatizations for probabilistic finite-state behaviors. In: Sassone, V. (ed.) FoSSaCS 2005. LNCS, vol. 3441, pp. 110–124. Springer, Heidelberg (2005). https://doi.org/10.1007/978-3-540-31982-5_7

7. Fu, Y.: Checking equality and regularity for normed BPA with silent moves. In: Fomin, F.V., Freivalds, R., Kwiatkowska, M., Peleg, D. (eds.) ICALP 2013, Part II. LNCS, vol. 7966, pp. 238–249. Springer, Heidelberg (2013). https://doi.org/10.1007/978-3-642-39212-2_23

8. Fu, Y.: A uniform approach to random process model (2019). https://arxiv.org/pdf/1906.09541.pdf

9. Giacalone, A., Jou, C.C., Smolka, S.A.: Algebraic reasoning for probabilistic concurrent systems. In: Proceedings of IFIP TC2 Working Conference on Programming Concepts and Methods. Citeseer (1990)

10. Glabbeek, R.J.: A complete axiomatization for branching bisimulation congruence of finite-state behaviours. In: Borzyszkowski, A.M., Sokołowski, S. (eds.) MFCS 1993. LNCS, vol. 711, pp. 473–484. Springer, Heidelberg (1993). https://doi.org/10.1007/3-540-57182-5_39

11. van Glabbeek, R.J., Smolka, S.A., Steffen, B.: Reactive, generative, and stratified models of probabilistic processes. Inf. Comput. **121**(1), 59–80 (1995)

12. van Glabbeek, R.J., Weijland, W.P.: Branching time and abstraction in bisimulation semantics. J. ACM **43**(3), 555–600 (1996)

13. Hansson, H., Jonsson, B.: A framework for reasoning about time and reliability. In: Proceedings of Real-Time Systems Symposium, pp. 102–111. IEEE (1989)

14. Hansson, H., Jonsson, B.: A calculus for communicating systems with time and probabilities. In: Proceedings of 11th Real-Time Systems Symposium, pp. 278–287. IEEE (1990)

15. Herescu, O.M., Palamidessi, C.: Probabilistic asynchronous π-calculus. In: Tiuryn, J. (ed.) FoSSaCS 2000. LNCS, vol. 1784, pp. 146–160. Springer, Heidelberg (2000). https://doi.org/10.1007/3-540-46432-8_10

16. Huang, M., Yin, Q.: Two lower bounds for BPA. In: 28th International Conference on Concurrency Theory, CONCUR 2017, 5–8 September 2017, Berlin, Germany, pp. 20:1–20:16 (2017). https://doi.org/10.4230/LIPIcs.CONCUR.2017.20

17. Jou, C.-C., Smolka, S.A.: Equivalences, congruences, and complete axiomatizations for probabilistic processes. In: Baeten, J.C.M., Klop, J.W. (eds.) CONCUR 1990. LNCS, vol. 458, pp. 367–383. Springer, Heidelberg (1990). https://doi.org/10.1007/BFb0039071

18. Kučera, A., Jančar, P.: Equivalence-checking on infinite-state systems: techniques and results. Theory Pract. Logic Programm. **6**(3), 227–264 (2006)

19. Larsen, K.G., Skou, A.: Bisimulation through probabilistic testing. Inf. Comput. **94**(1), 1–28 (1991)

20. Lowe, G.: Probabilities and priorities in timed CSP (1993)

21. Milner, R.: Communication and Concurrency, vol. 84. Prentice hall, New York (1989)

22. Milner, R.: A complete axiomatisation for observational congruence of finite-state behaviours. Inf. Comput. **81**(2), 227–247 (1989)

23. Philippou, A., Lee, I., Sokolsky, O.: Weak bisimulation for probabilistic systems. In: Palamidessi, C. (ed.) CONCUR 2000. LNCS, vol. 1877, pp. 334–349. Springer, Heidelberg (2000). https://doi.org/10.1007/3-540-44618-4_25

24. Stark, E.W., Smolka, S.A.: A complete axiom system for finite-state probabilistic processes. In: Proof, Language, and Interaction, pp. 571–596 (2000)

Compositional Verification of Heap-Manipulating Programs Through Property-Guided Learning

Long H. Pham[1(✉)], Jun Sun[2], and Quang Loc Le[3]

[1] Singapore University of Technology and Design, Singapore, Singapore
longph1989@gmail.com
[2] Singapore Management University, Singapore, Singapore
[3] School of Computing & Digital Technologies, Teesside University, Middlesbrough, UK

Abstract. Analyzing and verifying heap-manipulating programs automatically is challenging. A key for fighting the complexity is to develop compositional methods. For instance, many existing verifiers for heap-manipulating programs require user-provided specification for each function in the program in order to decompose the verification problem. The requirement, however, often hinders the users from applying such tools. To overcome the issue, we propose to automatically learn heap-related program invariants in a property-guided way for each function call. The invariants are learned based on the memory graphs observed during test execution and improved through memory graph mutation. We implemented a prototype of our approach and integrated it with two existing program verifiers. The experimental results show that our approach enhances existing verifiers effectively in automatically verifying complex heap-manipulating programs with multiple function calls.

1 Introduction

Analyzing and verifying heap-manipulating programs (hereafter heap programs) automatically is challenging [45]. Given the complexity, the key is to develop compositional methods which allow us to decompose a complex problem into smaller manageable ones. One successful example is the Infer static analyzer [1], which applies techniques like bi-abduction for local reasoning [36] to infer a specification for each function in a program to be analyzed.

While Infer generates function specifications for identifying certain classes of program errors, we aim to develop compositional methods for the more challenging task of verifying heap programs with data structures. In recent years, there have been multiple tools developed to verify heap programs in a compositional way, including Dafny [31], GRASShopper [43,44] and HIP [10]. These tools are, however, far from being applicable to real-world complex programs. One reason is that substantial user effort is needed. In particular, besides providing a specification to verify against, users must provide auxiliary specification to decompose the verification problem. For instance, Dafny, GRASShopper and HIP all require users to provide a specification for each function used in the program. Writing the function specification is highly non-trivial. It is thus desirable to develop approaches for verifying heap programs in a compositional way which requires minimum user effort.

© Springer Nature Switzerland AG 2019
A. W. Lin (Ed.): APLAS 2019, LNCS 11893, pp. 405–424, 2019.
https://doi.org/10.1007/978-3-030-34175-6_21

In this work, we propose to automatically generate function specifications for compositional verification of heap programs. Our approach differs from existing approaches like Infer in three ways. Firstly, because our goal is to verify the correctness of heap programs with *data structures*, our approach generates more expressive function specifications than those generated by Infer.

Secondly, we learn a specification of each function call (rather than each function) in a property-guided way. For instance, assume that we have the following verification problem (expressed in the form of a Hoare triple) $\{pre\}func(); func(); \{post\}$ where pre is a precondition, $post$ is a postcondition and $func(); func()$ are two consecutive calls of the same function. We automatically generate a program invariant inv after the first function call and before the second function call. As a result, we generate the specification $\{pre\}func()\{inv\}$ for the first function call and the specification $\{inv\}func()\{post\}$ for the second function call. The (smaller) problems of verifying these two Hoare triples thus replace the problem of verifying the original Hoare triple.

Thirdly, our invariant generation method is based on a novel technique, namely, a combination of classification and memory-graph mutation. We start with generating multiple random test cases (based on existing methods [37]). We then instrument the program and execute the test cases to obtain values of multiple features which are related to the memory graphs before and after each function call in the program. The obtained feature vectors are labeled according to the testing results (i.e., whether the postcondition is satisfied or not). Then we apply a classification algorithm [8] to find an invariant that separates the feature vectors with different labels. The invariant is an arbitrary boolean formula of the features, which is then used to decompose the verification problem.

There are two technical challenges which we must solve in order to make the above approach work. First, what features of the memory graphs shall we use? In this work, we adopt an expressive specification language for heap programs which combines separation logic, user-defined inductive predicates and arithmetic [10,23,27,45]. We then define a set of features based on the specification language. In addition, our approach allows users to define their own features. Secondly, how do we solve the problem of the lack of labeled samples, i.e., the test cases which we learn from may be limited. To overcome the problem, we mutate the memory graphs according to the learned invariant to validate whether the learned invariant is correct. We refine the invariant based on the validation result (if necessary) and repeat the process until the invariant is validated.

We implement our idea in a prototype, called SLearner, which takes a program to be verified as input, generates multiple invariants and outputs a set of decomposed verification tasks. We integrate SLearner with two existing state-of-the-art verifiers for heap programs, i.e., GRASShopper and HIP. Experiments are then performed on 110 programs manipulating 10 challenging data structures. The experimental results show that, enhanced with our approach, both GRASShopper and HIP are able to successfully verify programs with multiple function calls without user-provided function specifications.

The novelty of our work is in learning heap-related specification in a property-guided way and applying graph mutation to improve the learning process. The rest of the paper is organized as follows. Section 2 presents an illustrative example. Section 3 presents the details of our approach. Section 4 evaluates our approach. Section 5 reviews related work. Finally, Sect. 6 concludes.

```
1  public void main(int m, int n) {
2     //precondition : m ≤ n
3     Node x = createSLL(m);
4     Node y = createSLL(n);
5     getSum(x, y);
6     //postcondition : sll(x, _)*sll(y, _)
7  }
8  private Node createSLL(int n) {
9     if (n <= 0) return null;
10    else {
11       Node x = new Node(n, null);
12       x.next = createSLL(n − 1);
13       return x;
14    }
15 }
16 private int getSum(Node x, Node y) {
17    int sum = 0;
18    if (x != null) {
19       sum += x.data + y.data;
20       sum += getSum(x.next, y.next);
21    }
22    return sum;
23 }
```

Fig. 1. An illustrative example

2 An Illustrative Example

In this section, we illustrate our approach with an example. The program is shown as function main in Fig. 1, where function createSLL(n) returns a singly-linked list with length n and function getSum(x, y) returns the sum of the data in two disjoint singly-linked list objects (pointed to by the two pointers x and y). Note that both functions are recursively defined. The precondition and postcondition are shown at line 2 and 6 respectively. They are specified in an assertion language based on separation logic (refer to details in Sect. 3). The precondition is self-explanatory. The postcondition sll($x, \_$)*sll($y, \_$) intuitively means that x and y are two disjoint singly-linked list objects, i.e., sll(x, n) is an inductive predicate denoting that x is a singly-linked list object with n nodes, and * is the separating conjunction predicate specifying the disjointness in separation logic. Besides the postcondition, we assume that memory safety is always implicitly asserted and thus must be verified. For instance, we aim to verify that x.data at line 19 would not result in null-pointer de-referencing.

Our experiment shows that state-of-the-art verifiers like GRASShopper and HIP cannot verify this program. Only after specifications for both functions createSLL and getSum are provided manually, the program is verified. On one hand, providing a specification for every function called by the given program is highly nontrivial. On the other hand, part of the function specification may be irrelevant to verifying the given program. For an extreme example, if we change the postcondition of the program shown in Fig. 1 to true, a complete specification for singly-linked lists would not be necessary to verify the program.

Our approach is to automatically learn a just-enough invariant before and after each function call so that we can verify the program in a compositional way. For this example, we learn two invariants: inv_1 right after the first function call at line 3 and inv_2 right after the second function call at line 4. Next, we verify the program by verifying the following three Hoare triples: $\{m \leq n\}$createSLL(m)$\{inv_1[res/x]\}$; $\{inv_1\}$createSLL(n)$\{inv_2[res/y]\}$; and $\{inv_2\}$getSum$\{sll(x, \_)*sll(y, \_)\}$ with res is a special variable for the return value of a function and $inv_1[res/x]$ is a substitution of all variable x in inv_1 by variable res. As the program in each Hoare triple involves only one function, existing verifiers like GRASShopper and HIP can automatically verify the Hoare triples.

Table 1. Collected feature vectors and labels

	is_sll(x)	is_sll(y)	is_sll(x) $\wedge$ is_sll(y) $\wedge$ sep(x,y)	len_sll(x) $\leq$ len_sll(y)	label
m=1, n=0	true	true	true	false	negative
m=0, n=1	true	true	true	true	positive

To learn inv$_1$ and inv$_2$, we instrument the program to collect a set of features at the learning points and collect their values during test executions. For instance, Table 1 shows a few of the features and their values for the above program after line 4 for learning inv$_2$. The first row shows the features and the second and third rows show the values of the features given two test cases $\{m=1, n=0\}$ and $\{m=0, n=1\}$ respectively. The features are designed based on our assertion language. In particular, feature len_sll(x) is a numeric value denoting the length of a singly-linked list x which is extracted based on the user-defined predicate sll; feature is_sll(x) denotes whether x points to a singly-linked list, and feature sep(x, y) denotes whether x and y are disjoint in the heap. We label each feature vector with either *negative* or *positive*, where *negative* means that a memory error is generated, the postcondition is violated, or the test case likely runs into infinite loop (i.e., it does not stop after certain time units); and *positive* means otherwise.

Next, we apply a classification algorithm [8] to generate a predicate which separates the *positive* and *negative* feature vectors. The predicate takes the form of an arbitrary boolean formula of the features. Given the feature vectors in Table 1, the generated predicate is: len_sll(x) $\leq$ len_sll(y). Although this predicate is an invariant after line 4, it is not strong enough to verify the postcondition. This is in general a problem due to having a limited number of test cases. To solve the problem, we systematically mutate the memory graphs obtained during the test executions to obtain more labeled feature vectors with the aim to improve the predicate (see details in Sect. 3.5). In our example, with the additional feature vectors, the classification algorithm generates the following predicate for inv$_2$.

$$(\text{is\_sll}(x) \wedge \text{is\_sll}(y) \wedge \text{sep}(x, y) \wedge x\text{=null}) \vee$$
$$(\text{is\_sll}(x) \wedge \text{is\_sll}(y) \wedge \text{sep}(x, y) \wedge \text{len\_sll}(x) \leq \text{len\_sll}(y))$$

We obtain x=null $\vee$ (is_sll(x) $\wedge$ len_sll(x) $\leq n$) similarly for inv$_1$ after line 3.

Afterwards, inv$_1$ and inv$_2$ are translated into the formulas in our assertion language. Note that the translation is straightforward since the features are designed based on the assertion language. The last step is to verify three verification problems. This is done using state-of-the-art verifiers for heap programs. For instance, HIP solves the three verification problems automatically, which verifies the program.

For efficiency, in the verification step we perform the following two simplifications. First, for dead code detection, we invoke a separation logic solver (e.g., the one presented in [27,29]) to check the satisfiability of inferred invariant. Secondly, we identify and eliminate the frame of a Hoare triple before sending them to the verifiers. For example, for the Hoare triple $\{\text{inv}_1\}\text{createSLL(n)}\{\text{inv}_2[\text{res}/y]\}$, we find that x has not been accessed by the code, the occurrences of the singly-linked list x in both the precondition and postcondition of the triple are eliminated before sending it to the verifiers.

$$\Phi ::= \Delta \mid \Phi_1 \vee \Phi_2$$
$$\Delta ::= \exists \bar{v}\cdot (\kappa \wedge \pi)$$
$$\kappa ::= \text{emp} \mid r \mapsto c(\bar{t}) \mid P(\bar{t}) \mid \kappa_1 * \kappa_2$$
$$\pi ::= \text{true} \mid \phi \mid \neg\pi \mid \pi_1 \wedge \pi_2$$

$$\phi ::= i \mid v=\text{null}$$
$$i ::= a_1=a_2 \mid a_1 \leq a_2$$
$$a ::= k \mid v \mid k \times a \mid a_1+a_2 \mid -a$$

Fig. 2. Syntax: where c is a data type; k is an integer value; t_i, v, r are variables; and $\bar{t}$ is a sequence of variables

3 Our Approach

3.1 Problem Definition

Our input is a Hoare triple $\{pre\}prog\{post\}$, where pre is a precondition, $post$ is postcondition and $prog$ is a heap program which may invoke other functions. One example is the function `main` shown in Fig. 1. The precondition and postcondition are in an expressive specification language previously developed in [10,23,27,45]. The language supports separation logic, inductive predicates and Presburger arithmetic [19], which is shown to be expressive to capture many properties of heap programs.

The syntax of the language is presented in Fig. 2. In general, a predicate Φ in this language is a disjunction of multiple symbolic heaps. A symbolic heap Δ is an existentially quantified conjunction of a heap formula κ (i.e., a predicate constraining the memory structure) and a pure formula π (i.e., a predicate constraining numeric variables). A heap formula κ is an empty heap predicate emp, a points-to predicate $r \mapsto c(\bar{t})$ (where r is its root variable), a user-defined predicate $P(\bar{t})$, or a spatial conjunction of two heap formulas $\kappa_1 * \kappa_2$. User-defined predicates are defined in the same language. A pure formula π can be true, an (in)equality on variables, a Presburger arithmetic formula, negation of a formula, or their conjunction. We refer the readers to [19] for details on Presburger arithmetic. We note that $v_1 \neq v_2$ (resp. $v \neq \text{null}$) is used to denote $\neg(v_1=v_2)$ (resp. $\neg(v=\text{null})$) and we may use _ to indicate "don't care" values.

For instance, the following predicate $\text{sll}(x,n)$ defines a singly-linked list (with a root-pointer x and size n), which is used in the illustrative example.

$$\text{sll}(x, n) \equiv (\text{emp} \wedge x=\text{null} \wedge n=0)$$
$$\vee (\exists\, q, n_1\cdot x \mapsto Node(\_, q) * \text{sll}(q, n_1) \wedge n=n_1+1)$$

Our problem is to automatically verify the Hoare triple. Different from existing approaches, we aim to do that in a compositional way without user-provided function specifications.

3.2 Test Generation and Code Instrumentation

Given $\{pre\}prog\{post\}$, we first automatically generate a test suite S using existing test case generation methods like [37]. Note that we do not require the test cases to satisfy the precondition because negative feature vectors from invalid test cases will be filtered out by our learning process. Based on the testing results, we divide S into two disjoint sets. One set includes passed test cases that terminate normally without any memory error or violation of the postcondition, denoted as S^+. The other set contains the remaining ones, denoted as S^-. Note that we heuristically consider that a test case does not terminate after waiting for a threshold number of time units. Afterwards, we identify all function calls in $prog$ and add learning points before and after each call. At each learning point l, we identify a set of relevant variables, denoted as V_l. We apply static program slicing to remove the variables which are visible at l but irrelevant to the postcondition or memory safety. In the example shown in Fig. 1, the sets of relevant variables at learning point 1 and 2 are $\{x, n\}$ and $\{x, y\}$ respectively. For each learning point, we instrument the program to extract a vector of features from each test.

3.3 Feature Extraction

Central to our approach is the answer to the question: what features to extract? In this work, we view a program state as a memory graph and systematically extract two groups of features based on the memory graph. One group contains generic features of the memory graph and the other contains features which are specific to the verification task. Formally, a memory graph G is a tuple $(M, init, E, Ty, L)$ such that

- M is a set of heap nodes including a special node `null`;
- $init \in M$ is a special initial node;
- E is a set of labeled and directed edges such that $(s, n, s') \in E$ means that we can access heap node s' via a pointer named n from s. An edge starting from $init$ is always labeled with one of the variables in the program.
- Ty is a total labeling function which labels each heap node in M by a type;
- and L is a labeling function which labels a heap node of primitive type by a value.

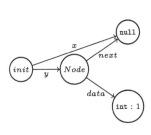

Fig. 3. A memory graph

Given a test case and a learning point, we represent the program state at the learning point during the test execution in the form of a memory graph $(M, init, E, Ty, L)$. Figure 3 shows the memory graph for our example at the learning point 2 with test input $m = 0$ and $n = 1$. Note that any rooted path of a memory graph represents a variable, e.g., the path with the sequence of labels $\langle y, next \rangle$ in the above memory graph is a variable $y.next$ at learning point 2. For complicated programs, the memory graph might contain many paths and thus many variables from which we can extract features. We thus set a bound on the number of de-referencing to limit the number of variables. For example, if we set the bound to be 2, we focus on variables $\{x, x.data, x.next, y, y.data, y.next\}$ at learning point 2 and similarly variables $\{x, x.data, x.next, n\}$ at learning point 1. With length bounded to 1, we focus only on $\{x, y\}$ at learning point 2 and $\{x, n\}$ at learning point 1.

We extract two groups of boolean features based on the memory graph. The first group contains generic heap-related features, which include the following.

- For each reference type variable x, we extract two features which represent if it is `null` or not, i.e, whether its corresponding path leads to the special node `null`.

Table 2. Features

#	feature	#	feature	#	feature
1	$x = \mathtt{null}$	10	$x \mapsto Node() \wedge \mathtt{is\_sll}(y) \wedge \mathtt{sep}(x,y)$	19	$\mathtt{len\_sll}(x) + \mathtt{len\_sll}(y) > 0$
2	$y = \mathtt{null}$	11	$\mathtt{is\_sll}(x) \wedge y \mapsto Node() \wedge \mathtt{sep}(x,y)$	20	$\mathtt{len\_sll}(x) - \mathtt{len\_sll}(y) > 0$
3	$x \mapsto Node()$ (a.k.a. $x \neq \mathtt{null}$)	12	$\mathtt{is\_sll}(x) \wedge \mathtt{is\_sll}(y) \wedge \mathtt{sep}(x,y)$	21	$-\mathtt{len\_sll}(x) + \mathtt{len\_sll}(y) > 0$
4	$y \mapsto Node()$ (a.k.a. $y \neq \mathtt{null}$)	13	$\mathtt{len\_sll}(x) > 0$	22	$-\mathtt{len\_sll}(x) - \mathtt{len\_sll}(y) > 0$
5	$x = y$	14	$\mathtt{len\_sll}(y) > 0$	23	$\mathtt{len\_sll}(x) + \mathtt{len\_sll}(y) = 0$
6	$x \neq y$	15	$\mathtt{len\_sll}(x) < 0$	24	$\mathtt{len\_sll}(x) - \mathtt{len\_sll}(y) = 0$
7	$\mathtt{is\_sll}(x)$	16	$\mathtt{len\_sll}(y) < 0$	25	$-\mathtt{len\_sll}(x) + \mathtt{len\_sll}(y) = 0$
8	$\mathtt{is\_sll}(y)$	17	$\mathtt{len\_sll}(x) = 0$	26	$-\mathtt{len\_sll}(x) - \mathtt{len\_sll}(y) = 0$
9	$x \mapsto Node() \wedge y \mapsto Node() \wedge \mathtt{sep}(x,y)$	18	$\mathtt{len\_sll}(y) = 0$		

- For each pair of reference type variables, we extract two features which represent if the two variables are aliasing or not, i.e., whether their corresponding paths lead to the same non-null node.
- For each pair of reference type variables, we extract a feature which represents whether two variables are separated in the memory. Assume that variables x and y lead to nodes n_x and n_y, x and y are separated, denoted as $\mathtt{sep}(x,y)$, if and only if all reachable nodes except $\mathtt{null}$ from n_x (including n_x) are not reachable from n_y and vice versa.
- For each pair of the numeric variables, we extract boolean features in difference logic and the octagon abstract domain [34], e.g., $\pm x \pm y > c$, $\pm x \pm y = c$, $\pm x > c$ or $x = c$ where c is a constant. We apply a heuristic to collect constants in conditional expressions in the given program as candidate values for c. The value 0 is chosen by default.

While general heap-related features are often useful, some programs can only be proven with features which are specific to the verification problem. Thus, we extract a second group of features based on user-defined predicates used to assert the correctness of the given program, which include the following.

- For every permutation of n variables, we extract a feature which represents whether the variables satisfy the predicate. For instance, given the user-defined predicate $\mathtt{sll}$ which has one reference type parameter, we extract a feature which represents whether x satisfies the predicate, for each reference variable x.
- For a pair of two sequences of variables X and Y which satisfy some user-defined predicates, we extract a feature which represents whether the variables are separated in the memory, i.e., all nodes reachable from any variable in X (except $\mathtt{null}$) are not reachable from any node in Y and vice versa. This feature is inspired by the separation conjunction operator $*$ in our assertion language. For instance, given x and y which both satisfy $\mathtt{is\_sll}$, this feature value is true if and only if all objects in the singly-linked list x and singly-linked list y are disjoint in memory. Note that this feature subsumes the feature $\mathtt{sep}(x,y)$ explained above.
- For each numeric parameter of the user-defined predicate, we use a variable to represent its value for each sequence of variables which satisfy the predicate. For instance, as $\mathtt{sll}$ has a numeric parameter, if variable x satisfies $\mathtt{sll}$, we use a fresh variable

(denoted as len_sll for readability) to represent the value of the numeric parameter. Boolean features of these numeric variables, together with existing numeric variables, are then extracted in the chosen abstract domains.

In general, user-defined predicates can be complicated. Existing heap program verifiers like GRASShopper and HIP maintain a library of commonly used predicates. We adopt the predicates in their library and define the corresponding functions to extract the above-mentioned features in the form of an extensible library for our approach. Note that this is a one-time effort. For instance, Table 2 shows the list of 26 features which we extract at learning point 2 for the program shown in Fig. 1.

3.4 Learning for Compositional Verification

In the following, we present our approach on learning an invariant based on the extracted feature vectors. Recall that we systematically instrument the program at every learning point, then extract a value for every feature we discussed above. In our implementation, each feature is extracted using a function which returns a boolean value. Afterwards, each test case is executed so that we collect a vector of boolean values (a.k.a. a feature vector) which represents an abstraction of the memory graph according to the chosen features. If the test case finishes successfully, the feature vector is labeled *positive*; otherwise, it is labeled *negative*. The labeled feature vectors can be organized into a matrix M whose rows are feature vectors and whose columns are the feature values in all test cases. To ensure all feature vectors have the same dimension, if a feature does not apply (e.g., a variable is not accessible in the test case), we set the corresponding feature value to a special default value. For instance, Table 3 shows the matrix where the features are sequenced in the same order of Table 2.

The first step in our learning process is normalising the matrix M. If there are two rows with the same feature values and same labels, one of them is redundant and removed. Next, we apply the algorithm in [8] to learn a boolean combination of features to separate positive and negative vectors. Informally, the algorithm considers each feature vector as a point in space and every positive point is connected to every negative point by a line. A feature 'cuts' a line if the corresponding positive point and negative point have different values for the feature. The goal is to find a list of features that can cut all the lines, i.e., separate all positive and negative points. The features are chosen using a greedy algorithm. At each step, the feature which cuts the most number of uncut lines is selected. After all lines are cut, the selected features partition the space into multiple regions, each of which contains either positive points only or negative points only. Each region can be characterised by a conjunction of the features and the disjunction of all the formulas characterising the positive regions is a boolean formula which separates all the positive and negative feature vectors.

The details are shown in Algorithms 1 and 2. In Algorithm 1, the input is a normalised matrix M and the output is the list of features K which can classify all positive and negative rows in M. K is initialised as an empty list (line 1). A list L is initialized to contain all pairs of rows (i, j) such that i is the index of a positive row and j is that of a negative row (line 1). During each iteration, the feature k that 'cuts' the most number of pairs in L is identified (line 3). Note that we do not consider the case

Table 3. Matrix of feature vectors

Vectors obtained from test cases

1	2	3	4	5	6	7	8	9	10	11	12	13	14	15	16	17	18	19	20	21	22	23	24	25	26	Label
1	0	0	1	0	1	1	1	0	0	1	1	0	1	0	0	1	0	1	0	1	0	0	0	0	0	positive
1	1	0	0	1	0	1	1	0	0	0	1	0	0	0	0	1	1	0	0	0	0	1	1	1	1	positive
0	0	1	1	0	1	1	1	1	1	1	1	1	1	0	0	0	0	1	0	1	0	0	0	0	0	positive
0	1	1	0	0	1	1	1	0	1	0	1	1	0	0	0	0	1	1	1	0	0	0	0	0	0	negative

Vectors obtained from memory graph mutation

1	2	3	4	5	6	7	8	9	10	11	12	13	14	15	16	17	18	19	20	21	22	23	24	25	26	Label
0	0	1	1	0	1	1	1	1	1	1	1	1	1	0	0	0	0	1	0	0	0	0	1	1	0	positive
0	0	1	1	0	1	0	1	1	1	0	0	N	1	N	0	N	0	N	0	N	N	N	N	N	N	negative
0	1	1	0	0	1	0	1	0	1	0	0	N	0	N	0	N	1	N	N	N	N	N	N	N	N	negative
0	0	1	1	0	1	1	1	1	1	1	1	1	1	0	0	0	0	1	1	0	0	0	0	0	0	negative
1	0	0	1	0	1	1	0	0	0	1	0	0	N	0	N	1	N	N	N	N	N	N	N	N	N	negative
0	0	1	1	0	1	1	0	1	0	1	0	1	N	0	N	0	N	N	N	N	N	N	N	N	N	negative
0	0	1	1	1	0	1	1	0	0	0	0	1	1	0	0	0	0	1	0	0	0	0	1	1	0	negative

Algorithm 1: Choose the list of features $\texttt{choose}(M)$

1   $K = \{\}$; $L = \{(i,j) \mid$ row i is positive and row j is negative$\}$;
2   **while** L *is not empty* **do**
3   Find k s.t. $\{(i,j) \in L \mid M_{ik} = 1 \wedge M_{jk} = 0\}$ is the largest;
4   **if** *the number of pairs* (i,j) *that* k *can classify is* 0 **then**
5   Stop and ask for user input for a new feature;
6   **else**
7   Remove (i,j) s.t. $M_{ik} = 1 \wedge M_{jk} = 0$ from L;
8   Add k to K;
9   Return K;

$M_{ik} = 0 \wedge M_{jk} = 1$ because it will create the negations of features, which may not be easily transformed into separation logic. We then remove from L the pairs that are classified correctly by k (line 7) and add the new feature k into K (line 8). The loop stops when L is empty (line 2) or the best feature at the current iteration cannot classify more pairs (line 4). In the former case, we return the list of features K (line 9). In the latter case, it means the features are not sufficient to distinguish all positive and negative rows. We thus stop and may ask users to provide a new feature (line 5).

Algorithm 2 then shows how a boolean formula that classifies all positive and negative rows in M is constructed from the chosen features. The input is a normalised matrix M and a list of features K chosen using Algorithm 1 and the output is a boolean combination of these features. Initially, the list of regions R is empty; PP and NP are the set of indexes of positive and negative rows respectively (line 1). Recall that each row can be seen as a point in space. All points in PP are marked as uncovered at line 2. Favoring simple hypothesis (which is a heuristics often applied in machine learning),

---

Algorithm 2: Combine the features `combine`(M, K)

---

1   $R = \{\}$; $PP = \{p \mid$ row p is positive$\}$; $NP = \{n \mid$ row n is negative$\}$;
2   Mark all $p \in PP$ as uncovered;
3   **for** $i = 1$ *to* $|K|$ **do**
4   Create all combinations C with i elements from the list of features K;
5   **for** *each combination* $c \in C$ **do**
6   **if** $\forall n \in NP \; \exists k \in c : M_{nk} = 0$ **then**
7             $CP = \{p \mid p \in PP$ and $\forall k \in c : M_{pk} = 1\}$;
8   **if** CP *contains at least one uncovered index* **then**
9   Remove from R the combinations that have the covered indexes are proper subsets of CP;
10   Add c to R; Mark all $p \in CP$ as covered;
11   **if** *all* $p \in PP$ *are covered* **then**
12   Return R;

---

we try the combination from 1 feature to $|K|$ (which is the number of features in K) features (line 3). At line 4, all the combinations of i features are created. For each combination (line 5), we check if the created region contains no negative points (line 6). If it is the case, we find a list of positive points that are covered by the region (line 7). If this region contains at least one uncovered point (line 8), we add this combination into R and mark the positive points in the region as covered (line 10). Line 9 simplifies the results by removing the chosen regions that only cover a proper subset of positive points in the new region. When all positive points are covered, we return the set of combinations R (lines 11 and 12). Each combination is a conjunction of features and the set of combinations is the disjunction of these conjunctions.

For our example, at the learning point 2, after removing redundant rows, we have a matrix with 4 rows and 26 columns, i.e., the bolded rows in Table 3. Rows 1, 2 and 3 are positive, whereas row 4 is negative. To separate these rows, two columns 1 and 4 are chosen. From this, we can form two regions, in particular, the first one with only column 1, the second one with only column 4. These two columns represent feature $x = $ `null` (column 1) and $y \neq$ `null` (column 4). As a result, we learn the predicate $x = $ `null` $\lor y \neq$ `null`. Note that this predicate is incorrect and it is to be improved later.

It can be shown that Algorithms 1 and 2 always terminate. The worst-case complexity of Algorithm 1 is $\mathcal{O}(Row^4 * Col)$ where Row and Col are the number of rows and columns in the input matrix respectively. For Algorithm 2, the worst-case complexity is $\mathcal{O}(2^{|K|} * (Row * Col + Row^3))$. While the worst-case complexity is high, these algorithms are often reasonably efficient (as we show in our empirical study). The main reason is that the number of features K (which dominates the overall complexity) is often small (average 1.05 in our experiments).

3.5   Automatic Memory Graph Mutation

Recall that we only need a correct predicate, which is an invariant at the learning point and sufficient to prove the postcondition. A fundamental limitation of using classification techniques is that the learned predicate is likely incorrect if the feature vectors (i.e., test cases) are insufficient. One way to solve this problem is to use a program verifier to check whether the predicate is correct. If it is not correct, the verifier would generate a counterexample and the learning process can continue with a new feature vector obtained from the counterexample. This approach is not ideal for two reasons. One is that verifying heap programs is often costly and thus we would like to avoid it as long as possible. The other is that it is highly nontrivial to construct counterexamples when verifying heap programs [5].

Because of that, in this work, to improve the learned predicate, we apply an idea similar in spirit to [11] to automatically mutate the memory graphs obtained from the test cases and generate more program states. For each learned predicate Φ, we systematically apply a set of mutation operators based on Φ. For each variable x in Φ, if it is a reference type, the following mutation operators are applied.

1. Point x to a freshly constructed object of the right type.
2. Point x to a heap node of the right type in the memory graph (including null).
3. Swap x with another reference type variable.

If x is a primitive type, we follow the idea in [42] and mutate it by setting it to a constant, increasing/decreasing its value with a pre-defined offset, or swapping it with another primitive variable. The number of mutants we generate depends on the current learned predicate.

These mutation operators are designed to create states which potentially invalidate the learned predicate. For instance, if the current predicate is $\texttt{is\_sll}(x) \wedge \texttt{is\_sll}(y) \wedge \texttt{sep}(x, y)$, where x and y are two reference variables, applying the mutation operators allows us to obtain memory graphs which invalidate $\texttt{is\_sll}(x)$, $\texttt{is\_sll}(y)$ and/or $\texttt{sep}(x, y)$. The expectation is that such a mutated program state would lead to violation of the postcondition and thus be labeled with *negative*. If our expectation is met, the predicate is now more likely to be correct; otherwise, the predicate is incorrect and is refined with the new feature vector.

In the extreme cases when all feature vectors are labeled *positive* or *negative*, the learned predicates are `true` or `false` respectively. We then apply all mutation operators to all variables at the learning point. In our implementation, the mutation is done automatically by instrumenting statements which mutate the according variables at the learning point. We then run the test suite with the mutated program, collect new feature vectors and new test results. These new feature vectors are added into the matrix to learn new predicates.

The mutation at a learning point in the middle of the program may result in program states which may not be reachable. As a result, the final learned predicate, which is expected to be an invariant, may be weaker than the actual one (if the mutated program state is labeled as *positive*). However, a weaker invariant may still serve our goal of verifying the program. To give an example, in the extreme case, if the postcondition is true (and there is no risk of memory error), it is sufficient to learn the invariant true. We repeat this process of mutation and learning until the learned invariant converges.

For our example, at the learning point 2, after obtaining the first predicate $x =$ null $\lor y \neq$ null, we apply mutation and obtain more feature vectors. The new feature vectors are shown in Table 3 where N is a special value denoting that the feature is not applicable. Next, applying Algorithm 1, the chosen features this time are $x =$ null, is_sll$(x) \land$ is_sll$(y) \land$ sep(x, y), len_sll$(x) <$ len_sll(y), and len_sll$(x) =$ len_sll(y) (column 1, 12, 21 and 24). From these 4 columns, we form 3 regions: $\{12, 1\}, \{12, 21\}$ and $\{12, 24\}$, which are transformed into the invariant inv_2 we show in Sect. 2. Similarly, with the help of state mutation, we improve the learned invariant at l_1 from $x =$ null $\lor n > 0$ to $x =$ null $\lor$ (is_sll$(x) \land$ len_sll$(x) \leq n)$.

The process of mutation and learning always terminates. As we only have a finite set of variables and features, the set of feature vectors is finite and thus the process of mutation converges eventually. Furthermore, matrix normalisation guarantees we do not have redundant rows in the matrix and, hence, the matrix is finite and the learning process always terminates.

3.6 Compositional Verification

Lastly, we show how we use the learned invariants to verify heap programs in a compositional way. Firstly, we transform each loop in the program into a fresh tail recursive function. Then the loop is replaced with a call to the corresponding function. Note that in the case of nested loops, we create multiple functions in which the function according to the outer loop will call the function according to the inner loop. This is a standard strategy adopted from existing program verifiers for heap programs [10]. We then treat loops in the same way as (recursive) function calls.

Secondly, we identify the learning points, i.e., before and after each function call statements and learn invariants at these points. Note that we do not learn before/after recursive function calls. This is because program verifiers for heap programs like GRASS-hopper and HIP support inductive reasoning and thus one specification for each recursive function is sufficient. Assume that the invariant learned before function call C_i is I_i and the one learned after C_i is I_{i+1}.

Thirdly, for each function call C_i, we generate a proof obligation in the form of a Hoare triple $\{I_i\}C_i\{I_{i+1}\}$, to prove that calling function C_i with I_i being satisfied results in a state satisfying I_{i+1}. Each proof obligation is submitted to a program verifier. Once the proof obligation is discharged, we replace the function call C_i with its now-established specification, i.e., two statements assert I_i; assume I_{i+1}. That is, we instrument the learned invariants into the program such that the invariant learned before/after C_i becomes an assert/assume-statement respectively.

Finally, we use an existing program verifier to verify the transformed program. Note that the program does not contain any function call (other than possibly a recursive call of itself) now. It is straightforward to see that the program satisfies the postcondition and is memory-safe with the precondition if all proof obligations are discharged and the transformed program is verified. If any part is not proved and a counterexample is constructed by the verifier, we use the counterexample to learn new invariants and then try to prove new Hoare triples.

Table 4. Results on GRASShopper (Gh)

Data structure	Functions	#Calls	#Progs	Gh		Gh+SLearner			Gh+SLearner-Mutation		
				#V	Time(s)	#V	Time(s)	L Time(s)	#V	Time(s)	L Time(s)
Singly-linked list	Traverse, Dispose, Insert, Remove, Concat	1	5	5	1.50	5	1.50	0	5	1.50	0
		2	12	0	-	12	4.97	202	0	-	32
		3	18	0	-	18	10.74	610	0	-	99
Sorted list	Traverse, Dispose, Insert	1	3	3	1.40	3	1.40	0	3	1.40	0
		2	6	0	-	6	4.94	152	4	2.71	12
		3	6	0	-	6	6.96	368	2	2.32	32
Binary tree	Traverse, Dispose, Insert	1	3	3	43.63	3	43.63	0	3	43.63	0
		2	6	0	-	4	90.23	134	4	90.23	12
		3	6	0	-	2	89.26	313	2	89.26	30

4   Implementation and Evaluation

Our approach has been implemented as a prototype, called SLearner, with 3070 lines of Java code. In the following, we evaluate SLearner to answer multiple research questions (RQ). All experiments are conducted on a laptop with one 2.20 GHz CPU and 16 GB RAM. To reduce the effect of randomness, we run each experiment 20 times with 10 random test cases each time.

RQ1: Can our approach enhance state-of-the-art verifiers for heap programs? We integrate SLearner into two state-of-the-art verifiers for heap programs: GRASShopper and HIP. Although GRASShopper and HIP target the same class of programs, their approaches differ in multiple ways, e.g., they provide a different library of user-defined predicates and they have different verification strategies. They thus allow us to check whether SLearner is general enough to support different program verifiers. We remark that alternative program verifiers like CPAChecker [6] and SeaHorn [20] target different classes of programs or program properties and hence are not applicable. The only other tool which is capable of verifying heap programs with heap-related specification is jStar [12], which is, however, no longer maintained.

We conduct two sets of experiments based on these two verifiers. Our first experiment is with GRASShopper. Although GRASShopper supports inductive predicates for describing data structures, unlike HIP, it does not support reasoning about separation logic directly. The inductive predicates in GRASShopper are defined based on first-order logic with some built-in predefined predicates. Due to GRASShopper's limitation, we conduct an experiment based on a set of benchmark programs in its distribution. All programs and experimental results are available at [2] and the tool is available at [3].

The GRASShopper distribution contains many functions for different types of data-structures. We focus on those non-trivial recursive functions with precondition and post-condition. To check how GRASShopper performs with and without SLearner, we generate a set of composite programs which randomly invoke one or more of these functions. The function call sequence is formed such that the postcondition of a previous function is identical (via syntactical checking) to the precondition of the subsequent function. The precondition of the composite program is composed from preconditions of invoked functions and the postcondition of the last function in the call sequence is the postcondition of the composite program. In total, we generate 65 composite programs containing 1, 2 and 3 function calls.

Table 5. Results on HIP

Data structure	Program	HIP			HIP+SLearner				HIP+SLearner-Mutation			
		Result	#Succ	Time(s)	Result	#Succ	Time(s)	L Time(s)	Result	#Succ	Time(s)	L Time(s)
Singly-linked list	Clean	Fail	0	-	Succ	20	0.37	17	Fail	0	-	3
	Clone	Fail	0	-	Succ	20	0.45	17	Fail	0	-	3
	Min	Fail	0	-	Fail	0	-	17	Fail	0	-	2
	Reverse	Fail	0	-	Fail	0	-	17	Fail	0	-	3
	Sort	Fail	0	-	Fail	0	-	17	Fail	0	-	3
	Insert	Fail	0	-	Succ	20	0.42	38	Fail	0	-	3
	Delete	Fail	0	-	Succ	20	0.42	37	Fail	0	-	2
	Append	Fail	0	-	Succ	20	0.45	90	Fail	0	-	6
	GetLast	Fail	0	-	Succ	20	0.42	17	Fail	0	-	3
	GetSum	Fail	0	-	Succ	15	1.02	77	Fail	0	-	6
	ToDll	Fail	0	-	Succ	20	0.30	17	Fail	0	-	3
Doubly-linked list	Clean	Fail	0	-	Succ	20	0.43	17	Succ	20	0.43	3
	Clone	Fail	0	-	Succ	20	0.67	17	Succ	20	0.67	3
	Min	Fail	0	-	Fail	0	-	17	Fail	0	-	3
	Reverse	Fail	0	-	Fail	0	-	17	Fail	0	-	3
	Sort	Fail	0	-	Fail	0	-	17	Fail	0	-	3
	Insert	Fail	0	-	Succ	20	0.58	18	Succ	19	0.58	3
	Delete	Fail	0	-	Succ	20	0.65	17	Succ	20	0.65	3
	Append	Fail	0	-	Succ	20	0.40	92	Fail	5	-	6
Sorted list	Clean	Fail	0	-	Succ	20	0.35	17	Succ	20	0.37	3
	Clone	Fail	0	-	Succ	20	0.37	17	Succ	18	0.35	3
	Min	Fail	0	-	Succ	20	0.37	17	Succ	19	0.37	3
	Travel	Fail	0	-	Succ	20	0.54	17	Succ	18	0.54	2
	Insert	Fail	0	-	Fail	0	-	16	Fail	0	-	3
	Delete	Fail	0	-	Fail	0	-	18	Fail	0	-	3
Cycle list	Clean	Fail	0	-	Fail	0	-	17	Fail	0	-	3
	Min	Fail	0	-	Fail	0	-	17	Fail	0	-	3
	Travel	Fail	0	-	Succ	20	0.30	17	Fail	0	-	3
	ToSll	Fail	0	-	Fail	0	-	17	Fail	0	-	3
Binary tree	InOrder	Fail	0	-	Succ	20	0.43	16	Succ	20	0.43	2
	PreOrder	Fail	0	-	Succ	20	0.46	17	Succ	20	0.46	3
	PostOrder	Fail	0	-	Succ	20	0.45	17	Succ	20	0.45	3
	Min	Fail	0	-	Succ	20	0.51	17	Succ	20	0.51	3
	Max	Fail	0	-	Succ	20	0.51	17	Succ	20	0.51	3
	Prec	Fail	0	-	Succ	20	0.57	17	Succ	20	0.57	3
	Succ	Fail	0	-	Succ	20	0.57	17	Succ	20	0.57	3
	Insert	Fail	0	-	Succ	20	0.67	17	Succ	20	0.67	3
	Delete	Fail	0	-	Fail	0	-	22	Fail	0	-	3
AVL tree	Insert	Fail	0	-	Fail	0	-	17	Fail	0	-	3
	Delete	Fail	0	-	Fail	0	-	24	Fail	0	-	3
Red-black tree	Insert	Fail	0	-	Fail	0	-	22	Fail	0	-	3
	Delete	Fail	0	-	Fail	0	-	38	Fail	0	-	3
MCF	Travel	Fail	0	-	Fail	0	-	17	Fail	0	-	3
Rose tree	Travel	Fail	0	-	Fail	0	-	17	Fail	0	-	3
Tll	SetRight	Fail	0	-	Succ	20	2.40	16	Succ	19	2.40	2

Table 4 shows the results, where the first four columns show the type of data structure, the involved functions, the number of function calls and the number of programs in the category. The next column shows the result of GRASShopper without the help of SLearner, i.e., the program is verified using GRASShopper without the specification of each invoked function in the program. We measure the number of verified programs (column #V) and the time taken. The next column shows the results of GRASShopper enhanced with SLearner. No additional user-defined predicates besides those provided in GRASShopper are used in our experiments. Note that we extract features automatically based on the user-defined predicates in GRASShopper in the experiment.

Without SLearner, GRASShopper only verifies 11 (out of 65) programs with 1 function call. For the remaining 54 programs which have 2 or 3 function calls, GRASShopper fails to verify any of them. This is expected as GRASShopper is unable to derive the necessary function specification automatically. Enhanced with SLearner, GRASShopper verifies 59 (out of 65) programs. For all these programs, we learn the correct invariants in every one of the 20 runs.

The second experiment is with HIP. We generate 45 programs based on common operations for 10 different data structures. Each program consists of multiple function calls. Each program starts with a call of a constructor which creates an object of the target data structure (e.g., a singly-linked list), or a function which reads the data structure (e.g., checking whether the root node is null, or traveling through the data structure). Lastly, a function supported by HIP for this data structure is called which may modify the data structure. The postcondition of the program is the postcondition of the last function. The precondition is manually written and checked to guarantee that the program terminates and satisfies the postcondition without any memory error.

Table 5 shows the results, where column *Program* shows the last function called in the program. Column *HIP+SLearner* shows the results using HIP enhanced with SLearner. Note that we may not be able to learn the same invariants every time due to randomness in generating the initial set of test cases. Thus, we add a column *#Succ* to show how many times, out of 20, we are able to learn the invariant and verify the program. No additional user-defined predicates besides those defined in HIP are used in our experiments. Column *HIP* shows that without SLearner, none of these programs is verified. With SLearner, HIP successfully verifies 27 programs. In all but 1 case (highlighted with bold) we are able to learn the same invariant consistently.

RQ2: Which features are useful in verifying heap programs? We learn invariants based on two groups of features, i.e., general heap-related features and those specific to user-defined predicates. The question is whether these two groups of features are useful and whether there are other features which we could learn based on.

In total, SLearner learned 104 invariants (74 with GRASShopper and 30 with HIP) to help solving the verification tasks. Among them, 93 invariants (66 with GRASShopper and 27 with HIP) contain only features extracted based on the user-defined predicates (e.g., $ds(x)$ or $ds(x)*ds(y)$ with ds being a user-defined predicate). The remaining 11 invariants are additionally constituted with generic features (e.g., $x = $ null or $x \neq $ null). None of the invariants is constituted with general heap-related features only. The results show that the user-defined predicates are important and invariants specific to a verification problem are needed for proving the program. Generic heap-related features are also necessary sometimes (in 11% of the cases).

A total of 24 programs (6 with GRASShopper and 18 with HIP) are not verified. There are two main reasons why they cannot be proved even with the help of SLearner. Firstly, some programs can only be verified with complex function specifications which require features that are not supported in SLearner. For example, to prove the remaining 6 programs in the experiment with GRASShopper, we need a feature characterizing the paths in the tree, which cannot be derived from user-defined predicates. This is similarly the case for experiments with HIP. One remedy is to extend our implementation with additional features through automatic lemma learning [28]. Secondly, there are programs that have a hierarchy of function calls, e.g., function calls within recursive functions. Some of the function calls occur under strict condition which is never satisfied by the test cases and thus we are unable to learn the specification of those function calls. This is a fundamental limitation of dynamic analysis approaches, which could be overcome with a comprehensive test suite from a systematic test case generation approach [39–41].

RQ3: Is memory graph mutation helpful? We compare the performance of the enhanced GRASShopper and HIP with and without memory graph mutation. The results are shown in the last columns of Tables 4 and 5. It can be observed that without memory graph mutation, the number of verified programs by GRASShopper is reduced from 59 to 23, and the number of verified programs by HIP is reduced from 27 to 17. It thus clearly shows that memory graph mutation helps to improve the correctness of the learned invariants. Furthermore, we observe that without memory graph mutation, it is more likely that different invariants are learned in different runs of the same experiments (refer to column *#Succ*). This is expected as without memory graph mutation, we cannot discard invariants which are the result of limited test cases.

RQ4: What is the overhead of invariant generation? We measure the time taken to learn the invariants. Columns *L Time* in Tables 4 and 5 show the results. In general, the learning time depends on the number of learning points, the complexity of the program and the initial test suite. Overall, the time required for learning is reasonable, ranging from seconds to minutes. In the most time consuming case, we spent 92 s to learn two invariants for program "doubly-linked list append". For most of the cases, the learning time is about 20 s for each learning point.

RQ5: Does our invariant generation approach complement existing ones? The most noticeable invariant generation tool for heap program is Infer [1]. However, Infer is not designed to support verification task. Instead, it generates generic specifications to capture the footprints of the pointers used in the functions based on bi-abduction. We apply Infer to generate specifications (e.g., pre/postconditions) for every function experimented above and notice that they are too weak for program verification.

Threats to Validity. Firstly, the set of programs used in our experiments are limited compared to real-world data-structure libraries. This is because state-of-the-art verifiers for heap programs are still limited to relatively simple programs due to the great difficulty in verifying heap properties. As our experiments show, SLearner successfully enhances the capability of state-of-the-art heap program verifiers so that programs with multiple functions can be automatically verified. Secondly, SLearner only works when we have the right features in the learning process. We expect that applying lemma synthesis could help us obtain more features and overcome this limitation.

5   Related Work

The closest to our work is approach for invariant inference using dynamic analysis with separation logic abstraction [30]. Similar to our work, it generates invariant based on user-defined predicates (i.e., features in our work). In contrast to ours, it made use of positive features only and did not support mutation. Close to our work are proposals for automatic program verification using black-box techniques adopted from the machine learning community. In particular, the method presented in [47] is based on user-supplied templates. It is designed to learn specification for heap programs which ensures no memory errors. The approach in [32] proposes to learn features from graph-structured inputs based on neural networks. The authors showed an application on verifying memory safety using the learning results. In contrast to [32], our goal is to learn invariants to compositionally verify the program against a given specification as well as ensure no memory errors. In [25], the authors presented a method to learn shared module codes and reuse them during an analysis. The work in [16] builds polynomial time active learning algorithms for automaton model of array and list structures. Our proposal also relies on a learning algorithm and actively improves the learned invariants. In [35], the authors proposed a learning method targeted lists only. This method learns the sequence of actions (remove or insert) from a program and infers the data structures manipulated by the program. However, it is hard to extend the method to support arbitrary heap programs. Similarly to ours, [7] guesses invariants from concrete program states and checks them by a theorem prover. However, their work only focuses on list-based programs. The ICE method proposed in [17, 18] supports inductive properties of loop invariant learning. Besides using the positive and negative points, ICE proposes additional implication points to encode the inductive checking for learning invariant. It is our future work to integrate the idea of ICE learning with our graph-based learning. The work in [38] presents an approach for precondition inference. The main contribution is feature learning for functional programs. It is interesting to apply the feature learning techniques in our future work.

Our work is also related to automatic and static analyzers for the shape analysis problems, e.g., TVLA [46] and separation logic [9,10,13,22,26], and for the verification problem of programs that requires both heap and data reasoning, e.g., PDR [24], interpolation [4] and template-based invariant generation [33]. To infer shape-based specification, while tools [9,13,26] are based on the bi-abduction technique, we use machine learning to obtain a generalized invariant from a set of concrete executions. In our implementation, we use GRASSHopper and HIP as external verification engines. As our approach is independent from the program verifiers, we plan to build a general framework so that different verifiers can be used. Lastly, this work is related to previous works on invariant generation, e.g., Daikon [14], or Houdini [15]. However, those works do not focus on learning invariants related to data structures like this one.

6   Conclusion

We have presented a novel learning approach to the automated and compositional verification of heap programs. The essence of our approach is an algorithm to infer invariants based on a set of memory graphs representing the program states obtained from concrete executing traces. We further enhance the precision of learned invariant with memory graph mutation. We have implemented a prototype tool and evaluated it over a set of programs which manipulate complex data structures. The experimental results show that our tool enhances the capability of existing program verifiers to verify nontrivial heap programs. In the future, we might apply our tool to more verifiers and more test subjects as well as compare our tool with other tools, e.g., Predator [13], Forester [21,22], S2 [26], and SLING [30].

Acknowledgments. This research is supported by MOE research grant MOE2016-T2-2-123.

References

1. Facebook Infer. https://fbinfer.com
2. https://figshare.com/s/ba1c12ad90c138fbb240
3. https://github.com/sunjun-group/Ziyuan
4. Albarghouthi, A., Berdine, J., Cook, B., Kincaid, Z.: Spatial interpolants. In: Vitek, J. (ed.) ESOP 2015, pp. 634–660 (2015). https://doi.org/10.1007/978-3-662-46669-8_26
5. Berdine, J., Cox, A., Ishtiaq, S., Wintersteiger, C.M.: Diagnosing abstraction failure for separation logic-based analyses. In: Madhusudan, P., Seshia, S.A. (eds.) CAV 2012, pp. 155–173 (2012). https://doi.org/10.1007/978-3-642-31424-7_16
6. Beyer, D., Keremoglu, M.E.: CPAchecker: a tool for configurable software verification. In: Gopalakrishnan, G., Qadeer, S. (eds.) CAV 2011, pp. 184–190 (2011). https://doi.org/10.1007/978-3-642-22110-1_16
7. Brockschmidt, M., Chen, Y., Kohli, P., Krishna, S., Tarlow, D.: Learning shape analysis. In: Ranzato, F. (ed.) SAS 2017, pp. 66–87 (2017). https://doi.org/10.1007/978-3-319-66706-5_4
8. Bshouty, N.H., Goldman, S.A., Mathias, H.D., Suri, S., Tamaki, H.: Noise-tolerant distribution-free learning of general geometric concepts. J. ACM **45**(5), 863–890 (1998). https://doi.org/10.1145/290179.290184
9. Calcagno, C., Distefano, D., O'Hearn, P.W., Yang, H.: Compositional Shape Analysis by Means of Bi-Abduction. J. ACM **58**(6), 26:1–26:66 (2011). https://doi.org/10.1145/2049697.2049700
10. Chin, W., David, C., Nguyen, H.H., Qin, S.: Automated verification of shape, size and bag properties via user-defined predicates in separation logic. Sci. Comput. Program **77**(9), 1006–1036 (2012). https://doi.org/10.1016/j.scico.2010.07.004
11. Cleve, H., Zeller, A.: Locating causes of program failures. In: Roman, G., Griswold, W.G., Nuseibeh, B. (eds.) ICSE 2005, pp. 342–351 (2005). https://doi.org/10.1145/1062455.1062522
12. Distefano, D., Parkinson, M.J.: jStar: towards practical verification for Java. In: Harris, G.E. (ed.) OOPSLA 2008, pp. 213–226 (2008). https://doi.org/10.1145/1449764.1449782
13. Dudka, K., Peringer, P., Vojnar, T.: Predator: a practical tool for checking manipulation of dynamic data structures using separation logic. In: Gopalakrishnan, G., Qadeer, S. (eds.) CAV 2011, pp. 372–378 (2011). https://doi.org/10.1007/978-3-642-22110-1_29

14. Ernst, M.D., Perkins, J.H., Guo, P.J., McCamant, S., Pacheco, C., Tschantz, M.S., Xiao, C.: The Daikon system for dynamic detection of likely invariants. Sci. Comput. Program **69**(1–3), 35–45 (2007). https://doi.org/10.1016/j.scico.2007.01.015

15. Flanagan, C., Leino, K.R.M.: Houdini, an annotation assistant for ESC/Java. In: Oliveira, J.N., Zave, P. (eds.) FME 2001, pp. 500–517 (2001). https://doi.org/10.1007/3-540-45251-6_29

16. Garg, P., Löding, C., Madhusudan, P., Neider, D.: Learning universally quantified invariants of linear data structures. In: Sharygina, N., Veith, H. (eds.) CAV 2013, pp. 813–829 (2013). https://doi.org/10.1007/978-3-642-39799-8_57

17. Garg, P., Löding, C., Madhusudan, P., Neider, D.: ICE: a robust framework for learning invariants. In: Biere, A., Bloem, R. (eds.) CAV 2014, pp. 69–87 (2014). https://doi.org/10.1007/978-3-319-08867-9_5

18. Garg, P., Neider, D., Madhusudan, P., Roth, D.: Learning invariants using decision trees and implication counterexamples. In: Bodík, R., Majumdar, R. (eds.) POPL 2016, pp. 499–512 (2016). https://doi.org/10.1145/2837614.2837664

19. Ginsburg, S., Spanier, E.: Semigroups, presburger formulas, and languages. Pac. J. Math. **16**(2), 285–296 (1966)

20. Gurfinkel, A., Kahsai, T., Komuravelli, A., Navas, J.A.: The SeaHorn verification framework. In: Kroening, D., Pasareanu, C.S. (eds.) CAV 2015, pp. 343–361 (2015). https://doi.org/10.1007/978-3-319-21690-4_20

21. Holík, L., Hruska, M., Lengál, O., Rogalewicz, A., Simácek, J., Vojnar, T.: Forester: from heap shapes to automata predicates - (competition contribution). In: Legay, A., Margaria, T. (eds.) TACAS 2017, pp. 365–369 (2017). https://doi.org/10.1007/978-3-662-54580-5_24

22. Holík, L., Lengál, O., Rogalewicz, A., Simácek, J., Vojnar, T.: Fully automated shape analysis based on forest automata. In: Sharygina, N., Veith, H. (eds.) CAV 2013, pp. 740–755 (2013). https://doi.org/10.1007/978-3-642-39799-8_52

23. Ishtiaq, S.S., O'Hearn, P.W.: BI as an assertion language for mutable data structures. In: Hankin, C., Schmidt, D. (eds.) POPL 2001, pp. 14–26 (2001)

24. Itzhaky, S., Bjørner, N., Reps, T.W., Sagiv, M., Thakur, A.V.: Property-directed shape analysis. In: Biere, A., Bloem, R. (eds.) CAV 2014, pp. 35–51 (2014). https://doi.org/10.1007/978-3-319-08867-9_3

25. Kulkarni, S., Mangal, R., Zhang, X., Naik, M.: Accelerating program analyses by cross-program training. In: Visser, E., Smaragdakis, Y. (eds.) OOPSLA 2016, pp. 359–377 (2016). https://doi.org/10.1145/2983990.2984023

26. Le, Q.L., Gherghina, C., Qin, S., Chin, W.: Shape analysis via second-order bi-abduction. In: Biere, A., Bloem, R. (eds.) CAV 2014, pp. 52–68 (2014). https://doi.org/10.1007/978-3-319-08867-9_4

27. Le, Q.L., Sun, J., Chin, W.: Satisfiability modulo heap-based programs. In: Chaudhuri, S., Farzan, A. (eds.) CAV 2016, pp. 382–404 (2016). https://doi.org/10.1007/978-3-319-41528-4_21

28. Le, Q.L., Sun, J., Qin, S.: Frame inference for inductive entailment proofs in separation logic. In: Beyer, D., Huisman, M. (eds.) TACAS 2018, pp. 41–60 (2018). https://doi.org/10.1007/978-3-319-89960-2_3

29. Le, Q.L., Tatsuta, M., Sun, J., Chin, W.: A decidable fragment in separation logic with inductive predicates and arithmetic. In: Majumdar, R., Kuncak, V. (eds.) CAV 2017, pp. 495–517 (2017). https://doi.org/10.1007/978-3-319-63390-9_26

30. Le, T.C., Zheng, G., Nguyen, T.: SLING: using dynamic analysis to infer program invariants in separation logic. In: McKinley, K.S., Fisher, K. (eds.) PLDI 2019, pp. 788–801 (2019). https://doi.org/10.1145/3314221.3314634

31. Leino, K.R.M.: Dafny: an automatic program verifier for functional correctness. In: Clarke, E.M., Voronkov, A. (eds.) LPAR 2010, pp. 348–370 (2010).https://doi.org/10.1007/978-3-642-17511-4_20

32. Li, Y., Tarlow, D., Brockschmidt, M., Zemel, R.S.: Gated graph sequence neural networks. CoRR abs/1511.05493 (2015)

33. Malík, V., Hruska, M., Schrammel, P., Vojnar, T.: Template-based verification of heap-manipulating programs. In: Bjørner, N., Gurfinkel, A. (eds.) FMCAD 2018, pp. 1–9 (2018). https://doi.org/10.23919/FMCAD.2018.8603009

34. Miné, A.: The octagon abstract domain. High. Order. Symbolic Comput. **19**(1), 31–100 (2006). https://doi.org/10.1007/s10990-006-8609-1

35. Mühlberg, J.T., White, D.H., Dodds, M., Lüttgen, G., Piessens, F.: Learning assertions to verify linked-list programs. In: Calinescu, R., Rumpe, B. (eds.) SEFM 2015, pp. 37–52 (2015). https://doi.org/10.1007/978-3-319-22969-0_3

36. O'Hearn, P.W., Reynolds, J.C., Yang, H.: Local reasoning about programs that alter data structures. In: Fribourg, L. (ed.) CSL 2001, pp. 1–19 (2001). https://doi.org/10.1007/3-540-44802-0_1

37. Pacheco, C., Lahiri, S.K., Ernst, M.D., Ball, T.: Feedback-directed random test generation. In: ICSE, vol. 2007, pp. 75–84 (2007). https://doi.org/10.1109/ICSE.2007.37

38. Padhi, S., Sharma, R., Millstein, T.D.: Data-driven precondition inference with learned features. In: Krintz, C., Berger, E. (eds.) PLDI 2016, pp. 42–56 (2016). https://doi.org/10.1145/2908080.2908099

39. Pham, L.H., Le, Q.L., Phan, Q.S., Sun, J.: Concolic testing heap-manipulating programs. In: FM 2019. To appear

40. Pham, L.H., Le, Q.L., Phan, Q.S., Sun, J., Qin, S.: Enhancing symbolic execution of heap-based programs with separation logic for test input generation. In: ATVA 2019. To appear

41. Pham, L.H., Le, Q.L., Phan, Q.S., Sun, J., Qin, S.: Testing heap-based programs with Java StarFinder. In: Chaudron, M., Crnkovic, I., Chechik, M., Harman, M. (eds.) ICSE 2018, pp. 268–269. ACM (2018). https://doi.org/10.1145/3183440.3194964

42. Pham, L.H., Thi, L.T., Sun, J.: Assertion generation through active learning. In: Duan, Z., Ong, L. (eds.) ICFEM 2017, pp. 174–191 (2017). https://doi.org/10.1007/978-3-319-68690-5_11

43. Piskac, R., Wies, T., Zufferey, D.: Automating separation logic with trees and data. In: Biere, A., Bloem, R. (eds.) CAV 2014, pp. 711–728 (2014). https://doi.org/10.1007/978-3-319-08867-9_47

44. Piskac, R., Wies, T., Zufferey, D.: GRASShopper - complete heap verification with mixed specifications. In: Ábrahám, E., Havelund, K. (eds.) TACAS 2014, pp. 124–139 (2014). https://doi.org/10.1007/978-3-642-54862-8_9

45. Reynolds, J.C.: Separation logic: a logic for shared mutable data structures. In: LICS, vol. 2002, pp. 55–74 (2002). https://doi.org/10.1109/LICS.2002.1029817

46. Sagiv, S., Reps, T.W., Wilhelm, R.: Parametric shape analysis via 3-valued logic. In: Appel, A.W., Aiken, A. (eds.) POPL 1999, pp. 105–118 (1999). https://doi.org/10.1145/292540.292552

47. Zhu, H., Petri, G., Jagannathan, S.: Automatically learning shape specifications. In: Krintz, C., Berger, E. (eds.) PLDI 2016, pp. 491–507 (2016). https://doi.org/10.1145/2908080.2908125

Logic and Automata

Pumping, with or Without Choice

Aquinas Hobor[1,2], Elaine Li[1(✉)], and Frank Stephan[2,3]

[1] Yale-NUS College, Singapore, Singapore
elaine.li@u.yale-nus.edu.sg
[2] School of Computing, National University of Singapore, Singapore
{hobor,fstephan}@comp.nus.edu.sg
[3] Department of Mathematics, National University of Singapore, Singapore

Abstract. We present the first machine-checked formalization of Jaffe and Ehrenfeucht, Parikh and Rozenberg's (EPR) pumping lemmas in the Coq proof assistant. We formulate regularity in terms of finite derivatives, and prove that both Jaffe's pumping property and EPR's block pumping property precisely characterize regularity. We illuminate EPR's classical proof that the block cancellation property implies regularity, and discover that—as best we can tell—their proof relies on the Axiom of Choice. We provide a new proof which eliminates the use of Choice. We explicitly construct a function which computes block cancelable languages from well-formed short languages.

Keywords: Pumping lemmas · Axiom of Choice · Coq

1 Overview

Pumping properties of formal languages have a rich history. Rabin and Scott provided a pumping lemma that displays properties of regular languages; Bar-Hilel, Perles, and Shamir did the same for context-free languages [17,24]. Pumping lemmas describe how words belonging to the relevant language L can be "pumped", *e.g.* if L is regular then a word $u \in L$ can be split into parts xyz ($vwxyz$ in the context-free case) such that for all $n \in \mathbb{N}$, $xy^n z \in L$ (respectively $vw^n xy^n z \in L$). Because pumping lemmas are often stated as *necessary* conditions of a language being regular or context-free, they are often used in modus tollens form to show that certain languages are *not* regular or context-free because they do not satisfy the pumping property. Pumping lemmas are also used to prove other properties of regular or context-free languages, *e.g.* that every context-free language over the unary alphabet $\{0\}$ is regular and that every automatic function increases the length of its input by at most a constant.

Aquinas Hobor is supported in part by Yale-NUS College grant R-607-265-322-121. Elaine Li is supported in part by Runtime Verification, Inc. Frank Stephan is supported in part by MOE AcRF Tier 2 grant MOE2016-T2-1-019/R146-000-234-112. Authors are ordered alphabetically.

A. W. Lin (Ed.): APLAS 2019, LNCS 11893, pp. 427–446, 2019.
https://doi.org/10.1007/978-3-030-34175-6_22

The converse question of whether pumping properties can also serve as *sufficient* conditions for a language to be regular or context-free is less straightforward. Sommerhalder [29] showed that even a more restrictive "matching" form of Rabin-Scott's pumping lemma—that both a language *and its complement* satisfy the pumping property—fails to precisely characterize regular languages because there are non-regular languages that satisfy it. Jaffe [18] was the first to provide a pumping lemma that precisely characterizes regularity, *i.e.* that gives *both* a necessary and a sufficient condition for regularity.

1.1   Jaffe's Pumping Lemma

Theorem 1 (Jaffe). *A language L is regular iff there is a constant k s.t.*

$$\forall x \in \Sigma^*. \ |x| = k \ \Rightarrow \ \exists u, v, w \in \Sigma^*.$$
$$x = uvw \ \wedge \ v \neq \epsilon \ \wedge \ \forall h \in \mathbb{N}, \ z \in \Sigma^*. \ (uvwz \in L \ \Leftrightarrow \ uv^h wz \in L)$$

Jaffe's pumping lemma is a reformulation of the Myhill-Nerode theorem [23]. The pumping constant k in Jaffe's pumping lemma refers to the length of word prefixes, equivalently the length of the language's derivative labels.

Definition 1 (Derivative). *The derivative of a language L with respect to a word $x \in \Sigma^*$, written L_x, is another language that accepts words y iff L accepts xy, i.e. $xy \in L \Leftrightarrow y \in L_x$.*

Theorem 2 (Myhill-Nerode). *A language L is regular iff it has a finite number of derivatives.*

1.2   The Block Pumping Lemma

Ehrenfeucht, Parikh and Rozenberg [14] provided a pumping property that gives a more sophisticated characterization of the regular languages.

Theorem 3 (EPR). *A language L is regular iff there is a constant k s.t. for any splitting of a word x into $k + 2$ blocks, i.e. $x = w, u_1, \cdots, u_k, w'$, one can find a an interval $u_i \cdots u_j$ of blocks that can be pumped any number h of times:*

$$\forall x, w, u_1, \cdots, u_k, w' \in \Sigma^*. \ x = wu_1 \cdots u_k w' \ \Rightarrow$$
$$\exists i, j \in \mathbb{N}. \ 1 \leq i < j \leq k \ \wedge \ \forall h \in \mathbb{N},$$
$$wu_1 \cdots u_{i+1} \cdots u_j \cdots u_k w' \ \in L \ \Leftrightarrow \ w \cdots (u_{i+1} \cdots u_j)^h \cdots u_k w' \in L$$

We call languages that satisfy EPR's "block pumping" property "block pumpable languages", and we write "L is block pumpable with k" to specify the block pumping constant. Furthermore, one can postulate that $u_1, \cdots, u_k$ are non-empty without changing the notion of block pumpable.

An advantage of block pumping over Rabin-Scott pumping is that it allows one to directly obtain block pumping constants for combined languages such as $L \cap H$, $L \cup H$ and $L \cdot H$ from the constants for L and H, as we will show in Sect. 3. Rabin-Scott pumping does not allow this: *e.g.* regular languages $L =$

$\{0^k 1^n 2^m : k = 1 \Rightarrow (n = m \bmod h)\}$ and $H = \{0\} \cdot \{1\}^* \cdot \{2\}^*$ both have pumping constant 2, but $L \cap H$ requires pumping constant $h + 1$, which is independent of the pumping constants of L and H.

To compare EPR's pumping property with Rabin-Scott's, Chak *et al.* [4] investigated languages that satisfy the block pumping property with the $\Leftrightarrow$ restricted to the $\Rightarrow$ direction only:

Definition 2 (One-sided block pumpable language). *A language L is one-sided block pumpable iff there is a constant k s.t.*

$$\forall x \in \Sigma^*.\ x \in L \ \Rightarrow\ \forall w, u_1 \cdots u_k, w' \in \Sigma^*.\ x = wu_1 \cdots u_k w' \ \Rightarrow$$
$$\exists i, j \in \mathbb{N}.\ 1 \le i < j \le k \ \wedge \ \forall h \in \mathbb{N},\ w \cdots (u_{i+1} \cdots u_j)^h \cdots u_k w' \in L$$

Chak *et al.* [4] showed that one-sided block pumpable languages not only need not be regular, but need not even be computable! Accordingly, these languages cannot be reasoned about in the same automata-theoretic way as other languages in the Chomsky hierarchy. Instead, proofs about one-sided block pumpable languages have a distinctly combinatorial flavor, relying critically on Ramsey theory.

1.3   Contributions

We present the first machine-checked proofs of the pumping lemmas of Jaffe and Ehrenfeucht, Parikh and Rozenberg in the Coq proof assistant. Jaffe's pumping lemma is straightforward to mechanize, but we present it nonetheless as a way to introduce the novelties of our setup. In particular, we use Myhill-Nerode to *define* the regularity of a language as having finitely many derivatives. We then present machine-checked proofs from block pumpable language theory that, to the best of our knowledge, are the first of formal language classes orthogonal to the Chomsky hierarchy. We introduce relevant definitions by presenting a mechanization of the closure properties of one-sided block pumpable languages: they are closed under intersection, union and concatenation [4, Thm 15].

We then proceed with EPR's more complex pumping lemma. This complexity is in part due to some omissions concerning the concept of "finiteness". We fill in the gaps of their proof and discover that it appears to require the Axiom of Choice to construct the inverse to a partial injective function.

Although not diehard constructivists, we find the Axiom of Choice a bit objectionable. One well-known consequence is the Banach-Tarski paradox [2]:

> Given a solid 3-D ball, one can decompose ("cut") it into five disjoint subsets ("pieces"), which can be reassembled using rigid motions (movements and rotations) to yield two identical copies of the original ball.

Coq offers a variety of flavors of the Axiom of Choice, but their use leads to the unfortunate (full or partial) collapse of the distinction between the set of mathematically true facts (Prop) and computationally decidable facts (Type) [3].

Accordingly, we present a new proof of EPR's pumping lemma that eliminates the Axiom of Choice by explicitly constructing the inverse function in question. This inverse function can compute block cancelable languages from well-formed input languages. The rest of this paper is organized as follows:

Section 2 We present our basic setup and prove Jaffe's pumping lemma.

Section 3 We define block pumpable languages and prove closure properties.

Section 4 We mechanize the original proof of EPR's pumping lemma. In the process we clarify several areas of the proof, in particular its treatment of finiteness. We show how EPR's proof uses the Axiom of Choice.

Section 5 We present our construction of an explicit inverse function and prove that it can enable a new choice-free proof of EPR's pumping lemma.

Section 6 We discuss related work before concluding in Sect. 7.

Along the way, we highlight aspects of our formalization which leverage features of Coq's type theory and/or contribute broadly applicable definitions and proofs for which we could not find existing alternatives. The present work includes results from the Capstone project of Li [21]. Our proofs are entirely machine-checked in Coq and available at

https://github.com/atufchoice/blockpump.

2   Regularity and Jaffe's Pumping Lemma

Here we present the first mechanization of Jaffe's pumping lemma, and with it the basics of our formal setup. We begin with the axioms we add to CiC:

1. Functional extensionality: $(\forall x.\ f(x) = g(x)) \Rightarrow (f = g)$
2. Propositional extensionality: $(P \Leftrightarrow Q) \Rightarrow (P = Q)$
3. Law of excluded middle: $P \vee \neg P$
4. Functional choice: $(\forall a.\ \exists b.\ aRb) \Rightarrow (\exists f.\ \forall a.\ aR(f(a)))$

Specifically: Jaffe (Sect. 2), EPR's original proof (Sect. 4), and our new EPR proof (Sect. 5) use functional and propositional extensionalities to prove language equivalence and (via proof irrelevance) equality on dependent types. Proofs about block pumping, *i.e.* closure properties for block pumpable languages (Sect. 3), EPR's original proof (Sect. 4) and our new Choice-free proof (Sect. 5) use the law of excluded middle due to the fact that block pumpable languages are not Turing-decidable, and as a result, we cannot check language membership computationally. Lastly, EPR's original proof (Sect. 4) uses functional choice.

We next present the basic mathematical definitions of alphabets, words, and languages. We use Σ to refer to a finite alphabet, and σ to refer to symbols in the alphabet. For simplicity in Coq, we use a three-letter alphabet (type T):

```
Inductive T : Type := aa | bb | cc.
```

We use variables x, y, z, w, v to denote words; $|w|$ to denote the length of w; and the symbol ϵ to denote the empty word. In Coq, words are just lists of letters:

```
Definition word := list T.
```

We use L, H to denote languages, *i.e.* sets of words:

```
Definition language : Type := word -> Prop.
```

We use functional and propositional extensionality to prove language equality:

```
Lemma language_equality : forall (l1 l2: language),
  l1 = l2 <-> forall (w: word), l1 w <-> l2 w.
```

Instead of using the standard representations of regular languages, *i.e.* finite automata or regular expressions, we use Myhill-Nerode's Theorem *definitionally* to represent regular languages as languages with finitely many derivatives. We write L_x to denote the derivative of a language with respect to a word x (sometimes L_σ with a single alphabet symbol), *i.e.*:

```
Definition derivative_of (L: language) (x: word) : language :=
  fun w => L (x ++ w).
```

We say that L_x is a derivative of L when there exists a derivative label x such that for all words w, L_x accepts w iff L accepts xw.

```
Definition is_deriv (L L_x: language) : Prop :=
  exists (x: word), forall (w: word), L_x w <-> L (x ++ w).
```

We leverage Coq's inductively defined lists to express the finiteness of a property in terms of the existence of a list of elements satisfying that property:

```
Definition is_finite {X: Type} (P: X->Prop) : Prop :=
  exists (L : list X), forall (x: X), In x L <-> P x.
```

A language L is regular iff it has finitely many derivatives:

```
Definition regular (L: language) : Prop :=
  is_finite (is_deriv L).
```

We define regularity in this way because (1) Coq formalizations of regular expressions, finite automata and their equivalence already exist [9,12,13,15]; and (2) Jaffe's and EPR's proofs critically rely on the exact notion of finiteness captured in our definition. Sometimes, for proof engineering purposes we use a dependently-typed notion of finiteness as follows:

```
Definition is_finite_dep {X: Type} (P: X->Prop) :=
  exists (L: list {x | P x}), forall (dep_x : {x | P x}), In dep_x L.
```

The following equivalence lets us use one or the other as locally convenient.

```
Lemma is_finite_equiv : forall {X: Type} (P: X->Prop),
  is_finite_dep P <-> is_finite P.
```

2.1   Jaffe's Pumping Lemma

Jaffe provides the following necessary and sufficient condition for regularity. The napp function performs word concatenation: napp h v is equivalent to v^h, or v concatenated to itself h times.

```
Definition jaffe_pumpable_with (k: nat) (L: language) :=
  forall (y: word), length y = k ->
    exists (u v w: word),
      y = u ++ v ++ w /\ v <> [] /\
        forall (h: nat) (z: word),
          L (u ++ napp h v ++ w ++ z) <-> L (y ++ z).
```

Jaffe's pumping lemma amounts to proving two theorems, the first of which is:

```
Theorem reg_to_jaffe : forall (L: language),
  regular L -> exists (k: nat), jaffe_pumpable_with k L.
```

From regularity we have a finite list of derivatives LD, from which we obtain the pumping constant $|LD| + 1$. Given y, we construct a list of derivatives of length $|LD| + 1$, which by the pigeonhole principle must contain a repeated derivative. We then split y based on the two prefixes of the repeated derivative language such that they correspond to u and u++v respectively.

The second theorem is the converse:

```
Theorem jaffe_to_reg : forall (k: nat) (L: language),
  jaffe_pumpable_with k L -> regular L.
```

The following helper lemma is required to prove the converse direction, and captures the central intuition of Jaffe's pumping lemma: for any Jaffe-pumpable with k language, every derivative is equivalent to some derivative with label length shorter than k. This lemma is proven via strong induction on $|x|$.

```
Lemma jaffe_helper : forall (k: nat) (L: language),
  jaffe_pumpable_with k L -> forall x, exists v,
    length v <= k /\ derivative_of L x = derivative_of L v.
```

We now prove that Jaffe's pumping condition implies regularity, *i.e.* that we can construct a list of finitely many derivative languages for L. The list LD we construct is the list of derivatives labeled by all words up to length k, where k is Jaffe's pumping constant. Proving that every language in LD is a derivative of L is direct by definition. Proving that every derivative L_x of L is in LD requires jaffe_helper and case analysis on the derivative label's length, *i.e.* $|x|$. When $|x| \leq k$, L_x is in LD by construction; when $|x| > k$, by jaffe_helper it is equivalent to some derivative whose label is shorter than or equal to k, which is in LD by construction.

3   Block Pumpable Languages and Their Closure Properties

In this section we define the block pumping and block cancellation properties, and prove that one-sided block pumpable languages are closed under union, intersection, and concatenation.

We use i, j to denote natural numbers and bp_1, bp_2 to denote breakpoints, *i.e.* indices into a word w. We define word parts in terms of indices of type nat rather than subwords of type list to allow Coq's omega tactic to automatically discharge associated proof goals. Pumping the empty word leaves it unchanged, so we can assume $|w| \geq 1$ and at least two possible breakpoints (0 and $|w|$). We use k to denote block pumping or cancellation constants. Therefore, k is at least 2, breakpoint sets are lists of k increasing, within-bounds indices into a word, and breakpoints are members of such lists. We leverage Coq's dependent types to track these technicalities as follows:

```
Definition block_pumping_constant := {p: nat | p >= 2}.
Definition breakpoint_set (k: block_pumping_constant) (w: word)
:= {bl: list nat | length bl = k
                /\ increasing bl
                /\ last bl d <= length w}.
Definition breakpoint {k: block_pumping_constant} {w: word}
  (bl: breakpoint_set k w) := {i: nat | In i bl}.
```

Recall from (Sect. 1, Theorem 3) EPR's block pumping property, *i.e.* in Coq:

```
Definition block_pumpable_matching_with (k: block_pumping_constant)
                                        (L: language) :=
  forall (w: word) (bl: breakpoint_set k w),
    exists (i j: breakpoint bl), i < j /\
      forall (m: nat),
      L w <->
      L (firstn i w++napp m (pumpable_block i j w)++skipn j w).
```

Here `firstn`, `napp`, `pumpable_block`, and `skipn` build the pumped word. EPR [14] also established a variant of the block pumping property called the block cancellation property: rather than repeating the word, we omit it. The last two lines of `block_pumpable_matching_with` are replaced with:

```
      L w <-> L (firstn i w++skipn j w).
```

While the one-sided block cancellation property is weaker than its pumping counterpart, the (two-sided) block cancellation and pumping properties are equivalent. Indeed, the block cancellation property plays a critical role in both EPR's theorem in Sect. 4, and the construction of our new Choice-free proof in Sect. 5.

3.1   Ramsey Theory

Proofs about block pumpable languages use Ramsey's theorem [28], a foundational result in combinatorics. Ramsey's theorem is typically stated on graphs.

Theorem 4 (Ramsey's theorem for graphs). *One can always find monochromatic cliques in any edge-coloring of a sufficiently large complete graph.*

We re-express Ramsey's theorem in terms of sets by representing vertices as elements of some set and edges as pairs of elements in the set as follows:

Theorem 5 (Ramsey's theorem for sets). *For every natural number k and finite set of colors Q, there exists a natural number $r(k)$ such that for every* *ordered set I with $r(k)$ elements and for every function mapping each pair (i,j) to a color $C(i,j)$, there exists a subset $J \subset I$ with k elements such that all pairs in J are mapped to the same color.*

We then formalize two-color Ramsey's theorem for sets in Coq using `bool` to represent two distinct colors:

```
Theorem Ramsey_single :
 forall (k: nat), k > 0 ->
  exists (rk: nat), rk >= k /\
   forall (l: list nat), length l = rk ->
   forall (f: nat -> nat -> bool),
     (exists (bl: list nat), length bl = k /\ subseq bl l /\
       forall (i j: nat), i < j < k ->
       f (nth i bl d) (nth j bl d) = true)
\/   (exists (bl: list nat), length bl = k /\ subseq bl l /\
       forall (i j: nat), i < j < k ->
       f (nth i bl d) (nth j bl d) = false).
```

We further specialize Ramsey to block pumping as follows:

```
Theorem Ramsey_single_prop :
 forall (k: block_pumping_constant),
  exists (rk: block_pumping_constant), rk >= k /\
   forall (w: word) (bps: breakpoint_set rk w)
         (P: nat -> nat -> Prop),
     exists (bps': breakpoint_set k w),
       sublist bps' bps /\
    ((forall (bp1 bp2: breakpoint bps'), bp1<bp2 -> (P bp1 bp2))
\/   (forall (bp1 bp2: breakpoint bps'), bp1<bp2 -> ~(P bp1 bp2))).
```

We use "Ramsey's constant" to refer to the existential witness $r(k)$ dependent on k given by Ramsey's theorem. Instead of a computable two-element coloring function, we use an arbitrary predicate P; for this reason the proof of this formulation of Ramsey requires LEM.

3.2   Closure Properties of One-Sided Block Pumpable Languages

We next formalize the results from [4] that one-sided block pumpable languages are closed under union, intersection and concatenation. The proofs turn on finding the right block pumping constant for the combined language. We present the definitions for combined languages, and refer the reader to our Coq development for statements of the closure properties. We use l1, l2 and k1, k2 to denote two languages and their pumping constants.

For union_lang l1 l2, the new pumping constant is max k1 k2. The proof follows directly from case analysis on whether the word is in l1 or in l2, and applying the block pumping property for the respective language.

For intersection_lang l1 l2, the new pumping constant is Ramsey's constant rk for max k1 k2. We know from Ramsey's theorem that every breakpoint set of size rk contains a subset bl of size k such that either all the breakpoint pairs form pumps for w into l1 or they do not. By the one-sided block pumping property for l1 and l2 we know that all breakpoint sets of size k contain *one* pair of breakpoints which form pumps for w into l1 and l2 respectively. In the case that bl contains all pumps for w into l1, we apply the one-sided block pumping property for l2 to obtain a pair of pumps for both l1 and l2. Otherwise, we find a contradiction.

For concat_lang l1 l2, the new pumping constant is k1+k2. For any word w=w1++w2, either all of w1's breakpoints are in itself, in which case we pump w1, or all of w2's breakpoints are in itself, in which case we pump w2. The proof proceeds by case analysis on the above two possibilities.

4   Ehrenfeucht, Parikh and Rozenberg's Pumping Lemma

Having presented all the relevant formal definitions, we move on to EPR's pumping lemma. EPR's pumping lemma states the following equivalence:

Theorem 6 (EPR's pumping lemma). *The block pumping property, the block cancellation property and regularity are equivalent.*

EPR's pumping lemma amounts to the commutative triangle in Fig. 1. The equivalence can be shown by proving either the clockwise or counterclockwise direction of the triangle. EPR choose regular → block pumping property → block cancellation property. We call languages that satisfy the block cancellation property (respectively the block pumping property) with pumping con-

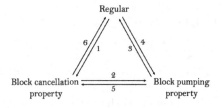

Fig. 1. The EPR commutative triangle

stant k "$BC(k)$ languages" (respectively "$BP(k)$ languages"). Of the three arrows, showing that the block cancellation property implies regularity (6) is by far the most difficult and involved.

Lemma 1 (EPR's Lemma 1). *Block cancellation property implies regularity.*

EPR splits this proof into three sub-lemmas:

Lemma 2 (EPR's Lemma 2). *$BC(k)$ languages are finite.*

Lemma 3 (EPR's Lemma 3). *If a language is $BC(k)$, so are all of its derivatives.*

Lemma 4 (EPR's Lemma 4). *Let P be some property of languages such that (i) there are only finitely many languages that P, and (ii) forall σ in Σ, if L has P then L_σ has P. Then P implies regularity.*

EPR's Lemma 4 follows directly from Myhill-Nerode [23], and Lemma 3 is straightforward. On the other hand, EPR's proof of Lemma 2 is a bit tricky to pin down. In [14], EPR claim that the following is sufficient to show that $BC(k)$ languages are finite.

Lemma 5 (EPR's Lemma 2-ish). *Two $BC(k)$ languages that agree on words shorter than $r(k)$, where $r(k)$ is Ramsey's constant, are equal.*

EPR's proof explains how to prove this lemma, but does **not** explain why it is sufficient, *i.e.* why it implies the finiteness of block cancelable languages. We complete EPR's proof by re-interpreting Lemma 2-ish as follows, and then using a classical set-theoretic fact about finiteness and injectivity which uses Lemma 2-ish to obtain the finiteness of block cancelable languages[1].

```
Definition is_short_lang (n: nat) (L: language) : Prop :=
   forall (w: word), L w -> length w <= n.
Definition filter_shortlang (n: nat) : language -> language :=
   fun L: language => (fun w: word => L w /\ length w <= n).
Theorem real_injectivity : forall (k: block_pumping_constant),
   exists (rk: block_pumping_constant),
   injective (block_cancellable_matching_with k)
             (is_short_lang rk)(filter_shortbclang k rk).
```

The definition of `injective` is standard and taken from Coq's Logic library, while `block_cancellable_matching_with` and `is_short_lang rk` describe the properties of the domain and codomain, *i.e.* block cancelable languages and short languages. The `filter_shortbclang` function is a dependently-typed version of the simpler `filter_shortlang` shown above which transforms languages in the domain into languages in the codomain by "shearing" off the long words. Thus, in set-theoretic terms, our formulation of EPR's Lemma 2-ish states that the shearing of a $BC(k)$ language down to a language containing only "short" words of length less than $r(k)$, where $r(k)$ is Ramsey's constant, is injective. Next, we use the following set-theoretic fact:

Lemma 6. *Every injective mapping onto some finite set is from a finite set.*

```
Theorem inj_finite {X Y: Type} :
   forall (P: X->Prop) (Q: Y->Prop) (f: {x | P x}->{y | Q y}),
     inhabited {x | P x} -> injective P Q f -> is_finite_dep Q ->
       is_finite_dep P.
```

---

[1] In our Coq development, we define `block_cancellable_matching_with` as the two-sided cancellation property, *i.e.* both L and L's complement satisfy it, while `block_cancellable_with` refers to the one-sided cancellation (pumping) property. The same applies for the block pumping property.

We know that the function which shears a block cancelable language down to short words is injective from EPR's 2-ish. We easily know that short languages containing length-bounded words are finite: there are exactly $2^{|\Sigma|^m}$ many of them, where $|\Sigma|$ is the size of the alphabet, and m is the length bound on words. Therefore, by the above fact, we know that block cancelable languages are finite.

We instantiate P with `block_cancellable_matching_with` k, Q with `is_short_lang` and f with our dependently-typed length-shearing function. We additionally prove that there is at least one $BC(k)$ language:

```
Lemma inhabited_bc : forall k : block_pumping_constant,
  inhabited (bc_language k).
```

This allows us to finally show that $BC(k)$ languages are finite:

```
Theorem bc_k_is_finite_dep: forall k : block_pumping_constant,
  is_finite_dep (block_cancellable_matching_with k).
```

Digression on the Axiom of Choice. The theorem `inj_finite` is classical because constructing a finite set from another finite set requires an inverse function of an injective function, which is constructed via the Axiom of Choice. As mentioned in Sect. 2, we use functional choice (`FunctionalChoice_on` from `Coq.Logic.ChoiceFacts`). It is conceivable that this is a little stronger than is required. While we cannot use constructive versions of Choice because the type of the domain is uncountable (sets of sets of words), it is plausible that with some additional gyrations we might be able to use the weaker Axiom of Description, *a.k.a.* the Axiom of No Choice (`FunctionalRelReification_on`):

$$(\forall a.\ \exists! b.\ aRb) \Rightarrow (\exists f.\ \forall a.\ aR(f(a)))$$

While weaker, relying on the Axiom of No Choice would still be unfortunate. We exorcise all forms of Choice by explicitly constructing the inverse in Sect. 5.

5   There and Back Again: An Explicit Inverse

We now present a Choice-free proof of EPR's Lemma 2. Our proof is comprised of three parts. First, we show that well-formed short languages are finite. Second, we explicitly construct a function that computes a characteristic function from a list of words. Finally, we prove correctness: that our function, when given a well-formed short language represented as a list of words, computes the block cancelable language that agrees with it on short words. We show that (i) when given a well-formed short language our function returns a block cancelable language; and (ii) every block cancelable language is in the image of our function.

5.1   Well-Formed Short Languages Are Finite

Our function must be computable so it inputs short languages as `list word` rather than `word -> Prop`. We require two properties of such lists to be suitable for building a block cancelable language: (P1) that they contain only "short" words, *i.e.* of length less than some $r(k)$; and (P2) that they agree with some $BC(k)$ language for all words up to length $r(k)$.

Informally, the fact that there are a finite number of sets containing words bounded by some length m is obvious: the cardinality is $2^{|\Sigma|^m}$. Proving this using Coq lists is less straightforward. Consider the following statement:

```
Lemma is_finite_shortlang_false : forall (rk: nat),
  exists (LW: list (list word)), forall (l: list word),
    In l LW <-> forall (w: word), In w l -> length w <= rk.
```

This statement is false because lists satisfying the right-hand side of the `<->` are infinite: they can contain duplicates. We must also contend with the hassles of permutations and ordering. We circumvent constructing and reasoning about duplicate-free, length-lexicographically sorted lists of words by proving the finiteness of a stronger property, and then weakening it to obtain the length property we require. We leverage Coq's inductive definitions to define a relation subseq, an order-preserving sublist relation of type `list -> list -> Prop`.

```
Inductive subseq (X: Type) : list X -> list X -> Prop :=
  | subseq_nil : forall (l: list X), subseq [] l
  | subseq_hm : forall (x: X) (l1 l2: list X),
    subseq l1 l2 -> subseq (x :: l1) (x :: l2)
  | subseq_hn : forall (x: X) (l1 l2: list X),
    subseq l1 l2 -> subseq l1 (x :: l2).
```

We can show that any list has a finite number of subseq lists, the proof of which proceeds by induction on the subseq relation.

```
Theorem subseq_finite: forall (l: list word),
  is_finite (fun s => subseq s l).
```

To show that there are finitely many lists containing words up to some length n, we want to instantiate l with the list containing *all* words up to length n. We define a function generate_words_of_length with correctness property:

```
Lemma generate_words_length_correct : forall (n: nat) (w: word),
  In w (generate_words_of_length n) <-> length w = n.
```

We then use it to define a function generate_words_upto_length with correctness property:

```
Lemma generate_words_upto_correct : forall (n: nat) (w: word),
  In w (generate_words_upto n) <-> length w <= n.
```

Now we can state the finiteness of (P1) using generate_words_upto:

```
Theorem is_finite_shortwords: forall (n: nat),
  is_finite (fun lw => subseq lw (generate_words_upto n)).
```

Next, we want to prune the lists that satisfy (P1) from is_finite_shortwords and keep only those that also satisfy (P2), i.e. that agree with some $BC(k)$ language up to some length. We first prove that any subset of a finite list is finite:

```
Lemma p_in_list_finite {X: Type}: forall (P: X->Prop) (L: list X),
  is_finite (fun l => P l /\ In l L).
```

This allows us to state that finiteness is preserved over conjunction:

```
Lemma is_finite_conj {X: Type} : forall (P: X->Prop) (Q: X->Prop),
  is_finite (fun l => P l) ->
  is_finite (fun l => P l /\ Q l).
```

Instantiating properties P and Q with (P1) and (P2) respectively, we obtain the finiteness of well-formed short languages and are ready to define our inverse function in Sect. 5.2.

```
Theorem is_finite_subseq_wf:
  forall (k rk: block_pumping_constant),
    is_finite (fun lw => subseq lw (generate_words_upto rk) /\
            exists (l : bc_language k), agreement_upto k rk l lw 0).
```

5.2 The **unshear** Function

Our unshear function inputs a list of words lw, and computes a characteristic function—*i.e.* a word membership decider—for a block cancelable language.

We begin with a bird's eye view description of unshear's behavior. unshear considers some arbitrary word w of length n. Starting with its input list lw_init, unshear incrementally considers sets of words of increasing length, adding those that pass some condition check until it has considered every word of length up to n. It then checks whether w is a member of the list computed so far, which we denote lw. The intuition behind unshear turns on the fact that block cancellation decreases word length, and that block cancelable languages are uniquely determined by a subset of words up to some length.

We follow with details of the function unshear. We accompany each computational function in bool with a correctness specification in Prop, and prove correctness: the _prop holds iff the function returns true.

A block canceled word with breakpoints i, j, is the word with the subword between the i-th and j-th symbol removed. We say that two indices cancel some word w into L if the block canceled word is a member of L. We build a block canceled word using firstn and skipn as follows:

```
Definition cancelled_word (w: word) (i j: nat) :=
  firstn i w ++ skipn j w.
```

First, we construct the function which checks words to be added to the list maintained by unshear. In particular, given some word w, we check for the existence of a k-size breakpoint set out of all possible k-size breakpoint sets for w, in which all pairs of breakpoints cancel w into some target list of words[2].

We first define a function which checks whether, for a given breakpoint set, all pairs of breakpoints cancel some word into a target list. The inner function are_all_pumps_helper takes one breakpoint hd and a list of breakpoints tl, and recursively traverses tl, pairwise checking the membership of the canceled word in the target list using a simple list membership checking function, is_member. We omit both functions for brevity.

---

[2] We postpone discussion of why this condition works until Sect. 5.3.

The outer function recursively traverses a list of breakpoints and calls the inner function with each head element on the rest of the list, thus guaranteeing pairs are checked in order. We express the ordered correctness property for this function in terms of list indexing:

```
Fixpoint are_all_pumps (w: word) (l: list word)
                                 (bps: list nat) :=
    match bps with
    | [] => true
    | hd :: tl => if are_all_pumps_helper w l hd tl
                  then are_all_pumps w l tl
                  else false end.
Definition are_all_pumps_prop (w: word) (l: list word)
                                 (bps: list nat) :=
    forall (i j : nat), i < j < (length bps) ->
      In (cancelled_word w (nth i bps d) (nth j bps d)) l.
```

We want to apply this function to all possible k-size breakpoint sets for some w. We generate all k-size breakpoint sets via an order-preserving `choose` function which chooses n elements from a list of greater than or equal to n elements.

```
Fixpoint choose {X: Type} (L: list X) (k: nat) {struct L} :=
 match k with
 | 0 => nil :: nil
 | S k' => match L with
           | nil => nil
           | h :: L' => (map (fun l => h :: l) (choose L' k'))
                     ++ (choose L' k) end end.
```

The list we give to `choose` is the list of all possible breakpoints for w, i.e. the list starting from 0 and ending at S (length w).

```
Definition get_k_bps (w: word) (k: nat) :=
    choose (iota 0 (S (length w))) k.
```

We use Coq's `existsb` function to check if there is a k-size breakpoint set in the list of all k-size breakpoint sets for which all pairs of breakpoints form pumps.

```
Definition exists_all_pumps_bps (w: word) (l: list word)
                                 (k: nat) :=
    existsb (are_all_pumps w l) (get_k_bps w k).
Definition exists_all_pumps_bps_prop (w: word) (l: list word)
                                 (k: nat) :=
    exists lp : list nat,
      are_all_pumps_prop w l lp /\ In lp (get_k_bps w k).
```

Thus far, we have built the condition checker for an individual word w to be added to lw maintained by unshear that is parameterized by a `list word`, *i.e.* the target list in which canceled word membership is checked. However, the role of lw in unshear is twofold: not only does it accept new words, it also serves as the target list to determine the acceptance of future new words. unshear considers individual words in batches of a certain length. When w contains words of length up to some m, unshear considers all words of length S m. lw helps unshear determine which new words of length S m to add, and then accepts the ones that pass, updating itself to now contain words of length up to S m.

We first define the function which considers all words of some length. Here, rk is the length bound of our initial list, n is the difference between the length of the candidate word and rk, and lref is our target list.

```
Definition chuck (k rk n: nat) (lref: list word) :=
  filter (fun w=>check w lref k) (generate_words_of_length (n+rk))
++ lref.
Definition chuck_prop (k rk n: nat) (lref: list word) (w: word) :=
  (exists_all_pumps_bps_prop w lref k /\ length w = n+rk)
\/ In w lref.
```

We then define the recursive function which adds words of *up to* some length to be structurally decreasing over word length nat.

```
Fixpoint chuck_length (k rk n: nat) (lref: list word) :=
  match n with
  | 0 => lref
  | S n' => chuck k rk n (chuck_length k rk n' lref) end.
```

We are now ready to define unshear, with return type word->Prop, or language. We include an intermediate representation unshear_bool with return type word->bool.

```
Definition unshear_bool (k rk: nat) (lref: list word) :=
  fun w => is_member w (chuck_length k rk (length w) lref).
Definition unshear (k rk: nat) (lref: list word) :=
  fun w => unshear_bool k rk lref w = true.
```

5.3   Functional Correctness of **unshear**

To use unshear to prove that there are finitely many block cancelable languages, we need to show that when given a well-formed short language represented as a list lw, unshear computes the block cancelable language that agrees with lw on short words. Proving the correctness of unshear thus amounts to proving the following theorem:

```
Theorem unshear_correctness: forall (k: block_pumping_constant),
  exists (rk: block_pumping_constant),
    forall (l: bc_language_dec k) (lw: list word),
      agreement_upto k rk l (chuck_length k rk lw 0) 0 ->
      (forall w, In w lw <-> (shear_language rk (unshear k rk lw)) w)
      /\ unshear k rk lw = (bc_language_dec_proj1 l).
```

The theorem states that for any decidable $BC(k)$ language L and list of words which agree with L up to length rk, (1) shear (unshear) lw = L, and (2) unshear (shear) L = lw, *i.e.* shearing an unsheared list returns us the input list, and unshearing a sheared language recovers us the language.

(1) amounts to showing unshear does not remove words from its input list or add words of length less than rk, and is straightforward.

(2) amounts to showing `unshear` recovers the block cancelable language L. This direction requires us to show the correctness of our `chucking` condition described above [Sect. 5.2], and involves Ramsey's theorem. In particular, we need to show that `chuck` preserves language agreement between `lw` and `L`, with language agreement defined as follows:

```
Definition agreement_upto (k rk: block_pumping_constant)
                          (l: bc_language_dec k)
                          (lw: list word) (m : nat) :=
  forall w, In w lw <-> (length w <= m + rk
                    /\ bc_language_dec_proj1 l w).
```

First, we show that given a list of words `lw` which agrees with some block cancelable language L up to length m, `chucking` in words of length m+1 results in a list which agrees with L up to length m+1. This further breaks down into two directions: (1) any word added by `chuck` must be in L and of length no more than m+1, and (2) any word in L and of length no more than m+1 must pass `chuck`'s condition check.

```
Lemma IH_chuck_step: forall (k: block_pumping_constant),
  exists (rk: block_pumping_constant),
    forall (l: bc_language_dec k) (lw: list word) (m: nat),
      agreement_upto k rk l lw m ->
       agreement_upto k rk l (chuck k rk (S m) lw) (S m).
```

For the first direction, we have a word w that is either in `lw` or newly `chucked` in, and we must show (i) $|w| \le$ `S m + rk` and (ii) L w. In the case that w is in `lw`, we are done. In the case that w is newly `chucked`, it satisfies the length requirement by definition. By our `chucking` condition, there exists a k-size breakpoint set `lp` with *all* breakpoint pairs forming pumps for w into `lw`. We apply L's block cancellation property with w and `lp` to obtain a cancelled word w′ which agrees with w on membership in L, use the induction hypothesis to obtain that w′ is in L, and thus complete the proof that w is in L.

For the second direction, we have a word w with (i) $|w| \le$ `S m + rk` and (ii) L w, and we must show that it is `chucked` in. This amounts to showing that it satisfies the `chucking` condition: that there exists a k-size breakpoint set containing all cancelable pumps for w into `lw`. This direction turns on Ramsey's theorem, as presented in (Sect. 2). From Ramsey's theorem, we know that for any r(k)-size breakpoint set, there exists a k-size breakpoint set with all pairs either forming cancelable pumps for L or cancelable pumps for L's complement. In the first case, we have exactly the `chucking` condition. In the negative case, we have a contradiction from L's block cancellation property.

`IH_chuck_step` can be seen as the inductive step for `chuck`'s correctness proof. We use it to prove `chuck_length`'s correctness theorem, which shows by induction that `chuck_length` preserves language agreement up to length m + `rk` for any arbitrary m, where `rk` is the length bound of `lw`.

```
Lemma IH_chuck:
 forall (k: block_pumping_constant),
  exists (rk: block_pumping_constant),
   forall (l: bc_language_dec k) (lw: list word) (m: nat),
    agreement_upto k rk l (chuck_length k rk 0 lw) 0 ->
    agreement_upto k rk l (chuck_length k rk m lw) m.
```

This completes the proof of the second obligation for unshear's correctness: unshear adds exactly the same words that its associated block cancelable language L accepts up to some length m + rk. Therefore, by language equality, the resulting language is equivalent to L.

6   Related Work

Automata Theory. Automata and formal languages have been foundational topics to computing since Turing's introduction of his Machine [30]. Chomsky, together with Marcel P. Schützenberger, introduced the Chomsky hierarchy [5,6] of regular, context-free, context-sensitive and recursively enumerable sets of strings. These classes of languages have been extensively studied over the decades since to yield results of both practical and theoretical interest [17].

Pumping Lemmas. Pumping lemmas connect the finite automata mechanism to the words such mechanisms can accept. The best-known pumping lemmas are by Rabin and Scott for regular languages and by Bar-Hilel, Perles, and Shamir for context-free languages [17,24]. Jaffe [18] and Ehrenfeucht, Parikh and Rozenberg [14] pioneered the study of pumping properties that characterize the regular languages. Follow-up work [29] provided evidence that other pumping conditions are insufficient to give a characterization. Varrichio [31] solved an open problem of EPR by establishing that the positive block pumping property (the pump can be repeated but not canceled) also characterizes regular languages. Chak, Freivalds, Stephan and Tan [4] studied the class of languages that are block pumpable but whose complement is not.

Constructive Mathematics. Brouwer originated the ideas of intuitionistic mathematics [16], which removes the Law of Excluded Middle as a universal reasoning principle. The generalized Axiom of Choice is not admitted by intuitionistic logic: Diaconescu's theorem shows that it leads to the Law of Excluded Middle [11].

Martin-Löf developed intuitionistic type theory [22] and the notion of dependent types, thereby contributing to many associated mechanized proof environments. Thierry Coquand took these ideas and built the calculus of constructions [8], which in turn led to the calculus of inductive constructions [27], the underlying logic of the Coq proof assistant [7]. Coq separates computation (*i.e.* Type) from mathematical truths (*i.e.* Prop). The Axiom of Choice, in a type-theoretical context, essentially erases this distinction.

Mechanizations of Automata Theory. Interest in mechanizing automata theory began over thirty years ago [20]. Existing work in formalizing automata theory focuses on languages in the Chomsky hierarchy: Kreitz [20] and Constable *et al.* [10] formalize finite automata-based regular language theory in NuPRL, Dockzal *et al.* [12,13] formalize regular language theory in Coq, Ramos *et al.* [26] formalize context-free language theory in Coq and Zhang *et al.* [32] formalize the Myhill-Nerode theorem using only regular expressions in Isabelle/HOL.

Some of these proofs are constructive, although in a few cases the authors assume that they are working in the Chomsky hierarchy to begin with. For example, Dockzal *et al.* [12] use the Coq type `word -> bool` to represent languages, rather than `word -> Prop` as we do, and then go on to prove Myhill-Nerode constructively. In a certain sense this begs the question, however.

There is also substantial existing work focusing on verified translation and decision procedures for representations of regular languages. Filliatre [15] constructively proves the expressive equivalence of regular expressions and finite automata in Coq, and extracts a functional program which translates a regular expression to a finite automata, Almeida et al. [1] prove the correctness of a partial derivative automata construction from regular expressions in Coq, Coquand and Nipkow et al. [9,25] verify a decision procedure for regular expression equivalence in Coq, and Krauss *et al.* [19] verify a regular expression equivalence checker in HOL/Isabelle etc.

7   Conclusion

To the best of our knowledge, the present work is the first mechanization of language classes, namely the one-sided block pumpable and one-sided block cancelable languages, that are orthogonal to the Chomsky hierarchy and furthermore, cannot be characterized algebraically or automata-theoretically. We have formalized two important and significantly different pumping lemmas which both characterize regularity: Jaffe's pumping lemma and EPR's block pumping lemma. We have also formalized closure properties of one-sided block pumpable languages. We have presented a new Choice-free proof of EPR's theorem by defining an inverse function from block cancelable to well-formed short languages.

References

1. Almeida, J.C.B., Moreira, N., Perira, D., de Sousa, S.M.: Partial derivative automata formalized in Coq. In: The 15th International Conference on Implementation and Application of Automata, pp. 10:59–10:68 (2010)
2. Banach, S., Tarski, A.: Sur la décomposition de ensebles de points en parties respectivement congruentes. Fundam. Math. **6**, 244–277 (1924)
3. Berardi, S., Bezem, M., Coquand, T.: On the computational content of the axiom of choice. J. Symbolic Logic **63**(2), 600–622 (1998)
4. Chak, C.H., Freivalds, R., Stephan, F., Yik, H.T.W.: On block pumpable languages. Theore. Comput. Sci. (2016)

5. Chomsky, N.: On certain formal properties of grammars. Inf. Control **2**(2), 137–167 (1959)
6. Chomsky, N., Schützenberger, M.P.: The algebraic theory of context free languages. Comput. Program. Formal Lang. (1963)
7. The Coq Development Team. The Coq Proof Assistant Reference Manual – Version8.10.0 (2019). http://coq.inria.fr
8. Coquand, T., Huet, G.: The calculus of constructions. Inf. Comput. **76**(2–3), 95–120 (1988)
9. Coquand, T., Siles, V.: A decision procedure for regular expression equivalence in type theory. In: Jouannaud, J.-P., Shao, Z. (eds.) CPP 2011. LNCS, vol. 7086, pp. 119–134. Springer, Heidelberg (2011). https://doi.org/10.1007/978-3-642-25379-9_11
10. Constable, R., Jackson, P.B., Naumov, P., Uribe, J.: Constructively formalizing automata theory. In: Proof, Language and Interaction (1998)
11. Diaconescu, R.: Axiom of choice and complementation. Proc. Am. Math. Soc. **51**, 176–178 (1975)
12. Doczkal, C., Kaiser, J.-O., Smolka, G.: A constructive theory of regular languages in Coq. In: Gonthier, G., Norrish, M. (eds.) CPP 2013. LNCS, vol. 8307, pp. 82–97. Springer, Cham (2013). https://doi.org/10.1007/978-3-319-03545-1_6
13. Doczkal, C., Smolka, G.: Regular language representations in the constructive type theory of coq. J. Autom. Reasoning (2018)
14. Ehrenfeucht, A., Parikh, R., Rozenberg, G.: Pumping lemmas for regular sets. SIAM J. Comput. **10**, 536–541 (1981)
15. Filliatre, J.-C.: Finite automata theory in Coq: a constructive proof of Kleene's theorem. Ecole Normale Supérieure de Lyon Research Report (1997)
16. Van Heijenoort, J.: From Frege to Godel: A Source Book in Mathematical Logic, 1879–1931. Harvard University Press (1967)
17. Hopcroft, J.E., Motwani, R., Ullman, J.D.: Introduction to Automata Theory, Languages and Computation, 3rd edn. Addison Wesley, Boston (2007)
18. Jaffe, J.: A necessary and sufficient pumping lemma for regular languages. ACM SIGACT News **10**(2), 48–49 (1978)
19. Krauss, A., Nipkow, T.: Proof pearl: regular expression equivalence and relation algebra. J. Autom. Reasoning **49**(1), 95–106 (2012)
20. Kreitz, C.: Constructive automata theory implemented with the Nuprl proof development system. Computer Science Technical Reports (1986)
21. Li, E.: Formalizing block pumpable language theory. Capstone Final Report for BSc. (Honours) in Mathematical, Computational and Statistical Sciences, Yale-NUS College (2019)
22. Martin-Löf, P.: An intuitionistic theory of types. Twenty-Five Years of Constructive Type Theory (1998)
23. Nerode, A.: Linear automaton transformations. Proc. Am. Math. Soc. **9**(4), 541–544 (1958)
24. Nijholt, A.: An annotated bibliography of pumping. Bull. EATCS **17**, 34–53 (1982)
25. Nipkow, T., Traytel, D.: Unified decision procedures for regular expression equivalence. Interact. Theorem Proving, 450–466 (2014)
26. Ramos, M.V.M., de Queiroz, R.J.G.B., Moreira, N., Almeida, J.C.B.: On the formalization of some results of context-free language theory. In: Väänänen, J., Hirvonen, Å., de Queiroz, R. (eds.) WoLLIC 2016. LNCS, vol. 9803, pp. 338–357. Springer, Heidelberg (2016). https://doi.org/10.1007/978-3-662-52921-8_21
27. Paulin-Mohring, C.: Introduction to the calculus of inductive constructions. In: Studies in Logic (Mathematical logic and foundations) (2015). 978-1-84890-166-7

28. Ramsey, F.P.: On a problem of formal logic. Proc. London Math. Soc. **s2**(30), 264–286 (1930)
29. Sommerhalder, R.: Classes of languages proof against regular pumping. RAIRO Informatique théorique **14**, 169–180 (1980)
30. Turing, A.M.: On computable numbers, with an application to the entscheidungsproblem: a correction. Proc. London Math. Soc. **43**(6), 544–546 (1937)
31. Varricchio, S.: A pumping condition for regular sets. SIAM J. Comput. **26**(3), 764–771 (1997)
32. Wu, C., Zhang, X., Urban, C.: A formalisation of the myhill-nerode theorem based on regular expressions (proof pearl). In: van Eekelen, M., Geuvers, H., Schmaltz, J., Wiedijk, F. (eds.) ITP 2011. LNCS, vol. 6898, pp. 341–356. Springer, Heidelberg (2011). https://doi.org/10.1007/978-3-642-22863-6_25

Simulations in Rank-Based Büchi Automata Complementation

Yu-Fang Chen[1], Vojtěch Havlena[2], and Ondřej Lengál[2(✉)]

[1] Academia Sinica, Taipei, Taiwan
[2] FIT, IT4I Centre of Excellence, Brno University of Technology,
Brno, Czech Republic
lengal@fit.vutbr.cz

Abstract. Complementation of Büchi automata is an essential technique used in some approaches for termination analysis of programs. The long search for an optimal complementation construction climaxed with the work of Schewe, who proposed a worst-case optimal rank-based procedure that generates complements of a size matching the theoretical lower bound of $(0.76n)^n$, modulo a polynomial factor of $\mathcal{O}(n^2)$. Although worst-case optimal, the procedure in many cases produces automata that are unnecessarily large. In this paper, we propose several ways of how to use the direct and delayed simulation relations to reduce the size of the automaton obtained in the rank-based complementation procedure. Our techniques are based on either (i) ignoring macrostates that cannot be used for accepting a word in the complement or (ii) saturating macrostates with simulation-smaller states, in order to decrease their total number. We experimentally showed that our techniques can indeed considerably decrease the size of the output of the complementation.

1 Introduction

Büchi automata (BA) complementation is a fundamental problem in program analysis and formal verification, from both theoretical and practical angles. It is, for instance, a critical step in some approaches for termination analysis, which is an essential part of establishing total correctness of programs [9,14,19]. Moreover, BA complementation is used as a component of decision procedures of some logics for reasoning about programs, such as S1S capturing a decidable fragment of second-order arithmetic [6] or the temporal logics ETL and QPTL [35].

The study of the BA complementation problem can be traced back to 1962, when Büchi introduced his automaton model in the seminal paper [6] in the context of a decision procedure for the S1S fragment of second-order arithmetic. In the paper, a doubly exponential complementation algorithm based on the infinite Ramsey theorem is proposed. In 1988, Safra [32] introduced a complementation procedure with an $n^{\mathcal{O}(n)}$ upper bound and, in the same year, Michel [28] established an $n!$ lower bound. From the traditional theoretical point of view, the problem was already solved, since exponents in the two bounds matched under

© Springer Nature Switzerland AG 2019
A. W. Lin (Ed.): APLAS 2019, LNCS 11893, pp. 447–467, 2019.
https://doi.org/10.1007/978-3-030-34175-6_23

the $\mathcal{O}$ notation (recall that $n!$ is approximately $(n/e)^n$). From a more practical point of view, a linear factor in an exponent has a significant impact on real-world applications. It was established that the upper bound of Safra's construction is 2^{2n}, so the hunt for an optimal algorithm continued [38]. A series of research efforts participated in narrowing the gap [15,23,24,39,41]. The long journey climaxed with the result of Schewe [33], who proposed an optimal rank-based procedure that generates complements of a size matching the theoretical lower bound of $(0.76n)^n$ found by Yan [41], modulo a polynomial factor of $\mathcal{O}(n^2)$.

Although the algorithm of Schewe is worst-case optimal, it often generates unnecessarily large complements. The standard approach to alleviate this problem is to decrease the size of the input BA before the complementation starts. Since minimization of (nondeterministic) BAs is a PSPACE-complete problem, more lightweight reduction methods are necessary. The most prevalent approaches are those based on various notions of *simulation-based reduction*, such as reductions based on *direct simulation* [7,36], a richer *delayed simulation* [12], or their *multi-pebble* variants [13]. These approaches first compute a simulation relation over the input BA—which can be done with the time complexity $\mathcal{O}(mn)$ [8,20,22,30,31] and $\mathcal{O}(mn^3)$ [12] for direct and delayed simulation respectively, with the number of states n and transitions m—and then construct a *quotient* BA by merging simulation-equivalent states, while preserving the language of the input BA. The other approach is a reduction based on *fair simulation* [18]. The fair simulation cannot, however, be used for quotienting, but still it can be used for merging certain states and removing transitions. The reduced BA is used as the input of the complementation, which often significantly reduces the size of the result.

In this paper, we propose several ways of how to exploit the direct and delayed simulations in BA complementation even further to obtain smaller complements and shorter running times. We focus, in particular, on the optimal *rank-based* complementation procedure of Schewe [33]. Essentially, the rank-based construction is an extension of traditional subset construction for determinizing finite automata, with some additional information kept in each macrostate (a state in the complemented BA) to track the acceptance condition of all runs of the input automaton on a given word. In particular, it stores the *rank* of each state in a macrostate, which, informally, measures the distance to the last accepting state on the corresponding run in the input BA. The main contributions of this paper are the following optimisations of rank-based complementation for BAs, for an input BA $\mathcal{A}$ and the output of the rank-based complementation algorithm $\mathcal{B}$.

1. *Purging*: We use simulation relations over $\mathcal{A}$ to remove some useless macrostates during the construction of $\mathcal{B}$. In particular, if a state p is simulated by q in $\mathcal{A}$, this puts a restriction on the relation between the ranks of runs from p and from q. As a consequence, macrostates that assign ranks violating this restriction can be purged from $\mathcal{B}$.

2. *Saturation*: We saturate macrostates with states that are simulated by the macrostate; this can reduce the total number of states of $\mathcal{B}$ because two or more macrostates can be mapped to a single saturated macrostate. This is

inspired by the technique of Glabbeek and Ploeger that uses *closures* in finite automata determinization [17].

The proposed optimizations are orthogonal to simulation-based size reduction mentioned above. Since the quotienting methods are based on taking only the symmetric fragment of the simulation, i.e., they merge states that simulate *each other*, after the quotienting, there might still be many pairs where the simulation holds in only one way, and can therefore be exploited by our techniques. Since the considered notions of simulation-based quotienting preserve the respective simulations, our techniques can be used to optimize the complementation *at no additional cost*. Our experimental evaluation of the optimizations showed that in many cases, they indeed significantly reduce the size of the complemented BA.

2   Preliminaries

We fix a finite nonempty alphabet Σ and the first infinite ordinal $\omega = \{0, 1, \ldots\}$. For $n \in \omega$, by $[n]$ we denote the set $\{0, \ldots, n\}$. An (infinite) word α is represented as a function $\alpha : \omega \to \Sigma$ where the i-th symbol is denoted as α_i. A finite word w of length $n + 1$ is represented as a function $w : [n] \to \Sigma$. The finite word of length 0 is denoted as ϵ. We abuse notation and sometimes also represent α as an infinite sequence $\alpha = \alpha_0 \alpha_1 \ldots$ and w as a finite sequence $w = w_0 \ldots w_{n-1}$. The suffix $\alpha_i \alpha_{i+1} \ldots$ of α is denoted by $\alpha_{i:\omega}$. We use Σ^ω to denote the set of all infinite words over Σ and Σ^* to denote the set of all finite words. For $L \subseteq \Sigma^*$ we define $L^* = \{u \in \Sigma^* \mid u = w_1 \cdots w_n \wedge \forall 1 \leq i \leq n : w_i \in L\}$ and $L^\omega = \{\alpha \in \Sigma^\omega \mid \alpha = w_1 w_2 \cdots \wedge \forall i \geq 1 : w_i \in L\}$ (note that $\{\epsilon\}^\omega = \emptyset$). Given $L_1, L_2 \subseteq \Sigma^*$, we use $L_1 L_2$ to denote the set $\{w_1 w_2 \mid w_1 \in L_1, w_2 \in L_2\}$.

A (nondeterministic) *Büchi automaton* (BA) over Σ is a quadruple $\mathcal{A} = (Q, \delta, I, F)$ where Q is a finite set of *states*, δ is a *transition function* $\delta : Q \times \Sigma \to 2^Q$, and $I, F \subseteq Q$ are the sets of *initial* and *accepting* states respectively. We sometimes treat δ as a set of transitions $p \xrightarrow{a} q$, for instance, we use $p \xrightarrow{a} q \in \delta$ to denote that $q \in \delta(p, a)$. Moreover, we extend δ to sets of states $P \subseteq Q$ as $\delta(P, a) = \bigcup_{p \in P} \delta(p, a)$. A *run* of $\mathcal{A}$ from $q \in Q$ on an input word α is an infinite sequence $\rho : \omega \to Q$ that starts in q and respects δ, i.e., $\rho_0 = q$ and $\forall i \geq 0 : \rho_i \xrightarrow{\alpha_i} \rho_{i+1} \in \delta$. We say that ρ is accepting iff it contains infinitely many occurrences of some accepting state, i.e., $\exists q_f \in F : |\{i \in \omega \mid \rho_i = q_f\}| = \omega$. A word α is accepted by $\mathcal{A}$ from a state $q \in Q$ if there is an accepting run ρ of $\mathcal{A}$ from q, i.e., $\rho_0 = q$. The set $\mathcal{L}_{\mathcal{A}}(q) = \{\alpha \in \Sigma^\omega \mid \mathcal{A} \text{ accepts } \alpha \text{ from } q\}$ is called the *language* of q (in $\mathcal{A}$). Given a set of states $R \subseteq Q$, we define the language of R as $\mathcal{L}_{\mathcal{A}}(R) = \bigcup_{q \in R} \mathcal{L}_{\mathcal{A}}(q)$ and the language of $\mathcal{A}$ as $\mathcal{L}(\mathcal{A}) = \mathcal{L}_{\mathcal{A}}(I)$. For a pair of states p and q in $\mathcal{A}$, we use $p \subseteq_{\mathcal{L}} q$ to denote $\mathcal{L}_{\mathcal{A}}(p) \subseteq \mathcal{L}_{\mathcal{A}}(q)$.

Without loss of generality, in this paper, we assume $\mathcal{A}$ to be complete, i.e., for every state q and symbol a, it holds that $\delta(q, a) \neq \emptyset$. A *trace* over a word α is an infinite sequence $\pi = q_0 \xrightarrow{\alpha_0} q_1 \xrightarrow{\alpha_1} \cdots$ such that $\rho = q_0 q_1 \ldots$ is a run of $\mathcal{A}$ over α from q_0. We say π is *fair* if it contains infinitely many accepting states. Moreover, we use $p \xrightarrow{w} q$ for $w \in \Sigma^*$ to denote that q is reachable from p over the word w; if a path from p to q over w contains an accepting state, we can write $p \overset{w}{\underset{F}{\leadsto}} q$. In this paper, we fix a complete BA $\mathcal{A} = (Q, \delta, I, F)$.

2.1   Simulations

We introduce simulation relations between states of a BA $\mathcal{A}$ using the game semantics in a similar manner as in the extensive study of Clemente and Mayr [26]. In particular, in a *simulation game* between two players (called Spoiler and Duplicator) in $\mathcal{A}$ from a pair of states (p_0, r_0), for any (infinite) trace over a word α that Spoiler takes starting from p_0, Duplicator tries to mimic the trace starting from r_0. On the other hand, Spoiler tries to find a trace that Duplicator cannot mimic. The game starts in the configuration (p_0, r_0) and every i-th round proceeds by, first, Spoiler choosing a transition $p_i \overset{\alpha_i}{\longrightarrow} p_{i+1}$ and, second, Duplicator mimicking Spoiler by choosing a matching transition $r_i \overset{\alpha_i}{\longrightarrow} r_{i+1}$ over the same symbol α_i. The next game configuration is (p_{i+1}, r_{i+1}). Suppose that $\pi_p = p_0 \overset{\alpha_0}{\longrightarrow} p_1 \overset{\alpha_1}{\longrightarrow} \cdots$ and $\pi_r = r_0 \overset{\alpha_0}{\longrightarrow} r_1 \overset{\alpha_1}{\longrightarrow} \cdots$ are the two (infinite) traces constructed during the game. Duplicator *wins* the simulation game if $\mathcal{C}^x(\pi_p, \pi_r)$ holds, where $\mathcal{C}^x(\pi_p, \pi_r)$ is a condition that depends on the particular simulation. In the current paper, we consider the following simulation relations:

- **direct** [11]: $\mathcal{C}^{di}(\pi_p, \pi_r) \overset{\text{def}}{\Longleftrightarrow} \forall i : p_i \in F \Rightarrow r_i \in F$,
- **delayed** [12]: $\mathcal{C}^{de}(\pi_p, \pi_r) \overset{\text{def}}{\Longleftrightarrow} \forall i : p_i \in F \Rightarrow \exists k \geq i : r_k \in F$, and
- **fair** [21]: $\mathcal{C}^f(\pi_p, \pi_r) \overset{\text{def}}{\Longleftrightarrow}$ if π_p is fair, then π_r is fair.

A maximal x-simulation relation $\preceq_x \subseteq Q \times Q$, for $x \in \{di, de, f\}$, is defined such that $p \preceq_x r$ iff Duplicator has a winning strategy in the simulation game with the winning condition $\mathcal{C}^x$ starting from (p, r). Formally, we define a strategy to be a (total) mapping $\sigma : Q \times (Q \times \Sigma \times Q) \to Q$ such that $\sigma(r, p \overset{a}{\to} p') \in \delta(r, a)$, i.e., if Duplicator is in state r and Spoiler selects a transition $p \overset{a}{\to} p'$, the strategy picks a state r' such that $r \overset{a}{\to} r' \in \delta$ (and because $\mathcal{A}$ is complete, such a transition always exists). Note that Duplicator cannot look ahead at Spoiler's future moves. We use σ_x to denote any winning strategy of Duplicator in the $\mathcal{C}^x$ simulation game. Let σ_x and σ_x' be a pair of winning strategies in the $\mathcal{C}^x$ simulation game. We say that σ_x is *dominated* by σ_x' if for all states p and all transitions $q \overset{a}{\to} q'$ it holds that $\sigma_x(p, q \overset{a}{\to} q') \preceq_x \sigma_x'(p, q \overset{a}{\to} q')$, and that σ_x is *strictly dominated* by σ_x' if σ_x is dominated by σ_x' and σ_x does not dominate σ_x'. A strategy is *dominating* if it is not strictly dominated by any other strategy. Strategies are also lifted to traces as follows: let π_p be as above, then $\sigma(r_0, \pi_p) = r_0 \overset{\alpha_0}{\longrightarrow} r_1 \overset{\alpha_1}{\longrightarrow} \cdots$ where for all $i \leq 0$ it holds that $\sigma(r_i, p_i \overset{\alpha_i}{\longrightarrow} p_{i+1}) = r_{i+1}$. The considered simulation relations form the following hierarchy: $\preceq_{di} \subseteq \preceq_{de} \subseteq \preceq_f \subseteq \subseteq_{\mathcal{L}}$. Note that every maximal simulation relation is a preorder, i.e., reflexive and transitive.

2.2   Run DAGs

In this section, we recall the terminology from [33] (which is a minor modification of the terminology from [24]). We fix the definition of the *run DAG* of $\mathcal{A}$ over a word α to be a DAG (directed acyclic graph) $\mathcal{G}_\alpha = (V, E)$ of vertices V and edges E where

- $V \subseteq Q \times \omega$ s.t. $(q, i) \in V$ iff there is a run ρ of $\mathcal{A}$ over α with $\rho_i = q$,
- $E \subseteq V \times V$ s.t. $((q, i), (q', i')) \in E$ iff $i' = i + 1$ and $q' \in \delta(q, \alpha_i)$.

Given $\mathcal{G}_\alpha$ as above, we will write $(p, i) \in \mathcal{G}_\alpha$ to denote that $(p, i) \in V$. We call (p, i) *accepting* if p is an accepting state. $\mathcal{G}_\alpha$ is *rejecting* if it contains no path with infinitely many accepting vertices. A vertex $(p, i) \in \mathcal{G}_\alpha$ is *finite* if the set of vertices reachable from (p, i) is finite, *infinite* if it is not finite, and *endangered* if (p, i) cannot reach an accepting vertex.

We assign ranks to vertices of run DAGs as follows: Let $\mathcal{G}_\alpha^0 = \mathcal{G}_\alpha$ and $j = 0$. Repeat the following steps until the fixpoint or for at most $2n + 1$ steps, where n is the number of states of $\mathcal{A}$.

- Set $rank_\alpha(p, i) := j$ for all finite vertices (p, i) of $\mathcal{G}_\alpha^j$ and let $\mathcal{G}_\alpha^{j+1}$ be $\mathcal{G}_\alpha^j$ minus the vertices with the rank j.
- Set $rank_\alpha(p, i) := j + 1$ for all endangered vertices (p, i) of $\mathcal{G}_\alpha^{j+1}$ and let $\mathcal{G}_\alpha^{j+2}$ be $\mathcal{G}_\alpha^{j+1}$ minus the vertices with the rank $j + 1$.
- Set $j := j + 2$.

For all vertices v that have not been assigned a rank yet, we assign $rank_\alpha(v) := \omega$. (Note that since $\mathcal{A}$ is complete, then $\mathcal{G}_\alpha^1 = \mathcal{G}_\alpha^0$.)

Lemma 1. *If* $\alpha \notin \mathcal{L}(\mathcal{A})$, *then* $0 \leq rank_\alpha(v) \leq 2n$ *for all* $v \in \mathcal{G}_\alpha$. *Moreover, if* $\alpha \in \mathcal{L}(\mathcal{A})$, *then there is a vertex* $(p, 0) \in \mathcal{G}_\alpha$ *s.t.* $rank_\alpha(p, 0) = \omega$.

Proof. Follows from Corollary 3.3 in [24].   □

3   Complementing Büchi Automata

We use as the starting point the complementation procedure of Schewe [33, Section 3.1], which we denote as COMPS (the 'S' stands for 'Schewe'). The procedure works with the notion of level rankings. Given $n = |Q|$, a *(level) ranking* is a function $f : Q \to [2n]$ such that $\{f(q_f) \mid q_f \in F\} \subseteq \{0, 2, \ldots, 2n\}$, i.e., f assigns even ranks to accepting states of $\mathcal{A}$. [1] For a ranking f, the *rank of* f is defined as $rank(f) = \max\{f(q) \mid q \in Q\}$. For a set of states $S \subseteq Q$, we call f to be *S-tight* if (i) it has an odd rank r, (ii) $\{f(s) \mid s \in S\} \supseteq \{1, 3, \ldots, r\}$, and (iii) $\{f(q) \mid q \notin S\} = \{0\}$. A ranking is *tight* if it is Q-tight; we use $\mathcal{T}$ to denote

---

[1]   Note that our basic definitions slightly differs from the ones in Sect. 2.3 of [33]. This is because of a typo in [33]; indeed, if the procedure from [33] is implemented as is, the output does not accept the complement (there might be a macrostate (S, O, f) where S contains accepting states and O is empty, and, therefore, the whole macrostate is accepting, which is wrong).

the set of all tight rankings. For a pair of rankings f and f', a set $S \subseteq Q$, and a symbol $a \in \Sigma$, we use $f' \leq_a^S f$ iff for every $q \in S$ and $q' \in \delta(q, a)$ it holds that $f'(q') \leq f(q)$.

The COMP$_S$ procedure constructs the BA $\mathcal{B}_S = (Q', \delta', I', F')$ whose components are defined as follows:

- $Q' = Q_1 \cup Q_2$ where
    - $Q_1 = 2^Q$ and
    - $Q_2 = \{(S, O, f, i) \in 2^Q \times 2^Q \times \mathcal{T} \times \{0, 2, \ldots, 2n - 2\} \mid$
        f is S-tight, $O \subseteq S \cap f^{-1}(i)\}$,
- $I' = \{I\}$,
- $\delta' = \delta_1 \cup \delta_2 \cup \delta_3$ where
    - $\delta_1 : Q_1 \times \Sigma \to 2^{Q_1}$ such that $\delta_1(S, a) = \{\delta(S, a)\}$,
    - $\delta_2 : Q_1 \times \Sigma \to 2^{Q_2}$ such that $\delta_2(S, a) = \{(S', \emptyset, f, 0) \mid S' = \delta(S, a),$
        f is S'-tight$\}$, and
    - $\delta_3 : Q_2 \times \Sigma \to 2^{Q_2}$ such that $(S', O', f', i') \in \delta_3((S, O, f, i), a)$ iff $S' = \delta(S, a), f' \leq_a^S f, rank(f) = rank(f'), f'$ is S'-tight, and
        * $i' = (i + 2) \mod (rank(f') + 1)$ and $O' = f'^{-1}(i')$ if $O = \emptyset$ or
        * $i' = i$ and $O' = \delta(O, a) \cap f'^{-1}(i)$ if $O \neq \emptyset$, and
- $F' = \{\emptyset\} \cup ((2^Q \times \{\emptyset\} \times \mathcal{T} \times \omega) \cap Q_2)$.

Intuitively, COMP$_S$ is an extension of the classical subset construction for determinization of finite automata. In particular, Q_1, δ_1, and I_1 constitute the deterministic finite automaton obtained from $\mathcal{A}$ using the subset construction. The automaton can, however, nondeterministically guess a point at which it will make a transition to a *macrostate* (S, O, f, i) in the Q_2 part; this guess corresponds to a level in the run DAG of the accepted word from which the ranks of all levels form an S-tight ranking, where the S component of the macrostate is again a subset from the subset construction. In the Q_2 part, $\mathcal{B}_S$ makes sure that in order for a word to be accepted by $\mathcal{B}_S$, all runs of $\mathcal{A}$ over the word need to touch an accepting state only finitely many times. This is ensured by the f component, which, roughly speaking, maps states to ranks of corresponding vertices in the run DAG over the given word. The O component is used for a standard cut-point construction, and is used to make sure that all runs that have reached an accepting state in $\mathcal{A}$ will eventually leave it (this can happen for different runs at a different point). The S, O, and f components were already present in [24]. The i component was introduced by Schewe to improve the complexity of the construction; it is used to cycle over phases, where in each phase we focus on cut-points of a different rank. See [33] for a more elaborate exposition.

Proposition 1 (Corollary 3.3 in [33]). $\mathcal{L}(\mathcal{B}_S) = \overline{\mathcal{L}(\mathcal{A})}$.

4 Purging Macrostates with Incompatible Rankings

Our first optimisation is based on removing from $\mathcal{B}_S$ macrostates $(S, O, f, i) \in Q_2$ whose level ranking f assigns some states of S an unnecessarily high rank.

Intuitively, when S contains a state p and a state q such that p is (directly) simulated by q, i.e. $p \preceq_{di} q$, then $f(p)$ needs to be at most $f(q)$. This is because in any word α and its run DAG $\mathcal{G}_\alpha$ in $\mathcal{A}$, if p and q are at the same level i of $\mathcal{G}_\alpha$, then the ranks of their vertices v_p and v_q at the given level are either both ω (when $\alpha \in \mathcal{L}(\mathcal{A})$), or such that $rank_\alpha(v_p) \leq rank_\alpha(v_q)$ otherwise. This is because, intuitively, the DAG rooted in v_p in $\mathcal{G}_\alpha$ is isomorphic to a subgraph of the DAG rooted in v_q.

Formally, consider the following predicate on macrostates of $\mathcal{B}_S$:

$$\mathcal{P}_{di}(S, O, f, i) \quad \text{iff} \quad \exists p, q \in S : p \preceq_{di} q \wedge f(p) > f(q). \tag{1}$$

We modify COMP$_S$ to purge macrostates that satisfy $\mathcal{P}_{di}$. That is, we create a new procedure PURGE$_{di}$ obtained from COMP$_S$ by modifying the definition of $\mathcal{B}_S$ such that all occurrences of Q_2 are substituted by Q_2^{di} and

$$Q_2^{di} = Q_2 \setminus \{(S, O, f, i) \in Q_2 \mid \mathcal{P}_{di}(S, O, f, i)\}. \tag{2}$$

We denote the BA obtained from PURGE$_{di}$ as $\mathcal{B}_S^{di}$. The following lemma, proved in Sect. 4.1 states the correctness of this construction.

Lemma 2. $\mathcal{L}(\mathcal{B}_S^{di}) = \mathcal{L}(\mathcal{B}_S)$

The following natural question arises: Is it possible to extend the purging technique from direct simulation to other notions of simulation? For *fair* simulation, this cannot be done. The reason is that, for a pair of states p and q s.t. $p \preceq_f q$, it can happen that for a word $\beta \in \Sigma^\omega$, there can be a trace from p over β that finitely many times touches an accepting state (i.e., a vertex of p in the corresponding run DAG can have any rank between 0 and $2n$), while all traces from q over β can completely avoid touching any accepting state. From the point of view of fair simulation, these are both unfair traces, and, therefore, disregarded.

On the other hand, *delayed* simulation—which is often much richer than direct simulation—can be used, with a small change. Intuitively, the delayed simulation can be used because $p \preceq_{de} q$ guarantees that on every level of trees in $\mathcal{G}_\alpha$ rooted in v_p and in v_q respectively, the rank of the vertex v_p is at most by one larger than the rank of vertex v_q (or by any number smaller). Formally, let $\mathcal{P}_{de}$ be the following predicate on macrostates of $\mathcal{B}_S$:

$$\mathcal{P}_{de}(S, O, f, i) \quad \text{iff} \quad \exists p, q \in S : p \preceq_{de} q \wedge f(p) > \lceil f(q) \rceil, \tag{3}$$

where $\lceil x \rceil$ for $x \in \omega$ denotes the smallest even number greater or equal to x and $\lceil \omega \rceil = \omega$. Similarly as above, we create a new procedure, called PURGE$_{de}$, which is obtained from COMP$_S$ by modifying the definition of $\mathcal{B}_S$ such that all occurrences of Q_2 are substituted by Q_2^{de} and

$$Q_2^{de} = Q_2 \setminus \{(S, O, f, i) \in Q_2 \mid \mathcal{P}_{de}(S, O, f, i)\}. \tag{4}$$

We denote the BA obtained from PURGE$_{de}$ as $\mathcal{B}_S^{de}$.

Lemma 3. $\mathcal{L}(\mathcal{B}_S^{de}) = \mathcal{L}(\mathcal{B}_S)$

The use of $\lceil f(q) \rceil$ in $\mathcal{P}_{de}$ results in the fact that the two purging techniques are incomparable. For instance, consider a macrostate $(\{p, q\}, \emptyset, \{p \mapsto 2, q \mapsto 1\}, 0)$ such that $p \preceq_{di} q$ and $p \preceq_{de} q$. Then the macrostate will be purged in PURGE_{di}, but not in PURGE_{de}.

The two techniques can, however, be easily combined into a third procedure PURGE_{di+de}, when Q_2 is substituted in COMPS with Q_2^{di+de} defined as

$$Q_2^{di+de} = Q_2 \setminus \{(S, O, f, i) \in Q_2 \mid \mathcal{P}_{di}(S, O, f, i) \vee \mathcal{P}_{de}(S, O, f, i)\}. \quad (5)$$

We denote the resulting BA as $\mathcal{B}_S^{di+de}$.

Lemma 4. $\mathcal{L}(\mathcal{B}_S^{di+de}) = \mathcal{L}(\mathcal{B}_S)$

4.1   Proofs of Lemmas 2, 3, and 4

We first give a lemma that an x-strategy σ_x preserves an x-simulation $\preceq_x$.

Lemma 5. *Let $\preceq_x$ be an x-simulation (for $x \in \{di, de, f\}$). Then, the following holds: $\forall p, q \in Q : p \preceq_x q \wedge p \xrightarrow{a} p' \in \delta \Rightarrow \exists q' \in Q : q \xrightarrow{a} q' \in \delta \wedge p' \preceq_x q'$.*

Proof. Let $p, q \in Q$ such that $p \preceq_x q$ and $p \xrightarrow{a} p' \in \delta$, and let π_p be a trace starting from p with the first transition $p \xrightarrow{a} p'$. From the definition of x-simulation, there is a winning Duplicator strategy σ_x; let $\pi_q = \sigma_x(q', \pi_p)$ and let $q \xrightarrow{a} q'$ be the first transition of π_q. Let $\pi_{p'}$ and $\pi_{r'}$ be traces obtained from π_p and π_r by removing their first transitions. It is easy to see that if $\mathcal{C}^x(\pi_p, \pi_r)$ then also $\mathcal{C}^x(\pi_{p'}, \pi_{r'})$ for any $x \in \{di, de, f\}$. It follows that σ_x is also a winning Duplicator strategy from (p', r'). $\qquad \square$

Next, we focus on delayed simulation and the proof of Lemma 3. In the next lemma, we show that if there is a pair of vertices on some level of the run DAG where one vertex delay-simulates the other one, there exists a relation between their rankings. This will be used to purge some useless rankings from the complemented BA.

Lemma 6. *Let $p, q \in Q$ such that $p \preceq_{de} q$ and $\mathcal{G}_\alpha = (V, E)$ be the run DAG of $\mathcal{A}$ over α. For all $i \geq 0$, it holds that $(p, i) \in V \wedge (q, i) \in V \Rightarrow rank_\alpha(p, i) \leq \lceil rank_\alpha(q, i) \rceil$.*

Proof. Consider some $(p, i) \in V$ and $(q, i) \in V$. First, suppose that $rank_\alpha(q, i) = \omega$. Since the rank can be at most ω, it will always hold that $rank_\alpha(p, i) \leq \lceil rank_\alpha(q, i) \rceil$.

On the other hand, suppose that $rank_\alpha(q, i)$ is finite, i.e., $\alpha_{i:\omega}$ is not accepted by q. Then, due to Lemma 1, $0 \leq rank_\alpha(q, i) \leq 2n$. Because $p \preceq_{de} q$, it holds that $\alpha_{i:\omega}$ is also not accepted by p, and therefore also $0 \leq rank_\alpha(p, i) \leq 2n$. We now need to show that $0 \leq rank_\alpha(p, i) \leq \lceil rank_\alpha(q, i) \rceil \leq 2n$.

Let $\{\mathcal{G}_\alpha^k\}_{k=0}^{2n+1}$ be the sequence of run DAGs obtained from $\mathcal{G}_\alpha$ in the ranking procedure from Sect. 2.2. In the following text we use the abbreviation $v \in \mathcal{G}_\alpha^m \setminus \mathcal{G}_\alpha^n$ for $v \in \mathcal{G}_\alpha^m \wedge v \notin \mathcal{G}_\alpha^n$. Since the rank of a node (r, j) is given as the number l s.t. $(r, j) \in \mathcal{G}_\alpha^l \setminus \mathcal{G}_\alpha^{l+1}$, we will finish the proof of this lemma by proving the following claim:

Claim. Let k and l be s.t. $(p, i) \in \mathcal{G}_\alpha^k \setminus \mathcal{G}_\alpha^{k+1}$ and $(q, i) \in \mathcal{G}_\alpha^l \setminus \mathcal{G}_\alpha^{l+1}$. Then $k \leq \lceil l \rceil$.

Proof: We prove the claim by induction on l.

- Base case: ($l = 0$) Since we assume $\mathcal{A}$ is complete, no vertex in $\mathcal{G}_\alpha^0$ is finite.

  ($l = 1$) We prove that if (q, i) is endangered in $\mathcal{G}_\alpha^1$, then (p, i) is endangered in $\mathcal{G}_\alpha^1$ as well (so both would be removed in $\mathcal{G}_\alpha^2$). For the sake of contradiction, assume that (q, i) is endangered in $\mathcal{G}_\alpha^1$ and (p, i) is not. Therefore, since $\mathcal{G}_\alpha^1$ contains no finite vertices, there is an infinite path π from (p, i) s.t. π contains at least one accepting state. In the following, we abuse notation and, given a strategy σ_{de} and a state $s \in Q$, use $\sigma_{de}((s, i), \pi)$ to denote the path $(s_0, i)(s_1, i + 1)(s_2, i + 2) \ldots$ such that $s_0 = s$ and $\forall j \geq 0$, it holds that $s_{j+1} = \sigma_{de}(s_j, r_{i+j} \xrightarrow{a_{i+j}} r_{i+j+1})$ where $\pi_x = (r_x, x)$ for every $x \geq 0$. Since $p \preceq_{de} q$, there is a corresponding infinite path $\pi' = \sigma_{de}((q, i), \pi)$ that also contains at least one accepting state. Therefore, (q, i) is not endangered, a contradiction to the assumption, so we conclude that $l = 1 \Rightarrow k = 1$.

- Inductive step: We assume the claim holds for all $l < 2j$ and prove the inductive step for even and odd steps independently.

  ($l = 2j$) We prove that if (q, i) is finite in $\mathcal{G}_\alpha^l$ (and therefore would be removed in $\mathcal{G}_\alpha^{l+1}$), then either $(p, i) \notin \mathcal{G}_\alpha^l$, or (p, i) is also finite in $\mathcal{G}_\alpha^l$. For the sake of contradiction, we assume that (q, i) is finite in $\mathcal{G}_\alpha^l$ and that (p, i) is in $\mathcal{G}_\alpha^l$, but is not finite there (and, therefore, $k > l$). Since (p, i) is not finite in $\mathcal{G}_\alpha^l$, there is an infinite path π from (p, i) in $\mathcal{G}_\alpha^l$. Because $p \preceq_{de} q$, it follows that there is an infinite path $\pi' = \sigma_{de}((q, i), \pi)$ in $\mathcal{G}_\alpha^0$ (π' is not in $\mathcal{G}_\alpha^l$ because (q, i) is finite there). Using Lemma 5 (possibly multiple times) and the fact that (q, i) is finite, we can find vertices (p', x) in π and (q', x) in π' s.t. $p' \preceq_{de} q'$ and (q', x) is not in $\mathcal{G}_\alpha^l$, therefore, $(q', x) \in \mathcal{G}_\alpha^e \setminus \mathcal{G}_\alpha^{e+1}$ for some $e < l$. Because $(p', x) \in \mathcal{G}_\alpha^l$ and it is not finite (π is infinite), it follows that $(p', x) \in \mathcal{G}_\alpha^f \setminus \mathcal{G}_\alpha^{f+1}$ for some $f > l$, and since $e < l < f$, we have that $f \not\leq e+1$, implying $f \not\leq \lceil e \rceil$, which is in contradiction to the induction hypothesis.

  ($l = 2j+1$) We prove that if (q, i) is endangered in $\mathcal{G}_\alpha^l$ (and therefore would be removed in $\mathcal{G}_\alpha^{l+1}$), then either $(p, i) \notin \mathcal{G}_\alpha^l$, or (p, i) is removed at the latest in $\mathcal{G}_\alpha^{l+1}$. For the sake of contradiction, assume that (q, i) is endangered in $\mathcal{G}_\alpha^l$ while (p, i) is removed later than in $\mathcal{G}_\alpha^{l+1}$. Therefore, since $\mathcal{G}_\alpha^l$ contains no finite vertices (they were removed in the $(l - 1)$-th step), there is an infinite path π from (p, i) s.t. π contains at least one accepting state. Because $p \preceq_{de} q$, there is a corresponding path $\pi' = \sigma_{de}((q, i), \pi)$ from (q, i) in $\mathcal{G}_\alpha^0$ that also contains at least one accepting state and moreover $\pi' \notin \mathcal{G}_\alpha^l$. Since π' has an infinite number of states (and at least one accepting), not all states from π' were removed in $\mathcal{G}_\alpha^{l-1}$, i.e., there is at least one node with rank less or equal to $l - 2$. Using Lemma 5 (also possibly multiple times) we can hence find states (p', x) in π and (q', x) in π' s.t. $p' \preceq_{de} q'$ and (q', x) is not in $\mathcal{G}_\alpha^l$ and has a rank less or equal to $l - 2$, therefore, $(q', x) \in \mathcal{G}_\alpha^e \setminus \mathcal{G}_\alpha^{e+1}$ for some $e < l - 1$. Because $(p', x) \in \mathcal{G}_\alpha^l$, it follows that $(p', x) \in \mathcal{G}_\alpha^f \setminus \mathcal{G}_\alpha^{f+1}$ for some $f \geq l$, and, therefore, $f \not\leq e + 1$, which is in contradiction to the induction hypothesis. ∎

This concludes the proof. □

Lemma 7. *Let $p, q \in Q$ such that $p \preceq_{di} q$ and $\mathcal{G}_\alpha = (V, E)$ be the run DAG of $\mathcal{A}$ over α. For all $i \geq 0$, it holds that $(p, i) \in V \wedge (q, i) \in V \Rightarrow rank_\alpha(p, i) \leq rank_\alpha(q, i)$.*

Proof. Can be obtained as a simplified version of the proof of Lemma 6.   □

We are now ready to prove Lemma 3.

Lemma 3. $\mathcal{L}(\mathcal{B}_S^{de}) = \mathcal{L}(\mathcal{B}_S)$

Proof. ($\subseteq$) Follows directly from the fact that $\mathcal{B}_S^{de}$ is obtained by removing states from $\mathcal{B}_S$.
($\supseteq$) Let $\alpha \in \mathcal{L}(\mathcal{B}_S)$. As shown in the proof of Lemma 3.2 in [33], there are two cases. The first case is when all vertices of $\mathcal{G}_\alpha$ are finite, which we do not need to consider, since we assume complete automata.
The other case is when $\mathcal{G}_\alpha$ contains an infinite vertex. In this case, $\mathcal{B}_S$ contains an accepting run

$$\rho = S_0 S_1 \ldots S_p (S_{p+1}, O_{p+1}, f_{p+1}, i_{p+1})(S_{p+2}, O_{p+2}, f_{p+2}, i_{p+2}) \ldots$$

with

- $S_0 = I, O_{p+1} = \emptyset$, and $i_{p+1} = 0$,
- $S_{j+1} = \delta(S_j, \alpha_j)$ for all $j \in \omega$,

and, for all $j > p$,

- $O_{j+1} = f_{j+1}^{-1}(i_{j+1})$ if $O_j = \emptyset$ or
  $O_{j+1} = \delta(O_j, \alpha_j) \cap f_{j+1}^{-1}(i_{j+1})$ if $O_j \neq \emptyset$, respectively,
- f_j is the S_j-tight level ranking that maps each $q \in S_j$ to the rank of $(q, j) \in \mathcal{G}_\alpha$,
- $i_{j+1} = i_j$ if $O_j \neq \emptyset$ or
  $i_{j+1} = (i_j + 2) \mod (rank(f) + 1)$ if $O_j = \emptyset$, respectively.

The ranks assigned by f_j to states of S_j match the ranks of the corresponding vertices in $\mathcal{G}_\alpha$.
⊛ Using Lemma 6, we conclude that ρ contains no macrostate (S, O, f, j) where $f(p) > \lceil f(q) \rceil$ and $p \preceq_{de} q$ for $p, q \in S$. Therefore, ρ is also an accepting run in $\mathcal{B}_S^{de}$. (We use ⊛ to refer to this paragraph later.)   □

Lemma 2. $\mathcal{L}(\mathcal{B}_S^{di}) = \mathcal{L}(\mathcal{B}_S)$

Proof. The same as for Lemma 3 with ⊛ substituted by the following:
⊛ Using Lemma 7, we conclude that ρ contains no macrostate (S, O, f, j) where $f(p) > f(q)$ and $p \preceq_{di} q$ for $p, q \in S$. So ρ is also an accepting run in $\mathcal{B}_S^{di}$.   □

Lemma 4. $\mathcal{L}(\mathcal{B}_S^{di+de}) = \mathcal{L}(\mathcal{B}_S)$

Proof. The same as for Lemma 3 with ⊛ substituted by the following:
⊛ Using Lemmas 7 and 6, we conclude that ρ contains no macrostate (S, O, f, j) where either $f(p) > f(q)$ and $p \preceq_{di} q$, or $f(p) > \lceil f(q) \rceil$ and $p \preceq_{de} q$ for $p, q \in S$. Therefore, ρ is also an accepting run in $\mathcal{B}_S^{di+de}$.   □

5   Saturation of Macrostates

Our second optimisation is inspired by an optimisation of determinisation of classical finite automata from [17, Section 5]. Their optimisation is based on saturating every constructed macrostate in the classical subset construction with all direct-simulation-smaller states. This can reduce the total number of states of the determinized automaton because two or more macrostates can be mapped to a single saturated macrostate. (In Sect. 5.2, we show why an analogue of their *compression* cannot be used.)

We show that a similar technique can be applied to BAs. We do not restrain ourselves to direct simulation, though, and generalize the technique to delayed simulation. In particular, in our optimisation, we saturate the S components of macrostates (S, O, f, i) obtained in COMPS with all $\preceq_{de}$-smaller states. Formally, we modify COMPS by substituting the definition of the constructed transition function δ' with δ'_{Sat} defined as follows:

- $\delta'_{Sat} = \delta_1^{Sat} \cup \delta_2^{Sat} \cup \delta_3^{Sat}$ where
    - $\delta_1^{Sat} : Q_1 \times \Sigma \to 2^{Q_1}$ with $\delta_1^{Sat}(S, a) = \{cl[\delta(S, a)]\}$,
    - $\delta_2^{Sat} : Q_1 \times \Sigma \to 2^{Q_2}$ with $\delta_2^{Sat}(S, a) = \{(S', \emptyset, f, 0) \mid S' = cl[\delta(S, a)]\}$, and
    - $\delta_3^{Sat} : Q_2 \times \Sigma \to 2^{Q_2}$ with $(S', O', f', i') \in \delta_3^{Sat}((S, O, f, i), a)$ iff $S' = cl[\delta(S, a)], f' \leq_a^S f, rank(f) = rank(f')$, and
        * $i' = (i + 2) \mod (rank(f') + 1)$ and $O' = f'^{-1}(i')$ if $O = \emptyset$ or
        * $i' = i$ and $O' = \delta(O, a) \cap f'^{-1}(i)$ if $O \neq \emptyset$,

where $cl[S] = \{q \in Q \mid \exists s \in S : q \preceq_{de} s\}$. We denote the obtained procedure as SATURATE and the obtained BA as $\mathcal{B}_{Sat}$.

Lemma 8. $\mathcal{L}(\mathcal{B}_{Sat}) = \mathcal{L}(\mathcal{B}_S)$

Obviously, as direct simulation is stronger than delayed simulation, the previous technique can also use direct simulation only (e.g., when computing the full delayed simulation is computationally too demanding). Moreover, SATURATE is also compatible with all PURGE$_x$ algorithms for $x \in \{di, de, di + de\}$ (because they just remove macrostates with incompatible rankings from Q_2)—we call the combined versions PURGE$_x$+SATURATE and the complement BAs they output $\mathcal{B}_{Sat}^x$.

Lemma 9. $\mathcal{L}(\mathcal{B}_{Sat}^{di}) = \mathcal{L}(\mathcal{B}_{Sat}^{de}) = \mathcal{L}(\mathcal{B}_{Sat}^{di+de}) = \mathcal{L}(\mathcal{B}_S)$

5.1   Proofs of Lemmas 8 and 9

We start with a lemma, used later, that talks about languages of states related by delayed simulation when there is a path between them.

Lemma 10. *For $p, q \in Q$ such that $p \preceq_{de} q$, let $L_\top = \{w \in \Sigma^* \mid p \overset{w}{\underset{F}{\rightsquigarrow}} q\}$ and $L_\perp = \{w \in \Sigma^* \mid p \overset{w}{\rightsquigarrow} q\}$. Then $L(q) \supseteq (L_\perp^* L_\top)^\omega$.*

Proof. First we prove the following claim:

Claim. For every word $\alpha = w_0 w_1 w_2 \cdots \in \Sigma^\omega$ where $w_i \in L_\top \cup L_\bot$, we can construct a trace $\pi = p \overset{w_0}{\leadsto} q_0 \overset{w_1}{\leadsto} q_1 \overset{w_2}{\leadsto} \cdots$ over α such that $p \preceq_{de} q_0$ and $q_i \preceq_{de} q_{i+1}$ for all $i \geq 0$.

<u>Proof:</u> We assign $q_0 := q$ and construct the rest of π by the following inductive construction.

- Base case: ($i = 0$) From the assumption it holds that $p \overset{w_1}{\leadsto} q_0$ and $p \preceq_{de} q_0$. From Lemma 5 there is some $r \in Q$ s.t. $q_0 \overset{w_1}{\leadsto} r$ and $q_0 \preceq_{de} r$. We assign $q_1 := r$, so $q_0 \preceq_{de} q_1$.
- Inductive step: Let $\pi' = p \overset{w_0}{\leadsto} q_0 \overset{w_1}{\leadsto} \cdots \overset{w_i}{\leadsto} q_i$ be a prefix of a trace such that $q_j \preceq_{de} q_{j+1}$ for every $j < i$. From the transitivity of $\preceq_{de}$, it follows that $p \preceq_{de} q_i$. From Lemma 5 there is some $r \in Q$ s.t. $q_i \overset{w_i}{\leadsto} r$ and $q \preceq_{de} r$. We assign $q_{i+1} := r$, so $q_i \preceq_{de} q_{i+1}$. ∎

Consider a word $\alpha \in (L_\bot^* L_\top)^\omega$ such that $\alpha = w_0 w_1 w_2 \ldots$ for $w_i \in L_\top \cup L_\bot$. We show that $\alpha \in \mathcal{L}(q)$. According to the previous claim, we can construct a trace $\pi = p \overset{w_0}{\leadsto} q = q_0 \overset{w_1}{\leadsto} q_1 \overset{w_2}{\leadsto} \cdots$ over α s.t. $p \preceq_{de} q_0$ and $q_i \preceq_{de} q_{i+1}$ for all $i \geq 0$. Since $p \preceq_{de} q$, from Lemma 5 it follows that we can construct a trace $\pi' = q \overset{w_0}{\leadsto} r_0 \overset{w_1}{\leadsto} r_1 \overset{w_2}{\leadsto} \cdots$ s.t. $q_i \preceq_{de} r_i$ for every $i \geq 0$. Because α contains infinitely often a subword from $L_\top$, there is some $\ell \in \omega$ such that $q_\ell \overset{w_\ell}{\leadsto} q_{\ell+1}$ and $r_\ell \overset{w_\ell}{\leadsto} r_{\ell+1}$ for $w_\ell \in L_\top$. Note that it holds that $p \preceq_{de} q_\ell \preceq_{de} r_\ell$. We can again use the claim above to construct a trace $\pi^\star = p \overset{w_\ell}{\leadsto} q = s_0 \overset{w_{\ell+1}}{\leadsto} s_1 \overset{w_{\ell+2}}{\leadsto} \cdots$ over $\alpha_\ell = w_\ell w_{\ell+1} w_{\ell+2} \ldots$ such that $p \preceq_{de} s_0$ and $s_i \preceq_{de} s_{i+1}$ for all $i \geq 0$. Since $p \preceq_{de} r_\ell$, we can simulate $\pi^\star$ from r_ℓ by a trace $\pi^{\star\prime}$, and because $p \overset{w_\ell}{\underset{F}{\leadsto}} q$, we know that $\pi^{\star\prime}$ will touch an accepting state in finitely many steps (this holds because w_ℓ is from $L_\top$, which are the words over which we can go from p to q and touch an accepting state). Consider $m \geq \ell$ such that s_m is the first state after the accepting state that is one of the $\{s_0, s_1, \ldots\}$ in $\pi^{\star\prime}$. This reasoning could be repeated for all occurrences of a subword from $L_\top$ in $\pi^\star$, therefore $\alpha \in \mathcal{L}(q)$. □

Next, we give a lemma used for establishing correctness of saturating macrostates with $\preceq_{de}$-smaller states.

Lemma 11. *Let $p, q, r \in Q$ such that $r \overset{a}{\to} q \in \delta$ and $p \preceq_{de} q$. Further, let $\mathcal{A}' = (Q, \delta', I, F)$ where $\delta' = \delta \cup \{r \overset{a}{\to} p\}$. Then $\mathcal{L}(\mathcal{A}) = \mathcal{L}(\mathcal{A}')$.*

Proof. ($\subseteq$) Clear.
($\supseteq$) Consider some $\alpha \in \mathcal{L}(\mathcal{A}')$ and an accepting trace π in $\mathcal{A}'$ over α. There are two cases:

1. (π contains only finitely many transitions $r \overset{a}{\to} p$)
   In this case, π is of the form $\pi = \pi_i \pi_\omega$ where π_i is a finite prefix $\pi_i = q_0 \overset{w_0}{\leadsto} r \overset{a}{\to} p \overset{w_1}{\leadsto} r \overset{a}{\to} p \overset{w_2}{\leadsto} \cdots \overset{w_n}{\leadsto} r \overset{a}{\to} p$, for $q_0 \in I$, and π_ω is an infinite trace from p that does not contain any occurrence of the transition $r \overset{a}{\to} p$. We construct

in $\mathcal{A}$ a trace $\pi' = q_0 \overset{w_0}{\leadsto} r \overset{a}{\to} q \overset{w_1}{\leadsto} r_1 \overset{a}{\to} q_1 \overset{w_2}{\leadsto} \cdots \overset{w_n}{\leadsto} r_n \overset{a}{\to} q_n.\pi'_\omega$ as follows. Let σ_{de} be a strategy for $\preceq_{de}$. We set $r_1 := \sigma_{de}(q, p \overset{w_1}{\leadsto} r)$, so $r \preceq_{de} r_1$. Since $r \overset{a}{\to} q \in \delta$, it follows that there is $r_1 \overset{a}{\to} q_1 \in \delta$ such that $p \preceq_{de} q_1$. For $i > 1$, we set $r_i := \sigma_{de}(q_{i-1}, p \overset{w_i}{\leadsto} r)$. By induction, it follows that $\forall 1 \le i \le n : p \preceq_{de} q_i$, in particular $p \preceq_{de} q_n$. We set $\pi'_\omega := \sigma_{de}(q_n, \pi_\omega)$. Since π_ω starts in p and contains infinitely many accepting states and π'_ω starts in q_n and $p \preceq_{de} q_n$, then π'_ω also contains infinitely many accepting states. It follows that π' is accepting, so $\alpha \in \mathcal{L}(\mathcal{A})$.

2. (π contains infinitely many transitions $r \overset{a}{\to} p$)
   In this case, π is of the form $\pi = q_0 \overset{w_0}{\leadsto} r \overset{a}{\to} p \overset{w_1}{\leadsto} r \overset{a}{\to} p \overset{w_2}{\leadsto} \cdots \overset{w_n}{\leadsto} r \overset{a}{\to} p \overset{w_\omega}{\leadsto} \cdots$, for $q_0 \in I$ and $\alpha = w_0 a w_1 a w_2 \ldots$ Since π is accepting, for infinitely many $i \in \omega$, we have $p \overset{w_i a}{\underset{F}{\leadsto}} p$ in $\mathcal{A}'$ and hence also $p \overset{w_i a}{\underset{F}{\leadsto}} q$ in the original BA $\mathcal{A}$. Using Lemma 10 and the fact that $p \preceq_{de} q$, we have $w_1 a w_2 a \cdots \in L(q)$ and hence $\alpha = w_0 a w_1 a w_2 a \cdots \in \mathcal{L}(\mathcal{A})$. $\square$

The following lemma guarantees that adding transitions in the way of Lemma 11 does not break the computed delayed simulation and can, therefore, be performed repeatedly, without the need to recompute the simulation.

Lemma 12. *Let $\preceq_{de}$ be the delayed simulation on $\mathcal{A}$. Further, let $p, q, r \in Q$ be such that $r \overset{a}{\to} q \in \delta$ and $p \preceq_{de} q$, and let $\mathcal{A}' = (Q, \delta', I, F)$ where $\delta' = \delta \cup \{r \overset{a}{\to} p\}$. Then $\preceq_{de}$ is included in the delayed simulation on $\mathcal{A}'$.*

Proof. Let σ_{de} be a dominating strategy compatible with $\preceq_{de}$ and σ'_{de} be a strategy defined for all $s \in Q$ such that $r \preceq_{de} s$ as $\sigma'_{de}(s, x) = \sigma_{de}(s, x)$ when $x \ne (r \overset{a}{\to} p)$ and $\sigma'_{de}(s, r \overset{a}{\to} p) = \sigma_{de}(s, r \overset{a}{\to} q)$. Note that σ'_{de} is also dominating wrt $\preceq_{de}$. This can be shown by the following proof by contradiction: Suppose σ'_{de} is not dominating; then there is a strategy ρ such that $\sigma'_{de}(s, r \overset{a}{\to} p)$ must be simulated by $\rho(s, r \overset{a}{\to} p) = t$. But then $\sigma_{de}(s, r \overset{a}{\to} q)$ must also (transitivity of simulation) be simulated by t, so σ_{de} is not dominating. Contradiction.

Further, let $t, u \in Q$ be such that $t \preceq_{de} u$. Let $\pi_t = t \overset{w_1}{\leadsto} t_f \overset{w_2}{\leadsto} r \overset{a}{\to} p.\pi'_t$ be a trace over $\alpha = w_1 w_2 a w_\omega \in \Sigma^\omega$ in $\mathcal{A}'$ such that t_f is an accepting state and $t_f \overset{w_2}{\leadsto} r$ does not contain any occurrence of $r \overset{a}{\to} p$. Further, let $\pi_u = u_0 \overset{w_1}{\leadsto} u_f \overset{w_2}{\leadsto} u_i \overset{a}{\to} u_{i+1}.\pi'_u$ be a trace corresponding to a run $u_0 u_1 u_2 \ldots$ over α in $\mathcal{A}$, where $u_0 = u$, constructed as $\pi_u = \sigma'_{de}(u, \pi_t)$.

Claim. There is a trace $\pi_v = t \overset{w_1}{\leadsto} v_f.\pi'_v$ over α such that π'_v contains an accepting state and π_v is $\preceq_{de}$-simulated by π_u at every position.

Proof: We have the following two cases:

- ($t \overset{w_1}{\leadsto} t_f$ does not contain any occurrence of $r \overset{a}{\to} p$)
  Let $\pi_v = t \overset{w_1}{\leadsto} t_f \overset{w_2}{\leadsto} r \overset{a}{\to} q.\pi'_v$ be a trace in $\mathcal{A}$ over α obtained from π_t by starting with its prefix up to r, taking $r \overset{a}{\to} q$, and continuing with $\pi'_v = \sigma'_{de}(q, \pi'_t)$. Since in π_v, it holds that t_f is at the same position as t_f in π_t, the first part of the claim holds. Further, π_u clearly $\preceq_{de}$-simulates π_v on

$t \overset{w_1}{\leadsto} t_f \overset{w_2}{\leadsto} r$, and because σ'_{de} simulates $r \overset{a}{\rightarrow} p$ by a transition to a state u_{i+1} such that $q \preceq_{de} u_{i+1}$ and π'_v is constructed using σ'_{de}, then also the second part of the claim holds.

- ($t \overset{w_1}{\leadsto} t_f$ contains at least one occurrence of $r \overset{a}{\rightarrow} p$)

  Suppose that π_t starts with $t \overset{w_{11}}{\leadsto} r \overset{a}{\rightarrow} p \overset{w_{12}}{\leadsto} t_f$ such that $t \overset{w_{11}}{\leadsto} r$ does not contain any $r \overset{a}{\rightarrow} p$. Then let us start building π_v such that it starts with $t \overset{w_{11}}{\leadsto} r \overset{a}{\rightarrow} q$. On this prefix, π_v is clearly $\preceq_{de}$-simulated by the corresponding prefix of π_u. We continue from q using the strategy σ'_{de}. In particular, the next time we reach $r \overset{a}{\rightarrow} p$ in π_t while we are at some state v_1 such that $r \preceq_{de} v_1$, we simulate the transition by $\sigma'_{de}(v_1, r \overset{a}{\rightarrow} p)$ and so on. We can observe that when we arrive to t_f in π_t, we also arrive to v_f in π_v such that $t_f \preceq_{de} v_f$. Therefore, π'_v contains an accepting state. Moreover, since σ'_{de} is dominating, the second part of the claim also holds. ∎

From the claim above, it follows that the trace $u_f \overset{w_2}{\leadsto} u_i \overset{a}{\rightarrow} u_{i+1}.\pi'_u$ contains an accepting state, so $\mathcal{C}^{de}(\pi_t, \pi_u)$. □

Finally, we are ready to prove Lemma 8.

Lemma 8. $\mathcal{L}(\mathcal{B}_{Sat}) = \mathcal{L}(\mathcal{B}_S)$

Proof. ($\subseteq$) Let $\alpha \in \mathcal{L}(\mathcal{B}_{Sat})$ and ρ be an arbitrary accepting run over α in $\mathcal{B}_{Sat}$ such that $\rho = S_0 S_1 \ldots S_{n-1}(S_n, O_n, f_n, i_n)(S_{n+1}, O_{n+1}, f_{n+1}, i_{n+1})\ldots$. For the sake of contradiction, assume that $\alpha \in \mathcal{L}(\mathcal{A})$, therefore, there is a run ρ' on α in $\mathcal{A}$ having infinitely many accepting states. From the fact that tight level rankings form a non-increasing sequence, we have that $f_n(\rho'(n)) \geq f_{n+1}(\rho'(n+1)) \geq \cdots$. This sequence eventually stabilizes and from the property of level rankings and the fact that ρ' is accepting, it stabilizes in some ℓ such that $f_\ell(\rho'(\ell))$ is even. This, however, means that the O component of macrostates in ρ cannot be emptied infinitely often, and, therefore, ρ is not accepting, which is a contradiction. Hence $\alpha \notin \mathcal{L}(\mathcal{A})$, so (from Proposition 1) $\alpha \in \mathcal{L}(\mathcal{B}_S)$.

($\supseteq$) Consider some $\alpha \in \mathcal{L}(\mathcal{B}_S)$. Let $\mathcal{A}'$ be a BA obtained from $\mathcal{A}$ by adding transitions according to Lemma 12. Then from Lemma 11, we have that $\mathcal{L}(\mathcal{A}) = \mathcal{L}(\mathcal{A}')$. Therefore, $\alpha \in \mathcal{L}(\mathcal{B}'_S)$ where $\mathcal{B}'_S$ is the BA obtained from $\mathcal{A}'$ using COMPS. It is easy to see that we can construct a run in $\mathcal{B}_{Sat}$ that mimics the levels of run DAG of α in $\mathcal{A}'$ (i.e., we are able to empty the O component infinitely often). Hence $\alpha \in \mathcal{L}(\mathcal{B}_{Sat})$. □

Lemma 9. $\mathcal{L}(\mathcal{B}_{Sat}^{di}) = \mathcal{L}(\mathcal{B}_{Sat}^{de}) = \mathcal{L}(\mathcal{B}_{Sat}^{di+de}) = \mathcal{L}(\mathcal{B}_S)$

Proof. ($\subseteq$) This part is the same as in the proof of Lemma 8.

($\supseteq$) Consider some $\alpha \in \mathcal{L}(\mathcal{B}_S)$. Let $\mathcal{A}'$ be a BA obtained from $\mathcal{A}$ by adding transitions according to Lemma 12. Then from Lemma 11, we have that $\mathcal{L}(\mathcal{A}) = \mathcal{L}(\mathcal{A}')$. Therefore, $\alpha \in \mathcal{L}(\mathcal{B}'_S)$ where $\mathcal{B}'_S$ is the BA obtained from $\mathcal{A}'$ using COMPS. It is easy to see that we can construct a run in $\mathcal{B}_{Sat}$ that mimics the levels of run DAG of α in $\mathcal{A}'$ (i.e., we are able to empty the O component infinitely often). Using Lemmas 7 and 6, we can conclude that the run contains no macrostate of the form (S, O, f, j), where $f(p) > f(q)$ and $p \preceq_{di} q$, or $f(p) > [\![f(q)]\!]$ and $p \preceq_{de} q$ for $p, q \in S$. Therefore, ρ is also an accepting run in $\mathcal{B}_{Sat}^{di+de}$. Hence $\alpha \in \mathcal{L}(\mathcal{B}_{Sat}^{di+de})$.   □

5.2   Remarks on Compression of Macrostates

An analogy to saturation of macrostates is their compression [17, Section 6], based on removing simulation-smaller states from a macrostate. This is, however, not possible even for direct simulation, as we can see in the following example.

Example 1. Consider the BA over $\Sigma = \{a\}$ given below.

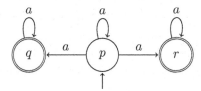

For this BA we have $q \preceq_{di} r$ and $r \preceq_{di} q$. If we compress the macrostates obtained in COMPS, there is the following trace in the output automaton:

$$\{p\} \xrightarrow{a} (\{p,q\}, \emptyset, \{p \mapsto 3, q \mapsto 2, r \mapsto 1\}, 0) \xrightarrow{a} (\{p,r\}, \{r\}, \{p \mapsto 3, q \mapsto 1, r \mapsto 2\}, 2)$$
$$\xrightarrow{a} (\{p,q\}, \emptyset, \{p \mapsto 3, q \mapsto 2, r \mapsto 1\}, 2) \xrightarrow{a} (\{p,r\}, \{r\}, \{p \mapsto 3, q \mapsto 1, r \mapsto 2\}, 0)$$
$$\xrightarrow{a} (\{p,q\}, \emptyset, \{p \mapsto 3, q \mapsto 2, r \mapsto 1\}, 0) \xrightarrow{a} \cdots$$

This trace contains infinitely many final states (we flush the O-set infinitely often), hence we are able to accept the word a^ω, which is, however, in the language of the input BA.   □

6   Use After Simulation Quotienting

In this short section, we establish that our optimizations introduced in Sects. 4 and 5 can be applied with no additional cost in the setting when BA complementation is preceded with simulation-based reduction of the input BA (which is usually helpful), i.e., when the simulation is already computed beforehand for another purpose. In particular, we show that simulation-based reduction preserves the simulation (when naturally extended to the quotient automaton). First, let us formally define the operation of quotienting.

Given an x-simulation $\preceq_x$ for $x \in \{di, de\}$, we use $\approx_x$ to denote the x-*similarity* relation (i.e., the symmetric fragment) $\approx_x = \preceq_x \cap \preceq_x^{-1}$. Note that since $\preceq_x$ is a preorder, it holds that $\approx_x$ is an equivalence. We use $[q]_x$ to denote the equivalence class of q wrt $\approx_x$. The *quotient* of a BA $\mathcal{A} = (Q, \delta, I, F)$ wrt $\approx_x$ is the automaton

$$\mathcal{A}/{\approx_x} = (Q/{\approx_x}, \delta_{\approx_x}, I_{\approx_x}, F_{\approx_x}) \tag{6}$$

with the transition function $\delta_{\approx_x}([q]_x, a) = \{[r]_x \mid r \in \delta([q]_x, a)\}$ and the set of initial and accepting states $I_{\approx_x} = \{[q]_x \in Q/\approx_x \mid q \in I\}$ and $F_{\approx_x} = \{[q]_x \in Q/\approx_x \mid q \in F\}$ respectively.

Proposition 2 ([7], [12]). *If $x \in \{di, de\}$, then $\mathcal{L}(\mathcal{A}/\approx_x) = \mathcal{L}(\mathcal{A})$.*

Remark 1 ([12]). $\mathcal{L}(\mathcal{A}/\approx_f) \neq \mathcal{L}(\mathcal{A})$

Finally, the following lemma shows that quotienting preserves direct and delayed simulations, therefore, when complementing $\mathcal{A}$, it is possible to first quotient $\mathcal{A}$ wrt a direct/delayed simulation and then use the same simulation (lifted to the states of the quotient automaton) to optimize the complementation.

Lemma 13. *Let $\preceq_x$ be the x-simulation on $\mathcal{A}$ for $x \in \{di, de\}$. Then the relation $\preceq_x^{\approx}$ defined as $[q]_x \preceq_x^{\approx} [r]_x$ iff $q \preceq_x r$ is the x-simulation on $\mathcal{A}/\approx_x$.*

Proof. First, we show that $\preceq_x^{\approx}$ is well defined, i.e., if $q \preceq_x r$, then for all $q' \in [q]_x$ and $r' \in [r]_x$, it holds that $q' \preceq_x r'$. Indeed, this holds because $q' \approx_x q$ and $r \approx_x r$, and therefore $q' \preceq_x q \preceq_x r \preceq_x r'$; the transitivity of simulation yields $q' \preceq_x r'$.

Next, let σ_x be a strategy that gives $\preceq_x$. Consider a trace defined as $[\pi_q]_x = [q_0]_x \xrightarrow{\alpha_0} [q_1]_x \xrightarrow{\alpha_1} \cdots$ over a word $\alpha \in \Sigma^\omega$ in $\mathcal{A}/\approx_x$. Then,

1. for $x = di$ there is a trace $\pi_q = q_0' \xrightarrow{\alpha_0} q_1' \xrightarrow{\alpha_1} \cdots$ in $\mathcal{A}$ s.t. $q_0' \in [q_0]_x$ and $q_i \preceq_x q_i'$ for $i \geq 0$. Therefore, if $[q_i]_x$ is accepting then so is q_i';
2. for $x = de$ there is a trace $\pi_q = q_0' \xrightarrow{\alpha_0} q_1' \xrightarrow{\alpha_1} \cdots$ in $\mathcal{A}$ s.t. $q_0' \in [q_0]_x$, $q_i \preceq_x q_i'$ for $i \geq 0$ and, moreover, if $[q_i]_x$ is accepting then there is q_k' for $k \geq i$ s.t. $q_k' \in F$.

Further, let $[q_0]_x \preceq_x^{\approx} [r_0]_x$. Then there is a trace $\pi_r = \sigma_x(r, \pi_q) = (r = r_0) \xrightarrow{\alpha_0} r_1 \xrightarrow{\alpha_1} \cdots$ simulating π_q in $\mathcal{A}$ from r. Further, consider its projection $[\pi_r]_x = [r_0]_x \xrightarrow{\alpha_0} [r_1]_x \xrightarrow{\alpha_1} \cdots$ into $\mathcal{A}/\approx_x$. For all $i \geq 0$, we have that $q_i \preceq_x r_i$, and therefore also $[q_i]_x \preceq_x^{\approx} [r_i]_x$. Since $\mathcal{C}^x(\pi_q, \pi_r)$, then also $\mathcal{C}^x([\pi_q]_x, [\pi_r]_x)$.

Finally, we show that $\preceq_x^{\approx}$ is maximal. For the sake of contradiction, suppose that $[r]_x$ is x-simulating $[q]_x$ for some $q, r \in Q$ s.t. $q \not\preceq_x r$. Consider a word $\alpha \in \Sigma^\omega$ and a trace $\pi_q = (q = q_0) \xrightarrow{\alpha_0} q_1 \xrightarrow{\alpha_1} \cdots$ over α in $\mathcal{A}$. Then there is a trace $[\pi_q]_x = [q = q_0]_x \xrightarrow{\alpha_0} [q_1]_x \xrightarrow{\alpha_1} \cdots$ over α in $\mathcal{A}/\approx_x$. According to the assumption, there is also a trace $[\pi_r]_x = [r = r_0]_x \xrightarrow{\alpha_0} [r_1]_x \xrightarrow{\alpha_1} \cdots$ such that $[\pi_r]_x$ is x-simulating $[\pi_q]_x$. But then there will also exist a trace $\pi_r = (r = r_0) \xrightarrow{\alpha_0} r_1' \xrightarrow{\alpha_1} r_1' \xrightarrow{\alpha_2} \cdots$ such that $r_i \preceq_x r_i'$ for all $i \in \omega$ and $\mathcal{C}^x(\pi_q, \pi_r)$ (see the previous part of the proof). Therefore, since $\preceq_x$ is maximal, we have that $q \preceq_x r$, which is in contradiction with the assumption. $\square$

7   Experimental Evaluation

We implemented our optimisations in a prototype tool [2] written in Haskell and performed preliminary experimental evaluation on a set of 124 random BAs with

---

[2] https://github.com/vhavlena/ba-complement .

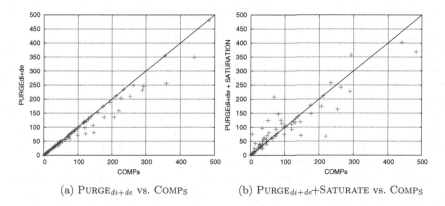

(a) $\text{P{\sc urge}}_{di+de}$ vs. C{\sc omps}   (b) $\text{P{\sc urge}}_{di+de}$+S{\sc aturate} vs. C{\sc omps}

Fig. 1. Comparison of the number of states of complement BAs generated by C{\sc omps} and our optimizations (lower is better)

a non-trivial language over a two-symbol alphabet generated using Tabakov and Vardi's model [37]. The parameters of input automata were set to the following bounds: number of states: 6–7, transition density: 1.2–1.3, and acceptance density: 0.35–0.5. Before complementing, the BAs were quotiented wrt the direct simulation for experiments with P{\sc urge}$_{di}$ and the delayed simulation for experiments with P{\sc urge}$_{de}$ and P{\sc urge}$_{di+de}$. The timeout was set to 300 s.

We present the results for our strongest optimizations for *outputs* of the size up to 500 states in Fig. 1. As can be seen in Fig. 1a, purging alone often significantly reduces the size of the output. The situation with saturation is, on the other hand, more complicated. In Fig. 1b, we can see that in some cases, the saturation produces even smaller BAs than only purging, on the other hand, in some cases, larger BAs are produced. This is expected, because saturating the S component of macrostates also means that more level rankings (the f component) need to be considered.

For outputs of a larger size (we had 11 of them), the results follow a similar trend, but the probability that saturation will increase the size of the result decreases. For some concrete results, for one BA, the size of the output BA decreased from 4065 (C{\sc omps}) to 985 (P{\sc urge}$_{di+de}$) to 929 (P{\sc urge}$_{di+de}$ +S{\sc aturate}), which yields a reduction to 24 %, resp. 22 %! Further, we observed that all P{\sc urge}$_x$ methods usually give similar results, with the difference of only a few states (when P{\sc urge}$_{di}$ and P{\sc urge}$_{de}$ differ, P{\sc urge}$_{di}$ usually wins over P{\sc urge}$_{de}$).

8   Related Work

BA complementation has a long research track. Known approaches can be roughly classified into Ramsey-based [34], determinization-based [29,32], rank-based [33], slice-based [23,39], learning-based [25], and the recently proposed subset-tuple construction [4]. Those approaches build on top of different concepts of capturing words accepted by a complement automaton. Some concepts can be translated into others, such as the slice-based approach, which can be translated to the rank-based approach [40]. Such a translation can help us get a deeper understanding of the BA complementation problem and the relationship between optimization techniques for different complementation algorithms.

Because of the high computational complexity of complementing a BA, and, consequently, also checking BA inclusion and universality (which use complementation as their component), there has been some effort to develop heuristics that help to reduce the number of explored states in practical cases. The most prominent ones are heuristics that leverage various notions of simulation relations, which often provide a good compromise between the overhead they impose and the achieved state space reduction. Direct [7,36], delayed [12], fair [12], their variants for alternating Büchi automata [16], and multi-pebble simulations [13] are the best-studied relations of this kind. Some of the relations can be used quotienting, but also for pruning transitions entering simulation-smaller states (which may cause some parts of the BA to become inaccessible). A series of results in this direction was recently developed by Clemente and Mayr [10,26,27].

Not only can the relations be used for reducing the size of the input BA, they can also be used for under-approximating inclusion of languages of states. For instance, during a BA inclusion test $\mathcal{L}(\mathcal{A}_S) \overset{?}{\subseteq} \mathcal{L}(\mathcal{A}_B)$, if every initial state of $\mathcal{A}_S$ is simulated by an initial state of $\mathcal{A}_B$, the inclusion holds and no complementation needs to be performed. But simulations can also be used to reduce the explored state space within, e.g., the inclusion check itself, for instance in the context of Ramsey-based algorithms [1,2]. Ramsey-based complementation algorithms [34] in the worst case produce $2^{\mathcal{O}(n^2)}$ states, which is a significant gap from the lower bound of Michel [28] and Yan [41]. The Ramsey-based construction was, however, later improved by Breuers et al. [5] to match the upper bound $2^{\mathcal{O}(n \log n)}$. The way simulations are applied in the Ramsey-based approach is fundamentally different from the current work, which is based on rank-based construction. Taking universality checking as an example, the algorithm checks if the language of the complement automaton is empty. They run the complementation algorithm and the emptiness check together, on the fly, and during the construction check if a macrostate with a larger language has been produced before; if yes, then they can stop the search from the language-smaller macrostate. Note that, in contrast to our approach, their algorithm does not produce the complement automaton.

9   Conclusion and Future Work

We developed two novel optimizations of the rank-based complementation algorithm for Büchi automata that are based on leveraging direct and delayed simulation relations to reduce the number of states of the complemented automaton.

The optimizations are directly usable in rank-based BA inclusion and universality checking. We conjecture that the decision problem of checking BA language inclusion might also bring another opportunities for exploiting simulation, such as in a similar manner as in [3]. Another, orthogonal, directions of future work are (i) applying simulation in other than the rank-based approach (in addition to the particular use within [1,2]), e.g., complementation based on Safra's construction [32], which, according to our experience, often produces smaller complements than the rank-based procedure, (ii) applying our ideas within determinization constructions for BAs, and (iii) generalizing our techniques for richer simulations, such as the multi-pebble simulation [13] or various look-ahead simulations [26,27]. Since the richer simulations are usually harder to compute, it would be interesting to find the sweet spot between the overhead of simulation computation and the achieved state space reduction.

Acknowledgement. We thank the anonymous reviewers for their helpful comments on how to improve the exposition in this paper. This work was supported by the Ministry of Science and Technology of Taiwan project 106-2221-E-001-009-MY3 the Czech Science Foundation project 19-24397S, the FIT BUT internal project FIT-S-17-4014, and The Ministry of Education, Youth and Sports from the National Programme of Sustainability (NPU II) project IT4Innovations excellence in science—LQ1602.

References

1. Abdulla, P.A., et al.: Simulation subsumption in Ramsey-based Büchi automata universality and inclusion testing. In: Touili, T., Cook, B., Jackson, P. (eds.) CAV 2010. LNCS, vol. 6174, pp. 132–147. Springer, Heidelberg (2010). https://doi.org/10.1007/978-3-642-14295-6_14

2. Abdulla, P.A., et al.: Advanced Ramsey-based Büchi automata inclusion testing. In: Katoen, J.-P., König, B. (eds.) CONCUR 2011. LNCS, vol. 6901, pp. 187–202. Springer, Heidelberg (2011). https://doi.org/10.1007/978-3-642-23217-6_13

3. Abdulla, P.A., Chen, Y.-F., Holík, L., Mayr, R., Vojnar, T.: When simulation meets antichains. In: Esparza, J., Majumdar, R. (eds.) TACAS 2010. LNCS, vol. 6015, pp. 158–174. Springer, Heidelberg (2010). https://doi.org/10.1007/978-3-642-12002-2_14

4. Allred, J.D., Ultes-Nitsche, U.: A Simple and optimal complementation algorithm for Büchi automata. In: Proceedings of the 33rd Annual ACM/IEEE Symposium on Logic in Computer Science, pp. 46–55. ACM (2018)

5. Breuers, S., Löding, C., Olschewski, J.: Improved Ramsey-based Büchi complementation. In: Birkedal, L. (ed.) FoSSaCS 2012. LNCS, vol. 7213, pp. 150–164. Springer, Heidelberg (2012). https://doi.org/10.1007/978-3-642-28729-9_10

6. Büchi, J.R.: On a decision method in restricted second order arithmetic. In: Proceedings of International Congress on Logic, Method, and Philosophy of Science 1960. Stanford University Press, Stanford (1962)

7. Bustan, D., Grumberg, O.: Simulation-based minimization. ACM Trans. Comput. Logic 4(2), 181–206 (2003)

8. Cécé, G.: Foundation for a series of efficient simulation algorithms. In: Proceedings of LICS 2017, pp. 1–12 (2017)

9. Chen, Y., et al.: Advanced automata-based algorithms for program termination checking. In: Proceedings of PLDI 2018, pp. 135–150. ACM (2018)
10. Clemente, L.: Büchi automata can have smaller quotients. In: Aceto, L., Henzinger, M., Sgall, J. (eds.) ICALP 2011. LNCS, vol. 6756, pp. 258–270. Springer, Heidelberg (2011). https://doi.org/10.1007/978-3-642-22012-8_20
11. Dill, D.L., Hu, A.J., Wong-Toi, H.: Checking for language inclusion using simulation preorders. In: Larsen, K.G., Skou, A. (eds.) CAV 1991. LNCS, vol. 575, pp. 255–265. Springer, Heidelberg (1992). https://doi.org/10.1007/3-540-55179-4_25
12. Etessami, K., Wilke, T., Schuller, R.: Fair simulation relations, parity games, and state space reduction for Büchi automata. SIAM J. Comput. **34**(5), 1159–1175 (2005)
13. Etessami, K.: A hierarchy of polynomial-time computable simulations for automata. In: Brim, L., Křetínský, M., Kučera, A., Jančar, P. (eds.) CONCUR 2002. LNCS, vol. 2421, pp. 131–144. Springer, Heidelberg (2002). https://doi.org/10.1007/3-540-45694-5_10
14. Fogarty, S., Vardi, M.Y.: Büchi complementation and size-change termination. In: Kowalewski, S., Philippou, A. (eds.) TACAS 2009. LNCS, vol. 5505, pp. 16–30. Springer, Heidelberg (2009). https://doi.org/10.1007/978-3-642-00768-2_2
15. Friedgut, E., Kupferman, O., Vardi, M.: Büchi complementation made tighter. Int. J. Found. Comput. Sci. **17**, 851–868 (2006)
16. Fritz, C., Wilke, T.: Simulation relations for alternating Büchi automata. Theor. Comput. Sci. **338**(1), 275–314 (2005)
17. van Glabbeek, R., Ploeger, B.: Five determinisation algorithms. In: Ibarra, O.H., Ravikumar, B. (eds.) CIAA 2008. LNCS, vol. 5148, pp. 161–170. Springer, Heidelberg (2008). https://doi.org/10.1007/978-3-540-70844-5_17
18. Gurumurthy, S., Bloem, R., Somenzi, F.: Fair simulation minimization. In: Brinksma, E., Larsen, K.G. (eds.) CAV 2002. LNCS, vol. 2404, pp. 610–623. Springer, Heidelberg (2002). https://doi.org/10.1007/3-540-45657-0_51
19. Heizmann, M., Hoenicke, J., Podelski, A.: Termination analysis by learning terminating programs. In: Biere, A., Bloem, R. (eds.) CAV 2014. LNCS, vol. 8559, pp. 797–813. Springer, Cham (2014). https://doi.org/10.1007/978-3-319-08867-9_53
20. Henzinger, M.R., Henzinger, T.A., Kopke, P.W.: Computing simulations on finite and infinite graphs. In: Proceedings of FOCS 1995, pp. 453–462. IEEE Computer Society (1995)
21. Henzinger, T.A., Kupferman, O., Rajamani, S.K.: Fair simulation. Inf. Comput. **173**(1), 64–81 (2002)
22. Ilie, L., Navarro, G., Yu, S.: On NFA reductions. In: Karhumäki, J., Maurer, H., Păun, G., Rozenberg, G. (eds.) Theory Is Forever. LNCS, vol. 3113, pp. 112–124. Springer, Heidelberg (2004). https://doi.org/10.1007/978-3-540-27812-2_11
23. Kähler, D., Wilke, T.: Complementation, disambiguation, and determinization of Büchi automata unified. In: Aceto, L., Damgård, I., Goldberg, L.A., Halldórsson, M.M., Ingólfsdóttir, A., Walukiewicz, I. (eds.) ICALP 2008. LNCS, vol. 5125, pp. 724–735. Springer, Heidelberg (2008). https://doi.org/10.1007/978-3-540-70575-8_59
24. Kupferman, O., Vardi, M.Y.: Weak alternating automata are not that weak. ACM Trans. Comput. Logic **2**(3), 408–429 (2001)
25. Li, Y., Turrini, A., Zhang, L., Schewe, S.: Learning to complement Büchi automata. In: Dillig, I., Palsberg, J. (eds.) Verification, Model Checking, and Abstract Interpretation. LNCS, vol. 10747, pp. 313–335. Springer, Cham (2018). https://doi.org/10.1007/978-3-319-73721-8_15

26. Mayr, R., Clemente, L.: Advanced automata minimization. In: Proceedings of POPL 2013, pp. 63–74 (2013)
27. Mayr, R., Clemente, L.: Efficient reduction of nondeterministic automata with application to language inclusion testing. Logical Methods Comput. Sci. 15, 12:1–12:73 (2019)
28. Michel, M.: Complementation is more difficult with automata on infinite words. In: CNET, Paris, vol. 15 (1988)
29. Piterman, N.: From nondeterministic Büchi and Streett automata to deterministic parity automata. In: Proceedings of LICS 2006. pp. 255–264. IEEE (2006)
30. Ranzato, F., Tapparo, F.: A new efficient simulation equivalence algorithm. In: Proceedings of LICS 2007, pp. 171–180 (2007)
31. Ranzato, F., Tapparo, F.: An efficient simulation algorithm based on abstract interpretation. Inf. Comput. 208(1), 1–22 (2010)
32. Safra, S.: On the complexity of ω-automata. In: Proceedings of FOCS 1988, pp. 319–327. IEEE (1988)
33. Schewe, S.: Büchi complementation made tight. In: Proceedings of STACS 2009, pp. 661–672. Schloss Dagstuhl-Leibniz-Zentrum fuer Informatik (2009)
34. Sistla, A.P., Vardi, M.Y., Wolper, P.: The complementation problem for Büchi automata with applications to temporal logic. Theor. Comput. Sci. 49(2–3), 217–237 (1987)
35. Sistla, A.P., Vardi, M.Y., Wolper, P.: The complementation problem for Büchi automata with applications to temporal logic. In: Brauer, W. (ed.) ICALP 1985. LNCS, vol. 194, pp. 465–474. Springer, Heidelberg (1985). https://doi.org/10.1007/BFb0015772
36. Somenzi, F., Bloem, R.: Efficient Büchi automata from LTL formulae. In: Emerson, E.A., Sistla, A.P. (eds.) CAV 2000. LNCS, vol. 1855, pp. 248–263. Springer, Heidelberg (2000). https://doi.org/10.1007/10722167_21
37. Tabakov, D., Vardi, M.Y.: Experimental evaluation of classical automata constructions. In: Sutcliffe, G., Voronkov, A. (eds.) LPAR 2005. LNCS (LNAI), vol. 3835, pp. 396–411. Springer, Heidelberg (2005). https://doi.org/10.1007/11591191_28
38. Vardi, M.Y.: The Büchi complementation saga. In: Thomas, W., Weil, P. (eds.) STACS 2007. LNCS, vol. 4393, pp. 12–22. Springer, Heidelberg (2007). https://doi.org/10.1007/978-3-540-70918-3_2
39. Vardi, M.Y., Wilke, T.: Automata: from logics to algorithms. Logic Automata 2, 629–736 (2008)
40. Vardi, M.Y., Wilke, T., Kupferman, O., Fogarty, S.J.: Unifying Büchi complementation constructions. Logical Methods Comput. Sci. 9, 1–25 (2013)
41. Yan, Q.: Lower bounds for complementation of ω-automata via the full automata technique. In: Bugliesi, M., Preneel, B., Sassone, V., Wegener, I. (eds.) ICALP 2006. LNCS, vol. 4052, pp. 589–600. Springer, Heidelberg (2006). https://doi.org/10.1007/11787006_50

Succinct Determinisation of Counting Automata via Sphere Construction

Lukáš Holík[1], Ondřej Lengál[1], Olli Saarikivi[2], Lenka Turoňová[1],
Margus Veanes[2(✉)], and Tomáš Vojnar[1]

[1] FIT, IT4Innovations Centre of Excellence, Brno University of Technology,
Brno, Czech Republic
[2] Microsoft Research, Redmond, USA
margus@microsoft.com

Abstract. We propose an efficient algorithm for determinising counting automata (CAs), i.e., finite automata extended with bounded counters. The algorithm avoids unfolding counters into control states, unlike the naïve approach, and thus produces much smaller deterministic automata. We also develop a simplified and faster version of the general algorithm for the sub-class of so-called monadic CAs (MCAs), i.e., CAs with counting loops on character classes, which are common in practice. Our main motivation is (besides applications in verification and decision procedures of logics) the application of deterministic (M)CAs in pattern matching regular expressions with counting, which are very common in e.g. network traffic processing and log analysis. We have evaluated our algorithm against practical benchmarks from these application domains and concluded that compared to the naïve approach, our algorithm is much less prone to explode, produces automata that can be several orders of magnitude smaller, and is overall faster.

1 Introduction

The *counting operator*—also known as the operator of *limited repetition*—is an operator commonly used in extended regular expressions (also called *regexes*). Limited repetitions do not extend expressiveness beyond regularity, but allow one to succinctly express patterns such as `(ab){1,100}` representing all words where `ab` appears 1–100 times. Such expressions are very common (cf. [3]), e.g., in the RegExLib library [20], which collects expressions for recognising URIs, markup code, pieces of Java code, or SQL queries; in the Snort rules [17] used for finding attacks in network traffic; or in real-life XML schemas, with the counter bounds being as large as 10 million [3]. This observation is confirmed by our own experiments with patterns provided by Microsoft for verifying absence of information leakage from network traffic logs. Counting constraints may also naturally arise

This work has been supported by the Czech Science Foundation (project No. 19-24397S), the IT4Innovations Excellence in Science (project No. LQ1602), and the FIT BUT internal project FIT-S-17-4014.

A. W. Lin (Ed.): APLAS 2019, LNCS 11893, pp. 468–489, 2019.
https://doi.org/10.1007/978-3-030-34175-6_24

in other contexts, such as in automata-based verification approaches (e.g. [11]) for describing sets of runs through a loop with some number of repetitions.

Several finite automata counterparts of regular counting constraints have appeared in the literature (e.g. [13,15,24,25]), all essentially boiling down to variations on counter automata with counters limited to a bounded range of values. Such counters do not extend the expressive power beyond regularity, but bring succinctness, exactly as the counters in extended regular expressions. In this paper, we call these automata *counting automata* (CAs).

The main contribution of this paper is a novel *succinct determinisation* of CAs. Our main motivation is in *pattern matching*, where deterministic automata allow for algorithms running reliably in time linear to the length of the text. However, the naïve determinisation of CAs (and counting constraints in general)—which encodes counter values as parts of control states, leading to classical nondeterministic finite automata (NFAs), which are then determinised using the standard subset construction—can easily lead to state explosion, causing the approach to fail. See, e.g., the CA in Fig. 1, for which the minimal deterministic finite automaton (DFA) has 2^{k+1} states with k being the upper bound of the counter. *Backtracking*-based algorithms, which can be used instead, are slower and unpredictable, may easily require a prohibitively large time, and are even prone to DoS attacks, cf. [19]. A viable alternative is *on-the-fly determinisation*, which determinises only the part of the given NFA through which the input word passes, as proposed already in [27]. However, the overhead during matching might be significant, and the construction can still explode on some words, much like the full determinisation, especially when large bounds on counters are used (which, in our experience, makes some regex matchers to give up already the translation to NFAs).

Our algorithm, which allows one to *succinctly* determinise CAs, is therefore a major step towards alleviating the above problems by making the determinisation-based algorithms applicable more widely. We note that this has been an open problem (whose importance was stressed, e.g., in [25]) that a number of other works, such as [13,15], have attempted to solve, but they could only cope with very restricted fragments or alleviate the problem only partially, yielding solutions of limited practical applicability only.

Our algorithm is general and often produces small results. Moreover, we also propose a version specialised to counting restricted to repetition of single characters from some *character class*, called *monadic counting* here (e.g., `[ab]{10}` is monadic while `(ab){10}` is not). This class is of particular practical relevance since we discovered that most of the regular expressions with counters used in practice are of this form. Our specialised algorithm can produce deterministic CAs exponentially more succinct than the corresponding DFAs and its worst-case complexity is only polynomial in the maximum values of counters (in contrast to the exponential naïve construction).

We have implemented the monadic CA determinisation and evaluated it on real-life datasets of regular expressions with monadic counting. We found that our resulting CAs can be much smaller than minimal DFAs, are less prone to explode, and that our algorithm, though not optimised, is overall faster than the naïve determinisation that unfolds counters. We also confirmed that monadic regexes present an important subproblem, with over 95% of regexes in the explored datasets being of this type.

Running Example. To illustrate our algorithms, consider the regex `.*a.{k}` where $k \in \mathbb{N}$. It says that the $(k+1)$-th letter from the end of the word must be a. The minimal DFA accepting the language has 2^{k+1} states since it must remember in its control states the positions of all letters a that were seen during the last $k+1$ steps. For this, it needs a finite memory of $k+1$ bits, which has 2^{k+1} reachable configurations. The regex corresponds to the nondeterministic CA of Fig. 1. In the transition labels, the predicates over the variable 1 constrain the input symbol, the predicates over c constrain the current value of the counter c, and the primed variant of c, i.e., c', stands for the value of c after taking the transition. The initial value of c is unrestricted, and the automaton accepts in the state r if the value of c equals k. Our monadic determinisation algorithm, presented in Sect. 4.2, then outputs the deterministic CA (DCA) of Fig. 2 (for $k=1$). Intuitively, it uses $k+1$ counters to remember how far back the last $k+1$ occurrences of a appeared. Depending on k, the resulting DCA has $k+2$ states, $4(k+1)+1$ transitions, and $k+1$ counters. That is, its size is linear to k in contrast to the factor 2^k in the size of the minimal DFA.   □

Fig. 1. A CA for the regex `.*a.{k}` with $k \in \mathbb{N}$, $I : \mathbf{s} = q$, $F : \mathbf{s} = r \wedge c = k$, and $\Delta : q\text{-}\{\top,\top\}\!\!\rightarrow\!q \vee q\text{-}\{1=a,c'=0\}\!\!\rightarrow\!r \vee r\text{-}\{c<k,c'=c+1\}\!\!\rightarrow\!r$.

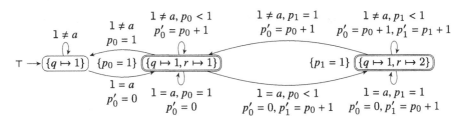

Fig. 2. The DCA generated from the CA of Fig. 1 for $k = 1$ by our algorithm for determinisation of monadic CA (Sect. 4.2).

2   Counting Automata

Preliminaries. We use $\mathbb{N}$ to denote the set of natural numbers $\{0, 1, 2, \ldots\}$. Given a function $f : A \to B$, we refer to the elements of f using $a \mapsto b$ (when $f(a) = b$). For the rest of the paper, we consider a fixed finite *alphabet* Σ of *symbols*. A word over Σ is a finite sequence of symbols $w = a_1 \cdots a_n \in \Sigma^*$. We use ϵ to denote the *empty word*.

Given a set of variables V and a set of constants Q (disjoint with $\mathbb{N}$), we define a *Q-formula over* V to be a quantifier-free formula φ of Presburger arithmetic extended with constants from Q and Σ, i.e., a Boolean combination of (in-)equalities $t_1 = t_2$ or $t_1 \leq t_2$ where t_1 and t_2 are constructed using $+$, $\mathbb{N}$, and V, and predicates of the form $x = a$ or $x = q$ for $x \in V$, $a \in \Sigma$, and $q \in Q$. An assignment M to free variables of φ is a *model* of φ, denoted as $M \models \varphi$, if it makes φ true. We use $\mathtt{sat}(\varphi)$ to denote that φ has a model.

Given a formula φ and a (partial) map $\theta : terms(\varphi) \to S$, where $terms(\varphi)$ denotes the set of terms in φ and S is some set of terms, $\varphi[\theta]$ denotes a *term substitution*, i.e., the formula φ with all occurrences of every term $t \in dom(\theta)$ replaced by $\theta(t)$. As usual, replacing a larger term takes priority over replacing its subterms (we treat primed variables and parameters as atomic terms, hence $(p' = 1)[\{p \mapsto q\}]$ is still $p' = 1$). The *substitution formula* φ_θ of θ is defined as the conjunction of equalities $\varphi_\theta \overset{\text{def}}{=} \bigwedge_{t \in dom(\theta)}(\theta(t) = t)$. Finally, the set of *minterms* of a finite set Φ of predicates is defined as the set of all satisfiable predicates of $\{\bigwedge_{\phi \in \Phi'} \phi \wedge \bigwedge_{\phi \in \Phi \setminus \Phi'} \neg\phi \mid \Phi' \subseteq \Phi\}$.

Labelled Transition Systems. We will introduce our counting automata, such as that of Fig. 1, as a specialisation of the more general model of labelled transition systems. This perspective and related notation allows for a more abstract and concise formulation of our algorithms than the more standard approach, in which one would define counting automata in a more straightforward manner as an extension of the classical finite automata.

A *labelled transition system* (LTS) over Σ is a tuple $T = (Q, V, I, F, \Delta)$ where Q is a finite set of *control states*, V is a finite set of *configuration variables*, I is the *initial Q-formula* over V, F is the *final Q-formula* over V, and Δ is the *transition Q-formula* over $V \cup V' \cup \{1\}$ with $V' = \{x' \mid x \in V\}$, $V \cap V' = \emptyset$, and $1 \notin V$. We call 1 the *letter/symbol variable* and allow it as the only term that can occur within a predicate $1 = a$ for $a \in \Sigma$, called an *atomic symbol guard*.[1] Moreover, 1 is also not allowed to occur in any other predicates in Δ. A *configuration* is an assignment $\alpha : V \to \mathbb{N} \cup Q$ that maps every configuration variable to a number from $\mathbb{N}$ or a state from Q. Let $\mathcal{C}$ be the set of all configurations. The transition formula Δ encodes the transition relation $[\![\Delta]\!] \subseteq \mathcal{C} \times \Sigma \times \mathcal{C}$ such that $(\alpha, a, \alpha') \in [\![\Delta]\!]$ iff $\alpha \cup \{x' \mapsto k \mid \alpha'(x) = k\} \cup \{1 \mapsto a\} \models \Delta$. We use $|\Delta|$ to denote the size of $[\![\Delta]\!]$. For a word $w \in \Sigma^*$, we define inductively that a configuration α' is a *w-successor* of α, written $\alpha \overset{w}{\to} \alpha'$, such that $\alpha \overset{\epsilon}{\to} \alpha$ for all $\alpha \in \mathcal{C}$, and $\alpha \overset{av}{\to} \alpha'$ iff $\alpha \overset{a}{\to} \bar{\alpha} \overset{v}{\to} \alpha'$ for some $\bar{\alpha} \in \mathcal{C}$, $a \in \Sigma$, and $v \in \Sigma^*$. A configuration α is *initial* or *final* if $\alpha \models I$ or $\alpha \models F$, respectively. The *outcome* of T on a word w is the set $out_T(w)$ of all w-successors of the initial configurations, and w is accepted by T if $out_T(w)$ contains a final configuration. The *language* $\mathcal{L}(T)$ of T is the set of all words that T accepts.

---

[1] To handle large or infinite sets of symbols symbolically, the predicates $1 = a$ may be generalised to predicates from an arbitrary effective Boolean algebra, as in [6].

Counting Automata. A *counting variable (counter)* is a configuration variable c whose value ranges over $\mathbb{N}$ and which can appear (within Δ, I, and F) only in *atomic counter guards* of the form $c \leq k, c \geq k$, (using $<, =, >$ as syntactic sugar) or *term equality tests* $t_1 = t_2$, and in *atomic counter assignments* $c' = t$ with t, t_1, t_2 being *arithmetic terms* of the form $d + k$ or k with $k \in \mathbb{N}$ and d being a counter. A *control state variable* is a variable s whose value ranges over states Q and appears only in *atomic state guards* $\mathsf{s} = q$ and *atomic state assignments* $\mathsf{s}' = q$ for $q \in Q$. A Boolean combination of atomic guards (counter, state, or symbol) is a *guard formula* and a Boolean combination of atomic assignments is an *assignment formula*.

A *(nondeterministic) counting automaton* (CA) is a tuple $A = (Q, C, I, F, \Delta)$ such that (Q, V, I, F, Δ) is an LTS with the following properties: (1) The set of configuration variables $V = C \cup \{\mathsf{s}\}$ consists of a set of counters C and a single control state variable s s.t. $\mathsf{s} \notin C$. (2) The transition formula Δ is a disjunction of *transitions*, which are conjunctions of the form $\mathsf{s} = q \wedge g \wedge f \wedge \mathsf{s}' = r$, denoted by $q\text{-}\{g, f\}\text{-}r$, where $q, r \in Q$, g is the transition's *guard formula* over $V \cup \{1\}$, and f is the transition's *counter assignment formula*, a conjunction of atomic assignments to counters, in which every counter is assigned at most once. (3) There is a constant $\boldsymbol{max}_A \in \mathbb{N}$ such that no counter can ever grow above that value, i.e., $\forall c \in C \ \forall w \in \Sigma^* \ \forall \alpha \in out_T(w) : \alpha \models c \leq \boldsymbol{max}_A$.

The last condition in the definition of CAs is semantic and can be achieved in different ways in practice. For instance, regular expressions can be compiled to CAs where assignment terms are of the form $c + 1$, 0, or c only, and every appearance of $c + 1$ is paired with a guard containing a constraint $c \leq k$ for some $k \in \mathbb{N}$. In this case, $\boldsymbol{max}_A = K + 1$ where K is the maximum constant used in the guards of the form $c \leq k$.

We will often consider the initial and final formulae of CAs given as a disjunction $\bigvee_{q \in Q}(\mathsf{s} = q \wedge \varphi_q)$ where φ_q is a formula over counter guards, in which case we write $I(q)$ or $F(q)$ to denote the disjunct φ_q of the initial or final formula, respectively. An example of a CA is given in Fig. 1.

A *deterministic counting automaton* (DCA) is a CA A where I has at most one model and, for every symbol $a \in \Sigma$, every reachable configuration α has at most one a-successor (equivalently, the outcome of every word in A is either a singleton or the empty set). Finally, in the special case when $C = \emptyset$, the CA is a (classical) nondeterministic *finite automaton* (NFA), or a deterministic finite automaton (DFA) if it is deterministic.

3   Determinisation of Counting Automata

In this section, we discuss an algorithm for determinising CAs. A naïve determinisation converts a given CA A into an NFA by hard-wiring counter configurations as a part of control states, followed by the classical subset construction to determinise the obtained NFA (the NFA is finite due to the bounds on the maximum values of counters). The state space of the obtained DFA then consists of all reachable outcomes of A. By determinising A in this way, the succinctness of using counters is lost, and the size of the DFA can explode exponentially not only in the number of control states of A but also in the number of reachable counter valuations, which makes the construction impractical. Instead, our construction will retain counters (though their number may grow) and represent possible word outcomes as configurations of the resulting DCA.

Spheres. In particular, the outcome of a word $w \in \Sigma^*$ in a CA $A = (Q, C, I, F, \Delta)$ can be represented as a formula φ over equalities of the form $c = k$ and $s = q$ where $q \in Q$, $c \in C$, $k \in \mathbb{N}$. Intuitively, disjunctions can be used to obtain a single formula for the possibly many configurations reachable in A over w. For example, the outcome of the word aab in Fig. 1 is $\varphi : s = q \vee (s = r \wedge (c = 1 \vee c = 2))$. Generally, the outcome of aab^i, for $0 \le i < k$, assuming $k > 2$, is $\varphi_i : s = q \vee (s = r \wedge (c = i \vee c = i + 1))$.

A crucial notion for our construction is then the notion of *sphere*. A sphere ψ arises from an outcome φ by replacing the constants from $\mathbb{N}$ by parameters drawn from a countable set $\mathcal{P}$ (disjoint from $\mathbb{N}$, V, Q, and $\{1, s\}$). In the example above, the sphere obtained from the φ is $\psi : s = q \vee (s = r \wedge (c = p_0 \vee c = p_1))$, and the same sphere arises from all outcomes φ_i with $0 \le i < k$.

Spheres will play the role of the control states of the resulting DCA. The idea of the construction is that the outcome of every word w in a DCA A^d will contain a single configuration (A^d is deterministic) consisting of a sphere ψ as the control state and a valuation of its parameters $\eta : \mathcal{P} \to \mathbb{N}$. The construction will ensure that $\psi[\eta]$ models the outcome $out_A(w)$ of w in A. In our example, the outcome of aab in A^d would contain the single configuration $\{s \mapsto \psi, p_0 \mapsto 1, p_1 \mapsto 2\}$, and the outcome of each φ_i, for $0 \le i < k$, would contain the single configuration $\{s \mapsto \psi, p_0 \mapsto i, p_1 \mapsto i + 1\}$. The example shows the advantage of our construction. Every outcome φ_i would be a control state of the naïvely determinised automaton, with a b-transition from each φ_j to φ_{j+1}, for $0 \le j < k - 1$. In contrast to that, all these states and transitions will be in A^d replaced by a single control state ψ with a single b-labelled self-loop that increments both p_0 and p_1. This structure can be seen in Fig. 2 (states are spheres, labelled by their multiset representation introduced in Sect. 4.2).

3.1   Determinisation by Sphere Construction

We now provide a basic version of our sphere-based determinisation, which can also be viewed as an algorithm that constructs parametric versions of the subsets used in subset-based determinisation. For this basic algorithm, termination is not guaranteed, but it serves as a basis on which we will subsequently build a terminating algorithm. Let us first introduce some needed additional notation.

Given a formula φ, we denote by $at(\varphi)$ and by $num(\varphi)$ the sets of assignment terms and numerical constants, respectively, appearing in φ. We will use the set $\mathcal{P}' = \{p' \mid p \in \mathcal{P}\}$ and the substitution $\theta_{unprime} = \{p' \mapsto p \mid p \in \mathcal{P}\}$. We say that a formula over variables $V \cup V' \cup \{1\} \cup \mathcal{P}$ is *factorised wrt guards* if it is a disjunction $\bigvee_{i=1}^{n}(g_i) \wedge (u_i)$ of factors, each consisting of a guard g_i over $V \cup \{1\} \cup \mathcal{P}$ and an update formula u_i over atomic assignments such that the guards of any two different factors are mutually exclusive, i.e., $g_i \land g_j$ is unsatisfiable for any $1 \leq i \neq j \leq n$.[2] For a set of variables U, we denote by $\exists U : \varphi$ a formula obtained by eliminating all variables in U from φ (i.e., a quantifier-free formula equivalent to $\exists U : \varphi$).[3]

Algorithm 1: Sphere-based CA determinisation (non-terminating)

   Input: A CA $A = (Q, C, I, F, \Delta)$.
   Output: A DCA $A^d = (Q^d, P, I^d, F^d, \Delta^d)$ s.t. $\mathcal{L}(A) = \mathcal{L}(A^d)$.

1   $Q^d \leftarrow Worklist \leftarrow \emptyset; \Delta^d \leftarrow \bot$;
2   $\psi_I \leftarrow I[\theta_{const}]$ for some total injection $\theta_{const} : num(I) \to \mathcal{P}$;
3   $I^d \leftarrow \mathsf{s} = \psi_I \land \varphi_{\theta_{const}}$;
4   add ψ_I to Q^d and to $Worklist$;
5   **while** $Worklist \neq \emptyset$ **do**
6      $\psi \leftarrow pop(Worklist)$;
7   Let $\bigvee_{i=1}^{n}(g_i) \land (u_i)$ be the formula $\exists C, \mathsf{s} : \psi \land \Delta$ factorised wrt guards;
8   **foreach** $1 \leq i \leq n$ **do**
9         $\psi_i \leftarrow u_i[\theta_{at}][\theta_{unprime}]$ for a total injection $\theta_{at} : at(u_i) \to \mathcal{P}'$;
10   add $\psi \text{-}\{g_i, \varphi_{\theta_{at}}\} \!\!\rightarrow\!\! \psi_i$ to Δ^d;
11   **if** $\psi_i \notin Q^d$ **then** add ψ_i to Q^d and to $Worklist$
12   $P \leftarrow$ all parameters found in Q^d;
13   $F^d \leftarrow \bigvee_{\psi \in Q^d} \mathsf{s} = \psi \land \exists C, \mathsf{s} : \psi \land F$;
14   $I^d \leftarrow ground(I^d); \Delta^d \leftarrow ground(\Delta^d)$;
15   **return** $A^d = (Q^d, P, I^d, F^d, \Delta^d)$;

The Algorithm. The core of our determinisation algorithm is the sphere construction described in Algorithm 1. It builds a DCA $A^d = (Q^d, P, I^d, F^d, \Delta^d)$ whose control states Q^d are spheres. Its counters are parameters from the set P that is built during the run of the algorithm. The initial formula I^d defined on line 3 assigns to s the initial control state ψ_I (obtained on line 2), which is a parametric version of I with integer constants replaced by parameters according to the renaming θ_{const}. Moreover, I^d also equates the parameters in ψ_I with the constants they are replacing in I. Hence, the formula $\psi_I[\theta_{const}^{-1}]$ models exactly the initial configurations of A.

---

[2]   A Boolean combination of atomic guards and updates can be factorised through (1) a transformation to DNF, yielding a set of clauses X; (2) writing each clause $\varphi \in X$ as a conjunction of a guard formula g_φ and an assignment formula f_φ; (3) computing minterms of the set $\{g_\varphi \mid \varphi \in X\}$; (4) creating one factor $(g) \land (f)$ from every minterm g where f is the disjunction of all the assignment formulae f_φ with $\varphi \in X$ compatible with g (i.e., such that $g \land f_\varphi$ is satisfiable).

[3]   We note that we only need to use a specialised, simple, and cheap quantifier elimination. In particular, we only need to eliminate counter variables c from formulae such that, in clauses of their DNF, c always appears together with a predicate $c = p$ where p is a parameter. Eliminating c from such a DNF clause is then done by simply substituting occurrences of c by p. We do not need complex algorithms such as the general quantifier elimination for Presburger arithmetic.

Example 1. In the running example (Fig. 1), whenever referring to some variable that is assigned multiple times during the run of the algorithm, we use superscripts to distinguish the different assignments during the run. On lines 1–4, the initial sphere ψ_I is assigned the formula $\mathbf{s} = q$, and the initial formula I^d is set to $\mathbf{s} = \psi_I$, which specifies that ψ_I is indeed the initial control state only (I does not constrain counters, hence I^d does not talk about parameters).   □

The remaining states of Q^d and transitions of Δ^d are computed by a worklist algorithm on line 5 with the worklist initialised with ψ_I. Every iteration computes the outgoing transitions of a control state $\psi \in$ *Worklist* as follows: On line 7, after eliminating $C \cup \{\mathbf{s}\}$ from the formula $\psi \wedge \Delta$, which describes how the next state and counter values depend on the input symbol and the current values of parameters, it is transformed into a guard-factorised form.

Example 2. When ψ_I is taken from *Worklist* as ψ^1 on line 6, its processing starts by factorising $\exists\{c, \mathbf{s}\} : \psi^1 \wedge \Delta$ on line 7. Here, $\psi^1 \wedge \Delta$ is the formula $\mathbf{s} = q \wedge (q\text{-}\{\top,\top\}\mapsto q \vee q\text{-}\{1=\mathtt{a},c'=0\}\mapsto r \vee r\text{-}\{c<k,c'=c+1\}\mapsto r)$, which can be also written as

$$\mathbf{s} = q \wedge (\mathbf{s}' = q \vee (1 = \mathbf{a} \wedge c' = 0 \wedge \mathbf{s}' = r)).$$

The elimination of $\{c, \mathbf{s}\}$ gives the formula $\mathbf{s}' = q \vee (1 = \mathbf{a} \wedge c' = 0 \wedge \mathbf{s}' = r)$. This formula is factorised into the following two factors:

$(F_1)\ (1 = \mathbf{a}) \wedge (\mathbf{s}' = q \vee (c' = 0 \wedge \mathbf{s}' = r))$,
$(F_2)\ (1 \neq \mathbf{a}) \wedge (\mathbf{s}' = q)$.   □

In the for-loop on line 8, every factor $(g_i) \wedge (u_i)$ is turned into a transition with the guard g_i; the mutual incompatibility of the guards guarantees determinism. The formula u_i describes the target sphere in terms of the parameters of the source sphere ψ, updated according to the transition relation. That is, it is a Boolean combination of assignments of the form $c' = p + k$ or $c' = k$ for $c \in C, p \in \mathcal{P}$, and $k \in \mathbb{N}$. Line 9 creates a sphere by substituting each of the assignment terms (of the form $p + k$ or k) with a parameter and replacing primed variables by their unprimed versions.[4] The corresponding assignment term substitution θ_{at} records how the values of the new parameters are obtained from the original values of the parameters occurring in ψ. It is used to define the assignment formula of the new transition that is added to Δ^d on line 10. The argument justifying that the construction preserves the language is the following: if reading $w \in \Sigma^*$ takes A^d to ψ with a parameter valuation η such that $\psi[\eta]$ is equivalent to $out_A(w)$, then reading a next symbol a using a transition newly created on line 10 takes A^d to ψ' with the parameter valuation η' such that $\psi'[\eta']$ models $out_A(wa)$.

---

[4] The choice of the parameters in the image of $\theta_{at} : at(u_i) \to \mathcal{P}'$ on line 9 is arbitrary, although, in practice, it would be sensible to define some systematic parameter naming policy and reuse existing parameters whenever possible.

Example 3. Factor F_1 of Example 2 above is processed as follows. A possible choice for θ_{at}^1 on line 9 is the assignment $\{0 \mapsto p_0\}$. Its application followed by $\theta_{unprime}$ creates

$$\psi_1^1 : \mathsf{s} = q \vee (c = p_0 \wedge \mathsf{s} = r).$$

From θ_{at}^1, we get the substitution formula $\varphi_{\theta_{at}^1} : (p_0' = 0)$ on line 10, and so the transition added to Δ^d is $(\mathsf{s} = q) \dashv_{\{1 = \mathsf{a}, p_0' = 0\}} (\mathsf{s} = q \vee (c = p_0 \wedge \mathsf{s} = r))$. The target ψ_1^1 of the transition is added to Q^d and to *Worklist* on line 11. Next, Factor F_2 generates the self-loop $(\mathsf{s} = q) \dashv_{\{1 \neq \mathsf{a}, \top\}} (\mathsf{s} = q)$, which ends the first iteration of the while-loop.

Let us also walk through a part of the second iteration of the while-loop, in which ψ_1^1 is taken from *Worklist* as ψ^2 on line 6. The formula $\psi^2 \wedge \Delta$ from line 7 is $((\mathsf{s} = r \wedge c = p_0) \vee \mathsf{s} = q) \wedge (q \dashv_{\{\top, \top\}} q \vee q \dashv_{\{1 = \mathsf{a}, c' = 0\}} r \vee r \dashv_{\{c < k, c' = c+1\}} r)$, which is equivalent to $(\mathsf{s} = q \wedge (\mathsf{s}' = q \vee (1 = \mathsf{a} \wedge c' = 0 \wedge \mathsf{s}' = r))) \vee (\mathsf{s} = r \wedge c = p_0 \wedge c < k \wedge c' = c + 1 \wedge \mathsf{s}' = r)$. The elimination of $\{c, \mathsf{s}\}$ on line 7 then gives the formula $(\mathsf{s}' = q \vee (1 = \mathsf{a} \wedge c' = 0 \wedge \mathsf{s}' = r)) \vee (p_0 < k \wedge c' = p_0 + 1 \wedge \mathsf{s}' = r)$, which is factorised into the following four factors:

(F_3) $(1 = \mathsf{a} \wedge p_0 < k) \wedge (\mathsf{s}' = q \vee (c' = 0 \wedge \mathsf{s}' = r) \vee (c' = p_0 + 1 \wedge \mathsf{s}' = r))$,
(F_4) $(1 \neq \mathsf{a} \wedge p_0 < k) \wedge (\mathsf{s}' = q \vee (c' = p_0 + 1 \wedge \mathsf{s}' = r))$,
(F_5) $(1 = \mathsf{a} \wedge p_0 \geq k) \wedge (\mathsf{s}' = q \vee (c' = 0 \wedge \mathsf{s}' = r))$, and
(F_6) $(1 \neq \mathsf{a} \wedge p_0 \geq k) \wedge (\mathsf{s}' = q)$.

In the for-loop on line 8, Factor F_3 is processed as follows. Let the chosen substitution θ_{at}^2 on line 9 be $\{p_0 + 1 \mapsto p_1, 0 \mapsto p_0\}$. Its application followed by $\theta_{unprime}$ generates

$$\psi_1^2 : \mathsf{s} = q \vee (c = p_0 \wedge \mathsf{s} = r) \vee (c = p_1 \wedge \mathsf{s} = r).$$

The substitution formula $\varphi_{\theta_{at}^2}$ on line 10 is $p_1' = p_0 + 1 \wedge p_0' = 0$, and so Δ^d gets the new transition $\psi_1^1 \dashv_{\{1 = \mathsf{a} \wedge p_0 < k, p_1' = p_0 + 1 \wedge p_0' = 0\}} \psi_1^2$. The evaluation of the while-loop would continue analogously.   □

In the final stage of the algorithm, when (and if) the while-loop terminates, line 12 collects the set P of all parameters used in the constructed parametric spheres of Q^d as new counters of A^d. Further, line 13 derives the new final formula by considering all computed spheres, restricting them to valuations where the original final formula is satisfied, and quantifying out the original counters. This way, final constraints on the original counters get translated to constraints over parameters in P.

Example 4. In our running example, for the spheres discussed above, we would have $F(\psi^1) : \bot$, $F(\psi_1^1) : p_0 = 1$, and $F(\psi_1^2) : p_0 = 1 \vee p_1 = 1$.   □

Finally, line 14 applies the function *ground* on the initial formula and the transition formula of the constructed automaton before returning it. This step is needed in order to avoid nondeterminism on unused and unconstrained counters. The function *ground* conjuncts constraints of the form $p = 0$ with the initial formula and with the guard of every transition for every parameter $p \in P$ that is so far unconstrained in the concerned formula. Moreover, it will introduce a reset $p' = 0$ to the assignment formula of every transition for every counter $p \in P$ that is so far not assigned on the concerned transition. The while-loop of Algorithm 1 needs, however, not terminate, as witnessed also by our example.[5]

Example 5. Continuing in Example 4, the DCA in Fig. 2 would be a part of the DCA constructed by Algorithm 1, its states being the spheres ψ^1, ψ^1_1, ψ^2_1 from the left, but the while-loop would not terminate, with ψ^2_1. Instead, it would eventually generate a successor of ψ^2_1, the sphere

$$\psi^3_1 : \mathsf{s} = q \vee (c = p_0 \wedge \mathsf{s} = r) \vee (c = p_1 \wedge \mathsf{s} = r) \vee (c = p_2 \wedge \mathsf{s} = r),$$

i.e., a sphere similar to ψ^2_1 but extended by a new disjunct with a new parameter p_2. Repeating this, the algorithm would keep generating larger and larger spheres with more and more parameters.   □

3.2   Ensuring Termination of the Sphere Construction

In this section, we will discus reasons for possible non-termination of Algorithm 1 and a way to tackle them. The main reason is that the algorithm may generate unboundedly many parameters that correspond to different histories of a counter c when processing the input word (including also impossible ones in which the counter exceeds the maximum value). The algorithm indeed "splits" a parameter appearing in a sphere into two parameters in the successor sphere when the transitions of A update the counter in two different ways.

In our terminating version of Algorithm 1, we build on the following: (1) distinguishing between histories that converge in the same counter value is not necessary, they can be "merged", and (2) the number of different reachable counter values is bounded (by the definition of CAs). We thus enforce the invariant of every reachable configuration of A^d that all parameters in the configuration have distinct values. The invariant is enforced by testing equalities of parameters and merging parameters with equal values on transitions of A^d. All transitions of A^d entering spheres with more than $max_A + 1$ parameters can then be discarded because the invariant implies that they cannot be taken at any configuration of A^d. Furthermore, we will also ensure that the algorithm does not diverge because of generating semantically equivalent but syntactically different spheres (because of different names of parameters or different formulae structure).

A terminating determinisation of CAs is obtained from Algorithm 1 by replacing lines 9–11 by the code in Algorithm 2. In order to ensure that parameters have pairwise distinct values, the transitions of A^d test equalities of the

---

[5] For this step to preserve the language of the automaton, we need to assume that the input CA does not assign nondeterministic values to live counters. We are refering to the standard notion: a counter is live at a state if the value it holds at that state may influence satisfaction of some guard in the future. Any CA can be transformed into this form, and CAs we compile from regular expressions satisfy this condition by construction.

values assigned to parameters and ensure that two parameters are never used to represent the same value. Different histories of counters are thus merged if they converge into the same value. To achieve this, Algorithm 2 enumerates all feasible equivalences of the assignment terms of u_i on line 16 and generates successor transitions for each of them separately. When deciding whether an equivalence $\sim$ on the assignment terms is feasible, the algorithm performs two tests: (1) The formula $\varphi_\sim \stackrel{\text{def}}{=} \bigwedge_{t_1 \sim t_2, t_1, t_2 \in at(u_i)}(t_1 = t_2) \wedge \bigwedge_{t_1 \not\sim t_2, t_1, t_2 \in at(u_i)}(t_1 \neq t_2)$ is tested for satisfiability, meaning that the equivalence is not trying to merge terms that can never be equal (such as, e.g., p and $p + 1$). (2) The number of equivalence classes should be at most $\boldsymbol{max}_A + 1$ since this is the maximum number of different values that the counters can reach due to the requirement that the values must be between 0 and $\boldsymbol{max}_A$.

Algorithm 2: Ensuring termination of sphere-based CA determinisation

---

16 **foreach** *equivalence* $\sim$ *on* $at(u_i)$ *s.t.* $\boldsymbol{sat}(\varphi_\sim)$ *and* $|at(u_i)/{\sim}| \leq \boldsymbol{max}_A + 1$
   do
17   **let** $\theta_{at} : at(u_i) \to \mathcal{P}'$ be an injection;
18     $\psi_i \leftarrow u_i[\theta_{at}][\theta_{unprime}]$;
19   **if** $\exists \theta_{rename} : \mathcal{P} \leftrightarrow \mathcal{P} \; \exists \sigma \in Q^d : \psi_i[\theta_{rename}] \Leftrightarrow \sigma$ **then**
20   add $\psi\text{-}\{g_i \wedge \varphi_\sim[\theta_{at}], \varphi_{\theta_{at}}[\theta'_{rename}]\}\!\mapsto\!\sigma$ to Δ^d;
21   **else**
22   add $\psi\text{-}\{g_i \wedge \varphi_\sim[\theta_{at}], \varphi_{\theta_{at}}\}\!\mapsto\!\psi_i$ to Δ^d;
23   add ψ_i to Q^d and to *Worklist*;

Line 17 builds a term assignment replacement θ_{at} that maps all $\sim$-equivalent terms to the same (future) parameter, and line 18 computes the target sphere, reflecting the given merge. The test on line 19 checks whether the target sphere is equal to some already generated sphere up to a parameter renaming (represented by a bijection $\theta_{rename} : \mathcal{P} \leftrightarrow \mathcal{P}$). If so, the created sphere is discarded, and a new transition going to the old sphere is generated on line 20; we need to rename the primed parameters used in the transition's assignment appropriately according to $\theta'_{rename} = \{p'_0 \mapsto p'_1 \mid p_0 \mapsto p_1 \in \theta_{rename}\}$. Otherwise, a transition into the new sphere is added on line 22, and the new sphere is added to Q^d and *Worklist*. In both cases, the guard of the generated transition is extended by the formula $\varphi_\sim[\theta_{at}]$, which encodes the equivalence $\sim$, and hence explicitly enforces that $\sim$ holds when the transition is taken.

Note that the test on the maximum number of equivalence classes can be optimised if finer information about the maximum reachable values of the individual counters is available. Such information can be obtained, e.g., by looking at the constants used in the guards of the transitions where the different counters are increased. For any counter, one should then not generate more parameters representing its possible values than what the upper bound on that counter is (plus one).

Theorem 1. *Algorithm 1 with the modification presented in Algorithm 2 terminates and produces a DCA with $\mathcal{L}(A) = \mathcal{L}(A^d)$ and $|Q^d| \leq 2^{|Q| \cdot (\boldsymbol{max}_A + 1)^{|C|}}$.*

Proof (idea). The fact that the algorithm indeed constructs a DCA is because line 7 of Algorithm 1 generates pairwise incompatible guards on transitions only. It is also easy to show by induction on the length of the words that the language is preserved. The termination then follows from the facts that (1) the algorithm has a bound on the maximum number of parameters in spheres (ensured by the condition over $\sim$ on line 16 of Algorithm 2) and (2) no spheres equal up to renaming are generated (ensured by the check on line 19). The bound on the size follows from the structure of spheres.   □

The number of equivalences generated on line 16 of Algorithm 2 (and therefore also the number of transitions leaving ψ) may be large. Many of them are, however, infeasible (cannot be taken in any reachable configuration of A^d), and could be removed. In most cases, the majority of such infeasible transitions may be identified locally, taking advantage of the invariant of all reachable configurations of A^d enforced by Algorithm 2: namely, values of distinct parameters are always pairwise distinct. Therefore, before building a transition for an equivalence $\sim$, we ask whether the $\sim$-equivalent assignment terms may indeed be made equivalent assuming that the constructed transition guard g_i and— importantly—also the distinctness invariant hold right before the transition is taken. Technically, we create new transitions only from those equivalences $\sim$ such that $\mathtt{sat}(\bigwedge_{p_1,p_2 \in P_\psi, dist(p_1,p_2)}(p_1 \neq p_2) \wedge g_i \wedge \varphi_\sim)$ where P_ψ is the set of parameters of ψ and $dist(p_1,p_2)$ holds iff p_1 and p_2 are distinct parameters.

3.3   Reachability-Restricted CA Determinisation

Above, we have described a terminating algorithm for CA determinisation. While it is witnessed by our experiments that the algorithm often generates much smaller automata than what could be obtained by transforming the automata into NFAs and determinising them, a natural question is whether the generated DCA is *always* smaller or equal in size to the DFA built by getting rid of the counters and using classical determinisation. Unfortunately, the answer to this question is no. The reason is that the transformation to a DCA needs not recognise that some generated transitions can never be executed and that some spheres are not reachable. To see this, it is enough to imagine a transition setting some counter c to zero and the only successor transition testing whether c is positive. The latter transition would not be executed when generating the DFA due to working with concrete values of counters, but it would be considered when constructing the DCA (since the construction does not know the values of the counters).

In our experiments with CAs obtained from real-life regexes, the above was not a problem, but we note that, for the price of an increased cost of the construction, one could further improve the algorithm by taking into account some reachability information. In an extreme case, one could first generate the DFA corresponding to the given CA and then use it when generating the DCA (as a hopefully more compact representation of the DFA). In particular, whenever adding some new sphere into the DCA being built, the algorithm can check whether there is a subset of states in the original CA represented as a state of the DFA that is an instance of the sphere. If not, the sphere is not added. The resulting DCA can then never be bigger than the DFA since each control state of the DFA (i.e., a subset of states of the original CA) is represented by a single sphere only, likewise each transition of the DFA is represented by a single transition of the DCA, and there are not any unreachable spheres or transitions that cannot be executed.

Notice that the reachability pruning is an alternative to Algorithm 2. Algorithm 1 equipped with the reachability analysis is guaranteed to terminate. For example, when run on the CA in Fig. 1, it would generate a DCA isomorphic to that from Fig. 2.

4   Monadic Counting

We now provide a simplified and more efficient version of the determinisation algorithm. The simplified version targets CAs that naturally arise from *monadic regexes*, i.e., regular expressions extended with counting limited to *character classes*. Their abstract syntax is

$$R ::= \emptyset \mid \varepsilon \mid \sigma \mid R_1 R_2 \mid R_1 + R_2 \mid R* \mid \sigma\{n, m\}$$

where σ is a predicate denoting a set of alphabet symbols, i.e., a *character class* (σ will be used to denote character classes from now on), and $n, m \geq 0$ are integers. The semantics is defined as usual, with $\sigma\{n, m\}$ denoting a string w with $n \leq |w| \leq m$ symbols satisfying σ.

The specialised determinisation algorithm is of a high practical relevance since the monadic class is very common, as witnessed by our experiments, where it covers over 95% of the regexes with counting that we found (cf. Sect. 5).

4.1   Monadic Counting Automata

Monadic regexes can be easily compiled to nondeterministic monadic CAs satisfying certain structural properties summarised below.[6] In particular, a (nondeterministic) *monadic counting automaton (MCA)* is a CA $A = (Q, C, I, F, \Delta)$ where the following holds:

1. The set Q of control states is partitioned into a set of *simple states* Q_s and a set of *counting states* Q_c, i.e., $Q = Q_s \uplus Q_c$.
2. The set of counters $C = \{c_q \mid q \in Q_c\}$ consists of a unique counter c_q for every counting state $q \in Q_c$.

---

[6] We note that we restrict ourselves to range sub-expressions of the form $\sigma\{n, n\}$ or $\sigma\{0, n\}$ only. This is without loss of generality since a general range expression $\sigma\{m, n\}$ can be rewritten as $\sigma\{m, m\}.\sigma\{0, n - m\}$.

3. All transitions containing counter guards or updates must be incident with a counting state in the following manner. Every counting state $q \in Q_c$ has a single *increment transition*, a self-loop $q \text{-} \{\sigma \wedge c_q < max_q, c'_q = c_q + 1\} \text{→} q$ with the value of c_q limited by the *bound* max_q of q, and possibly several *entry transitions* of the form $r \text{-} \{\sigma \wedge c'_q = 0\} \text{→} q$, which set c_q to 0. As for *exit transitions*, every counting state is either *exact* or *range*, where exact counting states have exit transitions of the form $q \text{-} \{\sigma \wedge c_q = max_q\} \text{→} s$, and *range* counting states have exit transitions of the form $q \text{-} \{\sigma, \top\} \text{→} s$ with $s \in Q$ s.t. $s \neq q$. That is, an exact counting state may be left only after exactly max_q repetitions of the incrementing transition (it corresponds to a regular expression $\sigma\{k\}$), while a range counting state may be left sooner (it corresponds to a regular expression $\sigma\{0, k\}$). We denote the set of range counting states Q_r and the set of exact counting states Q_e, with $Q_c = Q_r \uplus Q_e$.

4. The initial condition I is of the form $I : \bigvee_{q \in Q^I_s} \mathbf{s} = q \vee \bigvee_{q \in Q^I_c} (\mathbf{s} = q \wedge c_q = 0)$ for some sets of initial simple and counting states $Q^I_s \subseteq Q_s$ and $Q^I_c \subseteq Q_c$, respectively, with the counters of initial counting states initialised to 0.

5. The final condition F is of the form $F : \bigvee_{q \in Q^F_s \cup Q^F_r} \mathbf{s} = q \vee \bigvee_{q \in Q^F_e} (\mathbf{s} = q \wedge c_q = max_q)$ where $Q^F_s \subseteq Q_s$ is a set of simple final states, $Q^F_r \subseteq Q_r$ is a set of final range counting states, and $Q^F_e \subseteq Q_e$ is a set of final exact counting states. That is, final conditions on final states are the same as counter conditions on exit transitions.[7]

4.2 Determinisation of MCAs

Algorithm 2 can be simplified when specialised to monadic CAs. The simplification is based on the following observations. *Observation 1. Counters are dead outside their states.* To simplify the representation of spheres, we use the fact that every counter c_q of an MCA is "active" in the state q only, while c_q is "dead" in other states (i.e., its current value has no influence on runs of the MCA that are not in q). To represent different variants of c_q, we use parameters of the form $c_q[i]$ obtained by indexing c_q by an index i, for $0 \leq i \leq max_q$, while enforcing the invariant that, for distinct indices i and j, $c_q[i]$ and $c_q[j]$ always have different values. Since the value of c_q ranges from 0 to max_q, at most $max_q + 1$ variants of c_q are needed.[8] Since spheres only need parameters to remember values of live counters, every sphere can be equivalently written in the *normal form*

$$\psi \stackrel{\text{def}}{=} \bigvee_{q \in Q'_s} \mathbf{s} = q \vee \bigvee_{q \in Q'_c} \left(\mathbf{s} = q \wedge \bigvee_{0 \leq i \leq max'_q} c_q = c_q[i] \right)$$

---

[7] Notice that the guards $c_q < max_q$ on the incrementing self-loops of exact counting states could be removed without affecting the language since when c_q exceeds max_q, then the run can never leave q and has thus no chance of accepting. We include these guards only to conform to the condition on boundedness of counter values in the definition of CAs.

[8] Notice that maintaining a fixed association of a parameter to a counter is a difference from Algorithms 1 and 2, where one parameter may represent different counters.

for some $Q'_s \subseteq Q_s$, $Q'_c \subseteq Q_c$, and $\boldsymbol{max}'_q \leq \boldsymbol{max}_q$. That is, a sphere ψ records which states may be reached in the original MCA when ψ is reached in the determinised MCA and also which variants of the counter c_q may record the value of c_q when q is reached.

Observation 2. Variants of exact counting states can be sorted. For dealing with any exact counting state $q \in Q_e$, we may use the following facts: (1) If executed, the increment transition of q increments all variants of c_q whose values are smaller than $\boldsymbol{max}_q$. (2) New variants of c_q are initialised to 0 by the entry transitions. (3) Variants whose value is $\boldsymbol{max}_q$ can take an exit transition, after which they become dead and their values do not need to be propagated to the next configuration. It is therefore easy to enforce that the values of the variants $c_q[i]$ stay sorted, so that $i < j$ implies $\alpha(c_q[i]) < \alpha(c_q[j])$ in every configuration α of A^d. The sortedness invariant implies that the variant of c_q with the highest index, called *highest variant*, has the highest value. This, together with the invariant of boundedness by $\boldsymbol{max}_q$ and mutual distinctness of values of variants of c_q, means that the highest variant is the only one that may satisfy the tests $c_q = \boldsymbol{max}_q$ on exit transitions or fail the test $c_q < \boldsymbol{max}_q$ on the incrementing transition. Hence, the deterministic MCA does not need to test all variants of c_q but the highest one only.

Observation 3. Only the smallest variants of range counting states are important. For range counting states, we adapt the *simulation pruning* technique from [10]. The technique optimizes the standard subset-construction-based determinisation of NFAs by exploiting a *simulation* relation [7] such that any *macrostate* (which has the form of a set of states of the original NFA) obtained during the determinisation can be pruned by removing those NFA states that are simulated by other NFA states included in the same macrostate. The pruning does not change the language: the resulting DFA is bisimilar to the one constructed without pruning. For our DCA construction, we use the simulation that implicitly exists between configurations α and α' of A with the same range counting state $q = \alpha(\mathbf{s}) = \alpha'(\mathbf{s})$, where $\alpha(c_q) \geq \alpha'(c_q)$ implies that α' simulates α.[9] Hence, the spheres only need to remember the smallest possible counter value for every range counting state q, which may be always stored in $c_q[0]$, and discard all other variants.

Determinisation of MCAs. Observations 1–3 above allow for representing spheres using a simple data structure, namely, a multiset of states. By a slight abuse of notation, we use ψ for the sphere itself as well as for its multiset representation $\psi : Q \to \mathbb{N}$. The fact that $\psi(q) > 0$ means that q is present in the sphere (i.e., $\mathbf{s} = q$ is a predicate in the normal form of ψ), and for a counting state q, the counters $c_q[0], \ldots, c_q[\psi(q) - 1]$ are the $\psi(q)$ variants of c_q tracked in the sphere (i.e., $\psi(q) - 1 = \boldsymbol{max}_{q'}$ in the normal form of ψ).

---

[9] The fact that this relation is indeed a simulation can be seen from that both the higher and lower value of c_q can use any exit transition of q at any moment regardless of the value of c_q, but the lower value of c_q can stay in the counting loop longer.

The MCA determinisation is then an analogy of Algorithm 1 that uses the multiset data structure and preserves the sortedness and uniqueness of variants of exact counters. The initial sphere ψ_I assigns 1 to all initial states of I, and the initial configuration I^d assigns 0 to $c_q[0]$ for each counting state q in I. Further, we modify the part of Algorithm 1 after popping a sphere ψ from *Worklist* in the main loop (lines 7–11).

Let Δ_ψ denote the set of transitions of A originating from states q with $\psi(q) > 0$. Processing of ψ starts by removing guard predicates of the form $c_q < \boldsymbol{max}_q$ from increment transitions of exact counting states in Δ_ψ (since they have no semantic effect as mentioned already above). Subsequently, we compute minterms of the set of guard formulae of the transitions in Δ_ψ. Each minterm μ then gives rise to a transition $\psi\text{-}\{g,f\}\mapsto\psi'$ of A^d. The guard formula g, assignment formula f, and the target sphere ψ' are constructed as follows.

First, the guard g is obtained from the minterm μ by replacing, for all $q \in Q_c$, every occurrence of c_q by $c_q[\psi(q)]$, i.e., the highest variant of c_q. Intuitively, the counter guards of transitions of Δ_ψ present in μ will on the constructed transition of A^d be testing the highest variants of the counters. This is justified since (a) only the highest variant of c_q needs to be tested for exact counting states, as concluded in Observation 2 above, and (b) we keep only a single variant of c_q for range counting states (which is also the highest one), as concluded in Observation 3.

We then initialise the target multiset ψ' as the empty multiset $\{q \mapsto 0 \mid q \in Q\}$ and collect the set Δ_μ of all transitions from Δ_ψ that are compatible with the minterm μ (recall that increment self-loops of exact states in Δ_ψ have counter guards removed, hence counter guards do not influence their inclusion in Δ_μ). The transitions of Δ_μ will be processed in the following three steps.

Step 1 (simple states). Simple states with an incoming transition in Δ_μ get $\psi'(q) = 1$.

Step 2 (increment self-loops). For exact states with the increment self-loop in Δ_μ, $\psi'(q)$ is set to $\psi(q) - 1$ if an exit transition of q is in Δ_μ, and to $\psi(q)$ otherwise. Indeed, if (and only if) an exit transition of q is included in Δ_μ, and Δ_μ is enabled in some sphere, then the highest variant of c_q has reached $\boldsymbol{max}_q$ in that sphere, and the self-loop cannot be taken by the highest variant of c_q. The lower variants of c_q always have values smaller than $\boldsymbol{max}_q$, and hence can take the self-loop. The assignment f then gets the conjunct $c_q[i]' = c_q[i] + 1$ for each $0 \leq i < \psi'(q)$ since the variants that take the self-loop are incremented. For range states with the increment self-loop in Δ_μ, we set $\psi'(q)$ to 1, and $c_q[0]' = c_q[0] + 1$ is added to f (only one variant is remembered).

Step 3 (entry transitions). For each counting state q with an entry transition in Δ_μ, $\psi'(q)$ is incremented by 1 and the assignment $c_q[0]' = 0$ of the fresh variant of c_q is added to f. If the new value of $\psi'(q)$ exceeds $\boldsymbol{max}_q + 1$, then the whole transition generated from μ is discarded, since c_q cannot have more than $\boldsymbol{max}_q + 1$ distinct values. Otherwise, if q is an exact counting state, then f is updated to preserve the invariant of sorted and unique values of c_q: the increments of older variants of c_q are *right-shifted* to make space for the fresh variant, meaning that each conjunct $c_q[i]' = c_q[i]+1$ in f is replaced by $c_q[i+1]' = c_q[i] + 1$. If $q \in Q_r$, then if the assignment $c_q[0]' = c_q[0] + 1$ is present in f, it is removed (as the fresh variant has the smallest value 0).

Example 6. Determinising the CA from Fig. 1 using the algorithm described in this section would result in the DCA shown in Fig. 2. $\square$

The monadic determinisation has a much lower worst-case complexity than the general algorithm. Importantly, the number of states depends on $\boldsymbol{max}_A$ only polynomially, which is a major difference from the exponential bounds of the naïve determinisation and our general construction.

Theorem 2. *The specialised monadic CA determinisation constructs a DCA with* $|Q^d| \le (\boldsymbol{max}_A + 1)^{|Q|}$ *and* $|\Delta^d| \le |\Sigma| \cdot (4 \cdot (\boldsymbol{max}_A + 1))^{|Q|}$.

Proof (idea). The bound on the number of states is given by the number of functions $Q \to \{0, \ldots, \boldsymbol{max}_A\}$. The bound on the number of transitions is given by the fact, that if a sphere multiset maps a state q to n, then the successors of the sphere can map q to 0 (when q is not a successor), $n-1$, n, or $n+1$. Therefore, for every symbol from Σ and every macrostate from at most $(\boldsymbol{max}_A + 1)^{|Q|}$ many of them, there are at most $4^{|Q|}$ successors, and $|\Sigma| \cdot (\boldsymbol{max}_A+1)^{|Q|} \cdot 4^{|Q|} = (4 \cdot (\boldsymbol{max}_A + 1))^{|Q|}$. $\square$

5   Experimental Evaluation

The main purpose of our experimentation was to compare the proposed approach with the naïve determinisation and confirm that our method produces significantly smaller automata and mitigates the risk of the state space explosion causing a complete failure of determinisation (and the implied impossibility to use the desired deterministic automaton for the intended application, such as pattern matching). To this end, we extended the Microsoft's Automata library [18] with a prototype support for CAs, implemented the algorithm from Sect. 4 (denoted **Counting** in the following), and compared it to the standard determinisation already present in the library (denoted as **DFA**). For the evaluation, we collected 2,361 regexes from a wide range of applications—namely, those used in network intrusion detection systems (Snort [17]: 741 regexes, Yang [29]: 228 regexes, Bro [21]: 417 regexes, HomeBrewed [28]: 55 regexes), the Microsoft's security leak scanning system (Industrial: 17 regexes), the Sagan log analysis engine (Sagan [26]: 14 regexes), and the pattern matching rules from RegExLib (RegExLib [20]: 889 regexes). We only selected regexes that contain an occurrence of the counting operator, and from these, we selected only monadic ones (there were over 95% of them, confirming the fragment's importance). All benchmarks were run on a Xeon E5-2620v2@2.4 GHz CPU with 32 GB RAM with a timeout of 1 min (we take the mean time of 10 runs). In the following, we use μ, m, and σ to denote the statistical indicators mean, median, and standard deviation, respectively. All times are reported in milliseconds.

The number of timeouts was 110 for **Counting**, and 238 for **DFA**. The two methods were to some degree complementary, there were only 62 cases in which both timed out. This confirms that our algorithm indeed mitigates the risk of failure due to state space explosion in determinisation. The remaining comparisons are done only with respect to benchmarks for which neither of the methods timed out.

In Fig. 3, we compare the running times of the conversion of an NFA for a given regex to a DFA (the **DFA** axis) and the determinisation of the CA for the same regex (the **Counting** axis). If we exclude the easy cases where both approaches finished within 1 ms, we can see that **Counting** is almost always better than **DFA**. Note that the axes are logarithmic, so the advantage of **Counting** over **DFA** grows exponentially wrt the distance of the data point from the diagonal. The statistical indicators for the running times are $\mu = 110$, $m = 0.17$, $\sigma = 1,177$ for **DFA** and $\mu = 0.23$, $m = 0.13$, $\sigma = 0.09$ for **Counting**.

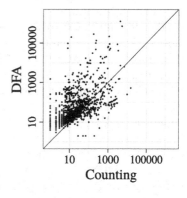

Fig. 3. Comparison of running times given in ms (the axes are logarithmic).

In Fig. 4, we compare the number of states of the results of the determinisation algorithms (DCA for **Counting** and DFA for **DFA**). Also here, **Counting** significantly dominates **DFA**. The statistical indicators for the numbers of states are $\mu = 4,543$, $m = 41$, $\sigma = 57,543$ for **DFA** and $\mu = 241$, $m = 13$, $\sigma = 800$ for **Counting**. To better evaluate the conciseness of using DCAs, we further selected 184 benchmarks that suffered from state explosion during determinisation (our criterion for the selection was that the number of states increased at least ten-fold in **DFA**) and explored how the CA model can be used to mitigate the explosion. Figure 5 shows histograms of how DCAs were more compact than DFAs and also how much

Fig. 4. Comparison of numbers of states (the axes are logarithmic).

the number of counters rose during the determinisation. From the histograms, we can see that there are indeed many cases where the use of DCAs allows one to use a significantly more compact representation, in some cases by the factor of hundreds, thousands, or even tens of thousands. Furthermore, the other histogram shows that, in many cases, no blow-up in the number of counters happened; though there are also cases where the number of counters increased by the factor of hundreds.

In terms of numbers of transitions, the methods compare similarly as for numbers of states, as shown in Fig. 6. We obtained $\mu = 14,282$, $m = 77$, $\sigma = 213,406$ for **DFA** and $\mu = 2,398$, $m = 23$, $\sigma = 8,475$ for **Counting**. (We emphasize

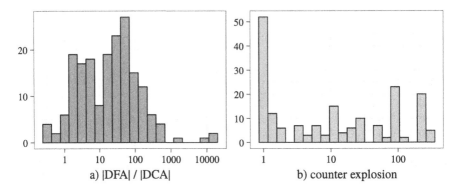

Fig. 5. Histograms of (a) the ratio of the number of states of a DFA and of the corresponding DCA (i.e., a bar at value x of a height h denotes that the size of the DCA was h times around x times smaller than the size of the corresponding DFA) and (b) the ratio of the number of counters used by a CA after and before determinisation. Note that the x-axes are logarithmic in both cases.

the number of states over the number of transitions in our comparisons since the performance and complexity of automata algorithms is usually more sensitive to the number of states, and large numbers of transitions are amenable for efficient symbolic representations [6,12,16].)

Benefits of the **Counting** method were the most substantial on the Industrial dataset. For the regex ".*A[^AB]{0,800}C[D-G]{43,53} DFG[^D-H]" (which was obtained from the real one, which is confidential, by substituting the used character classes by characters A–H), the obtained DFA contains 200,132 states, while the DCA contains only 12 states (and 2 counters), which is 16,667 times less. When minimised, the DFA still has 65,193 states. There were other regexes where **Counting** achieved a great reduction, in total two regexes had a reduction of over 10,000, three more regexes had a reduction of over 1,000, and 45 more had a reduction of over 100.

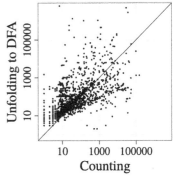

Fig. 6. Comparison of numbers of transitions (the axes are logarithmic).

Additionally, we also compared our approach against the naïve determinisation followed by the standard minimisation. Due to the space restrictions and since minimisation is not relevant to our primary target (preventing failure due to state space explosion during determinisation), we present the results only briefly. Minimisation increased the running times of **DFA** by about one half ($\mu = 150$, $m = 0.35$, $\sigma = 1,582$ for the running times of **DFA** followed by minimisation). The minimal DFAs were on average about ten times smaller than the original DFAs, and about ten times larger than our DCAs ($\mu = 385$, $m = 29$, $\sigma = 4,195$ for the numbers of states of the minimal DFAs).

6   Related Work

Our notion of CAs is close to the definition of FACs in [13], but our CAs are more general, by allowing input predicates and more complex counter updates. Also R-automata [1] are related but somewhat orthogonal to CAs because counters in R-automata do not need to have upper bounds and cannot be tested or compared. Counter systems are also related to CAs but allow more general operations over counters through Presburger formulas [2]. CAs can also be seen as a special case of extended finite state machines or EFSMs [5,22,24,25], but these already go beyond regular languages.

Extended FAs (XFAs) augment classical automata with so-called scratch memory of bits and bit-instructions [23,24], which can represent counters and also reduce nondeterminism. Regexes are compiled into deterministic XFAs by first using an extended version of Thompson's algorithm [27], then determinised through an extended version of the classical powerset construction, and finally minimised. Although a small XFA may exist, the determinisation algorithm incurs an intermediate exponential blowup of search space for inputs such as .*a.$\{k\}$ (cf. [23, Section 6.2]), i.e., the regex from our running example, and handling of such cases remained an open problem.

Regular expressions with counters are also discussed in [8,13,15]. The automata with counters used in [13], called FACs, correspond closely, apart from our symbolic character predicates and transition representation, to the class of CAs considered in our work. A central result in [13] is that for *counter-1-unambiguous* regexes, the translation algorithm yields deterministic FACs and that checking determinism of FACs can be done in polynomial time. There are also works on regular expressions with counting that translate deterministic regexes to CAs and work with different notions of determinism [4,9]. The related work in [14] studies membership in regexes with counting. None of these papers addresses the problem of determinising nondeterministic CAs.

7   Future Directions

Among future directions, we will consider optimisations of the current algorithm by means of avoiding construction of unreachable parts of DCAs or by finding efficient data structures, generalising the techniques used for monadic CAs to a larger class of CAs, and building a competitive pattern matching engine around the current algorithm. Since we believe that CAs have a lot of potential as a general succinct automata representation, we will work towards filling in efficient CA counterparts of standard automata algorithms, such as Boolean operations, minimisation, or emptiness test, that could also be used in other applications than pattern matching, such as verification and decision procedures of logics.

References

1. Abdulla, P.A., Krcal, P., Yi, W.: R-automata. In: van Breugel, F., Chechik, M. (eds.) CONCUR 2008. LNCS, vol. 5201, pp. 67–81. Springer, Heidelberg (2008). https://doi.org/10.1007/978-3-540-85361-9_9

2. Bardin, S., Finkel, A., Leroux, J., Petrucci, L.: FAST: acceleration from theory to practice. STTT **10**(5) (2008)
3. Börklund, E., Martens, W., Timm, T.: Efficient incremental evaluation of succinct regular expressions. In: Proceedings of CIKM 2015, ACM (2015)
4. Chen, H., Lu, P.: Checking determinism of regular expressions with counting. Inf. Comput. **241**, 302–320 (2015)
5. Cheng, K., Krishnakumar, A.S.: Automatic functional test generation using the extended finite state machine model. In: Proceedings of DAC 1993, ACM Press (1993)
6. D'Antoni, L., Veanes, M.: Minimization of symbolic automata. In: Proceedings of POPL 2014, ACM (2014)
7. Dill, D.L., Hu, A.J., Wong-Toi, H.: Checking for language inclusion using simulation preorders. In: Larsen, K.G., Skou, A. (eds.) CAV 1991. LNCS, vol. 575, pp. 255–265. Springer, Heidelberg (1992). https://doi.org/10.1007/3-540-55179-4_25
8. Gelade, W., Martens, W., Neven, F.: Optimizing schema languages for XML: numerical constraints and interleaving. In: Schwentick, T., Suciu, D. (eds.) ICDT 2007. LNCS, vol. 4353, pp. 269–283. Springer, Heidelberg (2006). https://doi.org/10.1007/11965893_19
9. Gelade, W., Gyssens, M., Martens, W.: Regular expressions with counting: weak versus strong determinism. In: Královič, R., Niwiński, D. (eds.) MFCS 2009. LNCS, vol. 5734, pp. 369–381. Springer, Heidelberg (2009). https://doi.org/10.1007/978-3-642-03816-7_32
10. van Glabbeek, R., Ploeger, B.: Five Determinisation algorithms. In: Ibarra, O.H., Ravikumar, B. (eds.) CIAA 2008. LNCS, vol. 5148, pp. 161–170. Springer, Heidelberg (2008). https://doi.org/10.1007/978-3-540-70844-5_17
11. Heizmann, M., Hoenicke, J., Podelski, A.: Software model checking for people who love automata. In: Sharygina, N., Veith, H. (eds.) CAV 2013. LNCS, vol. 8044, pp. 36–52. Springer, Heidelberg (2013). https://doi.org/10.1007/978-3-642-39799-8_2
12. Henriksen, J.G., et al.: Mona: monadic second-order logic in practice. In: Brinksma, E., Cleaveland, W.R., Larsen, K.G., Margaria, T., Steffen, B. (eds.) TACAS 1995. LNCS, vol. 1019, pp. 89–110. Springer, Heidelberg (1995). https://doi.org/10.1007/3-540-60630-0_5
13. Hovland, D.: Regular expressions with numerical constraints and automata with counters. In: Leucker, M., Morgan, C. (eds.) ICTAC 2009. LNCS, vol. 5684, pp. 231–245. Springer, Heidelberg (2009). https://doi.org/10.1007/978-3-642-03466-4_15
14. Hovland, D.: The membership problem for regular expressions with unordered concatenation and numerical constraints. In: Dediu, A.-H., Martín-Vide, C. (eds.) LATA 2012. LNCS, vol. 7183, pp. 313–324. Springer, Heidelberg (2012). https://doi.org/10.1007/978-3-642-28332-1_27
15. Kilpeläinen, P., Tuhkanen, R.: One-unambiguity of regular expressions with numeric occurrence indicators. Inf. Comput. **205**(6), 890–916 (2007)
16. Lengál, O., Šimáček, J., Vojnar, T.: VATA: a library for efficient manipulation of non-deterministic tree automata. In: Flanagan, C., König, B. (eds.) TACAS 2012. LNCS, vol. 7214, pp. 79–94. Springer, Heidelberg (2012). https://doi.org/10.1007/978-3-642-28756-5_7
17. Roesch, M., et al.: Snort: A Network Intrusion Detection and Prevention System. http://www.snort.org
18. Microsoft Automata Library: Automata and Transducer Library for .NET. https://github.com/AutomataDotNet/Automata

19. OWASP Foundation and Checkmarx: Regular Expression Denial of Service: ReDoS (2017)
20. RegExLib.com: The Internet's First Regular Expression Library. http://regexlib.com/
21. Sommer, R., et al.: The Bro Network Security Monitor. http://www.bro.org
22. Shiple, T.R., Kukula, J.H., Ranjan, R.K.: A comparison of Presburger engines for EFSM reachability. In: Hu, A.J., Vardi, M.Y. (eds.) CAV 1998. LNCS, vol. 1427, pp. 280–292. Springer, Heidelberg (1998). https://doi.org/10.1007/BFb0028752
23. Smith, R., Estan, C., Jha, S.: XFA: faster signature matching with extended automata. In: Proceedings of SSP 2008, IEEE (2008)
24. Smith, R., Estan, C., Jha, S., Siahaan, I.: Fast signature matching using extended finite automaton (XFA). In: Sekar, R., Pujari, A.K. (eds.) ICISS 2008. LNCS, vol. 5352, pp. 158–172. Springer, Heidelberg (2008). https://doi.org/10.1007/978-3-540-89862-7_15
25. Sperberg-McQueen, M.: Notes on Finite State Automata with Counters. https://www.w3.org/XML/2004/05/msm-cfa.html. Accessed 08 Aug 2018
26. The Sagan Team: The Sagan Log Analysis Engine. https://quadrantsec.com/sagan_log_analysis_engine/
27. Thompson, K.: Programming techniques: regular expression search algorithm. Commun. ACM 11(6), 419–422 (1968)
28. Češka, M., Havlena, V., Holík, L., Lengál, O., Vojnar, T.: Approximate reduction of finite automata for high-speed network intrusion detection. In: Beyer, D., Huisman, M. (eds.) TACAS 2018. LNCS, vol. 10806, pp. 155–175. Springer, Cham (2018). https://doi.org/10.1007/978-3-319-89963-3_9
29. Yang, L., Karim, R., Ganapathy, V., Smith, R.: Improving NFA-based signature matching using ordered binary decision diagrams. In: Jha, S., Sommer, R., Kreibich, C. (eds.) RAID 2010. LNCS, vol. 6307, pp. 58–78. Springer, Heidelberg (2010). https://doi.org/10.1007/978-3-642-15512-3_4

Author Index

Printed in the United States
By Bookmasters